# Operation AL-AQSA FLOOD

The Defeat of the Vanquisher

Jacques Baud

# OPERATION AL-AQSA FLOOD

## The Defeat of the Vanquisher

Max Milo

Max Milo, 2024
www.maxmilo.com
ISBN: 978-2-31501-986-1

# Contents

**Foreword** ................................................................................................ 15

**1. The Palestinian Question** ............................................................... 19
Historical Context .................................................................................. 19
    The Cold War .................................................................................. 27
    Resolution 181 ................................................................................. 28
    Resolution 242 ................................................................................. 34
The Boundary Problem ......................................................................... 36
The Question of Jerusalem ................................................................... 40
The Right to Return ............................................................................... 41
The Right to Resistance ........................................................................ 42

**2. Israel's Occupation Policy** ............................................................. 45
The Situation in the Occupied Territories ......................................... 45
The Question of the "Jewish State" ..................................................... 47
The Question of "Apartheid" ................................................................ 49
    Settlements in Occupied Palestinian Territories ...................... 52
    The Impossibility of Developing a Palestinian Economy ........ 53

**3. The Fight Against Palestinian Resistance** ................................. 55
Israeli Intelligence ................................................................................. 55
    Structural Weaknesses ................................................................... 61
    Overestimation ................................................................................ 62
    Underestimating your Opponent ................................................. 64
    *Taqiya* and the Surprise of October 7, 2023 ............................. 65
Israel's Counter-Terrorism Strategy .................................................... 67

| | |
|---|---|
| Failure to Develop Holistic Thinking | 70 |
| The Strategy of Deterrence | 74 |
| Doctrinal Apparatus Ill-Suited to an Asymmetrical Conflict | 77 |
| *The BETHLEHEM Doctrine* | 77 |
| *The DAHIYA Doctrine* | 80 |
| *The HANNIBAL Directive* | 82 |
| Extrajudicial Executions | 84 |

## 4. Gaza ................................................................................................93

| | |
|---|---|
| Gaza's Special Situation | 93 |
| The Israeli Presence Around Gaza | 98 |
| The Islamic Resistance Movement (HAMAS) | 101 |
| History of the Movement | 101 |
| *The Beginnings* | 101 |
| *The Emergence of Hamas* | 104 |
| *Hamas's Terrorist Strategy* | 106 |
| *The Impact of September 11, 2001* | 107 |
| *Hamas's Political Shift* | 108 |
| Hamas Doctrine | 112 |
| *The Hamas Charter* | 112 |
| *A Territorial and not a Religious War* | 114 |
| Islamic Resistance and Islamism | 117 |
| *The Nature of Palestinian Resistance* | 118 |
| *Our Understanding of Islamism* | 122 |
| Strategy and Operations | 124 |
| *Hamas's Approach to Resistance* | 124 |
| *Rockets* | 127 |
| *Incendiary Balloons* | 133 |
| *External Cooperation* | 133 |
| Structure | 134 |
| *The Political Component* | 136 |
| *The Military Component* | 137 |
| *Weapons* | 149 |
| Resources | 155 |
| Designation of Hamas as a Terrorist Organization | 160 |
| Other Palestinian Resistance Movements in Gaza | 166 |
| Sunni Movements | 167 |
| *Palestinian Islamic Jihad (PIJ)* | 167 |

      *Popular Resistance Movement (PRM)* ............................................. 170
      *Free Palestine Movement (MPL)* ................................................... 172
      *Humat al-Aqsa* ................................................................................ 173
   Shiite-Inspired Movements ................................................................... 174
      *Popular Resistance Committees (PRC)* ...................................... 174
      *Patients' Movement for Supporting Palestine (HESN)* ............ 175
      *Palestinian Mujahideen Movement (PMM)* .............................. 176
   Secular-Inspired Movements ............................................................... 179
      *Factions of the al-Aqsa Martyrs Brigad in Gaza* ...................... 179
      *The Popular Front for the Liberation of Palestine (PFLP)* ....... 181
      *The Democratic Front for the Liberation of Palestine (DFLP)*. 184
      *The Democratic Front for the Liberation of Palestine—General*
         *Command (PFLP-GC)* ................................................................ 186
   Other Armed Movements and Groups ............................................... 188
      *Jaysh al-Ummah, Bayt al-Maqdis Faction* ................................ 191
      *The Army of Islam (Gaza)* ........................................................... 191
      *The Army of the Partisans of Allah* ............................................ 193
      *The Unification and Jihad Legions* ............................................. 194
   Joint Conduct of Palestinian Resistance Factions ........................... 195

**5. Operation AL-AQSA** ............................................................................ 197
The Beginnings ............................................................................................. 197
   Expansion of Israeli Settlements in the West Bank ......................... 198
   Social Tensions in Gaza ........................................................................ 200
   Tougher Detention Conditions ........................................................... 201
   Desecration of the Haram al-Sharif (Esplanade of the Mosques) ..... 201
Objectives of the Operation ....................................................................... 204
   Strategic Objectives .............................................................................. 206
   Operational Objectives ........................................................................ 208
      *First Objective: The Gaza Division* ............................................. 208
      *Second Objective: Take Prisoners* .............................................. 209
   Tactical Objectives ................................................................................ 210
The Course of the Operation ..................................................................... 210
   Misinterpreted Clues ............................................................................ 212
   Israeli Conduct Overtaken by Events ................................................ 214
   New Tactics ............................................................................................. 221
      *"Zero Distance" Actions* ............................................................... 221
      *Combat Tunnels* ............................................................................ 224

  *Ambushes* ................................................................224
  *Dynamic Control Structures* ...........................226
War Crimes .......................................................................227
 Hostages or Prisoners? ............................................229
 Hamas' Treatment of Hostages ...............................231
 The Supernova Music Festival Attack ..................236
 The 40 Beheaded Babies ..........................................238
 Baby in the Oven .......................................................242
 The Disembowelled Woman ...................................244
 The Rapes .....................................................................245

## 6. The Israeli Response—Operation IRON SWORDS .............251
The Initial Response ........................................................251
The Plan of Action ............................................................252
Unclear Objectives ...........................................................252
 Preparatory Phase .....................................................254
 Phase 1: Takeover ......................................................256
  *The Hospital War* ..................................................256
  *The Tunnel War* ....................................................261
 Phase 2: Eliminating Pockets of Resistance .........264
  *Objective: Hamas Leadership* ............................264
 Phase 3: Restructuring the Gaza Strip ..................270
Matching Strategies ..........................................................272
Ill-Prepared Troops ..........................................................277
The Influence .....................................................................279
 Hasbara .........................................................................279
 Influence Operations .................................................282
 The War of Numbers ..................................................286
 The Quest for Success ...............................................288
The Use of Violence ..........................................................290
 The Right to Self-Defense ........................................291
 Rules of Engagement ................................................292
  *The Notion of "Civilian"* .....................................294
  *The Principle of Distinction* ...............................295
  *The Principle of Proportionality* ........................297
  *The Precautionary Principle* ...............................303
 An Unnecessarily Brutal Response ........................305
 Justifying the Use of Violence ..................................310

Human Shields .................................................................................. 311
Poor Tactics ........................................................................................... 315
Lack of Victories .................................................................................. 316
Reactions inside Israel ....................................................................... 317
Genocide, Ethnic Cleansing or Crimes Against Humanity? ............... 317
    Ethnic Cleansing ............................................................................ 318
    Genocide ......................................................................................... 322
        Incitement to Genocide .............................................................. 329
        South Africa's Lawsuit ................................................................ 330
        Order of the International Court of Justice (ICJ) ..................... 331
        The Israeli Response ................................................................... 334
        Military Operations Despite Suspicions of Genocide ............... 343
Negotiations and Concessions ........................................................... 345

## 7. Israel and its Neighbors ............................................................. 349
Israeli Security Policy .......................................................................... 349
A Less-Than-Faithful Ally .................................................................. 351
American Presence in the Middle East ............................................. 352
Syria ...................................................................................................... 354
Iran ........................................................................................................ 357
Lebanon ................................................................................................ 363
    Hezbollah's Raison d'Être ............................................................. 365
    Is Hezbollah a Terrorist Organization? ....................................... 368
    Hezbollah's Reaction After October 7, 2023 ............................... 370
Comparing the Security Policies of two Small Countries ............... 373

## 8. The Significance of the Palestinian Conflict for our Security ........ 377
Radicalization Fueled by our Policies ............................................... 381
Anti-Semitism ...................................................................................... 383
Mohammed Merah's Attacks in 2012 ............................................... 395

## 9. Conclusions .................................................................................. 399
The October 7th Response .................................................................. 400
The Absence of European Diplomacy ............................................... 401
An Arab World that has Forgotten its Brothers ............................... 403
Why are We Always Wrong? .............................................................. 403

## Appendix 1—The Hamas Charter .................................................... 409

**Appendix 2—United Nations Resolutions Condemning Israel**........ 417

**Appendix 3—Use of the Veto by the USA** ............................................ 437

**Appendix 4—Definition of Apartheid** .................................................... 439

*One of the mistakes some political analysts make is to think that their enemies must be our enemies.*

Nelson Mandela (1990)

# Foreword

If we are not careful, Israel could disappear.[1] Not because it does not fight Palestinian resistance, but precisely because it does.

The way Israel is fighting the Palestinians is leading to a loss of legitimacy that seems to be accelerating. It is accompanied—indeed amplified—by the decline in credibility of the Western world following the management of its wars, and in particular that of Ukraine. The complaint lodged by South Africa against Israel and the determination of the Houthis in Yemen to push the West to demand a ceasefire are markers of this evolution.

For many years, Israel has been criticized for its handling of the Palestinian conflict, but has enjoyed an impunity that no one has really tried to explain. In fact, this has no objective reason other than the sense of guilt of countries like Germany and France, which actively participated in the Holocaust during the Second World War. It is part of a form of supremacism cultivated by Europeans and exported to the Middle East by Israel, which accepts that, as in music, "one white woman is worth two black women," and which is reflected in various forms in French political discourse.

It is a system of thought that illustrates our transition from a "law-based international order" created at the end of the Second World War to avoid repeating the horrors seen there, to a "rules-based international order," which puts these rules into perspective. Even countries like Switzerland, which based its foreign policy on respect for the law, have now adopted the idea of basing it on "rules."

However, the "rest of the world" is attached to respect for the rule of law, which protects it from the voracity and foolishness of Western rulers. The conflict in Gaza thus stands as the hinge between two periods

---

1. Mark TRAN, "State of Israel could disappear, warns Olmert," *The Guardian*, November 29, 2007 (https://www.theguardian.com/world/2007/nov/29/israel)

and two worlds: the one that unbridled and thoughtless policies have progressively weakened, and the one that, seeking to survive in spite of everything, has become resilient and strengthened. The latter needed a locomotive, and it found it in the Eurasian bloc of China and Russia.

South Africa's action is not only a sign of political courage, it also highlights the ethical weakness of Western countries, which admire the move without daring to ask why they did not take the initiative.

The United Nations and humanitarian organizations regularly remind us that Israel violates international law. The regular use of torture, extra-judicial killings, the use of banned weapons, the sexual abuse of prisoners, the indefinite incarceration of children without charge, and arbitrary arrests form a sad catalog whose depth and density is equaled by no other country in the world. And yet, we act as if nothing happened, albeit with a certain guilty conscience, because in Switzerland, for example, military relations with Israel are regularly the subject of a special, confidential report to the government.

Our foreign policies have become gunboat policies, and we allow ourselves what we do not tolerate in others. This is nothing new. What is new is that the rest of the world is starting to apply our own rules to us.

Of course, we can argue about the way the Houthis show their support for a ceasefire in Gaza. But do they act any differently from the West when it unilaterally applies embargoes and boards ships to and from Russia? In this context, South Africa's claim of genocide marks a break with the past: it is a way for the South to regain power from the North.

Naturally, the Empire does not accept this show of independence and counters with strikes in Yemen. Should Yemen strike New York or Washington, too? We would call that "terrorism."

We cannot prejudge the decision of the International Court of Justice, and it is not impossible that it will get bogged down in procedural questions. But as for the substance, the notion of genocide is on everyone's mind, and honest experts in the field do not hesitate to be clear about it. This means that we are supporting a country that is committing genocide. Even Germany, which is struggling to come to terms with its historical complex and supports Israel, is accused of maintaining a continuity of genocidal policies.

J. Baud

*A conventional army loses if it doesn't win.*
*A guerrilla army wins if it doesn't lose.*

Henry Kissinger (*Foreign Affairs*, 1969)

# 1. The Palestinian Question

The Palestinian question revolves around four issues:
- Land distribution;
- The Jerusalem question;
- Israel's borders;
- The right to return.

## Historical Context

While the idea of the Jewish people having a homeland enjoys fairly broad support in itself, the Israeli authorities have made just about every mistake possible to delegitimize it. In seeking to impose itself by force, Israel has never sought to convince its neighbors of the added value it would represent in the region. This is why official Israeli discourse uses biblical tradition rather than international law to justify its existence. Debates about the antiquity of the name "Palestine" are sophisms in an attempt to justify non-compliance with United Nations decisions. Yet the Zionists themselves used the term before 1948.

Our aim is not to settle issues that are obviously both culturally and scientifically complex, and in which faith is interwoven with history, but to show that basing rights and policies on biblical texts inevitably exposes them to contestation. Like the question of creationism in the West, biblical justifications are in themselves vulnerable: the Bible has never been a history book or a land register, but the vehicle of a spiritual message. A few centuries ago, a literal reading of the Bible could serve as a substitute for science, enabling the Church to back up a political message. Today, with the development of science and archaeology, giving it a scientific character tends to undermine the political message it is intended to convey.

That said, without getting into a theological dispute that more competent experts could shed light on, even an examination of the Bible tends to vindicate the Palestinians. According to biblical tradition, God allotted the land of present-day Palestine to Abraham and *"his posterity."* According to tradition, this includes Ishmael, father of the Palestinian nation, and Isaac, father of the Israelite nation. The fact that Ishmael was Abraham's natural son makes no difference to the account, since according to Genesis, God says: *"I will also make a nation of the son of your handmaid; for he is your offspring"* (Genesis 21:13).[2] In other words, according to biblical tradition, the Jews have no more rights to the land of Palestine than the Palestinians, heirs to the tribes that have occupied the land ever since.

The idea of a Jewish state did not really arise in Europe until the end of the 19th century, with the emergence of Zionism in the context of a revival of nationalism in the wake of the Dreyfus Affair. This led to the Balfour Declaration in November 1917, in which Great Britain undertook to promote the establishment of a Jewish "national home" in Palestine, with a view to the dismemberment of the Ottoman Empire. By the end of the war, violence between Jewish and Arab factions in Palestine prompted the British to fulfill their promise.

In the 1920s-1930s, the Zionist movement split into two currents, which became the *World Zionist Organization* (WZO) and the *Revisionist Zionist Movement* (RZM) (which gave rise to the *World Union of Revisionist Zionists* in 1925). This *"revisionist"* current had absolutely nothing to do with today's revisionism, associated with the Holocaust. It demanded the "revision" of the British decision to grant Transjordan (today: Jordan) to the Hashemites (expelled from Mecca by Ibn Saud), to be added to the territory between the Mediterranean and the Jordan, to form the *"Jewish National Home."* The OSM was in the majority at the time and tended to the left, while the MSR was a right-wing organization, from which the Likud (to which Benjamin Netanyahu belongs today) was born in the 1950s.

---

2. https://www.bible.com/fr/bible/93/GEN.21.9-20.LSG

## The Irgun

*Figure 1—Irgun emblem, from the "Haganah B." The map in the background is that of "Greater Israel" as imagined by revisionist Zionists in the 1930s, comprising present-day Israel with the occupied Palestinian territories and Transjordan (present-day Jordan). It remains an old dream of certain circles on the Israeli far right, and explains why Israel has never clearly defined its borders. This is why movements like Hamas refuse to recognize the State of Israel today. Because recognizing it could mean ipso facto giving up Palestinian lands.*

Operationally, the armed wing of the OSM was the Haganah. In 1931, a revisionist armed wing split off from it, initially called the *Haganah Bet* ("Haganah B"), before becoming the *"Irgun Tzvai Leumi"* (National Military Organization), commonly known as *the Irgun,* in 1935. Extremely right-wing, its members were largely drawn from Betar, the youth organization of the MSR, which had political offices throughout Europe, notably in Paris, Warsaw, London and New York. The foundations of its doctrine were laid as early as 1923, in an article entitled, *"The Iron Wall,"* written by Vladimir Jabotinsky, leader of the revisionist movement.[3] It is based on the idea that the Zionist movement in Palestine is inherently colonial and that, as in every country in the world, the settlers, *"civilized or savage,"* will have to confront the indigenous population until they are no longer in a position to fight. Colonization would therefore have to be carried out under the shelter of an "iron wall," initially made up of military personnel. This was 25 years before Israel's independence!

In Germany, the Nazis came to power on January 30, 1933. The following day, in the *Jüdische Rundschau,* their official organ, the German Zionists

---

3. Vladimir JABOTINSKY, "O Zheleznoi Stene," *Rassvyet,* Berlin, November 4, 1923 (published in South Africa in 1937); *Zionism—A History of Zionism* (http://www.zionism-israel.com/zionism_history.htm)

asserted that they alone could ensure the defense of Jewish interests, and not the traditional Jewish organizations.[4] The German Zionists obviously did not share the Nazi ideology, but quickly realized that there was a convergence of interests that could be exploited: the Nazis wanted to "get rid" of the Jewish presence in Germany, and the Zionists wanted to populate Palestine. As early as March 16, they began negotiations with the new German government to examine ways of facilitating Jewish emigration.[5]

The "spontaneous" worldwide boycott against Germany, launched on March 23, 1933 by American Jewish movements,[6] was opposed by the Zionists, who were quick to send a telegram to Hitler, pointing out that *"Palestinian Jews have not proclaimed a boycott on German goods."*[7] On April 1st, 1933, Joseph Goebbels, Minister of Propaganda, responded with another boycott against Jewish businesses in Germany.[8]

At this stage, two strategies were developing in parallel in Germany:
- that of the Jewish community ("assimilationists"), who sought to influence German policy to allow normal coexistence with the Nazi authorities;
- that of the Zionist movement ("nationalists"), which believed that a policy of assimilation was not possible and that the time had come to create the Jewish national home promised by the Balfour Declaration by exploiting Nazi policy.

It is easy to imagine that for the Nazis, the idea of having a policy imposed on them by the Jewish community was far less acceptable than the idea of them leaving Germany. This explains why, after some hesitation, the Nazis finally accepted and exploited cooperation with the Zionists.

In the second half of 1933, the *Zionist Federation of Germany* (ZVfD)[9] invited Leopold von Mildenstein, an SS officer with the *Reich Central Security Office* (*Reichssicherheitshauptamt* or *RSHA*), to spend six months in Palestine. The aim was to promote Jewish nationalism, which

---

4. Edwin BLACK, *The Transfer Agreement—Pact between the Third Reich and Jewish Palestine*, Caroll & Graf, New York, 2001, p. 173.
5. Edwin BLACK, *The Transfer Agreement—Pact between the Third Reich and Jewish Palestine*, Caroll & Graf, New York, 2001, p. 82.
6. Edwin BLACK, "When Zionists Made Deal with the Nazis," *The Jerusalem Post*, September 23, 2009; "Judea Declares War On Germany," *Daily Express*, London, March 24, 1933, pp. 1-2; Holocaust-Referenz—Argumente gegen Auschwitzleugner (https://www.h-ref.de/feindbilder/juedische-kriegserklaerungen/daily-express-original.php)
7. Edwin BLACK, *The Transfer Agreement*, op. cit. p. 81.
8. Article "Anti-Nazi boycott of 1933," *Wikipedia*.
9. Zionistische Vereinigung für Deutschland.

the Zionists felt had been legitimized by the rise of German nationalism. Indeed, on June 21, the ZVfD sent a letter to the German government proposing extensive cooperation in the creation of a state in Palestine, citing their mutual nationalist objectives.[10]

Negotiations led to the promulgation of *Decree 54/33* of August 10, 1933, which authorized the creation of two clearing banks under the supervision of the ZVfD, to facilitate the financing of emigration to Palestine.[11] A bank in Germany, the *Palästina-Treuhandstelle zur Beratung deutscher Juden GmbH (PalTreu)*, and one in Palestine, the *Anglo-Palestine Bank*, were established. This arrangement enabled Jewish wealth to be transferred to Palestine, bypassing the boycott and currency export restrictions, while offering preferential exchange rates and tax breaks. It also circumvented immigration quotas to Palestine imposed by Great Britain for individuals who did not have £1,000 in cash with them. It worked as follows: when a Jewish person wanted to emigrate to Palestine, they realized their assets and deposited the funds with the *PalTreu*, which bought consumer goods and exported them to Palestine; on the spot, these goods were sold by the Palestinian bank and the proceeds paid back to the immigrants. The principle was not new, and is still used in the Middle East under the name of "hawala."

It was a "win-win" solution: for the Zionists, to encourage Jewish emigration to Palestine; and for Germany, to circumvent the boycott while encouraging the departure of the Jewish population. The mechanism was enshrined in the *Transfer Agreement* (Ha'Avara Agreement), signed between the ZVfD and the German government on August 25, 1933.[12] A small *Manual for Jewish Emigration* was published, to facilitate the process and provide advice on emigration.[13]

In 1933-1934, it appeared that Great Britain would not "revise" its policy in Palestine. Jabotinsky sought the support of another Mediterranean player: Fascist Italy, where he had lived for three years and whose language he spoke fluently. On March 29, 1936, the barracks of the

---

10. Lenni BRENNER, *51 Documents: Zionist collaboration with the Nazis*, Barricade Books, New Jersey, 2002.
11. Edwin BLACK, "When Zionists made deal with the Nazis," *The Jerusalem Post*, September 23, 2009 (https://www.jpost.com/features/when-zionists-made-deal-with-the-nazis)
12. Edwin BLACK, *The Transfer Agreement—Pact between the Third Reich and Jewish Palestine*, Caroll & Graf, New York, 2001.
13. *PhiloAtlas—Handbuch für die jüdische Auswanderung*, Philo GmbH, Jüdischer Buchverlag, Berlin, 1938, p. 283.

first Betar naval squadron were inaugurated at the Civitavecchia naval academy.[14] Apparently, a ship was allocated to him, with which he fought alongside the Italian navy in Abyssinia in 1935.[15]

In 1935, irritated by the slow pace of the Ha'Avara process, Hitler introduced a package of laws further restricting the rights of Jews in Germany (the Nuremberg Laws), to encourage them to emigrate.

In 1936, the Arabs of Palestine unleashed a violent revolt, led by Hajj Amin al-Husseini, Mufti of Jerusalem, which the British brutally repressed. This repression led to the disappearance of part of the Palestinian elite, which would be lacking ten years later at the time of the "partition." In July 1937, London sent a commission of inquiry, the Palestine Royal Commission (also known as the Peel Commission), which recommended the partition of the country and the creation of two states. Under arrest warrant, Amin al-Husseini found refuge in Germany. He asked the Führer to support the creation of an Arab state in Palestine?[16] But Hitler did not want to find himself caught up in a "ménage à trois:" he supported the Zionists not out of sympathy, nor out of concern to give them a state, but to "get rid of them" by circumventing the embargo imposed on him.

Two visions emerged among Nazi leaders: one was to continue the Ha'Avara process, expelling all Jews as a matter of priority, and later "solving" the problem of this Jewish state; the other—advocated by Adolf Eichmann—was to disperse the Jews throughout the world. Finally, in autumn 1937, Hitler chose to continue his cooperation with the Zionists.[17]

In 1938, embroiled in the Spanish Civil War, Mussolini needed to solidify his alliance with Germany. He therefore adopted racial laws, broke off his support for Jabotinsky's Zionists and expelled them from Italy. The result was heightened tension between Zionist "nationalists" and Jewish "assimilationists," who were blamed for the situation, and divisions within the Zionist movement itself.

---

14. Lenni BRENNER, *51 Documents: Zionist collaboration with the Nazis*, Barricade Books, New Jersey, 2002.
15. Article "Betar Naval Academy," Wikipedia (en.wikipedia.org/wiki/Betar_Naval_Academy); Alain Dieckhoff, *The Invention of a Nation: Zionist Thought and the Making of Modern Israel*, C. Hurst, 2003; Eric Kaplan, *The Jewish Radical Right: Revisionist Zionism and Its Ideological Legacy*, University of Wisconsin Press, 2005.
16. "Full official record: What the mufti said to Hitler," *The Times of Israel*, October 21, 2015.
17. Edwin BLACK, *The Transfer Agreement*, Carroll & Graf, New York, 2001 (p. 376)

But the Labor wing of the Zionists was not to be outdone. Between February 26 and March 2, 1937, Haganah intelligence officer Feivel Polkes was in Berlin (at RSHA expense) to develop contacts with the German secret service in exchange for improved terms of Jewish emigration to Palestine and funding for Haganah intelligence activities. After the assassination of Swiss Nazi party leader Withelm Gustloff (1936) and the attempted assassination of Konrad Henlein, head of the *Sudetendeutsche Heimatfront* in Czechoslovakia, Germany wanted to develop its intelligence capabilities on the activities of Jewish organizations abroad. Polkes thus became the Haganah's point of contact with the German intelligence services operating in Palestine under the cover of the German news agency DNB.[18] According to a CIA report (drawn up in 1960 on the occasion of the Eichmann trial), Polkes was paid £20 a month by the Germans.[19] His contact in Germany was none other than Adolf Eichmann, who visited Palestine in October 1937, before becoming one of the main architects of the deportations of Jews.[20]

But this was not the only factor. From July 6 to 15, 1938, the Evian Conference brought together 32 countries at the initiative of President Roosevelt, to find a solution to Jewish emigration. But none of the participating countries agreed to accept Jewish refugees. This failure was largely because of the Zionist organizations, including Golda Meir's, who feared that the initiative would undermine their efforts to encourage Jews to emigrate to Palestine.[21]

In early 1940, a radical group of revisionist Zionists led by Avraham Stern, opposed to the divorce with Italy, broke away from the Irgun. Initially called the *"Real Irgun,"* his faction became the *Lohamei Herut Israel* (Lehi) at the end of 1940, better known as the *"Stern Group."* Vladimir Jabotinsky was then overwhelmed by his right: the Stern Group deliberately engaged in terrorist violence, making itself responsible for several hundred Jewish and Arab deaths in Palestine.[22] For him, the British threat was greater than the Nazi threat. Indeed, after the French

---

18. Deutsche Nachrichtenbüro (DNB)
19. Memorandum addressed to the Director of the CIA, entitled "Adolf Eichmann, June 1960." "Uncovering the Architect of the Holocaust: The CIA Names File on Adolf Eichmann," The National Security Archives, Document 54 (https://nsarchive2.gwu.edu/NSAEBB/NSAEBB150/index.htm)
20. Lenni BRENNER, *51 Documents, op. cit.*
21. "évian, un crime prémédité en juillet 1938, la honte et la trahison," www.citedevian.fr, June 28, 2015 (https://www.citedevian.fr/conference-devian-de-juillet-1938/)
22. Arie PERLIGER & Leonard WEINBERG, *Totalitarian Movements & Political Religions*, Vol. 4, No. 3 (2003) 91-118.

defeat in 1940, Great Britain invaded Syria, fearing that it would fall into German hands, and thus extended its hold over the region. Through the German embassy in Beirut, the Stern Group offered to cooperate with the Third Reich in fighting the British in the Middle East.[23]

This unnatural closeness between the Zionists and the Nazi regime led to American mistrust of the Jewish community. As early as 1942, after the United States entered the war, the FBI feared the threat of Jewish espionage on behalf of the Nazis. The arrest of Herbert Karl Friedrich Bahr, a Jewish refugee suspected of working for the Gestapo, materialized American fears. He was sentenced to 30 years in prison. For this reason, during the war, the United States accepted very few Jewish refugees fleeing the Nazi regime.[24]

Particularly in France, the reading of the events of the Second World War is highly caricatured. As active players in the Holocaust, the French have never managed to escape from a binary vision of reality. The French government's association of "Judaism" with "Zionism" is one of the driving forces behind today's anti-Semitism, and makes it difficult to understand the complex situations in Ukraine and Palestine.

In October 2015, Benjamin Netanyahu declared:

> *At that time, Hitler didn't want to exterminate the Jews, he wanted to expel them.*[25]

He aroused international disapproval, but he was right. In the 1930s, the Nazis' priority was not to kill all Jews, but to expel them from Germany. Zionists then sought to align their goal of populating Palestine with Nazi policy. They simply applied a pragmatic strategy of allying themselves with those who could serve their cause. By 1940, the war in Europe and the Mediterranean made transfers to Palestine virtually impossible, forcing Germany to find a "final solution" to the Jewish question.

---

23. See Wikipedia, Lehi (militant group).
24. Daniel A. Gross, "The U.S. Government Turned Away Thousands of Jewish Refugees, Fearing That They Were Nazi Spies," *smithsonianmag.com*, November 18, 2015 (https://www.smithsonianmag.com/history/us-government-turned-away-thousands-jewish-refugees-fearing-they-were-nazi-spies-180957324/)
25. "Netanyahu: Hitler Didn't Want to Exterminate the Jews," *Haaretz*, October 21, 2015 (https://www.haaretz.com/israel-news/2015-10-21/ty-article/netanyahu-absolves-hitler-of-guilt/0000017f-dc2e-db22-a17f-fcbf7c1e0000)

On the other hand, when Netanyahu claimed that Hitler was inspired to exterminate the Jews by al-Husseini, in an attempt to blame the Palestinians for the Holocaust,[26] he was lying. The transcript of their discussion of November 28, 1941 exists and does not confirm this accusation.[27] Moreover, the Grand Mufti's participation in the Holocaust—mentioned by Dieter Wisliceny, one of Eichmann's deputies, during the Nuremberg trial—is today refuted by most historians, who believe that he was simply trying to save his skin.[28] As for the influence Amin al-Husseini may have had on Hitler, this is also denied by many historians.[29] That said, al-Husseini is said to have helped recruit volunteers for Bosnian units (created within the Waffen SS after the formation of a "Jewish Legion" in the British army), in order to fight Tito's Serbs in Yugoslavia, with no links to the Middle East. Moreover, the Nazis never supported the idea of Arab independence in Palestine: they were neither "pro-Jewish" nor "pro-Arab," but sought to reduce the influence and presence of the British Empire,[30] an objective—quite logically—shared with the Zionists.

## *The Cold War*

By 1945, the Mediterranean was largely in the hands of Britain and France. Stalin saw the creation of a Jewish state as an opportunity, both to combat British imperialism and to gain access to the Mediterranean Sea. He saw it as a fair return for the support he had given to the Jews during the war, and intended to rely on Zionist leaders in Palestine, such as Golda Meir, who were socialists and of Soviet origin. This is why, as early as 1946, he secretly supported the Jewish fighters against the British by supplying them with weapons. At the time, the USSR was one of the UN's most fervent supporters of the creation of a Jewish state.[31]

---

26. Jodi RUDOREN, "Netanyahu Denounced for Saying Palestinian Inspired Holocaust," *The New York Times*, October 21, 2015.
27. "Full official record: What the mufti said to Hitler," *The Times of Israel*, October 21, 2015 (https://www.timesofisrael.com/full-official-record-what-the-mufti-said-to-hitler/)
28. Raphael AHREN, "In Netanyahu's mufti-Holocaust allegation, echoes of his father's maverick approach to history," *The Times of Israel*, October 22, 2015.
29. See the Wikipedia article "Amin al-Husseini."
30. Sue SURKES, "Himmler had offered help to the Mufti of Jerusalem against 'Jewish intruders,'" *The Times of Israel*, March 30, 2017.
31. "Secrets Of War, The Cold War 05 Inside the KGB," *YouTube*, October 2, 2015 (https://youtu.be/ypuuxrxcVek)

## The shrinking of Palestinian territory

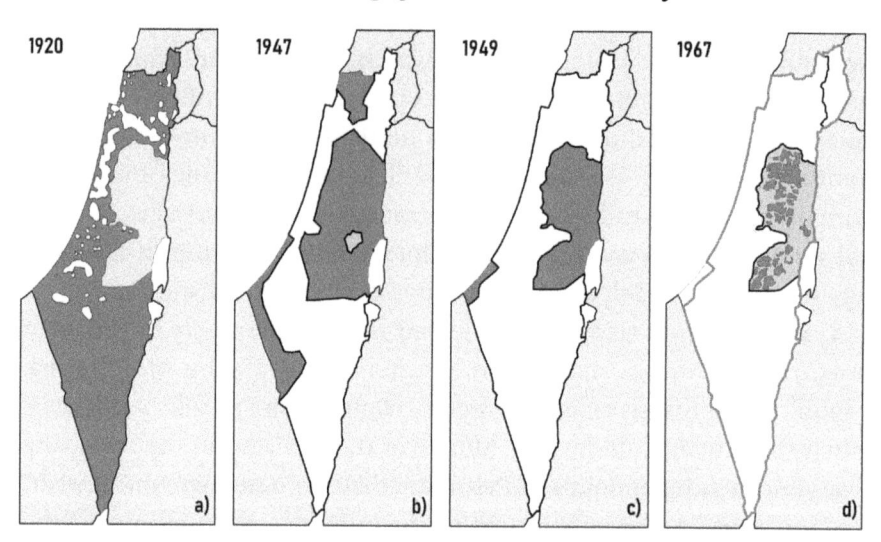

Figure 2—Israel's expansion. Until the 1920s, there was little Jewish presence in Palestine (a). The partition plan proposed by resolution 181 (b) was only a proposal. The borders currently accepted for Israel are those of the 1949 armistice (c). The war of June 1967, unleashed by Israel against countries that were not expecting it, led to the occupation of the Golan Heights, the West Bank and the Gaza Strip (d).

But after the creation of the State of Israel, its leaders showed a preference for the West, and the USSR began to support the Palestinians, who had been forced to abandon their land. This led to the emergence of a Marxist-based Palestinian resistance, dominated by the Palestine Liberation Organization and Fatah, which lasted until the late 1980s.

However, the relationship between the Jewish community and the USSR was still very much on everyone's mind. In the West, fear of the Communists was transferred to the Jewish community, which was the source of many of the Soviet spies of the period, such as the Rosenbergs and Rudolf Abel, who were later unmasked. The United States remained wary of Jewish asylum-seekers, and visas were granted sparingly. A situation that only served to underline the need to give them a state.

## Resolution 181

The CIA was dubious about the Jews' sincerity. On November 28, 1947, the day before the United Nations voted on the partition of Palestine, it published a SECRET report entitled, "*The Consequences of the Partition of Palestine."* It refers to the deployment of Jewish clandestine agents, as well as the transport of illegal immigrants and arms from the Black Sea to Palestine. Astonishingly perceptive, the CIA warns against accepting the partition plan and anticipates the violence that would ensue:[32]

> *In the long term, no Zionist in Palestine will be satisfied with the territorial arrangements of the partition plan. Even the most conservative Zionists will want all the Negev, the western part of Galilee, the city of Jerusalem and eventually all Palestine. The extremists will not only demand all of Palestine, they will want Transjordan.*
> *In the chaos that will follow the implementation of partition, atrocities will certainly be committed by fanatical Arabs; these actions will receive wide publicity and will even be exaggerated by Jewish propaganda. The Arabs will be accused of being the attackers, whatever the actual circumstances.*

This analysis was soon confirmed, and is still relevant today. But President Truman did not listen, and pushed his diplomatic corps to "convince" the countries that opposed the resolution: the United States brandished the suspension of its economic aid to decide against Haiti, and the Firestone company threatened Liberia that it would no longer buy latex from it!

On November 29, 1947, the United Nations General Assembly adopted *Resolution 181*, proposing the partition of Palestine into a Jewish state and an Arab state, with Jerusalem under international status. Intended to take effect on April 1st, 1948, this plan was not a decision, but merely a proposal that was not legally binding.

Resolution 181 did not aim to create a Jewish state, but proposed two states: a Jewish state and an Arab state. It envisaged that there would be Arabs living in Jewish territory and Jews living in Arab territory, that they would normally be integrated into the new states or be consulted, by virtue of the principle of self-determination of peoples; but it did not provide for any formal consultation mechanism. To understand resolution 181, we need to look back at what Palestine was at the time. The dismantling of the Ottoman Empire and the division of the Levant between France

---

32. *The Consequences of the Partition of Palestine (ORE 55)*, Central Intelligence Agency, October 5, 1947, p. 9 (https://www.cia.gov/readingroom/document/0000256628)

and Great Britain (the Sykes-Picot agreement) led to the creation of the "Mandatory State of Palestine," which then comprised present-day Israeli territory, the occupied Palestinian territories and present-day Jordan. This state had legal status. Golda Meir herself declared herself a Palestinian, and held a Palestinian passport.[33] Palestine even took part in the 1936 Olympic Games with a delegation.[34]

The reason why resolution 181 was only a proposal is that, according to the UN Charter, any change of borders or sovereignty must respect the right of peoples to self-determination. According to this principle, a referendum had to be held throughout Palestine to dissolve the Mandatory State of Palestine, in order to establish one or two new entities. Then, the people decide whether or not to partition Mandate Palestine. Eventual, because two visions clashed at this stage: the Jewish vision, which envisaged two separate states for Arabs and Jews, and the Arab vision, which foresaw a single state where Jews and Arabs would coexist. All this was to take place, if possible, before the departure of the British on May 15, 1948.

But the Jewish population was very much in the minority in Palestine, and the referendums provided for in "181" would certainly have gone in favor of the Arabs. For this reason, the Jewish population rejected this solution in favor of military action to seize the territories.

Arab fears were quickly confirmed: the populations were not consulted, and during the six months set aside for the implementation of the partition mechanism, Jewish militias felt authorized to appropriate Arab territory by force. The Palestinian villagers were quickly overtaken by these militias, made up mainly of seasoned former soldiers from the British army.[35] By the end of 1947, they had already committed 33 massacres against Palestinians, even before the Arab countries became involved in the conflict.[36] On March 10, 1948, Jewish leaders adopted Plan D ("Dalet" in Hebrew), which Israeli historian Ilan Pappé recalls.[37]

---

33. "Golda Meir. I am Palestinian.," *YouTube*, December 17, 2017 (https://youtu.be/I9M91iwP994)
34. https://www.jewishvirtuallibrary.org/israel-and-the-olympic-games
35. *Anglo-American Committee of Inquiry, Report to the United States Government and His Majesty's Government in the United Kingdom*, Lausanne, April 20, 1946.
36. Kathleen CHRISTISON, *Perceptions of Palestine: Their Influence on U.S. Middle East Policy*, University of California Press, Berkeley, 2000. (1st Ed.)
37. Ilan PAPPE, *The Ethnic Cleansing of Palestine*, Oneworld Publications Ltd, Oxford, 2011.

*The orders included a detailed description of the methods to be used to forcibly evict people: large-scale intimidation; besieging and bombing villages and population centers; burning houses, property and goods; eviction; demolition; and, finally, burying mines among the rubble to prevent the return of evicted inhabitants.*

From April 1, 1948, the Haganah and Palmach militias carry out several operations to create a "fait accompli" in the run-up to May 15, 1948, the day set for independence: operation NACHSHON (April 1), operation HAREL (April 15), operation MISPARAYIM (April 21), operation CHAMETZ (April 27), operation JEVUSS (April 27), operation YIFTACH (April 28), operation MATATEH (May 3), operation MACCABI (May 7), operation GIDEON (May 11), operation BARAK (May 12), operation BEN AMI (May 14), operation PITCHFORK (May 14) and operation SCHFIFON (May 14).[38]

Between the end of 1947 and the end of 1948, Jewish (and later Israeli) armed groups had conquered around 80% of the country, destroyed some 500 villages and driven more than a million people into exile.[39] The most famous episode was the brutal massacre of women and children at Deir Yassin—nicknamed the Palestinian Oradour-sur-Glane—by Lehi and Irgun units, then led by Menachem Begin,[40] on April 9, 1948. In 1950, Ben Gourion confessed:[41]

*Until the British left, not a single Jewish settlement, even a disused one, was seized or invaded by the Arabs, while the Haganah forcibly occupied several Arab positions and liberated Haifa and Tiberias, Jaffa and Safad.*
*So, on the decisive day, the part of Palestine where the Haganah had operated was almost completely cleared of Arab occupiers.*

This period is called "Nakba" (catastrophe) by the Palestinians. This term was be used by the Israelis to describe their response against Gaza

---

38. Rosemary Sayigh, *Palestinians: From Peasants to Revolutionaries*, Zed Press, October 1981, p. 74.
39. "Miko Peled Seattle. Oct. 1, 2012," *YouTube*, October 9, 2012 (www.youtube.com/watch?v=TOaxAckFCuQ)
40. Menachem Begin became Prime Minister of Israel (1977-1981) and was awarded the Nobel Peace Prize in 1979.
41. David Ben Gourion, *Rebirth and Destiny of Israel*, NY Philosophical Library, 1954, pp. 530-531.

in 2023. In fact, even before May 14, 1948, the date of the creation of the State of Israel, the Jews were already occupying more land than was provided for in the partition plan, and had expelled the Arabs who should have been cohabiting with the Jews on this land. This is true ethnic cleansing, which concerns the vast majority of Palestinian refugees, who remain to this day. It was for this reason—and not for a simple disagreement over the contours of the two countries, as experts and university professors claim—that the Arab populations took up arms the day after the proclamation of the State of Israel. This first conflict was superimposed by a second, which broke out on May 14 with the Arab countries seeking to prevent Jordan from annexing the Palestinian lands not yet taken by Israel. In 1949, at the end of this "second" war, an armistice determined Israel's "tolerated" borders, and around a million Palestinian refugees found themselves in Israel's neighboring countries and in Gaza.

The United Nations realized that the implementation of "181" would pose problems and appointed a mediator on May 20, 1948, Count Folke Bernadotte. He succeeded in negotiating a truce between Israelis and Palestinians, with the aim of setting up a democratic mechanism for the creation of the two states envisaged by Resolution 181. But he was assassinated on September 17, 1948, by an *"act of cowardice which appears to have been committed in Jerusalem by a group of criminal terrorists."*[42] This group was the *Lehi* (also known as the *"Stern Group"*), whose head of operations at the time was a certain Yitzhak Shamir, who went on to become Prime Minister of the Israeli state and was never tried for this crime.[43] But their behavior aroused indignation in the international Jewish community. On December 4, 1948, on the occasion of Menachem Begin's visit to the United States, Albert Einstein co-signed an open letter to the *New York Times*, denouncing Zionist crimes in Palestine.[44]

---

42. UN SC Resolution 57 (September 18, 1948) (https://digitallibrary.un.org/record/112002/files/S_RES_57(1948)-EN.pdf?ln=en)
43. https://www.jewishvirtuallibrary.org/the-assassination-of-count-bernadotte
44. "New Palestine Party," *New York Times*, December 4, 1948.

## Resolution 181 (1947)

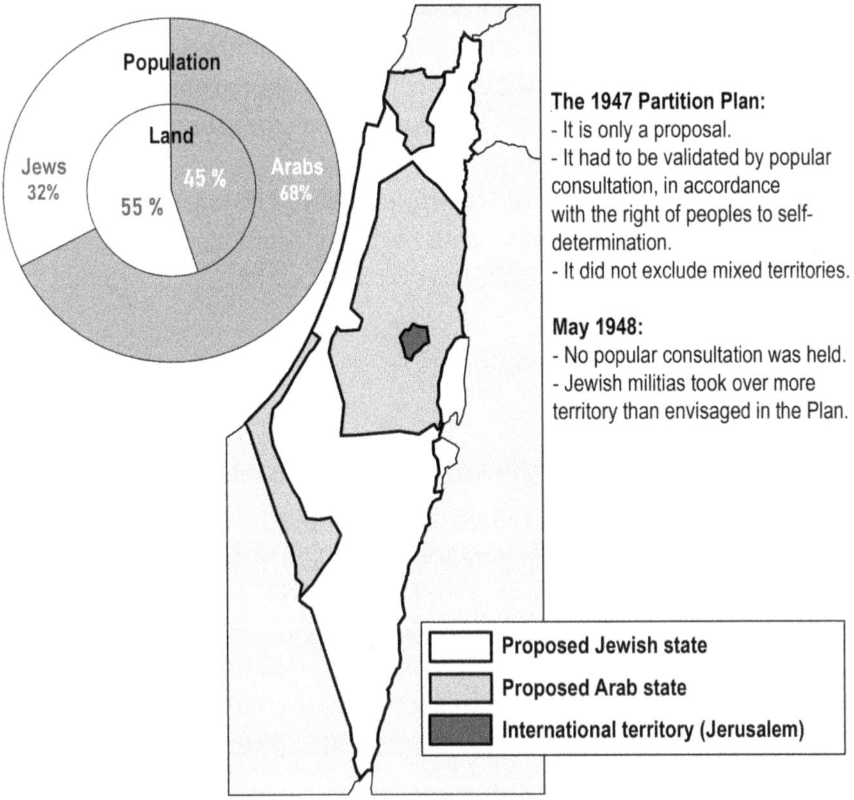

**Population**: Jews 32%, Arabs 68%
**Land**: 55% (Jews), 45% (Arabs)

**The 1947 Partition Plan:**
- It is only a proposal.
- It had to be validated by popular consultation, in accordance with the right of peoples to self-determination.
- It did not exclude mixed territories.

**May 1948:**
- No popular consultation was held.
- Jewish militias took over more territory than envisaged in the Plan.

Legend:
- Proposed Jewish state
- Proposed Arab state
- International territory (Jerusalem)

*Figure 3—Even before Resolution 181 came into force, Jewish militias had overstepped the proposed limits and driven out the Palestinian population. According to the Jewish Virtual Library, the Arab population fell from 1,324,000 in 1947 to 156,000 in 1948. The Jewish population then represented 32% of the population of Palestine, but was allocated 55% of the land. [Source: https://www.jewishvirtuallibrary.org/jewish-and-non-jewish-population-of-israel-palestine-1517-present]*

In the end, Resolution 181 was not even applied for a single day, since Israel had already annexed additional territories before independence. This triggered the 1948 war. Thus, the war actions that official history places *after* May 14, 1948, the day of Israel's declaration of independence, had begun long *before*, as confirmed by Miko Peled, son of Brigadier General Mattityahu Peled (one of Israel's pioneers in 1948).[45]

---

45. "Miko Peled Seattle. Oct. 1, 2012," *YouTube*, October 9, 2012 (www.youtube.com/watch?v=TOaxAckFCuQ)

While "181" provides a basis for Israel's existence, Zionists rarely refer to it, preferring to invoke biblical legitimacy. For example, the NGO *Concerned Women for America* published a leaflet entitled, *"Why Israel?,"* which never once mentioned the UN resolutions, but explained that *"this is an important issue for God."*[46] Perhaps because they themselves do not believe in a resolution they have never respected.

In short, while Resolution 181 clearly legitimized the right of the Jewish and Arab peoples to their own state in the land of Palestine, it did not justify the *way in* which this right was exercised, which is at the root of the Israeli-Palestinian conflict.

### Resolution 242

As the State of Israel has not defined its borders, the international community considers the 1949 armistice line to be the default. For this reason, reference is generally made to the borders of June 4, 1967. These are the borders that Hamas is prepared to recognize, as we shall see.

After the Six-Day War (June 1967), United Nations *Resolution 242* required Israel to withdraw from the territories it had conquered in a war of aggression: the West Bank, East Jerusalem and the Gaza Strip, which form the Occupied Palestinian Territories (OPT), and the Golan Heights. This resolution would enable the Palestinians to regain part of their land.

The problem is that the text of "242" is confusing. Its English translation imposes withdrawal *"from"* territories, a formulation which the British and Americans chose to counter the Soviet proposal to impose withdrawal *"from" the territories*. The latter, which corresponds to the interpretation then accepted by the members of the Security Council, had apparently been proposed on the instruction of Charles de Gaulle.[47]

---

46. https://concernedwomen.org/wp-content/uploads/2022/05/Concerned-Women-for-America-Why-Israel.pdf
47. Noam CHOMSKY, "The Israel-Arafat Agreement," *Z Magazine*, October, 1993 (http://www.chomsky.info/articles/199310--.htm)

### *Occupied Palestinian Territories (OPT)*

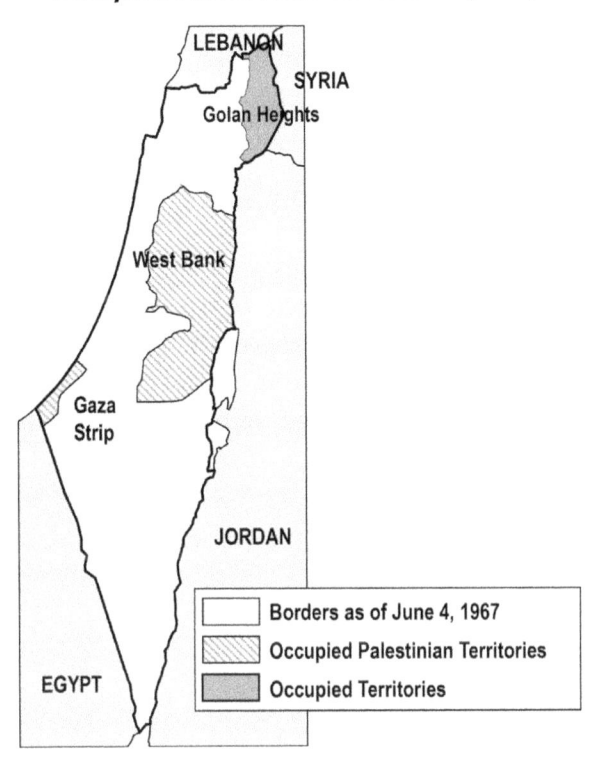

*Figure 4—The borders within which Israel exercises its sovereignty (solid line) do not conform to international law, as they include territories it occupies in violation of Article 2 of the United Nations Charter. The Occupied Palestinian Territories (OPT) are just one part of these. There are also territories in southern Lebanon that are too small to appear on this map. This is the reason for Hezbollah's persistence.*

The Israelis therefore prefer to invoke the English text (which allows them to determine for themselves what they want to leave), over the French text, which obliges them to leave *all the* occupied territories. This position gave rise to endless debate. However, at its meeting on November 16 1967, the Security Council adopted a final decision confirming that Israel must liberate *all* the occupied territories.[48] This discussion is specious, however, since "242" opens with the statement of a fundamental principle:

---

48. Document S/PV.1379, *Security Council*, November 16, 1967.

*The inadmissibility of acquiring territory through war.*

It is for these reasons that the Israelis today prefer to invoke the Bible rather than UN resolutions to justify their occupation of Palestinian land.

On November 27, 1967, at a press conference, General de Gaulle spoke of the events in Palestine with a prescience that our modern politicians seem to sorely lack:[49]

> *We know that France's voice was not heard, as Israel, having attacked, seized in six days of fighting the objectives it wanted to achieve. Now, in the territories it has taken, it is organizing the occupation that cannot go on without oppression, repression and expulsions, and a resistance to it that it in turn describes as terrorism.*

The whole history of Palestine in a few words.

## The Boundary Problem

In 2019, on the *RT France* channel, during a debate on anti-Semitism, journalist Martine Gozlan denounced the T-shirts worn by pro-Palestinian demonstrators in London, which showed a map of Palestine without Israel.[50] This may come as a shock, but she failed to mention that in Israel, a Knesset decision of October 14, 2007 bans the depiction of the "Green Line" (from 1949) as Israel's border in school textbooks.[51]

Under Ottoman rule, Christian, Muslim and Jewish communities coexisted peacefully in Palestine. As under the various caliphates, the Ottoman Empire had no real internal borders between communities. After its dissolution, the arrival of the West and its propensity to divide up territories on the basis of clear borders began to generate divisions in the Near and Middle East. The Balfour Declaration of 1917 promised

---

49. https://fresques.ina.fr/de-gaulle/fiche-media/Gaulle00139/conference-de-presse-du-27-novembre-1967.html
50. "Interdit d'Interdire—L'antisionisme est-il un antisémitisme comme un autre?," *RT France*, February 20, 2019.
51. "La Knesset bannit la ligne verte des écoles", *Le Figaro*, October 15, 2007.( https://www.lefigaro.fr/international/2007/01/02/01003-20070102ARTFIG90135-la_knesset_bannit_la_ligne_verte_des_ecoles.php)

to create a Jewish national home in Palestine by giving a territory over which the British had no authority, which they did not own and which was occupied by an Arab population.

As for the acquisition of land under the British mandate, this was largely carried out without regard to the law in force in these territories. The newcomers appropriated lands they considered "masterless," and confronted their rightful occupants.[52] At the root of the problem lay Muslim customary law, which defines land as the exclusive property of God. As is still the case today in many Muslim countries, one cannot own it; at most, one can pay a concession to the state (most often to the religious authorities responsible for administering the *Waqf*) for the benefit of social welfare.[53]

The declaration of independence of the State of Israel provides for[54]

> *the creation of a Jewish state in Eretz-Israel, to be known as the State of Israel.*

The State of Israel is therefore just one part of a larger space (*Eretz Israel*—generally translated as, *"Greater Israel"*). Israel is probably the only country in the world never to have defined its borders precisely. On May 12-14, 1948, just before the declaration of independence, Israel's provisional government debated the issue at length. But in the end, on Ben-Gurion's proposal, it decided by 5 votes to 4 not to define them, with the idea—already at this stage—of extending the borders defined by the United Nations.[55] This notion was interpreted by the countries of the region—rightly or wrongly—as a potential threat.

The 1949 armistice line—also known as the "Green Line"—is generally regarded as a "de facto" border—, but does not constitute an internationally recognized *de jure* border. Formally, the only internationally recognized borders of the State of Israel are those proposed by the United

---

52. Baptiste SELLIER, "L'usage du droit foncier par l'état d'Israël comme arme d'appropriation de l'espace Palestinien. What comparison with Colonial Algeria?," cnrs.fr (undated)
53. Haitam SULEIMAN & Robert HOME, "'God is an Absentee, Too': The Treatment of Waqf (Islamic Trust) Land in Israel/Palestine," *The Journal of Legal Pluralism and Unofficial Law*, n°41(59), January 2009, pp. 49-65 (DOI:10.1080/07329113.2009.10756629)
54. "Declaration of Establishment of State of Israel—14 May 1948," *Israel Ministry of Foreign Affairs* (mfa.gov.il)
55. Shelley KLEIMAN, *The State of Israel Declares Independence*, Israel Ministry of Foreign Affairs, April 27, 1999.

Nations General Assembly in November 1947. Israel maintained these borders until its offensive against the Arab countries in June 1967, which is why the date of June 4, 1967 is used as a reference today. Hamas's recognition of the 1967 borders is therefore a compromise that comes close to what the UN General Assembly advocated in 1947.[56]

## "Eretz Israel"

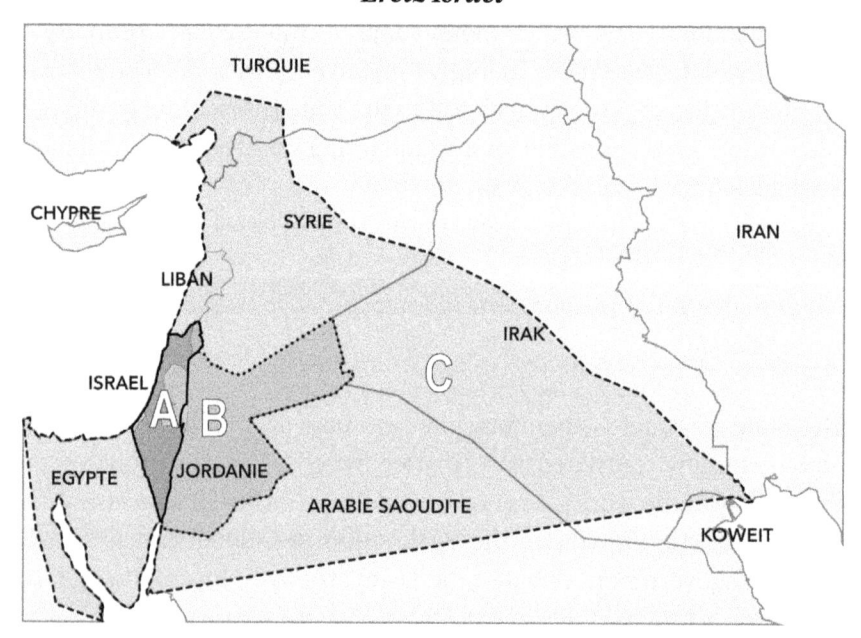

*Figure 5—"Greater Israel" is often evoked by Zionists. There are several definitions of what it could be. The minimum variant is present-day Israel (defined by the 1949 armistice line) plus the occupied territories (A). An intermediate variant, corresponding to what the revisionist Zionists wanted in the 1920s, which would include present-day Jordan (B). A maximum variant, which would include the territories on which Jews have lived according to biblical tradition (C), but which is only really mooted by certain ultra-Orthodox. Although this is probably just a dream for some, it explains why Israel is the only country in the world not to have defined its borders. It's also the reason why Palestinians are reluctant to recognize Israel, because under these conditions, recognition of Israel could ipso facto mean that Palestine no longer exists. Recognition of the Jewish state by the Palestinians can only be envisaged once Israel has defined its borders, as required by the UN.*

---

56. Barak RAVID, "Meshal Offers 10-year Truce for Palestinian State on '67 Borders," *Haaretz*, April 21, 2008 (https://www.haaretz.com/2008-04-21/ty-article/meshal-offers-10-year-truce-for-palestinian-state-on-67-borders/0000017f-db3d-d3ff-a7ff-fbbd77080000)

But Israel *never intended to* limit its ambitions to the borders proposed by Resolution 181, not even before its declaration of independence. The media pass over this problem in silence, even though it lies at the heart of the Palestinian question. Thus, the precondition for any discussion with Hamas is recognition of the State of Israel. But in the absence of a clear definition of its borders, such recognition is impossible: it could mean recognizing Israel's sovereignty over the occupied territories, and thus *ipso facto* losing the legitimacy to claim them. This is why the recognition of the existence of the State of Israel by Arafat's *Palestine Liberation Organization* (PLO) in 1993 was rejected by many Palestinian groups, who saw it as a veritable "blank check" for the Israeli occupier.

It is important to remember here that, although the Palestinians would probably have preferred Israel not to exist, they are not against its existence, as the Hamas charter testifies. What they do want, however, is for its territory to be clearly demarcated: legally, the Palestinian territories are occupied, but Israel rejects this terminology, as it would remove all legitimacy from the settlements and restrictions imposed in the West Bank and Gaza.

Our media and journalists do their utmost to promote an image of Hamas that rules out compromise. In 2006, the *Boston Review* reported on an interview with Dr. Mahmoud Ramahi, elected by Hamas to the Palestinian Legislative Council:[57]

> *We have made it clear that Israel is a state that exists and is recognized by many countries around the world. But the part that needs recognition is Palestine! The Israelis must recognize our right to have a state on all the territories occupied in 1967. After that, it should be easy to reach an agreement. They are asking us to recognize Israel without telling us what borders they are talking about! Let us discuss borders first, and then we will discuss recognition.*

In other words, Hamas is not prepared to give Israel a blank check over the whole of Palestine. Israel must first, in accordance with United Nations decisions, define the territory over which it declares its authority, and then it will be easy to recognize it. But it does not.

---

57. https://www.bostonreview.net/articles/helena-cobban-hamas-palestine/

## The Question of Jerusalem

Jerusalem takes its name from Salem, goddess of the Canaanites, ancestors of the... Palestinians. The epicenter of the world's three great monotheistic religions, it is considered a holy place by Israelites, Christians and Muslims.

Because of this complexity, Resolution 181 of 1947 provided for an international status for the city, which was then violently disputed by Jews and Arabs. In 1967, following the Six-Day War, Israel annexed Jerusalem, despite the injunctions of the United Nations (Resolution 267 [1969]).

Even today, the official position of the United Nations is that Jerusalem is Arab territory occupied by Israel.[58] This is why UNESCO decided in 2016 to maintain the Arabic names of the city's landmarks, triggering a storm, particularly in the ranks of the American far right.[59] Thus, the official name of the Temple Mount is Haram al-Sharif.

This is why Donald Trump's decision to recognize Jerusalem as Israel's capital and move the American embassy there is illegal under international law. In fact, the USA's foreign policy is not based on international law, but on *"rule-based international order,"* which it defines itself, such as recognizing Israel's right to annex the Golan Heights.

On December 14, 1981, the Knesset, the Israeli parliament, passed the "Golan Annexation Law." Three days later, in Resolution 497, the United Nations Security Council condemned this action, which violated Resolution 242 and international humanitarian law (IHL), and declared it *"null and void and without* international *legal effect."*[60] Yet this did not lead to any international protests or sanctions, and did not prevent Donald Trump from recognizing this annexation in 2019.[61]

Thus, we have players who do not respect international law, but who whine when others do.

---

58. https://www.un.org/unispal/wp-content/uploads/2016/07/The-Status-of-Jerusalem-English-199708.pdf; French: https://unispal.un.org/pdfs/97-24262f.pdf
59. "Resolution passed by UNESCO describes Temple Mount as Muslim site," *The Times of Israel*, October 13, 2016 (https://fr.timesofisrael.com/une-resolution-de-lunesco-decrit-le-mont-du-temple-comme-un-site-musulman/)
60. https://daccess-ods.un.org/access.nsf/Get?OpenAgent&DS=S/RES/497(1981)&Lang=F
61. Vanessa Romo, "Trump Formally Recognizes Israeli Sovereignty Over Golan Heights," *NPR*, March 25, 2019 (https://www.npr.org/2019/03/25/706588932/trump-formally-recognizes-israeli-sovereignty-over-golan-heights)

The situation was further aggravated by the project led by Jewish ultra-Orthodox[62] and fanatical American Christians[63] to rebuild Solomon's Temple on the Haram al-Sharif (Temple Mount), with the consequent destruction of Muslim holy sites.[64] The arrival in power of a far-right government backed by the ultra-Orthodox gave this project a boost.

Far from being anecdotal, this project was supported by the Israeli government and was the cause of numerous riots on the Esplanade of the Mosques in 2023[65] and is the root cause of the AL-AQSA FLOOD operation. It undermines a site that has been declared a World Heritage Site. Yet *France 24* only mentions it on its English pages, and not in French. More than Israel's response to Hamas's action, it is undoubtedly this project that is provoking Saudi Arabia's reluctance to put the so-called "Abraham Accords" into practice and renew lasting diplomatic relations with Israel.

## The Right to Return

Paradoxically, for a people who claim the right to return to a land they left voluntarily 2,000 years ago,[66] the Palestinians are forbidden to return to the land taken from them by force 75 years ago.

One of the problems is that the British, then the Israelis, have changed the rules of land acquisition, imposing laws that disregard the customary law under which the land was originally acquired. After forcibly evicting the inhabitants—some of whom still hold the keys to their homes—the Israelis gave them a deadline for reclaiming their property, without informing them. In a word, the Palestinians' land was stolen, and the theft was legally wrapped up.

Very early on, the United Nations became concerned about the fate of Palestinians who had been forcibly displaced and whose land had been stolen. Sent to Israel by the UN to find a solution to this issue, Count Folke

---

62. https://www.jewishvoice.org/read/article/update-building-third-temple
63. https://versebyverseministry.org/bible-answers/when-is-the-third-temple-built
64. https://thirdtemple.org/en/
65. "The Israelis set for new Jewish temple on Al-Aqsa site," *France 24*, June 5, 2023 (https://www.france24.com/en/live-news/20230605-the-israelis-set-for-new-jewish-temple-on-al-aqsa-site)
66. https://mondediplo.com/2008/09/07israel

Bernadotte was assassinated by an Israeli militia, one of whose leaders would go on to become Prime Minister of Israel.

In December 1948, the United Nations General Assembly, in its Resolution 194 (III):

> *11. Decides that refugees who so desire should be enabled to return to their homes as soon as possible and to live in peace with their neighbors, and that compensation should be paid for the property of those who decide not to return and for any property lost or damaged where, under the principles of international law or in equity, such loss or damage must be made good by the responsible Governments or authorities;*[67]

Note that it gives these tasks to the "*Governments or authorities responsible*," because the crimes were committed not only from 1948 onwards by the State of Israel, but also by the provisional authorities that ran the Jewish militias before its creation. Paragraph 11 is regularly recalled in all resolutions on this subject. The latest, at the time of writing, is December 7, 2023. In other words, for 75 years, Israel has refused to submit to the decisions of the United Nations.

## The Right to Resistance

The situation of the Palestinians has long been recognized. In December 1982, following the Israeli intervention in Lebanon to destroy the PLO, then headquartered in Beirut, in a move very similar to that seen in Gaza today, the United Nations General Assembly issued Resolution 37/43, which

> *Reaffirms the legitimacy of the struggle of peoples for their independence, territorial integrity and national unity, and for liberation from foreign colonial domination and foreign occupation by all available means, including armed struggle.*[68]

---

67. https://daccess-ods.un.org/access.nsf/Get?OpenAgent&DS=A/RES/194 (III)&Lang=F
68. https://digitallibrary.un.org/record/40572/files/A_RES_37_43-FR.pdf?ln=en

This principle is reaffirmed even more specifically in Resolution 45/130 of December 1990 on the *"Importance for the effective guarantee and observance of human rights of the universal realization of the right to self-determination and the speedy granting of independence to colonial countries and peoples,"* which states:

> *Recalling also the Geneva Declaration on Palestine and the Programme of Action for the Realization of Palestinian Rights, adopted by the International Conference on the Question of Palestine, Considering that the denial of the inalienable rights of the Palestinian people to self-determination, sovereignty, independence and return to Palestine, the brutal repression of the Intifada, the heroic uprising of the Palestinian population in the occupied territories, by Israeli forces, and Israel's repeated aggressions against the population of the region, pose a grave threat to international peace and security,*
> *Bearing in mind Security Council resolutions 605 (1987) of 22 December 1987, 607 (1988) of 5 January 1988 and 608 (1988) of 14 January 1988 and its own resolutions 43/21 of 3 November 1988, 43/177 of 15 December 1988 and 44/2 of 6 October 1989 concerning the deteriorating situation of the Palestinian people in the occupied territories,*
> *Deeply concerned and alarmed by the deplorable consequences of Israel's acts of aggression against Lebanon, its practices and continued occupation of parts of southern Lebanon, and its refusal to implement the relevant Security Council resolutions, in particular resolution 425 (1978) of March 19, 1978,*
> *1. Calls upon all States to implement fully and scrupulously all United Nations resolutions concerning the exercise of the right to self-determination and independence by peoples under colonial and alien domination;*
> *2. Reaffirms the legitimacy of the struggle of peoples to secure their independence, territorial integrity and national unity and to liberate themselves from colonial domination, apartheid and foreign occupation by all means at their disposal, including armed struggle;*[69]

---

69. https://documents-dds-ny.un.org/doc/RESOLUTION/GEN/NR0/567/77/IMG/NR056777.pdf?OpenElement

Palestinian resistance to Israeli occupation, including the use of force, is therefore legitimate. Of course, this legitimacy does not authorize everything, and certainly not terrorist acts against civilian populations.

The notion of "resistance" implies action against an occupying army. But in Palestine, things need to be nuanced: a great many exactions are carried out by settlers, who are armed civilians, who carry out their actions under the complacent eyes of the authorities; in the case of Gaza, the siege of the area makes it impossible for Gazans to resist in a "classic" way, since the military shoots at them from outside.

Terrorism is detestable and must be condemned. But it is up to each of us to put ourselves in the Palestinians' situation: what would we do in such a situation, where any negotiation process is out of the question, where the international community is uninterested in their fate, where Western politicians approve of the massacres they are suffering?

In the early 1990s, Jan Narveson, a specialist in anti-terrorism in the United States, noted:[70]

> *If the Israeli government simply allowed free trade on an equal basis with the Palestinians, would their inclination towards terrorism be as great?... Terrorism is probably wrong in all circumstances, but there are too many in which it may be understandable, perhaps even forgivable. We must do what we can to minimize "circumstances" of this kind.*

This is where an intelligent counter-terrorism strategy should come in. If Israel's real concern were to eliminate terrorism, it would have a strategy of encouraging economic and social development. But that is not the case, because that is not its aim. On the contrary, its aim is to make life impossible for the Palestinians, so that they leave their territories.

---

70. Jan NARVESON, "Terrorism and Morality," *Violence, Terrorism, and Justice*, Ed by R.G. Frey & Christopher W. Morris, Cambridge University Press, New York, 1991.

# 2. Israel's Occupation Policy

## The Situation in the Occupied Territories

Israel's presence in the occupied territories is governed by the Geneva Conventions, which define a framework for their governance and treatment of the population.

Firstly, an occupying power does not acquire sovereign rights over the occupied territory. It cannot, therefore, alter its status or intrinsic characteristics.

Secondly, occupation is a temporary situation. In this respect, the occupying power must maintain the *status quo ante* and must not adopt policies or measures which would introduce or bring about permanent changes, particularly in the social, economic and demographic fields. The aim is to maintain as normal a life as possible in the occupied territory and to administer the territory for the benefit of the local population.

Thirdly, the occupying power must permanently maintain a balance between its own security needs and the needs of the local population. Even if this balance is in favor of its own security needs, the law of occupation never allows it to completely ignore the needs of the local population.

Fourthly, the rules of the law of occupation do not permit the occupying power to exercise its authority to promote its own interests (other than its military interests), or to use the inhabitants, resources or other property of the territory it occupies for the benefit of its own territory or population.

Since 1947, Israel has occupied territories acquired by force, ethnically cleansing the Arab populations living in Palestine. Indeed, it was largely this population that came to form the population of the Gaza Strip. The

State of Israel that emerged from this first conflict in 1949 already had disputed borders, which today remain a *de facto* situation, but not a *de jure* one. Israel's attack on its neighbors in June 1967 was illegal under international law, and the resulting acquisition of territory is equally illegal under the United Nations Charter.

In August 2023, a report on the legality of the Israeli occupation of the Palestinian territories, produced for the United Nations,[71] provides a documented critique of the Israeli occupation. The dispersal of demonstrations using lethal weapons,[72] the designation of Palestinian human rights organizations as *"terrorist organizations,"*[73] mass arrests[74] and arbitrary detentions are regularly noted by the United Nations:

> *The systematic practice of administrative detention amounts to a war crime of deliberately depriving protected persons of the right to a fair and regular trial.*[75]

International law imposes obligations on the occupying powers of a country, but Israel does not respect them. It is Israel's failure to respect international law that is the cause of Palestinian resistance, and it is the accumulation of these repeated and unpunished violations that provokes terrorism.

A fundamental problem is that the West refuses to enforce international law. In 2015, a study commissioned by the European Parliament on compliance with IHL during the occupation of territories compared Crimea and the occupied territories in Palestine. It noted that Russia was immediately subject to sanctions, and recommended that these should

---

71. https://www.un.org/unispal/wp-content/uploads/2023/08/Study-on-the-Legality-of-the-Israeli-occupation-of-the-OPT-including-East-Jerusalem.pdf
72. "Report of the Independent International Commission of Inquiry on the Occupied Palestinian Territory, including East Jerusalem, and Israel," A/HRC/50/21, *United Nations*, May 9, 2022.
73. "UN experts Condemn Israeli Suppression of Palestinian Human Rights Organizations," *United Nations*, August 24, 2022. (https://www.ohchr.org/en/press-releases/2022/08/un-experts-condemn-israeli-suppression-palestinian-human-rights)
74. "Israeli Settlements in the Occupied Palestinian Territory, including East Jerusalem, and in the Occupied Syrian Golan Report of the United Nations High Commissioner for Human Rights," A/HRC/49/85, *United Nations Human Rights Council*, February 21, 2012 (https://documents-dds-ny.un.org/doc/UNDOC/GEN/G22/330/44/PDF/G2233044.pdf?OpenElement)
75. "Special Rapporteurs Demand Accountability for Death of Khader Adnan and Mass Arbitrary Detention of Palestinians," *United Nations*, May 3, 2023. (https://www.ohchr.org/en/press-releases/2023/05/israel-un-experts-demand-accountability-death-khader-adnan-and-mass)

also be applied to Israel, as part of a coherent policy.[76] But this was not be done. This difference in treatment fuels conspiracy theories and is one of the driving forces behind anti-Semitism in our country.

But security is not the only problem. In the occupied territories, access to water is a problem. The rules for digging wells and tapping water are different for settlers and Palestinians. In the West Bank, *Military Directive 158* of October 30, 1967 decreed that Palestinians could no longer dig wells without special authorization from Israel. By 1992, only 34 permits had been issued. In 1987, the *West Bank Data Base Project* forecast 137 m3 of water per Palestinian and 1,000 m3 per settler by 1990. At that time, Israel was exploiting around 85% of the groundwater for its own needs, thus depleting the Palestinians' own resources. As a result, Palestinian irrigation capacity dwindled, forcing Palestinians off their land, while Israeli settlements were able to fill their swimming pools.[77] In Gaza in 1984, Palestinians had an annual per capita consumption of 123 m3, while the Israeli occupiers had 2,326 m3, killing off Palestinian citrus farming.[78]

The situation has only deteriorated since the 1990s.

## The Question of the "Jewish State"

Israel does not have a Constitution, like the vast majority of states, but a set of fundamental laws that constitute a constitutional corpus. On July 19, 2018, the Knesset passed the Law *"Israel, Nation-State of the Jewish People,"* which defines the general principles that determine the governance and policy of the State of Israel.[79]

Until now, Israel has not defined itself as a "Jewish state," since almost 20% of its population is non-Jewish. Yet Benjamin Netanyahu has repeatedly declared[80] since 2001 that recognition of Israel as a "Jewish

---

76. *Occupation/annexation of territory: Respect for international humanitarian law and human rights and coherent EU policy in this area*, Directorate-General for External Policies—Thematic Department, European Parliament, June 2015 (https://www.europarl.europa.eu/thinktank/fr/document/EXPO_STU(2015)534995)
77. https://www.amnesty.org/en/latest/campaigns/2017/11/the-occupation-of-water/
78. Natasha BESCHORNER, "Water and Instability in the Middle East," Adelphi Paper 273, *International Institute for International Studies*, 1992.
79. https://www.jpost.com/Israel-News/Read-the-full-Jewish-Nation-State-Law-562923
80. Amos HAREL, Avi Issacharoff & Akiva Eldar, "Netanyahu Demands Palestinians Recognize 'Jewish State,'" *Haaretz*, August 16, 2009 (https://www.haaretz.com/2009-04-16/ty-article/netanyahu-demands-palestinians-recognize-jewish-state/0000017f-e368-d568-ad7f-f36b0d890000)

state"[81] was a prerequisite for any discussion with the Palestinians.[82] Paradoxically, as former SHABAK director Avi Dichter noted, Netanyahu was demanding that the Palestinians do what the Israelis themselves were not doing.[83]

Resolution 181 of 1947 already provided for the creation of a "Jewish state" and an "Arab state." Thus, this designation comes as no surprise. The problem is that the 2018 law has the effect of depriving the Palestinians of their rights. For Palestinians, who still want to return to the lands confiscated from them in 1947, Israel's exclusively Jewish character means they have no right of return. It even rules out the possibility of a single state for two peoples. This is why many Israeli intellectuals would have preferred Israel to be the "State of the Jews."[84]

The Palestinians therefore have two fundamental reasons to be cautious before recognizing Israel:

- By recognizing a State of Israel that has not defined its borders, they run the risk of losing all possibility of sovereignty over the territories considered occupied today.
- By recognizing Israel as a Jewish state, they close the door on the rights of Arabs living in Israel, and run the risk of abandoning a state for two nations.

This is also why Hamas refers to the "Zionist entity" in its charter and sometimes to the "Israeli entity" in its discourse. It is therefore false to claim that Hamas denies the existence of Israel: it refuses to recognize the sovereignty of a state that excludes from the outset any solution to the problems of borders and return. Conversely, Benjamin Netanyahu's reason for demanding recognition is that it would lock in the situation for the Palestinians.

As we can see, the Palestinians are very consistent and committed to international law. On these issues, the Israelis find it hard to compete, which is why they resort to religious discourse.

---

81. "Netanyahu: Recognition of Jewish state is key issue in peace talks," *The Times of Israel*, August 16, 2013. (https://www.timesofisrael.com/netanyahu-recognition-of-jewish-state-key-issue-in-peace-talks/)
82. Jodi RUDOREN, "Sticking Point in Peace Talks: Recognition of a Jewish State," *The New York Times*, January 1st, 2014 (https://www.nytimes.com/2014/01/02/world/middleeast/sticking-point-in-peace-talks-recognition-of-a-jewish-state.html)
83. David WAINER, "Is Israel the Jewish State? Not According to Its Own Laws," www.bloomberg.com, June 12, 2017.
84. Alexis VARENDE, "Un 'État juif' pour interdire un État palestinien," *Orient XXI*, March 4, 2014.

## The Question of "Apartheid"

In March 2017, a report commissioned by the United Nations concluded:

*Israel has set up an apartheid regime that dominates the Palestinian people as a whole.*[85]

Under pressure from the United States and Israel, the report was promptly removed from the website of the United Nations *Economic and Social Commission for Western Asia* (ESCWA), and its director resigned. In February 2022, *Amnesty International* published an explosive report on Israeli governance of the Occupied *Palestinian Territory (*OPT).[86] Its conclusions were confirmed in March by the report of an expert commissioned by the United Nations, who used the term "apartheid."[87]

The notion of apartheid is defined in the *"Apartheid Convention"* of November 30, 1973[88] and Israeli policy towards the Arab minority living on its territory corresponds to this definition (see appendix). In other words, Israel, which defines itself as a "Jewish state," grants different rights to its "citizens" depending on their ethnic and religious background. This is the same principle as Nazi Germany's so-called Nuremberg Laws of 1935.

That said, the word "apartheid," commonly translated as "separation" or "exclusion," originally referred to a policy adopted in South Africa that advocated the *"separate development"* (*"afsonderlike ontwikkeling"*) of the white, colored (*sic*) and black communities.[89] It was based on the premise that whites and blacks lived in different cultural contexts, and

---

85. *Israeli Practices towards the Palestinian People and the Question of Apartheid*, Palestine and the Israeli Occupation, Issue No. 1, Economic and Social Commission for Western Asia (ESCWA), 2017 (E/ESCWA/ECRI/2017/1) (https://opensiuc.lib.siu.edu/ps_pubs/9/)
86. "Israel's apartheid against the Palestinian population: a cruel system of domination and a crime against humanity," *Amnesty International*, February 1, 2022 (https://www.amnesty.org/fr/latest/news/2022/02/israels-apartheid-against-palestinians-a-cruel-system-of-domination-and-a-crime-against-humanity/) (https://www.amnesty.org/fr/wp-content/uploads/sites/9/2022/02/MDE1551412022ARABIC.pdf)
87. https://news.un.org/en/story/2022/03/1114702
88. https://treaties.un.org/doc/Publication/UNTS/Volume%201015/volume-1015-I-14861-French.pdf
89. There were three officially recognized communities: "Whites," "Coloreds" (of Asian or Indian origin) and "Blacks."

that their respective developments should therefore follow different rhythms. The reasoning is inherently racist, but it would be wrong to understand it through the prism of hatred. For, although there were many abuses, apartheid was driven more by a form of exacerbated paternalism, in the spirit of the colonialism of the late nineteenth and early twentieth centuries. With their Protestant tradition, South Africans felt responsible for the development of the black community. Despite discrimination and differentiated service provision for the various communities, the schools and hospital care available to the black population were far superior to those in neighboring countries. Moreover, illegal immigration *into* South Africa was massive, prompting the government to erect fences along the border with Mozambique and Zimbabwe, and to create autonomous zones ("Bantustan") to enable "self-management" of the black population. So, imperfect and racist though it was, there was the idea of a policy of development and assistance for the black population, which helped to shape the elites now at the helm of the country and probably contributed to a smooth transition to democracy in the early 1990s.

This qualification is refuted by Israel and has been the subject of numerous articles and discussions. Two situations need to be considered here:

- Israel's domestic situation, where citizens should be equal. In a democratic country, religion should not be a criterion for the enjoyment of rights. In Nazi Germany, the so-called "Nuremberg Laws" of 1935 assigned different rights to the inhabitants of the Reich, depending on their ethnic origin. In other words, rights were assigned according to who you were, not what you did. The 2018 *"Israel, Nation-State of the Jewish People"* law does exactly the same thing, giving Arabs living in Israel different rights from their Jewish fellow citizens. We are in a *de facto* apartheid situation.
- Occupied territories are distinct entities, one of which is occupied by the other. The relationship between occupier and occupied necessarily implies a difference in status. However, the occupier cannot "dispose" of the occupied as an exploitable resource. The Geneva Conventions are there precisely to provide a framework for occupation policy and prevent the occupier from abusing the situation. In other words, the laws and behaviors applied in the PTOs must also comply with international law. However, Israel tends to

regard the PTOs—particularly the West Bank—as an extension of its national soil, and settlements in the occupied territories are considered a *"national value."*[90]

The problem is that Israel treats the occupied territories as its own, taking water, resources and even applying the "Made in Israel" label to products from these territories, while continuing to apply a policy of occupation. Thus, if the term "apartheid" refers primarily to the policy applied on Israeli soil (domestic policy), it can probably also be applied to its policy in the OPT (occupying power).

In Palestine, the notion of *"separate development"* has never been invoked. Israel, as the occupying power, has never felt the need to help the Palestinians develop. Not even as part of a counter-terrorist strategy aimed at demobilizing Palestinian fighters. In the West Bank, construction and infrastructure improvements have been carried out almost exclusively for the benefit of settlers. In Gaza, when Israel withdrew in 2005, it even destroyed the infrastructure that would have enabled the territory's economic development.

In a democracy, it is the people, all the people, who are sovereign. But the Jewish nation-state law gives privileges, such as the right to self-determination, to Jewish citizens only, and not to Arab citizens. This is in response to Benjamin Netanyahu's statement.

We often hear that Israel is the only democracy in the Middle East. That was certainly the original intention. But it is just as certainly not the case today. Israel is not the country of all its citizens, but only of its Jewish citizens. Even if its institutions remind us of Western ones, the comparison tends to end there. Symptomatically, MP Zvika Fogel even declares:

> *First we'll destroy Hamas, then we'll deal with Hezbollah and, for dessert, we'll settle things at the Supreme Court. All in good time. Patience!*[91]

By placing Israel's Supreme Court on the same level as Hamas and Hezbollah, this MP shows us the value he places on his country's institutions!

---

90. https://www.timesofisrael.com/final-text-of-jewish-nation-state-bill-set-to-become-law/
91. "Far-right MK, ex-Shin Bet chief both panned for equating rivals to Israel's enemies," *The Times of Israel*, January 2, 2024 (https://www.timesofisrael.com/far-right-mk-ex-shin-bet-chief-both-panned-for-equating-rivals-to-israels-enemies/)

## Settlements in Occupied Palestinian Territories

The behavior of an occupying power in a territory is defined by the Fourth Geneva Convention, Section III. For example, it is forbidden to destroy, or make permanent alterations that affect the lives of people living in these territories.

The *"Israel, Nation-State of the Jewish People"* law defines Israel as a Jewish state, it changes the Arabic language from "official" to "special" status, and settlements in the occupied territories are considered a *"national value."*[92]

**Settlers in the West Bank**

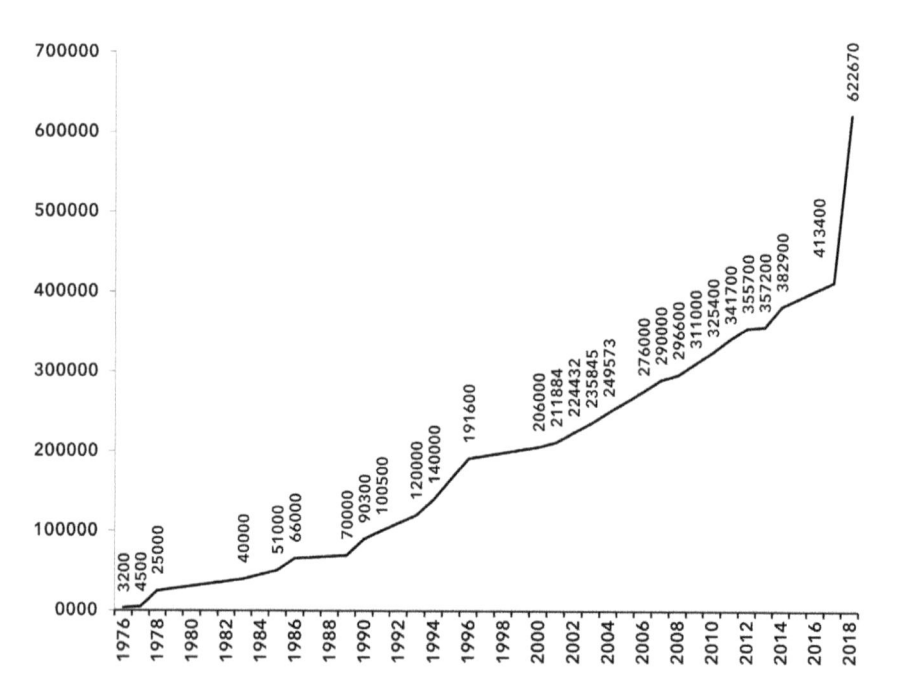

*Figure 6—Israel's settlement policy in the occupied territories contravenes several United Nations resolutions, notably 242 of 1967. Israel has adopted an aggressive settlement policy in response to Palestine's Arab majority. In forty years, the Jewish population of the West Bank has increased nearly 200-fold. [Source: B'Tselem, United Nations]*

The problem is that this constitution does not respect international law, as is repeated in virtually every United Nations resolution condemning

---

92. https://www.timesofisrael.com/final-text-of-jewish-nation-state-bill-set-to-become-law/

Israel (see appendix). In order to get around this difficulty, the Israeli government speaks of *"disputed territories,"* while the Supreme Court calls them *"belligerent possessions."* As is often the case with Israel, words are played with to avoid respecting principles. The fact is that, under international law, the Gaza Strip, the West Bank, East Jerusalem, the Golan Heights and a host of small territories along the Lebanese border (including the Shebaa Farms area) are "occupied territories."

Construction carried out in these territories under illegal jurisdictions is illegal. Thus, all settlements established by Israel in the occupied territories are illegal in the eyes of international law. But as part of its policy of occupation, Israel has defined those settlements which have authorization to set up ("legal" settlements) and those which do not ("illegal" settlements). There is thus a kind of double jurisdiction, rejecting both international law and Palestinian law.

## *The Impossibility of Developing a Palestinian Economy*

In addition to security and human rights issues, Israeli occupation contravenes the laws of war. A population under occupation has the right to engage in economic activity in order to meet its needs, such as agriculture or handicrafts. However, not only have changes to the terrain, such as the construction of separation walls in the West Bank and Gaza, considerably restricted the possibilities of cultivating the land (notably through the destruction of Palestinian irrigation networks), but this has led to the destruction of almost 100,000 olive trees for oil production.[93]

One of the problems of the Israeli occupation is that it has appropriated the work of the Palestinians, notably by considering their production as Israeli. For example, products from the occupied territories carry the same *"made in Israel"* label as goods produced in Israel.

According to the European Court of Justice,[94] consumers need to know clearly which products come from the State of Israel and which come from settlements in the occupied territories. These settlements are illegal under international law and constitute a presumed war crime under the Rome Statute. It is therefore justified that European consumers have precise information when they decide to buy products manufactured in

---

93. Azmi BISHARA, "The Wall: Its Implications And Dangers," *Al-Hayat*, (07.07.2003)
94. Judgment of the Court of Justice of November 12, 2019 in case C-363/18, *European Jewish Organization and Vignoble Psagot Ltd v Ministre de l'Économie et des Finances*, ECLI:EU:C:2019:954.

these areas.[95] The European Union is therefore requesting that products be labeled accordingly.[96]

This is the raison d'être of the "BDS" (*Boycott, Divestment and Sanctions*) movement, which calls for a boycott of Israeli products until the Hebrew state complies with international regulations. France is known for playing with international law, rather than applying it. For example, it condemns activists taking part in the BDS movement.[97]

The paradox is that the accumulation of these injustices, accompanied by confusing explanations, generates indignation. It is largely for this type of reason that France is the scene of more terrorist and anti-Semitic acts than other European countries. It is a deliberate choice.

---

95. https://www.europarl.europa.eu/doceo/document/E-9-2023-002978_EN.html
96. https://trade.ec.europa.eu/access-to-markets/en/news/new-code-y864-goods-imported-eu-preferential-origin-israel-16-may-2023
97. Ghislain Poissonnier & François Dubuisson, "Boycott des produits israéliens: la France persiste à y voir un délit en dépit de la décision de la CEDH," *actu-juridique.fr*, November 12, 2020 (https://www.actu-juridique.fr/administratif/libertes-publiques-ddh/boycott-des-produits-israeliens-la-france-persiste-a-y-voir-un-delit-contre-la-decision-de-la-cedh/)

# 3. The Fight Against Palestinian Resistance

## Israeli Intelligence

The basis of any strategy is understanding the problem. It is the role of intelligence to provide a reading of the security environment in order to *understand* the situation and thus facilitate decision-making. The Anglo-Americans use the word "*intelligence*," derived from the Latin verb "*intelligere*" *(to* understand), to designate intelligence activities.

The spectacular capture of Adolf Eichmann in 1960 gave the Israeli intelligence services their credentials. Indeed, their ability to track down and eliminate Palestinian terrorists around the world has been unrivalled. But that is not what intelligence is all about. It is even the least important part.

The primary role of intelligence is to provide relevant information for decision-making at political, strategic, operative and tactical (operational) levels. It is therefore an essential tool in the rule of law, where decisions are not discretionary but rational, based on the interests of the nation and not on particular interests. Its analytical product must constitute a reference, helping decision-makers to free themselves from misinformation, rumors and, therefore, external influences. That is why, to be relevant, intelligence must remain non-partisan and inform decision-making, while remaining free from political wrangling.

With the development of conflicts, whose asymmetrical logic we do not understand, and increasing bureaucratization, intelligence in all countries has been accompanied by an aversion to risk in terms of forecasting. The result, since the mid-1990s, has been two trends with perverse effects that affect all Western intelligence services: a shift towards police intelligence to the detriment of strategic intelligence, and the production of analyses that are more descriptive than predictive. The Israeli services are no exception to the rule. They failed to detect the preparations for the Egyptian offensive in October 1973; they failed to exploit Shiite support in Lebanon in 1982; and they seriously underestimated Hezbollah's defensive capabilities in 2006.

Our understanding of Israeli intelligence is often limited to a romanticized reading of Mossad's exploits. Mossad ("Institute") is the body responsible for strategic intelligence and clandestine actions. It is the equivalent of the CIA in the United States. Its director reports to the Prime Minister's Office. Its clandestine activities are not limited to assassinations (for which it is renowned), but also include *"second track diplomacy."* The advantage of a secret service is that it can approach "banned" interlocutors, such as movements considered to be terrorists, to reach an agreement. It was services such as the CIA and Mossad that paved the way for the Oslo agreement, and this is also why the CIA supported the establishment of the Palestinian Authority's security forces. In Warsaw, Mossad was negotiating the terms of a possible truce between Hamas and Israel, and a solution for the prisoners, with the USA, Qatar and the Central Intelligence Agency (CIA) at the end of 2023.[98] It was involved again in January 2024, in negotiations, in France, for a prisoner exchange.

That said, there were tensions within Israeli political leadership from the end of 2023 onwards. While Western countries *without exception* support Netanyahu's genocidal policy, the Israeli services seem to have a more nuanced approach to how to conduct the conflict. Mossad, for example, is probably the best equipped to obtain information on the fate of the hostages taken by Hamas. However, in December 2023, Benjamin Netanyahu forbade David Barnea, Director of Mossad, to have direct contact with Yoav Gallant, Minister of Defense, outside his presence.[99]

As is often the case, Western governments (notably the USA, Great Britain, Germany, Italy, France, Switzerland and Austria) systematically adopt the most extremist position of Israel's disputed far-right govern-

---

98. "CIA chief to meet Israeli, Qatari officials for hostage deal talks," *Reuters*, December 18, 2023 (https://www.reuters.com/world/cia-chief-meet-israeli-qatari-officials-monday-hostage-deal-talks-axios-2023-12-18/)
99. "PM said to bar Gallant from holding 1-on-1 discussions with Mossad head on hostages," *The Times of Israel*, December 26, 2023 (https://www.timesofisrael.com/pm-said-to-bar-gallant-from-holding-1-on-1-discussions-on-hostages-with-mossad-head/)

ment, while the Israeli intelligence services very often adopt a more moderate stance.

## The Israeli Intelligence Community

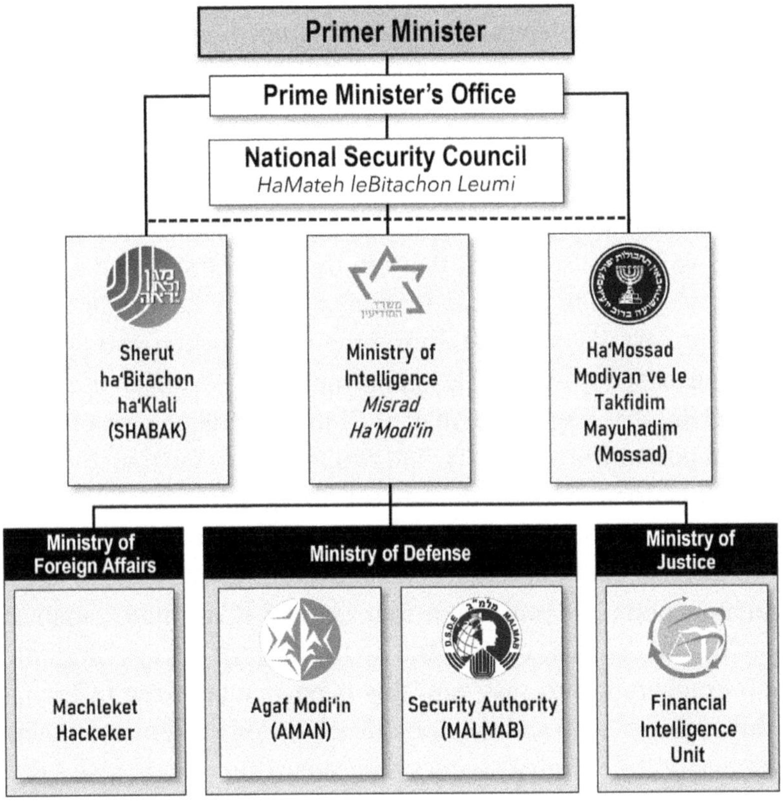

```
                    Primer Minister
                          |
                Prime Minister's Office
                          |
               National Security Council
                 HaMateh leBitachon Leumi
```

| Sherut ha'Bitachon ha'Klali (SHABAK) | Ministry of Intelligence *Misrad Ha'Modi'in* | Ha'Mossad Modiyan ve le Takfidim Mayuhadim (Mossad) |

| Ministry of Foreign Affairs | Ministry of Defense | Ministry of Justice |
|---|---|---|
| Machleket Hackeker | Agaf Modi'in (AMAN) / Security Authority (MALMAB) | Financial Intelligence Unit |

*Figure 7—Israeli intelligence has built up a solid reputation over the years. However, a more professional look requires a more critical eye. While the Israeli services have been excellent at tracking individuals around the world thanks to an incomparable network of "sayanim," the problem lies essentially in their analytical capabilities.*

Apart from Mossad, Israel's second "legendary" intelligence service is SHABAK, or Shin Beth or SBK. In fact, it is not an intelligence service, but a security service. It is the equivalent of France's *Direction Générale de la Sécurité Intérieure* (DGSI). It maintains networks of informers in Israel and the occupied territories. The division of tasks between Mossad and SHABAK with regard to the occupied territories is very pragmatic, depending on the case.

While Israel's approach to the Palestinian question relies exclusively on the use of violence, the analyses of Mossad and SHABAK, which we generally learn about belatedly, thanks to the confessions of their leaders, seem considerably more realistic and intelligent than what their political leaders or their intermediaries, such as Meyer Habib in France, feed us. We sometimes get the feeling that there is a total disconnect between the vision of the "services" and the political decision. In other words, discretionary power can lead to decisions that are inconsistent with official statements, as has been the case since October 2023.

That said, it is easy to criticize Israeli intelligence, which is on the ground and has considerable resources deployed around the Gaza Strip. However, we must also look at Western intelligence services, which are extremely weak when it comes to analyzing the situation in the Near and Middle East. We saw this during the crises in Iraq and Syria, and we see it again today with Gaza. For example, the American intelligence services claim that the basement of al-Chifa hospital housed the Hamas command post and arms depots.[100] In reality, it turns out that this was not the case. The problem here is that our services get their information from Israeli services. Thus, we have false information circulating on a loop.

As we can see, our knowledge of the movements we define as terrorist is extremely poor. The problem is that we tend to attribute capabilities to them not on the basis of facts, but on the basis of our own prejudices. It is no exaggeration to say—and this is particularly true in France—that the "experts" who show up on our television screens are the most dangerous for the country's security, because they tend to give a totally distorted image of the adversary just to have the "privilege" of being in the media. This is true of the vast majority of journalists, but also of so-called academic researchers.

---

100. Kevin LIPTAK, "White House says intelligence shows Hamas using al-Shifa hospital for command node, storing weapons," *CNN*, November 14, 2023 (https://edition.cnn.com/2023/11/14/politics/white-house-hamas-al-shifa/index.html)

## Israeli Military Intelligence

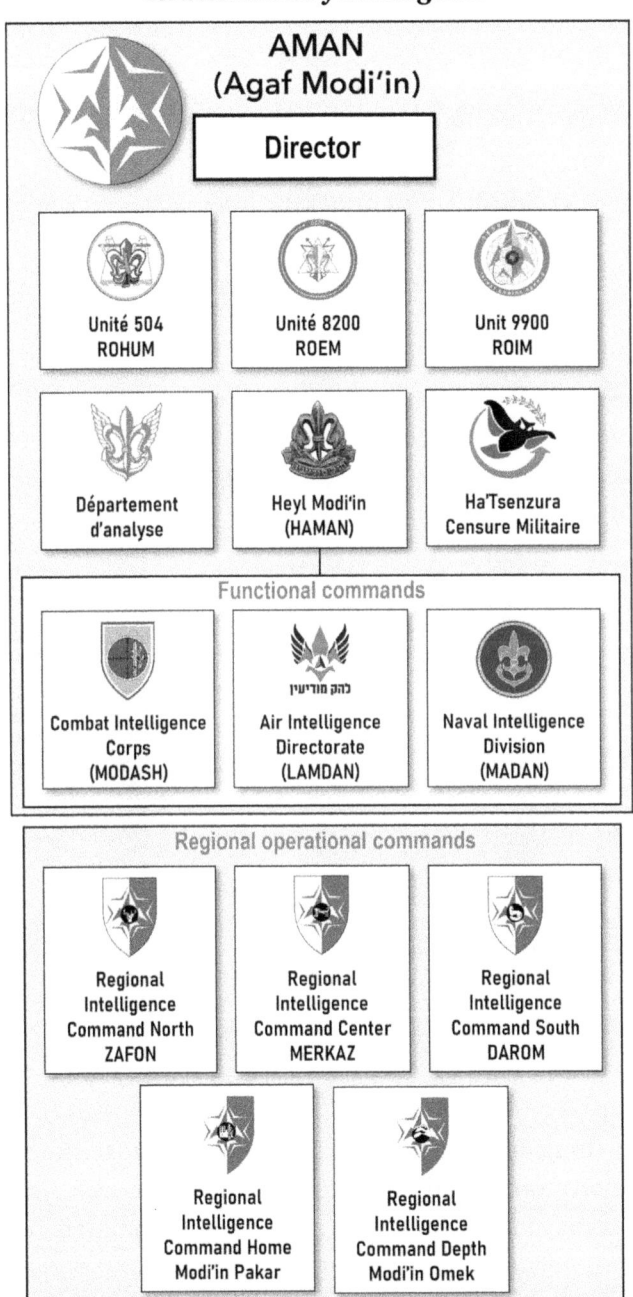

**AMAN (Agaf Modi'in)** — Director

- Unité 504 — ROHUM
- Unité 8200 — ROEM
- Unit 9900 — ROIM
- Département d'analyse
- Heyl Modi'in (HAMAN)
- Ha'Tsenzura Censure Militaire

**Functional commands**
- Combat Intelligence Corps (MODASH)
- Air Intelligence Directorate (LAMDAN)
- Naval Intelligence Division (MADAN)

**Regional operational commands**
- Regional Intelligence Command North — ZAFON
- Regional Intelligence Command Center — MERKAZ
- Regional Intelligence Command South — DAROM
- Regional Intelligence Command Home — Modi'in Pakar
- Regional Intelligence Command Depth — Modi'in Omek

*Figure 8—Israeli operational intelligence is closest to the ground. MODASH is responsible for information gathering. MADAN, which monitors the Mediterranean coast, and MERKAZ are the services most likely to detect Hamas preparations.*

3. The Fight Against Palestinian Resistance

## *Intelligence Support from Great Britain and the United States*

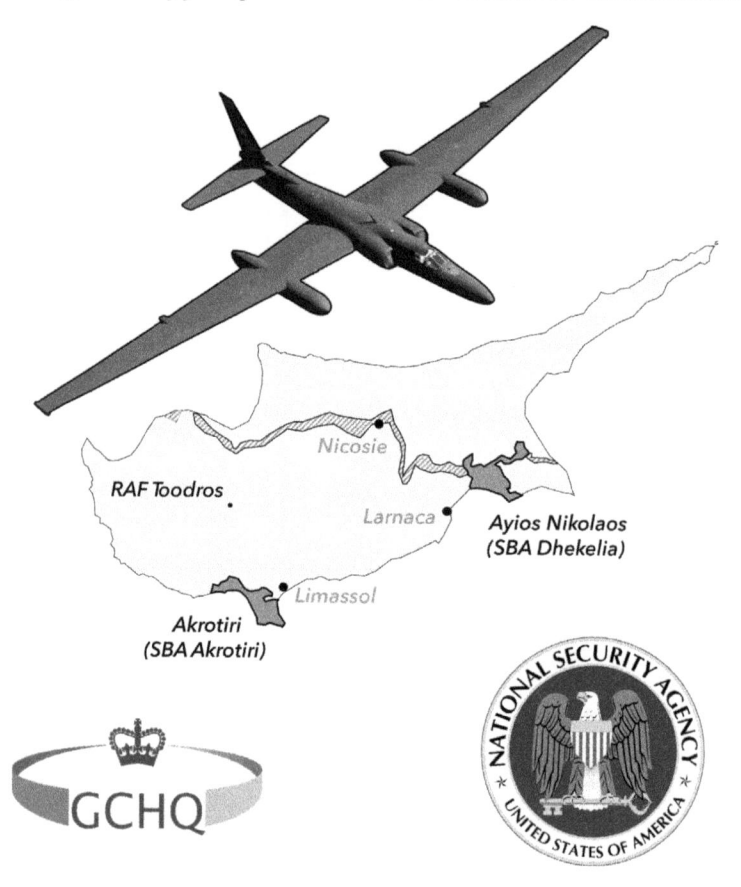

*Figure 9—During the crisis of the Palestinian operation, Israel received electronic and aerial intelligence support from CIA and Government Communication Headquarters (GCHQ) bases in Cyprus. These included electronic eavesdropping from the Toodros station, and electronic reconnaissance missions using American U-2 and British SHADOW R-1 aircraft from the Akrotiri and Ayios Nikolaos bases.*

The same thing happened with Ukraine: our governments relied on information from a single, non-independent source. This worked in Russia's favor, just as it is working in the Palestinian resistance's favor today.

## *Structural Weaknesses*

Highly effective at tracking down individuals, Israeli intelligence services have a very mixed record when it comes to assessing the threat. If the failure to detect the Egyptian attack in October 1973 and that of Hamas fifty years later are the most emblematic, the inability to assess the combative capabilities of Hezbollah in 2006, then those of Hamas after October 7, 2023, show profound analytical weaknesses. Like most Western services, the Israeli services believe that their failures could have been avoided with more information.

As a result, they have set up extensive and highly effective information-gathering systems. But this system is only effective at the tactical level—which is their preferred level of action against terrorism—but is not very effective in achieving strategic success. This explains the Israelis' repeated failures in their fight against the resistance.

One of the weaknesses of Israeli intelligence is the absence of a structure to harmonize the analyses of the various services. In the United States, this function is performed by the Director of National Intelligence (DNI), and in Great Britain by the Joint Intelligence Committee (JIC). In Israel, the Ministry of Intelligence created in 2009 was designed on the model of the American DNI. In reality, however, it operates more like France's Secrétariat Général de la Défense et de la Sécurité Nationale (SGDSN), which is part of the intelligence community, but is more a policy-making body than an intelligence body as such.

In Israel, the strategic analysis of the various departments is not really harmonized. This is an advantage insofar as it allows for diverse opinions. But it is often a disadvantage, as there are no synergies between departments and no consolidated reading of the situation at strategic level. It is a weakness that adds to the others as we shall see, and contributes to Israel's difficulty in gaining the upper hand in its Gaza operation.

It is also worth mentioning here that Palestinian counter-intelligence resources have been particularly developed in recent years. In the case of Gaza, it was probably the success of Palestinian counter-intelligence that led to the Israeli surprise on October 7, as we shall see. Conversely, one aspect of this development has been the establishment of Palestinian units capable of infiltrating the IDF.

In addition, the compartmentalization of Gaza has made Israeli intelligence work more complicated. The SHABAK, responsible for domestic intelligence, no longer has the same access to sources as in the West Bank. The hermetic sealing off of Gaza has *de facto* cut off services from Gazan society, where informers could be found.

## *Overestimation*

One weakness of Israeli intelligence is its highly overrated reputation. Certainly, the Israeli intelligence community has acquired a solid reputation worldwide, and some "experts" consider it to be the best in the world. While spectacular and successful operations to capture or eliminate war criminals and terrorists tend to lend credence to this reputation, it is highly overrated when it comes to strategic intelligence and anticipatory work.

Indeed, the performance of the Israeli services is mainly because of an excellent, tightly-knit network of informers *(sayanim)*, feeding them sources of information all over the world. Nearly six decades of conflict, war and counter-terrorism have given the Israelis unrivalled know-how in tactical and operational intelligence. Extra-judicial executions and special operations—such as the famous raid on Entebbe—are examples of their mastery of operational intelligence and its integration into tactical decision-making processes.

On the other hand, Israeli intelligence has proved mediocre—not to say bad—in its strategic analysis capabilities. Focused on threats that could directly affect Israel, Israeli intelligence lacks an overall vision. As in the United States, Great Britain, France and the vast majority of Western countries, the weakness of intelligence is analysis. In December 2003, the Knesset Committee for Foreign Affairs and Defense called for a commission of inquiry to examine the failings of Israeli intelligence prior to the war in Iraq.

According to Brigadier General Shlomo Brom, former Deputy Commander of the Planning Branch of the Israel Defense Forces, Israeli intelligence suffers from three main evils:[101] "*a dogmatic conception based on a one-dimensional image of the enemy,*" "*excessive anxiety*" and "*a lack of the necessary professionalism.*"

The greatest weakness of the Israeli services (like those of their Western counterparts) is their prejudiced approach. Convinced of their superio-

---

101. Brom SHLOMO, "The War in Iraq: An Intelligence Failure?," *Strategic Assessment*, Jaffee Center for Strategic Studies, Tel-Aviv University, Volume 6, No 3, November 2003.

rity, they have never been able to assess their adversary correctly. This partly explains why they are often forced to pick up a hammer to crush an ant. In October 1973, they were easily fooled by the misinformation of the Egyptian Operation BADR. Designed on the model of the Soviet *"maskirovka,"* this operation remains to this day a model of its kind, and arguably the best conceived and most sophisticated disinformation operation in history. Its complexity bears no comparison with the simplistic descriptions we hear from "experts" and other "journalists" about Russia. But it contains all the elements that enabled Hamas to keep its preparations off the radar of the Israeli services.

Influenced by the nature of the terrorist threat, Israeli services have become security services. A bit like at home. Worse still, they have adapted to "local" terrorism, as former Mossad director Efraim Halevy explains:[102]

> *We must remember that Israel has shown success in the fight against "local" terrorism. We must not forget that we have been present in the "territories," the main breeding ground for terrorism, for over 20 years... And yet, Israeli results on terror are debatable.*

In other words, the Israeli services fight against networks that evolve, but whose players remain relatively identical, unlike Islamist terrorism, whose networks appear and articulate themselves in unpredictable ways. Their results can be counted in body counts, but not in the reduction of terrorism. Operation AL-AQSA FLOOD demonstrates that Israeli strategy is based exclusively on firepower. There is no political strategy of appeasement, because the logic is confrontation. This can only end in the disappearance of the Arabs or the Israelis.

In the Israeli intelligence community, the Foreign Ministry's Political Research Department (MAMAD) is arguably the smallest of the Israeli services. Often in competition with the Ministry of Defense's AMAN, its analyses have generally proved to be of better quality. But its modest size does not give it a credible stature. When Ehud Barak was Foreign Minister, he preferred AMAN's analyses.

---

102. Efraim HALEVY, "In defence of the intelligence services," *The Economist*, July 31, 2004 (https://www.economist.com/by-invitation/2004/07/29/in-defence-of-the-intelligence-services)

## *Underestimating your Opponent*

The corollary of the previous weakness is the permanent underestimation of the Palestinians. This is a cultural phenomenon in Israel, which we find among some of our journalists, who feel they are superior to others and thus possess judgment that authorizes the obliteration of others.

Paradoxically, this state of mind goes a long way towards explaining the Palestinians' advantage. After the 9/11 attacks, attempts were made to explain terrorist acts in terms of mental disorders, and terrorists were portrayed as bloodthirsty psychopaths. In the early 2000s, I took part in a study on the psychology of Islamist terrorists as part of a NATO working group. We drew on the work of the Israelis, who had studied Palestinian Islamist fighters and the way in which suicide fighters (*shahids*) were recruited. This gives us a picture of the quality of Hamas at that time.

Unsurprisingly, we found that the "martyrs" were young. Around 67% of suicide bombers were aged between 17 and 23, with Hamas "martyrs" being older on average than those of Islamic Jihad. In Israel, the youngest Palestinian "martyr" was 16, but security forces have arrested volunteers as young as 13! On the other hand, their intellectual and educational level is high. In Israel, between September 2000 and June 2002, out of 149 "martyrs," 53 had a higher university education, 56 had a high school education and just 40 had only attended elementary school. This is partly because of the fact that Islamist movements, and Hamas in particular, recruited from al-Najah University in Nablus and the Islamic University of Gaza.[103]

In the early 2000s, Salah Shehada, then commander of the *Izz al-Din al-Qassam Brigades*, explained Hamas's recruitment policy:[104]

> *The choice is made according to four criteria: Firstly, diligent observance of religion. Secondly, we check that the young person obeys his parents' wishes, that he is loved by his family, and that his martyrdom will not affect the life of his family, i.e., that he is not the head of the family and that he has brothers and sisters—because we don't want to take on only children. Thirdly, his ability to carry out the mission and understand its gravity. Fourthly, his martyrdom*

---

103. Nachman TAL, "Suicide Attacks: Israel and Islamic Terrorism," *Strategic Assessment*, Volume 5, No.1, June 2002.
104. Salah SHEHADA, Commander of the Al-Qassam Brigades Interview on the Islam Online website, (May 29, 2002)

*must be able to encourage other martyrs and foster Jihad in people's hearts. We prefer unmarried people. It is the regional command of the Hamas military apparatus that proposes his candidacy and decides whether to accept him.*

Contrary to widespread opinion at the time, the future "martyrs" were not "brainwashed:" the abuses committed by the Israeli security forces provided a sufficiently strong motivation. Interrogations of young Palestinians arrested before committing their act showed that "suicide fighters" did not sacrifice themselves "for" religion, but that religion offered a cultural framework conducive to this mode of action. Motivations were most often linked to identity claims or a sense of national humiliation.[105]

Today, there is no indication that this picture has changed significantly. Israeli state propaganda aside, testimonies and videos tend to show competent, imaginative and disciplined fighters. A professional examination of the videos published by Hamas shows a skill at taking advantage of the mistakes and indiscipline of Israeli soldiers. Without going into detail here, we observe that Hamas fighters have been considerably better trained than the Israeli military. Their conduct is more intelligent, better constructed and better adapted to the context than that of their Israeli adversary, who appears overwhelmed by events in Gaza, as we shall see.

## Taqiya *and the Surprise of October 7, 2023*

The great surprise of the Hamas offensive was the inability of the Israeli services to detect its preparations, given that the border with Gaza is undoubtedly one of the most heavily guarded in the world, with ground radars and automatic firing installations.[106]

Thus how could Israel have been surprised? Our self-proclaimed "experts" have come up with every possible explanation—except the right one! In fact, that is exactly what our journalists and other military pseudo-experts have done during the Ukraine conflict: declaring Russia weak and incapable of waging war. There are several explanations.

---

105. NATO Research & Technology Organisation, "Report—Suicide Terrorism: The Strategic Threat and Countermeasures," NATO, August 2004.
106. Katrina MANSON, "Israel's Massive Failure Perplexes Ex-US Intelligence Officials," *Bloomberg*, October 10, 2023 (https://www.bloomberg.com/news/newsletters/2023-10-10/israel-s-massive-failure-perplexes-ex-us-intelligence-officials)

First of all, as they told *Reuters*,[107] the Palestinians have applied one of the fundamental principles of the art of war, enunciated by Sun Tzu over 2,500 years ago:

*When you're strong, look weak!*

In fact, they have largely contributed to this same strategy with Hamas. For example, Hamas did not retaliate against Israeli strikes after the Palestinian Islamic Jihad launched rockets in 2021-2022.

According to the *New York Times*, in 2022 the Israeli authorities received a 40-page document entitled "Walls of Jericho," which gave full details of Hamas' planning.[108] But the military did not believe it, and felt that Hamas did not have the capacity to implement it. Was this really Hamas planning, a simple assessment of its capabilities, or a "sky is falling" analysis? We do not know; but it seems that this document did not present concrete elements, but was a series of speculations.

According to press reports, Egyptian intelligence services had warned their Israeli counterparts of the imminence of *"something big"* that was due to hit Israel.[109] Added to this were the observations of military personnel stationed to monitor the Gaza Strip, who had warned their superiors of the possible risks.[110]

It has been suggested that Benjamin Netanyahu deliberately disregarded the warning in order to have a pretext for launching a decisive conflict that would enable him to retake the Gaza Strip. This is a possible scenario, but only a hypothesis at this stage.

What seems certain is that the information provided by Egypt (and others) was not "actionable." In intelligence jargon, we use the English

---

107. Samia NAKHOUL & Jonathan SAUL, "How Hamas duped Israel as it planned devastating attack," *Reuters*, October 10, 2023 (https://www.reuters.com/world/middle-east/how-israel-was-duped-hamas-planned-devastating-assault-2023-10-08/)
108. Ronen BERGMAN & Adam GOLDMAN, "Israel Knew Hamas's Attack Plan More Than a Year Ago," *The New York Times*, November 30, 2023 (updated December 2, 2023) (https://www.nytimes.com/2023/11/30/world/middleeast/israel-hamas-attack-intelligence.html)
109. "Egypt intelligence official says Israel ignored repeated warnings of 'something big," *The Times of Israel*, October 9, 2023 (https://www.timesofisrael.com/egypt-intelligence-official-says-israel-ignored-repeated-warnings-of-something-big/)
110. Shira SILKOFF, "Surveillance soldiers warned of Hamas activity on Gaza border for months before Oct. 7," *The Times of Israel*, October 26, 2023 (https://www.timesofisrael.com/surveillance-soldiers-warned-of-hamas-activity-on-gaza-border-for-months-before-oct-7/)

expression *"actionable intelligence"* to designate information that does not allow us to react concretely other than by seeking other information.

Playing on the Israelis' inordinate self-confidence, the Palestinians did not even need to disguise all their preparations. They even recreated a full-scale kibbutz in Gaza to train for urban combat. The thousand or so fighters who took part in the assault on October 7 were trained without knowing for what purpose. The way in which the Palestinians managed to "numb" Israeli surveillance is reminiscent of the Egyptian army's BADR operation in October 1973, described in my *Encyclopedia of Intelligence and Secret Services*.[111]

## Israel's Counter-Terrorism Strategy

The fight against an insurgency or resistance movement must begin long before it is in a position to use force. The inability to deal with violence before it emerges means that we are always one step behind. *A fortiori*, in a situation of occupation (as Israel has been since 1948, and even more so since 1967), an effective strategy had to be based on anticipation. The latter presupposes an understanding of the logic and mechanisms that generate and fuel terrorism.

However, the Israeli interpretation of the terrorist phenomenon is similar to that observed in France, and is based on a number of postulates that are accepted as fact.

*Postulate 1*: Terrorism as an inherent inevitability of the Muslim religion. In other words, as long as there are Arabs (and therefore Palestinians), there will be terrorism. This idea feeds into the concept of an Islamic project to conquer the world, imagined by Bat Ye'or (Gisèle Littman) in her book *Eurabia*,[112] which describes a Muslim plot to dominate the Western world and *"establish sharia law, the government of Allah over the whole of humanity."*[113] In fact, for Bat Ye'or it is more a question of a kind of revenge after the expulsion of her family from Egypt in 1956 in the wake of the "Lavon affair," which we will come back to later.

---

111. Jacques Baud, *Encyclopédie du Renseignement et des Services Secrets*, Lavauzelle, Panazol, 2002 (Article Maskirovka)
112. Bat Ye'or, *Eurabia*, éditions Jean-Cyrille Godefroy, Paris, 2006.
113. "Bat Ye'or interview on jihad," *Dreuz Info*, November 15, 2020.

However, this idea has inspired other works, such as *Conquest of the West* by Swiss journalist Sylvain Besson,[114] which, according to researchers at Sweden's Uppsala University, influenced Norwegian right-wing extremist Anders Behring Breivik[115] (perpetrator of the Utoya massacre on July 22, 2011), and this scenario is taken up by all the major far-right movements in Europe.[116] It dominates Israeli and Western thinking on the issue of Islamist terrorism.

In France, this idea has become very popular. In January 2018, in a documentary, made by Conspiracy Watch, entitled *Complotisme, les alibis de la terreur*[117] and broadcast on *France 3*, philosopher Jacob Rogozinski asserts:

> *Jihadism is also a movement that aims for sovereignty, for global power. There's a dream behind it, a crazy dream no doubt, but a dream of creating a caliphate, which would be a global caliphate, which will take over Rome, which will take over Europe, which will defeat America, which will establish a global network of true believers, united behind absolute sovereign power.*[118]

This type of conspiracy theory in the truest sense of the word spread rapidly after the 2015 attacks in France. Its "advantage" is to place Muslims in the position of eternal enemy, since terrorism is part of a global project. The Koran is presented as a war manual, as freelancer Antoine Hasday states.[119] It is the equivalent of the "global Jewish conspiracy" propagated by certain far-right movements. This type of theory targeting Muslims supports Israel's approach to fighting terrorism and systematically eradicating populations. This is why our media maintain the image of Hamas as an extension of the Islamic State, whose project is religious in nature, with the aim of destroying Israel. We add the equation

---

114. Sylvain BESSON, *La Conquête de L'Occident. Le Projet secret des islamistes*, éditions du Seuil, Paris, October 7, 2005.
115. Mattias GARDELL, "Crusader Dreams: Oslo 22/7, Islamophobia, and the Quest for a Monocultural Europe," *Terrorism and Political Violence*, 26:129-155, 2014.
116. Raphaël LIOGIER, "Le mythe de l'invasion arabo-musulmane," *Le Monde diplomatique*, May 2014, p. 8-9.
117. Rudy REICHSTADT & Georges BENAYOUN, *Complotisme, les alibis de la terreur*, YouTube, January 24, 2018, www.youtube.com/watch?v=d8e18NIqWiI
118. Jacob ROGOZINSKI in *Complotisme, les alibis de la terreur*, YouTube, January 24, 2018, (www.youtube.com/watch?v=d8e18NIqWiI), (31'20").
119. Antoine HASDAY, "La pensée djihadiste décryptée," *slate.fr*, November 6, 2017.

"Islam = Islamism" to assert that, since terrorism is inherent to Islam, to get rid of terrorism we need to eliminate Muslims.

The idea of genocide of the Palestinians is therefore not far off.

*Postulate 2*: The Israeli-Palestinian conflict is religious in nature and has nothing to do with territorial claims. This reformulation of the conflict has the advantage (for Israel) of ruling out any discussion or negotiation from the outset. This is why, from the early 2000s, Israel has sought to associate Palestinian terrorism with al-Qaeda terrorism. By decoupling the Palestinian question from the territorial problem and placing it in the perspective of a "global jihad,"[120] Israel went from actor to victim, thus justifying the impossibility of a counter-insurgency strategy.

Yet since 1947, Palestinians of all persuasions have consistently declared that their aim is to reclaim their land. The aim of the Palestinian resistance is to enforce United Nations resolutions in order to recover the territories unduly conquered since 1947 and which Israel must return.

*Postulate 3*: The land of Israel belongs to the Jewish people. By referring to the Bible (or Torah) and declaring that Palestine was given to it by God (or Yahweh), rather than invoking UN Resolution 181 (which it has never respected), Israel places God's law above that of men. This is exactly what we criticize the Salafists for. This logic is accentuated by theocratic governance, which legitimizes its actions in Palestine through religion. Benjamin Netanyahu is a representative of "religious Zionism," a form of Zionism based on the religious tradition,[121] which justifies the destruction of the Palestinians by comparing them to the biblical tribe of "Amalek." The war against Gaza thus becomes a kind of holy war.[122] We are thus faced with a type of governance similar to that of the Islamic State.

Benjamin Netanyahu explains the Israeli-Palestinian conflict as a "*struggle between the sons of light and the sons of darkness, between humanity and the law of the jungle.*"[123] This is not simply a personal view, but the expression of an official reading of the conflict, which he presented

---

120. https://www.inss.org.il/wp-content/uploads/sites/2/systemfiles/(FILE)1298359986.pdf
121. "Netanyahu: what is religious Zionism?," *BBC News*, November 8, 2022 (https://www.bbc.com/afrique/monde-63534134)
122. Joshua Krug, "Comparing Hamas to Amalek, our biblical nemesis, will ultimately hurt Israel," *The Jewish News of Northern California*, November 2, 2023 (https://jweekly.com/2023/11/02/comparing-hamas-to-amalek-our-biblical-nemesis-will-ultimately-hurt-israel/)
123. Sonam Sheth, "Netanyahu deleted a post on X about a struggle against 'children of darkness' around the time of a tragic hospital explosion in Gaza," *Business Insider*, October 17, 2023 (https://www.businessinsider.com/netanyahu-deleted-children-of-darkness-post-gaza-hospital-attack-2023-10?r=US&IR=T)

to the Knesset.[124] In official Israeli discourse, references to the Bible are superimposed on legal arguments. We therefore have a paradoxical situation where a state declaring itself to be Western, but legitimizing its actions on the basis of religion, and an organization (Hamas) declaring itself to be inspired by religion, but legitimizing its actions on the basis of international law.

*Postulate 4*: As a consequence of the previous postulates, Israel defends itself. At no point is there any mention of the possibility that Israeli policy generates indignation, anger and injustice which, in the absence of a mechanism for dialogue, takes the form of armed resistance, which may use the methods of terrorism.

The consequence of this reading is that we see terrorism as a fatality, whose occurrence is not because of our actions, but to what we are. In fact, this is what Manuel Valls, then Prime Minister, declared to the National Assembly on November 19, 2015, in order to mask his government's responsibility for the genesis of the terrorist acts that affected France:

> *Make no mistake: a totalitarianism has struck France not for what it does, but for what it is.*[125]

Israel has exactly the same position. In reality, there is no fatality. Islamist terrorism is *always* a response to violent action, and is almost always the result of an unfortunate decision taken at home. If, at the end of the day, the terrorist is the one who commits the crime, then our governments, ministries and parliamentarians are all responsible for creating the right conditions for this threat to emerge.

This is what the world is discovering about Israel, and this is what is imposing a strategic defeat on it, even if, in the end, the Palestinian population will be the victim.

### *Failure to Develop Holistic Thinking*

Our journalists' comments on Israel's action in Gaza tend to suggest that terrorism can only be fought by strikes. Media outlets such as *CNews*, *BFMTV*, *LCI* in France, *RTS* in Switzerland and other far-right

---

124. https://www.gov.il/en/departments/news/excerpt-from-pm-netanyahu-s-remarks-at-the-opening-of-the-knesset-s-winter-assembly-16-oct-2023
125. "Speech to the National Assembly—Manuel Valls: "A risk of chemical or bacteriological weapons"," www.parismatch.com, November 19, 2015.

American media never mention other ways of resolving an insurrectionary situation.

With Yasser Arafat officially abandoning the use of terrorism, the Palestinians are seeking to embark on a more political path. But their efforts went unrewarded. Thus was born the first Intifada, essentially a movement of civil disobedience, which claimed the lives of 16 civilians and 11 soldiers on the Israeli side, and 1,100 Palestinians, according to Israeli sources.[126]

This incredible disproportion stems from the strategy adopted by the Israelis: deterrence. The idea is to strike brutally in order to terrorize the population and dissuade them from taking part in the riots. While perhaps effective in Europe, such an approach is totally at odds with a counter-terrorist strategy in the Middle East.

On the face of it, firmness seems to be an effective tool against insurrectionary violence: if nothing else, it reduces the number of troublemakers—initially. But this is a simplistic calculation that can only work when the targeted group is small and does not enjoy significant popular support. In Palestine, the situation is very different, and resonates with cultural elements, such as the notion of jihad, which we shall examine later. As a result, Israel's strategy has amplified the problem rather than calming it down. With their Western culture, the Israelis have created the conditions for the emergence of jihadist terrorism. This is what happened with the emergence of Hamas in 1987.

In a system where disobedience is punishable by death, an Islamist-inspired doctrine associated disobedience with victory. This was one of the reasons for the emergence of Hamas at that time.

Since the early 2000s, it has been difficult to discern a coherent strategy for combating Palestinian resistance to occupation. On the one hand, the expansion of settlements increased tensions and the determination of Palestinians to take back by force what had been taken from them by violence. On the other, we are multiplying strikes that hit the civilian population hard, without really affecting the conduct of resistance movements.

While counter-insurgency strategies seek to play with "the carrot and the stick," the Israelis use only the stick. It seems that Israel is unable to break out of a single pattern to overcome Palestinian resistance, which is

---

126. https://www.jewishvirtuallibrary.org/first-intifada

gaining strength not only in terms of operational capabilities, but also in terms of political support.

Drawing on Mao Zedong's famous expression that the guerrilla must *"be in the civilian population like a fish in water,"* we can outline some possible strategies for fighting resistance.

### *Possible Counter-Insurgency Strategies*

| Strategy | Description | Applicability in Palestine |
|---|---|---|
| **Fishing for fish** | This is essentially how the West and Israel are trying to combat terrorism. It is simply a matter of destroying the terrorist structure. It is the most satisfying for vengeful minds, but it is the least effective in the long term, because it does not address the problem holistically. It requires a remarkable knowledge of the "fish" and their behavior. Its effectiveness is all the greater when the terrorist group or movement does not enjoy strong popular support. *This is how Action Directe* in France, the *Cellules Communistes Combattantes* in Belgium and the *Rote Armee Fraktion* in Germany were neutralized. | This is the strategy the Israelis have been trying to apply in Gaza since October 7, 2023 to eliminate Hamas. But to work, such a strategy must rely on the use of special forces and agents infiltrated into insurgent structures. Israel has none. As in all Western countries, its "special forces" have become "commando" forces used as intervention forces. Many Hamas fighters will be eliminated, but the movement will not be eradicated, because its popular support is too strong. |
| **Remove water** | The idea is to separate the rebels from the population in which they operate. It is a highly effective strategy when the resistance movement lacks broad popular support or divides public opinion. The British were very successful with this strategy in the 1960s-1970s. There are several ways to achieve this result: - Physically separate the rebels from the population. This is what the British did in Malaya, with the "New Villages" strategy. - "Charm" civilian populations so that they no longer see any point in supporting the resistance. These are the "hearts & minds" operations, tools of the war of influence, which aim to win the hearts of populations. | The real problem is that the Israelis are not fighting terrorists, but Palestinians. That is why the Israeli variant of this strategy is to carry out ethnic cleansing and force the entire population out of Gaza. In fact, this is the aim of the settlements in the West Bank and East Jerusalem. |

| | | |
|---|---|---|
| **Feed the fish enough so that it loses its aggressiveness** | The aim is to ensure that certain requirements are met, in order to remove the desire—and legitimacy—to fight. This method has been very effective in some Latin American countries, such as Venezuela in the 1970s, but requires excellent knowledge of the opponent. It must necessarily be integrated into a negotiation process, which is often enough on its own to put an end to violence. | It could have been used in Gaza, after Hamas's electoral victory in 2006. Israel's (and the international community's) rejection of the election results proved that Hamas had the right strategy. Israel thus helped boost its popularity. The problem is that, contrary to popular opinion, the Israelis know very little about their opponents. |
| **Add another fish** | The aim is to introduce a competing rebel movement that neutralizes the existing one. This new player thus becomes a state auxiliary. There are two operating variants: 1. The new group does the government's work and is supplied by it. 2. The rivalry between the two groups and the difference in treatment withdraws popular support from the first group and thus pushes it towards a political solution. It implies that the government must keep control of the situation, otherwise it can generate new problems just as big as the initial one. | This is what the Israelis tried to do, first by encouraging the emergence of Hamas. Then, in a second phase, by trying to take away its electoral victory in 2006, in order to encourage rivalry with Fatah. But Israel totally lost control of the situation. This strategy might have worked had it been able to demonstrate that Fatah's path was politically successful and more promising. But by closing the door to both rivals at the same time, Israel merely demonstrated that the Hamas path was the only possible one. |
| **Remove water and fish** | In essence, this is the strategy often evoked by Israel—in part already applied with the mass deportations of 1948—to find a solution to Palestinian terrorism, by seeking to drive the entire Palestinian population out of the occupied territories. In international law, this is known as "ethnic cleansing." | In a way, this strategy is already being implemented by the slow nibbling away of the occupied territories by settlements and the security fence, the construction of which was initiated in 2002. |

In the West, the only countries to have faced a situation approaching that of Israel in Palestine are Great Britain (in Northern Ireland), Italy (during the "lead years") and Spain (in the Basque country). Yet these countries have managed to control terrorism without destroying entire cities or massacring civilians and children by the thousands. Thus it is perfectly possible, if one wants.

The main weakness of Israel's approach to counter-terrorism is that it is based on the principle of revenge, not anticipation and prevention. In short, it is a responsive (anti-terrorist) strategy, not a pro-active (counter-terrorist) one, which eliminates terrorists, but not terrorism.

Worse: when we kill innocents instead of terrorists, or along with terrorists, we generate terrorism. As I demonstrated in my book on asymmetrical warfare,[127] Israel daily creates the threat it is fighting against.

This leads us to a number of key observations that shed light on the situation at the end of 2023:

- The reason why Britain, Italy and Spain have kept terrorism under control is that these countries realized that at some point they would have to live with the populations that supported terrorism. In Israel, this perspective simply does not exist: it considers that it will never share the land of Palestine with the Palestinians. This explains its approach based solely on the use of violence.
- For the Palestinians, the logical consequence of this realization is that the State of Israel must disappear. For years, Hamas spoke of its destruction, but since 2017, it no longer does so and envisages another form of state, which does not exclude collaboration with the Israelis.
- Not only is Israel the only country in the world unable to rid itself of terrorism in over 75 years, but its policies have steadily increased hostility towards it in Palestine and abroad.
- Israel seems incapable of conceiving of the fight against terrorism other than through the use of violence, and has a cultural inability to change its approach when the former does not work.
- Mostly foreign to the Middle East, Israelis have failed to understand the cultural mechanisms that govern the conflicts and terrorism that affect them.
- Contrary to official rhetoric, the Israeli objective is not to eliminate terrorism, but to have no more "competitors" on the land of Palestine. In other words, it is fighting the Palestinian population under the guise of fighting terrorism.

## The Strategy of Deterrence

Until the early 1950s, Israel sought to control Palestinian terrorism in the same way as civilized countries: by using police force.

The doctrines of the Palestinian movements were inspired by Marxism. Terrorism is seen as a stage in a revolutionary process and a means of gaining the support of the popular masses in a bid for success. This is the

---

127. Jacques BAUD, *La Guerre asymétrique ou la Défaite du vainqueur*, Éditions du Rocher, 2003.

same process seen in Northern Ireland and the Basque Country, where independence/separatist movements also saw themselves as being under occupation.

In Palestine, the aim was to create a situation that would have prompted Arab countries to intervene, as in 1948. The Israelis then understood that they were embarking on a recursive process that could lead to the end of the state. There were therefore at least two possible courses of action: to accommodate the Palestinians' legitimate demands, implement the UN resolutions and integrate them into a single state where the two communities would live in harmony—or to engage in confrontation.

But we were in the middle of the Cold War, and negotiating with Moscow-backed movements at a time when Tel Aviv was trying to ingratiate itself with Washington was not really on the agenda. In 1955, Lieutenant-Colonel Moshe Dayan sketched out a strategy that is still applied today:

> *We can't protect every water pipe from bursting and every tree from being uprooted. We cannot prevent the murder of a worker in an orchard or a family in bed. But it is within our power to set a high price for our blood, a price too high for the Arab community, the Arab army or the Arab government to consider worth paying.*[128]

The idea is to punish every action of the resistance disproportionately, in order to deter them. The problem is that there comes a point where the punishment is so severe that it legitimizes the terrorist action, and the military strategy becomes a kind of mafia vendetta. We then enter a cycle of violence that never stops.

Up until the early 2000s, Israel fought the Resistance largely by means of special forces and infiltrators, enabling relatively targeted actions against Resistance cadres. This is still a deterrent dynamic, but one that remains within certain limits, even if the collateral damage is enormous, without eliciting any reaction from the Israeli population in whose name these crimes are committed.

The situation changed with the *"War on Terror"* unleashed by George W. Bush in the wake of 9/11. It seems that the fight against terrorism allows for all kinds of excesses. The Israelis did everything in their

---

128. https://politikon.iapss.org/index.php/politikon/article/download/127/126/258

power to associate Palestinian resistance with global jihadism, so as to legitimize disproportionate action based on the American model. Their strategy was to isolate the Palestinians by building security walls and fences in the West Bank (from 2002), then in Gaza (from 2006), and to combat "terrorism" with air strikes.

The word "terrorism" is placed here in quotation marks for two reasons. The first is that the Palestinians understood at this time that the terrorist method tended to do them a disservice internationally, because of the association with "al-Qaeda," and there was a shift in Palestinian strategy towards more political action. The second is that, just like the occupying forces of the Third Reich in Europe, the resistance is invariably described as "terrorist," even when no terrorist strategy is employed.

These strikes, based on the American model, cause a disproportionate number of collateral casualties. They have several distinctive counter-insurgency features:

- Because they are practiced at a distance, they are perceived as cowardly and a refusal to fight "man to man."
- Because of their inability to target isolated individuals clearly identified as the enemy, they kill many civilians, accentuating the will to resist the occupation.
- They force resistance fighters to fight from a distance too, and to respond with means that will also create collateral damage. In Palestine, the Israeli strategy led the various movements to use rockets in *response to* air strikes.

In short, fighting terrorism from a distance using only air strikes, as Israel does, is without doubt the least effective of all possible strategies. The only reason to use such an ineffective strategy is if it has a genocidal, ethnic cleansing objective.

On a more tactical level, this kind of dissuasive strategy tends not to be effective in an Islamic environment, as we have seen above. The difficulty for Israel is that, despite its thousand-year-old claim to belong to this land, it does not have the cultural keys to understand this environment. The Israeli population is predominantly of Western and European culture, which is not capable of understanding the complexity of the Middle East.

## Doctrinal Apparatus Ill-Suited to an Asymmetrical Conflict

### The BETHLEHEM Doctrine

This doctrine was developed by Daniel Bethlehem,[129] legal advisor to Benjamin Netanyahu and then to British Prime Minister Tony Blair. It postulates that states are entitled to *preventive self-defense* against an "imminent" attack. The difficulty here is to determine the "imminent" nature of an attack, which implies that the terrorist action is close in time and that there is a body of evidence to confirm it.

In February 2013, *NBC News* released a Department of Justice "White Paper" defining "imminent:"[130]

> *the imminent threat of a violent attack against the United States does not require the United States to have proof that a specific attack against American persons or interests will take place in the immediate future.*

While the principle appears legitimate, it is the interpretation of the word "imminent" that poses a problem. In intelligence circles, the "imminence" of an attack is defined in terms of its proximity in time and the likelihood of it taking place. But, according to Daniel Bethlehem, this is no longer the case here:

> *It must be right that states should be able to act in self-defense in circumstances where there is evidence of imminent attacks by terrorist groups, even if there is no specific evidence of where such an attack will take place or of the precise nature of the attack.*[131]

---

129. Daniel BETHLEHEM, "Principles Relevant to the Scope of a State's Right of Self-Defense against an Imminent or Actual Armed Attack by Non-state Actors," *The American Journal of International Law*, volume 106, 2012.
130. *Lawfulness of a Lethal Operation Directed Against a U.S. Citizen Who Is a Senior Operational Leader of Al-Qa'ida or an Associated Force*, Department of Justice White Paper, February 4, 2013.
131. Daniel BETHLEHEM QC, "Written evidence submitted by Daniel Bethlehem QC, Director of Lauterpacht Research Centre for International Law, University of Cambridge, International Law And The Use Of Force: The Law As It Is And As It Should Be," Lauterpacht Research Centre for International Law, June 7, 2004, https://publications.parliament.uk/pa/cm200304/cmselect/cm-faff/441/4060808.htm

In this way, a terrorist attack can be considered "imminent," even if the details and timing are unknown. This makes it possible, for example, to launch an air strike simply on the basis of suspicions of an imminent attack.

In November 2008, while a ceasefire was in force, an Israeli commando raid killed six people in Gaza. The explanation given by the Israeli army illustrates the BETHLEHEM doctrine:[132]

> *This was a targeted operation to prevent an immediate threat... There was no intention to break the ceasefire; rather, the aim of the operation was to eliminate an immediate and dangerous threat posed by the Hamas terrorist organization.*

This doctrine is similar to the one enunciated in 2001 by Dick Cheney, then Vice President of the United States, also known as the *"Cheney doctrine"* or the *"1% doctrine:"*

> *If there's a 1% probability that Pakistani scientists are helping terrorists to develop or build weapons of mass destruction, we have to treat that as a certainty, in terms of response.*[133]

It is the strategic/operational version of the Wild West "hip shot." It is symptomatic of the way we understand the law and the way we wage war: without values and without honor.

The problem with the BETHLEHEM doctrine is that it has been systematically used by Israel to justify ceasefire violations. This is true of extra-judicial killings, which are not considered ceasefire violations.[134] A study of Palestinian rocket attacks shows that they are always carried out in response to an Israeli attack, which does not generally appear in our media. From this stems our perception that Palestinian organizations—Palestinian Islamic Jihad and Hamas in particular—wantonly attack Israel with their rockets, and therefore engage in terrorist practices.

---

132. Rory McCarthy, "Gaza truce broken as Israeli raid kills six Hamas gunmen," *The Guardian*, November 5, 2008 (https://www.theguardian.com/world/2008/nov/05/israelandthepalestinians)
133. Ron Suskind, *The One Percent Doctrine: Deep Inside America's Pursuit of Its Enemies Since 9/11*, Simon & Schuster, May 15 2007.
134. "Senior official: 'Israel didn't agree to halt targeted killings for ceasefire," *Times of Israel*, November 15, 2019 (https://www.timesofisrael.com/senior-official-israel-didnt-agree-to-halt-targeted-killings-for-ceasefire/)

In its February 2018 report, the *Human Rights Council* (HRC) reports that during the Gaza border protests (Return Marches), the Israeli army shot dead 183 civilians, including 154 who were unarmed and 35 children.[135] In February 2019, it reported that the Israeli army *"intentionally"* shot children, medical personnel (wearing badges and shot in the back!),[136] journalists and disabled people.[137] The Palestinian children shot by Israeli snipers with fragmentation bullets[138] while simply standing in front of the border in Gaza in 2018,[139] or the handcuffed and blindfolded Palestinian youth shot in the back in April 2019,[140] are war crimes.

Israel's supporters claim *self-defence*,[141] but this is fallacious, as the videos published by the United Nations[142] show. Firstly, because the victims were in a 150 m security strip *inside* Gaza,[143] separated from Israel by a fence and a wide berm, from which Israeli snipers fired. Secondly, because those killed were "armed" only with stones, and thirdly, because some of those hit (notably children) were shot in the back.[144]

So much for the world's most moral army, which the United Nations has asked to stop shooting children.[145]

---

135. *Report of the UN Commission of Inquiry on the 2018 protests in the OPT*, www.ohchr.org /EN/HRBodies/HRC/CoIOPT/Pages/Report2018OPT.aspx
136. Ali Abunimah, "Gaza nurse killed by Israel was shot in the back," www.aurdip.org, June 3, 2018.
137. *Report of the independent international commission of inquiry on the protests in the Occupied Palestinian Territory*, (A/HRC/40/74), Human Rights Council, February 25, 2019.
138. Pierre Stambul, "Gaza: silence, on tue," *Union juive française pour la paix (UJFP)*, April 23, 2018; "Over 100 bullet fragments in brain of Palestinian child shot by Israel soldier," *Middle East Monitor*, July 15, 2019.
139. Noa Landau, "UN Council: Israel Intentionally Shot Children and Journalists in Gaza," *Haaretz*, February 28, 2019 (https://www.haaretz.com/israel-news/2019-02-28/ty-article/un-council-israel-intentionally-shot-children-and-journalists-in-gaza/0000017f-f02b-d497-a1ff-f2ab3be90000)
140. Tamar Pileggi, "IDF shoots handcuffed, blindfolded Palestinian suspect during escape attempt," *The Times of Israel*, April 22, 2019 (https://www.timesofisrael.com/idf-shoots-handcuffed-blindfolded-palestinian-suspect-during-attempted-escape/)
141. *Ibid.*
142. "COI on Gaza Protests: Lethal force against demonstrators not posing imminent threat," *UN Human Rights Council/YouTube*, April 3, 2019.
143. Initially 50 m wide, according to the Oslo Accords, it has varied between 100 and 500 m over the years, without the Israeli authorities explicitly defining or marking it; OCHA, "*The humanitarian impact of restrictions on access to land near the perimeter fence in the Gaza Strip*," August 3, 2018 cited in *Human rights situation in Palestine and other occupied Arab territories—Report of the detailed findings of the independent international Commission of inquiry on the protests in the Occupied Palestinian Territory*, Human Rights Council, Document A/HRC/40/CRP.2, March 18, 2019.
144. Ahmad Nafi & Chloé Benoist, "Gaza: The Palestinians who died during the Great March of Return," *Middle East Eye*, December 28, 2018 (https://www.middleeasteye.net/news/gaza-palestinians-who-died-during-great-march-return)
145. "UN envoy tells 'outrageous' Israel to stop shooting children in Gaza," *The Times of Israel*, April 20, 2018 (https://www.timesofisrael.com/un-envoy-tells-outrageous-israel-to-stop-shooting-children-in-gaza/)

## The DAHIYA Doctrine

The Israeli army deliberately ignores the principles of international humanitarian law and applies the *"Dahiya doctrine,"* drawn up by General Gadi Eisenkot, now Chief of the General Staff. It advocates the use of *"disproportionate force"* to create maximum damage and destruction,[146] and considers that there are *"no civilian villages, these are military bases... This is not a recommendation. It is a plan."*[147]

It is a doctrine that presents itself as a deterrent, but contrary to *Wikipedia's* assertion,[148] it is a tactic that can only work in a symmetrical context, i.e., when the action has a linear effect on weakening the adversary. In an asymmetrical context, where the determination of combatants depends on the brutality of their adversary, such destruction only serves to stimulate the will to resist and the determination to use a terrorist approach. This is the essence of jihad.

In fact, the very existence of this doctrine shows that the Israelis have failed to understand their adversaries and their operating logic. This explains why Israel is the only country in the world not to have mastered terrorism in three-quarters of a century.

In October 2023, the same logic was applied. The British newspaper *The Telegraph* quoted Rear Admiral Daniel Hagari, spokesman for the Israeli army, as saying that for the strikes *"the emphasis is on damage, not precision,"* the aim being to reduce Gaza to a *"tent city"* by the end of the campaign.[149]

---

146. Gabi Siboni, *"Disproportionate Force: Israel's Concept of Response in Light of the Second Lebanon War,"* Institute for National Security Studies (INSS), Insight no. 74, October 2, 2008; https://wikileaks.org/plusd/cables/08TELAVIV2329_a.html
147. "Israel warns Hezbollah war would invite destruction," *Reuters*, October 3, 2008 (https://www.reuters.com/article/idUSL3251393/)
148. Wikipedia, "Dahiya Doctrine" article.
149. James Rothwell, "Israel abandons precision bombing in favour of 'damage and destruction,'" *The Telegraph*, October 11, 2023 (https://www.telegraph.co.uk/world-news/2023/10/11/israel-abandon-precision-bombing-eliminate-hamas-officials/)

## Comparison of the Lethality of Military Action between Ukraine[150] and Gaza[151]

| From | Visit | Number of days | Civilians killed | Average per day | Children killed | Average per day |
|---|---|---|---|---|---|---|
| 24.02.2022 | 04.12.2023 | 648 | 6702 | 10,3 | 386 | 0,6 |
| 07.10.2023 | 08.12.2023 | 63 | 17487 | 277,6 | 7729 | 122,7 |

*Figure 10—Comparison of death tolls between the Ukrainian theater of operations and Gaza. This comparison stops at the beginning of December, because until December 8, the Office for the Coordination of Humanitarian Action (OCHA) gives precise figures for the number of children killed. From that date onwards, only a percentage (70% of civilian deaths) is provided by OCHA.*

## Justified by the Bombing of Dresden (1945)

**Michael Tracey** @mtracey

Israeli ambassador to the UK cites the firebombing of Dresden in 1945 (deliberate aerial incineration of civilian population centers by US and UK) as precedent for what Israel is about to do in Gaza

BREAKING NEWS — Heappey: Challenge is complete destruction of Hamas
0:05 / 1:06

11:20 AM · Oct 16, 2023 · 297.5K Views

436 Reposts  169 Quotes  1,111 Likes  177 Bookmarks

*Figure 11—The Israeli ambassador to Britain threatens to use the same strategies of bombing civilians in Gaza as in Dresden in 1945. [Source: https://twitter.com/mtracey/status/1713847432935510354].*

---

150. https://www.ohchr.org/en/news/2022/12/ukraine-civilian-casualty-update-5-december-2022
151. https://www.ochaopt.org/content/hostilities-gaza-strip-and-israel-reported-impact-day-63

*Figure 12—Former Prime Minister Naftali Bennett speaks of using the same strategy that the British used at Dresden in 1945. [Source: https://twitter.com/mtracey/status/1713864692559429745]*

The problem here is that condemning Palestinian actions in the strongest possible terms, without saying a word about Israel's, means supporting the Hebrew state's violations of international law.

## The HANNIBAL Directive

Our media never mention the "HANNIBAL directive," which came into force in 1986 in the Israeli army, designed to prevent Israeli prisoners from being used as bargaining chips by the Palestinians.[152] It stipulated that those holding the prisoner were to be destroyed by any means necessary (including at the cost of the prisoner's own life and that of civilians in the area). Applied during Operation PROTECTIVE EDGE, it was behind the

---

152. https://en.wikipedia.org/wiki/Hannibal_Directive

total destruction of a Rafah neighborhood on August 1st, 2014, an event known in Palestine as *Black Friday*.[153]

This directive seems to be still in use, naturally without much publicity. It explains why the Israelis are not concerned about the hostages taken by Hamas:

> *The European diplomats were also struck by the lack of interest shown by the Israeli government in prioritizing the lives of the hostages held in Gaza.*[154]

Very soon after the start of the Hamas operation, Israel announced the deaths of 1,400 Israeli civilians. This number became a *leitmotif* for refusing any dialogue with Hamas and other Palestinian groups. But this number was revised downwards after 200 charred bodies were recognized as those of Hamas fighters. Then, on December 2, 2023, it was lowered again to 1,000 in a tweet from the Israeli government.[155]

An Israeli air force colonel would later confirm that on October 7, a "free fire" was ordered from the air force, described as a "mass HANNIBAL."

The HANNIBAL directive is applied not only in cases of hostage-taking, but also when soldiers are at risk of capture. For example, on January 24, 2024, near Khan Yunis, a tank was damaged by rocket fire, and the Israeli military was unable to approach it to retrieve the three wounded crewmen. The general staff therefore preferred to bomb the tank and its occupants rather than risk them falling into the hands of Hamas.

In any case, we can see that the Israeli army applies the precautionary principle neither to the Palestinians nor to its own men. One could say with a certain cynicism that, at least here, Palestinians and Israelis are treated equally.

In mid-December 2023, the discovery of three bodies in a tunnel in Gaza sparked controversy. They were three men held by Hamas, whom the Israeli army spokesman had declared killed by the Palestinian organization. They had no apparent injuries and appeared to have been killed by

---

153. Raf SANCHEZ, "Israel ends the 'Hannibal Directive'—military policy to kill your own troops rather than let them be captured," *The Telegraph*, June 29, 2016; https://blackfriday.amnesty.org/report.php; *The Hannibal Directive—Featured Documentary, Al Jazeera/YouTube*, October 8, 2016.
154. Gideon RACHMAN, "Western diplomats are walking an impossible tightrope with Israel," *Financial Times*, October 13, 2023 (https://www.ft.com/content/e803f827-f1dd-4bbe-af76-55436e3db587)
155. https://twitter.com/IsraelinUSA/status/1731131639089041788

poisoning. Were they killed by the deliberate use of a combat toxicant or accidentally by toxic fumes from explosions (such as carbon monoxide)? We do not know, but the mother of one of them, Ron Sherman, believes he was deliberately sacrificed by the army.[156] In any case, this illustrates the Israeli army's failure to respect the precautionary principle.

### *Extrajudicial Executions*

Extra-judicial executions are an important element in Israel's policy of deterrence against Palestinian movements. They consist of eliminating militants outside the judicial process, using killers or "one-off" strikes such as air attacks. Legally questionable, they are often strategically ineffective. Three countries use them regularly: the United States, Israel and France. Presented as a preventive measure, they are generally carried out in a punitive manner, like Sicilian vendettas, without any real assessment of their strategic consequences. In practice, they fuel a growing process of violence and are a source of legitimacy for terrorism. In fact, they often reflect a lack of real counter-terrorist strategy.

The archetype of this mode of action is Operation ANGER OF GOD (*Mivtza Za'am Ha'el*), also known as Operation BAYONET, carried out by the Mossad to punish the perpetrators of the attack on the Israeli Olympic team in Munich in 1972 (Operation BERIM & IKRIT). Within a year, almost the entire Palestinian commando was eliminated: Wae Zwaiter (Rome, October 16, 1972), Mahmoud Hamchari (Paris, January 9, 1973), Abd El-Hir (Nicosia, January 24, 1973), Basil Al-Kubaissi (Paris, April 6, 1973), Ziad Muchassi (Athens, April 12, 1973), Mohammed Boudia (Paris, June 28, 1973), Kamal Nasser, Mahmoud Najjer and Kamal Adouan (Beirut, April 9, 1973). Its leader, Ali Hassan Salameh, was killed in Beirut on January 22, 1979, followed by his second-in-command, Khalil al-Wazir (alias Abou Djihad), on April 16, 1988 in Tunis. In the end, only one member of the group, Jamal al-Gasheï, seems to have escaped the wrath of GOD,[157] while an innocent man was mistakenly killed in Lillehammer (Norway).

These actions are punitive operations. What our countries and Israel consider part of the game is called terrorism when others do it. By accepting

---

156. Yuval ABRAHAM, "A hostage's mother says toxic gas from Israeli bombs killed her son. Is she right?," +972 *Magazine*, January 31, 2024 (https://www.972mag.com/weapons-toxic-gas-gaza-hostages/)
157. Simon REEVE, *One Day in September*, Arcade Publishing, London, 1998.

it from Israel, we create a permissive environment that could well legitimize the elimination of some of our political leaders. Which could happen.

Since 1988, Israel has been using specially trained units to operate clandestinely in the occupied territories. Known as *"mista'aravim"* or YAMAS, these are *ad hoc* formations that operate clandestinely (in Arab clothing—hence their name) in the occupied territories for reconnaissance missions, commando actions or extra-judicial executions. *Mista'aravim* actions are mainly carried out in the West Bank by Sayeret Duvdevan (Unit 217).

The best-known of these was Mossad's attempt to poison Khaled Mashal, political leader of Hamas in Jordan, in 1997. It ended in failure: the two Israeli agents carrying Canadian passports were arrested; then Israel had to provide an antidote and release Sheikh Ahmed Yassin in exchange for the release of his agents. The result was Israel's loss of credibility with the international community and the mistrust of Jordan—with which Israel has a peace treaty.

*Mista'aravim* are the equivalent of the *Groupe Antiterroriste de Libération* (GAL) units used in Spain in the 1980s, which are considered a form of state terrorism. However, the advantage of this type of action is that it can eliminate an individual without razing an entire neighborhood or destroying entire families. But it requires agents who are all the more competent and courageous because the Palestinians have strengthened their counter-espionage and internal security capabilities. This is why this type of operation has become almost impossible to carry out in Gaza, but is still common practice in the West Bank. In Gaza, Israel prefers to carry out its actions "at a distance," using more sophisticated means such as drones or guided missiles, which have a devastating effect on the civilian population.

With some 2,300 known assassinations, Israel rivals the United States as the country that regularly assassinates opponents and terrorists.[158] When carried out on foreign soil, an "elimination" is a complex operation, relying on a network of local informers (*"sayanim"*), most often recruited from the Jewish diaspora. But this has a perverse effect: it turns the previously well-integrated Jewish community into an object of distrust, perceived as a "5th column" in many countries of the Near and Middle East.

---

158. Ronen Bergman, *Rise and Kill First: The Secret History of Israel's Targeted Assassinations*, Random House, January 30, 2018; Charles Glass, "'Rise and Kill First' Explores the Corrupting Effects of Israel's Assassination Program," *The Intercept*, March 11, 2018.

But extra-judicial executions not only carry a significant political risk if unsuccessful, they tend to legitimize illegal violence and terrorism, as evidenced by the *Arabian Peninsula Jihad Base*'s (APJB) *Inspire* magazine:[159]

> *[The assassination of leaders of the civil and military unbelievers] is one of the most important arts of terrorism and one of the most advantageous and deterrent types of operation. These methods are also used by the enemies of Allah. The CIA has authorization from the US government to assassinate presidents, if it is in the national interest of the United States, and they have used it more than once. In the CIA, there is a special department for that! So I do not know why we are prevented from doing it?*

This is a case of Islamist asymmetry: the "cure" is worse than the "disease." The assassination of leaders has no dissuasive effect. It makes the dead a martyr and an example to follow. It hardly ever leads to the end of terrorist action, but keeps the flame of resistance alive and takes on more varied forms.

With highly decentralized structures, the elimination of cadres does not necessarily weaken the terrorist group, but it does force its hierarchy to renew itself more rapidly and apply new methods and policies of action. This is what happened with Hamas.

But on August 21, 2003, Israeli forces eliminated Ismaïl Abou Shanab. At the time, he was considered a Hamas moderate, and his assassination triggered widespread condemnation and an unprecedented mobilization of the Palestinian population. Attacks resumed in step with the eliminations carried out by Israel.

In September 2023, on the *LCI* channel, where journalist Darius Rochebin praises the assassinations carried out by the Ukrainian secret services, General Christophe Gomart explained that France also carries them out. He is a perfect illustration of the Western way of thinking. Like the Israelis, he thinks it is useful to shoot a leader *"because in fact it is the leaders who decide, and it takes longer to train a leader than it does to train an ordinary soldier,"* so:[160]

---

159. Abu Musab AL-SURI, "The Jihadi Experiences: Individual Terrorism Jihad and the Global Islamic Resistance Units," *Inspire*, no. 5, Spring 2011, p. 32.
160. https://youtu.be/Mf3OgKg6vhc

*We destabilize, we disorganize, and the idea in war is to disorganize the adversary in order to weaken him and make it possible to win, and therefore to overthrow him... that's what we did in the Sahel against the terrorist leaders: we sought to disorganize the terrorist or jihadist "Katibats."*

## Targeted Eliminations that Generate the Use of Terrorist Methods (non-exhaustive list)

| Date | Target | Group | Answer | Victims of the response (deaths) | Comment |
|---|---|---|---|---|---|
| 06.01.1996 | Yahya Ayyash | Hamas | 25.02.1996<br>25.02.1996<br>03.03.1996<br>04.03.1996 | 1<br>27<br>20<br>13 | This elimination is at the origin of the biggest wave of human bombs. |
| 31.07.2001 | Jamal Mansour | Hamas | 09.08.2001 | 15 | |
| 23.11.2001 | Mahmoud Abou Hanoud | Hamas | 01.12.2001<br>02.12.2001 | 11<br>15 | |
| 14.01.2002 | Raed al-Karmi | Fatah | 27.01.2002<br>16.02.2002<br>02.03.2002 | 1<br>2<br>11 | This elimination led the Al-Aqsa Brigades to use human bombs. |
| 23.07.2002 | Salah Shahada | Hamas | 04.08.2002 | 9 | The Israeli action left 14 people dead. |
| 26.12.2002 | 6 militants | Fatah, PIJ | 05.01.2003 | 22 | |
| 15.08.2003<br>21.06.2003 | Mohammed Sidr<br>Abdallah 'Awashmeh | Al-Quds Brigades<br>Hamas | 19.08.2003 | 21 | Joint response from the Al-Quds Brigades and Hamas. |
| 08.08.2003 | Fayez al-Sadr | Al-Qassam Brigades | 12.08.2003 | 2 | |
| 22.03.2004<br>17.04.2004 | Ahmed Yassine Abd el-Rantissi | Hamas | 31.08.2004 | 16 | The Israeli assassinations caused 9+2 deaths and provoked a double suicide attack in Be'er-Sheva. |
| 09.03.2012 | Zohair al-Qaisi | Popular Resistance Committees (PRC) | 09.03.2009 | - | 15 innocent dead. Response: 300 rockets fired, wounding 23 Israelis. |

*Figure 13—The "human bomb" technique is not a "tradition" of Palestinian movements. It was used between 1994 and 2005-2006, in response to Israeli extra-judicial executions. [Note: only deaths are mentioned here].*

Not only does this illustrate a tactical approach to the fight against terrorism, but it is not valid for highly decentralized insurgent structures, made up of small, quasi-autonomous groups. This partly explains the operational and strategic failure of French action in the Sahel.

This somewhat childish vision of war may work in a conventional conflict, but not in an unconventional context, and certainly not in a jihadist one. It flies in the face of what a British SAS officer told me during my counter-terrorism training in Britain during the war in Northern Ireland in the mid-1980s. The British had extremely detailed files and information on the various commanders of the *Irish Republican Army* (IRA), down to knowing their every move. When I asked why they did not eliminate them, the officer replied:

> *Because we know them. We know their psychology, their families, their networks, their way of fighting, and we can better anticipate their actions, even pre-empt them. If we kill them, others will come along, perhaps more effective, more aggressive, and we'll know nothing about them.*

Of course, such an answer is only possible when you have studied your opponent thoroughly and know him in great detail. The fact is that today, we know very little about our opponents. Even public figures like Vladimir Putin are so poorly known that he is diagnosed with illnesses he does not have. It is the same in Palestine.

Experience shows that extra-judicial executions have no operational effect. On the contrary, they encourage the spirit of vengeance and tend to mobilize the spirit of resistance. This phenomenon is all the stronger when civilians are killed in the process. They inspire contempt rather than admiration, as they represent a success not achieved in face-to-face combat. Moreover, as in the case of Operation AL-AQSA FLOOD, the Israeli military are not fighting a "brave" battle. This is why these executions become a substitute for real success against terrorism. They therefore appear more as proof of weakness and incapacity than as a demonstration of effectiveness.

According to some (unconfirmed) reports, SHABAK has set up a clandestine unit, code-named INDIGO, whose mission is to hunt down the perpetrators of the crimes of October 7, 2023. But with evidence mounting that the vast majority of these crimes were the result of errors of conduct, the question of the extent to which this group will punish the real perpetrators of the massacres remains open.

## *Consequences of Israeli Eliminations (non-exhaustive list)*

| Israeli action | Consequences |
|---|---|
| On April 16, 1988, the assassination of Khalil al-Wazir (alias Abu Jihad), Yasser Arafat's right-hand man and considered operational leader of the first Intifada, was intended to put an end to the Palestinian uprising. | Not only was this not the case, but Arafat was deprived of a wise advisor. |
| February 16, 1992, the elimination of Sheikh Abbas Moussaoui, Secretary General of Hezbollah. | This allowed the more radical Hassan Nasrallah to become Hezbollah's leader. |
| The elimination of Fathi Shikaki, leader of Islamic Jihad, on October 26, 1995, had been decided on the assumption that his probable successor, Abdallah Ramadan Sallah, would not have the qualities required to lead the organization, and would thus have constituted a less ferocious adversary. | The Israeli services' analysis was wrong: the number and effectiveness of Islamic Jihad attacks increased after his death. |
| On January 6, 1996, the elimination of Yahya Ayyash (alias "the engineer"), an explosives specialist, while he was observing a truce with Israel. | This undermined Yasser Arafat's credibility, discouraged the Hamas moderates who were counting on a political process, and led to the biggest wave of suicide attacks in Israel's history. |
| On August 27, 2001, Abu Ali Moustafa, Secretary General of the Popular Front for the Liberation of Palestine (PFLP), was eliminated in response to an attack that killed three Israeli soldiers.[161] | This action led to the assassination of the Minister of Tourism, Rehavam Ze'evi, on October 10, 2001, and the launch of a campaign of suicide attacks, which the PFLP had never carried out before. In the end, the Israeli action indirectly caused two Israeli deaths and 48 injuries.[162] |
| On March 22, 2004, the assassination of Sheikh Ahmed Yassine,[163] the spiritual and historical leader of Hamas, was aimed at weakening the movement. | On the contrary. It pushed Abd el-Rantissi, more virulent than his predecessor, to its head, who was to be eliminated in his turn on April 17. On August 31, 2004, a double suicide attack in Beer-Shev'a, killing 16 people, was claimed in the name of Hamas, to avenge the deaths of Sheikh Yassin and Abd el-Rantissi.[164] |

---

161. NOA: in fact, the attack was carried out by a commando of the *Democratic Front for the Liberation of Palestine* (DFLP)!
162. The subsequent attacks carried out by the PFLP on April 24, 2003 (which was also claimed by the *Al-Aqsa Brigades*) and May 22, 2004 can probably no longer be associated with this process.
163. He was eliminated a week after a double suicide attack on an ammonia depot in the port of Ashdod. This attack—which left ten Israelis dead—was seen as an attempted chemical attack and was interpreted as a new level of terrorist action.
164. *Jerusalem Post*, September 1, 2004.

| On March 9, 2012, Israel eliminated Zohair al-Qaisi, secretary general of the Popular Resistance Committees (PRC), killing some fifteen innocent civilians.[165] | The French government's support for this operation motivated Mohammed Merah's attacks on March 22. |
|---|---|

*Figure 14—What appears to be an intelligence success is in fact an intelligence failure. More precisely, it's a tactical intelligence success and a strategic intelligence failure.*

These eliminations illustrate the characteristic feature of the Israeli services: a great ability to locate their targets, but a profound inability to understand their enemies, which is the fundamental criterion for judging a service's capabilities. The result is that, far from weakening their adversaries, the Israelis have strengthened their fighting spirit, discouraging the efforts of moderates within Hamas and Fatah. In short: tactical success, strategic failure.

The counter-productive nature of extra-judicial executions is even greater and more systematic when they are carried out during a negotiation process or a truce: a recurrent practice of the Israelis. In fact, Israel does not consider targeted eliminations or drone attacks as ceasefire violations.[166] Thus, Palestinian rocket attacks, always presented by the Western press as demonstrations of mood, almost *always* take place *after* raids or ceasefire violations by Israel.[167]

### *Israeli Actions and Targeted Eliminations during a Peace Process or Truce*

| Date | Target | Group | Comments |
|---|---|---|---|
| 06.01.1996 | Yahya Ayyash | Hamas | His elimination led Hamas to create a special group, the Jerusalem Group (Majmuat al-Quds), to carry out revenge operations, resulting in the deaths of over 60 Israelis. |
| 31.07.2001 | Jamal Mansour | Hamas | The Israeli action broke an almost two-month ceasefire. |
| 23.11.2001 | Mahmoud Abou Hanoud | Hamas | The Israeli action rendered null and void the agreement between Hamas and Fatah not to attack targets in Israel after "9/11." |

---

165. *The Guardian* and *The Washington Post*, March 10, 2012.
166. "Senior official: 'Israel didn't agree to halt targeted killings for ceasefire,'" *The Times of Israel*, November 15, 2019.
167. http://blog.thejerusalemfund.org/2012/12/israeli-ceasefire-violations-in-gaza.html

| | | | |
|---|---|---|---|
| 23.07.2002 | Salah Shahada | Hamas | The Israeli action left 14 people dead, just hours before a widely-heralded ceasefire between Tanzim and Hamas was because of take effect. |
| 26.12.2002 | 6 militants | Fatah, PIJ | The Israeli action comes as representatives of Fatah, Hamas and other factions negotiate a ceasefire on attacks on Israeli civilians in Cairo. |
| 23.08.2003 | Ismaïl Abou Shanab | Hamas | His assassination broke a truce agreed on June 29 and triggered an unprecedented mobilization of the Palestinian population. Terrorist attacks resumed. |
| 05.11.2008 | 6 militants | Hamas | Israel breaks the ceasefire in force since June 19. Hamas responds by firing 35 rockets. This marked the start of Operation DURCI LEAD.[168] |
| 09.03.2012 | Zohair al-Qaisi | Popular Resistance Committees (PRC) | Breach of the ceasefire agreed during Operation PLOMB DURCI. This is an act of treachery which the French government has declared its solidarity with,[169] angering Mohammed Merah. |
| 15.11.2012 | Ahmed al-Jabari | Hamas | The Israeli action left 9 people dead, and Hamas's response was the pretext for the start of Operation PILARS OF DEFENSE.[170] |
| 01.08.2014 | | Hamas | While a ceasefire has been agreed by both sides, Israel begins to blow up Hamas tunnels.[171] Benjamin Netanyahu declares that he will do so "with or without a ceasefire."[172] |
| 18.08.2014 | Unknown chef | Hamas | Just as a new ceasefire was agreed on August 18, Israel launched an air strike against a Hamas leader, killing 3 people including a woman and a child. Hamas retaliated with a salvo of 40 rockets.[173] |
| 02.01.2024 | Salah Al-Ahrouri | Hamas | Al-Arouri was assassinated in Beirut while negotiations were underway through Egypt and Qatar. The process was interrupted. |

*Figure 15—Impact of extra-judicial executions on negotiations. More recent comparisons are difficult given, on the one hand, the abandonment of negotiation processes and, on the other, the different nature of the Palestinian resistance's means of action.*

---

168. Rory MCCARTHY, "Gaza truce broken as Israeli raid kills six Hamas gunmen," *The Guardian*, November 5, 2008 (https://www.theguardian.com/world/2008/nov/05/israelandthepalestinians)

169. "Press release—Israel and occupied Palestinian territories. All parties must protect civilians in Gaza and Israel following ceasefire announcement," *Amnesty International*, March 13, 2012.

170. Harriet SHERWOOD, "Hamas says 'gates of hell opened' as Israel kills military leader in Gaza," *The Guardian*, November 15, 2012 (https://www.theguardian.com/world/2012/nov/14/israel-assassinates-hamas-military-chief)

171. Sudarsan RAGHAVAN, William BOOTH & Griff WITTE, "How a 72-hour truce in Gaza fell apart in less than 2 hours," *The Washington Post*, August 1st, 2014 (https://www.washingtonpost.com/world/israel-hamas-agree-to-72-hour-humanitarian-cease-fire/2014/08/01/059f1ff8-194e-11e4-9e3b-7f2f110c6265_story.html)

172. "Gaza ceasefire crumbles as Israel resumes military operations," *France 24*, August 1, 2014 (https://www.france24.com/en/20140801-gaza-ceasefire-crumbles-israel-hamas-palestinians-usa-un-military)

173. https://www.reuters.com/article/uk-mideast-gaza-idUKKBN0GI12R20140819

As *Haaretz* noted, since 2019, as part of its *"divide and rule"* policy, the Israeli government has been carrying out targeted eliminations against the *Palestinian Islamic Jihad* (PIJ) that are far from surgical. On November 12, 2019, for example, Israel launched a strike against Bahaa Abou al-Ata, commander of the PIJ, which had originally been scheduled in 2017 (indicating that there was no emergency situation). As the *New York Times* notes, this attack comes *"after a period of relative calm"*[174] and in the midst of a bitter struggle over the composition of the Israeli government, suggesting a domestic political objective.

These eliminations do nothing to improve security. Intuitively, one might see an arithmetical reduction in the threat, and some studies have attempted to demonstrate that these eliminations have reduced the number of suicide attacks.[175] But in reality, the opposite is true. The gradual disappearance of this type of attack from 2005 onwards is the result of a change in strategy initiated in 2002 by Mohammed al-Deif, leader of the *Kata'ib Izz al-Din al-Qassam*. Linked to the construction of the Israeli "barrier," the aim was to move away from "haphazard" terrorism towards a more structured resistance struggle, including the use of rockets and mortars as a means of action.

---

174. Isabel Kershner, Iyad Abuheweila & David M. Halbfinger, "Israel Kills Senior Islamic Jihad Commander in Gaza," *The New York Times*, November 12, 2019 (https://www.nytimes.com/2019/11/12/world/middleeast/israel-gaza-islamic-jihad.html)
175. Ophir Falk, "Measuring the Effectiveness of Israel's 'Targeted Killing' Campaign," *Perspectives on Terrorism*, vol 9, no 1, 2015.

# 4. Gaza

## Gaza's Special Situation

The Gaza Strip is not only the area where, in ancient times, the Philistines, ancestors of today's Palestinians, were located. It was part of Mandate Palestine until 1948, when the survivors of the Nakba found refuge there after being expelled from their villages and homes. Since the Israeli aggression of 1967, the Palestinian population has lived under occupation. In 2005, Israel "disengaged" from the Gaza Strip under the Oslo Accords.

Since then, Israel has claimed that it has left the Gaza Strip and that it is no longer an occupied territory, as Alain Finkielkraut says on *LCI*[176] or journalist Pascal Praud on *CNews*.[177] This is why Israel considers its conflict with Hamas to be an international conflict,[178] and why it claims the *"right to defend itself,"* to which we will return later. But this is not true. In fact, not only does the international community, like the European Union,[179] consider Gaza to be an occupied territory, it also considers the blockade of the territory to be illegal.[180]

---

176. https://youtu.be/ARABP7GwjFw?t=186
177. https://youtu.be/FnXH4WNu7W4?t=488
178. https://unwatch.org/item-7/claim/claim-6-israels-blockade-of-gaza-is-illegal/
179. Andrew Rettman, "Israel's siege of Gaza is illegal, EU says," *euobserver.com*, October 10, 2023 (https://euobserver.com/world/157534)
180. "U.N. experts say Israel's blockade of Gaza illegal," *Reuters*, September 13, 2011 (https://www.reuters.com/article/idUSTRE78C59R/)

## International Institutions that Consider Gaza an Occupied Territory
### (non-exhaustive list)

| Institution (alphabetical order) | References |
|---|---|
| Amnesty International (AI) | https://www.amnesty.org/en/latest/campaigns/2017/06/israel-occupation-50-years-of-dispossession/ |
| United Nations General Assembly | https://www.un.org/unispal/document/assistance-to-the-palestinian-people-ga-resolution-a-res-76-126-2/ |
| B'Tselem | https://www.btselem.org/duty_to_end_occupation |
| ICC Pre-Trial Chamber I | https://www.icc-cpi.int/sites/default/files/CourtRecords/CR2021_01165.PDF |
| International Committee of the Red Cross (ICRC) | https://www.icrc.org/en/document/ihl-occupying-power-responsibilities-occupied-palestinian-territories |
| United Nations International Independent Investigation Commission on the Occupied Palestinian Territory | https://undocs.org/en/A/78/198 |
| International Criminal Court (ICC) | https://www.icc-cpi.int/sites/default/files/itemsDocuments/palestine/210215-palestine-q-a-eng.pdf |
| International Federation for Human Rights (FIDH) | https://www.fidh.org/en/region/north-africa-middle-east/israel-palestine/50th-anniversary-of-israel-s-military-occupation-of-palestine |
| Global Centre for the Responsibility to Protect | https://www.globalr2p.org/countries/israel-and-the-occupied-palestinian-territory/ |
| Human Rights Watch (HRW) | https://www.hrw.org/report/2021/04/27/threshold-crossed/israeli-authorities-and-crimes-apartheid-and-persecution |
| Doctors Without Borders (MSF) | https://www.msf.org/photo-story-living-under-occupation-palestine |
| ICC Office of the Prosecutor | https://www.icc-cpi.int/sites/default/files/CourtRecords/CR2020_00161.PDF |
| African Union (AU) | https://archives.au.int/bitstream/handle/123456789/6461/EX CL 1115 (XXXIV) _E.pdf |
| European Union (EU) | https://www.eeas.europa.eu/node/41718_en |

*Figure 16—Unlike our media, international organizations consider Gaza to be a territory under occupation. The criterion is not the presence or absence of the Israeli military in the Gaza Strip, but the control Palestinians have over their own lives.*

When *CNews'* Vincent Hervouët asserted that Gaza *"is autonomous,"* he demonstrated the level of ignorance and incompetence of our media: Israel bans the import of "coriander, sage, jam, chocolate, French fries, dried fruit, fabrics, notebooks, empty flower pots and toys."[181]

---

181. Amira HASS, "Why Won't Israel Allow Gazans to Import Coriander?," *Haaretz*, May 7, 2010 (https://www.haaretz.com/2010-05-07/ty-article/why-wont-israel-allow-gazans-to-import-coriander/0000017f-f866-d887-a7ff-f8e6fc210000)

Occupation is defined by Article 42 of the 4th *Hague Convention*:[182]

> *A territory is considered occupied when it is in fact placed under the authority of the enemy army. Occupation extends only to territories where this authority is established and capable of being exercised.*

As a result, even though Israeli troops are no longer stationed in the Gaza Strip, they are able to impose on it conditions of existence that have nothing to do with those of a free country. As a result,

> *The ICRC considers that the Gaza Strip remains an occupied territory because Israel continues to exercise key elements of its authority there, notably over its borders (airspace, sea and land—with the exception of the border with Egypt). Although Israel no longer maintains a permanent presence inside the Gaza Strip, it remains bound by certain obligations under the law of occupation which are proportional to the degree of control it exercises over the Gaza Strip.*[183]

Even the *Atlantic Council*, an organization associated with NATO, considers that, whatever the terminology used, Israel has the duties of an occupying power towards the Gaza Strip and should concentrate its efforts on protecting the civilian population.[184]

When the Israelis withdrew from Gaza in 2005, they systematically destroyed the infrastructure (houses, roads, airport, etc.), leaving the Palestinian Authority with a field of ruins.[185] Today, the blockade of Gaza and the limitation of fishing zones help to keep Palestinians away from a certain prosperity that could deter them from fighting.

In 2007, after Hamas won the legislative elections, Israel decided to set up a blockade around the territory. The official aim was to prevent terrorist attacks against the surrounding Israeli population, located in an area known as the "Gaza envelope."

---

182. https://ihl-databases.icrc.org/fr/ihl-treaties/hague-conv-iv-1907
183. https://www.icrc.org/en/document/ihl-occupying-power-responsibilities-occupied-palestinian-territories
184. Celeste Kmiotek, "Israel claims it is no longer occupying the Gaza Strip. What does international law say?," *Atlantic Council*, October 31, 2023 (https://www.atlanticcouncil.org/blogs/menasource/gaza-israel-occupied-international-law/)
185. "Israel destroys homes as Gaza pullout nears end," *CNN*, August 22, 2005 (https://edition.cnn.com/2005/WORLD/meast/08/21/gaza.pullout/index.html)

While the concern for security is understandable, the method appears unconvincing. Not only is it illegal under international law,[186] but by preventing the economic development of the territory, Israel is encouraging it to carry out terrorist actions.

## Map of the Gaza Strip

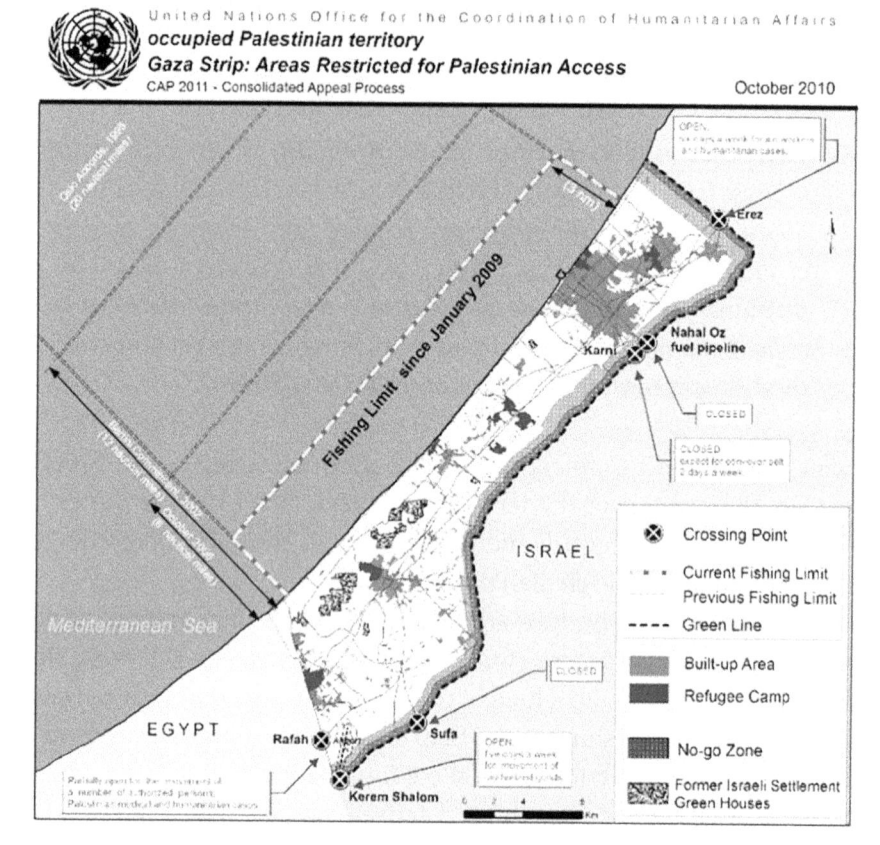

*Figure 17—Map of the Gaza Strip by the United Nations Office for the Coordination of Humanitarian Affairs (OCHA). The restrictions imposed on Gazans by Israel mean that the United Nations considers the Gaza Strip to be under occupation, even though there are no Israeli troops physically deployed in the territory.
[Source: https://www.unocha.org/attachments/11fc4a3f-1f13-3f4d-b52d-673176533390/645600582A81E1B4852577F2005CE77E-map.pdf]*

---

186. "U.N. experts say Israel's blockade of Gaza illegal," *Reuters*, September 13, 2011 (https://www.reuters.com/article/us-un-gaza-rights/u-n-experts-say-israels-blockade-of-gaza-illegal-idUS-TRE78C59R20110913/)

As a result, the Gaza Strip, described as an "open-air prison,"[187] has become a gigantic refugee camp surrounded by watchtowers and walls that go down into the ground to a "classified" depth, but probably more than 40 m, to prevent Gazans from building tunnels to communicate with the outside world. The Israeli authorities only let in food up to a per capita level of 2,279 calories.[188] By way of comparison, according to the *Encyclopedia of the Holocaust, in* 1941, in Nazi concentration camps, Russian prisoners were allowed 2,200 calories per day.[189] According to *Amnesty International*, the water reaching Gaza is 90-95% unsuitable for consumption, and the Israeli authorities do not allow the transfer of water from the West Bank, where the Israelis have appropriated water resources:[190]

> *In November 1967, the Israeli authorities issued Military Directive 158, which stipulated that Palestinians could not build new water supply facilities without first obtaining a permit from the Israeli army. Since then, tapping water from any new source or building any new water supply infrastructure has required permits from Israel, which are virtually impossible to obtain.*

The 2015 US State Department report on human rights practice in Israel and the Occupied Territories, acknowledges *"institutional and societal discrimination"* against Israeli Arabs, *"particularly in access to equal opportunity and employment."*[191]

The treatment of Gaza by the Israeli authorities is a source of violence on the ground and a primary cause of current anti-Semitism in the West. But it is also at the root of a growing disaffection with Israel among (young) American Jews, as evidenced by Anna Baltzer's remarkable report *"Life*

---

187. "Special Rapporteur Says Israel's Unlawful Carceral Practices in the Occupied Palestinian Territory Are Tantamount to International Crimes and Have Turned it into an Open-Air Prison," *ohchr.org*, July 10, 2023 (https://www.ohchr.org/en/news/2023/07/special-rapporteur-says-israels-unlawful-carceral-practices-occupied-palestinian)
188. Mark Weiss, "Israel sets calorie limit for Gaza residents," *The Irish Times*, October 18, 2012 (https://www.irishtimes.com/news/israel-sets-calorie-limit-for-gaza-residents-1.553966)
189. https://encyclopedia.ushmm.org/content/en/article/the-treatment-of-soviet-pows-starvation-disease-and-shootings-june-1941january-1942
190. "The Occupation of Water," *Amnesty International*, November 29, 2017 (https://www.amnesty.org/en/latest/campaigns/2017/11/the-occupation-of-water/)
191. 2015 Country Reports on Human Rights Practices—Israel and The Occupied Territories, Bureau of Democracy, Human Rights, and Labor, State Department, April 13, 2016.

in Palestine"[192] or the interview with Dr. Gabor Maté, Holocaust survivor and father of American journalist Aaron Maté.[193]

## The Israeli Presence Around Gaza

Surveillance of the Gaza Strip and protection of the "Gaza envelope" are the responsibility of the "Gaza Division" (Ugdat Aza), which is subordinate to the Israel Defense Forces Southern Command. Since August 2022, it has been commanded by Brigadier General Avi Rosenfeld.

It provides permanent surveillance of the fence surrounding the Gaza Strip. This is a double fence, with observation towers and firing towers placed at regular intervals. The towers are equipped with optronic observation equipment, enabling them to monitor activity near the fence day and night. The firing towers are equipped with remote-controlled machine guns, some of which can be activated automatically.

The Gaza Division's system is completed by the SIGINT electronic intelligence station based at Urim,[194] 17 km from the Gaza Strip border. Known by the code name YARKON, it is operated by a detachment of Unit 8200 of AMAN, Israel's military intelligence service.[195] This detachment, known as the *National Warning Unit,* constantly monitors all Palestinian electronic activity. Its *raison d'être* is the threat to the territories adjacent to the Gaza Strip, commonly known as the "Gaza envelope."

In November 2018, an Israeli commando from the elite "Sayeret Matkal" unit was intercepted in Khan Yunis by Hamas operatives and its infiltration attempt failed. The Hamas intelligence service, *Djihaz Al-Amn*, then recovered the commando's transmission equipment and managed to break the encryption algorithms. This enabled the Palestinians to gather information on the troops of the Gaza Division, responsible for surveillance of the Gaza Strip. This success enabled them to understand how the Israelis operated and to adopt transmission procedures that rendered Israeli electronic eavesdropping inoperative. This is why, in

---

192. "Life in Occupied PALESTINE by Anna Baltzer," *YouTube*, August 10, 2014 (https://youtu.be/Q_MDC2Gty4I)
193. "Gabor Maté on the misuse of anti-Semitism and why fewer Jews identify with Israel," *The Grayzone/YouTube*, November 6, 2019 (https://youtu.be/8TBBhPUwrCU)
194. https://virtualglobetrotting.com/map/urim-sigint-base/view/google/
195. https://www.tabletmag.com/sections/israel-middle-east/articles/unit-8200

2022, Unit 8200 stopped intercepting and decrypting Hamas telephone conversations,[196] as this was considered a waste of time.[197]

***Articulating Intelligence around Gaza***

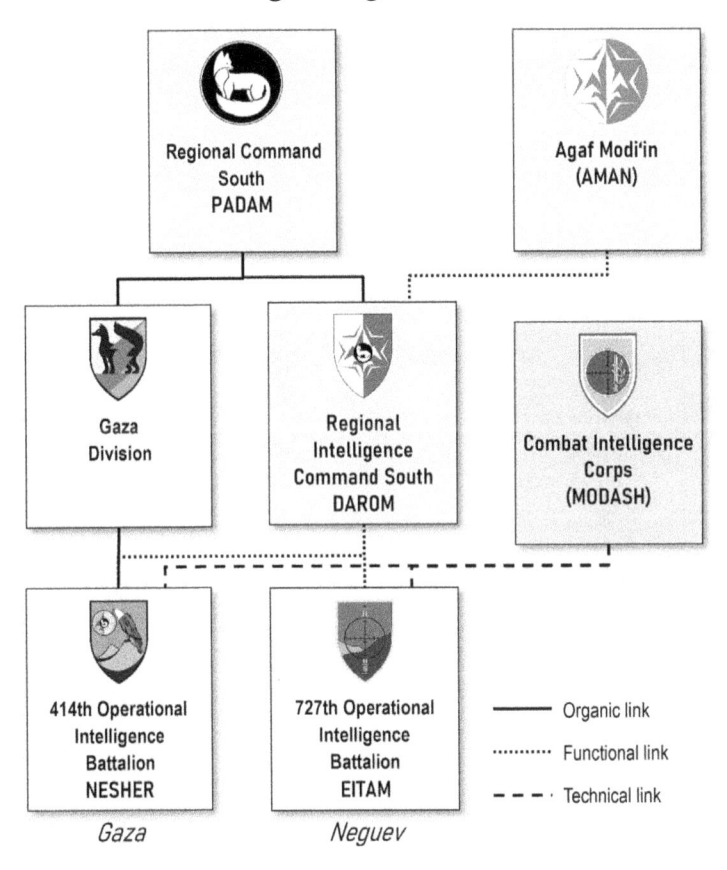

*Figure 18—Operational intelligence in Israel's southern sector. Surveillance of Gaza is the responsibility of the NESHER Battalion, which reports organically to the Southern Regional Command. The battalion is part of the Operational Intelligence Corps, created in 2009 following the events in southern Lebanon.*

---

196. Uri BAR-JOSEPH, "Israel's Deadly Complacency Wasn't Just an Intelligence Failure," *Haaretz*, November 11, 2023 (https://www.haaretz.com/israel-news/2023-11-11/ty-article-magazine/.highlight/israels-deadly-complacency-wasnt-just-an-intelligence-failure/0000018b-b9ea-df42-a78f-bdeb298e0000) (https://archive.ph/sAr2l)

197. Ronen BERGMAN, Mark MAZZETTI & Maria ABI-HABIB, "How Years of Israeli Failures on Hamas Led to a Devastating Attack," *The New York Times*, October 29, 2023 (updated November 1, 2023) (https://www.nytimes.com/2023/10/29/world/middleeast/israel-intelligence-hamas-attack.html)

But the most important information gathered by Hamas concerns the Urim base. It enabled ten men from *Group 17* of the Hamas Special Forces (*Wahdat Al-Khassa*) to reach and penetrate YARKON, in order to seize documents, on October 7, 2023.

As we have seen, Gaza is an occupied territory, with the distinctive feature that this occupation is exercised from a distance. In other words, resistance actions can only be carried out outside the territory, in the so-called "Gaza envelope," where the military is interwoven with the Israeli civilian population.

*Israeli Intelligence around Gaza*

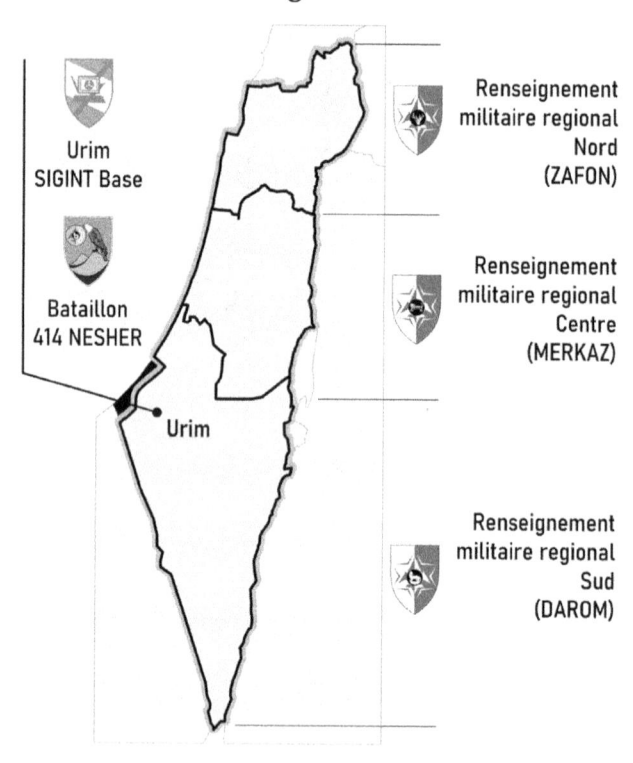

Figure 19—Israeli intelligence around Gaza is probably one of the most extensive in the world over such a small area. It is organized around the Regional Military Command South. It includes the AMAN intelligence resources assigned to this command. It also includes the Urim electronic intelligence base, located 17 km from the Gaza border. This is one of the largest listening bases in the world and is managed by a detachment of Unit 8200, which is responsible for electronic intelligence for the Israeli government. Human intelligence is provided by the NESHER battalion (Unit 414). Note the border of Israel according to the military (in gray), which includes the occupied territories (except Gaza) (in black).

The problem is that Israeli security forces try to avoid direct contact with the Palestinian resistance, preferring to keep it at a distance. This is what happened with the siege of Gaza. This meant that, in order to assert their right to resistance, the Palestinians *had to* leave their territory to strike at the Israeli forces located in the envelope of Gaza, where there are also civilian populations.

*Electronic Surveillance of the Gaza Strip*

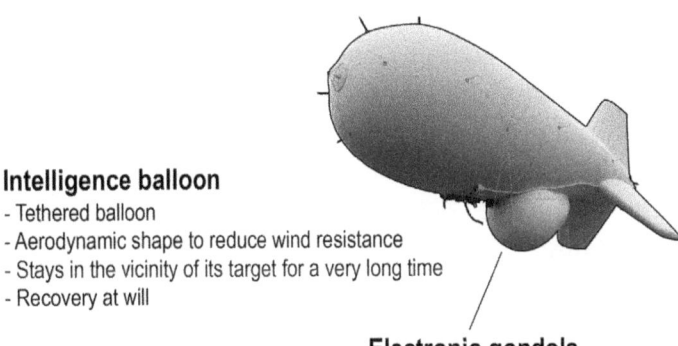

**Intelligence balloon**
- Tethered balloon
- Aerodynamic shape to reduce wind resistance
- Stays in the vicinity of its target for a very long time
- Recovery at will

**Electronic gondola**

*Figure 20—The Gaza Strip is closely monitored by one of the world's most sophisticated intelligence complexes, located at the Urim base, 17 km from the border. Led by AMAN Unit 8200, Israel employs a range of relatively "conventional" systems. Less well known is the use of "spy balloons." They bear no resemblance to what the "experts" in our media presented to us during the Chinese "spy balloon" incident, which was merely a sounding balloon. Three of these tethered balloons are normally used for electronic surveillance of the Gaza Strip. Apparently, all three were inactive on October 7, 2023.*

## The Islamic Resistance Movement (HAMAS)

### History of the Movement

#### The Beginnings

Hamas stands for *Harakat al-Mouqawamah al-Islamiya (Islamic Resistance Movement)*, which also means *"Enthusiasm."* It was founded on December 14, 1987 in Gaza, five days after the start of the first Intifada. Its historical and spiritual leader was Sheikh Ahmed Yassine,[198] who was killed by Israeli helicopter fire on March 22, 2004.

---

198. Sheikh Ahmed YASSINE, imprisoned in Israel from 1989 to 1997, released following the Mossad blunder in Jordan. He was eliminated on March 22, 2004 by an Israeli rocket attack.

Hamas grew out of *Al-Mujamma al-Islami,* a movement founded in 1967 and legally registered in Israel in 1978 by Sheikh Ahmed Yassin. The seven founding members of Hamas are Ahmed Yassine, 'Abd al-Fattah Dukhan, Mohammed Shama', Ibrahim al-Yazuri, Issa al-Najjar, Salah Shahadah and 'Abd al-Aziz Rantissi. Ismaïl Abou Shanab was also one of the movement's early disciples.

In the 1960s-1970s, the Palestinian movement was divided. Largely supported by the USSR and Eastern European countries, its approach was essentially anti-imperialist and Marxist. It is one of many pawns in the international struggle against so-called Western imperialism. Palestinian groups are numerous, with very different strategies of action, and carry out operations all over the world, with Israel as their target. The most infamous of these terrorist actions was the attack on Israeli athletes at the Munich Olympics in 1972, which brought worldwide condemnation of the Palestinians.

At this stage, the main bearer of the Palestinian struggle was Yasser Arafat's PLO. On November 13, 1974, he scored a decisive political success by addressing the United Nations General Assembly in New York. He pledged to abandon international terrorism and concentrate his efforts in Palestine. He wore his revolver on his belt, to underline the importance of armed struggle. The PLO gained observer status at the UN. Finally, in 1988, Yasser Arafat renounced terrorism. This more political orientation stimulated international support for the Palestinian cause, and Israel saw it as a threat.

As soon as the Likud party came to power in 1977, the Israeli objective was to marginalize the PLO and divide the Palestinian movement, by encouraging the emergence of rival movements.[199] Contacts between *Al-Mujamma* leaders and Israeli officials increased. Brigadier-General Yitzhak Segev, then military governor of Gaza, would later confess that he had funds at his disposal to finance the construction of mosques[200] and thus encourage the emergence of an Islamist movement that would become Hamas.[201]

---

199. Yossi Melman, "Hamas: When a Former Client Becomes an Implacable Enemy: Israel: The Likud government originally saw this Muslim fundamentalist organization as a welcome alternative to the PLO," *Los Angeles Times,* December 20, 1992 (https://www.latimes.com/archives/la-xpm-1992-12-20-op-4428-story.html)
200. Richard Sale, "Hamas history tied to Israel," *UPI,* June 18, 2002.
201. Robert Dreyfuss, *Devil's Game—How the United States Helped Unleash Fundamentalist Islam,* New York, 2005, p. 169.

The phenomenon is well known, but largely ignored by the French-speaking media, who prefer to forget the nuances:[202] they do not like contradictions that could fuel criticism of Israel. Yet this policy has been maintained over the years, as Benjamin Netanyahu himself confirmed at a meeting of a Likud faction in March 2019. This has led former Defense Minister Avigdor Liberman to say that Israel *"finances terrorism against itself."*[203]

In the 1970s-1980s, Israel saw the PLO as its main threat. Its strategy was therefore to create a sort of counter-fire to the PLO in order to divide the Palestinian movement.[204] The various Palestinian movements were gradually all driven out of Palestine. Israel then found itself in the same strategic situation as Hamas in 2023: it had an adversary operating at a distance, which it was unable to fight from its own territory. Thus, it did what Hamas would do forty years later—it intervened.

Hamas benefited from Yasser Arafat's international failures. The relocation of the PLO leadership to Lebanon and then Tunisia in 1982 left a vacuum in the occupied territories, which *Al-Mujamma* was quick to fill.

Sheikh Yassin created the *Al-Madjahadoun Al-Filistinioun*, a parallel group fighting both the Israelis and rival Palestinian movements. At first, his struggle was essentially political, but he acquired weapons to extend his field of action. In 1984, the discovery of this group by the Israeli services led to the arrest of Sheikh Yassin and thirteen of its main leaders. Weapons hidden at the Islamic University of Gaza were seized. In 1985, the *Al-Moujamma* numbered some 2,000 militants, mainly recruited from this university.[205]

During the Gulf War (1990-1991), Hamas condemned Yasser Arafat's support for Saddam Hussein and advocated the withdrawal of Iraq and the United States from Kuwait and Saudi Arabia. After the war, Saudi aid initially earmarked for PLO social works was redirected to Hamas. From

---

202. Ishaan Tharoor, "How Israel helped create Hamas," *The Washington Post*, July 30, 2014; "Hamas Israel's own creation," *The Times of Israel*, December 3, 2018.
203. Lahav Harkov, "Netanyahu: Money to Hamas part of strategy to keep Palestinians divided," *Jerusalem Post*, March 12, 2019.
204. "Grave accusation by Tzipi Livni: 'Netanyahu's government supports Hamas in order not to solve the Palestinian problem,'" *Infos-Israel.news*, September 2, 2018; "Hamas Israel's own creation," *The Times of Israel*, December 3, 2018.
205. Founded in the mid-1980s from a religious college, following the closure of the Egyptian university after the signing of the Camp David Accords, the Islamic University of Gaza is the main university in the occupied territories, with some 4,500 students. It is the object of struggles between secularists and religionists, notably over the wearing of veils by women.

then on, some US$28 million a year was channeled into Hamas' social work, enabling it to consolidate its presence among the Palestinian population.

Hamas was thus able to weave an alternative and parallel social and political structure to that of the PLO in a very short space of time. Its base of supporters gradually expanded from the Gaza Strip.

## *The Emergence of Hamas*

The first Intifada in 1987 was essentially a movement of civil disobedience against the expansion of settlements in the West Bank and East Jerusalem. But Israel's strategy of dissuasion by firing live ammunition at demonstrators meant that the dead became martyrs. This strategy opened the door to a jihadist approach, which integrates the ultimate sacrifice into the process of resistance.

In 1988, the political approach of Yasser Arafat's Fatah and its renunciation of terrorism were welcomed by the Palestinians, but did not lead to an easing of Israeli repression or a political solution to the question of the territories. At the same time, the Marxism on which the Palestinian resistance was based was fading, and Islam became the bearer of revolutionary hopes in Palestine and elsewhere.

Gradually, the absence of tangible results was showing the Palestinians that Israel was not sincere about reaching a solution that satisfies both parties, and that action was needed.

The tacit "cooperation" between Israel and Hamas deteriorated after the kidnapping and murder of two Israeli soldiers (Avi Sasportas, in February 1989, and Ilan Sa'adon, in May of the same year). Hamas was officially banned in December 1989.

Since 1989, Hamas has agreed to submit to the decisions of the *Palestinian National Council* (PNC), while actively collaborating with other Palestinian movements, including the *Popular Front for the Liberation of Palestine (PFLP)*, which is opposed to Fatah. Nevertheless, the Israeli strategy of division worked, and clashes between Hamas and Fatah were numerous and brutal, notably in Nablus in June 1991 and Gaza in July 1992. Curiously enough, while Israel could have benefited from these fratricidal clashes, it made no attempt to differentiate between the two organizations and fought them both.

After what the Palestinians called the "Al-Aqsa Mosque Massacre" on October 8, 1990, Hamas hardened its position, declaring that every Israeli soldier was a potential target. The United States, a little more far-sighted than it is today, understood that the situation was ready to degenerate and put pressure on the United Nations to condemn Israel.[206] But Israel's policy remained unchanged.

This situation, where no mechanism other than force can achieve results, favors Hamas's terrorist strategy. If not concrete results, at least the feeling of having acted. This is exactly what "jihad" means.

On December 21, 1992, in an unprecedented move in Israel, Israeli television broadcast an interview with Sheikh Yassin, the historic leader of Hamas. The interview was part of the movement's demands to spare the life of Sergeant Nissim Toledano, kidnapped on December 12. It was clearly a success for Hamas strategy: Yasser Arafat would not be given a real interview on the Israeli media until after the signing of the Oslo Accords in 1993.

In the early 1990s, the rapid rise of Hamas in the occupied territories led to a weakening of the PLO's influence. It was undoubtedly this phenomenon that prompted Yasser Arafat to seek success on the international stage, and to accept negotiations and then an agreement with Israel, which Hamas continues to oppose.

As soon as the Oslo Accords were signed in 1993, the PLO regained legitimacy and credibility on the international scene. It regained external funding, enabling it to develop its social action and thus regain ground on Hamas, which tended to be in the minority among the Palestinian population. But Israel's attitude towards the Palestinian leadership—and in particular the personal "rivalry" between Ariel Sharon and Yasser Arafat—played a major role in undermining the peace process and—indirectly—vindicating hardliners like Hamas.

Israel's divide-and-rule policy was not translating into improved security. The Palestinian Authority was unable to reduce terrorist activity resulting from rivalry between Palestinian groups. As a result of Israel's strategy, the Palestinian Authority was perceived as incapable of ensuring the security of Palestinians, thus playing into the hands of Hamas. To be credible, the fraternal enemies had to work together. To coordinate their actions in the Intifada in the occupied territories, Hamas and the PLO set up a joint command in March 1993.

---

206. Paul Lewis, "Mideast Tensions; U.S. Presses The U.N. To Condemn Israel," *The New York Times*, October 10, 1990 (https://www.nytimes.com/1990/10/10/world/mideast-tensions-us-presses-the-un-to-condemn-israel.html)

## Hamas's Terrorist Strategy

Before the first Intifada, then known as "*al-Mujamma al-Islami*," the movement still had an ideology close to that of the Muslim Brotherhood, and directed its activities against heretics and deviants of Islam. But it was increasingly moving away from the "Brotherhood" doctrine, and its focus shifted from ideological considerations to more operational engagements against members of the armed or security forces.

In 1992, Hamas marked its ideological and institutional break with the Muslim Brotherhood by creating its own political leadership mechanisms with its own Consultative Council (*Majlis al-Shura*) and Political Bureau (*Maktab al-Siyasi*).

The situation gradually changed after the signing of the Oslo Accords. Hamas' influence waned, while the Palestinian Authority (PA), under international pressure, had to demonstrate that it could constitute the embryo of a state. Violent clashes between the PA and Hamas in Gaza in 1994 led to a refocusing of Hamas activities on the West Bank. The head of Hamas's political office in Jordan, Mousa Abu Marzooq, implicitly recognized the state of Israel and advocated a return to the 1948 borders, with the release of Palestinian prisoners. In early 1994, Sheikh Yassin offered a ceasefire (*hudna*) in exchange for an Israeli withdrawal from the occupied territories, the release of Palestinian prisoners and the dismantling of settlements.

On February 25, 1994, Israeli terrorist Baruch Goldstein killed 29 Palestinians praying in a Hebron mosque. Goldstein was revered as a hero in Israel, but he prompted Hamas to adopt the tactic of suicide bombings, making its operations extremely deadly. Between 2000 and 2002 in Palestine, suicide attacks accounted for 1% of attacks, but 44% of victims.[207] Hamas bombs were designed by Yahya Ayyash (alias Al-Muhandis), who was eliminated by Mossad on January 5, 1996 using a booby-trapped cell phone.

In the 1990s, internal differences emerged within the movement: the political leadership based abroad and the military wing were opposed to any compromise with Israel, while the political leadership in Palestine was more ready. In July 1999, however, Mousa Abu Marzooq, former

---

207. Pape ROBERT A., *The Strategic Logic of Suicide Terrorism*, unpublished manuscript (18.02.2003) cited in report to Congress "Terrorists and Suicide Attacks," *Congressional Research Service*, 28.08.2003.

head of the Hamas political bureau, declared that the movement was open to negotiations with other "forces of the Palestinian people."

At this stage, Hamas's strategy was hardline, in response to the Palestinians' disappointment with the political path advocated by Yasser Arafat. Volunteers for Hamas suicide operations were numerous:

> *We cannot offer [all our volunteers] a martyrdom operation because the number of targets is limited and the enemy objectives we would like to reach are highly fortified.*[208]

## The Impact of September 11, 2001

Contrary to popular opinion, the Palestinians did not rejoice at 9/11. The event triggered mistrust of Palestinian movements and contributed to the drying up of certain sources of funding that did not want to be assimilated with "al-Qaeda" financing.

On December 22, 2001, Hamas issued a communiqué announcing that it would no longer carry out operations *"in the Palestinian territories occupied since 1948, including mortar attacks."*[209] This decision followed the recommendations of the special session of the United Nations General Assembly[210] and negotiations between Hamas and Yasser Arafat. It would only be maintained, however, if Israel abandoned its policy of targeted eliminations.[211]

On June 29, 2003, in application of the "road map," Hamas and its military wing, the *Izz al-Din al-Qassam*, agreed to a three-month ceasefire (*hudna*). But on August 21, 2003, Israeli forces eliminated Ismail Abu Shanab. At the time, he was considered a Hamas moderate, and his assassination triggered widespread condemnation and an unprecedented mobilization of the Palestinian population. Attacks resumed in step with the eliminations carried out by Israel.

On March 22, 2004, Sheikh Ahmed Yassin, the historic leader of Hamas, was killed by Israeli helicopter fire. He was succeeded at the head of the

---

208. Salah Shehada, Commander of the Al-Qassam Brigades, Interview on the Islam Online website, May 29, 2002.
209. http://edition.cnn.com/2001/WORLD/meast/12/24/mideast.bethlehem/index.html
210. https://www.ohchr.org/en/press-releases/2009/10/general-assembly-emergency-session-occupied-palestinian-territories-calls
211. *BBC News*, December 22, 2001.

movement by Abd al-Aziz Rantissi, who was also shot dead on April 17, 2004. Khaled al-Mash'al replaced him and remained the movement's political leader until 2017. To avoid his elimination, his name was initially kept secret.

During its early years, Israeli operations made Hamas the "true" bearer of the Palestinian struggle, and gave it unprecedented popularity. The attacks of September 11, 2001, the launch of the "War on Terror" by George W. Bush and the association made between Hamas and "al-Qaeda" by the Israelis discouraged Arab countries from actively supporting Hamas. As a result, Hamas shifted its focus to more political fields, and regained international credibility.

Israel's abandonment of the Gaza Strip in 2005 marked a decisive turning point in the movement's policy. Now almost the sole master of the territory, it took its responsibilities into its own hands and sought to move from a resistance movement limited to armed struggle to a more political movement, capable of competing with Fatah.

### Hamas's Political Shift

Hamas joined the ceasefire that concluded the second Intifada in February 2005[212] and ceased its terrorist activities.[213] It then became involved in associative and trade union activities. It took part in the municipal elections of 2005, then in the legislative elections of January 2006.

The British daily *The Guardian* noted that Hamas, "*after four years of violence against Israel, is now considering refocusing on the* political dimension."[214]

In June 2002, President Bush urged the Palestinians to find a successor to Yasser Arafat.[215] In February 2005, Mahmoud Abbas was elected President of the Palestinian Authority. This success prompted the Americans to call for legislative elections, convinced of Fatah's victory. The idea was to have an interlocutor with whom to pursue dialogue.

---

212. Mark Oliver, "Sharon and Abbas agree ceasefire," *The Guardian*, February 8, 2005 (https://www.theguardian.com/world/2005/feb/08/israel4)
213. "Analysis: Palestinian suicide attacks," *BBC News*, January 29, 2007 (http://news.bbc.co.uk/1/hi/world/middle_east/3256858.stm)
214. Conal Urquhart, "Hamas hints at ceasefire as the Palestinians vote," *The Guardian*, January 9, 2005 (https://www.theguardian.com/world/2005/jan/09/israel)
215. https://georgewbush-whitehouse.archives.gov/news/releases/2002/06/20020624-3.html

But the Israelis had another strategy: to apply a differentiated regime between Gaza and the West Bank, thereby encouraging the division of the Palestinian movement. This was the background to the Gaza disengagement plan approved by the Israeli government on June 6, 2004. It led to a withdrawal of settlers which ended on September 12, 2005. However, Gaza's infrastructure was carefully destroyed by the Israeli army before leaving, and access to the territory was strictly controlled. The Palestinians thus had a territory that was nothing more than a vast refugee camp.

At this stage, the Oslo process was dead, but the Gazans saw this restitution as the result of their armed resistance. In other words, they felt that between Fatah's political approach and Hamas's armed one, the latter was more promising. The lack of political progress between Fatah and the Israeli authorities seems to confirm this conclusion. This was what allowed Hamas to establish its authority. On January 26, 2006, Hamas won the legislative elections, for which the European Union's election observation mission concluded:[216]

> *The conduct of these elections was a model for the entire Arab region, and clearly demonstrated the Palestinian people's commitment to democracy.*

It won 74 of the 132 seats in the Palestinian Parliament. It thus became the main Palestinian political force, ahead of Fatah (45 seats). But this result took the international community by surprise. In 2016, the Anglo-American press published a statement made by Hillary Clinton the day after the election:[217]

> *I don't think we should have pushed for elections in the Palestinian territories. I think it was a big mistake... And if we wanted to push for an election, we should have tried to do something about who was going to win.*

This change of direction could then have been exploited by Israel and the international community to push Hamas definitively into a more political role. But this was not the option chosen.

---

216. https://www.un.org/unispal/document/auto-insert-194881/
217. https://www.dailymail.co.uk/news/article-3885072/We-did-determine-going-win-Hillary-Clinton-heard-tape-making-stunning-argument-fixed-2006-Palestinian-election.html

Instead of exploiting this momentum to put Hamas against the wall and try to find a solution, the international community refused to deal with the new Palestinian government it was leading. Worse still, disappointed by the outcome, President George W. Bush approved a clandestine action to use Fatah to attempt a "coup" against Hamas:[218]

> *After failing to anticipate Hamas's victory over Fatah in the 2006 Palestinian elections, the White House has concocted a new, scandalously secretive and self-destructive debacle in the Middle East: a mixture of Iran-contra and Bay of Pigs. Using confidential documents corroborated by outraged former and current U.S. officials, the author reveals how President Bush, Condoleezza Rice and Deputy National Security Advisor Elliott Abrams supported an armed force led by Fatah strongman Muhammad Dahlan, triggering a bloody civil war in Gaza and leaving Hamas stronger than ever.*

The result was violent clashes between Hamas and Fatah supporters in 2006-2007, which turned into a civil war and led to Fatah's withdrawal from Gaza, leaving Hamas in total control of the area.

Israel used this pretext to lay siege to Gaza, surrounding it with a fence and placing the territory under close surveillance and total control. The Gaza Strip thus became an "open-air prison," condemning Hamas to further military action.

But our media are not short of lies, and the Swiss *RTS* claimed: "*Hamas took power in Gaza in June 2007 in a coup de force at the expense of the Palestinian Authority.*"[219] This is exactly the opposite of what happened! The media's portrayal of the crisis deliberately ignored a whole series of Israeli events and decisions, which systematically closed the door to a solution to the conflict. The Palestinians were pushed further and further into a corner, condemned to the sole use of force to assert their rights.

The myth of Iranian financial support for Hamas began with the parliamentary elections in January 2006. Following the election victory, Hamas began consultations with Fatah to form a coalition movement.

---

218. David Rose, "The Gaza Bombshell," *Vanity Fair*, March 3, 2008 (https://www.vanityfair.com/news/2008/04/gaza200804)
219. "Gaza: Salafists crushed by Hamas," rts.ch, June 28, 2010 (https://www.rts.ch/info/monde/1056172-gaza-les-salafistes-ecrases-par-le-hamas.html)

The international community froze aid, the United States declared an embargo against the enclave and Israel blocked United Nations aid. On February 21, 2006, President Mahmoud Abbas officially asked Hamas to form a government. Under American pressure, Fatah decided not to participate, but a sort of partnership agreement was established between the two rival groups for the management of a certain number of services.

On February 22, Iran offered to financially compensate the Palestinian government for this loss,[220] followed by the European Union in June.[221] It is important to note that Iran was supporting the Palestinian *government* and not *Hamas*, even though the latter was in charge. The reason for Iran's gesture was the existence of a Shiite minority in Gaza. By trying to isolate Hamas, the United States has opened the door to Iran, which also saw an opportunity to take a dig at Israel and its Palestinian policy.

Since its political turnaround in 2005-2006, Hamas's military thinking had been moving towards a more conciliatory policy, incorporating the notion of a long-term truce (*hudna*) and putting armed struggle to one side. Hamas's Dr. Ahmed Youssef advocated a "hudna" strategy:

> *The hudna goes beyond the Western concept of a ceasefire and obliges the parties to use this period to seek a permanent, non-violent solution to their differences... Whereas war dehumanizes the enemy and makes him easier to kill, the hudna offers the opportunity to humanize one's adversaries and understand their position, with the aim of resolving the inter-tribal or international dispute.*[222]

The *hudna* is defined as follows:

> *In Islamic law, the hudna is equivalent to an "international treaty" in modern terminology. Its purpose is to suspend the legal effects of hostilities and provide the preconditions for peace between Muslims and non-Muslims, without the latter's territory becoming part of dar al-Islam. The Koran provides for Muslims not only the possibility of concluding a peace agreement with the enemy, but also the*

---

220. *BBC News*, February 22 2006 (http://news.bbc.co.uk/2/hi/middle_east/4739900.stm).
221. "L'Europe doit peser de tout son poids pour sauver Gaza du chaos," *lefigaro.fr*, July 2 2007.
222. Ahmed Yousef, "Pause for Peace," *The New York Times*, November 1, 2006 (https://www.nytimes.com/2006/11/01/opinion/01yousef.html)

*obligation to respect the terms of the agreement until the end of its specified period.*[223]

Another term used in January 2024 during ceasefire negotiations was "*tadiyah,*" which corresponds to the notion of a military truce.[224] Apparently, during the negotiations in Paris, the PIJ indicated that the Palestinians would agree to a "permanent *tadiyah.*" This was to be an intermediate situation, leading to a permanent ceasefire.

The problem is that Israel's policy has never been aimed at creating the conditions for peace and harmonious development of the two peoples side by side, but at driving the Palestinians into exile by making life impossible for them.

In May 2018, Yahya Sinwar, head of the Hamas Political Bureau in Gaza, declared that his movement was participating in the "Marches of Return" and could move to a strategy of civil disobedience under the aegis of the Palestinian Authority.[225] As we can see, this was not a strategy of violence at all costs, as our media would have us believe.

## Hamas Doctrine

### The Hamas Charter

In October 2023, to reinforce the idea of the religious dimension of Hamas, our media evoke the Hamas Charter. On *Sud Radio*, philosophy professor Raphaël Einthoven recalls its reference to the *Protocol of the Elders of Zion*, a highly controversial document in the West (but widely read in the rest of the world), which attributes to the Jews a project of global conquest.[226] Similarly, carefully selected extracts from this charter can be found on the website of the Israeli Consulate General in New York,[227] which refers to Hamas's refusal to recognize Israel's existence and its desire to destroy it. In fact, this is disinformation and conspiracy.

---

223. Mohammed Khadduri, Article "Hudna," Encyclopedia of Islam, (CD-ROM Edition v.1.1.) Koninklijke Brill NV, Leiden, 2001.
224. Dag Tuastad, "Hamas's Concept of a Long-term Ceasefire—A Viable Alternative to Full Peace?," *Peace Research Institute Oslo (PRIO)*, November 2010 (https://www.files.ethz.ch/isn/144215/Hamas Concept of a Long-term Ceasefire, PRIO Paper 2010.pdf)
225. https://www.memri.org/tv/hamas-leader-yahya-sinwar-our-people-took-off-their-uniforms-and-joined-the-marces
226. https://youtu.be/yePvAADcc9w?t=178
227. https://embassies.gov.il/NEW-YORK/ABOUTISRAEL/Pages/Hamas-Covenant.aspx

As the Consulate General himself says: *"Nothing is more monstrous than trying to explain barbarity."*[228]

Our media systematically refer to these selected extracts, like Stéphanie de Muru on *Sud Radio*, who claims that Hamas seeks to *"eradicate the State of Israel and the Jews"* (terms that are not found in any version of the Hamas charter), while her interlocutor, Aurélien Taché (despite being a critic of Israel) declares that it is a "genocidal" movement.[229] Whether for or against the Palestinian cause, the ignorance and stupidity of our commentators alone explain why the problem persists.

In fact, the Charter that our media invariably quote is the one from 1988. However, this has been completely rewritten and replaced by a new Charter, published on May 1st, 2017. Even Wikipedia only cites and describes the Charter of August 18, 1988, hastily mentioning that it was *"completed"* in 2017.[230] But this is not true. The content and articulation of the document clearly show that it is an entirely new document.

Among other changes, contrary to what our journalists claim, it does not call for the destruction of the State of Israel and marks its distance from the doctrine of the Muslim Brotherhood. It merely formalizes the change in approach that took place after the second Intifada and the end of the Oslo process. Today, Hamas no longer has anything in common with the Muslim Brotherhood. To give everyone an idea of the Charter, it is published in the appendix.

Hamas' objectives are set out in its new charter of May 1, 2017. Essentially, they are to re-establish Arab sovereignty over the entire territory of Palestine. Hamas refutes the Balfour Declaration (1917), the partition plan for Palestine (Resolution 181 of 1947) and the documents derived from them.

The refutation of these documents is not totally incongruous. Hamas' view is that these documents should be replaced by the implementation of the right of peoples to self-determination. This was what was envisaged by Resolution 181, which was only a "plan"—and not a decision—which was to be put to a referendum of the populations concerned. But this was neither done by the British before they left, nor by the Israelis.[231]

---

228. https://youtu.be/5rLzghDJ6Xs?t=414
229. https://youtu.be/ZkrSl7gufpg
230. https://fr.wikipedia.org/wiki/Charte_du_Hamas
231. https://avalon.law.yale.edu/20th_century/res181.asp

That said, the Hamas Charter establishes a link between Islam and the liberation of the occupied territories, which limits, if not excludes, any compromise on the occupied territories that would be interpreted as a concession on Islam itself.

## A Territorial and not a Religious War

The official Israeli and Western line is that the Palestinian struggle *"is not a war of territory, it is a war of religion."*[232] This is not true. Apart from the fact that it has long been steeped in Marxism, the Palestinian cause has so little to do with Islam that it has found no support from the jihadists of the Islamic State. In fact, by placing the Palestinian approach within a broader religious project, Israeli rhetoric rules out any political solution, since it situates the conflict within the religious sphere.

The problem is that Israel does not see the conflict with the Palestinians as being linked to their right to self-determination, and therefore to the territorial question, but to the idea that the countries around it want Israel to disappear. In other words, Israel sees it more as a question of external security policy than a problem of internal security. This no doubt explains why it has never really developed a counter-terrorism strategy.

With Operation AL-AQSA FLOOD, our media and politicians have adopted the Israeli narrative of a religious conflict. For example, on October 11, 2023, *CNews* journalist Pascal Praud asserted that Hamas *"wants the destruction of the Jews."*[233] Where does he get this allegation from? A mystery. Because no Hamas document says so, and certainly not the Hamas Charter, which says exactly the opposite in article 16:

> *Hamas claims that its conflict is with the Zionist project, not with Jews because of their religion. Hamas is not fighting against Jews because they are Jews, but against the Zionists who occupy Palestine. Yet it is the Zionists who constantly identify Judaism and Jews with their own colonial project and illegal entity.*

This is why Zionist circles (but not Jewish movements) are trying to impose equality between "anti-Semitism" and "anti-Zionism." It is

---

232. "Meyer Habib: 'un attentat quasiment tous les jours' en Israël," *CNews/YouTube*, November 18, 2014 (00'45") (https://youtu.be/4UA2tlNP_Ik)
233. https://youtu.be/x4Z5XjKOYC4?t=311

exactly the same logic as establishing an equivalence between "Islam" and "Islamism:" the aim is to make problems of a political (and therefore negotiable) nature dependent on a higher (religious) and inescapable logic. This absolves us of any responsibility for finding solutions, and locks us into perpetual conflict.

Contrary to the message that Israel tries to convey in order to demonstrate the impossibility of negotiating with Hamas, the latter's positions are considerably more realistic. Thus, in 2003, Ismail Abu-Shanab declared:

> *Let's be frank. We cannot destroy Israel. The practical solution for us is to have a state. When we build a Palestinian state, we won't need these militias anymore; all the need to attack will cease. Everything will be transformed into civilian life.*[234]

On the Israeli side, there has long been a desire to slide the problem into religious confrontation. This was the aim of the massacre of Palestinians at prayer in the Mosque of Abraham (Tomb of the Patriarchs, for the Jews) on February 25, 1994, which was to be the starting point for Hamas's suicide attacks.

Unlike the Palestinians, who systematically invoke the return to the 1948 lands and the application of UN resolutions, Israel prefers to invoke the Bible. Since October 7, Benjamin Netanyahu has multiplied references to the Bible to justify his military operations in Gaza.[235] He has even decided to change the name of his operation in Gaza (SWORDS OF IRON) to the biblical "GENESIS."[236]

On October 25, 2023, at a press conference, Benjamin Netanyahu spoke of the fulfillment of Isaiah's prophecy.[237] Four days later, he declared:

---

234. Jeroen GUNNING, "Peace with Hamas? The Transforming Potential of Political Participation," *International Affairs*, Volume 80, Issue 2, March 2004, Pages 233-255, (https://doi.org/10.1111/j.1468-2346.2004.00381.x)

235. "Netanyahu's references to violent biblical passages raise alarm among critics," *NPR.org*, November 7, 2023 (https://www.npr.org/2023/11/07/1211133201/netanyahus-references-to-violent-biblical-passages-raise-alarm-among-critics)

236. Shirit Avitan COHENM "Exclusive: Iron Swords or Genesis? The behind-the-scenes effort to rename war," Israel Hayom, December 29, 2023 (https://www.israelhayom.com/2023/12/29/exclusive-iron-swords-or-genesis-the-behind-the-scenes-effort-to-rename-war/)

237. "Netanyahu: Defeating Hamas will make prophecy of Isaiah a reality," *The Christian Post*, October 25, 2023 (https://www.christianpost.com/news/netanyahu-defeating-hamas-will-make-prophecy-of-isaiah-a-reality.html)

*You must remember what Amalek did to you, says our Holy Bible. 1 Samuel 15:3 "Go and strike Amalek, destroy everything he owns and do not spare him; kill men and women, children and infants, oxen and sheep, camels and donkeys."*[238]

This discourse, imbued with a divine mystique, aims to give a religious logic to the conflict, which rules out any possible political solution. Thus, the conflict can only end in the destruction of one or other of the protagonists. Not only is this discourse genocidal in substance (these quotations will be retained by the International Court of Justice), but it contradicts what the United Nations says about the conflict.

In December 2000, speaking to Swiss journalist Malika Nedir, Sheikh Yassin, founder of Hamas, declared:[239]

*The conflict is not religious. We respect all religions and we have good relations with all religions. The issue is one of aggression. There is an aggressor who has attacked us, who has exiled us, who has confiscated our homes and our land. We must resist and we must reclaim our rights.*

Like Israel, Hamas claims sovereignty over the entire territory between the Mediterranean Sea and the Jordan River. It has remained very consistent on this line, but its leaders have repeatedly admitted that Palestinian independence within the 1967 borders (in fact, the 1949 armistice line or "Green Line") would be acceptable for negotiation, suggesting that Hamas is not seeking the annihilation of Israel:[240]

*If Israel withdraws to the 1967 borders, including Jerusalem, recognizes the right of return, lifts its siege, dismantles settlements [in the occupied territories] and releases prisoners, then it is possible for us Palestinians and Arabs to take a serious step in favor of the Zionists.*

Hamas repeated this commitment in its 2017 charter. It thus recognizes the existence of a *"Zionist entity"* or *"Israeli entity."* On the other hand, as

---

238. https://www.livemint.com/news/world/pm-netanyahu-invokes-amalek-theory-to-justify-gaza-killings-what-is-this-hebrew-bible-nation-11698555324918.html
239. Cheikh Yassine, interview for Radio Suisse Romande, by Malika Nedir (December 2000)
240. "Khaled Meshaal, political leader of Hamas," *Reuters*, May 3, 2006.

we have seen, it cannot formally recognize a State of Israel, which has still not defined its borders, despite the injunctions of the United Nations.

## *Islamic Resistance and Islamism*

On October 11, 2023, *CNews* journalist Pascal Praud relayed the speech made the previous day by MP Meyer Habib at the French National Assembly, who asserted that the war was *"between our civilization and barbarism."* *"Hamas wants a state in place of Israel, not next to it,"* and declared that *"Hamas is the Islamic State."*[241] This is low-level propaganda. To understand the Islamic dimension of Palestinian resistance, we need to go back to history.

The main consequence of the First World War was the disappearance of the great European empires and the emergence of states based on the idea of nationhood. The inter-war period was one of instability, leading to the emergence of dictatorships. In the Middle East, the Western powers rushed to take the place left vacant by the Ottoman Empire, triggering resistance movements throughout the Mashreq.

But these movements, divided by their ethnic and tribal components, failed to achieve the critical mass to drive out the occupiers. The idea of "nation" could hardly be associated with a territory, as in Europe.

In Egypt, to mobilize the population, Hassan al-Banna advocated a form of nationalism based not on territory, but on religious community. In 1928, he created the Muslim Brotherhood movement. In fact, he applied exactly the same reasoning as Theodor Herzl, founder of Zionism a few years earlier: to bring together a people separated by geography, you have to rely on what they have in common: religion. In fact, the two nationalisms that clash today in Palestine both have their origins in the emergence of nationalism in the late 19th and early 20th centuries.

In Palestine, resistance to the colonial power took a particular form. In 1920, the League of Nations gave Great Britain the mandate to administer Palestine. The Balfour Declaration of 1917 promised the Jews a "national home" in Palestine, but the British were slow to respect it in the face of opposition from the Arab population, who had occupied the country since biblical times. This gave rise to an anti-British resistance movement on the part of the Jewish community, while the Arabs saw the British more as protectors.

---

241. https://www.dailymotion.com/video/x8oqkr9

After the Second World War, Jewish militants received help from the USSR, before turning to the West once independence was achieved in May 1948. The USSR helped the Palestinian movement in its struggle against Western imperialism. But by the mid-1980s, the Palestinian movement was threatened by geographical and ideological fragmentation. The unifying element was no longer Marxist anti-imperialism.

The pan-Arabism of the 1950s-1960s, a blend of nationalism and Marxism, was fundamentally secular and oriented towards modernism. But it did not "speak" to an essentially rural population whose daily life remained very traditional. To unite Palestinians around their cause and win the support of Arab peoples, Hamas borrowed the idea of Islamic nationalism from the Muslim Brotherhood.

That is why Hamas has tried—successfully—to keep its struggle within Palestine, to avoid alienating international public opinion. This was a mistake made by the Palestinian liberation movements of the 1960s-1970s, which advocated an internationalist struggle within a Marxist ideological framework.

## The Nature of Palestinian Resistance

The events of October 2023 were an opportunity for the French media and politicians to appropriate Hamas as a national security issue. To achieve this intellectual exercise, it is necessary to claim that Islam is Islamism, as Manuel VALLS says,[242] therefore Hamas is the Islamic State, as Benjamin Netanyahu and Anthony Blinken say,[243] and therefore "*France has been a victim of Hamas*," according to Damien Rieu, French MP.[244] Such nonsense would be laughable if these "intellectuals" were not politicians. This artificial association between Hamas and the Islamic State explains how and why our politicians are intellectually incapable of dealing with the issue of terrorism.

In France, our "experts" describe Islamism as "political Islam." A notion that has never really been defined. It is loosely understood as an approach that aims to impose certain behaviors, such as the wearing of the Islamic veil, adapted menus in school cafeterias or separate times for men and women in swimming pools. This is simplistic. The former has a more

---

242. Manuel VALLS, "Grand Jury" program, RTL, *LCI* and *Le Figaro*, November 26, 2017.
243. https://www.state.gov/secretary-antony-j-blinken-and-israeli-prime-minister-benjamin-netanyahu-after-their-meeting-2/
244. https://youtu.be/VshpTRd_QeA?t=1779

traditional than religious origin, the latter was a long-established practice in the airline industry, and the latter began in France with demands from the Jewish community in the late 1970s.[245]

Particularly in France, where inappropriate policies have generated a feeling of rejection of Arab populations, individual behavior (Islamic veils, etc.) is more a question of identity than Islamism. In English-speaking countries, where they have not been exacerbated by passion as in France, these individual practices do not pose a problem.

Like any entity involved in a crisis, revolutionary or resistance movements are defined by values. These values are a combination of cultural, religious, societal and political elements. In a limited geographical space, these values are relatively homogeneous and understood by all. But this is not the case when it comes to bringing together a globally dispersed community, which does not have a homogeneous set of values. Some have therefore sought to rally around the "lowest common denominator"—religion. This is what Theodor Herzl did with Zionism, and what Hassan al-Banna did with the Islamism of the Muslim Brotherhood.

In fact, Islamism can be defined as Muslim nationalism. It developed exponentially after the wars waged by the West in the Near and Middle East from the early 2000s, which revived—and even created—the feeling of an Islamic identity in solidarity with the populations affected by the conflicts.

Just as the French felt solidarity after the attacks of 2015-2016, just as the Israelis felt solidarity after October 7, 2023, Muslims have felt solidarity with populations attacked by Westerners since 2001. This solidarity reinforced the feeling of belonging to the Muslim nation, generating a Muslim nationalism—Islamism.

In terms of security, Islamism essentially provides what is known in computing as an "operating system" in tune with the population's culture. It adds to the military notion of *resistance* (*muqawama*) that of *jihad*, which has nothing to do with a "holy war." The term "jihad" derives from the verb "to resist" or "to strive." It implies that we do not give up in the face of difficulties, but that we maintain the will to confront them.

Etymologically, and in the daily practice of every Muslim, jihad (then called *Great Jihad*) aims to resist temptations to deviate from God's path.

---

245. Muriel BERNARD, "Des créneaux réservés aux élèves des écoles juives," *ledauphine.com*, October 20, 2011.

It therefore has an essentially spiritual and cultural dimension. But it can also take a more physical form in response to aggression (military or otherwise). In this case, one speaks of a *Small Jihad*.

This notion of jihad resonates with that of *"sumud"* (resilience),[246] which emerged in Palestine after the June 1967 war as a form of passive individual resistance that has passed into popular culture.

### Three Forms of Resistance in Palestine

| Arabic term | Translation | Meaning | Operational significance |
|---|---|---|---|
| Muqawama | Resistance | Action of wearing down and harassing the opponent. | Resistance in the military sense of the word. |
| Jihad | Moral resistance | Refusal to bow our heads, to bow to difficulty. | Active personal involvement in the Resistance. |
| Sumud | Resilience | Resist and endure. | Passive form of personal resistance. |

*Figure 21—Palestinian resistance is fueled by a superposition of military, religious and cultural elements that reinforce each other and give it its robustness.*

The Palestinians know that the numerical advantage is in Israel's favor. The contribution of an Islamist mindset enables them to approach victory in a way that escapes the Western (and Israeli) notion of victory based on the balance of power. Thus, for an Islamist, the notion of victory is not linked to the destruction of the adversary, but to the refusal to give up the fight. In fact, this is what Abu Mohammed al-Adnani, head of operations for the Islamic State, said in June 2015:[247]

*Real defeat is the loss of willpower and the desire to fight.*

For an Islamist, victory is above all a victory over oneself. For this reason, he can find victory despite an unfavorable balance of power: the will to resist is already a victory. This explains why, even when he dies, the resistance fighter is victorious, and explains the longevity of the Palestinian resistance.

---

246. https://www.monde-diplomatique.fr/mav/157/PIRONET/58319
247. Speech by Abu Mohammed al-Adnani, June 2015.

This is why, for example, Palestinian rockets are not intended to kill, but to be fired. Actions such as incendiary balloons, carried out by various groups in the Gaza Strip, are not intended to kill, but to demonstrate the will to resist. By responding with strikes, the Israelis are only encouraging the Palestinians' will to resist. For this reason, they will not succeed in resolving the problem in this way.

Once you understand how this logic works, you understand the absurdity of Darius Rochebin's remark on *LCI*:

> *Do you agree that it's a good idea to kill every single Islamist to prevent them from doing any harm?*

The reason why Islamism and Jihadism have developed so rapidly in recent years is the multiplication of wars against Muslim populations around the world. In Palestine, Islamism is simply an expression of resistance to the illegal occupation of territories acquired through a war of aggression in 1967. Even with the demise of Hamas, this resistance will not disappear. Israeli and Western discourse avoids talking about "resistance," preferring to evoke "terrorism" born of hatred of the Jew and understood as inevitable. It is essential to understand that Islam does not provide Hamas with an objective, but with a *modus operandi*.

It is therefore technically, politically, intellectually and security-wise wrong to equate Hamas with the Islamic State.[248] The only thing they really have in common is their response to aggression, which has been condemned by the international community, but against which it has done nothing. Had the international community acted to prevent, deter or condemn such aggression, these movements would probably have had no need to resort to violence. For everyone agrees that, from 2001 to the present day, our interventions have been unjustified, pointless and totally stupid.

The recipe for combating Islamism is simple: fight fewer wars, respect international law that we ourselves set up, stop getting involved in the internal politics of Muslim countries. In short, do not do what Israel did. In October 2023, it was not the actions of Hamas that stimulated anti-

---

248. Monica MARKS, "What the World Gets Wrong About Hamas," *TIME Magazine*, October 30, 2023 (https://time.com/6329776/hamas-isis-gaza/)

Semitic acts in France, but the government's inability to step back from Israel and demand that it comply with UN resolutions.

## Our Understanding of Islamism

We are used to describing different terrorist groups under the common label of "Islamist," and we have a very homogenous image of them. In reality, this term covers very different realities:

- Al-Qaeda has never been an organization, but a movement to which a number of jihadist groups have attached themselves. Its "Islamism" was based on the United States' refusal to fulfill its promise to leave Saudi territory (considered sacred) after the first Gulf War. Its "jihadism" aimed to make them leave;
- the Islamic State, seeks to create a state (caliphate) in southeastern Syria (a territory that does not belong to it). Its "Islamism" here served to mobilize the Muslim community against Western strikes, and its "jihadism" was aimed at fighting foreign interventions (France, Belgium or the United States) that prevented it from fully realizing this project. For Western countries did not seek to prevent the Islamic State from taking root in Syria, but to prevent it from taking the place of the Kurds;
- Hamas uses Islamism to associate the Muslim community with the Palestinian cause, which threatened to be forgotten after the fall of communism. Its "jihadism" drives resistance to Israeli occupation.

As we can see, Hamas and the Islamic State rely on Islamic nationalism, but not to the same ends. Hamas puts it at the service of a strictly Palestinian nationalism, in order to reclaim occupied land, while the Islamic State sees it as the foundation of the caliphate it wishes to create on the territory of a sovereign Arab country. This is why the West has not really fought the Islamic State, but has used it to destabilize the Syrian government.[249]

It should be noted here that the Islamic State considers the apostasy of Arab countries to be a more important and urgent problem than the threat posed by infidels. Abu Musab al-Zarqawi, one of the precursors

---

249. Brad Hoff, "West will facilitate rise of Islamic State 'in order to isolate the Syrian regime': 2012 DIA document," *Foreign Policy Journal*, May 21, 2015; see also: http://www.judicialwatch.org/wp-content/uploads/2015/05/Pg.-291-Pgs.-287-293-JW-v-DOD-and-State-14-812-DOD-Release-2015-04-10-final-version11.pdf

of the Islamic State, had himself declared that the destruction of Israel was not a priority (as confirmed by Major General Aharon Zeevi, head of Israeli military intelligence in 2006).[250] This is why, in 2016, at the height of the EI, Moshe Ya'alon, Defense Minister at the time, declared:[251]

> *In Syria, if the choice is between Iran and the Islamic State, I choose the Islamic State.*

Our governments wanted to use the IS to fight Bashar al-Assad, but they lost control of the situation, which is why they made it an absolute threat. Israelis have a much less dramatic perception of it. Benjamin Netanyahu's comparison between Hamas and the Islamic State is nothing but "fodder" for ignorant Europeans.

Often referred to—wrongly—as the Palestinian branch of the Egyptian *Muslim Brotherhood*, Hamas is not a religious movement. While there are *Muslim Brothers* in Egypt (*Jamaat al-Ikhwan al-Muslimin fi Misr*), Syria (*Ikhwan al-Muslimin fil-Suriya*), Jordan (*Jamiat Jama'at al'Ikhwan al-Muslimin fil'Urdun*), Sudan and Turkey, there is no "*Muslim Brotherhood in Palestine*." For the link between the two movements stops at the initial idea of Muslim nationalism. This does not prevent the *Muslim Brotherhood in Jordan from* supporting the struggle of the Palestinian people.[252]

Muslim Brotherhood doctrine advocates strengthening Islam in Muslim countries before embarking on a process of liberation or independence. Hamas, on the other hand, believes that liberation against the Israeli occupiers must come first, followed by the consolidation of Islam and its values. This question of the place of ideology in the revolutionary process is far from unique to Hamas. It can be found in most Marxist groups of the 20th century. In this respect, we might compare Hamas' approach to that of Che Guevara in Latin America. It is this fundamental difference in strategic approach that distinguishes Hamas from the Muslim Brotherhood.

---

250. https://www.jcpa.org/jl/vp538.htm
251. "Ya'alon: I prefer Islamic State in Syria than Iran," *The Times of Israel*, January 19, 2016 (https://www.timesofisrael.com/liveblog_entry/yaalon-i-prefer-islamic-state-in-syria-than-iran/)
252. https://nabd.com/s/126896291-5810f4/جمعية-الإخوان-المسلمين-تتمثن-عاليا-خطاب-جلالة-الملك-في-قمة-القاهرة-للسلام

In France, the Muslim Brotherhood is seen as the link between Hamas and the jihadist Islamic State. This gives rise to the idea that Hamas is a religious movement aiming to recreate the Caliphate and impose Sharia law. For example, Damien Rieu, a politician from the ultra-nationalist *Reconquête* movement, claims that *"France has been the victim of Hamas."*[253] Not only is this a blatant display of a lack of education, it is also factually untrue. Our politician is therefore engaged in disinformation. In the February 2016 edition of its *Dar al-Islam* magazine, the Islamic State criticized the Palestinian Hamas quite severely,[254] and even declared war on it because it is not fighting for religion but for a land![255]

The fundamental difference between Hamas and the Islamic State is that the latter's objective is to seize (with Western help!)[256] territory that does not belong to it (in Syria) in order to create a state in the form of a caliphate. Hamas is a movement that aims to liberate Israeli-occupied territories and preserve the integrity of the Muslim heritage in Jerusalem, notably the Haram al-Sharif (known to the Israelis as the Temple Mount) and the Al-Aqsa Mosque, Islam's third holiest site. This role explains why, after the attempted occupation by Israeli "ultras" in June-October 2023,[257] the Palestinians named their operation "AL-AQSA FLOOD." This is a totally different model from that of the Islamic State.

## Strategy and Operations

### Hamas's Approach to Resistance

In the early 1990s, Hamas carried out terrorist knife attacks against isolated individuals, often soldiers, on buses or bus shelters. This was similar to what Resistance fighters did in France during the Second World War. This method can be practised by anyone with no particular prepa-

---

253. https://youtu.be/VshpTRd_QeA?t=1779
254. "How to know the truth," *Dar al-Islam*, no. 8, p. 61, Rabi ath-Thani 1437, January-February 2016.
255. Iyad ABUHEWEILA & Isabel KERSHNER, "Islamic State declares war on Hamas as Gaza families disown sons in Sinai," *The Irish Times*, January 11, 2018 (https://www.irishtimes.com/news/world/middle-east/islamic-state-declares-war-on-hamas-as-gaza-families-disown-sons-in-sinai-1.3351899)
256. Brad HOFF, "West will facilitate rise of Islamic State "in order to isolate the Syrian regime: 2012 DIA document," *Foreign Policy Journal*, May 21, 2015; see also: http://www.judicialwatch.org/wp-content/uploads/2015/05/Pg.-291-Pgs.-287-293-JW-v-DOD-and-State-14-812-DOD-Release-2015-04-10-final-version11.pdf
257. "The Israelis set for new Jewish temple on Al-Aqsa site," *France 24*, June 5, 2023 (https://www.france24.com/en/live-news/20230605-the-israelis-set-for-new-jewish-temple-on-al-aqsa-site)

ration or logistics, but it tends to transform political action into an act of personal vengeance. It creates insecurity among Israelis, but without political coherence. That is why this method was quickly abandoned.

In 1994, the massacre at the Mosque of Abraham (Tomb of the Patriarchs) in the middle of prayer marked a new phase for Palestinian resistance. This was the period of suicide bombings. They enabled the occupation forces (such as checkpoints and patrols) to be targeted more effectively. Although these attacks often resulted in collateral civilian casualties, they were still part of a resistance struggle against a military occupation.

"Resistance" expresses the determination to fight an occupation. The method of achieving this may involve "terrorism." The difference between an act of terrorism and another act of resistance is, to put it simply, the nature of the objective: when it is military, it is an act of resistance; when it is civilian, it is terrorism. This is one of the criteria used by the United States,[258] which explains why the Taliban are not considered terrorists.

But in Palestine, the situation is complicated for three reasons. The first is that in the West Bank, civilians are armed and organized into paramilitary militias.[259] The second is that the liberalization of access to weapons by the new far-right government certainly enables citizens to defend themselves, but this makes them legitimate targets for acts that would fall under the heading of terrorism, especially in a climate of high tension.[260] The third is that the Israeli army is a conscript army, and during their leave, soldiers must keep their individual weapons. Adopted in February 2016, this measure had been criticized as potentially dangerous for society.[261]

The militarization of the population and the right of Israelis to open fire on Palestinians without being questioned by the courts[262] is not only a serious breach of the rule of law, which tends to confirm the idea of

---

258. https://2001-2009.state.gov/s/ct/info/c16718.htm
259. Dan WILLIAMS, "Israel arms civilian security squads, fearing internal strife," *Reuters*, October 22, 2023 (https://www.reuters.com/world/middle-east/fearing-internal-strife-gaza-war-israel-arms-civilian-security-squads-2023-10-22/)
260. William BOOTH & Sufian TAHA, "'Guns are everywhere' in Israel, occupied territories as violence spikes," *The Washington Post*, February 4, 2023 (https://www.washingtonpost.com/world/2023/02/04/israel-palestine-guns-violence-attacks/)
261. Judah ARI GROSS, "Rather than saving lives, arming off-duty soldiers could bring greater risk," *The Times of Israel*, February 23, 2016 (https://www.timesofisrael.com/rather-than-save-lives-arming-off-duty-soldiers-could-bring-greater-risk/)
262. "Israeli Settlers Killing Palestinians: A History of Impunity," *Haaretz*, August 27, 2023 (https://www.haaretz.com/israel-news/2023-08-27/ty-article-magazine/.premium/settlers-killing-palestinians-a-history-of-impunity/0000018a-2875-d700-a7ef-faf5d7f40000)

"apartheid,"[263] but it has created a situation where "civilians" are not really civilians. For example, in Jerusalem in November 2023, Yuval Castleman, an Israeli citizen who had just opened fire on Palestinians, was shot dead by an Israeli soldier who thought he too was a Palestinian.[264]

## Interplay between Israeli and Palestinian Strategies

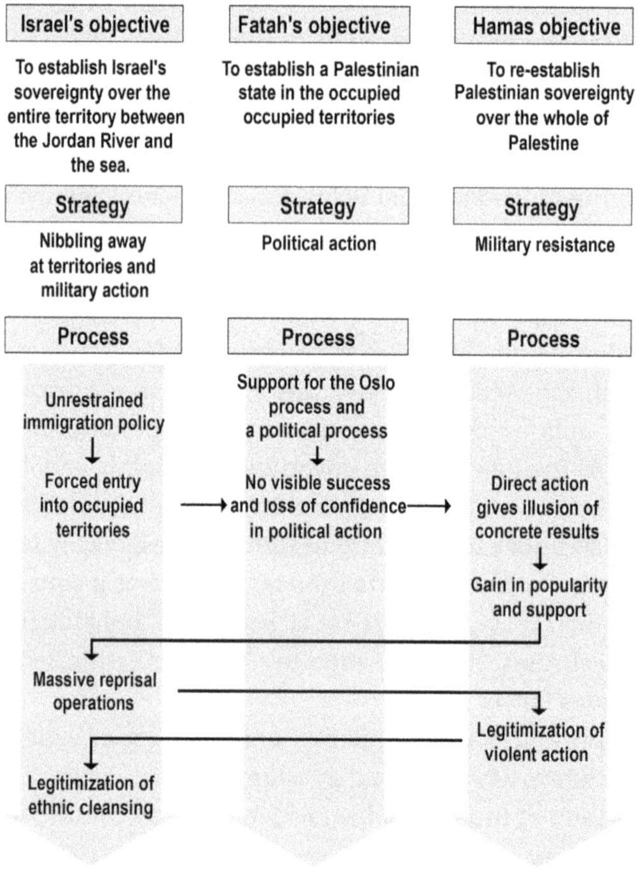

| Israel's objective | Fatah's objective | Hamas objective |
|---|---|---|
| To establish Israel's sovereignty over the entire territory between the Jordan River and the sea. | To establish a Palestinian state in the occupied occupied territories | To re-establish Palestinian sovereignty over the whole of Palestine |
| **Strategy** | **Strategy** | **Strategy** |
| Nibbling away at territories and military action | Political action | Military resistance |
| **Process** | **Process** | **Process** |
| Unrestrained immigration policy ↓ Forced entry into occupied territories | Support for the Oslo process and a political process ↓ No visible success and loss of confidence in political action | Direct action gives illusion of concrete results ↓ Gain in popularity and support |
| ↓ Massive reprisal operations ↓ Legitimization of ethnic cleansing | | Legitimization of violent action |

*Figure 22—Comparison of the strategies of the various players in the Israeli-Palestinian conflict. As can be seen, they all fit together. Israel's strategy can only be explained by the complete eradication of the Palestinian people. Technically, this is what is known as ethnic cleansing.[265]*

---

263. "Israel/OPT: Impunity reigns for perpetrators of settler violence," Amnesty International, March 3, 2023 (https://www.amnesty.org/en/latest/news/2023/03/israel-opt-impunity-reigns-for-perpetrators-of-settler-violence/)
264. "Death of Israeli man who fired on Palestinian attackers fuels criticism of excessive force," PBS.org, December 3, 2023 (https://www.pbs.org/newshour/world/death-of-israeli-man-who-fired-on-palestinian-attackers-fuels-criticism-of-excessive-force)
265. https://press.un.org/en/2021/gapal1439.doc.htm

The notion of "terrorism" takes on a whole new dimension. Indeed, this is what seems to have happened on October 7: some young people had their weapons in the trunk of their car and exchanges of fire took place, even though civilians *were not* Hamas's target.

That said, Hamas has repeatedly declared that it is abandoning terrorist methods. Particularly after the communal elections of 2005, Hamas sought to embark on a political path. But there was no intention of having a form of governance in Gaza capable—in the long term—of taking over from Fatah and taking a firm stance on Israel. This is why the United States organized a coup against Hamas in 2006, which resulted in a civil war in Gaza in 2006-2007, as we have seen.

## Rockets

The containment policy adopted by Israel in the early 2000s, notably through the construction of "walls" around the Palestinian territories, led to the use of new methods. Rockets quickly proved their worth, applying the same logic as Israel—strike from a distance.

The asymmetrical nature of this notion of victory is clearly illustrated by Palestinian rocket fire from the Gaza Strip. Since the erection of the "Wall" between Israel and the occupied territories in 2000, the possibility of carrying out attacks on Israeli soil has been considerably reduced. Initially, the number of planned attacks against Israel rose sharply to compensate for the difficulty of carrying them out, but as the number of attacks prevented also increased, the Palestinians opted for another mode of action—firing rockets.

The Palestinian rockets that continue to strike southern Israel have no military effectiveness: the number of deaths they cause is minimal,[266] but they do testify to the determination of the Palestinian resistance. As the American website *Stratfor*[267] puts it:

> *The rocket fire from Gaza into the heart of Israel, alarming as it may seem to the residents of Tel Aviv, Jerusalem and Hadera, is a political tactic, not a military one.*

---

266. There were 33 Israeli deaths between 2001 and 2015 (figure as at June 1, 2015) and around 4,600 Palestinian victims—at least—because of Israeli strikes.
267. https://worldview.stratfor.com/article/examining-hamas-rockets

## Palestinian Rocket Fire (2001-2021)

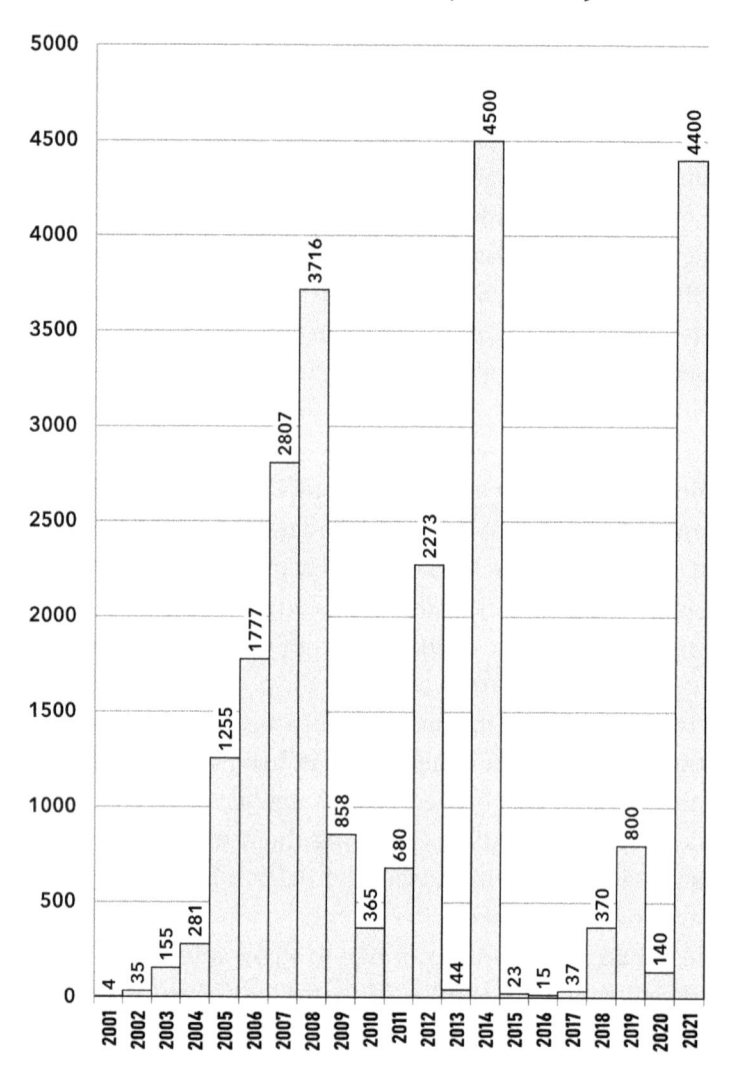

| Year | Rockets |
|---|---|
| 2001 | 4 |
| 2002 | 35 |
| 2003 | 155 |
| 2004 | 281 |
| 2005 | 1255 |
| 2006 | 1777 |
| 2007 | 2807 |
| 2008 | 3716 |
| 2009 | 858 |
| 2010 | 365 |
| 2011 | 680 |
| 2012 | 2273 |
| 2013 | 44 |
| 2014 | 4500 |
| 2015 | 23 |
| 2016 | 15 |
| 2017 | 37 |
| 2018 | 370 |
| 2019 | 800 |
| 2020 | 140 |
| 2021 | 4400 |

*Figure 23—With the construction of the wall in the West Bank and the sealing off of the Gaza Strip, Palestinian organizations began to use rockets rather than "conventional" attacks. Thus, the "barrier" did not "break" the Palestinians' determination. In asymmetrical and jihadist terms, this is already a Palestinian victory. In over 60 years of war, the Israelis have never managed to understand their adversary's logic: it's the only country in the world that hasn't found a solution to its terrorist problem. [Figures: Israeli Ministry of Foreign Affairs]*

## Hamas Rockets

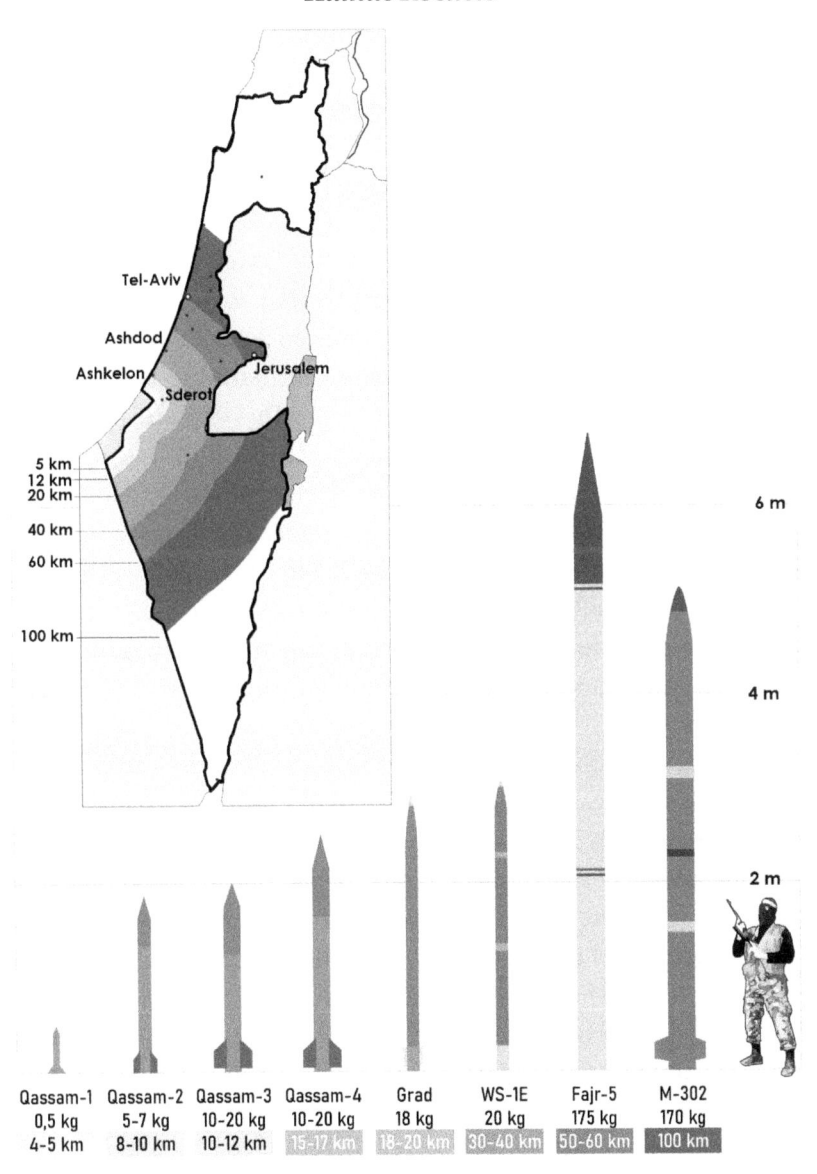

| Qassam-1 | Qassam-2 | Qassam-3 | Qassam-4 | Grad | WS-1E | Fajr-5 | M-302 |
|---|---|---|---|---|---|---|---|
| 0,5 kg | 5-7 kg | 10-20 kg | 10-20 kg | 18 kg | 20 kg | 175 kg | 170 kg |
| 4-5 km | 8-10 km | 10-12 km | 15-17 km | 18-20 km | 30-40 km | 50-60 km | 100 km |

*Figure 24—With the construction of separation walls around the West Bank and Gaza Strip, rockets have become one of the main modes of action of Hamas and other Palestinian groups. However, they are generally only used in response to Israeli strikes.*

On the other hand, the 140 times greater losses inflicted by Israeli retaliation keep the will to resist alive, encourage international support for the Palestinian cause and thus have a strategic effect—they help generate a dynamic that is increasingly less favorable to Israel on the international stage. Israel maintains the illusion of victory in Palestine, at the cost of a political legitimacy that is deteriorating by the day, even with its greatest ally: the United States.

In fact, the Palestinians have realized that Israel needs to maintain terrorist activity in order to carry out its plan to seize the whole of Palestinian territory. They therefore adopted a strategy of response, avoiding spectacular terrorist aggression and shifting the burden of the conflict's unpopularity onto Israel alone. This explains their abandonment of international terrorism in the 1970s, followed by suicide attacks in the 2000s. By firing rockets—spectacular, but causing very few casualties—in response to Israeli strikes, the Palestinians have clearly won over international opinion. For their part, the Israelis have pursued a deliberately disproportionate policy of repression, contrary to international law, supported only by the US government, but widely condemned by public opinion around the world, including American Jews.[268]

Two years following Ariel Sharon's decision to evacuate the Gaza Strip, the Egyptian services quickly established themselves as an essential partner in preventing Gaza from becoming a terrorist state. In June 2004, General Suleiman, head of the Egyptian intelligence services, entered into negotiations with *Hamas* and *Islamic Jihad* to halt the firing of *Qassam* rockets against Israel and set up a mechanism to prevent the development of violence in the Gaza Strip: the training of Palestinian Authority officers in Egypt, the confiscation of illegal weapons, the dismantling of Palestinian militias and an information campaign to promote the rule of law.[269] Ariel Sharon's policies, personally directed against Yasser Arafat, were to undermine these efforts.

For the Palestinians, the simple fact of resisting, whatever the methods or weapons used, gives the satisfaction of "victory." This explains the dazzling success of Hamas in the occupied territories: its attacks fuel—in small steps—a sense of victory by refusing to give up the fight, whereas

---

268. Jonathan Cook, "Can young Jews in US turn tide against Israel?," *The National*, June 26, 2017.
269. *Jerusalem Post*, June 23, 2004.

Fatah, oriented towards a negotiation process, gives the impression of "giving ground."

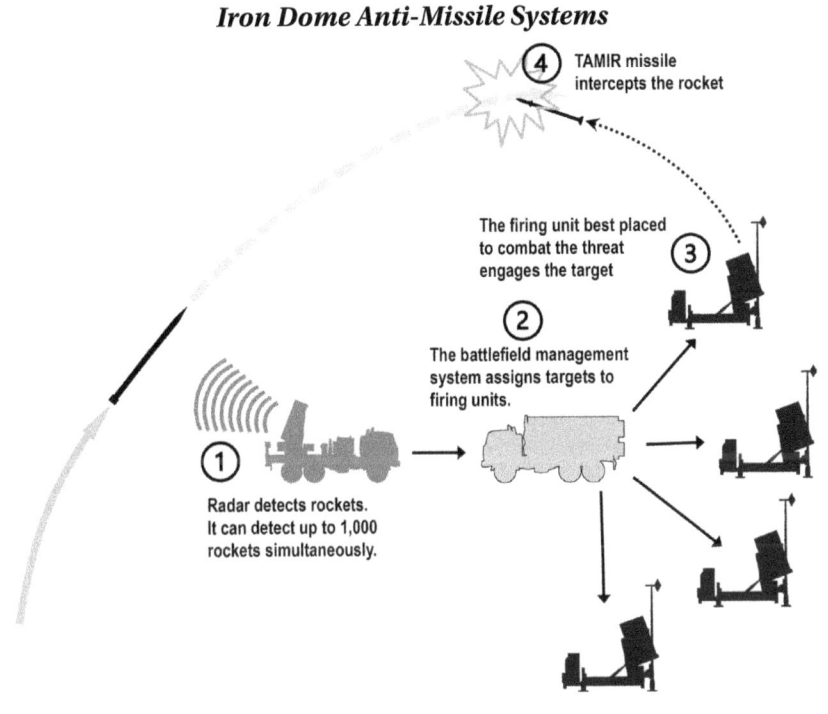

### Iron Dome Anti-Missile Systems

① Radar detects rockets. It can detect up to 1,000 rockets simultaneously.

② The battlefield management system assigns targets to firing units.

③ The firing unit best placed to combat the threat engages the target

④ TAMIR missile intercepts the rocket

*Figure 25—The DÔME DE FER system was designed to combat Palestinian rockets.*

The Palestinians are not trying to kill as many people as possible, but to show that they are not giving up their resistance. This very Middle Eastern logic is not always understood in the West. That is why Israel tends more often than not to fudge the numbers to show that the Palestinians are out to destroy the Jewish people. For example, during the May 2021 incidents in Jerusalem and Gaza, the 10:1 ratio of Palestinian to Israeli casualties was explained by the fact that Israel had intercepted 90% of Palestinian rockets with its IRON DOME system. The balance was thus apparently restored. But this is not true. In fact, the Iron Dome is not as effective as the Israeli authorities claim. According to CNN, by May 2021, the system intercepted only 1,200 missiles out of 2,650, i.e., 45%,[270] which is

---

270. Tim LISTER, "Israel's Iron Dome doesn't chase every rocket it sees," *CNN*, May 18, 2021.(https://www.cnn.com/2021/05/18/middleeast/israel-iron-dome-defense-gaza-rockets-intl-cmd/index.html)

in line with estimates of the system's actual effectiveness. What is more, the system is only deployed around certain sensitive sites and is not, for example, deployed in the Sderot sector, close to the Gaza Strip. In other words, this shows that the Palestinian rockets are not aimed at killing as many people as possible, and that there is a real disproportion in the resources deployed on both sides.

Generally speaking, as we saw before and since October 7, the Palestinians—and Hamas in particular—understand their enemy better than the Israelis. This is why the Palestinians, though outnumbered, will always be able to stand up to the Israelis.

## *Number of Palestinian Suicide Attacks (1994-2008)*

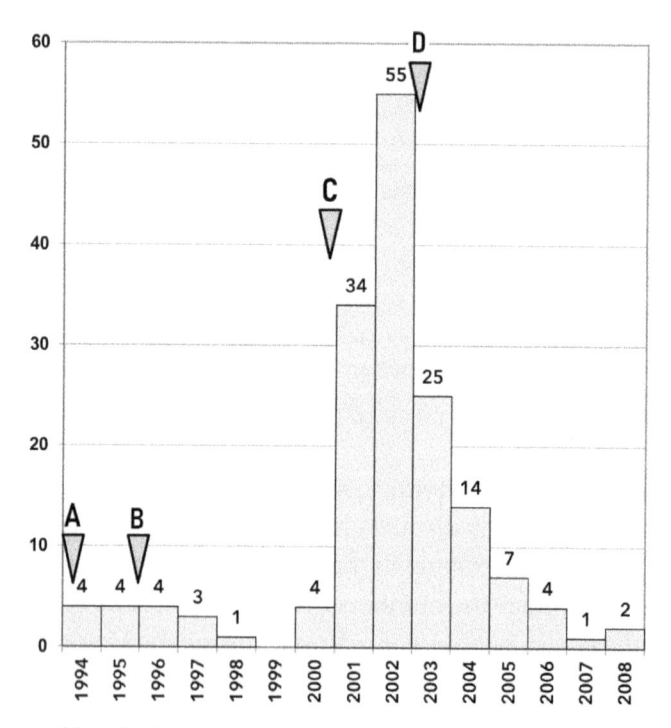

*Figure 26—Although a formal link between most suicide attacks and Israel's targeted eliminations is sometimes difficult to detect, a correlation is observable. The first suicide attacks, in 1994, were triggered by the attack on the Tomb of the Patriarchs (February 25, 1994) (A). Those of 1996 were triggered by the elimination of Yahya Ayyash (January 4, 1996) (B). There was a radical increase in attacks following the official resumption of Israel's policy of targeted eliminations (November 9, 2000) (C). The construction of the protective barrier between the West Bank and Israel (D) forced Hamas to change its strategy, abandoning suicide bombings in favor of the use of rockets in response to Israeli attacks.*
*[Figures: Israeli Ministry of Foreign Affairs].*

## Incendiary Balloons

Balloons carrying small incendiary charges, to set fire to the fields surrounding the Gaza Strip, are part of the resistance's panoply. As with rockets, although these devices can be potentially dangerous, they are not a strategy designed to kill.

August 30, 2020 statement on balloon throwing by the Al-Aqsa Martyrs Phalanx:

> *We inform you that no decision has been taken to stop the incendiary balloons, and we in the Al-Aqsa Unit continue to intensify the work by launching incendiary and booby-trapped balloons against the enemy rapists in the Gaza envelope until all the demands of our people are represented in the complete lifting of the siege on the Gaza Strip, and we continue to work and we will not leave the field yet.*

The idea here is to show a willingness to defend. In the logic of jihad, it is not the effect on the opponent that counts, but the demonstration of determination.

## External Cooperation

Contrary to the claims of the Israeli government, Hamas does not appear to have a policy of collaboration with international Islamist movements. The fight against Israeli occupation is still perceived as a strictly Palestinian problem, and Hamas carries out its actions in the territory of Mandatory Palestine. The Arab revolutions in Egypt, Libya and Syria did not seem to have had any significant repercussions in Palestine in terms of strategic coordination. The rise of jihadism in Syria has not stimulate action by Hamas, probably deliberately, so as not to provoke an Israeli reaction that would become a kind of "final solution" to the Palestinian question.

On the other hand, it seems that outside Sunni jihadists have encouraged the radicalization of some Palestinians, who have embraced jihadism and set up cells in the occupied territories. Israel's strategy of blaming Hamas has only served to reinforce the emergence of extremist cells by complicating the role of Hamas, which is trying to play a more political than militant role. At the same time, the Israeli blockade of the Gaza Strip and the virtual impossibility of viable economic activity there have made Palestinians as a whole—and armed movements in particular—dependent on clandestine channels for supplies, discouraging cooperation with Israel and encouraging contacts beyond the control of the authorities.

Hamas is certainly supported by Iran, which supplies it with weapons through Hezbollah and Palestinian cells in southern Lebanon. Israel regularly strikes Iranian forces that have come to support the Syrian government, so it is logical that Iran should do the same. This explains why Iran has resumed its support for the Palestinian resistance. But it would be wrong to claim that Iran "controls" Hamas. What is surprising is that the Israelis have failed to exploit the rivalries between the Sunni movements and the very small Shiite minority (around 1%) in the Gaza Strip. These have resulted in clashes between militias, the closure by Hamas of offices of Iranian-funded charitable organizations—such as the *al-Baqiyat al Salihat* association, in 2011—and the arrest of Shiite activists.

### *Structure*

Hamas is run by an advisory council *(Majlis al-Shura)* chaired since May 2017 by Ismail Haniyeh (who succeeded Sheikh Ahmed Yassine, Dr Abd el-Aziz Rantisi, then Khaled al-Mash'al in this position). The exact number of members of this council remains confidential.

The *Majlis al-Shura* is a consultative body made up of members of the four "regional" *shuras*, elected by Hamas members in Gaza, the West Bank and the diaspora, and by prisoners in Israeli jails. Initially dominated by religious figures, the *shuras* now include political and social figures, whose identities are usually kept secret.

The general structure of Hamas comprises the national political bureau and four "regional" political bureaus: for the West Bank, Gaza, the diaspora and prisoners. The national political bureau is made up of 15 members elected by the *Majlis al-Shura* every four years, while the members of the regional offices are elected by "regional" *shuras*.

The *Political Bureau* (*Maktab al-Siyasi*) is the executive body of Hamas. Its authority is granted by the *Majlis al-Shura*. It determines social, political and military policies, in consultation with the *Majlis al-Shoura*. Until 2011, it was based in Syria. The Sunni revolution forced it to move to Qatar. In May 2017, Ismail Haniyeh succeeded Khaled Mashal at its head.

Since March 2021, the Hamas Political Bureau for Gaza has been headed by Yahya Al-Sinwar, who is responsible for the movement's operational leadership in the territory. He is credited with the AL-AQSA FLOOD operation and is currently the most wanted man in Palestine.

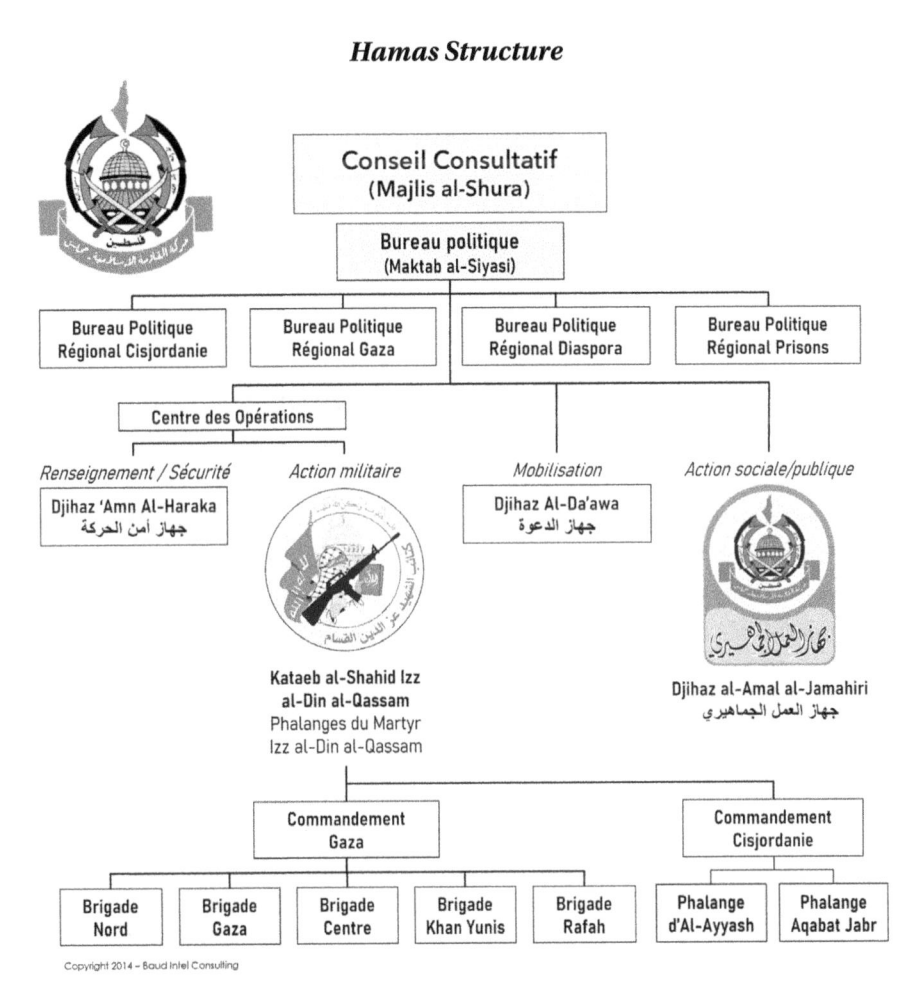

## *Hamas Structure*

*Figure 27—Structure of Hamas. The armed wing of the movement is relatively well known, but not its political and civil wing. It is by combining "successful" military action with social action that Hamas has made itself popular. Its strategy is reminiscent of Che Guevara's in Latin America in the 1960s. The inability of the Israelis to understand its strategy and to counter it with an antagonistic strategy has helped to strengthen Palestinian support for the movement.*

## The Political Component

The essence of Hamas is resistance, and its military activities are naturally the best known. But in the early 2000s, the movement realized that it could take advantage of Israel's simplistic strategy based on the use of violence. The result was an asymmetrical approach to the conflict, with the consequence that Israel's actions backfire. Israel's strategy has become a weapon that contributes to the popularity of Hamas among Palestinians for and in the world.[271] Nothing new here. As I described in 2003, in my book, *La guerre asymétrique ou la défaite du vainqueur*:[272] its tactical successes become strategic defeats. This is what we saw in the wake of Hamas's action in October 2023.

To exploit Israel's weakness, Hamas needed to be able to target the Palestinian population and international opinion. It thus developed two instruments to implement this approach:

- An *"Advocacy Unit"* (*Jehaz al-Dawa*) whose function is to mobilize support for the movement. It works with humanitarian organizations and helps to highlight Hamas's actions on behalf of the Palestinian population and Israel's crimes. It works intensively with international organizations to raise funds to support the victimized population. It has a social structure called the *Coalition of the Good (Itilaf al-Khayr)*, which coordinates the activities of some fifty charitable organizations in the occupied territories.[273] Since November 12, 2008, the *Coalition for Good* has been considered by the US Treasury Department as an organization financing terrorism.[274]

- A *"Public Action Unit"* (*Jehaz al-Amal al-Jamahiri*) whose function is to assist local authorities and the civilian population in concrete activities. This involves, for example, rebuilding infrastructure, so that every attack by Israel becomes a political argument for Hamas.

---

271. Justin Curtis, "Why Hamas: The Socioeconomic and Political Foundations of the Islamists' Popularity," Lecture, Harvard University, 2016 (http://projects.iq.harvard.edu/expose/book/why-hamas-socioeconomic-and-political-foundations-islamists'-popularity)

272. Jacques Baud, *La guerre asymétrique ou la défaite du vainqueur*, Éditions du Rocher, 2003.

273. It is estimated that 75-80% of the Hamas budget is used to finance social and medical assistance, the construction of medical infrastructures and orphanages. (David H. Gray & Larson John Bennett, "Grass Roots Terrorism: How Hamas' Structure Defines a Policy of Counterterrorism," *Research Journal of International Studies*, November 2008.

274. https://home.treasury.gov/news/press-releases/hp1267

Surprisingly enough, Israel, no doubt bolstered by Western support, has never considered the political consequences of its failure to comply with international law and of its actions.

For example, in the occupied territories, Israel seeks to drive out the Palestinian population by destroying residential houses, with punitive (1% of cases), administrative, judicial or military (e.g., when they are too close to settler settlements or military installations) justifications (20% of cases). According to the *Israeli Committee Against House Demolitions*, 56,445 houses were destroyed between 1967 and September 2023.[275]

Israeli policy gives the appearance of a virile takeover of the terrorist problem and presents itself as a deterrent. But it is an illusion. Not only has this policy only stimulated Palestinian resistance, it has also brought about a qualitative change in its strategy. For the Israeli authorities did not foresee that, deprived of a roof over their heads, these families are more often than not taken in by charitable organizations associated with Hamas, which it had the foresight to create as early as October 2000. Palestinian families are thus thrust into the open arms of Hamas, even when they were not necessarily previously affiliated with it. In other words, Israel has not only increased hatred of its occupation, but has also helped to boost the popularity and ranks of Hamas. Ultimately, these punitive demolitions have the effect of fanning the flames of violence without deterring terrorist attacks.[276] In military terms, Israel has undermined its own strategic posture with a tactical measure.

## *The Military Component*

The military wing of Hamas is the heir to the *Jehaz Aman*, which was responsible for the security of the *Al-Mujamma al-Islami*. Its main function was internal security, including tracking down potential traitors, those who collaborated with the Israeli authorities and those who broke the movement's rules (such as selling narcotics).

In 1987, the armed wing of Hamas had two main components:
- The *Majmuat al-Jihad w-l-Dawa*, also known by its acronym *(al) Majd (Glory)*, led by Yahya Sinwar and Rawhi Mushtaha.

---

275. https://icahd.org/2021/04/26/statistics-on-house-structure-demolitions-november-1947-march-2021/
276. Meir Margalit, *"The Truth behind Formal Statistics—Demolition of illegal houses in the West Bank during 2004,"* Israeli Committee Against House Demolition, April 2005.

- *Al-Mujahidin al-Filastinun,* created in 1982 after the Sabra and Chatila massacres in Lebanon. It is responsible for clandestine activities (acquisition of weapons and explosives) and bombings. It was led by Nizar Abd el-Qadir Rayyan (until his death on January 1, 2009).

Apparently, several cells were formed to carry out violent actions against the Israeli occupation forces. The first cell formed was called Group 101 and was led by Muhammad Al-Sharatha.

In 1991, these two components were integrated into the *Brigades of the Martyr Izz ad-Din al-Qassam* (which we will refer to here as *the Al-Qassam Brigades*), created by Walid Zakaria Akel, then Hamas's military chief in Gaza. However, it was not until January 1, 1992 that the name of the Brigades was revealed in their first official communiqué. Mainly based in the Gaza Strip, they also have elements in the West Bank. Their numbers are not known, but it is estimated that there are 30,000 fighters trained in urban guerrilla warfare. Initially, they were the smallest branch of Hamas. They were made up of small autonomous cells, very difficult to locate and penetrate by Israeli security forces. Until 1994, they carried out attacks with handguns and knives.

The phalanx (brigade) leadership structure was unveiled in 2005. It consists of a Commander-in-Chief, flanked by a Military Council, whose composition seems to vary. At the end of November 2023, it comprised: Mohammed Al-Deif, Mohammed Sinwar, Raed Saad and Marwan Issa. Three members of the Council were then eliminated by Israel: Abu Shamala, Ahmed Al-Jaabari, commander of the Al-Qassam Brigades for the Gaza Strip, and Ahmed Al-Ghandour (commander of the Northern Brigade).

As in Syria and Iraq, the designation of the military formations of Palestinian groups is sometimes confusing for Westerners accustomed to precise nomenclature. Resistance groups generally refer to themselves as "*kata'ib,*" which is usually translated as "brigades." But some major movements have "brigades" (*liwa*), structured into battalions (*kata'ib*). This seems contradictory. In fact, most Arab resistance groups were created as an unstructured collection of "battalions" (*kata'ib*). Thus, in most cases, it is a generic, "historical" appellation with no structural significance. We will translate it here as simply "brigades," to avoid confusion.

## Generic Structure of Palestinian Resistance Groups

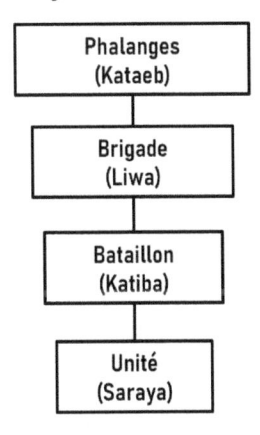

```
Phalanges
(Kataeb)
   │
Brigade
(Liwa)
   │
Bataillon
(Katiba)
   │
Unité
(Saraya)
```

*Figure 28—The designation of Palestinian groups has often been overtaken by their evolution. What was once a battalion has become a small army. The result is a confusion of terms. Examination of the documents issued by these groups shows that, despite their apparent vagueness, they have very precise structures.*

Since 2018, the Al-Qassam Brigades have been led by Mohammed Diab Ibrahim Al-Masri "Al-Deif," whose *nom de guerre* is "Abu Khaled." His second-in-command is Marwan Issa.

In 2003, on the advice of Salah Shahadah, Hamas decided to create a popular militia, a sort of reserve, separate from the Al-Qassam Brigades. Called *Al-Murabitun*,[277] its strength is the subject of much speculation and could number in the tens of thousands. It was involved in clashes with Fatah in the Gaza Strip in 2006-2007.

After the attack on January 14, 2004, carried out by Reem Salah al-Riyashi, an activist from the *Al-Aqsa Martyrs' Brigades*, Hamas decided to create a women's unit whose commitment to suicide bombing was authorized by a fatwa signed by Nizar Abd el-Qadir Rayyan. Today, the Al-Qassam Brigades have adopted the tactic of firing rockets from the West Bank and Gaza Strip. In principle, they no longer carry out suicide attacks, but they retain the capacity to do so, giving "*priority to men and young people.*"[278]

---

277. Not TO BE confused with the *Brigades of the Mourabitoun Committee in Palestine (Kata'ib al-Murabitun fil'Filastin)*, created in 2004 by members of the *Popular Front for the Liberation of Palestine (PFLP)* in Khan Yunis.

278. https://alkhanadeq.com/post/4780/استشهاديات-كتائب-القسام-دور-عسكري-أي-أرض-للم

## Operational Units of the Kata'ib of Martyr Izz Al-Din al-Qassam in Gaza

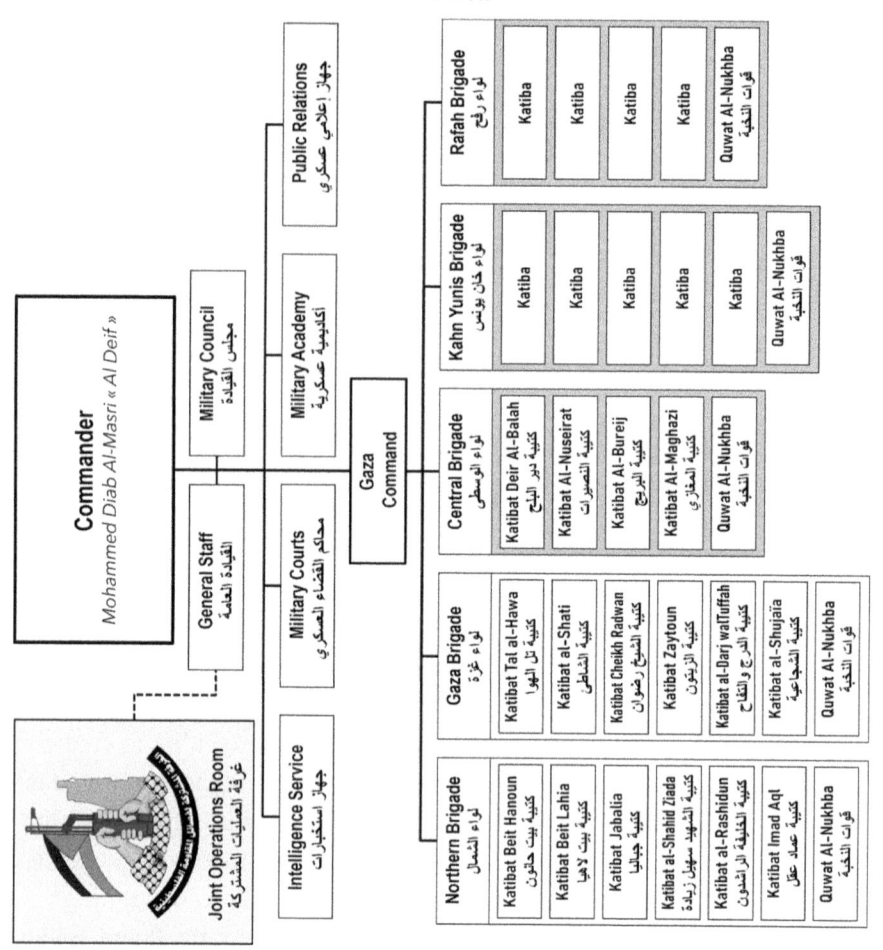

*Figure 29—Al-Qassam Brigade commands in Gaza. Strategic reserve units in grey. For October 7 and the weeks that followed, units from the Northern and Gaza brigades were committed. This engagement plan shows that Hamas commanders anticipated the Israeli decision very well.*

In April-May 2006, shortly after its victory in the legislative elections, Hamas created an *Executive Force (Tanfithya)* responsible for security in the Gaza Strip.

Operationally, Hamas is divided into two commands: one for the Gaza Strip—which constitutes the bulk of the movement's military potential—and the second for the West Bank.

## Deployment of the Martyr Izz Al-Din al-Qassam Kata'ib (2023)

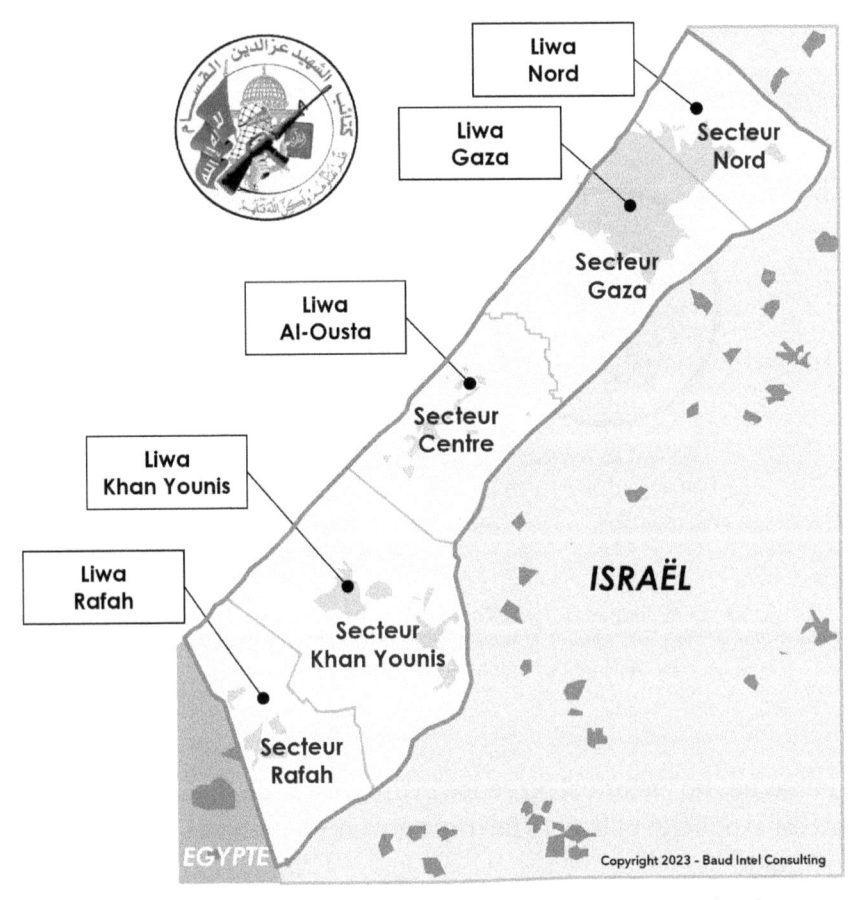

*Figure 30—Schematic deployment of Brigades Al-Qassam brigades (Liwa).*

In Gaza, the battalions (*kata'ib*) are subdivided into five brigades (*liwa*), organized according to the territory's administrative structures: North, Gaza, Center, Khan Yunis and Rafah. They are placed under the command of the Gaza forces, under the political leadership of Yahya Sinwar. Each brigade is said to have around 8,000 fighters, giving a total strength of 40,000 men in Gaza. The brigades are made up of battalions (*katiba*), whose strength ranges from 800 to 1,500 men.

## Hamas Command in the West Bank

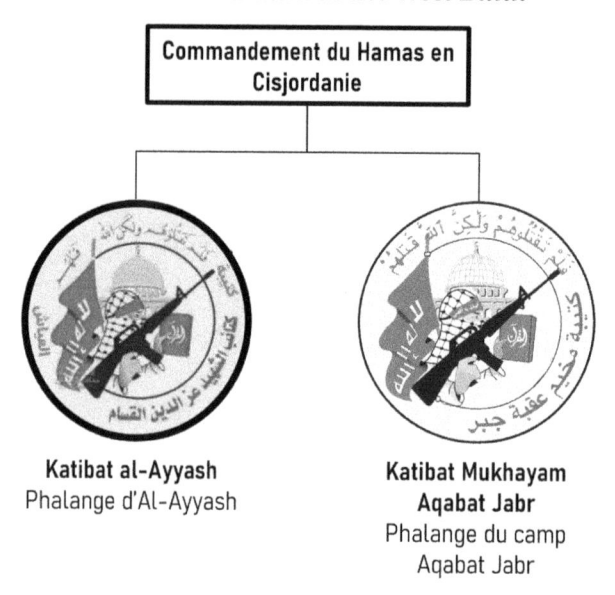

```
         Commandement du Hamas en
                 Cisjordanie
         ┌──────────────┴──────────────┐
   Katibat al-Ayyash          Katibat Mukhayam
  Phalange d'Al-Ayyash            Aqabat Jabr
                                Phalange du camp
                                   Aqabat Jabr
```

*Figure 31—By early 2023, Hamas has two active phalanxes in the West Bank, cooperating actively with Fatah's Al-Aqsa Martyrs Phalanx and Palestinian Islamic Jihad's Al-Quds Units, notably as part of the Jenin Battalion.*

Hamas has no historical presence in the West Bank, but with the more aggressive policies of Israel's far-right government, it has begun to gain a foothold.

*Katibat Al-Ayyash* (named after the Hamas "engineer" eliminated in 1996) depends organically on the Hamas command in the West Bank, but operationally it is integrated into the Jenin Battalion of the *Palestinian Islamic Jihad*.

### Hamas's Military Branches

Hamas' branches bear witness to its capabilities, some of which were revealed by Operation AL-AQSA FLOOD.

## Hamas Branches

**Martyr Izz Al-Din al-Qassam Kata'ib**
كتائب الشهيد عز الدين القسام
*Mohammed al-Deif*
*Marwan Issa*

| وحدة المشاة<br>Wahdat al-Mushat<br>Infantry | الوحدة الخاصة<br>Wahdat al-Khassa<br>Special Forces | الضفادع البشرية البحرية<br>Al-Dhafadi' al-Bashariat Al-Bahriah<br>Combat Swimmer Unit |
|---|---|---|
| وحدة الدروع<br>Wahdat al-Doru<br>Motorized unit | وحدة الدفاع الجوي<br>Wahdat al-Difa' al-Javviyah<br>Air defense unit | وحدة المدفعية<br>Wahdat al-Midfa'yah<br>Artillery unit (mortars) |
| وحدة الهندسة<br>Wahdat al-Hindisa<br>Engineering unit | وحدة الحرب الالكترونية<br>Wahdat al-Harb al-Alektrunia<br>Electronic warfare unit | وحدة الظل<br>Wahdat al-Zili<br>Ghost unit |
| وحدة القناصة<br>Wahdat al-Qanasa<br>Sniper unit | وحدة الإسناد<br>Wahdat al-Isnad<br>Support unit | وحدة الصواريخ<br>Wahdat al-Sawarikh<br>Rocket unit |
| وحدة التعبئة والتوجيه<br>Wahdat al-Taebiat wal-Tawjih<br>Mobilization and orientation unit | وحدة المسعفين الحربيين<br>Wahdat al-Museifin al-Harbiayn<br>Military medical unit | وحدة الإشارة والاتصالات<br>Wahdat al-Isharat wal-Aytisalat<br>Transmission and communication unit |
| القوات الجوية<br>Quwat al-Jawiat<br>Air force | وحدة مضادة للدروع<br>Wahdat Mudadat lil-Durue<br>Anti-tank unit | وحدة الاستشهاديين<br>Wahdat al-Aistishhadiine<br>Martyrs unit |

*Figure 32—Types of forces available to Hamas*

4. Gaza

## Infantry

Infantry troops (*Wahdat al-Mushat*) make up around 85% of the Kata'ib al-Qassam's strength.

## Anti-Aircraft Defense

The anti-aircraft troops (*Wahdat al-Difa' al-Javviyah*) are designed to combat or deter the many strikes carried out by Israel. They use DShK 12.7 mm machine guns, ZPU 14.5 mm machine guns and portable missiles SA-7 (9K32 Strela2), SA-18 (9K38 IGLA) and the locally-produced MUTABAR1 missile system.

*Anti-Aircraft Troops*

*Figure 33—Badge of the Hamas anti-aircraft missile unit. It represents the MUTABAR-1 anti-aircraft missile system, produced in the Gaza Strip.*

Revealed in Hamas videos, the MUTABAR-1 system is one of the surprises of the AL-AQSA FLOOD operation. The system was designed and produced in Gaza. It testifies to the ability of Palestinians, despite very precarious conditions, to create, design and produce defense systems.[279]

However, it seems that only the carriage is produced in Gaza. The missile itself seems to have come from outside, but the model is not known with certainty. It is not a homing missile, but one guided by the radar operator and detonated at a specific altitude. Its function seems to be to make it more difficult for combat helicopters to fire at. According to Palestinian sources, the MUTABAR-1 caused damage to four Israeli helicopter

---

279. https://english.iswnews.com/30776/military-knowledge-mutabar-1-air-defense-system/

gunships in the early days of Operation AL-AQSA FLOOD, but this has not been confirmed. To what extent this system is capable of hitting a target despite powerful Israeli countermeasures is an open question.

The launcher is remote-controlled and several firing units can be engaged simultaneously. The total number of units available to Hamas is not known at this stage.

The MUTABAR-1 is probably more of a "propaganda" weapon, designed more to show the determination of the Palestinians to resist Israeli forces, than to actually destroy aircraft.

## The MUTABAR-1 Anti-Aircraft System

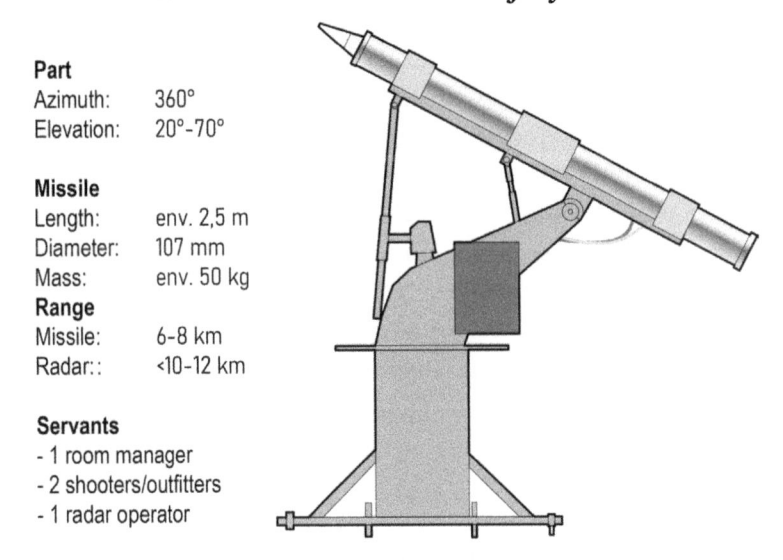

**Part**
Azimuth: 360°
Elevation: 20°-70°

**Missile**
Length: env. 2,5 m
Diameter: 107 mm
Mass: env. 50 kg

**Range**
Missile: 6-8 km
Radar:: <10-12 km

**Servants**
- 1 room manager
- 2 shooters/outfitters
- 1 radar operator

*Figure 34—Unveiled at the start of Operation AL-AQSA FLOOD, the MUTABAR-1 anti-aircraft system was one of the surprises of the operation. It is a remote-controlled missile system using numerous external components, assembled in Hamas workshops.*

## Special Forces

The Special Forces (*Wahdat al-Khassa*) are trained to carry out raids on Israeli territory. They are known generically as *Quwat al-Nukhba* (Elite Force). They total between 5,000 and 7,000 fighters spread across the five Al-Qassam Brigades in Gaza.

The fighters are trained for one to two years, probably in southern Lebanon, where there is still a large Palestinian community. To what extent this training is carried out by Hezbollah units is open to debate.

Apparently, they were not involved in the first phase of Operation AL-AQSA FLOOD on October 7. Trained in close combat and guerrilla warfare, they are the ones fighting the Israeli forces who intervened in the Gaza Strip.

**Combat Swimmers**

Marine commando or combat swimmer formations (*al-Dhafadi' al-Bashariat al-Bahriah*), distributed throughout the five territorial commands. They are part of the Elite Forces (*Quwat al-Nukhba*) and are considered the best-trained of the Al-Qassam Brigades. Created in 2014, they have already carried out operations against the Israeli naval base of Zikim in that year, prompting the Israeli army to reinforce its posture along the coast adjacent to the Gaza Strip. The activities of its *Unit 916*, responsible for securing coastal sites, were stepped up and, in 2018, a barrier was built to protect the base. It is 200 meters long and 6 meters high. Reputedly impenetrable, it is equipped with motion detectors both underwater and on land.[280] This did not prevent Hamas commandos from attacking the base again on October 7, 2023, and holding out until October 24.[281] By November 2021, Palestinian media were already talking about its preparations for a "*strategic strike*" against Israel in its "*next military battle*" with an "*operation similar to the previous one*." This is exactly what happened on October 7, 2023[282] with a landing in the Ashkelon area.[283]

**Motorized Ultralight Air Unit**

October 7 saw the unveiling of the "SAQR" (Falcon) squadron (القوات الجوية—سرب الصقر), which constitutes the movement's air force. It is equipped with motorized ultralight aircraft of the "paraglider" type, which have been used to cross the fence that surrounds the Gaza territory.[284] It appears to have been formed solely for the launch of operation AL-AQSA FLOOD.

---

280. https://adnanabuamer.com/post/3207/israels-increasing-concern-about-hamas-growing-naval-capabilities
281. https://en.wikipedia.org/wiki/Battle_of_Zikim
282. https://alkhanadeq.com/post.php?id=1514
283. https://english.almayadeen.net/news/politics/al-qassam-brigades-executes-beach-landing-in-occupied-territ
284. https://alkhanadeq.com/post/6006/مفاجآت-القسام-للخطلوف-الأقصى-حتى-الآن

## Engineer Troops

Engineering units (*Wahdat al-Hindisa*) are responsible for digging and maintaining the tunnel networks on which supplies to the Gaza Strip depend. On October 7, these troops blew up parts of the barrier surrounding the Gaza Strip, and bulldozed the openings to allow Hamas vehicles through.

## Artillery

The artillery formations (*Wahdat al-al-Midfa'yah*) are responsible for firing al-Qassam rockets.

### RAJUM Multiple Rocket Launcher

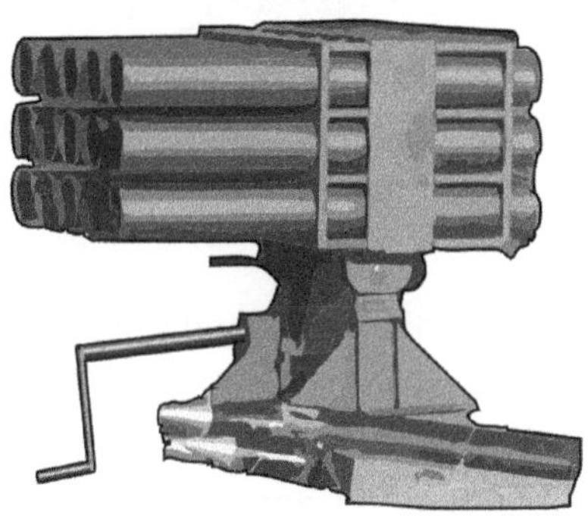

*Figure 35—The RAJUM multiple rocket launcher fires series of 15 114 mm rockets.*

Another technical surprise of the AL-AQSA FLOOD operation was the appearance of the locally manufactured RAJUM multiple rocket launcher, inspired by the Chinese 107 mm rocket launcher concept of the 1960s-1970s. It is an effective weapon, launching unguided projectiles with a range of 8-9 km. It has been used to strike Israeli army installations in the Deir al-Balah and Beit-Hanoun areas of the Gaza Strip. As well as military targets located in the Gaza envelope, in Re'im, Nissim, Kissufim and Amitai, at a distance of 2-3 km from the border with Gaza.

## Cyberwar

The Electronic Warfare Unit (*Wahdat al-Harb al-Alektrunia*) is the most recent branch of the Al-Qassam Brigades. Its existence was revealed on October 13, 2022. Hamas had been working since 2014 to set up this unit with Muhammad Al-Tawashi (eliminated by Israel), then with Jumaa

Al-Tahla, a Hamas engineer (eliminated by the Israeli army in May 2021 before he could realize his *"Jerusalem Electronic Army"* [*Jaïsh al-Quds al-Alektrunii*] project), which was to mobilize capabilities outside the Gaza Strip to carry out attacks against Israeli forces.[285]

### *Electronic Warfare Unit*

*Figure 36—Hamas cyberwarfare unit logo*

According to Hamas, the unit penetrated observation tower operating systems and military transmissions in the "Gaza envelope" area of Nir Oz. It also penetrated the headquarters of the Southern Command, as well as those of the Northern and Central Commands, and the Nevatim, Hatzrim, Palmachim and Ramat David airbases. Difficult to verify, but numerous reports from Israel tend to confirm the Hamas unit's track record.[286] Over and above these successes—whether proven or not—this shows that the Palestinian resistance has capabilities that are undoubtedly greater than those presented to us by our media.[287]

### "Phantom" Unit

The so-called "phantom" unit (*Wahdat al-Zili*) was created in 2006 to capture the Israeli soldier Gilad Shalit, who would be exchanged for 1,027 Palestinian prisoners. The existence of this unit was only revealed in 2016 on the express authorization of Mohammed Deif, leader of

---

285. https://www.arab48.com/فلسطينيات/أخبار/2022/10/13/كتائب-القسام-تكشف-عن-وحدة-سايبر-تستهدف-إسرائيل-من-8-سنوات

286. https://www.calcalist.co.il/internet/articles/0,7340,L-3744073,00.html

287. https://alkhanadeq.com/post/3921/سايبر-حماس-القسام-البنية-التحشيةلية-الإسرائيلية-التي-تم-الاستهداف-فيها

the al-Qassam Brigades. Its role is to hide prisoners with a view to an exchange and prevent them from being recovered by the Israelis.[288]

### *Hamas "Phantom" Unit*

Figure 37—Logo of the unit responsible for securing prisoners or hostages. This is the most secret unit of the Al-Qassam Brigades.

This unit was responsible for guarding and moving the prisoners on October 7. The latter, released at the end of November 2023, testified to the good behavior and humane treatment they had received from the members of this unit, responsible for their protection. Unfortunately, the Palestinian prisoners released by the Israelis at the time could not say the same.

## Weapons

### Anti-Tank Weapons

The use of armored vehicles, notably MERKAVA battle tanks and NAMER and ACHZARIT infantry fighting vehicles, to suppress riots in the occupied territories, has prompted the Palestinians to develop their anti-tank capabilities. Hamas has a unit capable of producing rockets for the RPG-7V anti-tank rocket launcher.

---

288. https://www.alaraby.com/news/أسرار-وحدة-الظل-كيف-تستطيع-حماس-إخفاء-الأسرى-عن-إسرائيل

## The Al-Yassin 105 Anti-Tank Rocket

*Figure 38—The AL-YASSIN 105 anti-tank grenade, produced in Hamas workshops. Hamas propaganda claims that these grenades are manufactured by the movement itself. This is possible, but it is more likely that they are simply assembled and packaged by Hamas in the occupied territories.*

The YASSIN-105 is a copy of the Russian PG-7VR (105 mm) rocket, mass-produced in Hamas workshops.[289] It consists of two hollow charges in tandem: one of 64 mm caliber and one of 105 mm. The first is designed to pierce additional armor (what the Germans called "Schürzen" on their tanks during the Second World War), which is intended to detonate the shaped charge prematurely, while the second charge pierces the main armor. This type of grenade also works against reactive armor or other systems, such as the TROPHY fitted to MERKAVA tanks, NAMER tracked and EITAN wheeled personnel carriers.

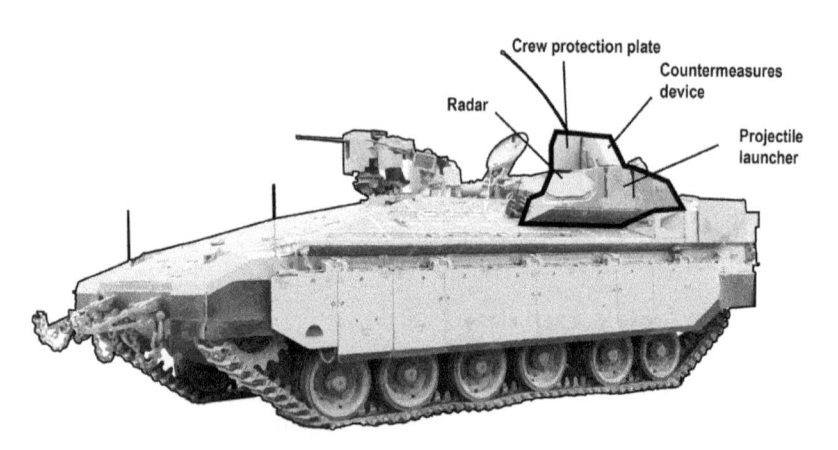

*Figure 39—The NAMER armored personnel carrier with the TROPHY device (also used on MERKAVA tanks) designed to neutralize anti-tank rockets. The Palestinians use AL-YASSIN-105 rockets to combat this system. More recently, since Israeli forces entered Gaza, Palestinians have been using so-called "zero-distance" weapons.*

---

289. https://english.iswnews.com/31801/military-knowledge-al-yassin-105-anti-tank-rocket-the-zionists-nightmare-in-gaza/

Hamas also produces a copy of the Russian TBG-7V thermobaric grenade, designed to be fired from an RPG-7 rocket launcher. It is used in urban areas against personnel. The 105 mm diameter grenade dissipates a cloud of hydrocarbon-based aerosol which is then ignited, creating a deadly fireball. Numerous videos show them being used against Israeli army teams ambushed on the floors of buildings.

**Drones**

Since 2006, with the recruitment of Mohammed Zouari, a Tunisian engineer, the Al-Qassam Bigades have created a whole range of combat drones. They officially announced the use of their first ABABIL A1a model on July 14, 2014.[290]

Their technology seems relatively simple, but given the tight surveillance and import restrictions imposed on Gaza, their realization remains a technical feat.[291] They are inspired by the Israeli drones shot down over the Gaza Strip, and the aircraft used by Hezbollah in Lebanon. According to Israeli sources, it is unlikely that Iran or Hezbollah supplied components for these devices.[292]

### *The ABABIL A1a Drone*

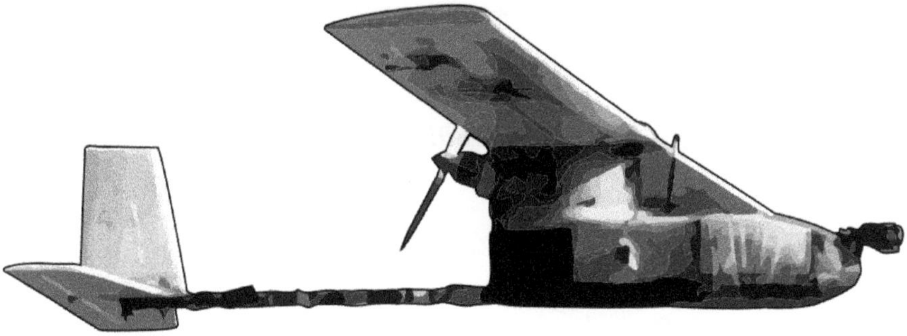

*Figure 40—The ABABIL A1a drone is a reconnaissance vehicle equipped with a portable GoPro-type camera.*

---

290. https://www.echoroukonline.com/des-drones-ababil-1-de-la-resistance-terrifient-israel
291. https://alkhanadeq.com/post.php?id=1685
292. https://www.jpost.com/operation-protective-edge/hamas-our-drones-have-collected-intel-over-kirya-military-hq-in-tel-aviv-362705

### The ABABIL A1b Drone

Figure 41—The ABABIL A1b is a multi-purpose drone, which can be used for reconnaissance missions, thanks to a camera placed under its nose. It can also be used to drop bombs or fire small missiles.

### The SHEHAB Drone

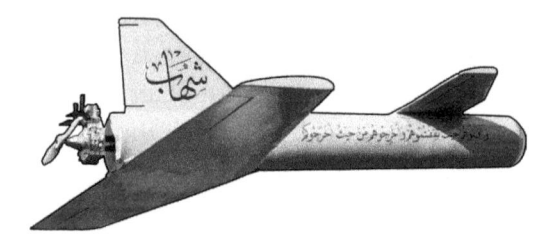

Figure 42—The SHEHAB was first presented in 2018. It is a suicide drone, whose guidance system is not publicly known.

### The ZOUARI Suicide Drone

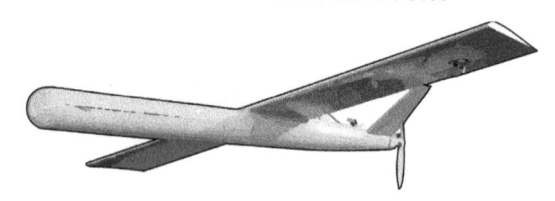

Figure 43—Presented on Twitter on October 12, 2023, the Zouari is the latest Hamas drone. It is named after Mohammed Zouari, the Tunisian engineer recruited by Hamas in 2006 to develop the drone program. Zouari was eliminated by Israeli services in 2016. This is a suicide drone that can be used against infantry or artillery positions.[293] Its guidance system is not publicly known. More recent versions appear to have pylons for carrying bombs or rockets.[294] Hamas is reported to have used 35 of these drones in the early days of its operation AL-AQSA DELUGE.[295]

---

293. https://twitter.com/timand2037/status/1711094206880714960
294. https://english.almayadeen.net/news/politics/hamas-drone-spurs-israeli-fear-over-hezbollahs-advanced-arse
295. https://english.almayadeen.net/news/politics/al-qassam:-al-zouari-suicide-drones-played-key-role-in-the-o

The ZOUARI drone is one of the surprises of this conflict.[296]

## The ZOUARI Suicide Drone

Figure 44—The Izz al-Dine al-Qassam Brigades released a video of ZOUARI drone engagements, which were used on October 7, 2023 to attack military targets in the "Gaza envelope," which are primarily Gaza Division facilities. [Source: https://twitter.com/timand2037/status/1711094206880714960]

Gaza's industrial capacity is very modest, and imports of the necessary technologies are very limited, making drone production difficult and giving it an operational impact that is more symbolic than military.

### Anti-Tank Drones

The first challenge faced by the Hamas fighters on October 7 was to cross the security fence and neutralize the automatic firing installations, which

---

296. https://www.eurasiantimes.com/hamas-reveals-zouari-kamikaze-drone-that-can-potentially-rain/

are located every 500 m or so. Palestinian engineers therefore produced drones carrying PG-7 anti-tank grenades, equipped with a camera that enables the rocket to be dropped with great precision. The system can of course be used against armored vehicles, but is ideal for destroying the security fence's surveillance systems.

### Surveillance and Firing Installations—Hamas' First Targets on October 7

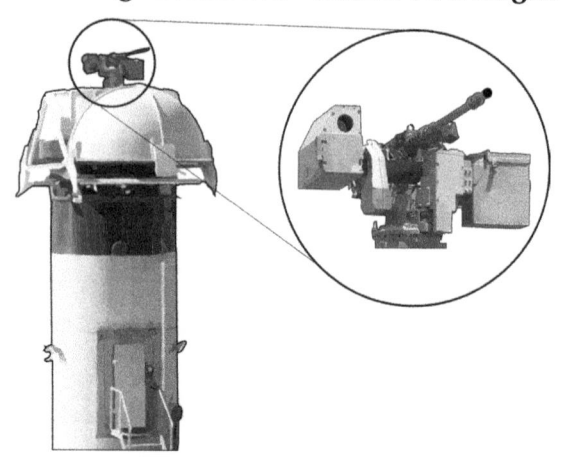

*Figure 45—Automatic/remote-controlled firing installation along the security fence around Gaza. The RCWS (Remote Controlled Weapons System) firing system is protected by two half-shells, in order to neutralize the system. The idea is to release a rocket-piercing grenade exactly at the vertical position of the tower.*

### Anti-Tank/Anti-Tower Control Drone

*Figure 46—Drone used to drop an anti-tank grenade on the top of a tank (its most vulnerable part).*

**Naval Drones**

Hamas also presented the AL-ASIF underwater drone system, designed to combat Israeli coastal surveillance vessels. It closely resembles the devices developed in Ukraine to attack the Russian fleet. The exact purpose of such a device is not entirely clear.

*AL-ASIF Underwater Drone*

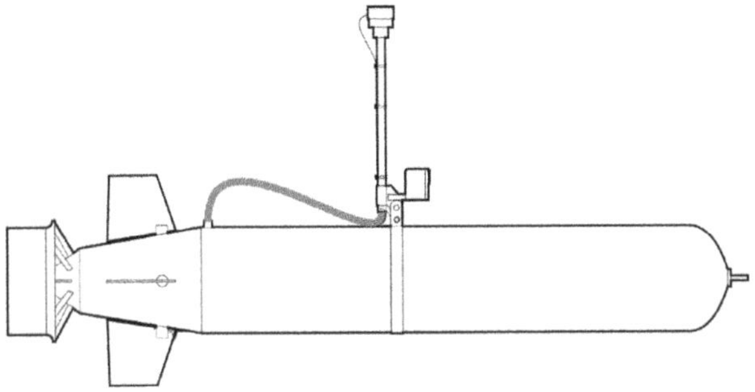

*Figure 47—The AL-ASIF underwater drone seems to have been inspired by the work carried out in Ukraine. It is a kind of guided torpedo.*

## *Resources*

To understand Hamas's funding mechanisms, we need to remember that with the Oslo Accords, the Palestinian Authority (PA) became the main recipient of international aid. Hamas enjoys broad support among Muslim countries, but with these agreements, it became Fatah's main partner within the Palestinian Authority.

Qatar largely finances the Palestinian Authority, because the West is reluctant to do so because of the presence of Hamas within it. Of the $480 million in aid earmarked for Palestine, Qatar contributes $300 million. In total, since the beginning of 2010, Qatar has provided some $1.5 billion in aid to the Palestinian Authority.[297]

Contrary to what our media suggest, there is no evidence that this aid is financing Hamas's military activities. In fact, it is part of an Egyptian mediation between Hamas and the Israeli government. Under UN supervision, Hamas receives $8.2 million a month from Qatar. It was the reallocation of some of these funds to other projects in Gaza that provoked

---

297. Zvi BAR'EL, "Qatar's ATM for the Palestinians Is Fed by the War in Ukraine," *Haaretz*, September 16, 2022 (https://www.haaretz.com/middle-east-news/2022-09-16/ty-article/.premium/qatars-atm-for-the-palestinians-is-fed-by-the-war-in-ukraine/00000183-4085-d070-abef-e497b7780000)

social unrest in Hamas ranks in May 2023, contributing to instability in the Gaza Strip.

As for Iran, it is inaccurate to claim that it supports Hamas. The Palestinian question is not an issue in Iranian policy. On the other hand, there is a small Shiite minority in the Gaza Strip supported by Iran. It is in this context that Iran supports the governance provided for in the Oslo Accords.

Like the European Union, Iran provided financial support for the Palestinian Authority (PA). As a result, Hamas was able to open a liaison office in Tehran as early as 1993. But the political leadership of the movement is based in Qatar.

Following Hamas's victory in the 2006 legislative elections, described by the European Union as a *"model for the entire Arab region,"*[298] and Fatah's withdrawal from the PA, Western funding ceased, making it impossible to manage the occupied territories. But Iran did not stop funding the PA and thus became the sole backer of the Palestinian government.[299] It was easy for Western propagandists to claim that Iran was funding Hamas. As for Hamas, with no other resources, it reluctantly accepted Iranian aid, as *The Guardian* pointed out:[300]

> *Our relations with Iran have irritated Saudi Arabia, but sometimes we have no choice. We would prefer to have closer relations with Saudi Arabia, but perhaps that will come.*

In reality, then, it was the West that brought about the somewhat unnatural rapprochement between Hamas and Iran, after an election result they had not foreseen. But this in no way means that Hamas is an instrument of Iranian foreign policy. Indeed, the neo-conservative US *Council of Foreign Relations* notes that Iran has no direct control over the Palestinian movement.[301]

---

298. https://www.un.org/unispal/document/auto-insert-194881/
299. "Iran to give Palestinian government $50 million," *NBC News*, April 16, 2006 (https://www.nbcnews.com/id/wbna11100857)
300. Conal URQUHART, "Iran replaces EU as top Palestinian donor in Gaza City," *The Guardian*, January 15, 2007 (https://www.theguardian.com/world/2007/jan/15/israel.iran)
301. Bernard GWERTZMAN, "Iran Supports Hamas, but Hamas Is No Iranian 'Puppet,'" *Council of Foreign Relations*, January 7, 2009 (https://www.cfr.org/interview/iran-supports-hamas-hamas-no-iranian-puppet)

Since 2007, Iranian diplomatic efforts have been aimed at supporting the reconstruction of a national unity government in the Palestinian Authority. Iran's policy is not motivated by an identity of view with the Sunni movement, but by the desire to maintain Palestinian unity.

This policy runs exactly counter to the Israeli strategy, which seeks, on the contrary, to maintain a division in the Palestinian resistance. At a Likud congress in 2019, Benjamin Netanyahu clearly stated:

> *Those who want to prevent the creation of a Palestinian state should support the strengthening of Hamas and the financing of Hamas. This is part of our strategy, which is to create a differentiation between Palestinians in Gaza and Palestinians in Judea and Samaria [the West Bank].*[302]

In 2011, the Sunni Islamist revolution supported by Saudi Arabia, France and the USA began to tear Syria apart. In April, the Hamas security service closed down the offices of the Iranian-funded Shiite charity *al-Baqiyat al Salihat*[303] and hunted down activists from Gaza's Shiite minority (around 1% of the population).[304] This is why, in August 2011, after the political leadership of Hamas officially sided with the Syrian rebellion and left Damascus, Tehran stopped funding the Hamas-dominated PA.[305] On the other hand, it began to fund Shiite militias in the Gaza Strip, leading to the emergence of Palestinian Shiite resistance groups, such as the Sabreen Movement.

---

302. Jonathan Freedland, "Warning: Benjamin Netanyahu is walking right into Hamas's trap," *The Guardian*, October 20, 2023 (https://www.theguardian.com/commentisfree/2023/oct/20/benjamin-netanyahu-hamas-israel-prime-minister)
303. Jamestown Foundation, *Shiite Militancy Makes Inroads in Sunni Gaza*, 17 June 2011, *Terrorism Monitor*, no. 24, (https://www.refworld.org/docid/4e3fdb7e2.html) [accessed September 18, 2019]
304. Avi Issacharoff, "Hamas Brutally Assaults Shi'ite Worshippers in Gaza," *Haaretz*, January 17, 2012.
305. "Iran Cuts Hamas Funding for Failing to Show Support for Assad," *Reuters/ Haaretz*, August 21, 2011 (https://www.haaretz.com/2011-08-21/ty-article/iran-cuts-hamas-funding-for-failing-to-show-support-for-assad/0000017f-ecfa-dc91-a17f-fcffc83a0000)

## The United States Brings out the old Wild West Formulas.

*Figure 48—A $10 million reward is offered to those who can provide information on Hamas funding. As we can see, neither Israeli nor American intelligence services are familiar with these networks.*

With the restoration of the situation in Syria and the failure of the revolution encouraged by the West, relations between Iran and the Gaza Strip have warmed up. On November 27, 2018, for example, Iran reportedly offered to provide compensation for victims of the violence in Gaza following the "Great March of Return."

The financing of Hamas as a movement is the subject of much speculation. The amounts it receives and the way in which they are channeled (suitcases of cash!) are often pure invention on the part of our "experts." So little is known about these mechanisms that in early January 2024, the *US Department of Justice* published virtual "fliers" requesting public assistance in identifying financing networks.[306] In other words, we know extremely little about these Palestinian movements, and what we are served by our media are more often than not constructions poorly informed by prejudice.

Its funding mechanisms operate largely on the principle of small streams making large rivers. The main source of funding is *zakat*, which is collected in Gaza. There are also reports of funding mechanisms using virtual currencies on the Internet (Bitcoin); but in reality, we know absolutely nothing about this. Hamas is also said to have a vast network of charitable organizations and social associations in the occupied territories, which it uses to raise funds. However, here too the accusations are often gratuitous, as in the case of the *Comité de Bienfaisance et de Secours aux Palestiniens*, falsely accused by the *Conseil Représentatif des Institutions Juives de France* of helping to support Hamas.[307]

The difficulty of getting a clear picture of Hamas funding stems largely from the fact that Israel (and therefore the USA) regard Hamas humanitarian activities as terrorist activities. In reality, funding for Hamas aid organizations, including victim assistance, support for widows and orphans, and housing reconstruction, is fairly well monitored and known.

The difficulty in identifying Hamas's sources of funding is largely because of Israel's policy of perpetuating the idea of an international conspiracy against it, and thus highlighting links between Hamas and Iran. In fact, the Shiite presence in Palestine is very weak; the Lebanese Hezbollah and Hamas do not pursue the same basic objectives (even if they have the same adversary), and armed Shiite groups regularly confront Sunni groups by force of arms.

In October 2023, it was fashionable to declare that Hamas is supported by Iran. It is hard to see why Shiite Iran would specifically support Hamas, a Sunni movement that does not act according to its interests in Syria, for a cause that is not its own.

---

306. https://www.telegraph.co.uk/news/2024/01/06/10m-reward-for-information-on-top-five-hamas-backers/
307. https://fr.wikipedia.org/wiki/Comité_de_bienfaisance_et_de_secours_aux_Palestiniens

*Financing Hamas with Cybercurrency*

مكافأة لحد 10 ملايين دولار لمعلومات
تؤدي إلى تعطيل الشبكات المالية لحماس

تولّد حماس مبالغ هائلة من الإيرادات من خلال محافظها الاستثمارية السرية لتمويل هجماتها الإرهابية. إذا كانت لديك معلومات عن شبكات حماس المالية، فأرسلها إلينا عبر سغنال أو تلغرام أو واتساب أو خط تبليغ المستند إلى متصفح تور أدناه. قد تكون مؤهلا للحصول على مكافأة أو تحويل.

Tor Link: he5dybnt7sr6cm32xt77pazmtm65flqy6irivtflruqfc5ep7eiodiad.onion

U.S. Department of State
Diplomatic Security Service
Rewards for Justice

+1-202-294-1037
@REWARDS4JUSTICE

*Figure 49—It is claimed that Hamas uses digital financial tools to finance itself. In reality, our knowledge is extremely limited and largely speculative. So much so, that the U.S. Department of Justice has to appeal to the public for information. The text asks: "Hamas generates enormous revenues through its secret investment portfolios to finance its terrorist attacks. If you have information about Hamas's financial networks, please send it to us via Signal, Telegram, WhatsApp or via the information line based..."*
*[Source: https://twitter.com/RFJ_USA/status/1735730255539650631]*

## Designation of Hamas as a Terrorist Organization

It is tempting to try and resolve the Hamas issue by labelling it "terrorist" in order to justify its destruction and the refusal of any dialogue. But we must remain cautious and avoid a simplistic approach.

First of all, the notion of "terrorism" is essentially political in nature, with criteria that differ from country to country. Thus, the French Resistance fighters of the Second World War were described as terrorists by the Germans. Similarly, the rioters in Washington on January 6, 2021 were also called terrorists. The fact is, there is no officially or internationally recognized definition of terrorism.

Each country defines terrorism according to its own political stakes, with the result that we have never succeeded in eradicating this method. This lack of understanding is reflected in the number of definitions used around the world, and explains the inability to define coherent strategies for dealing with it.

If we were to apply Western definitions to the State of Israel, we would no longer speak to it, and could condemn all those who supported it.

For not only did Jewish terrorism cause the British to withdraw from Palestine and abandon the League of Nations mandate, it was also behind the creation of the State of Israel.[308] What is more, a number of its leaders have been bloodthirsty terrorists, and it continues to apply a terrorist policy towards the Palestinian population,[309] a policy which meets the definition of state terrorism.

In 1994, there were 212 definitions of terrorism in use around the world, 90 of which were in official use.[310] After 9/11, the number literally exploded, and often several different definitions are used in the same country. Work on a universal definition began in 1937, within the League of Nations, with the drafting of the *Convention for the Prevention and Suppression of Terrorism*,[311] but never came to fruition.

In simple terms, the debate is between two main camps:
- Western countries, which tend to define terrorism in terms of its modes of action and effects, emphasizing its criminal nature.
- The "Global South," and in particular the member countries of the *Organization of Islamic Cooperation (OIC)*, which prefers a definition that takes account of its causes, without attributing to it *a priori* a criminal character. This position is explained by the struggles for independence against considerably more powerful Western forces, and by the Israeli-Palestinian conflict, which is seen from the same perspective.

We could sum it up by saying that the Western vision allows us to condemn terrorism, but not to fight it; whereas the vision of the rest of the world would allow us to fight it, but not to condemn it. This discussion is particularly visible in France, where our journalists strive to obtain "condemnations" of Hamas without *ever* proposing a solution to the underlying problem.

The risk, of course, is that including causes in a definition of terrorism only serves to justify it:

---

308. John L. Peeke, "Jewish -- Zionist Terrorism and the Establishment of Israel," *Naval Postgraduate School Monterey CA*, 1977 (https://apps.dtic.mil/sti/pdfs/ADA047231.pdf)
309. https://www.eeas.europa.eu/eeas/israelpalestine-statement-spokesperson-latest-developments-west-bank_en
310. Jeffrey D. Simon, *The Terrorist Trap*, Indiana University Press, Bloomington, 1994.
311. *Convention for the Prevention and Suppression of Terrorism*, League of Nations, November 16, 1937, N°C.546.M.383.1937.V

*As for the legal definition of "terrorism," the Israeli representative said that some countries still maintain that an act of terrorism—a car bomb in a crowded market, for example—should not be considered terrorism, if it was claimed in the context of national liberation. He said that terrorism was defined by "what you do, not why you do it." To defend an attack on innocent people in the name of the fight for freedom is incomprehensible.[312]*

The Israeli representative is right; in principle, even a just cause does not justify terrorism. But here again, there are nuances. The reason why Western countries fight terrorism with such virulence is that they claim to be democracies. In other words, a claim (political or otherwise) can be expressed through mechanisms that are defined and accepted by all. Terrorism is then a way of bypassing these mechanisms and attempting to impose decisions by force, going against the very democratic process, which—in addition to its criminal nature—justifies fighting it.

The problem arises when the state no longer offers any space for this demand to be expressed, heard or taken into consideration. The state itself then falls into a form of denial of democracy. This is what happens with Israel, which refuses to implement international humanitarian law and offers no space for Palestinian demands to be taken into account. This is why Yasser Arafat's political approach failed to improve the situation, paving the way for more radical Islamist movements.

The simple effect of the "terrorist" label is to exclude any dialogue with the entity (individual or organization) in question. This is why, in 2021, the United Nations condemned Israel for labelling Palestinian human rights organizations in this way.[313] This is because Israel's strategy has systematically been to cut off all channels of communication with the Palestinians, as if to encourage them to resort to violence.

The position of the "rest of the world" is based on the fact that terrorism is sometimes the last resort in a war against a technologically or numerically superior adversary. Terrorism is then seen as a method of combat,

---

312. Summary record of *the 29th session of the 6th Committee of the United Nations*, November 15, 2000 (GA/L/3169)
313. "UN experts condemn Israel's designation of Palestinian human rights defenders as terrorist organisations," *ohchr.org*, October 25, 2021 (https://www.ohchr.org/en/press-releases/2021/10/un-experts-condemn-israels-designation-palestinian-human-rights-defenders

which can serve the most diverse, but also the most legitimate, objectives and causes, and is part of a "weak to strong" strategy:

*As long as we are unable to distinguish between terrorism and the right to defend one's land, we cannot agree on what terrorism is.[314]*

The problem is that in Palestine, the possibilities for expressing discontent are so limited that the choice of possible strategies tends to be reduced to terrorism, thus giving it legitimacy.

Added to this is the problem of state terrorism (indiscriminate bombings,[315] assassinations,[316] torture,[317] arbitrary arrests,[318] etc.), which tends to become a strategy in the fight against terrorism, and which only reinforces those who advocate a violent struggle.

With the revolutionary movements of the 1960s-1980s, we slowly began to see terrorism as an ideology in itself, and thus introduced an antagonism between "freedom fighter" and "terrorist." And yet, semantically speaking, these are two fundamentally different things: the "freedom fighter" (or "resistance fighter") is defined in terms of a goal, while the "terrorist" is defined in terms of a mode of action.

It is in this complex context that Hamas is considered a terrorist organization by the Western world, i.e., essentially by the United States[319] and the European Union,[320] but not by the rest of the world. In fact, Hamas defines itself as a national liberation movement, fighting against the occupation of Palestine and for the restoration of the rights of the Palestinian people. It has no ambitions and poses no threat beyond the borders of Palestine.

The West's definition of Hamas as a terrorist group reflects both a misunderstanding of its nature and a desire to express support for Israel. In so doing, we renounce our role as mediator in the conflict. This is why Western diplomacy is powerless. Today, the Palestinian resistance

---

314. *Iran News*, reported by AFP, September 30, 2001.
315. https://www.amnesty.org/en/latest/news/2023/10/damning-evidence-of-war-crimes-as-israeli-attacks-wipe-out-entire-families-in-gaza/
316. https://casebook.icrc.org/case-study/israel-targeted-killings-case
317. https://www.amnesty.org/en/latest/news/2023/11/israel-opt-horrifying-cases-of-torture-and-degrading-treatment-of-palestinian-detainees-amid-spike-in-arbitrary-arrests/
318. https://www.ohchr.org/en/press-releases/2022/06/un-experts-condemn-israels-arbitrary-detention-and-conviction-palestinian
319. https://www.state.gov/foreign-terrorist-organizations/
320. https://bit.ly/2L6szt9

is caught between the State of Israel, which refuses to implement international law and negotiate, Westerners who have prevented themselves from negotiating with Hamas, and an Arab world that refuses to get involved for fear of reprisals and American and European sanctions. As a result, the only option left is violent action.

On October 17, 2023, on *Sud Radio*, journalist Jean-Jacques Bourdin sought to undermine a French politician by asking her whether Hamas was a terrorist or resistance organization.[321] Known for his manipulative and perverse tendencies,[322] the journalist demonstrates profound incompetence and dishonesty. The expressions "resistance" or "freedom fighter" are based on the movement's purpose. Terrorism," on the other hand, is a method (or one of the methods) of achieving it. Comparing apples and oranges is like asking the question, "Is this a journalist or a fool?" Obviously, one does not exclude the other (and very rarely does).

In France, this kind of manipulation is a method of governance. On October 18, Interior Minister Gérald Darmanin filed a complaint against the politician for "*apology for* terrorism."[323] One gets the feeling that the Minister was seeking to fan the flames of communitarianism. In the United States, the website of the *Director of National Intelligence* (DNI) mentions Hamas on its list of terrorist movements, but states that the movement practices "*armed resistance*," which is compatible with resolution 45/130 (1990).[324]

On a more technical level, defining Hamas as a terrorist movement only serves to condemn it politically, but does not solve the problem. Legally speaking, terrorism has no internationally accepted definition. In other words, it does not provide a basis for joint action in line with international law. This is why Western interventions in the Near and Middle East have all been either illegal or illegally diverted from their original purpose.

---

321. https://youtu.be/T2hr6hHyNT0
322. https://www.public.fr/News/Jean-Jacques-Bourdin-vire-de-RMC-apres-des-accusations-de-harcelement-sexuel-le-journaliste-se-dit-libere-1711956
323. Nathalie Segaunes, "Danièle Obono calls Hamas a 'resistance movement', Gérald Darmanin takes legal action for 'apologie du terrorisme'," *Le Monde*, October 18, 2023 (https://www.lemonde.fr/politique/article/2023/10/18/daniele-obono-qualifie-le-hamas-de-mouvement-de-resistance-gerald-darmanin-saisit-la-justice-pour-apologie-du-terrorisme_6195084_823448.html)
324. https://www.dni.gov/nctc/ftos/hamas_fto.html

## Countries Designating Hamas as Terrorist

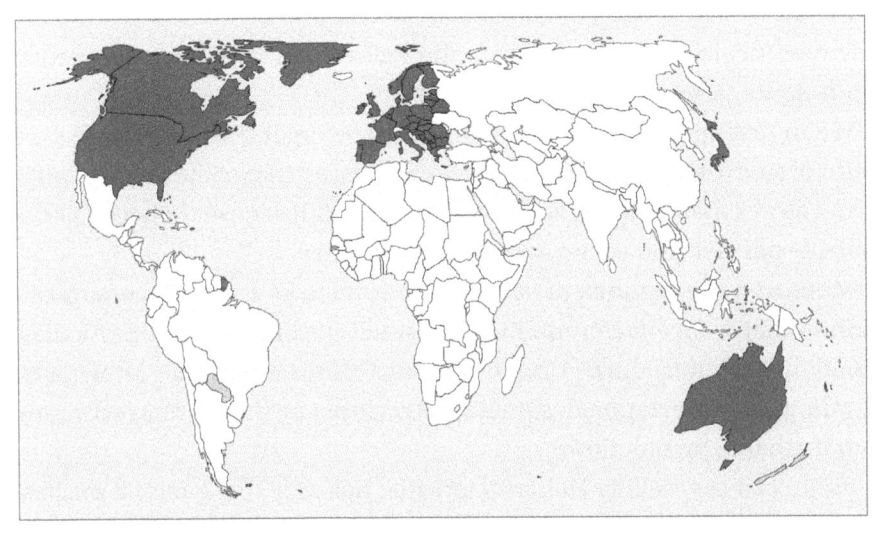

*Figure 50—Countries designating Hamas as terrorist. In dark gray, countries designating the entire movement; in light gray (Paraguay and New Zealand), countries designating only the Al-Qassam Brigades.*

The problem is that Western countries have systematically sought to create problems for themselves. It is obvious that when you have a problem with terrorism on your territory, such as ETA in Spain, or the PKK in Turkey, you define it as terrorist so that you can apply a jurisdiction that corresponds to this type of threat. When Israel has a problem with the Palestinian resistance, and this resistance—as its name suggests—"resists" and is not active in other parts of the world, there is no reason why third countries, such as Switzerland or even the European Union, should adopt this designation.

Designating Hamas as a terrorist movement will have absolutely no impact on our security, or even on Israel's security. In fact, its only effect is to exclude any possibility of negotiating or mediating with Hamas. In Palestine, the State of Israel has systematically sought to link the resistance to the global jihadist movement, so as to legitimize its non-compliance with international law. This is part of a general Western tendency to operate within an international order governed by "rules" rather the "law."

The nature of Palestinian resistance has changed significantly since 2005-2006. With the help of the American "War on Terror," the Palestinians realized that offensive terrorist acts did not bring them more support, and that the asymmetry of Israeli actions could work in their favor in an asymmetrical context. As a result, the Palestinian resistance adopted a more strategic and political approach.

When dealing with Hamas, we must never forget that Israel itself was born of a terrorism whose brutality far surpassed that of the Palestinians. It has struck at its allies as well as its enemies. It has never behaved like a reliable partner, and yet we are talking to it today.

Moreover, the paradox of designating Hamas as a terrorist organization is that it *ipso facto* outlaws the Israeli government (in particular Benjamin Netanyahu). Under US anti-terrorism laws, knowingly funding an organization designated as terrorist by the Secretary of State is punishable by sanctions!

As we can see, calling Hamas a terrorist has only one effect: it pushes Israel to use the American, British or French methods of fighting terrorism, i.e., the massacre of civilians. Those who dream of banishing Israel from the international community can rejoice, as this is exactly what is happening. One has to wonder whether the talking-heads in our media are not the real anti-Semites.

Terrorism is not inevitable. Hamas has demonstrated that it knows how to renounce violence and is open to a politically negotiated solution. The Israeli-Palestinian conflict will not be resolved by invective or sterile qualifications. War crimes, if any, must be judged and condemned on both sides, while a dialogue must be opened. Our journalists should be helping politicians find bridges, rather than building walls with pointless "condemnations." But can they?

## Other Palestinian Resistance Movements in Gaza

Palestinian resistance movements are all influenced to varying degrees by Islamism. But it would be wrong to see in them civilizational objectives or the expression of anti-Western radicalism, as tends to be understood in France. It is more a question of a shared vision of how to conduct resistance against the Israeli occupation. Notions of personal sacrifice, individual determination, victory or the refusal to abandon a cause are at the heart of this doctrinal choice.

On the other hand, although we have given an indication of the religious or philosophical leanings of the groups here, it must be interpreted with nuance, as we see very diverse tendencies intertwined within Palestinian groups. Clearly, the Palestinian resistance as a whole is guided by the aim of liberating a territory, not achieving a religious objective. This is why we find Shiite fighters in Sunni groups and vice-versa. It is very important to understand that religion is not the objective, but a cultural contribution to the way of fighting.

Even secular movements are driven by Muslim culture. The distinction made in the West, which stems from our inability to admit our own responsibility for the rise of violence in the Middle East, leads us to understand Palestinian violence as the expression of a religious project. This simplistic approach is also found among French politicians. It is wrong, and it is the reason why we are failing to prevent terrorism.

## Sunni Movements

### Palestinian Islamic Jihad (PIJ)

The *Palestinian Islamic Jihad Movement (Harakat al-Jihād al-Islāmi fi Filastīn)* (PIJ) is a Sunni-based Palestinian movement founded by students at the Islamic University of Gaza in 1982. But it became effectively operational under the leadership of Fathi Abd al-Aziz al-Shaqaqi[325] and Sheikh Abd al-Aziz Awda. Today, it is the second largest resistance movement in the Gaza Strip.

Its aim is the "liberation" of historic Palestine and the creation of an Islamic Palestinian state, with Jerusalem as its capital. It advocates a *"Palestine—from the river [Jordan] to the sea—an Arab, Islamic country whose law forbids ceding an inch of its territory."*[326] However, although it campaigns for the liberation of the whole of Palestine, its current objectives are limited to the pre-June 1967 borders. In May 2002, Dr. Ramadan Abdallah Shalah, the movement's secretary-general, stated: *"With the current Intifada, all Palestinian factions, including Islamic Jihad, agree*

---

325. Fathi Abd al-Aziz al-Shiqaqi, originally from Rafah, studied medicine. He was assassinated on October 26, 1995 in Malta by a Mossad commando.
326. "Introduction to the movement and its vision," www.qudsway.com (quoted by Human Rights Watch: https://www.hrw.org/reports/2002/isrl-pa/ISRAELPA1002-05.htm

*that the objective of the Palestinian resistance today is to unconditionally drive back the Israeli occupation of the West Bank and Gaza."*[327]

## The Palestinian Islamic Jihad Movement

*Figure 51—PIJ logo.*

Today, its armed wing is made up of the Al-Quds Units (or Jerusalem Units). They were created by Mahmoud Arafat Al-Khawaja, according to some versions, or by Ziad Nakhalah according to others. During the first Intifada, they were known as the "Saif al-Islam Brigades." Later, they were renamed the "Islamic Mujahideen Forces," commonly known as the "Department." Their epicenter is Jenin in the West Bank.

In 2019, during the citizen protests in the Gaza Strip against the Israeli siege, the PIJ warned that if civilians were killed, it could lead to war.[328] And that is where we are now.

The *Al-Quds Units* (Jerusalem Units) are its armed wing. They originate from the Gaza Strip, but have also established a military presence in the West Bank. Their remarkable organization has made them a benchmark among PTOs.

The Al-Quds Units began with small-scale actions, often knife attacks, and gradually moved on to more structured actions by armed groups. They pioneered the use of rockets against Israel. Their first home-made

---

327. Ibrahim HAMIDI, "Islamic Jihad reiterates possibility of end to attacks on civilians," *Daily Star*, Beirut, May 16, 2002.
328. https://www.timesofisrael.com/islamic-jihad-warns-israel-of-war-if-civilians-killed-during-protests/

rocket was fired against Ashkelon on November 15, 2002. Initially called "Jenin," their rockets were renamed "Al-Quds."

### Saraya al-Quds

*Figure 52—al-Quds Units logo.*

Many of the movement's leaders were assassinated by Israeli forces. These include Fathi al-Shaqaqi, the movement's historic leader, assassinated on October 26, 1995 in Malta by an Israeli commando; Khaled Al-Dahdouh "Abu Al-Walid," commander of the Gaza Phalanx, assassinated in March 2006 by a car bomb; Hossam Jaradat, eliminated in August 2006 by the Israeli army during the assault on the Jenin camp, or Baha Abu Al-Ata, commander of the Al-Quds Units in Gaza, killed along with his family by an air strike in 2019. Following numerous elimination-attempts by the Israeli services, the PIJ no longer communicates the names of its leaders.

After the assassination of Fathi Shaqaqi, the PIJ was led by Dr. Ramadan Abdullah Shallah, the movement's secretary-general, who died of an illness on June 6, 2020. Its current secretary-general is Ziyad al-Nakhalah.

The PIJ participated in the *Joint Operations Room* and was a partner in the AL-AQSA FLOOD operation alongside Hamas.

Akram Al-Ajouri is believed to be the head of the Al-Quds Units, responsible for its logistics in the manufacture of rockets and various weapons, as well as for the training of its members abroad. He is said to be a member of the movement's political bureau and Shura Council, and to have played a leading role in its financing and arming. Israel attempted to assassinate him in Syria in 2019, but the attempt failed.

**PIJ Combat Units**

**Mouvement du Djihad Islamique en Palestine**

**Sarayat al-Quds**
Unité Jérusalem

| Katibat Jenin | Katibat Nablus | Katibat Toubas | Katibat Tulkarem |
|---|---|---|---|
| Phalange de Jenine | Phalange de Naplouse | Phalange de Toubas | Phalange de Tulkarem |

*Figure 53—Palestinian Islamic Jihad originated in Gaza, where its Al-Quds units operate. It has recently created phalanxes in the West Bank. The Jenin Phalanx is a combined unit, which also includes Hamas' Al-Ayyash battalion.*

## *Popular Resistance Movement (PRM)*

The People's Resistance Movement (*Harakat al-Muqawama al-Sha'biyya*) grew out of the People's Resistance Committees. It is headed by Zakaria Dughmush "Abu al-Qasim," who is its Secretary General. Its military wing, the *Al-Nasser Salah al-Din Brigades* (*Kata'ib Al-Nasser Salah al-Din*), *was* created in 2000.

## Popular Resistance Movement

*Figure 54—The PRM is an Islamist group, as the details of its logo show.*

In October 2022, the al-Nasser Salah al-Deen Brigades, the military wing of the Popular Resistance Movement in Palestine, announced the launch of their first West Bank operation from the city of Jenin.[329] Almost all the Palestinian groups in Gaza are expanding into the West Bank.

## Kata'ib al-Nasser Salah al-Din

*Figure 55—Logo of the al-Nasser Salah al-Deen Brigades.*

---

329. https://qudsnet.com/post/542001/اشتباك-بين-عناصر-من-كتائب-القسام-وقوات-الاحتلال-في-جنين

## Free Palestine Movement (MPL)

The Free Palestine Movement is a small resistance movement led by Khaled Abu Hilal "Abu Adam," its Secretary General. The number of its fighters is not known precisely, but should be around 1,000.

**Free Palestine Movement**

*Figure 56—Logo of the Free Palestine Movement. The historical symbolism of Palestinian movements (the map and flag of Palestine from the Mediterranean to the Jordan) and that of Islamist movements can be seen.*

**Kata'ib al-Ansar**

*Figure 57—The Brigades of the Supporters take up the graphic elements of Sunni movements found in Syria, for example, such as the two swords. On the other hand, the traditional Palestinian symbolism (map and Haram Al-Sharif mosque) underlines the movement's national character.*

## *Humat al-Aqsa*

Humat al-Aqsa (Protectors of Al-Aqsa) is a Sunni-inspired Islamist group founded in April 2006 by Fathi Hamad as an offshoot of Hamas. In 2018, its activities included incendiary balloon attacks against the "Gaza envelope."

**Houmat Al-Aqsa**

*Figure 58—Houmat al-Aqsa logo.*

**Liwa Khan Yunis**

*Figure 59—Logo of the Khan Yunis Brigade of the Humat al-Aqsa Brigades.*

## Shiite-Inspired Movements

### Popular Resistance Committees (PRC)

**Popular Resistance Committees (PRC)**

Figure 60—PRC logos (variants).

The *Popular Resistance Committees in Palestine* (PRC) (*Lijān al-Muqāwama al-Sha'biyya fi Filastin*) are the third largest armed group in the Gaza Strip. They were founded on September 28, 2000, at the start of the second Intifada, by Jamal Abu Samhadana, Yasser Zanoun, Mubarak Al-Hasanat and Abu Yusuf Al-Quqa, all of whom have since been assassinated.

**Liwa al-Nasser Salah al-Deen**

Figure 61—Logo of the al-Nasser Salah al-Deen Brigade, the armed wing of the PRC in the Gaza Strip.

On March 9, 2012, Israel's elimination of Zuhir al-Qaisi, PRC secretary general, led to the deaths of some 15 innocent civilians, provoking rocket fire. This triggered an escalation of violence, which was then welcomed by the French government, provoking Mohammed Merah's outrage in France.

The PRC regularly cooperates with Hamas and the Palestinian Islamic Jihad. After winning the 2006 elections, Hamas placed former PRC executive Jamal Abu Samhadana at the head of its paramilitary executive force.

The *al-Nasser Salah al-Deen Brigade* is the armed wing of the PRC. It is said to have been formed in the south of the Gaza Strip by former members of the Al-Aqsa Martyrs' Brigades (AMB) opposed to the Palestinian Authority (PA) and the Oslo Accords. The *Economist*'s former Palestine correspondent, Graham Usher, reported that *"the bulk of the fighters come from the Tanzims, including officers from the PA's intelligence and police forces."* It operates autonomously in the Gaza Strip. It produces and operates NASSER and NASSER-3 rockets.

In April 2001, Yasser Arafat reportedly ordered the disbanding of the PRC and the return of its fighters to their original groups. However, PRC leaders refused to comply. It seems that the PRC also includes former PFLP members.

PRC doctrine is influenced by Islamic nationalism. Although the group does not participate in PA or PLO politics and advocates armed resistance, it supports the creation of a Palestinian state based on the pre-June 1967 borders. Israel accuses Iran of supporting and financing the PRC.

The PRCs took part in joint military operations with the IQB, including the capture and detention of PFLP members.

## Movement of the Patient ones in Support for Palestine (HISN)

*Harkat al-Sabireen Nasran li-Filastin (HISN)*, also known as the *Sabireen Movement* or *"Fortress" Movement*, is a Shiite movement that emerged in the Gaza Strip in 2014. It resulted from the detachment of a faction of the *Palestinian Islamic Jihad* (PIJ) led by Hisham Salim. Its emergence was the result of tensions between Shiites and Sunnis generated by the attempt by the United States and France to destabilize Syria, and their support for the Muslim Brotherhood's Free Syrian Army (ASL). The disappearance of the ASL in favor of jihadist groups has fanned the flames of rivalry between Sunni and Shiite groups, even in the Gaza Strip.

The Sabireen Movement is said to be financed by Iran and has been listed as a terrorist movement by the United States.[330] The insistence of Western countries and our media on equating Gazans and Hamas with the Islamic State has obscured the existence of a small Shiite minority in the Gaza Strip. It is this minority that is financed by Iran.

*Harakat "Al-Sabireen"*

Figure 62—The emblem of the Patients' Movement is clearly inspired by that of the Lebanese Hezbollah. It is said to benefit from Iranian funding, following the development of Sunni Islamist forces in Syria, which have the political backing of Hamas.

In July 2015, Hamas shut down the movement's activities and banned it.[331] The unstable relations between Hamas and the Shiite movements in the Gaza Strip explain Iran's relations with the latter. Contrary to what some experts claim, Iran has sought to maintain a form of stability in the territory that takes account of the Shiite minority.

### *Palestinian Mujahideen Movement (PMM)*

The *Palestinian Mujahideen Movement* (*Harkat-ul-Mujahideen al-Falastini*) is a Shiite movement originally from Gaza, which began deploying units in the West Bank in late 2022-early 2023. It appears to be close to the *Popular Resistance Movement* (MRP).

---

330. Matthew LEVITT, "New Palestinian and Egyptian Designations Highlight Iran and the Muslim Brotherhood," *The Washington Institute*, January 31, 2018 (https://www.washingtoninstitute.org/policy-analysis/new-palestinian-and-egyptian-designations-highlight-iran-and-muslim-brotherhood)
331. https://howiyapress.com/9451-2/

It defines itself as an Islamic reformist movement, whose aim is the liberation of the entire territory of Palestine. Its links with Tehran and the Lebanese Hezbollah earned it a place on the 2018 US list of terrorist movements.[332]

### Palestinian Mujahideen Movement (PMM)

*Figure 63—The MMP logo.*

### Kata'ib al-Mujahideen

*Figure 64—Logos of the Brigades of the Moudjahidin.
The symbolism is reminiscent of that of the Martyrs of Al-Aqsa Brigades.*

---

332. https://alkhanadeq.com/post.php?id=2349

The armed wing of the MMP emerged in 2000 from a split in Fatah's Brigades of the Al-Aqsa Martyrs. It was created by Omar Abu Sharia under the name of *Mujahidin Battalions* (*Khatib Al-Mujahidin*). In 2006, it officially became the military wing of the MMP and was renamed *"Brigades of the Mujahidin"* (*Khatib Al-Mujahidin*), under the leadership of Assad Abu Sharia (alias "Abu Al-Sheikh"). Currently, the Brigade is led by Nael Abu Odeh, head of the MMP's political bureau in Gaza.

The MMP possesses locally-made missiles, such as the "Sa'ir" and "Hafs al-Mutawwar" missiles, 107 mm and 122 mm GRAD rockets, as well as SA-16 portable anti-aircraft missiles (MANPADS). It also has its own network of tunnels, which it uses in its combat and organizational activities.

### Interior Martyrs Unit during the Occupation

*Figure 65—Logo of the Occupation Martyrs' Unit of the Palestinian Mujahideen Movement (MRP).*

The Interior Martyrs Unit during the Occupation (DAHIM Unit) is a secret unit of volunteers who infiltrate Israeli forces. On May 22, 2022, Israeli security arrested Shihada Abu Al-Qia'an, one of these infiltrators, who was supplying information to the resistance.[333]

---

333. https://alkhanadeq.com/post.php?id=4713

## Secular-Inspired Movements

Secular resistance movements are heirs to the historic Marxist-inspired Palestinian resistance of the 1960s-1970s. As a rule, they remain secular and very much in the minority. Strangely enough, Israel and the West have not tried to support these movements, and have instead allowed Islamist movements to develop. For example, the expulsion from France of Mariam Abu Daqqa, a 73-year-old PFLP activist, in October-November 2023, shows the absence of a strategy for Palestine.

That said, the rhetoric is evolving over time and drifting towards that of Islamist movements. Notions of "success" and "victory" are difficult to sustain in the secular Marxist logic of the 20th century. The lack of political prospects offered by the occupying power is slowly pushing the Palestinian resistance towards an Islamist approach, which makes it easier to manage the hopes and expectations of the population. This is one of the reasons why Israel's strategy encourages it to engage in tougher confrontation.

## Factions of the al-Aqsa Martyrs Brigade in Gaza

The *al-Aqsa Martyrs Brigades* (AMB) are Fatah's armed wing. They are mainly present in the West Bank. But despite the attempted coup financed by the United States in 2006-2007, which led to deadly clashes with Hamas, understanding between the two movements in the Gaza Strip is good. Fatah maintains several cooperating factions in the territory, including participation in the *Joint Operations Room*.

### Liwa Gaza

*Figure 66—Logo of the Gaza Brigade. It coordinates the various factions of the Brigades of the al-Aqsa Martyrs on Gaza territory.*

## Factions of the al-Aqsa Martyrs Brigades in Gaza

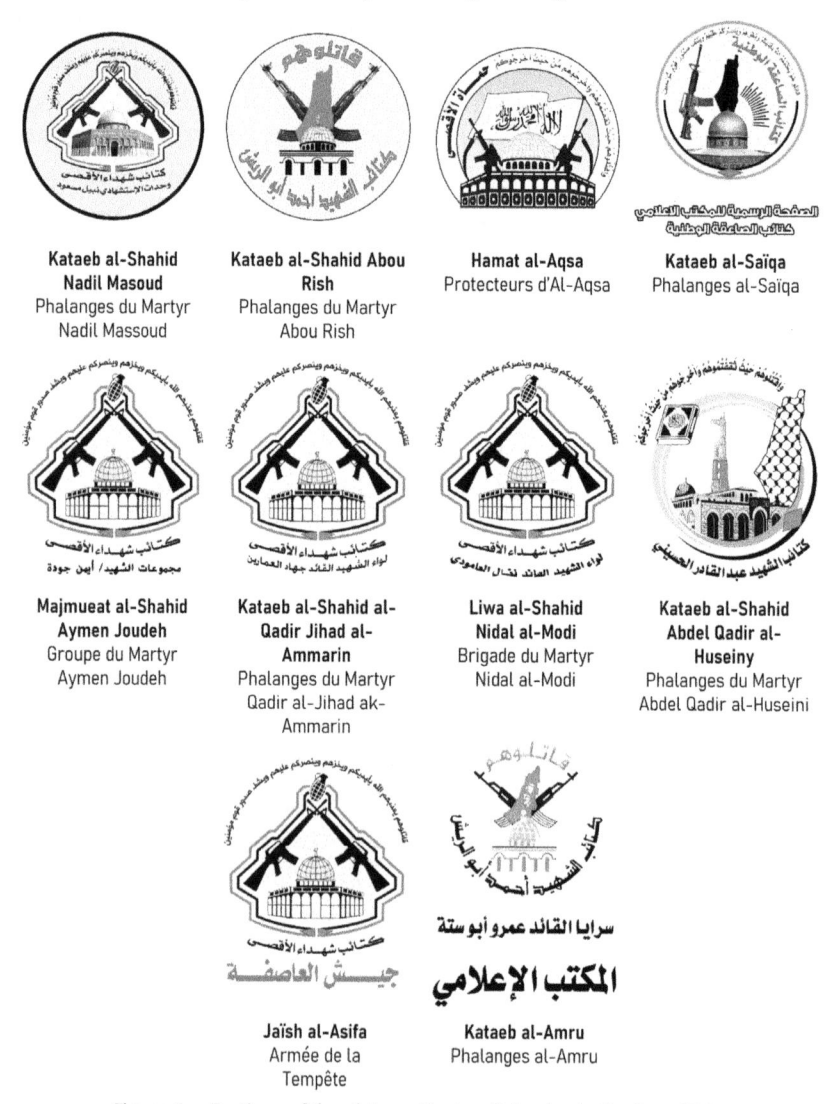

**Kataeb al-Shahid Nadil Masoud**
Phalanges du Martyr Nadil Massoud

**Kataeb al-Shahid Abou Rish**
Phalanges du Martyr Abou Rish

**Hamat al-Aqsa**
Protecteurs d'Al-Aqsa

**Kataeb al-Saïqa**
Phalanges al-Saïqa

**Majmueat al-Shahid Aymen Joudeh**
Groupe du Martyr Aymen Joudeh

**Kataeb al-Shahid al-Qadir Jihad al-Ammarin**
Phalanges du Martyr Qadir al-Jihad ak-Ammarin

**Liwa al-Shahid Nidal al-Modi**
Brigade du Martyr Nidal al-Modi

**Kataeb al-Shahid Abdel Qadir al-Huseiny**
Phalanges du Martyr Abdel Qadir al-Huseini

**Jaïsh al-Asifa**
Armée de la Tempête

**Kataeb al-Amru**
Phalanges al-Amru

*Figure 67—Factions of the al-Aqsa Martyrs Brigades in the Gaza Strip.*

The AMBs were originally small armed resistance groups that emerged in 2000, during the second Intifada. Their *raison d'être* is the fight against West Bank settlements, which regularly expel Palestinians from their land. On March 27, 2002, they were placed on the US State Department's list of terrorist organizations.

Initially, their actions were directed at settlers in the occupied territories. With the increase in evictions in East Jerusalem, the AMBs stepped up their action inside Israel. It should be noted here that arming settlers in the West Bank and Jerusalem turned civilians into military targets.

The Brigades claimed responsibility for the first suicide attack carried out by a woman in Palestine. On January 14, 2004, Reem Salah al-Riyashi detonated the bomb she was carrying at the Erez checkpoint at the entrance to the Gaza Strip. This action set a precedent. A women's unit was created within the *al-Aqsa Martyrs Brigades*. The example was soon followed by the *Palestinian Islamic Jihad* and the *Al-Qassam Brigades*.

Since 2013, *Al-Qassam Brigade* units in the Gaza Strip have been under the command of the Gaza Brigade (Liwa Gaza).[334] They participate in the joint command of Palestinian forces, along with Hamas and Palestinian Islamic Jihad. Their numbers are not precisely known.

## *The Popular Front for the Liberation of Palestine (PFLP)*

**Popular Front for the Liberation of Palestine (PFLP)**

*Figure 68—PFLP logo.*

The PFLP (*al-Jabha al-Shabiyah li-Tahrir Filastin*) is a Marxist-Leninist movement created in December 1967 from elements of the *Palestine Liberation Front (PLF)* and the *Arab Nationalist Movement (ANM)*. Until July 2000, it was led by its founder, Dr George Habash. His successor,

---

334. https://alkhanadeq.com/post/545/كتائب-القسام-ألاءشهداء-بى-عمواقة-معسكرية-في-الضفة

Abu Ali Mustapha, was assassinated by an Israeli missile on August 27, 2001. Since October 3, 2001, it has been led by Ahmad Sa'adat, arrested by Israeli security forces in 2002. Its political leadership is based in Damascus (Syria), and its operational presence is centered on Nablus, in the West Bank, and within the Palestinian Christian community.

The PFLP grew out of the *Arab Nationalist Movement (ANM) (Harakat al-Qawmiyyin al-Arab)*, a nationalist movement—but already oriented towards the Palestinian question—founded in Beirut in 1952 by George Habash with Abd al-Karim Hamad, Ahmad al-Yamani and Wadie Haddad. The movement, whose slogan was "unity, liberation, revenge," enjoyed a certain success among Arab youth.[335] In 1964, the movement became the *National Front for the Liberation of Palestine* and carried out several terrorist operations against Israel at the end of the same year.

After the 1967 war, it changed its name to the *Popular Front for the Liberation of Palestine* and moved to Jordan. Attempting to publicize the Palestinian cause abroad, it acquired a notorious reputation for hijacking airplanes. In February 1969, after its annual conference, the left wing of the movement, led by Nayef Hawatmeh, seceded and created the *Popular Democratic Front for the Liberation of Palestine (PFLP)*.[336] The PFLP continued its struggle and advocated the overthrow of Hashemite rule, leading to the fierce fighting of September 1970, which saw the expulsion of the Palestinian resistance from Jordan. It boycotted meetings of the Palestinian National Council and the PLO Executive Committee, but remained faithful to the principle of Palestinian national unity and the maintenance of the PLO.

Thus, in 1972, the PFLP renounced "external operations" and concentrated on Israel and the Occupied Territories. After 1973, the PFLP opposed the PLO's new moderate orientation. Differences between the PFLP and Fatah remained profound, and resurfaced after the 1982 Lebanon war.

In September 1974, the PFLP withdrew from the *PLO Executive Committee* (which it did not rejoin until 1987) and formed The Rejectionist Front, rejecting all negotiations with Israel, as well as its right to exist. Publicly displaying its differences with Yasser Arafat, the PFLP spawned a large number of radical, often murderous splinter groups. The PFLP is

---

335. The MNA had a South Arab branch in Yemen as early as 1959.
336. Which became the *Democratic Front for the Liberation of Palestine (DFLP)*.

opposed to the 1993 Israeli-Palestinian agreement (Oslo Accords) and the Wye Plantation Agreement.

In the 1970s-1980s, the PFLP collaborated closely with the *Democratic Front for the Liberation of Palestine* (DFLP), and was one of the Arab movements most closely linked with European terrorism (including the Irish Republican Army (IRA)). It subcontracted its actions to other groups, such as the *Red Eagles*, led by Samir Shaas (1993).

### Kata'ib Abu Ali Mustafa

*Figure 69—Brigades Abu Ali Mustafa.*

In April 2000, George Habash resigned as secretary-general for health reasons, but remained politically active. He was replaced in July by the movement's number two, Abu Ali Mustafa, who had reinstalled the PFLP office in Ramallah in August 1999. During the second Intifada, the PFLP carried out attacks against Israel and the settlements. On August 27, 2001, Abu Ali Moustafa was eliminated by Israeli forces, in response to an attack on a military post—carried out by a commando of the *Democratic Front for the Liberation of Palestine (DFLP)*—which had killed three Israeli soldiers. In response, the movement's armed wing was renamed *the Abu Ali Mustafa Brigades*. On October 17, 2001, the latter carried out an operation targeting an Israeli minister for the first time: one of its commandos eliminated Rehavam Zeevi, in Jerusalem, the Minister of Tourism and member of Israel's far-right Moledet party.

The Palestinian Authority has tried to limit the actions of radical Palestinian movements, notably the *Abu Ali Mustafa Brigades*. On

January 14, 2002, following the attack on Minister Zeevi, the Palestinian Authority arrested Ahmed Saadat, secretary-general of the PFLP. On March 14, 2006, Ahmed Saadat and Ahed Ghulmeh, leader of the Abu Ali Mustafa Brigades, were captured by Israel.

## The Democratic Front for the Liberation of Palestine (DFLP)

The FDLP (*al-Jabha al-Dīmūqrāṭiyya li-Taḥrīr Filasṭīn*) was founded by Nayef Hawatmeh under the name of *Popular Democratic Front for the Liberation of Palestine (FDPLP) (Jabhat al-Shabiya al-Dīmūqrāṭiyya li-Taḥrīr Filasṭīn)*. It is Maoist-leaning and less Nasserist than the PFLP, opposes the internationalization of terrorism and has concentrated its operations in Israel itself.

**Democratic Front for the Liberation of Palestine (DFLP)**

*Figure 70—Variants of the FDLP logo.*

Formed by disappointed Fatah supporters, it split from the *Popular Front for the Liberation of Palestine* (PFLP) in May 1969. It is notably responsible for the spectacular and controversial Ma'alot school massacre (Israel) in 1974. It changed its name to the DFLP in August 1974. Despite its criticism of Yasser Arafat, the DFLP continues to support PLO unity. It is represented on the PLO Executive Committee by Taysir Khaled (alias, Mohammad Sa'adeh Odeh). It accepts the idea of the existence of a Jewish nation, but denies the role of the Hebrew state in instituting true democracy.

It took a violent part in the internal struggles of the Palestinian movement, notably against the PFLP, and carried out attacks in Jordan and Egypt. It maintains relations with Cuba, the People's Republic of China, Iraq and, in the past, the USSR. Iraq provided financial support until 1974. After the Ma'alot massacre, Libya supported the DFLP. In 1991, it split into two factions: one pro-Syrian, led by Hawatmeh—who joined the opposition in Syria—and the other more pro-Arafat, led by Yasser Abed Rabbo.

### DFLP Forces in Gaza

**Kataeb al-Muqawamat al-Wataniat al-Filastinia**
Phalanges de la Résistance Nationale Palestinienne

**Quwat al-Shahid Omar al-Qassi**
Force du Martyr Omar al-Qassi

*Figure 71—DFLP units operating in the Gaza Strip.*

The Abed Rabbo faction supported the PLO leader's negotiations with the United States. In July 1999, the DFLP declared itself open to negotiations with a view to joining Yasser Arafat's movement and the peace process. It developed as a reformist movement within the PLO from 1990-91, forming the *Palestinian Democratic Union* (*Al-Ittihad al-Dimuqrati al-Filastini—FIDA*), which asserted itself in 1993.

The DFLP's armed forces are the *National Resistance Brigades* (NRB) (*Katā'ib al-Muqāwamah al-Waṭanīyah*), based in Gaza. In June 2003, the NRB called for the unity of Palestinian resistance forces and increased operations against Israel. Its operations mainly target Israeli military security forces.

## The Democratic Front for the Liberation of Palestine—General Command (PFLP-GC)

The PFLP-CG *(al-Jabhat al-Shaebiat li-Tahrir Filastin—al-Aiadat Aleama) is* a dissident faction of the PFLP, created and led by Ahmed Jibril in late 1968, close to Hafez al-Assad's Syria. During the 1970s-1980s, it had its headquarters on the outskirts of Damascus (Syria), and an operational command post in Deir Zenoun, Lebanon.

The PFLP-GC is on the list of entities declared terrorists by the United States under Executive Order 13224.[337]

**PFLP—General Command**

*Figure 72—The PFLP-GC logo. As with the logos of the Palestinian movements of the 1960s-1970s, there are no Islamic symbols. This is the logic of a national liberation movement. Israeli policy will only encourage the radicalization of these movements.*

As early as 1959, Ahmed Jibril founded the *Front for the Liberation of Palestine (FLP)*, which carried out its first attacks against Israel in 1965. In 1967, the FLP merged with George Habash's FPLP. But while Habash saw the struggle from a political angle, Jibril advocated purely military action. As a result of these tensions, the two movements split and the FPLP-CG was created in 1968. A member of the *Palestine Liberation Organization (PLO)*, the PFLP-CG systematically opposed the political direction given to the Palestinian struggle by Yasser Arafat, and gradually withdrew from the PLO Executive Committee and the *Palestine Central Council*. It nevertheless accepted the decision of the *Palestinian National*

---

337. https://www.state.gov/executive-order-13224/#state

*Council*—in which it continued to participate—in June 1974 to abandon international terrorism.

In 1983, Fatah was the target of an internal rebellion led by radical elements opposed to Yasser Arafat's political process. Syria supported Abu Musa, leader of *Fatah Provisional Command (Fatah-CR)*, and Jibril, who broke with the PLO. In 1985, Fatah-CR and PFLP-GC joined the *Palestinian National Salvation Front (PNSF)*.

From 1988 onwards, Arafat's efforts to contain the first Intifada and impose recognition of UN resolutions 242 and 338, consummated the split between Jibril and the PLO.

Until 1989, the PFLP-CG had links with Libya, where it maintained bases. After being expelled from Libya, the PFLP-CG moved to Syria and Lebanon in 1990.

***PFLP-GC Forces***

*Figure 73—Logo of the Brigades of the Martyr Jihad Jibril. It can be seen that the assassinations carried out by the Israelis led to the formation of new combat units.*

From the early 1990s, PFLP-GC activities declined. In 1991, it carried out an attack on American forces in Germany. Syria, which had lost the patronage of the Soviet Union with the fall of the Berlin Wall, tried to rehabilitate itself in the eyes of the Western community. It took part in the coalition against Iraq and tried to limit the activities of the PFLP-GC. The latter concentrated its activities against Palestinian movements aligned with Arafat's policies.

In 1999, Syria entered into negotiations with Israel to renounce the use of terrorism. But the outbreak of the *Al-Aqsa Intifada* and severe Israeli repression upset the talks, and Syria continued its discreet support for the PFLP-GC.

Since the Israeli withdrawal from southern Lebanon, the PFLP-GC has remained relatively inactive. By 2001, however, there was a resumption of cross-border activities against Israel. The most significant attack was undoubtedly the use of nine 107 mm missiles against Israeli electronic surveillance installations on Mount Hermon on April 4, 2002. This was followed on April 8 by further rocket attacks on the town of Kiryat Shmona.

On May 20, 2002, Ahmed Jibril's son, Mohammed Jihad Ahmed Jibril, was assassinated by a car bomb. Although the attack was claimed by a mysterious *"Lebanese Nationalist Movement,"* it is widely believed to have been an extra-judicial execution carried out by the Israeli Mossad. At his funeral, Ahmed Jibril stated that the PFLP-GC trained Hamas fighters in its camps in Lebanon.[338] Today, the PFLP-GC's armed faction in Gaza bears Ahmed Jibril's name.

## *Other Armed Movements and Groups*

Most of the "other" armed groups in Gaza are radical factions that have emerged from more "traditional" movements, such as Hamas, Fatah or the PIJ, formed by those disappointed by an approach that had failed to deliver a solution. They emerged in the early 2000s, simultaneously with the Western-led "war on terror," which revived a virulent Islamic nationalism.

Since 9/11, Western strategy in the Middle East has been driven more by revenge than by a rational strategy to eliminate terrorism. In fact, the West attacks terrorists, but not terrorism, with the result that terrorism has only grown and spread. The Palestinian resistance has been no exception. After the failure of various attempts at a political solution, political violence appears to some as a possible solution. Israeli—and therefore Western—policy has only contributed to radicalizing Palestinian resistance.

But Palestinian leaders of all persuasions are often more rational than the Israelis. They realize that violence alone cannot provide a solution. This is why Hamas attempted a political shift in 2005, but was prevented from doing so by Israel and the international community. It was at this

---

338. *An-Nahar*, May 25, 2002.

time that Salafist jihadist movements began to emerge, particularly in the Gaza Strip. As the *Jerusalem Post* explains:[339]

> *The complex relationship between Hamas and Jihadist-Salafist militant groups dates back to 2006, when Hamas took part in democratic elections. Many Jihadist-Salafist fighters were once part of Hamas. However, participation in the elections and Hamas' governance, which refuses to apply a Salafist interpretation of Sharia law, put Hamas at odds with Jihadist-Salafist ideology. This is why Jihadist-Salafist groups in Gaza often refer to the Hamas government as "apostate."*

As we can see, the statements heard on the French media, such as *CNews*, *BFMTV*, and members of certain political parties, such as Rassemblement National or Reconquête, aimed at equating Hamas with Salafist Jihadist movements, or even with the Islamic State, are pure lies as well as a desire to generate tension between the country's religious communities.

In reality, Hamas has always tried to avoid the radicalization of movements in the Gaza Strip. The problem is that, with the Israelis' repeated strikes, the acceleration of colonization in the occupied territories, the repeated failure of any attempt at negotiation and Israel's repeated violations of international law, the Palestinians tend to become radicalized.

In fact, you only need to read *Dabiq*, the official magazine of the Islamic State[340] to be convinced:

> *The various leaders and branches of Hamas have been proclaiming to wage jihad against the Jews for years. The reality is that this militia is a nationalist entity, actively embracing democracy as a vehicle for change since "2005." Hamas has engaged in municipal, presidential and legislative elections, taken part in law-making and the execution of man-made laws. This democratic ideology was propagated by its leadership even before "2005," since the time of Ahmed Yassin.*

---

339. Dov LIEBER, "Powerful militant group in Gaza allegedly pledges allegiance to ISIS," *The Jerusalem Post*, September 11, 2015 (https://www.jpost.com/Middle-East/ISIS-Threat/Powerful-militant-group-in-Gaza-allegedly-pledges-allegiance-to-ISIS-415869)
340. "From Jihad to Fasad," *Dabiq Magazine*, n°11, p.27.

Despite repeated accusations of collusion with "al-Qaeda," Hamas has systematically distanced itself from any jihadist tendencies that may have emerged in Palestine. This is true of *Jaish al-Islam, which was* brutally dismantled by Hamas security forces in September 2008, and of several radical groups that emerged in Gaza in the wake of the rise of jihadism in Syria and Egypt, also dismantled between 2013 and 2015. For example, on May 4, 2015, the Hamas headquarters was the target of a bomb attack by Salafist militants from the *Ansar Beit al-Maqdis* group aimed at securing the release of one of its leaders arrested by Hamas.[341] In the same month, the Islamic State's official magazine reported that its forces had attacked the *Aknaf Beit al-Maqdis* group, the local Hamas militia,[342] which protects Palestinians in the Yarmouk refugee camp near Damascus in Syria.[343]

Despite Hamas's efforts to suppress them, these groups remain, and have taken advantage of Operation AL-AQSA FLOOD to attack Israel as well. This explains why Israeli forces were able to seize jihadist flags[344] and accuse Hamas of being a jihadist movement.

### *Islamic State Flag*

*Figure 74—The presence of Salafist elements in the Gaza Strip has been known for a long time, but despite Hamas's attempts to eradicate them, it seems that they were able to interfere in the AL-AQSA FLOOD operation, as "stowaways."*

---

341. "Explosion targets Hamas security headquarters in Gaza," *24 Heures/ATS*, May 4, 2015.
342. This militia was created during the rebellion against the Syrian government.
343. "The Yarmūk Camp," *Dabiq Magazine*, No. 9, Shaban 1436 (May 2015).
344. https://jcpa.org/hamas-raises-the-isis-banner-in-its-invasion-of-israel/

Contrary to what our journalists claim, Hamas has nothing to do with Salafist-inspired movements. In fact, Israel's *Meir Amit Intelligence and Terrorism Information Center* notes that Hamas is actively fighting against Salafist movements.[345]

## Jaysh al-Ummah, Bayt al-Maqdis Faction

Jaysh al-Ummah is a Salafist-inspired jihadist group that emerged in 2008 in Khan Yunis (Gaza). It is close to the international jihadist movement known as al-Qaeda.

**Jaysh al-Ummah, Bayt al-Maqdis**

*Figure 75—Jaysh al-Ummah logo. Note that it uses a symbolism that differs fundamentally from that of the logos of other Palestinian movements.*

It is opposed to Hamas, which it considers too moderate, and criticizes it for failing to apply Sharia law in the Gaza Strip. It is responsible for firing rockets against Israel and took part in the fighting against Israeli forces during the Gaza wars of 2012 and 2014.

## The Army of Islam (Gaza)

Jaysh al-Islam is a Salafist-inspired jihadist group. It emerged around 2006 in Gaza following a split in Hamas. In addition to refusing to apply Sharia law, the group criticizes Hamas for oppressing Muslims and working for the *"interests of the Jews."*

---

345. https://www.terrorism-info.org.il/ar/20094/

Led by Mumtaz Dughmush, it is one of the oldest and most powerful jihadist-Salafist groups in the Gaza Strip. It became famous after kidnapping BBC reporter Alan Johnston in Gaza on March 12, 2007. The journalist was freed less than four months later, thanks to a Hamas intervention.[346] The group was brutally dismantled by Hamas security forces in September 2008, but re-formed during the conflict in Syria, with the support of Western countries against the government of Bashar al-Assad.

### Jaysh al-Islam (Gaza)

*Figure 76—Jaysh al-Islam logo. Like other Salafist groups, its symbolism uses none of the markers of Palestinian resistance.*

Initially close to the jihadist movement commonly known as "al-Qaeda," the group took part in the fighting against the Alawite government in Syria, before further radicalizing its position. In September 2015, the *Jerusalem Post* reported that the group had officially pledged allegiance to the Islamic State.[347]

The US State Department placed *Jaysh al-Islam* on its list of terrorist organizations in May 2011, followed by its leader in August 2011.[348] But, rather symptomatically, in May 2016, the United States, Great Britain and France rejected a Russian proposal to place the group on the United

---

346. Conal URQUHART, "BBC reporter Alan Johnston freed in Gaza," *The Guardian*, July 4, 2007 (https://www.theguardian.com/media/2007/jul/04/middleeastthemedia.israel2)
347. Dov LIEBER, "Powerful militant group in Gaza allegedly pledges allegiance to ISIS," *The Jerusalem Post*, September 11, 2015 (https://www.jpost.com/Middle-East/ISIS-Threat/Powerful-militant-group-in-Gaza-allegedly-pledges-allegiance-to-ISIS-415869)
348. https://www.dni.gov/nctc/ftos/army_of_islam_fto.html

Nations list of terrorist organizations.[349] At the time, these three countries were instrumentalizing the Islamic State in an attempt to overthrow the Syrian government.

### The Army of the Partisans of Allah

*Jund Ansar* Allah is a Salafist jihadist group close to the al-Qaeda movement that emerged in Gaza in June 2009 with an attack on the Karni checkpoint.

**Jund Ansar Allah (Gaza)**

*Figure 77—Jund Ansar Allah logo. In the background is a world map, not a map of Palestine. The ideological context is therefore very different from that asserted by the Israeli government and its relays in the West, who seek to equate Hamas with a Salafist movement.*

In August, the proclamation of an "Islamic State of Palestine" by Latif Moussa, the group's leader, from the Rafah mosque, triggered a sharp response from Hamas, which left 22 people dead, including the group's leader himself.

---

349. "U.S., Britain, France block Russia bid to blacklist Syria rebels," *Reuters*, May 11, 2016 (https://www.reuters.com/article/us-mideast-crisis-syria-sanctions-idUSKCN0Y22F8/)

**Flag of the Islamic State of Palestine**

*Figure 78—Banner of the Islamic State of Palestine—Gaza Governorate, proclaimed in 2009 by Jund Ansar Allah. It features the same components as the banners of the Arabian Peninsula Jihad Base (APJB).*
*[https://ctc.westpoint.edu/militant-imagery-project/0329/]*

### The Oneness and Jihad Legions

The *The Leigions of Oneness and Jihad in Palestine (Jahafil Al-Tawhid Wal-Jihad fi Filastin)* are said to have emerged in Gaza in 2008. They carried out their first action against Israeli forces on November 5 of the same year.[350]

The Legions grew out of the *Tawhid wal-Jihad (Oneness and Jihad)* movement, which was the main Salafi-inspired jihadist movement in the Sinai Peninsula. It was founded in 1997 by Khaled Masaad and Nasser Khamees El-Malakhi, and appears to have emerged in the Gaza Strip in 2007.[351]

Like the other Salafist groups in the Gaza Strip, these are small groups with no real influence on the operations of the more traditional Palestinian groups. The aim of these groups is to create an Islamic entity where Sharia law would be applied in all its rigor.

---

350. Jonathan FIGHEL, "Tawhid and Jihad Legions in Palestine: A New Global Jihad Oriented Organization in Gaza," *International Institute for Counter-Terrorism* (ICT), December 22, 2008 (https://ict.org.il/tawhid-and-jihad-legions-in-palestine-a-new-global-jihad-oriented-organization-in-gaza/)
351. https://timep.org/2014/07/22/tawhid-wal-jihad/

### Tawhid wal-Jihad

*Figure 79—Tawhid wal-Jihad logo—Beit al-Maqdis Faction.*

## Joint Conduct of Palestinian Resistance Factions

In May 2006, Hamas and the Palestinian Islamic Jihad signed a National Agreement Document aimed at *"forming a unified front to resist the occupation, coordinate its actions and provide a common political reference."* Initially, this coordination concerned only the Izz al-Deen Al-Qassam Brigades and the Al-Quds Martyrs Brigades. The main aim was to coordinate their actions and, above all, to try to curb rocket fire and integrate them into a political approach.

But in 2018, with the "Marches of Return" and their severe repression by Israel, a dozen resistance groups and movements in the Gaza Strip decided to create a "Joint Operations Room" (JOR).

The function of this JOR is to pool operational planning resources, benefit from synergies between groups and create doctrinal coherence in operations. The underlying idea is that these currently disparate groups could form the embryo of a Palestinian national army in the future. It also harmonizes communication between the different groups and issues joint communiqués.

Hamas is naturally the dominant force in this association. However, it provides technical and military assistance to groups with fewer resources.[352]

---

352. https://www.aljazeera.net/politics/2021/5/28/غرفة-العمليات-المشتركة-للمقاومة-في

# Gaza Joint Operations Room

| | | |
|---|---|---|
| Kataeb al-Shahid Izz al-Din al-Qassam | Sarayat al-Quds | Kataeb al-Shahid Abou Ali Moustafa |
| Kataeb al-Shahid Nidal Al-Amoudi | Kataeb al-Shahid Aymen Joudah | Martyr Abdul Qader Brigades Al-Husseini |
| Brigades de Résistance Nationale Palestinienne | Kataeb al-Shahid Jihad Jibril | Kataeb al-Ansar |
| Kataeb al-Moudjahidin | Kataeb Al-Nasser Salah al-Deen | Kataeb Shuhada al-Aqsa Jaïsh al-Asifa |

*Figure 80—Since 2006, the Palestinian resistance has formed a coordinating body in Gaza. Twelve factions are directly involved. Hamas forces are among them, alongside Fatah formations and other historic Palestinian resistance movements.*

# 5. Operation AL-AQSA

## The Beginnings

Operation AL-AQSA FLOOD did not come out of the clear blue sky. Since 2021, tensions between Palestinians and Israelis had been on the rise, but our media have remained silent on the actions of the Israeli far right against Arab populations. Yet, since Benjamin Netanyahu's return to power, incidents have multiplied: expulsions in the West Bank, incursions by ultra-Orthodox militants on the Mosque Esplanade, tougher detention conditions for Palestinians in Israeli prisons, and the withdrawal of funding from the Palestinian administration.

Numerous tensions had built up since the end of 2022 and throughout 2023, punctuated by violence and violations of international law against which the international community—focused on the Ukrainian conflict—failed to react. The main causes of the outbreak of violence in October 2023 are:

- Social tensions in Gaza.
- The violent expansion of settlements in the West Bank.
- The extension of imprisonment and the tightening of detention conditions.
- Repeated violations of the Haram al-Sharif by the Orthodox Jewish community.
- The Gaza blockade and its humanitarian consequences.
- The normalization of relations between Israel and certain Arab states, promoted by the United States, which ignores the Palestinian cause.

These events took place against a backdrop of decades-long discontent, such as restrictions on economic activity. It is also important to understand that the revolt in Gaza is also linked to the situation in the West Bank.

### *Expansion of Israeli Settlements in the West Bank*

Israel's settlement policy has obviously intensified in the West Bank. The Basic Law "Israel, Nation-State of the Jewish People," adopted on July 19, 2018 by the Knesset, defines settlements in the occupied territories as a "national *value.*"[353] The problem is that they are contrary to international law, of which they violate two main rules:
- The principle of "*the inadmissibility of the acquisition of territory by war,*" recalled by Security Council Resolution 242.
- Non-compliance with the Geneva Convention relative to the Protection of Civilian Persons in Time of War, dated August 12, 1949.

The situation deteriorated dramatically in 2023 under Benjamin Netanyahu's government.

Not only did expulsions of Palestinians from their land multiply, but they became increasingly violent, while repression against those who did not express their satisfaction at being expelled hardened.[354]

In June, Israeli settler attacks on Palestinians escalated into deadly clashes.[355] Even the very pro-Israeli *Anti-Defamation League* (ADL) took offence at the aggressiveness and violence of the settlers and called on the Israeli authorities to do more to protect the lives and property of Palestinians.[356] In France, Switzerland and Belgium, none of the extreme right-wing media reported these crimes.

---

353. https://www.timesofisrael.com/final-text-of-jewish-nation-state-bill-set-to-become-law/
354. https://twitter.com/ExtSpoxEU/status/1719437318874927513
355. Yaniv Kubovich, Hagar Shezaf & Ido Efrati, "Four Israelis Killed, Four Wounded in West Bank Shooting Attack," *Haaretz*, June 20, 2023 (https://www.haaretz.com/israel-news/2023-06-20/ty-article/at-least-1-israeli-wounded-in-suspected-west-bank-shooting/00000188-d8fb-d5fc-ab9d-dbfb7e9e0000)
356. Hagar Shezaf, Jack Khoury, Ben Samuels & Amir Tibon, "Palestinian Shot Dead as Dozens of Jewish Settlers Torch Homes, Vehicles in West Bank," *Haaretz*, June 21, 2023 (https://www.haaretz.com/israel-news/2023-06-21/ty-article/.premium/dozens-of-jewish-settlers-set-fire-to-palestinian-homes-vehicles-in-west-bank-town/00000188-ddba-df52-a79d-ddbbf2310000)

***Even the ADL Speaks Out against the Treatment of Palestinians***

> **ADL** ✡
> @ADL
>
> We strongly condemn the violent rampage by extremist Israeli settlers targeting Palestinian villages in the West Bank. There's no excuse for violence. Israeli security forces must go after all those involved and do more to protect Palestinian individuals and property.
>
> 4:42 PM · Jun 21, 2023 · **18.7K** Views
>
> 33 Reposts  13 Quotes  163 Likes  6 Bookmarks

*Figure 81—Even the very pro-Israeli Anti-Defamation League criticizes the use of violence in the occupied territories. It is quite significant that European media, which claim to respect our values, blindly support the extreme right-wing policies of the Israeli government, which are contested by its own population. [Source: https://twitter.com/ADL/status/1671529084696903681]*

On September 6, 2023, at a time when settlement building had been declared illegal under the Geneva Conventions, Bezalel Smotrich, Israel's Finance Minister, decided to legalize the three new settlements, "Avigail" and "Asael" in the southern West Bank and "Beit Hogla" in the Jordan Valley region.

This situation was obviously exacerbated by the AL-AQSA FLOOD operation. As noted by the Israeli media +972, the events of October 2023 only stimulated the violence of Jewish ultra-nationalists in the West Bank.[357] Not only have expulsions multiplied, but violence and pogroms against Palestinians themselves have multiplied, accompanied by massacres, including children. At the end of October 2023, for example, in a single week, armed settlers (i.e., civilians) killed 51 Palestinians, including children.[358] Even the European Union (which "unconditionally" supports Israel) seemed alarmed by this increase in violence—but does nothing.[359]

---

357. Oren Ziv, "Palestinians recount settler, army torture amid surge in West Bank expulsions," +972 *Magazine*, October 30, 2023 (https://www.972mag.com/wadi-siq-settler-army-torture-expulsion-palestinians/)
358. Yuval Abraham, "Settlers take advantage of Gaza war to launch West Bank pogroms," +972 *Magazine*, October 13, 2023 (https://www.972mag.com/settler-attacks-west-bank-gaza-war/)
359. https://www.eeas.europa.eu/eeas/israelpalestine-statement-spokesperson-latest-developments-west-bank_en

## Social Tensions in Gaza

In May 2023, the *World Food Programme* (WFP) warned that the Gaza Strip was heading for a humanitarian crisis, as food supplies were no longer being financed. The Israeli newspaper *Haaretz* even declared that foreign diplomats in Israel were aware of the situation and of the possible drift from a humanitarian crisis to a security crisis. The lack of funding is because of the fact that European countries are redirecting planned aid to Palestine to Ukraine, as they can no longer sustain the financial effort promised to Zelensky. The lack of prospects in this conflict discourages Western countries, which prefer to finance the illusion of success in Ukraine. As the newspaper reports, diplomats explain:[360]

> *In Israel, there's a government that doesn't want to do anything about the Palestinian question, but as soon as there's a humanitarian crisis, it sends emissaries to ask us to increase our financial support.*

This brings us back to the incredible incompetence of Israelis at all levels to understand the nature of their problem and to find lasting solutions. In fact, *"the Israeli strategy is to maintain the status quo and sporadically repeat the same cycles of violence."*[361]

Added to this already tense situation is a social crisis. In September 2023, Qatar paid only 55% of the amount it was supposed to, leaving 50,000 Hamas employees without pay, generating social unrest and demonstrations in Gaza.[362] At the same time, Egyptian and Qatari mediators asked Israel to grant more permits for Gaza workers, in order to ease tension at the border.[363]

---

360. Amir Tibon, "Low on Cash, UN Warns of Looming Humanitarian Disaster in Gaza. Israel Aware of Crisis 'For Weeks'," *Haaretz*, May 31, 2023 (https://www.haaretz.com/israel-news/2023-05-31/ty-article/.premium/low-on-cash-un-warns-of-humanitarian-crisis-in-gaza-israel-aware-of-crisis-for-weeks/00000188-71e6-d2d1-afbe-7defd48a0000)
361. Jack Khoury, "Five Days and 35 Dead Later, Back to the Hopeless Status Quo in Gaza," *Haaretz*, May 14, 2023 (https://www.haaretz.com/israel-news/2023-05-14/ty-article/.highlight/back-to-the-hopeless-status-quo-in-gaza/00000188-16a7-d8d1-aff8-bef7e2f20000)
362. Jack Khoury, "Hamas Wary of Gaza Conflict With Israel, but Humanitarian Crisis May Lead to Flare-up," *Haaretz*, September 20, 2023 (https://www.haaretz.com/middle-east-news/palestinians/2023-09-20/ty-article/.premium/hamas-seeks-to-prevent-escalation-on-gaza-border-by-quelling-protests/0000018a-b205-d818-afce-fa77e0dd0000)
363. Amos Harel, "Israel Hoped a Better Gaza Economy Would Quell Violence. Hamas Has Other Plans," *Haaretz*, September 28, 2023 (https://www.haaretz.com/israel-news/2023-09-28/ty-article/.premium/economic-improvement-in-gaza-fails-to-stop-violent-resistance-against-israel/0000018a-d825-d476-abcf-fae734330000)

## Tougher Detention Conditions

In parallel with the tightening of the occupation policy, detention conditions have been tightened. This is one of the most important reasons behind Operation AL-AQSA FLOOD. After the breakdown of negotiations concerning prisoners between Hamas and the Israeli authorities, with the mediation of Qatar and Egypt, the Palestinians realized that the only way to free them was to capture the occupying soldiers and then carry out an exchange. This was one of the main objectives of Operation AL-AQSA FLOOD.

Significantly, the prisoners released by the Israelis on the occasion of the exchanges agreed in November 2023 were released naked. Their treatment in Israeli jails[364] has been the subject of protests by human rights organizations for years.

## Desecration of the Haram al-Sharif (Esplanade of the Mosques)

With the advent of Benjamin Netanyahu's new government, ultra-Orthodox provocations have multiplied. The project to build Solomon's Third Temple on the Temple Mount has gained new momentum, provoking multiple incursions of hundreds, even thousands, of demonstrators onto the Mosque Esplanade.

The crux of the matter is the construction of Solomon's Third Temple in place of the Al-Aqsa Mosque:[365]

> *According to Jewish law, the ashes of a red heifer (young female cow)... must be scattered on the Haram al-Sharif (mosque esplanade) before the Jews can ascend it and build the Third Temple. While the red cow hunt has long been considered a fringe initiative touted by Temple Mount activists, new research shows that the Israeli government is now involved in the project.*
>
> *Despite the Israeli government's promise to maintain the status quo at Al-Aqsa, the settlers involved in the red heifer project stress that the objective is the Jewish ascent on the Haram al-Sharif in order to*

---

364. Dominic WAGHORN, "Israel-Hamas war: 'We were treated like dogs'—released Palestinian prisoners complain of mistreatment," *SKY News*, November 27, 2023 (https://news.sky.com/story/israel-hamas-war-we-were-treated-like-dogs-released-palestinian-prisoners-complain-of-mistreatment-13017228)

365. https://profidecatholica.com/2023/09/10/les-trumpistes-derriere-le-mystere-de-la-genisse-rousse-incineree-qui-conduira-a-lantechrist/

*build the Third Temple—which implies the destruction of the Dome of the Rock.*

This project involves the destruction of the Al-Aqsa Mosque, and the denaturing of the Haram al-Sharif, Islam's third holiest site, which Palestinians see as a mark of their identity, and of which Hamas feels itself to be the protector, as stated in its 2017 charter (appended).[366] In September 2023, around 4,500 settlers stormed the Al-Aqsa mosque.[367] The scale of these clashes aimed at changing the religious purpose of Islam's third holiest site could not fail to have consequences.

Indeed, Palestinian Islamic organizations had warned as early as May 2022 that this project, led by Bezalel Smotrich, the far-right Finance Minister, threatened many "red lines."[368] In September-October 2023, informed observers (from whom our journalists can be removed) warned that these riots could lead to greater violence.[369]

Thus we knew that the situation was explosive, and that the Palestinians would seize the opportunity of the ultra-nationalist incursions into the Haram al-Sharif to demonstrate.[370] Apparently, in early October, the Israeli government became concerned about the possible impact of incidents linked to the social situation of Palestinians in Gaza on the agreement with Saudi Arabia.[371] Moreover, it is likely that the situation of the Haram al-Sharif was also of concern to other Arab countries, first and foremost Saudi Arabia, custodian of Islam's first two holy sites. It is likely that even without the Hamas operation, these countries would not have ratified the Abraham Accords.

---

366. "The Israelis set for new Jewish temple on Al-Aqsa site," *France 24*, June 5, 2023 (https://www.france24.com/en/live-news/20230605-the-israelis-set-for-new-jewish-temple-on-al-aqsa-site)

367. https://alkhanadeq.org.lb/post/6261/اهلام-حرب-طوفان-الأقصى-كنتست-قروض-من-تنظيم

368. Crispian Balmer & Nidal Al-Mughrabi, "Hamas says Israel must rethink flag march or face violence," *Reuters*, May 26, 2022 (https://www.reuters.com/world/middle-east/hamas-says-israel-must-rethink-flag-march-or-face-violence-2022-05-26/)

369. Jack Khoury, "Egyptian Mediators: Continued Jewish Ascent to Temple Mount Will Lead to Escalation," *Haaretz*, October 3, 2023 (https://archive.ph/MElOz)

370. Jack Khoury & Nir Hasson, "Palestinians Say Will Freeze Gaza Border Protests After Vowing to Resume Them Over Jews at Temple Mount," *Haaretz*, October 1, 2023 (https://www.haaretz.com/israel-news/2023-10-01/ty-article/.premium/palestinians-announce-resumption-of-gaza-border-protests/0000018a-eae3-dfa2-a99e-eaebcedc0000)

371. Amir Tibon, Jonathan Lis & Yaniv Kubovich, "Amid Border Escalation, Netanyahu Gov't Weighs Aid to Calm Gaza for Sake of Israeli-Saudi Deal," *Haaretz*, October 2, 2023 (https://archive.ph/ZoTyM#selection-445.0-600.0)

In 2023, Israel mainly attacked the PIJ, which is probably Iran's main ally in Gaza, both to divide the Palestinians among themselves and to provoke Iran. Hamas refrained from entering this bilateral struggle between the PIJ and Israel, so as not to jeopardize its funding, which was largely dependent on Israel, and not to incite Israel to withdraw the work permits and licenses it had granted for the reconstruction of Gaza.

*The Old City of Jerusalem*

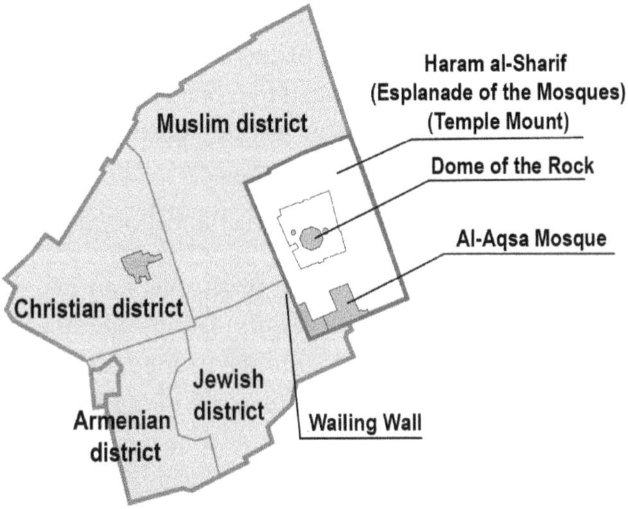

*Figure 82—The configuration of the sites in Jerusalem makes the problem of assigning sovereignty to one or other of the communities inextricable. This is why Resolution 181 (1947) provided for it to be placed under international jurisdiction, corresponding to its status as part of the World Heritage of Mankind and as the meeting point of the world's three great monotheistic religions. Donald Trump's decision to recognize the Holy City as the capital of the State of Israel clearly aggravated an already tense situation.*

Our journalists' profound disdain for the Arab population in general, and for the situation of the Palestinians in particular, led to acceptance of the human rights violations against them. Thus, our media did not report these violations, but they were well perceived in Israel. The *Haaretz* newspaper was already suggesting a week before the Palestinian operation that events in Jerusalem and the West Bank, as well as the stricter conditions imposed on Palestinian security prisoners in Israel, could have a direct impact on events along the Gaza border.

## Objectives of the Operation

As we have seen, there are countless reasons for Gazans to revolt. The question is: "Why now?"

At first glance, the objectives of Operation AL-AQSA FLOOD are unclear. The Israeli narrative, faithfully reproduced by the Western media, tends to obscure the Palestinians' motives. We find ourselves in much the same situation as at the start of the Russian offensive in Ukraine, where analysis of the facts was totally overwhelmed by a narrative fabricated in the West. This has led to a misunderstanding of the real reasons for the Russian intervention, and ultimately, this narrative became a trap for Ukraine. The same phenomenon can be seen in the Palestinian operation: not only is Israel failing to achieve its objectives, it is also confronted with the contradictions of its narrative *vis-à-vis* its own population and the international community.

In fact, the situation in the occupied territories had been explosive for many months. On October 3, 2023, the Israeli newspaper *Haaretz* expressed concern at the growing number of incursions by ultra-Orthodox militants and settlers on the Esplanade of the Mosques (Haram al-Sharif). It reported that the Egyptian authorities were alarmed by the consequences on the Gaza border.[372] It was therefore a combination of problems and accumulated tensions that created the conditions for the launch of Operation AL-AQSA FLOOD. The breakdown of negotiations on prisoner exchanges at the end of 2021 certainly triggered the decision to carry out a large-scale operation to force Israel back to the negotiating table.

Initially, only the statements made by the operation's two main protagonists, Hamas and the PIJ, make it possible to identify the objectives of the operation.

On January 22, 2024, Hamas published a 16-page booklet entitled "*Our narrative—Operation AL-AQSA FLOOD,*"[373] explaining its action and objectives. The late arrival of this document can no doubt be explained

---

372. Jack Khoury, "Egyptian Mediators: Continued Jewish Ascent to Temple Mount Will Lead to Escalation," *Haaretz*, October 3, 2023 (https://www.haaretz.com/israel-news/2023-10-03/ty-article/.premium/egyptian-mediators-continued-jewish-ascent-to-temple-mount-will-lead-to-escalation/0000018a-f474-d12f-afbf-f5751d620000)

373. https://www.lbcgroup.tv/uploadImages/ExtImages/Images2/Our Narrative-Operation Al-Aqsa Flood-Web_compressed (1).pdf

by Israeli and Western accusations of crimes and atrocities committed by Hamas fighters on October 7, 2023. It seems that Hamas leaders wanted to have a clear idea of what really happened before expressing a position. Indeed, the document makes numerous references to the Israeli press, suggesting that Hamas sought to understand before reacting.

While this delay has allowed the Israeli and Western narrative to take hold, it has also enabled events to be presented from a more coherent angle. What Hamas has lost in presence in our media, it has gained in credibility in the hearts of the public. The Hamas version is consistent with the observations, analyses and findings of researchers and analysts, particularly in the United States, and with the testimonies that have appeared in the Israeli press. When it comes to information warfare, Israel probably has small tactical victories, but Hamas has definitely won strategically.

***Hamas Publication***

Figure 83—Absent from our media, and arriving very late, Hamas's explanation of its operation confirms the analyses of many serious commentators in the West.

Operation AL-AQSA FLOOD seems a bit like the explosion of a pressure cooker. It was probably the accumulation of problems, broken promises and day-to-day abuses (with the complacency of Western countries and despite the recommendations of the United Nations), which led to this explosion of violence. The corollary of this observation is that the Gazans seemed to have focused a whole series of objectives on this operation.

### Strategic Objectives

Over and above the historical objectives of Palestinian resistance, which are aimed at creating a Palestinian state or returning to the land taken from them, the objectives of Operation AL-AQSA FLOOD essentially concerned the situation in Gaza.

***Palestinian Victims of the "Marches of Return" in Gaza (2018-2019)***

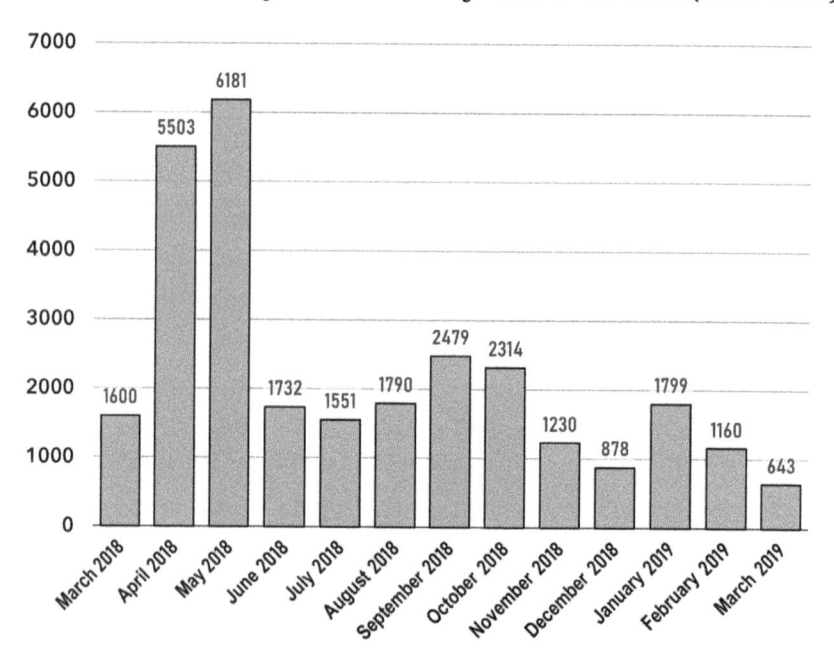

| Month | Victims |
|---|---|
| March 2018 | 1600 |
| April 2018 | 5503 |
| May 2018 | 6181 |
| June 2018 | 1732 |
| July 2018 | 1551 |
| August 2018 | 1790 |
| September 2018 | 2479 |
| October 2018 | 2314 |
| November 2018 | 1230 |
| December 2018 | 878 |
| January 2019 | 1799 |
| February 2019 | 1160 |
| March 2019 | 643 |

Figure 84—The Marches of Return were intended to draw the world's attention to the living conditions of Palestinians in Gaza. The number of civilian casualties (dead and wounded) shot from outside the fence showed that it was not possible to achieve a result by peaceful means. [Source: https://www.theguardian.com/world/ng-interactive/2019/mar/29/a-year-of-bloodshed-at-gaza-border-protests]

The operation's central strategic objective was to end the blockade of the Gaza Strip and restore normal living conditions for the population. This includes the end of permanent surveillance by Israeli forces, restrictions on trade in goods, and measures that prevent economic and social development. This objective followed on from the "Marches of Return," which were led by civil society, but were met with sniper fire.

Achieving this goal involved *enabling* objectives, the most important of which was to bring the Palestinian question back onto the international stage. In November 2012, the United Nations General Assembly granted Palestine the status of "non-member observer state of the United Nations."[374] Since then, however, no progress has been made in dealing with the Palestinian question, and the situation has even deteriorated with the arrival of Israel's ultra-nationalists in power.

The second intermediate objective was to interrupt the normalization process between Israel and certain Arab countries. Not because of normalization itself, but because it sidelined the Palestinian question. The Palestinians had always wanted these issues to be linked, so that there would be leverage to force Israel to implement UN decisions.

The third intermediate objective was to rally the Muslim community around the issue of the future of the Esplanade of the Mosques (or Temple Mount), which is closely linked to the Palestinian question.[375] As Ihsan Ataya, a member of the political bureau of the *Palestinian Islamic Jihad* (PIJ) and head of the PIJ's Arab and International Relations Department[376] states:

> *The aim of Operation AL-AQSA FLOOD has been stated from the outset: to prevent the Al-Aqsa Mosque (in Jerusalem) from being attacked, Muslim religious rites from being insulted or defamed, our women from being assaulted, efforts to Judaize the Al-Aqsa Mosque and normalize its occupation by Israel from being implemented, or the mosque from being divided in time and space.*

---

374. https://press.un.org/en/2012/ga11317.doc.htm
375. https://english.almayadeen.net/news/politics/hamas-head-announces-operation-al-aqsa-flood-responding-to-i
376. Ali Bou JBARA, "Palestinian Islamic Jihad: 'Al-Aqsa Flood was a preemptive strike against the enemy," *The Cradle*, October 30, 2023 (https://new.thecradle.co/articles/palestinian-islamic-jihad-al-aqsa-flood-was-a-preemptive-strike-against-the-enemy)

It has to be said that, while the blockade of Gaza has not been lifted, these three intermediate strategic objectives have been at least partially achieved. To what extent they will lead to a lasting and just solution to the Palestinian question is an open question, but Hamas has clearly underlined the responsibility of the international community to enforce the decisions it has taken.

## *Operational Objectives*

### *First Objective: The Gaza Division*

The first objective was to destroy the elements of the Gaza Division and the surveillance installations encircling the Gaza Strip. On October 12, Abu Obeida, spokesman for the Al-Qassam Brigades, explained:

> *Operation AL-AQSA FLOOD was aimed at destroying the Gaza Division, which was attacked at 15 points, followed by 10 more. We attacked the Zikim site and several other settlements outside the Gaza Division headquarters.*

This objective may seem outdated to us, since it was clear from the outset that the Palestinian operation could not maintain its momentum for very long, and that the fighting would necessarily continue in the Gaza Strip itself. Consequently, the destruction of infrastructure could only be temporary, but highly symbolic.

To understand this, one has to put oneself in the Palestinians' mindset. Victory is not achieved by destroying the adversary, but by maintaining the determination to resist. In other words, whatever the Israelis do, however much destruction and death they cause, the Palestinians have already emerged victorious from this operation. Faced with a numerically and materially stronger adversary, victory in the Western sense of the term is not possible. On the other hand, overcoming fear and feelings of powerlessness is already a victory. This is the very essence of the notion of jihad.

Consequently, all the humiliations the Israelis can inflict on their prisoners or the civilian population can only make the Palestinians feel better, and lower the military's thirst for vengeance. In fact, this is what is happening around the world—the Israelis are obliged to use their censorship to hide the crimes committed by their soldiers, and the idea of "*the most moral army in the world*" is now totally discredited.

## Second Objective: Take Prisoners

The second objective was to seize prisoners in order to exchange them for those held by Israel. Very quickly, testimonies in the Israeli press showed that the aim of the Hamas and Palestinian Islamic Jihad (PIJ) fighters was not to carry out a "pogrom," but to seize soldiers in order to exchange them for Palestinians held by Israel. The aim was to gain leverage to resume the negotiations interrupted by the Israeli government in November 2021. Since then, it has been known that Hamas would carry out such an operation.[377] The deputy chief of staff of the Al-Qassam Brigades, Marwan Issa, had declared that "*the prisoners' file will be the surprise of the enemy's next surprises.*"[378]

Clearly, the aim was not to kill civilians, but rather to obtain a bargaining chip for the release of some 5,300 prisoners held by Israel.[379] Eyewitness accounts in the Israeli press suggest that the original idea was to take only military prisoners (who are "more valuable" than civilians for an exchange). These same accounts show that the Palestinians were surprised to find so few military personnel on site, which can be explained by the fact that part of the garrisons had been redeployed to the West Bank a few weeks earlier. Yasmin Porat's testimony, mentioned above, shows that Hamas fighters stayed with civilians in their homes, waiting for the security forces to intervene. The testimonies indicate that the Palestinian fighters left with civilian prisoners only after the Israeli military had intervened, firing indiscriminately into the houses with their tanks. It therefore appears that the capture of civilians was more the result of a combination of circumstances than a decision taken in advance.

The death of civilians was therefore not an objective, and the fact that the freed hostages declared that they had been treated with respect, and

---

377. Abdelrahman NASSAR, "Resistance threatens to take more Israeli captives if prisoner swap stalls," *The Cradle*, November 15, 2021 (https://new.thecradle.co/articles/resistance-threatens-to-take-more-israeli-captives-if-prisoner-swap-stalls)
378. https://alkhanadeq.com/post.php?id=1659
379. Robert INLAKESH & Sharmine NARWANI, "What really happened on 7th October?," *The Cradle*, October 24, 2023 (https://new.thecradle.co/articles/what-really-happened-on-7th-october)

even in a friendly manner, tends to confirm that this was not a "pogrom" against the Israeli population.

The prisoner exchanges of November 2023 illustrate Hamas's strategy, at the heart of which were military prisoners, not civilians. That is why the Palestinians released the women and children first, and kept the military (especially the top brass) for later. We will come back to this later.

## *Tactical Objectives*

The Hamas attack targeted 25 military objectives located in the "Gaza envelope." The three main tactical objectives of the operation were:
- the Zikim naval base in the north of the Gaza Strip, which was attacked by Hamas marine commandos, who resisted Israeli counter-attacks for several days;
- the Erez checkpoint, in the north of the Gaza Strip, which manages part of the fence's surveillance facilities;
- the Gaza Division command post at the Re'im site, where the heaviest fighting will take place on October 7; and
- the Urim intelligence center some 17 km from the Gaza Strip, in order to damage Israeli surveillance installations.

A document discovered near Kibbutz Mefalsim, 2 km from the Gaza Strip, containing data on the number of soldiers and security forces, shows that the operation was meticulously prepared and directed against military installations.

## The Course of the Operation

Operation AL-AQSA FLOOD (literally: *Battle of the Al-Aqsa Flood*) was a joint operation by the various Palestinian groups that make up the *Jerusalem Axis*, also known as the *"Axis of Resistance."* They were coordinated by the *Joint Operations Room (JOR)* in Gaza. *Hamas* was the largest group, followed by the *Palestinian Islamic Jihad* (PIJ), the *Popular Resistance Committees* (PRC) and the *Popular Front for the Liberation of Palestine* (PFLP).

Its preparations seem to have taken just under two years. Apparently, as early as May 2022, the Israelis detected them,[380] but were unable to

---

380. https://www.israeldefense.co.il/node/54653

interpret them and understand exactly the nature and extent of what they indicated. The fact that the operation took place almost 50 years after the start of the Yom Kippur War (October 6, 1973) is probably no more than a coincidence. What is no coincidence, however, is that it was launched on a Saturday morning. Anyone who has been involved in warning intelligence knows that the best times for military offensives are holidays (Christmas, Easter, New Year, etc.) and public holidays (Sabbath, Sundays, etc.).

The operation was launched on Saturday, October 7, 2023 at 6:26 a.m., with several hundred rockets fired at targets in the Gaza envelope. Around 5,000 rockets were fired that day.

Under the leadership of Hamas, between 1,000 and 1,500 Palestinian fighters crossed the perimeter fence at six points[381] and went on the attack in a vast joint operation. Twenty-five military targets in the "Gaza envelope" were attacked by land, sea and air. Documents found on the attackers show that Hamas had very detailed knowledge of each target and the forces responsible for protecting them. So much so that some have speculated that sources deep inside the Israeli army may have provided information.[382]

The overall plan was quite simple.

In the first phase, the aim was to simultaneously attack the outposts and bases of the Gaza Division and the police in order to destroy them or render them inoperative, blocking communications channels to slow the arrival of reinforcements, after disabling surveillance cameras and other defense systems.

In a second phase, the commandos were to seize military prisoners and bring them back to the Gaza Strip, to be exchanged later.

In the third phase, the aim was to lure Israeli forces into the Gaza Strip so as to fight them on favorable ground and inflict maximum damage. By exploiting an immense network of "attack tunnels," designed to move within the territory, the Palestinians were able to multiply their attacks and ambushes against the Israelis.

---

381. Victoria BEAULE, "A detailed look at how Hamas secretly crossed into Israel," *ABC News*, October 12, 2023 (https://abcnews.go.com/International/detailed-hamas-secretly-crossed-israel/story?id=103917182)

382. Patrick KINGSLEY & Ronen BERGMAN, "The Secrets Hamas Knew About Israel's Military," *The New York Times*, October 13, 2023 (https://www.nytimes.com/2023/10/13/world/middleeast/hamas-israel-attack-gaza.html)

## Misinterpreted Clues

On January 12, 2024, Ronen Bergman and Yoav Zitun, two journalists from the Israeli media *YNet*, who have excellent contacts in military and intelligence circles, recounted the events of October 7. Without complacency, they showed us the dysfunctions of the Israeli forces, somewhat lost in the face of a situation they had not really foreseen.[383]

Apparently, during the night of October 6-7, 2023, signals were picked up indicating that something was afoot in Gaza. But neither SHABAK nor the IDF were able to interpret these signals and place them in a pattern. In fact, it was more the quantity of the signals than their nature that worried Israeli officials and prompted them to hold several conference calls during the night.

At first, Israeli officials thought that a small commando had made an incursion with an as yet unidentified goal. The SHABAK director ordered the deployment of a TEQUILA intervention team made up of SHABAKL and IDF commandos.

*Logo of the AL-AQSA FLOOD Operation (معركة طوفان الأقصى) (TUFAN AL-AQSA).*

*Figure 85—Logo for Operation AL-AQSA FLOOD, which appeared the day after the start of the operation. It uses the same graphic elements as the logo of the Izz al-Dine al-Qassam Brigades.*

---

383. https://w.ynet.co.il/yediot/7-days/time-of-darkness?externalurl=true

## Operation AL-AQSA FLOOD

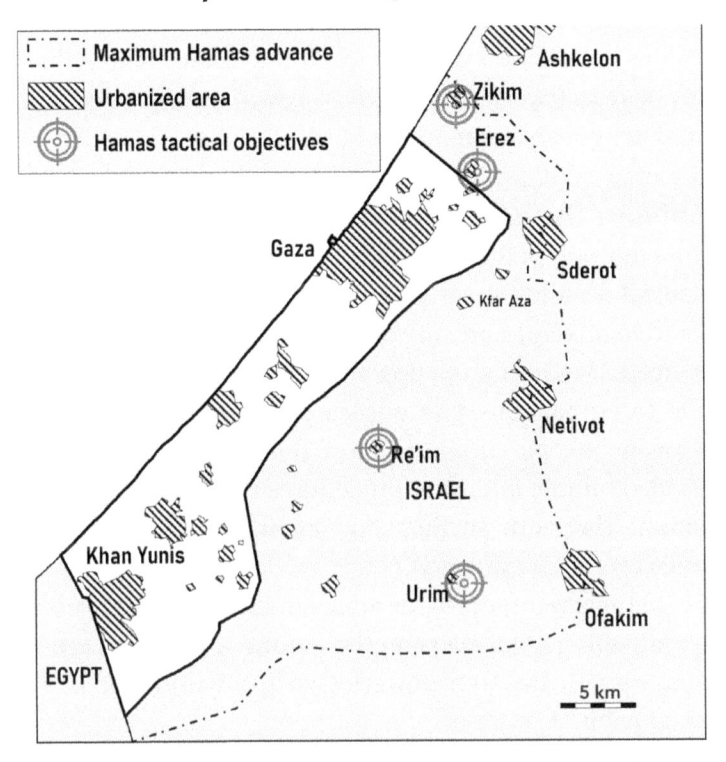

*Figure 86—Despite its impact, the Hamas operation was never able to endanger Israel.*

The first difficulty was to achieve a surprise effect, despite the fence and the warning and security devices (including automatic fire installations) surrounding the Palestinian territory. To this end, the operation was carried out with perfect timing. First, drones attacked the surveillance and automatic fire towers, destroying the RCWS SAMSON systems.

At the same time, commandos from the SAQR squadron crossed the barrier from the air with their microlights, surprising the Israeli military.[384] The operation took the world by surprise, but in reality it was not the first time that the Palestinian resistance had used microlights. On November 25, 1987, the PFLP-General Command carried out such an operation from southern Lebanon against an Israeli army base. The

---

384. Nataliya VASILYEVA, "Paragliding Hamas terrorists bring terror to streets of Israel," *The Telegraph*, October 7, 2023 (https://www.telegraph.co.uk/world-news/2023/10/07/israel-gaza-rockets-hamas-idf-tel-aviv-palestine/)

operation was named AL-QIBYA PLANTERS, after the Palestinian village bombed in 1953 by the Israeli air force near Ramallah.[385]

Amphibious commando units attacked the Zikim military base. They held out for at least a week. The Israeli army was disorganized and clearly unprepared to fight an action of this kind.

### *Israeli Conduct Overtaken by Events*

In the first minutes of the operation, as they crossed the security fence, Hamas special forces (*Quwat al-Nukhba*) neutralized 40% of the Gaza Division's transmission and surveillance installations with snipers and attack drones, as well as detonating relays. Whether by chance or Hamas action, the three balloons that ensure permanent surveillance of the Gaza Strip were not operational. In short, the Israeli command was blind. But it was also blindly following procedures that were not designed for this situation. Therefore an incursion by small groups of Palestinian commandos was to be exptected.

Two F-16 fighters were sent to the area. But their task was to monitor the airspace, and with no observers on the ground to describe the situation and designate goals, they were powerless to do anything, circling over the operation zone for 45 minutes.

On the ground, the Palestinian fighters were trying to reach the Re'im base which houses the Gaza Division command. They had been carefully briefed before the operation—they should walk as much as possible and avoid running, so that surveillance drones could not identify them too quickly. According to journalists from the Israeli media *YNet*, this ruse worked for much of the morning of October 7, until the order was given to shoot at any potential target, even if it was not clearly identified.

On their way, some groups came face to face with the young people at the music festival, which took place just between the base and the Gaza Strip. Confused, some of the Hamas fighters asked the festival-goers for directions. As it turned out, the festival should have ended on Friday evening, but in view of its success the organizers asked for an extension until Saturday morning.

Very quickly, combat drones were dispatched to the scene, without any prior knowledge of the situation. In the absence of precise orders,

---

385. https://alkhanadeq.com/post/1797/م‌ع‌م‌ل‌ي‌ة-ال‌ط‌ل‌ائ‌ع‌-ال‌ش‌ر‌اع‌ي‌ة-م‌و‌اج‌ه‌ة-م‌ب‌اش‌ر‌ة-ف‌ي-م‌ع‌س‌ك‌ر-ال‌ا‌ح‌ت‌لال‌.

operators engaged them without coordination or instructions from air force command. Normally, air support is carried out on the instructions of observers on the ground. But here, it was civilians who were giving instructions to helicopter and drone pilots. In all, more than a hundred missions were carried out by the drones, mainly on Israeli territory, but with virtually no coordination.

Helicopter gunship units were immediately alerted, and the first APACHE helicopter gunships arrived on the scene at around 7 am. These aircraft came from Ramon air base, not far from the Gaza Strip. However, the bulk of the helicopters were redeployed to the north of the country, because of the threat from the Lebanese border. The bulk of the helicopters would not arrive until around 10am. Once in the area, the pilots tried to contact the Gaza Division command. But the latter, deprived of its means of transmission, remained mute. The pilots then tried to make contact with the kibbutz security forces using their cell phones. The use of private telephone networks goes against all military procedures, but the collapse of military transmission networks forced the fighters on the ground to conduct the air raid from their cell phones.

### *Vehicles Targeted by APACHE Attack Helicopters*

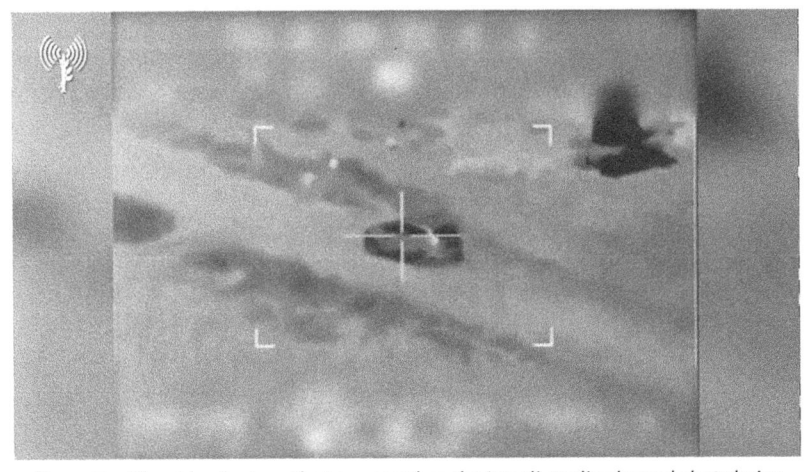

*Figure 87—The video footage that appeared on the Israeli media showed shots being fired at vehicles, which were clearly not positively identified as Hamas. By their own admission, the pilots shot at vehicles fleeing the combat zone, without really knowing who was inside. It turned out that a great many young Israelis were in those cars.*
*[Source: IDF]*

At this stage, the Gaza Division command was inoperative and the baton passed to the Southern Command and the Armed Forces Command in Tel Aviv. But they were totally blind and had no idea of the real situation on the ground. They interpreted it as a series of small-scale incursions and then began to understand that it was a major operation. Staff then resorted to the *Telegram* social networks and tried to understand the situation from the channels used by Hamas, as well as from the local press.

The military leadership was totally disorganized. The soldiers were unable to react in a coordinated fashion. At the Erez checkpoint, clashes quickly turned to the advantage of the Palestinian fighters. On October 20, the *Haaretz* newspaper described the situation:

> *The coordination and liaison office was attacked on October 7, as were all the outposts along the division's sector. A large Hamas force seized the Erez crossing, which was closed for the holiday of Simhat Torah. From there, in a matter of minutes and without resistance, they advanced into the military base, killing and kidnapping soldiers from the civilian administration, although a few of them managed to shoot back before being hit... Brigadier General Rosenfeld entrenched himself in the division's underground war room with a handful of soldiers, men and women, desperately trying to rescue and organize the attacked sector. Many soldiers, most of them non-combatants, were killed or wounded outside. The division was forced to request air intervention against the base itself in order to repel the terrorists.*[386]

From his underground command post in the Gaza Division at Re'im, Brigadier-General Avi Rosenfeld launched air strikes against his own positions, indiscriminately hitting Palestinians and Israeli soldiers, who were among the October 7 victims attributed to Hamas. Hamas fighters held out until the afternoon.

---

386. Amos Harel, "Failures Leading Up to the Hamas Attack That Changed Israel Forever," *Haaretz*, October 20, 2023 (https://www.haaretz.com/israel-news/2023-10-20/ty-article/.premium/underprepared-and-overconfident-israel-failed-to-spot-the-signs-of-impending-disaster/0000018b-4976-d03a-afcb-697edb020000)

## APACHE fire on civilians

*Figure 88—Examination of the images produced by the Israeli forces and published in the Israeli media, such as this SUV just before it was destroyed, shows that the helicopters fired on civilians. Were they Palestinians or Israelis? Nobody knows, but the images clearly show the absence of weapons, such as assault rifles, while the young girl trying to jump onto the vehicle suggests that they were young Israelis. In any case, the precautionary principle imposed by IHL has not been respected.*

At around midday, according to *YNet* media, the Israeli supreme command ordered the prevention of the capture of prisoners *"at any price."* According to the two journalists, this was the triggering of a HANNIBAL directive, which was not, however, named directly.

Apparently, the Palestinians also burned car tires, not to set fire to houses, but to create a screen against helicopter attacks. This made it more difficult for the APACHE to identify and hit the right target. This technique, which had already been widely used (or tested?) during the 2018 Marches of Return in the Gaza Strip, had already borne fruit against surveillance and firing installations. The Palestinians thus helped create the "fog of war" that affected Israeli conduct at this crucial moment.

An interview on Israeli radio with a survivor from the Be'eri kibbutz shows that the Israeli army fired indiscriminately at Hamas fighters and its own citizens.[387]

---

387. https://youtu.be/gi-ESUGUUMk

## *Destruction Incompatible with Palestinian Arming*

> **Israel** ישראל ✡ ✅ 🌐
> @Israel
>
> 8 weeks ago today, over 1,000 of our loved ones were murdered by Hamas terrorists.
>
> Israeli woman and girls were brutally raped and tortured.
>
> Children and Holocaust survivors were kidnapped to Gaza.
>
> Shabbat has never been the same since then.
>
> 3:12 PM · Dec 2, 2023 · **598.3K** Views

*Figure 89—Tweet from the Israeli government. The level of destruction shows that it was not the result of Hamas action but of Israeli command panic and disproportionate use of force.*[388]

In the Be'eri kibbutz, a MERKAVA tank unit intervened. But without knowing what was really going on or where the Hamas fighters were, they fired at both Israelis and Palestinians, as a young tank commander confessed. Whether or not the HANNIBAL directive (described in my book *Vaincre le terrorisme djihadiste*)[389] was being applied, what emerges from these sad events is the panic-stricken Israeli conduct. Very clearly, the Israeli command had no contingency plan. Tactical-level commanders were totally left to their own devices. The initiative was left to inexperienced non-commissioned officers and junior officers, who had no overview of the situation.

---

388. https://twitter.com/Israel/status/1730953051609981300
389. Jacques BAUD, *Vaincre le terrorisme djihadiste*, ÉDITIONS Max Milo, Paris, 2022.

## A "Mass HANNIBAL"

**Max Blumenthal** ✓
@MaxBlumenthal

Israeli Col. Nof Erez described a "mass Hannibal" targeting by the Israeli military of Hamas militants AND Israeli citizens on October 7 to prevent captives from getting to Gaza

See: the Hannibal Dorective

[Col. Nof Erez video: "what we saw here was a MASS HANNIBAL. There were many openings in the fence, thousands of people on many different vehicles with hostages and without."]

From **D A**

8:17 PM · Nov 20, 2023 · **70.5K** Views

*Figure 90—Colonel Nof Erez explains that on October 7, in the absence of a clear vision of the situation and in view of the mass of Palestinian attackers, the general staff authorized shooting on sight at all targets that presented themselves, without first determining whether they were enemies or friends. He refers to the application of a "mass HANNIBAL" directive, although the term itself is not used by the Israeli general staff. Max Blumenthal is one of the best investigative journalists currently working on the Gaza question.*

Without knowing the exact nature of the attack or the actual situation on the ground, the Tel Aviv command ordered the mobilization of reservists, who were met by Hamas special forces when they arrived at the assembly points. The scenario on which the Israeli staff were working was an infiltration from tunnels dug under the barrier surrounding the Gaza Strip, but not a crossing of the barrier at several points. In other words, the Israeli plan was geared towards protecting Israeli kibbutzes and villages, but not towards more offensive action at the crossing points.

Israeli units were fighting without knowing what was happening in adjacent areas. According to the *YNet* media, at 8 a.m., more than an hour and a half after the launch of the operation, the Tel Aviv headquarters had still not realized the scale of the attack.

In the absence of orders, the combat helicopter units decided to abandon all procedures and open firing freely "on anything that looks threatening or the enemy." With no observers on the ground, the pilots drew up their own list of targets. They logged on to *Whatsapp* networks and used their cell phones to communicate directly with kibbutz civilians, who pointed out the targets. But this was far from a military target designation protocol—it was all about approximation and imprecision.

The Palestinian fighters were suspected of having come to take prisoners in order to exchange them later for Palestinians in captivity. This is the case of the HANNIBAL directive, which empowers everyone to shoot in order to prevent the capture of an Israeli, even at the cost of his or her life. This is what happened. The order was given to shoot at all vehicles, "*even if they were feared to contain hostages*," as reported by *YNet*. This is what happened—the helicopters fired indiscriminately at all the vehicles, most of which contained young people seeking to flee the area. An Israeli Air Force colonel spoke of a "mass *HANNIBAL*."[390]

In fact, the Israelis had not expected an operation of this scale. Their contingency plans were calibrated for operations carried out by very small commandos infiltrating Israeli territory from tunnels or holes in the fence. The intervention units dispatched to the area were quickly overwhelmed by the mass of fighters. Israeli observation and control posts were quickly neutralized. Drone operators were forced to use kibbutz WhatsApp groups to get civilians to point out targets.

Tanks were dispatched, with crews of very (too?) young women, clearly with no real experience. Interviewed, the young tank commander explained that she did not really know what to do, and ended up firing on targets designated by local civilians. The crew opened fire with their 120 mm cannon on houses without knowing if there were any civilians inside. There were, and the images of the house later show that it was these shots that caused the destruction. A drone captured the scene on video.

It is therefore possible that Hamas fighters committed war crimes that day. But all the evidence suggests that the panic of the young soldiers, with no real leadership from the higher echelons, was most probably the real cause of that day's massacre.

---

390. "Mass Hannibal—We killed Israelis on 7 October, says Israeli air force colonel," *YouTube*, December 5, 2023 (https://youtu.be/r63nmfbIUBA).

### *The Testimony of a Young Tank Commander*

*Figure 91—This young MERKAVA tank commander admits quite simply that she opened fire on houses in a kibbutz on the instructions of a civilian, without knowing whether there were Israeli civilians with the Hamas fighters.*

There is every reason to believe that Hamas carried out a planned and prepared military operation against the targets of the occupying forces.

## New Tactics

After October 7, Israeli troops pushed into the Gaza Strip. This is what the Palestinians wanted—they were prepared for guerrilla warfare on their territory. The Israelis simply had to take the bait. The Israelis were then confronted with combat techniques for which they were not prepared.

## "Zero Distance" Actions

The Palestinian groups managed to hold out despite the numerical and material superiority of the Israelis. So-called "zero-distance" actions, i.e., actions carried out by infantrymen in direct contact with Israeli tanks, are both highly effective and highly publicized.

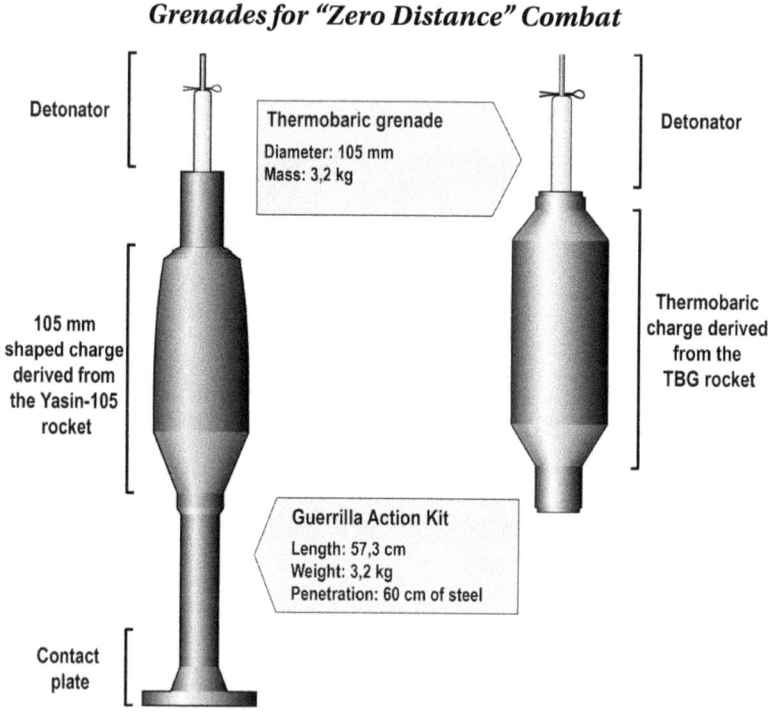

**Grenades for "Zero Distance" Combat**

- Detonator
- Thermobaric grenade
  Diameter: 105 mm
  Mass: 3,2 kg
- Detonator
- 105 mm shaped charge derived from the Yasin-105 rocket
- Thermobaric charge derived from the TBG rocket
- Guerrilla Action Kit
  Length: 57,3 cm
  Weight: 3,2 kg
  Penetration: 60 cm of steel
- Contact plate

*Figure 92—The Guerrilla Action Kit is nothing more than an AL-YASSIN-105 grenade with a magnetic contact plate attached. Hamas fighters attach these grenades to the rear door of MERKAVA tanks. The explosion causes a projectile of molten copper to be projected, causing extensive damage to the passenger compartment. The thermobaric grenade is used against groups of infantrymen in enclosed spaces.*

Ill-prepared technically, tactically and psychologically for guerrilla combat, the Israeli military were in a permanent climate of insecurity. The result was that they did not get out of their tanks, and sought to remain under the protection of their armor and active protection systems, such as the WINDBREAKER (also known as the TROPHY).

Taking advantage of armor blind spots, and the minimal distances required to activate TROPHY systems, Palestinian fighters had developed weapons designed to be engaged in direct contact ("zero distance") with armor. These are charges which are applied against the armor and explode, causing considerable damage.

To protect against "zero range" weapons, Israeli tanks have been fitted with an anti-magnetic coating designed to prevent the attachment of an explosive device. This is the same solution adopted during the Second World War on German tanks (Zimmerit).

### *"Zero Distance" Explosives*

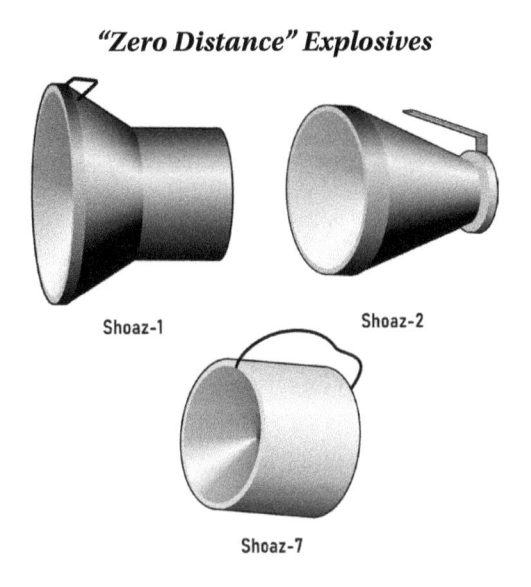

*Figure 93—SHOAZ explosives are zero-distance weapons, deployed in close proximity to Israeli tanks. Using attack tunnels, Hamas fighters can emerge from the ground close to the Israelis to deposit their explosive charge, then disappear by the same route.*

SHOAZ destruction charges are part of the arsenal developed by the Palestinians. These are shaped charges that are placed in the immediate vicinity of armored vehicles, or charges that propel copper plates that deform in flight to form powerful, destructive projectiles. Known as *Explosive Formed Penetrators* (EFP), these weapons had already been observed in Iraq in the early 2000s.

The explosives used in these devices come from unexploded Israeli bombs and shells, whose explosives are extracted and recovered. The "dud" rate for Israeli explosive projectiles is around 15%, according to Israeli intelligence.[391]

---

391. Maria ABI-HABIB & Sheera FRENKEL, "Where Is Hamas Getting Its Weapons? Increasingly, From Israel" *The New York Times*, January 28, 2024 (updated January 29, 2024) (https://www.nytimes.com/2024/01/28/world/middleeast/israel-hamas-weapons-rockets.html)

## TV Kit

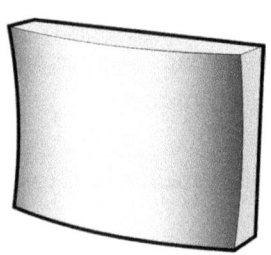

Figure 94—The TV kit, so named because of its resemblance to a television set, is the local Gaza-made version of the American CLAYMORE mine used in Vietnam. It is considerably more powerful and is used to carry out ambushes inside buildings or tunnels, for example. It is detonated by a simple remote control.

### Combat Tunnels

The subsoil of the Gaza Strip has been pierced by a multitude of small tunnels whose sole function is to enable Palestinian fighters to move around unseen and to pop up close to Israeli troops. These tunnels show that Hamas is first and foremost a defensive resistance organization. But it also shows that its leaders have anticipated very well how and where Israeli forces would intervene in the territory. Clearly, the Israeli army is predictable, and this is a major vulnerability for which the Israeli military has paid a high price since entering Gaza.

The Hamas propaganda videos show well-trained tactics, applied with discipline as early as October 7. These include attacks on armored vehicles, with the first team immobilizing the tank with AL-YASSIN-105 rockets before quickly disappearing into a tunnel, while a second team takes the shocked Israeli soldiers prisoner.

This means that tunnel networks are extremely extensive, diversified and spread over several levels.

### Ambushes

Ambush tactics are as old as the hills. But for the Israeli army, it is a new situation. Operation SWORDS OF IRON is to a large extent the first operation in which the IDF has been confronted with resistance action in the classical sense of the term. The classic tactics of resistance are all being used imaginatively.

### *Extremely Realistic Training*

*Figure 95—Hamas fighters have been practicing ambushes with life-size models. Here, a MERKAVA IV battle tank, followed by a NAMER infantry fighting vehicle and another MERKAVA. The routines drilled in training are being precisely reproduced today against Israeli troops. [Source: Hamas propaganda]*

Hamas fighters are clearly well trained for guerrilla warfare. Videos showing their training on life-size, highly realistic tank models explain their dexterity.

### *Houses Become Multiple Rocket Launchers*

*Figure 96—View of the interior of the house, the six 107 mm rockets, wedged in place with cinder blocks. [Source: Saraya Al-Quds]*

*Figure 97—View of the front of the house with the six openings. [Source: Saraya Al-Quds]*

In Gaza, Israeli tanks are crippled. The Palestinians fight with an almost uninterrupted series of ambushes. One can at times speak of "staggered ambushes:" a first Israeli group falls into an ambush and then, when reinforcements arrive, they are greeted by a new ambush. Up to three ambushes have been observed nested in this pattern.

Israeli forces do try to claim that the Palestinians are using the homes of the civilian population to fire rockets, and that this is why they have been forced to bomb populated areas. But this excuse has been "debunked" and the house in question, located in Zeitoun, had been bombed before and the area had been evacuated by civilians.[392]

## Dynamic Control Structures

After 120 days of intense conflict, the Palestinians appeared to be far from loosing their leadership and leadership structures. Not only have the Palestinians managed to maintain a presence throughout the territory occupied by the Israeli army, but it seems that the coordination and conduct of their operations are totally intact. In fact, Palestinian fighters are sharing feedback between the north and south of the Gaza Strip.

This means that the leadership structures are highly decentralized, but retain the ability to coordinate their actions. In other words, the image

---

392. https://twitter.com/EekadFacts/status/1744810655524212829

propagated by Israel of command centers hidden under hospitals was false, because they did not exist; but, more seriously, the Israelis still have not understood how the Palestinians conduct their operations. In other words, they do not understand how Palestinian resistance works. This corresponds to the way Israel has been fighting the Palestinians for 75 years: they seek to destroy individuals, but are incapable of bringing down the Palestinian "system."

In other words, the Israelis can only achieve tactical objectives, while the Palestinians can achieve an operational victory and have already achieved a strategic victory.

## War Crimes

Very quickly, on October 7, the Israeli authorities announced 1,400 deaths on the Israeli side. This figure was later revised downwards, but it is still widely cited by the media as a measure of Hamas's crimes, and is associated with genocidal intent.

Despite the fact that in law no crime can justify another, the narrative of Hamas's war crimes has become the cornerstone of Israeli strategy, as we saw during the preliminary hearings at the International Court of Justice.[393] It is therefore essential to understand what really happened that day, because the vagueness surrounding that day is exploited by our media to make the brutality of the Israeli response "acceptable."

The images broadcast by Israel after October 7 seem to lend credence to the accusation of war crimes against Hamas. In November 2023, the Israeli government edited the videos allegedly taken by Hamas fighters. The result was a 47-minute film that was shared with all Israeli representations abroad and shown to a selected audience by invitation. British journalist Owen Jones, known for his support of Israel, was invited to see it and noted:

> *There are no scenes of decapitation of living individuals. There are no elements to document the accusation of torture. There are*

---

393. https://www.youtube.com/watch?v=939hSvcH0qM

*no scenes of rape or sexual violence. There are no scenes of Hamas killing children.*[394]

The Israeli and Western narratives soon showed their weaknesses. Testimonies published in the Israeli press gave a totally different picture of the situation. The many accounts published in the Israeli media (but not in the West!), describing a chaotic Israeli military response, showed that the nature and extent of the crimes Hamas is accused of are far from clear. The nature of the destruction and damage caused that day suggests that it was caused by weapons considerably more powerful than those available to the Palestinians.

While some crimes can be attributed to Hamas, it appears that the most heinous crimes mentioned by media outlets such as *LCI*, *BFMTV* or *CNews* in France never took place, such as the 40 beheaded babies or the oven-baked baby. The problem is that this Israeli narrative is used by our media to justify the massacre of Gaza's civilian population.

Only an independent, international and impartial investigation would enable an honest judgement to be made. As soon as the protagonist who claims to be the victim refuses such an investigation, which would enable an objective and irrefutable accusation to be made, the question arises as to his or her good faith. In the past, in the cases of the MH-17, the Bucha massacre or the sabotage of Nord Stream 1 & 2, the authorities of the victim-countries have systematically refused international investigations, preferring to substitute national ones. This is usually the sign of a profound gap between the narrative and the reality of the facts. October 7 seems to be no exception to the rule: the Israeli government refuses to authorize an international inquiry[395] and, after a heated debate on whether or not to conduct a national inquiry, Netanyahu finally agreed to an internal investigation by the armed forces.[396] Clearly, Israel seems worried about the possible conclusions of an impartial and independent international inquiry.

---

394. https://youtu.be/mc5iG3DX7ho
395. "UN seeks Israel access for Hamas sexual violence investigation," *France 24*, December 6, 2023 (https://www.france24.com/en/live-news/20231206-un-seeks-israel-access-for-hamas-sexual-violence-investigation)
396. Neri Zilber, "Benjamin Netanyahu's allies turn on IDF over its October 7 inquiry plans," *The Financial Times*, January 5, 2024 (https://www.ft.com/content/2dc0aa94-bc8e-4a48-90e3-d4fae91a0e52)

Justifying the disproportionality of the Israeli response has become a central element of communication for the Israeli government and the mainstream European media. Depending on the decisions of the International Court of Justice, these media, which know all the facts of the case, could be accused of supporting or even inciting genocide.

## *Hostages or Prisoners?*

In July 2023, the Special Rapporteur of the Office of the United Nations High Commissioner for Human Rights reported that Israel was holding around 5,000 Palestinians, including 160 children and 1,100 detainees against whom no charges had been brought.[397] These prisoners, held without charge, are used by Israel to put pressure on their families. They are therefore hostages, and no one in the West talks about them.

As early as 2021, Hamas had asked Egyptian mediators to open negotiations for the release of these prisoners, particularly those against whom no charges had been brought.[398] But at the end of the year, Israel broke off the talks.

In the absence of international support for the settlement of this dispute, one of Hamas's objectives was to take prisoners in order to gain leverage for resuming negotiations for the release of Palestinians held by Israel in conditions that have been repeatedly denounced by humanitarian organizations. Here again, if the international community had taken an interest in this issue, Hamas no doubt would not have had a reason to launch its operation.

The Hamas plan, however, encountered two unexpected developments: the absence of the Israeli military and the music festival. The Hamas commandos had expected to fight soldiers, but part of the Gaza Division had been redeployed to the West Bank and they were confronted by civilians. So, unable to take military prisoners, the Palestinians had to fall back on civilians. This is why, after entering the kibbutz, the Palestinians initially waited for the soldiers in the houses. According to some accounts, they even encouraged civilians to call the security forces. When the first Israeli soldiers appeared, with tanks, the

---

397. "Special Rapporteur Says Israel's Unlawful Carceral Practices in the Occupied Palestinian Territory Are Tantamount to International Crimes and Have Turned it into an Open-Air Prison," *Office of the High Commissioner for Human Rights*, July 10, 2023 (https://www.ohchr.org/en/news/2023/07/special-rapporteur-says-israels-unlawful-carceral-practices-occupied-palestinian)
398. https://alkhanadeq.com/post.php?id=1677

situation was totally confused. The tanks fired on the houses, killing all the Palestinian and Israeli occupants, and the commandos withdrew with civilian prisoners.

Capturing civilians in order to carry out a prisoner exchange with an occupying force is certainly not in conformity with International Humanitarian Law (IHL), but this same right would imply that prisoners of the Israelis also benefit from this right, and that channels for dialogue exist. Yet not only are Palestinian prisoners subjected to torture and ill-treatment, but the channels for negotiation no longer exist, for the reasons mentioned above. What is more, deliberately shooting civilians to prevent their capture is hardly in line with IHL. The problem—which affects the whole Palestinian question—is that Israel has created a lawless zone, of which it is a victim today.

None of this excuses Hamas for capturing civilians. But when there is no instrument to resolve the problem of hostages taken by Israel (i.e., Palestinians captured without charge, and incarcerated solely to put pressure on their families), when Israel closes all channels of discussion, when the international community refuses to enforce the rules of law, Hamas is left with nothing but the use of force.

Technically speaking, the term "hostage" is appropriate for civilians captured by Palestinian militants, and could constitute a war crime, even if the aim is to force Israel to negotiate. With regard to military personnel, on the other hand, we should speak of prisoners of war, whose capture is perfectly legal, which is consistent with Netanyahu's declarations that "Israel is at war."[399]

On November 24, 2023, a prisoner exchange was organized between Hamas and Israel. The latter released 39 prisoners: 15 minors and 24 women, against whom no charges had been brought. Everyone can judge for themselves the nature of a state that makes arbitrary arrests. But what is most interesting is that the Palestinians were not allowed to celebrate the return of these prisoners, lest they be branded terrorists.[400]

---

[399]. "Netanyahu on massive Hamas attack: 'We are at war,'" *The Times of Israel*, October 7, 2023 (https://www.timesofisrael.com/liveblog_entry/netanyahu-on-massive-hamas-attack-we-are-at-war/)
[400]. https://youtu.be/voXlir19xpA

## Hamas' Treatment of Hostages

On France 5's "C à vous" program on November 14, 2023, former French Foreign Minister Jean-Yves Le Drian tried to convince us that Hamas was using its prisoners as human shields under a hospital, as Israel then claimed:[401]

> It's a method used by all terrorist groups. Your colleague Didier François, when he was kidnapped by DAESH, was under a hospital.

Thus, if we are to believe what the Israeli army and Le Drian are telling us, Hamas treats its prisoners well and holds them in the place least likely to be hit: a hospital. Le Drian thus confirms that Israel does not respect IHL. But apparently Hamas knows this too, and is seeking to preserve the lives of these "hostages" so that they can negotiate. This explains why no concrete indication has been found that the hostages were held in hospitals: Hamas is trying to preserve them.

In fact, ex-hostage testimonies all agree that Hamas fighters treated their prisoners with respect and without animosity.

Yocheved Lifschitz, 85, who was kidnapped on October 7, recounted after her release that on that day, the prisoners were visited by Yahya Sinwar, Hamas's operational leader in the Gaza Strip, who reassured them and explained the reason for their abduction and that they would soon be exchanged. She even reproached him for kidnapping people who, like her, were in favor of peace between Israelis and Palestinians, and he did not respond.[402]

A "Complément d'enquête" documentary entitled, *Hamas, du sang et des armes* (Hamas, Blood and Arms) is an example of how inaccuracies follow lies in a work that has nothing whatsoever to do with journalism. A Franco-Israeli survivor gives a testimony clearly driven by emotion, which contrasts with that of Yasmin Porat, who declared on an Israeli radio station that it was the Israeli military who killed most of the Israeli civilians along with Hamas militants.[403]

---

401. https://youtu.be/GVUINzGxz8c?t=274
402. "'I Asked Him How He Isn't Ashamed': 85-year-old Israeli Hostage Says She Confronted Hamas Chief Sinwar in Gaza Tunnel," *Haaretz*, November 29, 2023 (https://www.haaretz.com/israel-news/2023-11-29/ty-article/85-year-old-freed-israeli-hostage-confronted-hamas-chief-sinwar-in-gaza-tunnel/0000018c-1ad5-d4e4-a1df-3edd611c0000)
403. https://youtu.be/gi-ESUGUUMk

Yasmin Porat, a mother of three who had fled the Supernova rave before being captured by Hamas militants, said she and other civilians had been detained for several hours and treated *"humanely."* A recording of her interview, on the public Kan channel,[404] on the *Haboker Hazeh* ("This morning") radio program hosted by Aryeh Golan, circulated on social networks, but not on our media, which are busy stirring up trouble:

> *They didn't treat us badly. They treated us very humanely.*
> *By that I mean they looked after us... They gave us drinks here and there. When they saw we were nervous, they calmed us down. It was very scary, but nobody treated us violently. Fortunately, what I heard in the media*[405] *didn't happen to me.*

On Israeli TV *Channel 12*, she declared:

> *They were very humane towards us... [Quoting a Palestinian fighter, who spoke Hebrew] He said to me: "Look at me carefully, we're not going to kill you. We want to take you to Gaza. We're not going to kill you. So stay calm, you're not going to die." That's what he said to me, in those words.*
> *I was calm because I knew nothing would happen to me.*
> *We were the ones who called the police at the same time as the kidnappers, because they wanted the police to arrive. Their aim was to kidnap us and take us to Gaza.*[406]

Although there were only a dozen Israeli prisoners, Ms. Porat was instructed to tell the Israeli police that 40 of them were being held by Hamas fighters, who themselves numbered between 40 and 50 men, most of them in their twenties, according to Ms. Porat's estimates. They were young and scared themselves," she told *Channel 12*.

On October 26, 2023, octogenarian hostage Yocheved Lifschitz, freed by Hamas a few days earlier, gave a press conference on her conditions of detention and release. She stated that *"the prisoners received medical care and were fed the same bread, cream cheese and cucumber meal as*

---

404. https://www.kan.org.il/content/kan/kan-b/p-9969/
405. https://www.youtube.com/watch?v=gi-ESUGUUMk
406. https://youtu.be/fghF54maONw

*their 'friendly' guards."* The Hamas fighters treated their female prisoners with respect, dignity and care. This did not stop the state media *France 24* from headlining that she *had "been through* hell."[407] This Israeli woman was dragged through the mud and called a liar by the Israeli and Western media. But at the end of November, testimonies from other hostages confirmed her claims. On Israeli *Channel 13*, military analyst Alon Ben David confirmed:

> *She was telling the truth exactly as these [captives] said it. I sat with them and heard exactly the same story from their mouths.*[408]

But these statements undermine the Israeli narrative. In the wake of Yocheved Lifschitz's statements, Jonathan Pollard, a former US intelligence officer convicted in the United States of spying for Israel and pardoned by Donald Trump in 2016, declared that we should *"shut the mouths of the families of the hostages"* released.[409]

Chen Goldstein-Almog, who was released with her three children at the end of November, said that *"she and her children were held together, treated 'with respect' and not* mistreated."[410] She even stated that during air strikes, Hamas fighters protected them with their bodies and that when she asked one of them if they were going to kill them, he replied *"We'll die before you."*[411]

After the prisoner exchanges, in November 2023, Danielle Aloni, a former Hamas prisoner with her daughter, wrote a letter to her captors thanking them for the *"extraordinary humanity"* with which she and her daughter had been treated. It sparked an outcry in Israel, where it was claimed to be propaganda[412] written under duress. However, the psycho-

---

407. https://www.france24.com/en/live-news/20231024-freed-israeli-says-beaten-by-abductors-then-well-treated-in-gaza
408. https://www.middleeastmonitor.com/20231128-israel-freed-captives-testify-to-being-treated-extremely-well-by-hamas/
409. "Pollard: Israel should've 'shut the mouths of hostage families,'" *i24 News*, November 23, 2023 (https://www.i24news.tv/en/news/israel-at-war/1700759005-pollard-israel-should-ve-shut-the-mouths-of-hostage-families)
410. Anat SCHWARTZ, "Apology, Tears and Terror: A Former Hostage Recounts a 7-Week Ordeal," *The New York Times*, December 15, 2023 (https://www.nytimes.com/2023/12/15/world/middleeast/hamas-israel-hostage.html)
411. https://www.trtworld.com/middle-east/freed-israeli-hostage-says-hamas-protected-them-during-israels-air-strikes-16374456
412. https://nypost.com/2023/11/28/news/danielle-aloni-letter-praising-hamas-is-propaganda-family/

logical experts who examined the letter found no evidence of coercion or falsification.[413]

Obviously, this letter contradicts the official propaganda, but it would probably be more interesting to reflect on the reasons that led Ms. Aloni to write it. For the way the *Wahdat al-Zili* militants treated their hostages, shattered years of propaganda unleashed to portray the Palestinians and Hamas as bloodthirsty brutes. The testimonies of those freed show that they were surprised and impressed by the friendliness and thoughtfulness of the Palestinians.

On *Channel 13*, Israeli military analyst Alon Ben David, who was able to speak to the hostages freed by Hamas, testified:

> *[Hamas fighters] put the members of each kibbutz together, which made them feel more comfortable.*
> *[The prisoners] suffered no violence or insults, and Hamas members tried to provide them with food, painkillers and their usual medicines as much as possible, in dangerous and difficult security conditions underground and inside the tunnels... They sat and talked together... This encouraged them to persevere.*[414]

In late November 2023, in the *Jerusalem Post*, a member of Ruth Munder's family stated:

> *Fortunately, they did not suffer bad conditions during their captivity; they were treated humanely... Contrary to what we feared, they did not live through the horrible stories we had imagined... They were not harmed.*[415]

This is a far cry from Meyer Habib's[416] *"mobs galvanized by Jew hatred."* The Hamas prisoners were treated with dignity. So dignified, in fact, that the Israeli government has taken steps to ensure that the freed hostages no longer speak out in the media. Nothing to do with the Palestinian priso-

---

413. https://forward.com/culture/571714/hostage-letter-danielle-aloni-hamas-morality/
414. "Israel: freed captives testify to being treated 'extremely well' by Hamas," *Middle East Monitor*, November 28, 2023 (https://www.middleeastmonitor.com/20231128-israel-freed-captives-testify-to-being-treated-extremely-well-by-hamas/)
415. Uri Sella & Erez Harel, "What were Israeli hostages' conditions upon release from Gaza?," *The Jerusalem Post*, November 25, 2023 (https://www.jpost.com/breaking-news/article-775018)
416. https://youtu.be/MRntn41zKek

ners released by the Israelis, threatened with rape, bruised and with even broken arms, six of whom died in the seven weeks prior to their release.[417] The Israeli media claimed that the injuries of young Mohammed Nazzal (arrested without any grounds in August 2023) were false and produced a video (in degraded quality) showing that he was doing very well and that it is Palestinian propaganda. But *France 24* investigated and it turned out that the Israeli video was a fake and showed another individual, in a different circumstance.[418] Liars.

As always in these situations, where the "terrorists" behave better than the "liberators," it is claimed that the ex-hostages were victims of *Stockholm syndrome*.

The reality is more prosaic: the Israeli military considers that Palestinians have no rights, as one military official told the father of a young Palestinian American.[419]

*Stockholm syndrome* is a behavior attributed to hostage-takers, who become dependent on their captors and develop a form of affection for them. In reality, this phenomenon does not exist. It was invented by a Swedish police psychologist in 1973, to discredit a hostage's critics, after a particularly brutal assault by Swedish police.[420] As in Stockholm fifty years ago, this "syndrome" is used to discredit Hamas fighters, who have shown themselves to be—in fact—more respectful than the Israeli military.

We knew that "animals" had "human" feelings. We now know that *"human animals"* have a considerably higher level of morality and ethics than certain peoples who claim to be superior.

The Israelis treat prisoners like animals. Ghandi said:

> *The degree of civilization of a people can be recognized by the way they treat their animals.*

Everyone will be the judge.

---

417. Lucy WILLIAMSON, "Released Palestinians allege abuse in Israeli jails," *BBC News*, December 1, 2023 (https://www.bbc.com/news/world-middle-east-67581915)
418. https://www.youtube.com/watch?v=ZH7gVpNBaLY
419. Jay GRAY & Doha MADANI, "13-year-old Palestinian American was shot by Israeli soldiers and detained, his family says," *NBC News*, December 22, 2023 (https://www.nbcnews.com/news/world/13-year-old-palestinian-american-was-shot-israeli-soldiers-detained-fa-rcna130797)
420. Rebecca ARMITAGE, "Is Stockholm syndrome a myth? The terrifying crime behind psychology's most famous—and dubious—term," *ABC News*, August 22, 2023 (https://www.abc.net.au/news/2023-08-23/is-stockholm-syndrome-a-myth/102738084)

### The Supernova Music Festival Attack

The *Supernova* festival, which took place near Re'im—where the Gaza Division headquarters were located—was the scene of many of the deaths on October 7, and remains—rightly so—the greatest object of resentment on the part of the Israeli population. The Western media claim that Hamas fighters deliberately killed the fleeing youth.

The reality is that, in the absence of an international and impartial investigation, it will be difficult to establish the exact circumstances of this massacre. However, certain elements and eyewitness accounts give an idea of what happened and how it unfolded.

The magnitude of the damage, including the destruction of cars and the intense heat that burned the bodies to the point where the Israelis themselves mistook the corpses of young Israelis for Hamas fighters, suggests that it was caused by the Israeli army.

Moreover, it is now clear that the Palestinians' objective was not the "rave party," as our media would have us believe, but the Re'im military base to which the festival was attached. In fact, the festival was due to end on Friday evening, but at the request of the organizers, it was allowed to continue until Saturday. Investigations carried out by the Israeli police tend to confirm that the Palestinian fighters did not think they were going to come upon the festival and had no intention of attacking the festival-goers. It was therefore an unfortunate combination of circumstances that led to the music festival being hit by the fighting.[421] The investigation and images of the massive damage also show that it was Israeli APACHE helicopters that killed most of the young people.[422]

The charred bodies, presented by our media as a Hamas massacre, are in fact victims of HELLFIRE missiles fired by helicopters, to the extent that the authorities were only belatedly able to identify 200 charred bodies of Palestinian fighters among the 1,400 victims on October 7.[423]

Speaking before the Foreign Affairs Committee of the French National Assembly, expert Gilles Kepel associated the AL-AQSA FLOOD operation with a "razzia" in the "Muslim *religious imagination*"[424] where "*we arrive,*

---

421. https://www.aljazeera.com/news/2023/11/18/hamas-had-not-planned-to-attack-israel-music-festival-israeli-report-says
422. https://www.haaretz.co.il/news/politics/2023-11-18/ty-article/0000018b-e1a5-d168-a3ef-f5ff4d070000
423. https://twitter.com/muhammadshehad2/status/1725464800157749598
424. "Hearing of Mr. Gilles Kepel on the situation in Israel and the Palestinian territories," LCP—Assemblée nationale, November 10, 2023 (https://youtu.be/yUDaC2Z-JHg?t=1744)

*we take, we kill as many people as possible… in a rather irrational way."* This is not true.

Firstly, he attributes the phenomenon of "razzia" to Islam, whereas it is a practice that predates the arrival of Islam and is widely observed in North Africa. Secondly, he sees it as a totally irrational act whose aim is to kill, for which he attributes responsibility to Iran, in a desire to avenge the death of General Soleimani. In particular, he associates the al-Quds units (of the Palestinian Islamic Jihad), which are Sunni, with the Shiite Iranian Revolutionary Guards…

Another problem during the rave party was that many of the young people had weapons in their cars and rushed to get them. This explains why the Palestinian fighters shot at people near their vehicles. But, once again, it will only be possible to make a definitive judgement once a serious investigation has been carried out.

If the Palestinians' aim had been to kill civilians, they would have had plenty of time to do so. But in reality, they occupied the ground for hours, in some areas for days, before being dislodged. During this period, testimonies indicate that the Palestinians were friendly with Israeli civilians.

An Israeli woman called Rotem describes her first contact with a Hamas militant in her kibbutz, and how he asked her permission to have a banana, before leaving.[425] This is a far cry from what Benjamin Netanyahu and his relays in France, such as *CNews* and *BFMTV,* were telling us.

On December 18, three Israeli prisoners of war managed to escape and approach Israeli lines. They are bare-chested to show that they were unarmed and carrying no explosives. On a white flag they wrote a message in Hebrew asking for help. They called their brothers-in-arms in Hebrew, so as not to be mistaken for Palestinians. However, they were shot dead by the Israeli military[426] who were in charge of "retrieving" them.[427]

Not only is it a war crime to shoot down unarmed people who surrender carrying a white flag, it is a further demonstration of the indiscipline that reigns in the IDF.

---

425. https://www.youtube.com/watch?v=rD7NI0tGbp8
426. "Israel Gaza: Hostages shot by IDF put out 'SOS' sign written with leftover food," *BBC News,* December 18, 2023 (https://www.bbc.com/news/world-middle-east-67745092)
427. Michael Rios, "Israeli military report reveals new failures in mission to rescue mistakenly killed hostages," *CNN,* December 29, 2023 (https://edition.cnn.com/2023/12/29/middleeast/israel-hostages-killed-military-report-intl-hnk/index.html)

### The 40 Beheaded Babies

On October 10, 2023, journalist Nicole Zedek posted on her Twitter account that *"Soldiers told me they believed 40 babies/children had been killed. The exact number of dead is still unknown, as the army continues to go house to house and find more Israeli victims."*[428]

#### The Invention of the 40 Babies Massacre

Figure 98—Tweet from Nicole Zedeck, October 10, 2023.

Israeli army spokesperson Eden Tal confirmed that children have been beheaded.[429] However, no image or form of confirmation whatsoever was

---
428. https://twitter.com/nicole_zedek/status/1711721433968111855
429. https://www.dailymotion.com/video/x8oqg9t

published. In fact, she knew absolutely nothing about it and was lying to confirm the rumor. This easily verifiable lie has certainly leave its mark on people's memories, but it also contributes to the Israeli government's loss of credibility.[430]

Tal Heinrich, spokesman for Benjamin Netanyahu's far-right government, confirmed the news.[431] However, already on October 10, the Israeli armed forces (IDF) announced that they were unable to confirm this information.[432] The American website *The Intercept* repeated that the IDF had been unable to confirm the massacre, and stressed that *"the level of misinformation—and disinformation—appears* unprecedented*."*[433]

In fact, even President Joe Biden claimed to have seen the photos of the beheaded babies, but the White House had to backtrack to declare that this was not the case.[434] A president who has practically lied all his life, who fabricates to justify Israeli strikes against Palestinian civilians. Such is the image of American democracy.

Israeli journalist Oren Ziv visited the site of Kfar Aza, where the tragedy is said to have taken place, and spoke to IDF soldiers. On October 11, he tweeted, *"The soldiers I spoke with yesterday in Kfar Aza did not talk about 'beheaded babies.'"*[435] The Israeli army announced that it was not confirming the crime and would not open an investigation.[436] It turns out that the story was false—but it persists, as noted by the Turkish news agency *Anadolu*, which states that Jerusalem-based French journalist Samuel Forey said he was in the settlement of Kfar Aza on Tuesday, but

---

430. "New U.S. Poll Raises Questions about Americans' Support for Israel's War against Hamas," *Jerusalem Center for Public Affairs*, December 31, 2013 (https://jcpa.org/new-u-s-poll-raises-questions-about-americans-support-for-israels-war-against-hamas/)
431. https://edition.cnn.com/middleeast/live-news/israel-hamas-war-gaza-10-11-23/h_a63b0fd 57f2df717147ea8e26a2f758c
432. https://twitter.com/anadoluagency/status/1711812910035407131
433. Alice Speri, "'Beheaded Babies' Report Spread Wide and Fast—but Israel Military Won't Confirm It," *The Intercept*, October 11, 2023 (https://theintercept.com/2023/10/11/israel-hamas-disinformation/)
434. Farrah Tomazin, "White House walks back Biden's claims over Hamas baby beheadings," *The Sidney Morning Herald*, October 12, 2023 (https://www.smh.com.au/world/north-america/white-house-walks-back-biden-s-claims-over-hamas-baby-beheadings-20231012-p5ebob.html)
435. https://twitter.com/OrenZiv_/status/1712039990610260177
436. Joshua Zitser, "IDF says it won't back up its claim that Hamas decapitated babies in Israel because it is 'disrespectful for the dead,'" *Business Insider*, October 11, 2023 (https://web.archive.org/web/20231011205950/https://www.businessinsider.com/idf-says-wont-back-up-beheaded-babies-disrespectful-2023-10)

that no one had mentioned the alleged beheadings and that the military *"did not witness any such* atrocities."[437]

### Western Media and Incitement to Violence

*Figure 99—On October 10, the Turkish media outlet* Anadolu *reported that the Israeli army had no confirmation of the horrors reported in our media. At the very least, this information would encourage caution and restraint in an explosive environment. This was not be the case... [Source: https://www.aa.com.tr/en/middle-east/israeli-army-says-it-does-not-have-confirmation-about-allegations-that-hamas-beheaded-babies-/3014787]*

But Swiss *RTS* ignored these calls for caution. On the Forum program of October 11, 2023, Stéphane Amar, *RTS* correspondent in Jerusalem, spoke of the *"barbarity of Hamas,"* with *"children's throats slit, dismemberments, deaths by the hundreds, often at point-blank range."*[438] In its evening news of October 11, the Swiss channel gave the floor to an Israeli:

> *I know the Americans will help us, because they realize what's going on here. We've been through a little Shoah. A Shoah. They killed babies, women. No country in the world can stand this. We have to put an end to this.*[439]

---

437. Mehmet Solmaz & Enes Calli, "Despite refutations from Israeli military, headlines that Hamas 'beheaded babies' persist," *Anadolu*, October 11, 2023 (updated October 12, 2023) (https://www.aa.com.tr/en/middle-east/despite-refutations-from-israeli-military-headlines-that-hamas-beheaded-babies-persist/3016167)
438. https://www.rts.ch/play/tv/-/video/-?urn=urn:rts:video:14383406&startTime=330
439. https://www.rts.ch/play/tv/-/video/-?urn=urn:rts:video:14383466&startTime=40

But in the article published on the *RTS* website, the text became:

*I know the Americans will help us, because they realize what's going on here. We've been through a little Shoah. A Shoah. They slit the throats of babies and women. No country in the world can put up with that. We have to put an end to this.*[440]

**Near and Middle East Media Set the Standard**

Figure 100—*Turkish media outlet* Anadolu *was the first to declare that the story about the beheaded babies was false. But our media, which had already been carriers of false information about Ukraine, repeat the claimm, the aim being to justify the ongoing genocide in Gaza. [Source: https://www.aa.com.tr/en/middle-east/despite-refutations-from-israeli-military-headlines-that-hamas-beheaded-babies-persist/3016167]*

In fact, there are no official reports of children having their throats slit, and it seems that only one baby was killed on October 7 (Mila Cohen, 10 months), apparently by Israeli fire, according to the *Jewish News Syndicate*.[441]

---

440. https://www.rts.ch/info/monde/14381098-le-hamas-affirme-avoir-libere-une-otage-et-ses-deux-enfants.html
441. Etgar LEFKOVITS, "Three generations wiped out by Hamas in Kibbutz Be'eri," *Jewish News Syndicate*, October 23, 2023 (https://www.jns.org/three-generations-wiped-out-by-hamas-in-kibbutz-beeri/)

The Swiss state media, known for developing conspiracy theories[442] and whose journalists even inspired the far-right terrorist Anders Breivik,[443] not only propagated unconfirmed information, but altered the content of texts to incite hatred and genocide against Palestinians.

*Age Distribution of Israeli Victims on October 7, 2023*

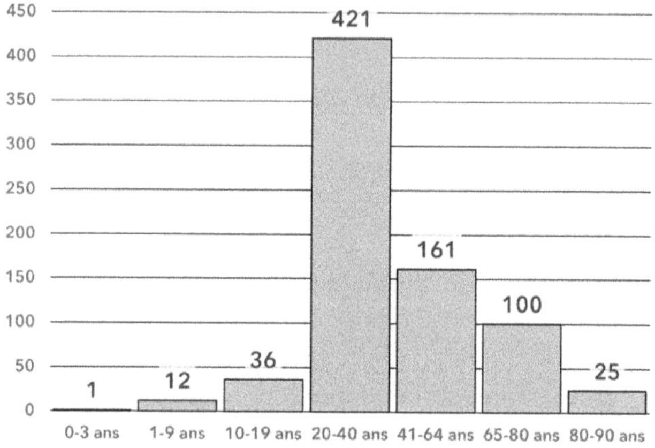

|  |  |
|---|---|
| 0-3 ans | 1 |
| 1-9 ans | 12 |
| 10-19 ans | 36 |
| 20-40 ans | 421 |
| 41-64 ans | 161 |
| 65-80 ans | 100 |
| 80-90 ans | 25 |

*Figure 101—The age breakdown published by the* Times of Israel *on December 4, 2023 shows that only one baby died that day. This baby was killed on Kibbutz Be'eri, apparently with its father and grandmother, by Israeli tank fire. [Source: The Times of Israel][444]*

## Baby in the Oven

The story of a baby burned in an oven on October 7 by Hamas fighters quickly made the rounds. In France, Warda A., an influencer who ironized this "event," was indicted for *"apology for terrorism."*[445] In reality, she was mocking the baseless accusations circulating whose the sole aim was to incite hatred.

For while her joke is in bad taste, to say the least, it is not about the crime itself, but about the misinformation that the event constitutes. Indeed, it soon became clear that the story was false, as reported in the *Jerusalem Post* on November 8:[446]

---

442. https://youtu.be/bEv4-IJsl9k?t=414
443. Mattias GARDELL, "Crusader Dreams: Oslo 22/7, Islamophobia, and the Quest for a Monocultural Europe," *Terrorism and Political Violence*, 26:129-155, 2014.
444. https://www.timesofisrael.com/14-kids-under-10-25-people-over-80-up-to-date-breakdown-of-oct-7-victims-we-know-about/
445. https://www.tf1info.fr/justice-faits-divers/en-direct-proces-warda-anwar-influenceuse-ironisant-sur-la-mort-d-un-bebe-dans-un-four-israel-hamas-jugee-a-paris-aujourd-hui-2277029.html
446. https://www.jpost.com/israel-news/article-772181

*The story of the Israeli baby whose body was found in the oven has been circulating for 24 hours, with serious consequences. The story was first circulated by pro-Israeli accounts to describe the dimensions of the massacre perpetrated on 7/10, but very quickly the trend was reversed and the story was used to promote Hamas propaganda and claim that Israel is fabricating evidence and inflating the number of people murdered.*

Two lessons can be drawn from this case. The first is that we have uneducated, short-sighted magistrates who encourage misinformation and incitement to hatred, and discourage those who are critical of information. They act impulsively and without foresight—exactly the opposite of what their deontology should dictate, because it is behavior like theirs that is the root cause of radicalization.

### *The Baby in the Oven*

Figure 102—Quite unwittingly, our magistrates highlighted one of the most heinous crimes committeed by the Jews. It was carried out in 1948, during the massacre of the village of Deir Yassin, by Jewish militias, as testified by a survivor. [Source: https://youtu.be/Bwy-Rf15UIs?t=1498]

The second, more ironic, is that it allowed us to point the finger at a particularly heinous crime that did take place, but was committed by Jews. In fact, it is the French magistrates who should be condemned for apology for genocide, war crimes and terrorism.

### The Disemboweled Woman

On October 18, human rights lawyer Brooke Goldstein shared a video of a disemboweled woman on social networks, accompanied by a warning comment: *"This is the worst video I've ever seen in my life. This is what the Palestinian Hamas Nazis are doing to a pregnant woman."*

#### Video of the Disemboweled Woman

**Brooke Goldstein** ✓
@GoldsteinBrooke

WARNING: this is the worst video I have every seen in my life. This is what Palestinian Hamas Nazis do to a pregnant woman. Share it so the world sees what Israel must eliminate. Share it so that the Hamas Holocaust deniers are shown as frauds. Share it before it's taken down. Share it so the world sees what pro-Hamas groups on college campuses and on the street are celebrating. #HamasHolocaust

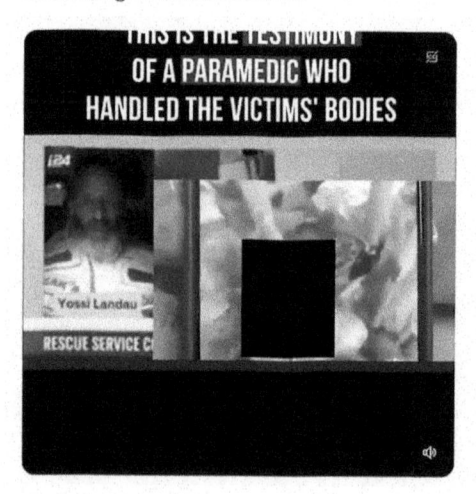

THIS IS THE TESTIMONY OF A PARAMEDIC WHO HANDLED THE VICTIMS' BODIES

Yossi Landau
RESCUE SERVICE C

9:20 PM · 18/10/2023 · **178K** Views

*Figure 103—Widely quoted and repeated in our media, the story of the disemboweled pregnant woman did not take place during the Hamas attack. It is based on a video dated January 17, 2018, which shows a criminal act committed by the Mexican organization "La Guardia Guerrerense." The post was subsequently deleted, but the rumor about this incident continues to circulate, particularly on TV platforms in France.*[447]

---

447. https://www.altnews.in/2018-mexico-video-falsely-viral-as-hamas-killing-pregnant-woman-unborn-child/

In fact, the only person who claims to have seen the disemboweled woman is Yossi Landau, a member of ZAKA, an Orthodox Jewish self-help organization,[448] who also claimed to have seen the babies' throats slit. But no one saw a disemboweled woman. Even officials at Kibbutz Be'eri, where the incident is said to have taken place, confirmed to the *Haaretz* newspaper that no one had any knowledge of it:

> *The kibbutz adds that "the story of the pregnant women reported by Zaka is not relevant to Be'eri." The police say they are not aware of the case, and a doctor at the Shura military base told Haaretz that he was not aware of the case.*[449]

The problem is that many of the accusations of atrocities against Hamas come from ZAKA. Yet this organization, seen by some Israeli journalists as a "militia,"[450] is notorious in Israel for fabrications and spreading false information.[451]

## *The Rapes*

Women and children are always the main innocent victims of conflict. They are indirect victims, through the effects of conflict on their living conditions, but often also direct victims of the effects of weapons and sexual violence. Violence against women in war is as old as mankind itself, and unfortunately we do not seem to have evolved much in this area (or in others).

It is a recurring theme in the information warfare of recent conflicts, and one that calls for a certain caution. In the context of Operation AL-AQSA FLOOD, the question of serial rape appeared rather late in our media, at the end of November 2023, which raises certain questions. The American media outlet *The Intercept* investigated and found that, curiously enough,

---

448. https://youtu.be/fX5s5yIdzS8?t=366
449. Nir HASSON, Liza ROZOVSKY, "Hamas Committed Documented Atrocities. But a Few False Stories Feed the Deniers," *Haaretz*, December 4, 2023 (https://www.haaretz.com/israel-news/2023-12-04/ty-article-magazine/.premium/hamas-committed-documented-atrocities-but-a-few-false-stories-feed-the-deniers/0000018c-34f3-da74-afce-b5fbe24f0000)
450. https://www.ynet.co.il/articles/0,7340,L-3046198,00.html
451. https://www.the7eye.org.il/29123

nothing was done the day after the Palestinian attack to accumulate evidence to support the Israeli government's accusations.[452]

Israeli feminist organizations accused the United Nations of ignoring the plight of women raped by Hamas. But this is irrelevant. As early as October 10, the United Nations set up a commission of inquiry into the crimes committed on October 7,[453] which called for testimonies, particularly concerning sexual violence.[454] On October 13, UN Women, the UN women's agency, issued a statement condemning the violence of October 7, without mentioning any rapes.[455] A week later, in a note assessing the humanitarian situation, UN Women made no mention of rape or sexual violence.[456]

For its part, Israel does not seem to be making it easy for those seeking to find evidence of sexual violence. Not only does Benjamin Netanyahu refuse the truces proposed by Hamas to exchange prisoners who could have saved women from possible ill-treatment,[457] but no measures are being taken to preserve possible evidence.[458] In early November, the Israeli media *YNet* noted that no effort was being made to collect evidence and preserve crime scenes for investigation.[459]

As *CNN* noted, what is special here is the absence of victims for the investigators, and the number of second- and third-hand accounts.

---

452. Judith LEVINE, "There Was No Cover-Up of Hamas's Sexual Violence on October 7," *The Intercept*, December 24, 2023 (https://theintercept.com/2023/12/24/feminism-sexual-violence-hamas-israel/)
453. Commission of Inquiry collecting evidence of war crimes committed by all sides in Israel and Occupied Palestinian Territories since 7 October 2023, United Nations, 10 October 2023 (https://www.ohchr.org/en/press-releases/2023/10/commission-inquiry-collecting-evidence-war-crimes-committed-all-sides-israel)
454. https://www.ohchr.org/en/hr-bodies/hrc/co-israel/call-submissions-international-crimes-7-october-2023
455. https://www.unwomen.org/en/news-stories/statement/2023/10/un-women-statement-on-the-situation-in-israel-and-the-occupied-palestinian-territory
456. https://www.unwomen.org/sites/default/files/2023-10/un-women-rapid-assessment-and-humanitarian-response-in-the-occupied-palestinian-territory-en.pdf
457. Ruth MICHAELSON, Julian BORGER & Emine SINMAZ, "Netanyahu rejected ceasefire-for-hostages deal in Gaza, sources say," *The Guardian*, November 9, 2023 (https://www.theguardian.com/world/2023/nov/09/netanyahu-rejected-ceasefire-for-hostages-deal-in-gaza-sources-say)
458. Bethan McKERNAN, "Israel women's groups warn of failure to keep evidence of sexual violence in Hamas attacks," *The Guardian*, November 10, 2023 (https://www.theguardian.com/world/2023/nov/10/israel-womens-groups-warn-of-failure-to-keep-evidence-of-sexual-violence-in-hamas-attacks)
459. https://www.ynet.co.il/news/article/yokra13660087#autoplay

*Police Superintendent Dudi Katz said officers had collected more than 1,000 statements and over 60,000 video clips about the attacks, including testimonies from people who had seen women being raped. He added that investigators did not have first-hand accounts, and it was unclear whether the rape victims had survived.[460]*

In other words, we have thousands of testimonies, but no victims. This is confirmed by the *Times of Israel*, which stated in early November that there was no evidence of rape and that the forensic doctors who examined the corpses had not detected any traces of rape:

*But in the wake of this event of unprecedented scale, no physical evidence of sexual assault has been collected from the corpses by Israel's overburdened forensic services, as part of efforts to identify those killed, most of whose bodies were mutilated and burned.[461]*

So apparently, not only are there no living victims, no post-mortem examinations, no videos made by witnesses whose reliability has not even been verified to confirm accusations of rape.

Behind this accusation of rape and the Israelis' inability to find proof of it lies the fact that the bodies were burnt *en masse*, indicating the use of weapons considerably more powerful than those used by Hamas. The extremely degraded state of the bodies and the difficulty of identifying them indicate that they were indeed victims of the Israeli army. Ironically, this accusation of rape is unfounded and reveals Israeli, not Palestinian, crimes.

On December 28, 2023, the *New York Times*[462] published an article on the October 7 rapes. Based on around 150 interviews, the article focuses on Gal Abdush, described as "the woman in the black dress." But at the beginning of January, the family of the main witness asked that the article be withdrawn, as the story had been invented:

---

460. https://www.cnn.com/2023/11/17/world/israel-investigates-sexual-violence-hamas/index.html
461. Carrie KELLER-LYNN, "Amid war and urgent need to ID bodies, evidence of Hamas's October 7 rapes slips away," *The Times of Israel*, November 9, 2023 ( (https://www.timesofisrael.com/amid-war-and-urgent-need-to-id-bodies-evidence-of-hamass-october-7-rapes-slips-away/)
462. Jeffrey GETTLEMAN, Anat SCHWARTZ & Adam SELLA, "'Screams Without Words': How Hamas Weaponized Sexual Violence on Oct. 7," *The New York Times*, December 28, 2023 (https://www.nytimes.com/2023/12/28/world/middleeast/oct-7-attacks-hamas-israel-sexual-violence.html)

> We knew nothing about the rape. We only found out after a reporter from the New York Times contacted us. They said they had compared the evidence and concluded that she had been sexually assaulted.[463]

Finally, after violent controversy both inside and outside the paper, the *New York Times* quietly withdrew the articles linked to these accusations.[464] We have documents showing that Hamas fighters fired on civilians, we have evidence that they captured civilians, but there is no document, evidence or test result to confirm the accusation of rape. It is possible that there were rapes that day, but there is no evidence to support it. This is the case of "Sapir," who is said to be the only witness who herself saw *"three other women being raped and terrorists carrying the severed heads of three other women."*[465] Yet not only, according to *Haaretz*, have the Israeli police been unable to identify and locate the victims of these rapes,[466] but there are no reports of any women being beheaded on October 7. American journalists Max Blumenthal and Aaron Maté of the alternative American media *The Grayzone* investigated these allegations and found them to be fabricated.[467]

Mass rape is an accusation often made in the information war, but rarely proven. We recall the case of Lyudmila Denisova, Ukrainian Commissioner for Human Rights,[468] who made such accusations against Russia in 2022. At the time, Swiss *RTS* claimed that these crimes had been carefully verified.[469] However, it was all false[470] and Denisova was sacked

---

463. https://www.ynet.co.il/news/article/hyfwvej006
464. Daniel Boguslaw & Ryan Grim, "New York Times Puts 'Daily' Episode on Ice Amid Internal Firestorm Over Hamas Sexual Violence Article," *The Intercept*, January 28, 2024 (https://theintercept.com/2024/01/28/new-york-times-daily-podcast-camera/)
465. Jeffrey Gettleman, Anat Schwartz & Adam Sella, "'Screams Without Words': How Hamas Weaponized Sexual Violence on Oct. 7," *The New York Times*, December 28, 2023 (updated January 25, 2024) (https://www.nytimes.com/2023/12/28/world/middleeast/oct-7-attacks-hamas-israel-sexual-violence.html)
466. https://www.haaretz.co.il/news/law/2024-01-04/ty-article/.premium/0000018c-d3e4-ddba-abad-d3e502980000?gift=0d660f6ae8134267b732f295253d7d35
467. https://thegrayzone.com/2024/01/10/questions-nyt-hamas-rape-report/
468. https://www.francetvinfo.fr/monde/europe/manifestations-en-ukraine/guerre-en-ukraine-apres-le-massacre-de-boutcha-les-temoignages-glacants-des-victimes-de-viols-commis-par-l-occupant-russe_5145007.htm
469. https://www.rts.ch/audio-podcast/2022/audio/multiplication-des-accusations-de-viols-en-ukraine-interview-de-lea-rose-stoian-25813937.html
470. https://hromadske.ua/posts/deputati-zibrali-pidpisi-za-vidstavku-ombudsmenki-denisovoyi-vona-nazivaye-mozhlive-zvilnennya-nezakonnim

because her accusations were not proven and her allegations damaged Ukraine's image, according to Ukrainian media outlet *Ukrinform*.[471]

In the case of Gaza, we seem to be in the same situation once again. The problem here is that the Israeli authorities understand that their only way of justifying their disproportionate reaction is to show that their adversary is even more brutal. Behind these allegations lies a strategic issue, which explains why Israel refuses to investigate these crimes.

It is likely that these investigations will only uncover lies. The testimonies of victims who came into contact with Hamas fighters seem to contradict a criminal intent and uncontrolled brutality. What is more, the Hamas attack was short-lived and of an intensity that probably did not give the fighters the "leisure" to indulge in such crimes.

---

471. https://www.ukrinform.fr/rubric-ato/3496821-la-commissaire-aux-droits-de-lhomme-ukrainienne-demise-de-ses-fonctions.html

# 6. The Israeli Response —Operation SWORDS OF IRON

## The Initial Response

The initial response to the Palestinian attack on October 7 was chaotic, with no plan of action, and improvised adaptations of orders and procedures designed for a much smaller threat.

More than the surprise effect—which can never be totally avoided—the inability to react is a sign of intelligence that is profoundly ignorant of the reality of the Palestinian movements and their capabilities, and of conduct that lacks flexibility.

A contingency plan is not a precise forecast of what might happen, but rather the preparation of orders, usually simplified, to react to uncertain developments in the situation. The disorganized reaction to the Palestinian action was all the more inexcusable in that the structure of the forces involved in monitoring the "Gaza envelope" had been altered by redeployment to the West Bank. It was this series of errors of conduct that caused the vast majority of the day's deaths, rather than Hamas.

Such was the chaos that the Israeli authorities were unable to count the number of Hamas fighters killed that day, and it took them more than a month to realize that there were at least 200 Palestinians among the charred victims of that day.

## The Plan of Action

In the two weeks following October 7, Israel had no strategy and clearly no contingency plan. The response was limited to massive air and artillery strikes. By this stage, the Israelis had killed more than three times the number of children killed in 20 months of war by the Ukrainians and Russians combined.

After hesitating to intervene with troops in the Gaza Strip, the Israeli government has defined a three-phase strategy:[472]

- The first phase is to take control of the northern part of the Gaza Strip, including Gaza City, where Hamas is believed to have its leadership structure. The aim is to destroy this leadership structure, first with air strikes, then with a ground assault.
- The second phase is the elimination of pockets of resistance through infantry combat.
- The third phase is the installation of new structures in the Gaza Strip, and the withdrawal of Israeli forces.

## Unclear Objectives

Every strategy needs objectives. But these objectives have never been very clear: there is talk of freeing the hostages, decapitating Hamas (i.e., eliminating its leaders), destroying Hamas (i.e., destroying its military and civilian capabilities), destroying the Al-Qassam Brigades (i.e., destroying Hamas's military capabilities), eliminating the population of Gaza and moving them to a third country. In short, we can see that the Israeli leadership is vacillating between feasibility, acceptability and ideology in its approach to the issue.

On October 14, 2023, on the *LCI* television channel, Bernard-Henri Lévy declared that the Israeli military had "*all*" told him they had three objectives: to decapitate Hamas, save the hostages and spare the civilian population of Gaza.[473] However, at the end of December, Hamas still had

---

472. Emanuel FABIAN, "Israel sets out 3 phases of war; will seek new 'security regime' once Hamas vanquished," *The Times of Israel*, October 20, 2023 (https://www.timesofisrael.com/gallant-says-after-hamas-vanquished-israel-will-seek-new-security-regime-in-gaza/)
473. https://youtu.be/C27c31qr9A8

full leadership capacity,[474] the only dead hostages had been killed by the Israeli army,[475] and not only had the civilian population of Gaza suffered the most violent strikes seen anywhere in the world for two decades, but they had been hit in areas declared "safe" by the Israeli army.

> *On Thursday, an Israeli strike destroyed a house in Muwasi, a small rural strip on Gaza's southern coast that the Israeli army had declared a safe zone. The explosion killed at least 12 people, according to Palestinian hospital officials. Among the dead were a man and his wife, seven of their children and three other children aged between 5 and 14, according to a list of the dead that arrived at Nasser Hospital in the nearby town of Khan Yunis.*[476]

The problem with Israel's response is that it is short-term. When it comes to fighting terrorism, violence may seem tempting, but the question always remains: "What next?"

In fact, unlike Western countries, the United States was quick to become concerned about the nature of Israeli planning in response to the Palestinian operation.[477] Despite the fact that they actively support Israel, notably by supplying arms, the Americans are concerned about the turn of events. They have always had an ambiguous attitude towards Israeli policy. Anxious to maintain good relations with the Gulf monarchies, they have been the main driving force behind the various peace initiatives in the region, but have also always been unconditional supporters of Israel.

This is why, apparently, the United States had approved an initial Israeli plan to push the Gazan population towards Egypt, then raze Gaza to the ground in order to eliminate all Palestinian fighters once and for all. But faced with firm opposition from Arab countries, the USA urged Israel to scale down its ambitions.

---

474. "Hamas 'far from collapsing' in north Gaza: Israeli media," *The Cradle*, November 27, 2023 (https://new.thecradle.co/articles-id/13815)
475. "Hamas armed wing: More than 60 hostages are missing due to Israeli airstrikes," *Reuters*, November 4, 2023 (https://www.reuters.com/world/middle-east/hamas-armed-wing-more-than-60-hostages-are-missing-due-israeli-airstrikes-2023-11-04/)
476. Najib Jobain, Julia Frankel & Jack Jeffery, "Israeli defense minister lays out vision for next steps of Gaza war ahead of Blinken visit," *Associated Press*, January 5, 2024 (https://apnews.com/article/israel-hamas-war-news-01-03-2024-3b77b0c36bf2cd9922b7a484234bef5f)
477. Helene Cooper, Adam Entous & Eric Schmitt, "U.S. Raises Concerns About Israel's Plan of Action in Gaza, Officials Say," *The New York Times*, October 23, 2023 (updated October 31, 2023) (https://www.nytimes.com/2023/10/23/us/politics/israel-us-gaza-invasion.html)

## Preparatory Phase

Immediately after the start of the Hamas operation, it was clear that Israel had to retaliate. The problem is how. In Ukraine, civilians had left Bakhmut, a small pre-war town of some 50,000 inhabitants, before the fighting. But in Gaza, a vast urbanized area measuring 10x36 km on each side and home to between 2 and 3 million people, the situation is more complex.

The Israelis took the immediate step of laying siege to the Palestinians. Yoav Gallant, Minister of Defense, ordered a "complete siege" of the Gaza Strip: "*no electricity, no food, no fuel, everything is* closed:"[478]

*We fight human animals and act accordingly.*

These words rightly shocked the Arab world and the world at large—he used exactly the same terms as Heinrich Himmler did for the Jews.[479]

Although Israel did not define it as such, this phase was intended to configure the battlefield for the subsequent phases of Operation SWORDS OF IRON. In essence, the aim was to push the civilian population southwards, so that they would not interfere with military operations, and thus ensure that the only Palestinians on the ground were combatants.

But the brutality of the Israeli response prompted the international community, and the United States in particular, to call for the creation of humanitarian corridors to enable civilians to evacuate the Gaza City area. This did not prevent the Israeli army from striking these humanitarian convoys attempting to flee to the south.[480] Here again, the balance between tactical and strategic objectives did not seem to influence Israeli conduct. This would be fatal for them in January 2024, with the decision of the International Court of Justice.

---

478. Emanuel FABIAN, "Defense minister announces 'complete siege' of Gaza: No power, food or fuel," *The Times of Israel*, October 9, 2023 (https://www.timesofisrael.com/liveblog_entry/defense-minister-announces-complete-siege-of-gaza-no-power-food-or-fuel/)
479. https://www.jewishvirtuallibrary.org/remarks-by-himmler
480. Paul BROWN & Jemimah HERD, "Strike on civilian convoy fleeing Gaza: What we know from verified video," *BBC News*, October 16, 2023 (https://www.bbc.com/news/world-middle-east-67114281)

## Operation SWORDS OF IRON—Preparatory Phase

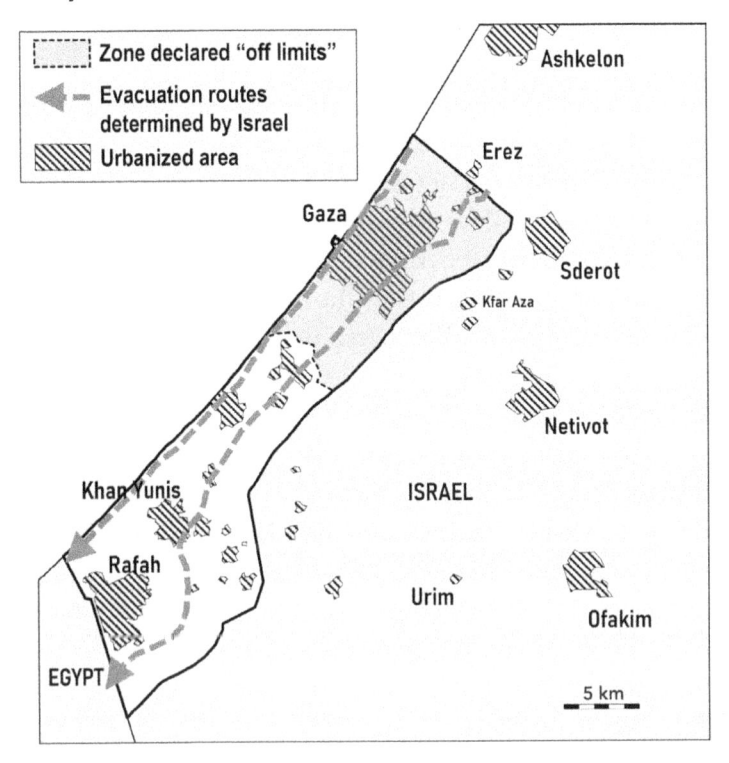

*Figure 104—In preparation for phase 1, the Israelis sought to push the Gazans southwards. The northern part of the Gaza Strip was declared "off-limits" and massive bombardments were carried out simultaneously.*

Although our media only mention Hamas fighters, Palestinian defenders were drawn from all the militias and groups we have seen above. The groups coordinated by the JOR acted according to an overall plan, while the other groups appeared to act independently according to local coordination, based on personal relationships.

The problem for the Israelis was that not all civilians were willing or able to move. Fear of not returning to their homes, or of abandoning elderly relatives unable to move, meant that entire families remained in the northern part of the territory.

## Phase 1: Takeover

The aim of this phase was to destroy Hamas's leadership structures, which the Israeli services had located in Gaza City.

Initially, Israeli troops targeted Gaza's hospitals, which were supposedly used by Hamas as bases for operations. Indiscriminate bombardments were then carried out against Gaza City and the northern part of the territory.

The ground offensive followed two axes: one from north to south along the coast in the direction of the Al-Shifa refugee camp, and the other from east to west to the south of Gaza City; the aim was to cut the city off from the rest of the Gaza Strip in order to trap the Hamas leadership.

### The Hospital War

For reasons that are unclear, Israel was convinced that a *"large number"* of Palestinians used hospitals *"as bases for planning terrorist activities and carrying out attacks."*[481] This is possible, but until the end of January 2024, Israeli forces failed to find evidence of this allegation after taking control of hospitals in the northern Gaza Strip. Apart from the fact that this tends to demonstrate faulty military intelligence, their repetition reasonably suggests that this is no more than a pretext to justify acts contrary to international law.

From the outset of Operation SWORDS OF IRON, the Israeli aim was to "empty" the Gaza Strip of its occupants—first the civilian population, then the Palestinian fighters. The problem was that, with the Israeli strikes, hospitals had become an essential infrastructure holding back the population. They therefore had to be destroyed or rendered inoperative in order to push the Gazans southwards.

Israel claimed that the Indonesian hospital housed a base used by Hamas to launch rockets into Israel.[482] This information was firmly denied by the Indonesian government, which funds its operation, and MER-C, the charitable organization that runs it.[483]

---

481. "Cisjordanie: un commando israélien tue trois membres du Hamas et du Jihad islamique dans un hôpital," *franceinfo / AFP*, January 30, 2024 (https://www.francetvinfo.fr/monde/proche-orient/israel-palestine/cisjordanie-occupee-trois-terroristes-palestiniens-tues-dans-un-raid-israelien-sur-un-hopital_6334144.html)
482. Emanuel Fabian, "IDF releases new intel detailing Hamas use of Gaza hospitals for terror purposes," *The Times of Israel*, November 5, 2023 (https://www.timesofisrael.com/idf-releases-new-intel-detailing-hamas-use-of-gaza-hospitals-for-terror-purposes/)
483. "IDF says Hamas using Indonesian Hospital to hide terror base; Jakarta pushes back," *AFP/ The Times of Israel*, November 7, 2023 (https://www.timesofisrael.com/jakarta-pushes-back-as-idf-says-hamas-using-indonesian-hospital-to-hide-terror-base/)

On October 17, the explosion of a missile in the immediate vicinity of the al-Ahli Arab hospital[484] caused between a few dozen and more than 500 casualties. Israel was suspected of having targeted the hospital, but quickly responded that it was a Palestinian Islamic Jihad (PIJ) missile that had malfunctioned. In support of its allegations, the Israeli government showed an image of a PIJ rocket salvo taken at 6.58 pm.[485] This was the version used by our media.[486]

Because, of course, they only listen to Israel. They failed to mention that just after the attack, Hananya Naftali, former adviser to Benjamin Netanyahu, declared on his X account that *"the Israeli air force struck a Hamas base located in a hospital in Gaza."* Her tweet was quickly deleted.

On a more technical level, the strike took place at 7.20 pm, around twenty minutes after the video presented by the Israeli forces. This is why their tweet was deleted and replaced by another without video,[487] indicating potential manipulation.[488]

Our media naturally also failed to mention that this same hospital was hit directly three days earlier by Israeli aircraft.[489] According to the Archbishop of Canterbury, head of the Anglican Church in charge of the hospital, Israeli soldiers had telephoned the hospital on October 15 to order its evacuation.[490] His words were confirmed by Hosam Naoum, Anglican Bishop of Jerusalem, who stated that the hospital had received evacuation orders before the explosion on October 17.[491] Such orders were given to all hospitals in the Gaza Strip, and on October 14, the World Health Organization (WHO) issued a statement declaring that *"Israel's*

---

484. https://english.iswnews.com/31150/israel-or-palestinian-resistance-who-is-responsible-for-air-strike-on-al-ahli-arab-hospital/
485. https://www.facebook.com/IsraelinSwitzerland/videos/idf-spokespersonfrom-the-analysis-of-the-operational-systems-of-the-idf-an-enemy/1312447709392892/
486. https://www.rts.ch/info/monde/14396268-des-centaines-de-victimes-suite-a-une-frappe-sur-un-hopital-de-gaza-annonce-le-hamas.html
487. https://twitter.com/Israel/status/1714371894521057737?lang=en
488. "Deleted Israeli Video Adds to Confusion Around Gaza Hospital Blast," *Newsweek*, October 17, 2023 (updated October 18, 2023) (https://www.newsweek.com/deleted-israeli-video-adds-confusion-around-gaza-hospital-blast-1835596)
489. "Anglican-run al-Ahli Arab Hospital in Gaza damaged by Israeli rocket fire as war continues," *Anglican Communion News Service*, October 16, 2023 (https://www.anglicannews.org/news/2023/10/anglican-run-al-ahli-arab-hospital-in-gaza-damaged-by-israeli-rocket-fire-as-conflict-continues.aspx)
490. https://www.channel4.com/news/who-was-behind-the-gaza-hospital-blast-visual-investigation
491. https://apnews.com/article/israel-palestinians-gaza-hospital-explosion-3d255725997c4e-2757372b3ee2fc8859

*orders to evacuate hospitals in the northern Gaza Strip are a death sentence for the sick and wounded,*" and that it would not be possible to carry them out within the timeframe ordered and with the means available.[492] Thus we knew that Israel was planning to hit these hospitals.

In order to present their version of events, the Israeli forces published a short video which brought together the various incriminating elements.[493] On the basis of these elements and the available videos of the incident, *Forensic Architecture,* from the University of London, was able to reconstruct a 3D model and demonstrate that it was indeed an Israeli strike.[494]

In addition, a sound analysis of the projectile's arrival at the hospital was carried out by the NGO *Earshot.ngo*, which specializes in investigating humanitarian issues. The analysis is based on the Doppler effect, which makes it possible to determine the direction of the projectile's trajectory.

Finally, the "proof" provided by the Israeli authorities was the recording of a telephone conversation allegedly between two Hamas officials who noted the failed firing of a rocket and who then attribute it to the PIJ.[495] *Earshot.ngo*'s forensic analysis shows that this recording exhibits such a level of manipulation that its evidential value is hardly credible.[496] Clearly, the Israeli authorities were lying.

The Israelis were trying to prove that the medical infrastructure in the Gaza Strip was used by Hamas for military purposes. They needed to find legitimacy to strike indiscriminately at hospitals, places of worship and the entire population.

Soon enough, their attention turned to the al-Shifa hospital, located close to the coast and not far from the al-Shati refugee camp. Israel claimed it housed Hamas' main command post.[497]

The reason they were so sure is that they knew it well. The hospital was built in 1946 under the British mandate and then modernized by the Egyptians. From June 1967, the Gaza Strip was occupied by the Israelis, who built a command post under al-Shifa hospital—to use their own

---

492. https://www.who.int/news/item/14-10-2023-evacuation-orders-by-israel-to-hospitals-in-northern-gaza-are-a-death-sentence-for-the-sick-and-injured
493. https://youtu.be/nEe8pawDMBo
494. https://youtu.be/wVk7c125pMM
495. https://twitter.com/IDFSpokesperson/status/1714541413944250869
496. https://twitter.com/Channel4News/status/1715437877604049094
497. Kevin Liptak, "White House says intelligence shows Hamas using al-Shifa hospital for command node, storing weapons," *CNN*, November 14, 2023 (https://edition.cnn.com/2023/11/14/politics/white-house-hamas-al-shifa/index.html)

population as human shields.[498] This is why the Israelis accused Hamas of using these facilities in every operation they carried out against the Gaza Strip, as in 2009[499] and 2014.[500] But Hamas has always denied using Gaza's health infrastructure for military purposes. Despite this, Israeli army spokesman Daniel Hagari asserted:

> *The IDF has published extensive and irrefutable evidence of Hamas's misuse of the Al-Shifa hospital complex for terrorist purposes and clandestine terrorist activities.*[501]

To convince us of this, the Israeli army produced a 3D animation showing a sophisticated command post located beneath the hospital. It was also claimed that a network of tunnels leading to the command post and various Hamas facilities were accessible from inside the hospital. The case is reminiscent of Osama bin Laden's underground command post at Tora-Bora, which nobody has ever found. But the important thing is that morons believe it. Such is the case with David Pujadas, who did not hesitate to say that *"this is one of Hamas' headquarters!"*[502] Despite his affirmative tone, he did not know a thing about it and was merely repeating disinformation, the only effect of which was be to ridicule Israel later on.

Demonstrating this violation of IHL by Hamas was of strategic importance to Israel, whose bombing campaign was beginning to arouse disgust and criticism around the world. Israeli troops were therefore pushing rapidly towards the hospital to prove their allegations.

Initially, they tried to break through from the north along the coast. But with the resistance encountered at the refugee camp, they attempted a breakthrough from the south.

The Israeli army shot a video after taking the hospital, in order to justify the attack on the medical center. According to Swiss *RTS*, the video was unedited.[503] But this is not true. In fact, the final version of this video was cut

---

498. https://www.tabletmag.com/sections/news/articles/top-secret-hamas-command-bunker-in-gaza-revealed
499. https://www.nytimes.com/2009/01/11/world/middleeast/11hamas.html
500. https://www.wnd.com/2014/07/hamas-leaders-believed-hunkered-underneath-gaza-hospital/
501. Louisa Loveluck, Evan Hill, Jonathan Baran, Jarrett Ley & Ellen Nakashima, "The case of al-Shifa: Investigating the assault on Gaza's largest hospital," *The Washington Post*, December 21, 2023 (https://www.washingtonpost.com/world/2023/12/21/al-shifa-hospital-gaza-hamas-israel/)
502. https://youtu.be/nJGwggFlyVI?t=42
503. https://www.rts.ch/play/tv/-/video/-?urn=urn:rts:video:14475793&startTime=838

by 20 seconds, because the computer "discovered" by the Israeli military showed the image of a young Israeli military woman in the background![504] But our media would remain very discreet about this falsification.

In another video, the Israeli army spokesman shows us around:[505] two toilets, a small kitchen, a few empty air-conditioned rooms. No access to the tunnel from the hospital was shown. What the Israeli officer did show us was that the soldiers had to dig to access the hospital, and that its exit was blocked by scree. In other words, Hamas militants could not have used it, and the empty premises seemed to demonstrate that Hamas was not lying and was not using these tunnels. In fact, the Israeli news channel *i24 News* itself stated that the *"access shafts to the tunnels or basements inside the hospital were blocked with concrete by Hamas. The army brought in tanks to guard the area and bulldozers to try to open these shafts."*[506] This means that the Israeli army attacked the Al-Shifa hospital without knowing what was inside it, purely on the basis of presumptions. In terms of international humanitarian law, this is clearly a war crime.

As the *Washington Post*[507] noted:
- The parts connected to the network of tunnels discovered by IDF troops showed no evidence of military use by Hamas.
- None of the five hospital buildings identified by Daniel Hagari appeared to be connected to the tunnel network.
- There is no indication that the tunnels can be accessed from inside the hospital wards.

Not surprisingly, the narrative quickly collapsed. The video produced by the Israeli army[508] showed a few Kalashnikov rifles (which could very well had been placed there by the Israeli military themselves), military equipment for one (1!) Hamas fighter, a laptop on (whose background has been "blurred") and a stack of CD-ROMs. Problems: in an earlier version of the Israeli film, the screen was not blurred and we recognize—an Israeli soldier! As for the laptop, it is a *Lenovo ThinkPad TP490*—which has no CD-ROM drive.

---

504. https://www.youtube.com/watch?v=I4nIQPQIgvw
505. https://youtu.be/TUeZ5HKSfIo
506. https://twitter.com/i24NEWS_EN/status/1725034772760498244
507. Louisa Loveluck, Evan Hill, Jonathan Baran, Jarrett Ley & Ellen Nakashima, "The case of al-Shifa: Investigating the assault on Gaza's largest hospital," *The Washington Post*, December 21, 2023 (https://www.washingtonpost.com/world/2023/12/21/al-shifa-hospital-gaza-hamas-israel/)
508. https://youtu.be/QFmYWkquozk

The video of a crying nurse claiming that Hamas was operating in al-Shifa hospital and stealing food and medicine was a "fake" created by the Israeli army, as demonstrated by the *France 24* TV channel.[509] In reality, even after several days of Israeli occupation, there was no evidence that the hospital housed a Hamas command post. The documents presented by the Israeli army were very primitive falsifications.[510] As a *BBC* journalist who was able to visit the site (but who was not authorized to speak to hospital staff)[511] put it, Israel is clearly seeking to justify its war crimes.

In a word, the Israelis did not find anything; but the point was to provide an explanation for cutting off the hospital's electricity and bombing it repeatedly. As the Chinese strategist Sun-Tsu said 2,500 years ago, it is always dangerous to think your opponent is stupider than you. The existence of this "command post" is so well known that Hamas did not use it. Quite simply.

President Biden had supported the action by Israeli troops against the hospital[512] because of the presence of the Hamas command center.[513] But faced with the failure of the Israeli action, the White House back-pedaled and declared that it had never given Netanyahu the green light to attack the hospital.[514]

The Israeli insistence on demonstrating the Hamas presence in al-Shifa hospital obscured the fact that Israel specifically targets hospitals in the occupied territories.

## *The Tunnel War*

Every time Israel strikes a medical facility where women and children are being treated, it justifies its fire by claiming that Hamas fighters are

---

509. https://youtu.be/nQ-CxCEELmQ
510. https://youtu.be/5edJmnbe0h0
511. https://youtu.be/qNzWbP64Nmw
512. Nidal AL-MUGHRABI & Trevor HUNNICUTT, "U.S. backs claim Hamas uses Gaza hospitals as military cover amid hopes for hostages' release," *Reuters*, November 15, 2023 (https://www.reuters.com/world/middle-east/biden-says-gaza-hospitals-must-be-protected-2023-11-14/)
513. "Israel-Gaza war: US says Hamas has command center under Al-Shifa hospital," *BBC News*, November 14, 2023 (https://www.bbc.com/news/world-middle-east-67414091)
514. Sarah KOLINOVSKY, "White House denies US OK'd Israeli raid on Al Shifa Hospital in Gaza," *ABC News*, November 15, 2023 (https://abcnews.go.com/Politics/white-house-denies-us-okd-israeli-raid-al/story?id=104816260)

hiding there. This is particularly true of the Indonesian hospital. An accusation firmly refuted by Indonesia.[515]

In fact, it seems that the networks are more complex than the Israeli military imagined. There are relatively large tunnels, which are also intended to enable the civilian population to escape from the rubble of destroyed buildings. There are networks of logistical tunnels, housing strategically-placed ammunition depots and workshops. Finally, there are combat tunnels, which are a kind of underground trench used to get from one part of the battlefield to another. These battle tunnels are often dug very quickly, depending on the position of the Israelis.

By definition, tunnels are defensive installations, demonstrating that Hamas is a resistance organization.

In early December, the Israeli command decided to flood the underground tunnels with seawater. Despite the reluctance of some, concerned about the lives of the hostages, pumps were brought to the Gaza beach. But the quantities of water required were enormous, and the Israelis were unable to complete the project, despite enthusiastic declarations.[516] In January 2024, the *Wall Street Journal* noted that these attempts had failed, as Palestinian engineers had placed watertight doors in the tunnels to prevent flooding and the use of toxic products.

In fact, the tunnels are located at a wide range of depths, up to more than 80 m below ground, and the effect of bombing is virtually nil at these depths. At the end of January 2024, the *Wall Street Journal* and the Israeli newspaper *Israel Hayom* reported that 80% of the tunnel network was intact. In other words, the Israelis had destroyed thousands of homes and killed tens of thousands of innocent people for absolutely nothing at all—and they knew it.[517]

In the end, the Israeli military found nothing. We were shown an empty tunnel, leading nowhere, which the Israeli military were only able to access after blowing up the concrete slab covering the entrance: there were two toilets and a small kitchen, nothing resembling a headquar-

---

515. "IDF says Hamas using Indonesian Hospital to hide terror base; Jakarta pushes back," *The Times of Israel*, November 7, 2023 (https://www.timesofisrael.com/jakarta-pushes-back-as-idf-says-hamas-using-indonesian-hospital-to-hide-terror-base/)

516. Emanuel FABIAN, "IDF trial of flooding Hamas tunnels with seawater proves successful, ToI to," *The Times of Israel*, December 15, 2023 (https://www.timesofisrael.com/idf-trial-of-flooding-hamas-tunnels-with-seawater-proves-successful-toi-told/)

517. "WSJ: 80% of Hamas tunnel system remains intact ", *i24NEWS/Israel Hayom*, January 28, 2024 (https://www.israelhayom.com/2024/01/28/wall-street-journal-80-of-hamas-tunnel-system-remains-intact/)

ters.[518] A few videos shot in hospital basements attempted to demonstrate their use as command posts, but the demonstration was unconvincing and elicited mockery.[519] Parodies flourish on the net, and Israel failed to justify its violent bombing campaign.

As early as November, Israel claimed that the Hamas leadership center was in Khan Yunis and began an operation in the area. Apparently, it found nothing there either. Clearly, not only did Israel have no strategy, it did not know where to strike.

### The Israelis were Certain that the Hostages were in the Hospitals.

> **Aviva Klompas** @AvivaKlompas
>
> Found in the basement of Rantisi Children's Hospital in Gaza, a schedule showing the names of Hamas terrorists who guarded the hostages.
>
> Every name on this list is a dead man walking.
>
> 1:01 PM · 11/13/23 from Earth · **110K** Views

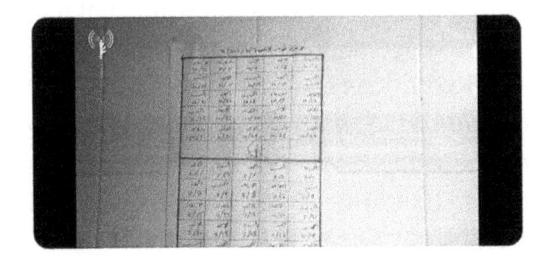

Figure 105—According to Israeli propaganda, this work plan represents the Hamas terrorists' guard towers for the hostages. Aviva Klompas even adds that "every name on this list is a death waiting to happen." But a closer look reveals that these are simply the days of the week...
[Source: tweet by Aviva Klompas—deleted]

It soon became clear that the Israelis were losing ground. They had a clear material and numerical superiority, but were unable to control the areas they occupied. The total length of the tunnel network is estimated

---

518. https://youtu.be/9IwwSNLaRtw
519. https://www.youtube.com/shorts/KjBCcjb9PG4

at 500 km, of which only 20% has been affected by Israeli operations, according to the *Wall Street Journal*.[520]

## Phase 2: Eliminating Pockets of Resistance

### Objective: Hamas Leadership

One of the Israeli government's objectives is the destruction of Hamas's leadership structure, in order to eradicate the organization. However, a little under two months later, when Israeli strikes had killed some 16,000 people, Israeli troops occupied a large part of Gaza City and had taken over what they consider to be the Hamas headquarters under the Al-Shifa hospital, a ceasefire agreement was reached.

Hamas's weapons then fell silent simultaneously throughout the area of operations. Next, Hamas was able to collect prisoners for exchange, then release them in a perfectly coordinated fashion at different points in the ruined city.

This means that not only does Hamas have a highly decentralized leadership structure that has nothing to do with what the Israeli military has in mind, but that it is perfectly operational, despite Israeli destruction and war crimes. In military terms, this means that its C3I (*Command, Control, Communications & Intelligence*) is perfectly functional. The Palestinians communicate via wired telephone networks, invulnerable to Israeli electronic countermeasures. Paradoxically, their simplicity makes them more robust.

In other words, once again, Israeli intelligence was unable to understand its adversaries' way of thinking. This is largely the reason why, three months after the start of Operation SWORDS OF IRON, despite the destruction and claims of "absolute operational control" in certain areas of northern Gaza, the Israeli army was unable to maintain a permanent presence there.

In some cases, Israeli soldiers saw the rockets leave just a few meters from their position to strike Israel. We can see that:
- The Palestinian fighters did not seem to be handicapped by the Israeli presence and seem to move freely in a terrain they know very well.
- The Palestinian leadership structures seem to be working perfectly. Ambushes and other actions against Israeli troops are perfectly

---

520. "WSJ: 80% of Hamas tunnel system remains intact," *Israel Hayom*, January 28, 2024 (https://www.israelhayom.com/2024/01/28/wall-street-journal-80-of-hamas-tunnel-system-remains-intact/)

coordinated. Complex actions, such as ambushes carried out by several commandos against Israeli units in tunnels 30 m underground, are perfectly coordinated with troops on the surface. There are even concentric ambushes on Israeli troops from several separate tunnel networks, indicating intact leadership capabilities.

As a result, Israel has no control over the situation anywhere in the northern Gaza Strip. In fact, on January 1st, 2024, one minute after midnight, Hamas fired 27 rockets against Tel Aviv from this area. Al-Quds Units attacked an Israeli base with six rockets. The base was equipped with electronic listening and detection systems. The Ali Abu Mustafa Brigades attacked an APACHE attack helicopter in the same area.

As the Israeli operation progresses, one gets the feeling that the Palestinian forces are in their element. They have drawn the Israelis into their territory and seem to be able to move quite freely to their rear. They film all their engagements by means of rifle- or head-mounted cameras. In some cases, a cameraman follows the fighter—they use the same tunnel to approach the Israelis and then leave again.

On January 6, 2024, Lieutenant-General Herzi Halevi, Chief of Staff of the IDF, and Ronen Bar, Director of SHABAK, were in Khan Yunis to visit a Hamas tunnel,[521] to demonstrate the successes of the Israeli army. Hamas chose this moment to launch a massive rocket attack on Tel Aviv from Khan Yunis. Its usual tactic is to fire once, then quickly leave the position before Israeli counter-battery fire. But this time, the Palestinians fired their rockets, slowly, one after the other, as if to show that despite the presence of Israel's top generals, they had complete control of the area.

On January 29, the 115th day of the operation, the Palestinians fired 15 rockets from an undisclosed location in Gaza against Tel Aviv and central Israel. In other words, the Palestinians show that their operational capabilities have not been reached. In other words, Israel's strategy has failed—it has only led to the stigmatization of unsavory practices contrary to international law, without providing a military solution. This illustrates the point of this book—that Israel and the West have never been able to devise effective strategies against insurgencies in the Near and Middle East, other than by massacre.

---

521. Yonah Jeremy Bob & Gadi Zaig, "IDF, Shin Bet chiefs visit tunnels in heart of Khan Yunis," *The Jerusalem Post*, January 6, 2024 (https://www.jpost.com/israel-hamas-war/article-781089)

In fact, we can see that the individual training of the Israeli military has not prepared them for this type of combat. Urban combat, particularly in a city like Gaza, is extremely demanding both physically and mentally. It often turns into individual combat, where you have to be attentive to every detail, as any object or debris can constitute a danger.

Israeli soldiers are trained to fight in small units, but not in individual combat. This explains why, when we analyze the ranks of Israeli soldiers killed, we find a high proportion of cadres (officers 26%, non-commissioned officers 19%)[522] eliminated by Palestinian snipers. Whereas the Palestinians operate with a highly decentralized leadership, Israeli soldiers lack individual initiative and tend to group together, making them easy targets for Hamas guerrillas.

Ill-prepared, soldiers tend to stay in their armored vehicles for hours on end. But an unprotected armored vehicle in an urban area becomes easy prey, especially for Hamas's "zero range" weapons.[523]

## Step 1: Isolating Gaza

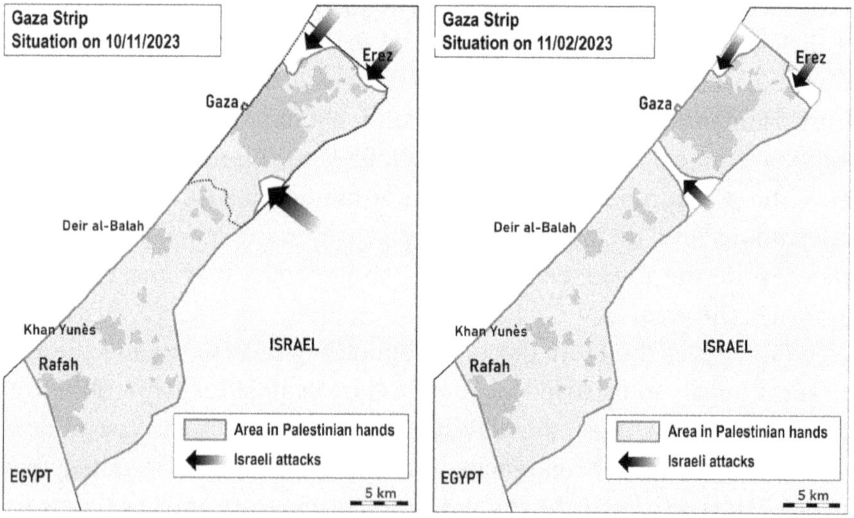

*Figure 106—Initially, the Israeli army sought to isolate Gaza City, where it believed it would find the leadership of Hamas. It advanced along the coast and into the uninhabited part of the Gaza Strip.*

---

522. https://www.timesofisrael.com/authorities-name-44-soldiers-30-police-officers-killed-in-hamas-attack/

523. https://alkhanadeq.org.lb/post/6364/ال‬‎‫التحام-الجيش-الاسرائيلي-المتكارث-الفشل-في-ضمن-ضغي

## The Push to Hospitals

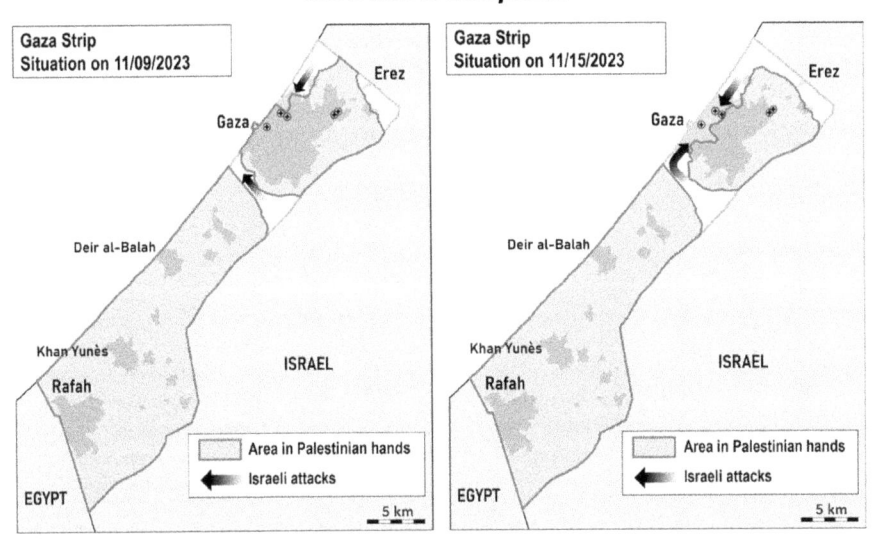

*Figure 107—Convinced that the Hamas leadership was hiding in the hospitals (black dots), the Israelis pushed towards Al-Shifa hospital, the city's largest.*

## Cleaning up Gaza City

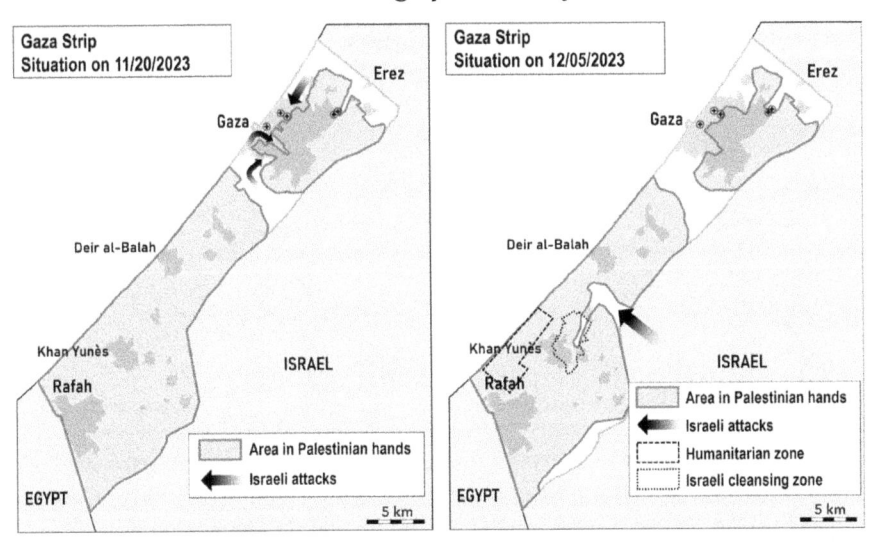

*Figure 108—With the occupation of the hospitals proving that Hamas's statements were correct, despite a vast propaganda campaign that attracted more ridicule on social networks than conviction, Israel was attempting to do the same in the Khan Yunis sector, where the population had taken refuge.*

## Cleaning up Khan Yunis

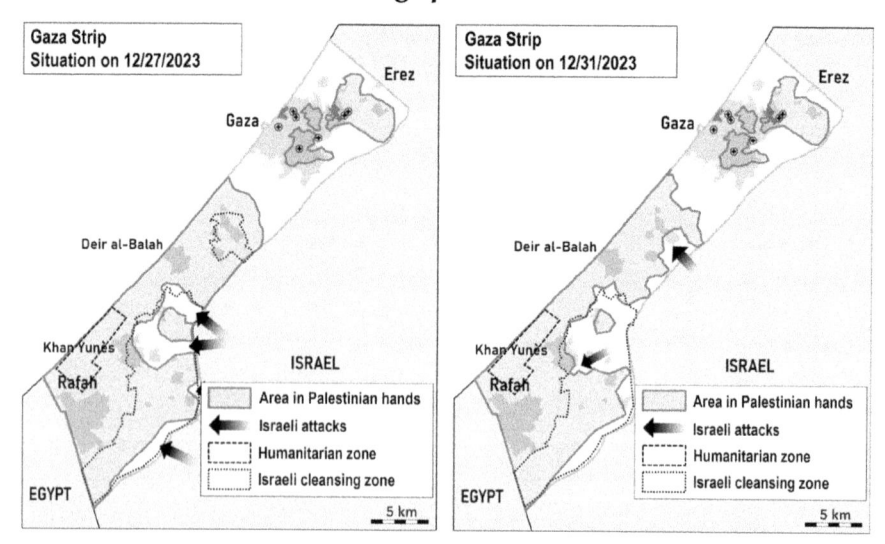

Figure 109—In Khan Yunis, Israeli forces faced fierce and remarkably agile resistance.

## The Failure of Khan Yunis and the Beginnings of a Gaza Withdrawal

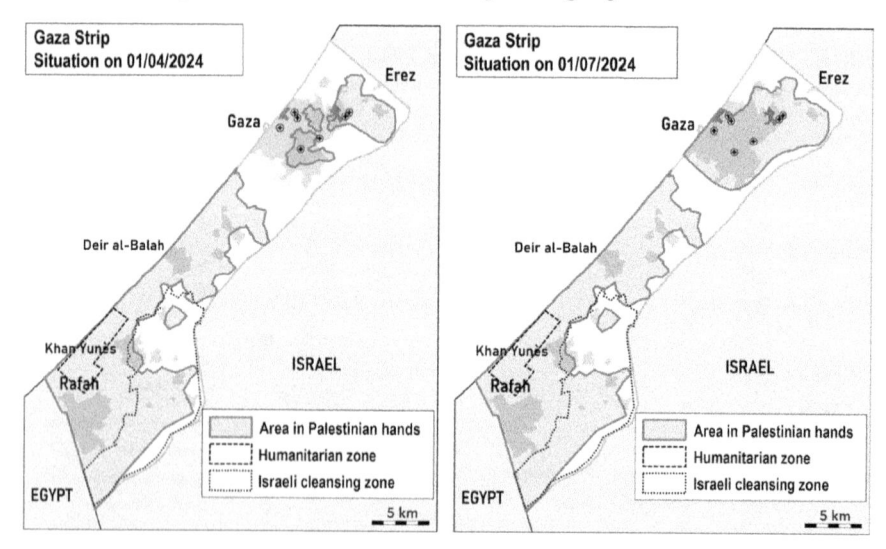

Figure 110—The cost of the operation is high for Israel. Not only was it unable to free the hostages, but Hamas and the other Palestinian resistance movements retain their full operational capacity and are acting in a perfectly coordinated fashion.

The Israeli army fights according to conventional patterns, but is unprepared for guerrilla warfare, where its soldiers are drawn into traps and pockets of fire ("killing zones"). These pockets of fire operate on the same principle as the Russian pockets of fire in Ukraine, with the difference that they are in "3D:" the Palestinian fighters let the Israeli soldiers advance, then emerge from their tunnels to strike them from behind.

Unexploded aviation bombs are reused to booby-trap buildings in which Israeli soldiers take up positions. A kind of return to sender, they have caused dozens of deaths in the Israeli ranks.

Analysis of the memory of downed Israeli drones enabled Hamas to geolocate Israeli positions in order to strike them.

On November 8 2023, the Israeli High Command stated that Hamas had lost control of the northern Gaza Strip.[524] Two months later, on January 7, 2024, it announced that it had *"completed the dismantling of Hamas structures in the north of the Gaza Strip."*[525] However, on February 3, the Israeli media announced that Hamas had reinvested northern Gaza.[526]

On February 5, 2024, the Israeli Ministry of Defense declared that 18 of the 24 Hamas *kata'ib* had been dismantled and were no longer operational.[527] But the facts tell a different story. On *CBS News*, General Frank McKenzie, former commander of US CENTCOM, declared that the Israelis' success was "very limited" and that the set objectives of destroying Hamas' political and military leadership structures had not been achieved. He noted that what Israel lacks is a strategy.[528] He confirmed what we have said in this book.

The Israelis then claimed to have killed 10,000 Hamas fighters.[529] But this figure is simply the number of men killed in Gaza, not the number of Hamas fighters. In fact, according to the UN, a total of 27,000 people died in Gaza, 70% of them women and children (just under 19,000).

---

524. "Israel's military spokesperson says Hamas has lost control in northern Gaza," *Reuters*, November 8, 2023 (https://www.reuters.com/world/middle-east/israels-military-spokesperson-says-hamas-has-lost-control-northern-gaza-2023-11-08/)
525. "Hamas command in north Gaza destroyed, Israel says," *BBC*, January 7, 2024 (https://www.bbc.com/news/world-middle-east-67904259)
526. "Hamas moves to reassert power in Gaza City areas from which Israeli forces withdrew," *The Times of Israel*, February 3, 2024 (https://www.timesofisrael.com/hamas-moves-to-reassert-power-in-gaza-city-areas-from-which-israeli-forces-withdrew/)
527. https://www.understandingwar.org/backgrounder/iran-update-february-6-2024
528. https://www.cbsnews.com/news/frank-mckenzie-former-chief-central-command-face-the-nation-transcript/
529. Yonah Jeremy Bob, "Israel defeats Hamas in Khan Yunis, over 10,000 Gazan terrorists killed," *The Jerusalem Post*, February 1, 2024 (https://www.jpost.com/israel-hamas-war/article-784787)

So, the Israeli figure is clearly messaging. What is more, we see a lot of footage of the destruction of buildings by the Israeli military, but very little combat action.

This contrasts with the images produced by the Palestinians, which tend to lend credibility to their communication. For example, in early February, Hamas claimed to have destroyed or heavily damaged some 1,108 armored vehicles (i.e., battle tanks, infantry fighting vehicles and assault bulldozers). The figure is difficult to verify, but seems consistent with the images circulating.

When you see Israeli soldiers exulting at the destruction of the University of Gaza,[530] you have to realize that this building had been used a few days earlier as their own headquarters. In other words, they knew that there are no tunnels and that it did not house a Hamas command post. In short, this was wanton destruction. A pure act of revenge. Militarily speaking, this is exactly how you *should not* fight a popular resistance movement.

The Israeli army is tactically driven. This was possible because the objective was the destruction of the Palestinian population: no need for strategy, just strike, and Operation AL-AQSA FLOOD offered the opportunity for Israeli leadership. But South Africa's complaint reshuffled the deck. By highlighting the plausibility of genocide, it shows the absence of a strategy to find a solution to the conflict. For it is clear that there can be no military solution to this conflict. We have allowed Israel to "play" with the Palestinians, but now it has its back to the wall.

### *Phase 3: Restructuring the Gaza Strip*

The details of this phase have never really been explained by the Israeli command, and it seems to be more an ellipsis to express an exit strategy than a clear plan.

The sequence of events in northern Gaza probably gives us an idea of what constitutes this third phase. Apparently, Israel is seeking to reconfigure the terrain so as to improve its warning capabilities. This involves re-establishing a "buffer zone" 500-1,000 m deep along the Gaza border, in which buildings are systematically destroyed, to create a sort of "no man's land" in which any movement can be detected. This area should also be covered by observation posts and detection systems. This is a way of further reducing the territory of the Gaza Strip.

---

530. https://www.youtube.com/shorts/XoABM-HylV4?feature=share

## Setting up a "Buffer Zone"

*Figure 111—The grey band roughly represents the buffer zone set up by the Israeli army. On January 24, 2024, 21 soldiers from the 261st brigade of the Gaza Division, who were preparing to destroy a group of buildings southeast of the Al-Maghazi camp, were killed when their own explosives were detonated by a YASSIN-105 rocket fired by Hamas fighters at the tank protecting them.[531]*

But apparently, the increase in operations by Palestinian groups in this area is probably intended to show the Israeli military that this area will remain a zone of resistance.

Israel claimed that Gaza City housed the Hamas command center, then, after finding nothing there, declared that the center was located in Khan Yunis, where Israeli forces also found nothing. This is why, in mid-February, Netanyahu called for an offensive to be planned on Rafah, with the consequence of requiring a new displacement of the Palestinian population into an undetermined area. Two things are clear. The first is that the Israelis are groping their way forward and have no

---

531. James SHOTTER, "Israel demolishes buildings to create buffer zone within Gaza," *Financial Times*, January 24, 2024 (https://www.ft.com/content/0694ab13-a291-4b4a-81c2-53ec91ae1cad)

idea of Hamas's leadership structure and locations. The second is that, as the Israelis advance, the population is not allowed to return to its original areas, but is systematically pushed southwards. The conclusion is that, contrary to official rhetoric, not only has the Israeli army still not achieved its objectives of freeing the hostages and destroying Hamas, but it is methodically applying what appears ever more clearly to be a strategy of ethnic cleansing.

That is why, "Genocide Joe" Biden sees his Democratic electorate melting away, and that he declares the Israeli offensive on Rafah *"beyond the pale."*[532]

## Matching Strategies

Fighting a resistance movement is a particularly complex task, if one wishes to remain in line with international humanitarian law (formerly known as the law of war). The main difficulty is that the combatant evolves within a society, moving fluidly from combatant to civilian status. The second challenge is to combat the combatant while minimizing the damage to the innocent people around him. The third difficulty is to accomplish all this without creating a feeling that stimulates the will to resist.

An analysis of Israel's strategy for defeating Hamas shows that it is out of step with reality on the ground. The problem is that, while it was possible in the 1940s to carry out vast campaigns of sweep and elimination, the interconnected world of 2024 no longer allows for this. Israel must therefore choose between a strategic victory without destroying Hamas, or a tactical victory against Hamas while losing international support.

To analyze the respective centers of gravity of Hamas and Israel, we use Clausewitz's definition:

> *...the center of all power and movement, on which everything depends; the characteristic, capacity or location from which enemy*

---

532. "Biden calls Israeli response in Gaza 'over the top', strikes on Houthis, Rafah bombing," Euronews/AP, February 9, 2024 (https://www.euronews.com/2024/02/09/israel-pounds-rafah-with-air-strikes-as-biden-calls-response-over-the-top)

*and friendly forces derive their freedom of action, physical strength or will to fight.*[533]

Thus it is not simply a "center of power." It is a tangible or intangible element from which a protagonist draws his strength and his ability to fight or achieve his objective. Nor is it its strategic objective, as some understand it. On the other hand, it is his opponent's objective.

*Elements of the Protagonists' Strategy for Gaza*

|  | Hamas | Israel |
|---|---|---|
| Strategic objective | Establish decent living conditions for the people of Gaza | Guaranteeing Israel's security |
| Desired end state | Having a trading platform | The Palestinian population of the West Bank and Gaza is expelled |
| Operational objective | Restoring its authority in the Gaza Strip | Destruction of Hamas and its leadership structures |
| Center of gravity | Tunnel network Support for the people of Gaza | Narrative to legitimize the brutality of its action |

Figure 112—Comparison of the strategic components of Hamas and Israel. The end state sought is the situation probably expected by both protagonists at the end of the current confrontation, triggered on October 7, 2023.

The legitimacy of Israel's action was soon called into question by the international community. No one disputed the fact that Israel had responded to the attack on October 7, but the form of its response, in defiance of IHL, aroused unanimous disapproval in the civilized world (as distinct from the Western world!).

---

533. "The hub of all power and movement upon which everything depends; that characteristic, capability, or location from which enemy and friendly forces derive their freedom of action, physical strength, or the will to fight," *Glossary*, FM 100-5 (German: *Schwerpunkt*). We also find: "... characteristic(s), capability(ies), or locality(ies) from which a nation, an alliance, a military force or other grouping derives its freedom of action, physical strength, or will to fight," Office of the Joint Staff, *DOD Dictionary of Military and Associated Terms*, Joint Publication 1-02 (Washington DC, 1984) p. 188.

## Study of Centers of Gravity

|  | Hamas | Israel |
|---|---|---|
| Center of gravity | Tunnel network supporting the people of Gaza | Narrative to legitimize the brutality of its action |
| Critical functions | Maintaining operational activity | Mastering narrative in Western media |
| Critical resources | Support from the people of the West Bank. The weather | U.S. support |
| Critical vulnerabilities | The humanitarian situation in Gaza | Testimony of survivors of October 7 and Israeli media. The weather |

*Figure 113—A comparison of Hamas's and Israel's centers of gravity shows that Israel is heavily dependent on the narrative propagated by our media, while Hamas depends only on the support of a population that is generally favorable to it. This is why, as in the case of Ukraine, our media must ensure that messages are aligned with the Israeli discourse.*

Israel's center of gravity is therefore the narrative, for it is on this that it relies to justify the disproportionality of its response. The problem is that it threatens to collapse. Thus, according to a Harvard-Harris poll in December 2023, 51% of young Americans would be prepared to *"end Israel and give it to Hamas."*[534]

Admittedly, at this stage, the age groups that make up the decision-makers remain overwhelmingly supportive of Israel, but this support is waning and is having an impact on American domestic policy. The majority of Democrats no longer support Joe Biden because of his Middle East policy.[535] Yet the composition of the Democratic electorate in the USA is one of the foundations of this policy. In other words, the benefits of supporting a country whose criminal actions keep it out of the international community are no longer very attractive.

This is why narrative is essential for Israel, in order to maintain a critical resource for its project: American support. The weakening of Israel's image in the world means that time is a critical vulnerability. This explains

---

534. https://harvardharrispoll.com/wp-content/uploads/2023/12/HHP_Dec23_KeyResults.pdf
535. Tony Czuczka, "Biden's Support of Israel Alienates More Democrats in New Poll," *Bloomberg*, December 10, 2023 (https://www.bloomberg.com/news/articles/2023-12-10/biden-s-support-of-israel-alienates-more-democrats-in-new-poll)

the efforts being made in Israel and elsewhere to maintain control of the narrative and prevent alternative narratives.

For the Palestinians, there are two centers of gravity: the first at the operational level, the network of tunnels that enables it to strike at Israeli forces at virtually any point in the Gaza Strip, and the second at the strategic level, which is support for the Gazan population, whom Israel is holding hostage by limiting their access to food and medical care.

## *The Asymmetrical Dimension of Conflict*

a) Symmetrical situation

| Enemy destruction | Enemy destruction |

b) Asymmetrical situation

| Enemy destruction | Enemy destruction |

c) Asymmetrical situation

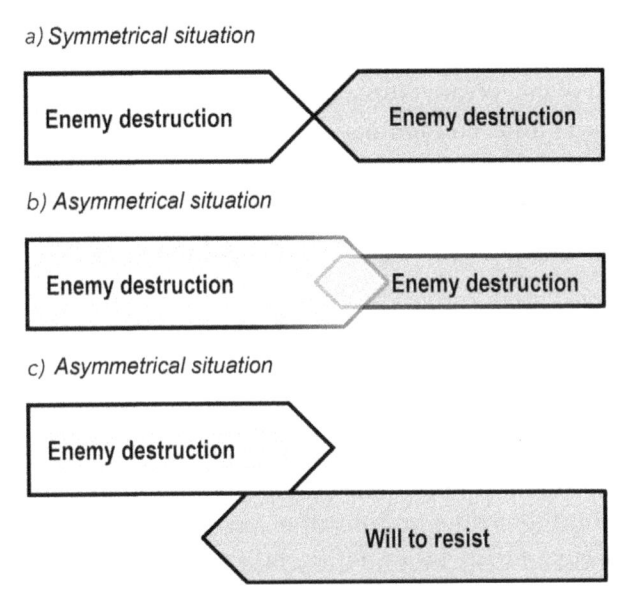

| Enemy destruction |
| Will to resist |

*Figure 114—In an asymmetrical situation, the strategy of one protagonist favors that of the other. The more homes the Israelis destroy and the more civilians they kill, the more they reinforce the Palestinians' victory. Here, the adversary can be compared to a "non-Newtonian" fluid: the greater the energy applied to it, the harder and more resistant to deformation it becomes. This is "the defeat of the vanquisher."*

If the Palestinians had a Western way of thinking, they would certainly already have the feeling of having lost: the destruction, the civilian deaths and probably the deaths of combatants give the feeling of failure. But in an Islamic approach, it is the loss of will to fight, not the number of deaths or destruction, that defines defeat. We can see that the Palestinians have gained considerable support by confronting an adversary more powerful than themselves. This is the asymmetrical dimension of the conflict that

Westerners seem to want to ignore, but which is crucial to understanding how Muslims understand the struggle, whether political or military.

On a more operational level, while one of the objectives of the Israelis is to obtain the release of the hostages,[536] it will take Israel more than a month to accept negotiation towards this objective. In other words, it took Israel more than a month to understand that the objective could be achieved by means other than the massive destruction that would justify South Africa's complaint to the International Court of Justice (ICJ). This means that for Israel, tactical objectives are more important than strategic ones, or that tactical objectives are aligned with other objectives that have nothing to do with appeasing the situation. In fact, Israel could have rid itself of the terrorist threat many years ago, with far less destruction and international condemnation.

The cuts in electricity, water and food supplies decided by the government from October 10, 2023, are illegal measures, as Josep Borrell, head of European Union foreign policy[537] also points out:

> *Israel has the right to defend itself, but it must do so in compliance with international law... cutting off water, electricity and food supplies to a civilian population is contrary to international law.*

None of our mainstream media picked up on this declaration of illegality, contributing to the impunity that surrounds the Hebrew state and stimulates anti-Semitism around the world.

Since 1948, the Israelis' problem has been to find a balance between military and political issues. Today, their objective is the destruction of Hamas's military potential, but clearly this will not solve the problem. It is merely an act of revenge, which will only stimulate the emergence of new volunteers to fight Israel more virulently. It is regrettable that Western countries did not advise the Israeli government better to protect its strategic interests. We find ourselves in a situation similar to that of Ukraine, where our "Arabophobia" tends to take precedence over the interests of our allies.

---

536. Raphaël JERUSALMY, "The first mission in Gaza is to rescue the hostages," *i24news*, October 9, 2023 (updated October 10, 2023) (https://www.i24news.tv/en/news/israel-at-war/1696834325-analysis-the-first-mission-in-gaza-is-to-rescue-the-hostages)
537. Andrew RETTMAN, "Israel's siege of Gaza is illegal, EU says," *EU Observer*, October 10, 2023 (https://euobserver.com/world/157534)

On February 9, 2024, the *New York Times* reported that U.S. intelligence believed that Israel was *"far from being able to eliminate Hamas."*[538] One of the problems cited is the inability to prioritize two objectives that tend to be mutually exclusive: freeing the hostages and eliminating Hamas.

## Ill-Prepared Troops

On October 7, the Israeli response showed troops ill-prepared for the scale of the Palestinian operation. We have already seen above the failure of Israel's operational control system. But this was compounded by the obvious inexperience of the troops. The list of Israeli soldiers killed that day, published by the *Haaretz* newspaper, shows a median age of 21, meaning they had virtually no experience.

The videos posted online by the Israelis during the fighting in the ruins of Gaza bear witness to a great lack of preparation and extremely inadequate training. Soldiers moving into the line of fire of their comrades, or standing in front of the weapons of those who should be covering them, are evidence of very rudimentary basic training. This level of training is consistent with the testimonies of October 7, which suggest troops in panic, whose situational *awareness* is virtually non-existent and who act in a disordered manner. This tends to confirm Israeli media findings that 20% of Israeli soldiers killed were killed by their own comrades (*"blue on blue."*)[539]

We can therefore quickly conclude that the Israeli troops engaged on October 7 were not trained for delicate situations in which the presence of civilians (hostages) had to be taken into account. This was also the case for the very young MERKAVA tank crews who arrived quickly on the scene, but who, in the absence of a concrete mission, simply followed the "orders" of civilians, without really knowing the nature of their objectives.

This very poor level of training, as shown by the testimonies of October 7 and the subsequent videos of Israeli soldiers, lends credence to Hamas's claims—without ruling out crimes committed by its fighters—that the majority of victims were caused by the Israeli forces themselves.

---

538. https://www.nytimes.com/live/2024/02/09/world/israel-hamas-war-gaza-news#us-intelligence-officials-tell-congress-that-israel-is-not-close-to-eliminating-hamas

539. Chantal Da Silva, "Nearly one-fifth of Israeli soldiers killed in Gaza died due to friendly fire and other accidents, IDF says," *NBC News*, December 12, 2023 (https://www.nbcnews.com/news/world/nearly-15-israeli-soldiers-killed-gaza-died-due-friendly-fire-accident-rcna129285)

Add to this the application of the HANNIBAL doctrine, which assumes that a soldier can expect to become a target for his comrades if he gets into trouble, and it is easy to see why morale is so low. Indeed, the state of mental health of the Israeli military is a cause for alarm in the general staff. Uriel Busso, Minister of Health, declared that this is the most serious mental health crisis the Israeli army has ever experienced.[540] The Palestinians, used to living under bombs and in difficult situations, are more robust than young Israelis fresh from a comfortable life in Tel Aviv or Haifa. The videos that Israeli soldiers post on Tik-Tok show concerns that seem completely out of step with reality on the ground, such as how to take care of one's skin in combat or how to keep one's nail polish.

After their intervention at Khan Yunis, just a few kilometers deep, Israel was unable to secure its logistical lines, despite the short distance and a terrain largely destroyed by bombardment. Parachute drops had to be made to supply the troops. This means that the Palestinians have a considerably better command of the terrain than the Israeli forces.

Moreover, while the Israeli objective was to destroy the Hamas infrastructure, the Palestinians have managed to move almost unhindered through the Israeli lines, attacking the troops from behind. For their part, Israeli soldiers seem reluctant to leave their armored vehicles, in which they feel protected. This has enabled the Palestinians to carry out so-called "zero-distance" attacks, i.e., to get as close as possible to the tanks and attach explosives.

It is also clear that some Israeli military personnel are questioning the relevance of the government's decisions, and since July 2023,[541] there has already been some unease among the pilots, which has had repercussions on Operation SWORDS OF IRON.[542]

---

540. Ran REZNIK, "The mental health crisis in the war is the most serious in Israeli history," *Israel Hayom*, November 5, 2023 (https://www.israelhayom.com/2023/11/05/the-mental-health-crisis-in-the-war-is-the-most-serious-in-israeli-history/)
541. Josh KAPLAN, "Why elite Israeli combat pilots are refusing to serve until judicial reforms are abandoned," *The Jewish Chronicle*, September 21, 2021 (https://www.thejc.com/news/why-elite-israeli-combat-pilots-are-refusing-to-serve-until-judicial-reforms-are-abandoned-hi81j9e1)
542. "Outrage as far-right minister suggests some pilots refusing air support for Gaza troops," *The Times of Israel*, December 31, 2023 (https://www.timesofisrael.com/outrage-after-far-right-minister-suggests-some-pilots-refusing-to-support-gaza-troops/)

## The Influence

As their name suggests, influence operations are designed to modify perceptions. In fact, they are often described as "perception management operations." Their function is to shape the image we have of the protagonists in the conflict, as well as of the course of operations.

Generally speaking, they have a strategic function, as they determine the quality and intensity of a protagonist's support. This function is all the more crucial when the protagonist is totally dependent on external support, whether political or material. This is why they played a decisive role in Ukraine, and why they are at the heart of Israeli strategy.

The importance of Israel's image is not a new problem, but it has taken on a considerable dimension in recent years, particularly with the arrival of Benjamin Netanyahu's government. Netanyahu's immunity from prosecution for corruption and all manner of malfeasance means that he escapes the courts. To stay in power, he has had to ally himself with parties whose extremism is at a level unseen in Europe for almost 80 years. As in Ukraine, where the problem of neo-Nazi militias is affecting the country's image and support, Israel has had to put in place a mechanism to control the narrative surrounding its actions in the occupied territories.

To carry out this task, Israel has at its disposal both civilian mechanisms, such as the "Hasbara," and military ones, such as influence operations and military censorship.

### *Hasbara*

We still know very little about the exact events of October 7, and it will only be possible to establish the facts through an impartial, multilateral and factual investigation. In the absence of such a process, we are reduced to relying on eyewitness accounts, which more often than not give a very different picture from the one propagated by the Israeli government and our media (which is the same).

The problem is that these events were immediately exploited to justify a heavy-handed and even disproportionate Israeli response. What is known is that:
- The 1,400 deaths announced by the Israeli authorities included at least 200 Hamas fighters who could not be identified until three

weeks later, given their degree of charring. The official death toll has now been reduced to 1,200.[543]
- On December 2, this number was reduced to *"more than 1,000 dead,"*[544] according to the Israeli Embassy in the United States.
- As of December 4, 369 military or security personnel were counted among the dead on that day.[545]

This means that 369 soldiers, plus around 100 armed security guards and police, died in combat, which does not in itself constitute a war crime.

This would put the number of civilian casualties attributable to Hamas at between 600 and 700. But testimonies appearing in the Israeli media show that a large proportion of these casualties were caused by the Israeli armed forces themselves. It is likely and probable that Hamas fighters committed war crimes that day. The question is to what extent. Amplifying the role of Hamas tends to serve as a pretext for the Israeli response (which is disproportionate in any case).

In order to justify a disproportionate response strongly condemned by the international community—with the exception of European countries and France in particular—Hamas' action must be presented as particularly inhuman. This has led to the emergence of stories that rival the far-fetched for horror. We have known since mid-October that children *"cut in half,"* their *"slit throats,"* *"decapitated,"* *"hung from wires"* or *"put in ovens"* and *"disemboweled women"* are fictions *deliberately* broadcast to justify the intensive bombardment of Gaza and its population.

As in Ukraine, Israel seeks to base the legitimacy of its military action on a certain narrative. To this end, it uses a form of public diplomacy called *Hasbara*,[546] which aims to promote its interests on social networks and the Internet.

It is interesting to note that in the French media, journalists like Ruth Elkrief or Darius Rochebin spend more energy protecting a narrative and justifying the response against Hamas, than questioning Israel's inability to solve its 75-year terrorism problem. The Israeli response to South Africa's accusations of genocide at the preliminary hearings of the ICJ[547]

---

543. https://www.timesofisrael.com/israel-revises-death-toll-from-oct-7-hamas-assault-dropping-it-from-1400-to-1200/
544. https://twitter.com/IsraelinUSA/status/1731131639089041788
545. https://www.aa.com.tr/en/middle-east/2-more-israeli-soldiers-killed-in-gaza-bringing-troop-deaths-to-7-in-one-day/3074133
546. https://hasbaraisrael.com/
547. https://youtu.be/H6CEKVSjg7o

was not focused on the substance of the accusation, but on the threat posed by Hamas. In strategic terms, the narrative has become Israel's center of gravity in its response to Operation AL-AQSA FLOOD.

And yet, in criminal law as in international law, no crime whatsoever, including genocide, can be a justification for other crimes, as our journalists suggest. In fact, this reasoning can be found in the discipline of language proposed by Israel: it is not a question of discussing Israel's policy or strategy, but only Hamas's crimes. On October 23, 2023, for example, MP Meyer Habib made this point on *La Chaîne Parlementaire*.[548]

The problem is that Israel knows it is fundamentally wrong. The Western politicians who declare "unconditional support" also know that they are supporting a plausible genocide. They feel protected by the impunity Israel has enjoyed for decades, thanks to the support of the United States.

The desire to minimize the plausibility of genocide in Gaza is, in fact, a way of covering up Israel's action, which is—genocide or not—illegal in substance. On December 10, 2023, far-right politician Christian Estrosi criticized the media for showing "*images of mothers crying with a plastic baby, making it look like a dead baby.*" A complaint would be lodged against him for "*serious and misleading statements.*"[549] For this "information," widely disseminated on social networks and "debunked" in October,[550] is notoriously false and serves only to dehumanize the Palestinians, in order to make the massacres more acceptable.[551]

Those who deviate from the official line, who condemn Israel's violations of IHL or who are pro-Palestinian are conspiratorial or "*linked to Russia.*"[552] Those who speak out on our TV channels have such a caricatured and simplistic vision that we have a right to wonder whether they are really serving Israel's cause.

Israel's problem is its steadily declining credibility in the world. Indeed, since the early 2000s, its policy of colonizing the occupied terri-

---

548. https://youtu.be/vYT7FEEGq5A
549. https://france3-regions.francetvinfo.fr/provence-alpes-cote-d-azur/alpes-maritimes/nice/christian-estrosi-vise-par-une-plainte-pour-avoir-accuse-les-medias-de-diffuser-les-images-d-un-faux-bebe-mort-a-gaza-2888390.html
550. https://www.altnews.in/4-yr-old-killed-in-gaza-israel-govt-falsely-claims-video-shows-a-doll-not-a-child/
551. https://www.lemonde.fr/les-decodeurs/article/2023/12/16/pallywood-en-plein-carnage-a-gaza-le-mythe-des-fausses-morts-palestiniennes_6206188_4355770.html
552. Aileen GRAEF, "Pelosi faces criticism for suggesting some pro-Palestinian protesters are connected to Russia," *CNN*, January 28, 2024 (https://www.cnn.com/2024/01/28/politics/pelosi-criticism-palestinian-gaza-protests-russia/index.html)

tories has become extremely unpopular worldwide, making it the most condemned country in the world by the United Nations. It is therefore no longer possible to justify policies and strategies that have not only been condemned, but are recognized as being largely ineffective in the fight against terrorism. The very fact that Israel is not changing its strategy means that its objective goes far beyond the fight against terrorism.

### The Essence of Israeli Storytelling

**DO NOT explain Israel's policy**

The issue here is not the Israeli-Palestinian conflict as a whole. It is very difficult for us to win there. October 7 is about war crimes committed by Hamas, an organization that people abroad for some reason do not perceive as terrorists, no matter how much we try to say that they are. Now there is proof. It's our 9/11, and that's a relatable analogy for most Westerners.

**DO NOT Explain Israel's Policy**

The problem here is not the Israeli-Palestinian conflict as a whole. It is very difficult for us to win in this area. October 7 is about the war crimes committed by Hamas, an organization that foreigners, for one reason or another, do not perceive as terrorists, even if we try to make them believe that they are. We now have the proof. It is our 9/11, and it is an understandable analogy for most Westerners.

Figure 115—Extract from the communication policy recommended by the "Israel Under Fire" website, which outlines the main lines of its communication on social networks; Israel is perfectly aware that its policy towards the Palestinians is indefensible. This is why its arguments revolve exclusively around the evocation of crimes committed by Hamas. Take the case of the 40 babies allegedly decapitated: our media have spent more time discussing this fictitious incident than the more than 7,000 Palestinian children killed in Gaza. [Source: https://israelunderfire.net/best-practices/]

## *Influence Operations*

Influence has always been part of conflict, and Gaza is no exception. We are seeing some of the same characteristics as influence operations in the Ukrainian theater of operations. On the one hand, we have Palestinian movements that communicate very little, both for technical and cultural reasons, but also because of their philosophy: they talk about facts rather than constructing a narrative. That is why most Palestinian communication is based on videos made by the fighters themselves during their operations, and quickly posted on Instagram or Telegram.

On the Israeli side, information is much more sophisticated, with draconian censorship against stories that might give a positive image of Hamas. For example, Facebook and Instagram[553] censor images showing Israeli hostages embracing Hamas fighters upon their release.[554] After Yocheved Lifschitz's release in October 2023, the Israeli government realized that her statements in the press were harming the national interest,[555] which was then to strike disproportionately at the Palestinian population.

Israeli propaganda can be bafflingly naive. The lies about the 40 beheaded babies or the "proof" of the use of the Al-Shifa hospital basements are the most striking illustrations (and the most mocked on the Internet). That is why we need a French minister to lodge a complaint against those who condemn this disinformation.

The image of the Israeli military on social networks is far from flattering. Confident of their impunity, they shamelessly film their war crimes. For example, in an interview with *Sky News*, Isaac Herzog, the Israeli president, claimed that a USB stick was found on a Hamas member, containing detailed instructions on the creation of chemical weapons from a "*2003 Al-Qaeda terrorist organization manual*," the cover of which he showed, indicating a link with Hamas.[556] But he is a liar. In reality, it is an over-the-counter brochure widely sold in the Middle East.[557]

Within the Operations Directorate of the Israeli General Staff is the *Department of Influence* (DI), responsible for influencing perceptions in Israel and abroad about the Palestinian conflict. It is obviously very active on social networks. For example, it runs a *Telegram* channel entitled "72 virgins—No Censorship," created on October 9, 2023, which glorifies the war crimes committed by the Israeli military. It shows the destruction of buildings, vehicles driving over the corpses of Palestinians, the ransacking of Palestinian homes and businesses in Gaza, and many

---

553. https://www.instagram.com/mertaloba/p/C0F5F0crvG4/?img_index=1
554. https://www.anews.com.tr/gallery/world/facebook-and-instagram-censor-images-of-released-hostages-and-hamas-members
555. Jonathan Lis, Yael Freidson & Michael Hauser Tov, "Freed Israeli Hostage's Remarks Seen by Government Officials as Damaging to Israeli Interests," *Haaretz*, Oct. 24, 2023 (https://www.haaretz.com/israel-news/2023-10-24/ty-article/.premium/freed-hostages-remarks-were-seen-by-government-as-damaging-to-israeli-interests/0000018b-628c-d288-afef-f2dc7ad60000)
556. https://www.gov.il/en/departments/news/ironswords231020233
557. https://www.noor-book.com/en/ebook-%D8%B1%D9%85%D8%B2%D9%8A-%D9%8A%D9%88%D8%B3%D9%81-pdf

other horrors.⁵⁵⁸ Thus, according to *Haaretz*, photos of Gazans trapped and dead are accompanied by comments such as *"Exterminate the cockroaches... exterminate the Hamas rats... Share this wonder!"*⁵⁵⁹ The aim here is to stir up hatred and stimulate the basest instincts, while dehumanizing Palestinians. On October 11, a post declared:

> *Burning their mother... You won't believe the video we got! You can hear the crunch of their bones. We're putting it online now, so get ready!*⁵⁶⁰

This is "the most moral army in the world," according to Meyer Habib. Everyone will judge.

The DI has also created a fake Hamas website designed to show Hamas crimes. *Euronews* investigated this site, which clearly appears to be an Israeli creation designed to show a fictitious reality of Hamas.⁵⁶¹ Very well done, it presents a caricatured reality of Hamas, whose messages are incidentally not very different from what we hear on the *LCI* or *BFMTV* channels in France.

In fact, Israeli communications are quite consistently geared towards highlighting Hamas's crimes, as these—according to the authorities—provide the legitimization for a massive response. In line with this logic, the Military Censorship (*Ha'tzenzura Ha'tzva'it*) (part of military intelligence) has issued a directive on the subjects on which it is forbidden to communicate:⁵⁶²

1. The hostages
2. Operation details
3. Intelligence
4. Weapons systems

---

558. "IDF says it ran unauthorized '72 Virgins—Uncensored' Telegram channel," *The Jerusalem Post*, February 6, 2024 (https://www.jpost.com/israel-hamas-war/article-785378)
559. Yaniv Kubovich, "Israeli Army Admits Running Unauthorized Graphic Gaza Influence Op," *Haaretz*, February 4, 2024 (https://www.haaretz.com/israel-news/security-aviation/2024-02-04/ty-article/.premium/israeli-army-its-admits-staff-was-behind-graphic-gaza-telegram-channel/0000018d-70b4-dd6e-a98d-f4b6a9c00000)
560. "'Roaches to Be Exterminated': Israel Military Admits Running Racist Telegram Group Against Palestinians," *The Wire*, February 8, 2024 (https://thewire.in/world/roaches-to-be-exterminated-israel-military-admits-running-racist-telegram-group-against-palestinians)
561. https://www.euronews.com/my-europe/2023/12/04/fact-check-did-hamas-create-a-website-boasting-about-massacring-israeli-civilians
562. https://www.gov.il/BlobFolder/news/8swordsofiron101023/en/operation Swords of Iron.pdf

5. Rocket attacks
6. Cyber attacks
7. VIP visits
8. Cabinet meeting information

As is obvious, the aim is to focus communication on Hamas's crimes. Even hostages (including those who have been released) are among the areas censored, as there is a fear of statements which might indicate that Hamas respects its prisoners.

### The Fake Hamas Website

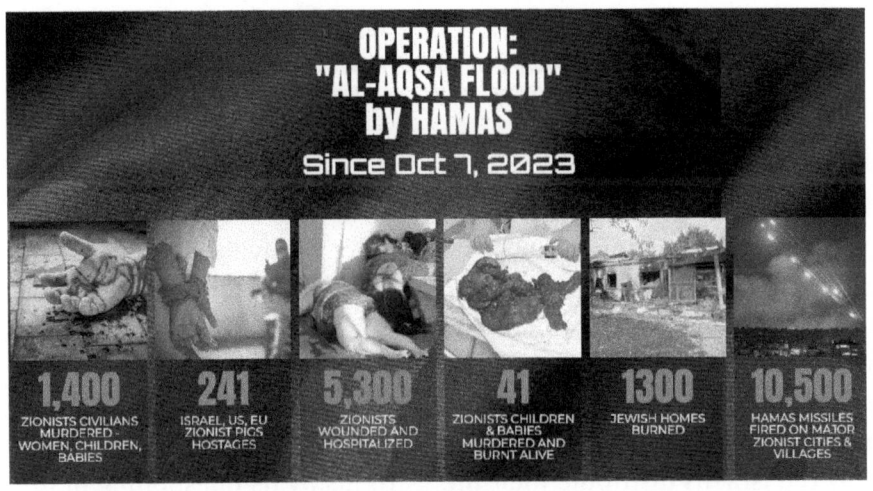

Figure 116—Hamas.com, a totally fake site designed to present Hamas as a terrorist organization and proud of it. [Source: hamas.com]

On several occasions, organizations of—real—journalists have denounced Israel's actions to prevent journalists from carrying out their work.[563] From the outset of their operations in Gaza, the Israeli military told *Reuters* and *Agence France Press* (AFP) that they could not guarantee the safety of journalists.[564] In other words, Israeli forces recognize that their surgical strikes are a myth.

---

563. "Journalist casualties in the Israel-Gaza war," *Committee to Protect Journalists*, February 2, 2024 (https://cpj.org/2024/02/journalist-casualties-in-the-israel-gaza-conflict/)
564. "Israeli military says it can't guarantee journalists' safety in Gaza," *Reuters*, October 28, 2023 (https://www.reuters.com/world/middle-east/israeli-military-says-it-cant-guarantee-journalists-safety-gaza-2023-10-27/)

*Journalists Killed in Gaza*

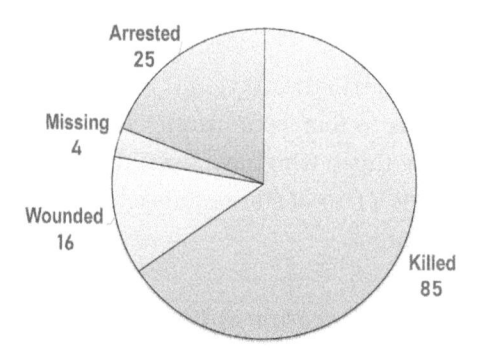

Figure 117—Number of journalists killed by Israeli forces in Gaza on February 2, 2024. Of the 85 journalists killed, 78 were Palestinians, 4 Israelis and 3 Lebanese. [Source: Committee to Protect Journalists].

## The War of Numbers

At the end of October 2023, the number of civilians, women and children killed by Israel was out of all proportion. Israeli authorities and our media, such as *Libération*,[565] *France Info*,[566] *La Croix*,[567] suggested that Palestinian casualty figures are unreliable. The *Washington Institute* made a "study" of the question, but it focused on differences in the number of men killed over a few days, without taking into account the way the Israelis distribute their fire.[568] To justify its questioning of the Palestinian figures, the French daily *La Dépêche*[569] refered to President Joe Biden's doubts.[570] The "award" undoubtedly goes to Caroline Fourest, on *BFMTV* (of course!) who declared on October 29 that the figures come from a *"single terrorist source"* and that *"the figures must*

---

565. https://www.liberation.fr/checknews/victimes-des-bombardements-sur-gaza-peut-on-en-core-faire-confiance-aux-chiffres-du-hamas-20231021_XDGED3XCTRGTTPYWU3AUTUHTSU/
566. https://www.francetvinfo.fr/monde/proche-orient/israel-palestine/guerre-entre-le-hamas-et-israel-les-chiffres-sur-le-nombre-de-victimes-a-gaza-sont-ils-fiables_6149955.html
567. https://www.la-croix.com/international/Morts-Gaza-peut-fier-chiffres-Hamas-2023-10-20-1201287694
568. https://www.washingtoninstitute.org/policy-analysis/how-hamas-manipulates-gaza-fatality-numbers-examining-male-undercount-and-other
569. Anne-Laure DE CHALUP, "Guerre Israël-Hamas: fake news, manipulation... pourquoi la fiabilité des informations est un enjeu majeur du conflit," *La Dépêche*, November 1, 2023 (https://www.ladepeche.fr/2023/11/01/guerre-israel-hamas-fake-news-manipulation-pourquoi-la-fiabilite-des-informations-est-un-enjeu-majeur-du-conflit-11551309.php)
570. https://youtu.be/h42Nm05zF-w

*be divided if not by five at least by* ten."[571] But intellectual honesty is not her main virtue.

As for the source of the figures, our media rather slavishly adopt the narrative coming from Israel, like the Swiss *RTS*, which claimed that these figures were *"provided by* Hamas."[572] This is disinformation. For, on October 26, Belgium's *RTBF* pointed out that *"the Palestinian Authority endorses these figures as emanating from its administration, the Ministry of Health located, among other places, in Gaza. It is therefore correct to refer to these figures as 'figures from the Palestinian Ministry of Health,' and not 'from Hamas.'"*[573]

As for the figures themselves, there is nothing to suggest that they are five or ten times higher than the reality. Certainly, there is no guarantee of their accuracy, even though the health authorities have provided the UN with lists of names and identity numbers for each victim.

Yet, according to the *Huffington Post*, official State Department reports regularly use these figures.[574] The American media outlet even quotes an American "official" as saying that *"according to UN and NGO reports, the real numbers are probably much higher."* This is exactly what the *Wall Street Journal* suggested on November 11.[575]

In fact, contrary to what our media claim, the figures announced by Gaza's health authorities are generally reliable, as confirmed by the prestigious British medical journal *The Lancet*, in a study published in December 2023.[576] What is more, the British journal even analyzed mortality in Gaza between October 7 and 26, 2023, on the basis of information given on the victims. Its authors noted that the data provided by the

---

571. https://www.bfmtv.com/replay-emissions/c-est-pas-tous-les-jours-dimanche/caroline-fourest-nous-avons-800-actes-antisemites-depuis-le-7-octobre-29-10_VN-202310290362.html
572. https://www.rts.ch/info/monde/14422799-parfois-mis-en-doute-les-bilans-de-victimes-publies-par-le-hamas-resteraient-globalement-fiables.html
573. https://www.rtbf.be/article/guerre-israel-gaza-les-chiffres-des-victimes-a-gaza-non-recoupes-une-premiere-dans-lhistoire-du-conflit-11277724
574. Akbar Shahid Ahmed, "Biden Cast Doubt On Gaza's Death Statistics—But Officials Cite Them Internally," *The Huffington Post*, October 26, 2023 (https://www.huffpost.com/entry/joe-biden-gaza-death-toll-state-department_n_653a80f3e4b0783c4ba0491f)
575. Vivian Salama, "State Department Says Gaza Death Toll Could Be Higher Than Reported," *The Wall Street Journal*, November 11, 2023 (https://www.wsj.com/livecoverage/israel-hamas-war-gaza-strip-2023-11-08/card/state-department-warns-gaza-death-toll-could-be-higher-than-reported-RWmIIiwHT4DfsOaJrZji)
576. Benjamin Q Huynh, Elizabeth T Chin & Paul B Spiegel, "No evidence of inflated mortality reporting from the Gaza Ministry of Health," *The Lancet*, December 6, 2023 (DOI:https://doi.org/10.1016/S0140-6736(23)02713-7) (https://www.thelancet.com/journals/lancet/article/PIIS0140-6736(23)02713-7/fulltext)

Palestinians is consistent with the demographics of the Gaza Strip, and is most likely not exaggerated. On the contrary, the experts concluded that the death toll is probably underestimated because of communication difficulties and the existence of corpses under the rubble of homes.[577]

So Caroline Fourest, *BFMTV*, *RTS* and the rest are talking nonsense. In fact, not only are the "Hamas" figures reliable, but they are even used by Israeli intelligence services in their internal briefings!

### Israeli Services use "Hamas figures"

> **Yuval Abraham** יובל אברהם
> @yuval_abraham
>
> Israeli intelligence secretly surveilled officials in Gaza's Health Ministry to check if their data on the number of civilians killed in Gaza is 'reliable', Israeli intelligence sources told us.
>
> The army found the numbers are reliable and now regularly uses them internally in intelligence briefings.
>
> According to two sources, Israeli intelligence has no good independent

*Figure 118—Our media systematically seek to discredit the figures given by the Palestinians. Yet apparently, according to Israeli journalist Yuval Abraham, even the Israeli intelligence services consider their figures to be reliable. [Source: https://twitter.com/yuval_abraham/status/1750123648533324158]*

The danger with these unscrupulous commentators and media is that their unsubstantiated and unproven assertions only serve to justify the disproportionality of the Israeli response.

## The Quest for Success

By the end of 2023, Operation SWORDS OF IRON was showing signs of weakness and tended to bog down without delivering the decisive blow Israel had promised. Hasbara began to turn against the Hebrew state, and its credibility plummeted. It is therefore necessary, on the one hand, to prevent the publication of what might look like Palestinian successes—for example, celebrating the return of their loved ones is considered

---

577. Zeina JAMALUDDINE, Francesco CHECCHI & Oona M R CAMPBELL, "Excess mortality in Gaza: Oct 7-26, 2023," *The Lancet*, November 26, 2023 (https://doi.org/10.1016/S0140-6736(23)02640-5)

to be support for terrorism and is forbidden to the families of released prisoners[578]—and, on the other hand, to try to find evidence of success.

### *The Return of the Undead with Swiss Newspaper* 20-Minuten

*Figure 119—The Swiss newspaper* 20-Minuten *published photos of Hamas cadres eliminated by Israel. Bottom left, the photo of Ayatollah Seyyed Ali Ghazi, who died in February 1947!*

The discovery of Yahya Sinwar's shoe in the ruins of his house was reported as a victory.[579] Images of destruction in Gaza have been widely circulated, including (hardly understandable in the context of the ICJ complaint) images of exactions against the Palestinian population by soldiers.

---

578. Dominic WAGHORN, "Israel-Hamas war: 'We were treated like dogs'—released Palestinian prisoners complain of mistreatment," *SKY News*, November 27, 2023 (https://news.sky.com/story/israel-hamas-war-we-were-treated-like-dogs-released-palestinian-prisoners-complain-of-mistreatment-13017228)

579. https://www.israelhayom.co.il/news/geopolitics/palestinians/article/15020647?utm_source=ground.news&utm_medium=referral

They even invented Hamas figures who have been eliminated by Israel, as in the Swiss-German newspaper *20-Minuten*, which resurrected an ayatollah who died in 1947!

## The Use of Violence

Western and Israeli discourse tends to make terrorism the central element in the Israeli-Palestinian conflict. It is a way of turning the accusation on its head. It is important to remember here that the United Nations recognizes the right of Palestinians to resist *"by all means at their disposal, including armed struggle."*[580] In other words, Palestinian resistance is a *response to* Israel's failure to comply with international law, as it arrogates to itself the right to dispose by force of territories occupied by Arab populations.

The use of terrorism by Hamas, while proven in certain situations prior to 2005, has been open to debate since it assumed political responsibility in the Gaza Strip. That said, the use of terrorism is undoubtedly reprehensible, but, as in other situations, if international law had been respected by Israel from the outset, the Palestinians would probably not have resorted to terrorism. Given the right to resist, when there is no alternative, there is only this one. If Israel really wanted to eliminate terrorism, there are dozens of possible strategies it could have used, but did not even try.

Three things are essential here:
- respect for international law is not limited to the issue of terrorism;
- respect for international law applies to all parties;
- one party's failure to comply with the law does not mean that the others can disregard it.

The problem with Israel's actions is that they will never have legal consequences. While our politicians accept, even encourage, Israel's muscular response, abuses will never be sanctioned. In other words, for 75 years, despite repeated reminders from the United Nations, we have been encouraging the punishment (even collective punishment) of the Palestinians, while knowingly accepting Israel's grave violations of human rights and international humanitarian law. Every one of our

---

580. https://www.un.org/unispal/document/auto-insert-184801/

politicians should be held accountable for every Palestinian civilian life lost.

The absence of criticism of Israeli policy is most apparent in the International Court of Justice's ruling on a possible case of genocide, where one gets the feeling that Israel could have escaped an unfavorable decision if its leaders had been more measured in their words. More on this later.

## *The Right to Self-Defense*

The right to self-defense is enshrined in the United Nations Charter. At the end of the Second World War, the aim of the Charter was to establish universal peace, and it condemned acts of war. But it also recognized that there were situations in which a country could be compelled to wage war, and that this could therefore be legitimate in certain cases. One such case is self-defense, as provided for in Article 51 of the Charter. This is a situation where a country is attacked by another and commits its armed forces to a defensive war, to avert an existential danger, against an adversary with comparable means at its disposal.

That said, even in this situation, military action must remain within the framework of international law, particularly with regard to the protection of civilian populations.

When Israel invoked this right with regard to the Palestinian resistance, it was not in this situation. First of all, Israel is officially an occupying power, and its presence in the Palestinian territories is illegal, according to UN Security Council Resolution 242 (1967). Consequently, resistance to this occupation is legal. This, moreover, is stated in UN General Assembly Resolution 45/130 (1990), which specifically gives Palestinians the right to resistance *"by all means at their disposal, including armed struggle."*[581] In the Gaza Strip, although there are no longer any troops on the territory itself, the population remains under occupation. Moreover, according to the Fourth Geneva Convention, Israel's internationally recognized status as occupying power obliges it to protect the Palestinian population and ensure its well-being.

Secondly, Israel naturally has the right to protect its own population. It is even one of its obligations. But as the occupying power, and with control over the Gazan population, the notion of defense is different from

---

581. https://www.un.org/unispal/document/auto-insert-184801/

an international conflict. To re-establish order, it must use appropriate means to protect civilians and the innocent. The situation on October 7 was quite simply the result of an occupation policy that has never been adapted to the situation, if we accept that the aim is not to drive the Palestinians into exile.

By trying to conduct a kind of "remote occupation," creating a sort of gigantic open-air concentration camp, Israel no longer has the necessary granularity of surveillance. As a result, the Hebrew state has completely lost control of the situation. But its legal position remains that of an occupying power.

Ironically, if Israel were to grant the Palestinians the right to a state, it could assert that right, wage a defensive war against it and thus eradicate Hamas.[582] This being the case, contrary to what journalists like Darius Rochebin on *LCI*[583] try to convince us, who seek to justify Israel's crimes, one crime cannot be justified by other crimes, whatever they may be.

### *Rules of Engagement*

Israel invokes the fight against terrorism to justify its use of violence. But when it comes to counter-terrorism, the use of force means that we have been unable to understand the mechanics of terrorism (in this case, jihadist terrorism) and to put in place strategies that could have dissuaded our adversary from going down the path of terrorism. Terrorism is not inevitable, and can be avoided *in all cases*.

The main reason for Israel's failure is its belief that terrorism is an inescapable phenomenon inherent to Islam.[584] This reading is not new, and tends to link Palestinian resistance to religious objectives, ruling out any possibility of negotiation on territorial issues. As a result, the solution can only lie in the use of violence. Very widespread in France and Belgium, this vision is conveyed by Islamophobic circles who refuse to question our foreign policies and actions. It is highly reductive and extremely dangerous, as it presents terrorism as a phenomenon that cannot be combated upstream through a holistic strategy, but only reactively through violence. Not only is this approach responsive and gives the

---

582. https://academic.oup.com/ejil/article-pdf/16/5/963/1337361/chi152.pdf
583. "Israel-Hamas war: 'France's position, I don't recognize it,' assures Zineb El Rhazoui," *LCI/YouTube*, November 18, 2023 (https://youtu.be/uJAGHp4r3zQ)
584. Antoine HASDAY, "La pensée djihadiste décryptée," *slate.fr*, November 6, 2017.

initiative to terrorists, it also "de-pluralizes" the causes of terrorism and encourages communitarianism. It is at the root of the spread of terrorism and our inability to deal with it.

An examination of Israel's approach to the fight against terrorism suggests that there is less real will to fight terrorism than to fight the Palestinians. In fact, the use of violence is only really effective against terrorism of a symmetrical nature. Terrorism of an asymmetrical nature (such as that based on an Islamic mindset) is encouraged by violence. But in three-quarters of a century, Israel still has not understood this.

In Afghanistan, the NATO command measured the effectiveness of Operation RESOLUTE SUPPORT by the number of insurgents killed.[585] In France, the "success" of Operation BARKHANE was measured by the number of militants killed.[586] However, these figures increasing did not reflect success: the situation was not improving, and hostility to the foreign presence grew. With no measurable objectives defined, all that remained to illustrate success was the number of adversaries killed.

The use of force in anti-terrorist action is a double-edged sword: it must achieve its objective without providing additional motivation for the terrorists. In 1990, a Vietnam War veteran declared:

> *The longer we stayed in Vietnam, the more Viet Cong there were, because we created them; we produced them... The Vietnamese hated me and I gave them every reason to hate me.*[587]

It is the same thing we are hearing today about Operation BARKHANE. On July 6, 2009, the High Command of the NATO force in Afghanistan (ISAF), recognizing—somewhat belatedly—the asymmetrical nature of the conflict, promulgated a directive stating:

---

585. Bill ROGGIO, "NATO command touts body count of 'Taliban irreconcilables,'" *The Long War Journal*, July 23, 2018.
586. "G5 Sahel: quelques succès militaires de Barkhane au milieu du chaos terroriste," *France 24*, February 15, 2021.
587. "Magnificent Storyteller Soldier Reveals What He Saw In Vietnam," *YouTube*, July 19, 2018, https://youtu.be/tixOyiR8B-8

*We must avoid the trap of winning tactical victories—but suffering strategic defeats—by generating excessive civilian casualties or damage, and thus alienating the population.*[588]

There is no rule to determine the "optimal level" of force to use to be effective against terrorism. There is a difficult balance to strike between eliminating a rebel or terrorist force, and alienating the populations that support them. This means that in all cases, the application of maximum force does not reduce the terrorist threat. Quite the contrary, in fact.

It is therefore best to work within the limits of common sense and international humanitarian law.[589] These are set by three basic principles for the planning and execution of military operations:
- the *principle of distinction*, which requires a distinction to be made between civilians and combatants. It prohibits indiscriminate attacks which are not aimed at a specific military objective, or which use a method or means of combat whose effects cannot be circumscribed;
- the *principle of proportionality*, which requires that the damage caused or the risk to civilians must be in proportion to the direct and concrete military benefit;
- the *precautionary principle*, which obliges the attacker to take all possible precautions to protect the civilian population and property against the effects of his attacks.

If, despite the application of these principles, there are civilian casualties, we can speak of "collateral damage." If these principles have not all been respected, we are talking about war crimes or more. This is the case with Israel, which is regularly singled out for its failure to respect these three basic principles.

## The Notion of "Civilian"

As a result, it is harder to reach your opponent than on a 17th-century battlefield. This is why fighting resistance requires sensitivity, imagina-

---

588. Jim GARAMONE, "Directive re-emphasizes protecting Afghan civilians," *American Forces Press Service*, July 6, 2009, www.af.mil/News/Article-Display/Article/119831/directive-re-emphasizes-protecting-afghan-civilians/
589. Protocol Additional to the Geneva Conventions of August 12, 1949, and relating to the Protection of Victims of International Armed Conflicts (Protocol I), June 8, 1977.

tion and creativity—three characteristics that the Israeli army has never demonstrated.

International humanitarian law[590] defines a civilian as follows:

> *In a non-international armed conflict, the term "civilian" refers to all persons who are neither members of the armed forces of the State nor members of an organized armed group.*[591]

And the civilian population:

> *The civilian population is made up of civilians. In international armed conflicts, the presence of individuals who do not meet the definition of civilians within the civilian population does not deprive the latter of its civilian character. Appropriate rules protect the entire population of a party to a conflict without any adverse distinction.*
>
> *In both international and non-international armed conflicts, the civilian population enjoys general protection against the dangers of military operations.*

## *The Principle of Distinction*

The principle of distinction is the easiest to apply. In 2006, after the Israeli intervention in southern Lebanon, the United Nations General Assembly's Commission on Human Rights noted:[592]

> *the systematic use of excessive, indiscriminate and disproportionate force by the Israel Defense Forces against Lebanese civilians and civilian property, without distinction between civilians and combatants and between civilian property and military objectives.*

Similarly, in May 2021, during the fighting in Jerusalem and Gaza, Israeli army spokesman Jonathan Conricus justified the number of Palestinian civilians killed by the intermingling of combatants and civi-

---

590. https://casebook.icrc.org/a_to_z/glossary/civilian-population
591. Additional Protocol I
592. "Report of the Commission of Inquiry on Lebanon pursuant to Human Rights Council Resolution S-2/1," *OHCHR*, November 10, 2006 (https://reliefweb.int/attachments/7d8261ec-f104-3a5e-a938-c3995d4edd47/C029ECF988517AFB4925722E0007C627-ohchr-lbn-10nov.pdf)

lians in Gaza. But this is a fallacious excuse, as the principle of distinction clearly forbids opening fire when one is unable to discriminate between military and civilian targets. Moreover, in the attack on Hamas executive Salah al-Arouri in Beirut on January 2, 2024, Israel succeeded in firing a relatively targeted shot. So it is possible. In other words, when a 1,000 kg bomb is used to hit an individual in a populated area, the aim is clearly to cause damage to the civilian population.

The choice of weapons plays a role here. Some of them are indiscriminate. Such is the case with white phosphorus incendiary weapons. Contrary to what some commentators say, the white phosphorus bombs used by Israel are not prohibited by international conventions. However, it is forbidden to use them against civilians, particularly in situations where it is impossible to distinguish between military personnel and civilians, such as in densely populated urban areas like Gaza. The use of these weapons is governed by Article 2 of Protocol III to the *Convention on Prohibitions or Restrictions on the Use of Certain Weapons*, which states:

> *2. It is prohibited in all circumstances to make a military objective located within a concentration of civilians the object of attack by means of incendiary weapons launched from aircraft.*[593]

Yet the Israeli army uses them in an area with one of the highest population densities in the world[594]. The same applies to the use of 1,000 kg bombs[595]. The United States seems to have understood this inadequacy, since it has asked Israel to use "smaller *bombs!*"[596]

To what extent the International Court of Justice will consider this a case of genocide is an open question at this stage. The fact remains, however, that these are clear violations of IHL to which our countries,

---

[593]. https://treaties.un.org/Pages/ViewDetails.aspx?src=TREATY&mtdsg_no=XXVI-2&chapter=26&clang=_fr

[594]. Philibert SLIBERT & Marija RISTIC, "Israel/OPT: Identifying the Israeli army's use of white phosphorus in Gaza," *Amnesty international*, October 13, 2023 (https://citizenevidence.org/2023/10/13/israel-opt-identifying-the-israeli-armys-use-of-white-phosphorus-in-gaza/)

[595]. Tamara QIBLAWI, Allegra GOODWIN, Gianluca MEZZOFIORE & Nima ELBAGIR, "'Not seen since Vietnam': Israel dropped hundreds of 2,000-pound bombs on Gaza, analysis shows," *CNN*, December 22, 2023 (https://edition.cnn.com/gaza-israel-big-bombs/index.html)

[596]. Adam ENTOUS, Eric SCHMITT & Julian E. BARNES, "U.S. Officials Outline Steps to Israel to Reduce Civilian Casualties," *The New York Times*, November 4, 2023 (https://www.nytimes.com/2023/11/04/us/politics/israel-gaza-deaths-bombs.html)

and the United States in particular, are contributing by supplying such weapons, knowing that they will be used against civilian populations.[597]

By December 5, 2023, Israel had killed around 2,000 Hamas fighters, with 12,000 bombs weighing between 150 and 1,000 kg. In other words, the Israelis hit targets where there were no Hamas fighters, and 10,000 bombs killed civilians.

When it is difficult, if not impossible, to distinguish between military personnel and civilians, another method must be used, such as fighting with the help of ground troops. This is no guarantee, however, that massacres will not occur: we all remember the massacre at Sabra and Shatila, near Beirut, during Operation PEACE IN GALILEE.

Numerous examples show that there is a clear intention to kill Palestinians. Israel has been repeatedly criticized by the United Nations for its failure to respect norms and international humanitarian law: soldiers simply kill for pleasure[598] or break the bones of captured young Palestinians.[599] In May 2021, according to Israeli media *Channel 12*, Israeli pilots confessed to destroying buildings in Gaza to *"vent their frustration."*[600]

In the fight against terrorism, the use of force must be rigorously integrated into a clear strategy. In Israel, the failure to resolve the Palestinian question gives the impression that the use of violence is nothing more than a kind of group therapy driven by a spirit of revenge.

## *The Principle of Proportionality*

The principle of proportionality is sometimes more difficult to determine. On December 5, 2023, on France 5, Samy Cohen, Director of Research Emeritus at Sciences Po's Center for International Studies and Research, declared:[601]

---

597. William CHRISTOU, Alex HORTON & Meg KELLY, "Israel used U.S.-supplied white phosphorus in Lebanon attack," *The Washington Post*, December 11, 2023 (https://www.washingtonpost.com/investigations/2023/12/11/israel-us-white-phosphorus-lebanon/)
598. "Israeli occupation soldiers kill Palestinian kids for fun,—Israeli soldiers cheer after shooting a Palestinian protester in the village of Madama," *B'Tselem/YouTube*, April 24, 2018.
599. Amira HASS, "Broken Bones and Broken Hopes," *Haaretz*, November 4, 2005. (https://www.haaretz.com/2005-11-04/ty-article/broken-bones-and-broken-hopes/0000017f-f6e1-d47e-a37f-fffda3b20000)
600. https://www.mako.co.il/pzm-magazine/Article-90031632ea98971027.htm?Partner=rss
601. https://youtu.be/mw83eoV8xd4?t=708

> *When we talk about disproportion, we have to be careful what we're talking about, because disproportion in terms of international law doesn't mean that we don't have the right to attack civilians. You have the right to attack them if they are close to a military target, provided that the military target is proportional to the casualties you are going to cause.*

This is not true. Contrary to what he claims, we do not have the right to attack civilians. Period. On the other hand, you can attack military targets, even if there are civilians nearby, as long as the weapons used do not hit them. For example, to eliminate a Hamas leader, one could use a sniper, with the certainty that there would be no collateral damage, or use missiles, as in the case of Sheikh Ahmed Yassin, leader of Hamas, eliminated in his wheelchair by a HELLFIRE missile in March 2004.[602] Ironically, it was the same type of missile that reduced the young people at the NOVA festival to ashes on October 7, 2013. Twenty years apart, the methods have not changed, but this time they eliminated dozens of young Israelis. We will come back to this.

As Colonel François-Régis Legrier of the French army noted with courage and lucidity after his mission in Syria:[603]

> *We have massively destroyed the infrastructure and given the population a detestable image of what Western-style liberation can be, leaving behind us the seeds of the imminent resurgence of a new adversary. We have by no means won the war.*

All the ingredients are there to generate terrorism, and that is exactly what Israel has been doing since 1947-1948. You only need to read my book *La guerre asymétrique ou la défaite du vainqueur*, published in 2003, to understand this.[604] "Collateral damage" then becomes yet another justification for terrorists, as the Islamic State puts it:

---

602. Stephen FARRELL & Richard BEESTON, "Out of the desert darkness came Hellfire," *The Times*, March 23, 2004 (https://www.thetimes.co.uk/article/out-of-the-desert-darkness-came-hellfire-3pnc2ll7rg7)
603. Clémence LABASSE, "Conflict in Syria A French colonel criticizes the Coalition's military strategy," *La Voix du Nord*, February 16, 2019.
604. Jacques BAUD, *La Guerre asymétrique ou la Défaite du vainqueur*, Éditions du Rocher, Monaco, 2003.

*Artillery, like terrorism, leads to the loss of non-combatant lives. A missile hitting a city, which is obviously not a precise weapon, is no different from a bomb in a city in a country that is at war with Muslims.*

*From this point on... it is clear that Muslims are entitled to target populations in countries that are at war with Muslims, with bombs, firearms or other forms of attack that inevitably lead to the death of non-combatants.*[605]

You only have to listen to former Israeli ambassador Mark Regev, to see that he has exactly the same argument as the Islamic State.[606]

The very principle of the deterrence strategy sketched out by Moshe Dayan in the early 1950s includes the notion of disproportionality that we find today in the DAHYA doctrine. The decision to strike with 1,000 kg bombs in densely populated areas contradicts the idea that civilians are not to be attacked. In fact, the aim of targeting civilians is to incite them to rebel against Hamas. This is a deliberate policy, comparable to that of the British in 1943-1945, who sought to provoke an uprising against the Nazi regime. This is why the Israeli government refers to the entire population of Gaza as "Nazis."[607] It is also for this reason that it repeatedly refers to the example of the bombing of Dresden, which had the same objective.[608]

By November 26, 2023, Israel had dropped 40,000 tons of bombs on Gaza,[609] killing 14,800 civilians[610] and killing between 1,000 and 2,000 Hamas fighters.[611] It is thus easy to verify that, at this stage, Israel

- kills about 10 civilians, including 6 children, per dead Hamas fighter;

---

605. *Inspire Magazine*, n°8, Fall 2011, p.42.
606. https://www.youtube.com/watch?v=VSlhB9X_cCY
607. Carrie KELLER-LYNN & Jacob MAGID, "'There are 2 million Nazis' in West Bank, says far-right Finance Minister Smotrich," *The Times of Israel*, November 28, 2023 (https://www.timesofisrael.com/there-are-2-million-nazis-in-west-bank-says-far-right-finance-minister-smotrich/)
608. "Gaza's destruction is "more or less" Germany's in World War II, says Josep Borrell," *Le Figaro / AFP*, December 12, 2023 (updated December 13, 2023) (https://www.lefigaro.fr/international/la-destruction-de-gaza-est-plus-ou-moins-celle-de-l-allemagne-lors-de-la-seconde-guerre-mondiale-selon-josep-borrell-20231212)
609. https://www.teletrader.com/40-000-tons-of-bombs-reportedly-dropped-on-gaza-since-octobe/news/details/61045294?internal=1
610. https://www.ochaopt.org/content/hostilities-gaza-strip-and-israel-flash-update-51
611. https://www.theguardian.com/world/2023/nov/26/idf-messaging-suggests-gaza-truce-unlikely-to-last-much-beyond-tuesday

- uses between 20 and 40 tons of bombs to kill one Hamas militant;
- uses more than 2 tons of bombs per civilian killed.

Israel's response thus appears to fail to respect the principle of proportionality. Yet these figures seem to satisfy the Israeli general staff, as evidenced by the statement of Jonathan Conricus, spokesman for the Israeli army:

> *I can say that if this is true—and I think our figures will be corroborated—if you compare this ratio to any other conflict in urban terrain between an army and a terrorist organization using civilians as human shields, and integrated into the civilian population, you will find that this ratio is formidable, extremely positive, and perhaps unique in the world.*[612]

In short, beyond the legal and humanitarian considerations, which are clear, the Israeli army is profoundly inefficient and ineffective. It is inefficient because the amount of ammunition and death required to achieve an objective is inordinate, and it is ineffective because, as we can see on the ground, the destruction and death it brings do not solve the problem.

Proportionality is expressed, on the one hand, in the relationship between the weapons used and the objective sought, as we have seen, and, on the other, in the relationship between the threat and the response to it. The ratio between the mortality of the Hamas attack and that of Operation SWORDS OF IRON is already an indicator of this disproportion. But examining the mortality rate between Palestinians and Israelis between 2008 and September 2023 shows that disproportion is part of the Israeli strategy, and that in a way, Israel is holding the Palestinian population hostage in order to put pressure on resistance movements.

---

612. Mitchell MCCLUSKEY & Richard Allen GREENE, "Israel military says 2 civilians killed for every Hamas militant is a 'tremendously positive' ratio given combat challenges," *CNN*, December 6, 2023 (https://edition.cnn.com/2023/12/05/middleeast/israel-hamas-military-civilian-ratio-killed-intl-hnk/index.html)

## Injured between 2008 and September 2023 in the Occupied Palestinian Territories

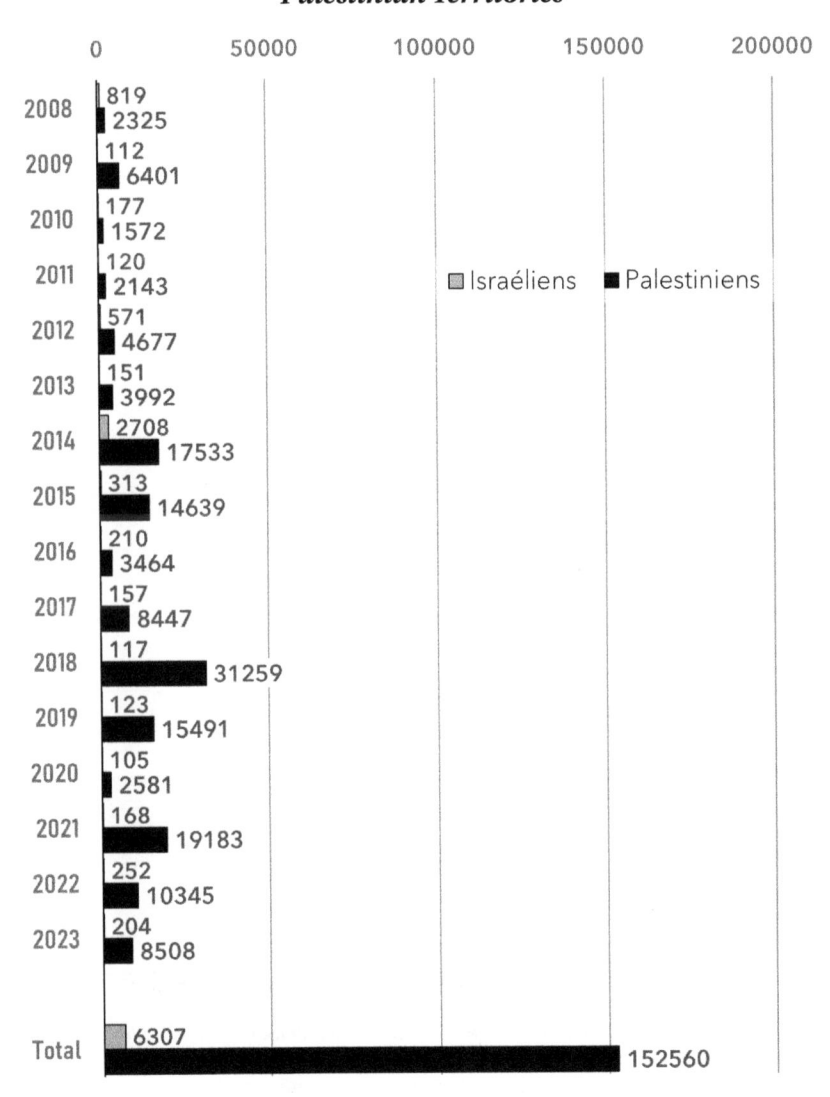

| Year | Israéliens | Palestiniens |
|---|---|---|
| 2008 | 819 | 2325 |
| 2009 | 112 | 6401 |
| 2010 | 177 | 1572 |
| 2011 | 120 | 2143 |
| 2012 | 571 | 4677 |
| 2013 | 151 | 3992 |
| 2014 | 2708 | 17533 |
| 2015 | 313 | 14639 |
| 2016 | 210 | 3464 |
| 2017 | 157 | 8447 |
| 2018 | 117 | 31259 |
| 2019 | 123 | 15491 |
| 2020 | 105 | 2581 |
| 2021 | 168 | 19183 |
| 2022 | 252 | 10345 |
| 2023 | 204 | 8508 |
| Total | 6307 | 152560 |

*Figure 120—Number of injuries per year between 2008 and September 19, 2023. In total, during this period, Israelis were wounded 6,307 times, while Palestinians were wounded 152,560 times. International law requires proportionality in military responses. Obviously, with a ratio of 24 to 1, it is hard to see proportionality! [https://www.ochaopt.org/data/casualties]*

## Killed between 2008 and September 2023 in the Occupied Palestinian Territories

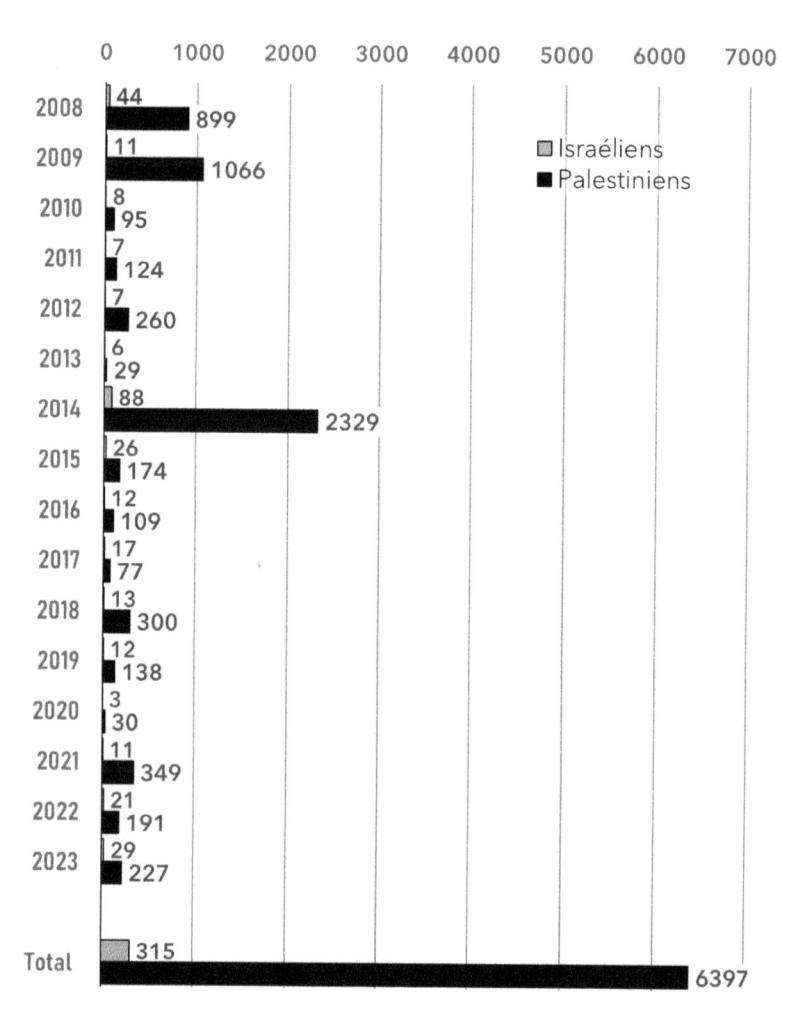

| Year | Israéliens | Palestiniens |
|---|---|---|
| 2008 | 44 | 899 |
| 2009 | 11 | 1066 |
| 2010 | 8 | 95 |
| 2011 | 7 | 124 |
| 2012 | 7 | 260 |
| 2013 | 6 | 29 |
| 2014 | 88 | 2329 |
| 2015 | 26 | 174 |
| 2016 | 12 | 109 |
| 2017 | 17 | 77 |
| 2018 | 13 | 300 |
| 2019 | 12 | 138 |
| 2020 | 3 | 30 |
| 2021 | 11 | 349 |
| 2022 | 21 | 191 |
| 2023 | 29 | 227 |
| Total | 315 | 6397 |

*Figure 121—The number of deaths between 2008 and September 19, 2023. Palestinians suffered 6,407 deaths and Israelis 308. It is this disproportion that shows that Israel is not only defending itself, but taking revenge on the Palestinian population, in the complete silence of the international community, and this is undoubtedly one of the driving forces behind Hamas's action on October 7, 2023. [https://www.ochaopt.org/data/casualties]*

## The Precautionary Principle

As for the precautionary principle, it presupposes an awareness of the importance of protecting the civilian population from the consequences of operations. But when Israeli President Isaac Herzog declares that:

> *A whole nation is responsible.*[613]

His words echo those of former Defense Minister Avigdor Liberman, who said in April 2018:

> *There are no innocents in Gaza.*[614]

We could also cite the example cited above of considering the population of Gaza as "2 million Nazis" as another way of showing that there is no distinction between civilians and combatants. In other words, the precautionary principle is rejected out of hand, suggesting, as the *Huffington Post* states, that the civilian population is considered a legitimate target.[615]

These statements, which will be retained by the ICJ to illustrate the "plausibility" of genocide, are not only damning, but will continue long after January 26, 2024, demonstrating the Israeli authorities' contempt for international institutions.

Another indication of non-compliance with the precautionary principle is the absence of a Battle Damage Assessment (BDA) mechanism, which would ensure that the same mistakes or crimes are not repeated.[616]

The broadcasting of messages urging the population to leave the areas to be bombed is certainly a preventive measure, but the precautionary principle implies that air strikes cannot be used in the absence of a duly conducted verification or in the event of suspicion of the presence, even residual, of civilians.

---

613. "'No Innocent Civilians in Gaza,' Israel President Says as Northern Gaza Struggles to Flee Israeli Bombs," *The Wire*, October 14, 2023 (https://thewire.in/world/northern-gaza-israel-palestine-conflict)

614. https://www.jpost.com/arab-israeli-conflict/there-are-no-innocents-in-gaza-says-israeli-defense-minister-549173

615. Paul BLUMENTHAL, "Israeli President Suggests That Civilians In Gaza Are Legitimate Targets," *The Huffington Post*, October 17, 2023 (https://news.yahoo.com/israeli-president-says-no-innocent-154330724.html?guccounter=1)

616. https://twitter.com/yuval_abraham/status/1750123648533324158

## The Contradictions of Israeli Discourse

*Figure 122—According to Israeli President Isaac Herzog, there are no innocents in Gaza. Not only does this denote a denial of the precautionary principle, but it contradicts the idea that Hamas "has taken its own people prisoner," as Caroline Fourest declares on BFMTV.[617] [Source: https://twitter.com/Sprinter99800/status/1713064886027063584]*

Our refusal to show Israel that it is mistaken in its approach to the problem means that it has never sought alternative strategies. Indeed, even our military has never had the imagination to fight terrorism with solutions that would spare civilians.

---

617. https://www.bfmtv.com/replay-emissions/c-est-pas-tous-les-jours-dimanche/caroline-fourest-nous-avons-800-actes-antisemites-depuis-le-7-octobre-29-10_VN-202310290362.html

### *An Unnecessarily Brutal Response*

The brutality of the Israeli response after October 7, 2023 is exceptional in its intensity, scale and media coverage, but there is nothing exceptional about it in itself. In fact, it corresponds to the feeling of having been beaten by a weaker person, a "human animal," "sub-humans." Thus, the need to react strongly. But on a less cultural and more political level, the need to strike hard stems from the philosophy of Israeli security policy, which is based on the balance of power. The myth of the "invincible army" is part of a national security approach based on discouraging potential enemies. After the 2008 incidents in the Gaza Strip, the *New York Times* noted:

> *Israel has a bigger concern: it fears that its enemies are less afraid of it today than they have been in the past, or than they should be. Israeli leaders believe that a show of force in Gaza could remedy this.*[618]

Israel is therefore in a deterrent mode, where the elimination of the Palestinians is a way of demonstrating its strength.

My observation of numerous combat situations and analysis of battles fought over more than a century show that brutality is inversely proportional to the quality of military leadership and planning.

The generic function of an army is to channel the use of force towards a common objective, thus preventing it from being dispersed against unimportant or individual objectives. It is therefore essential, in a crisis situation, to have at least one clear objective and the leadership capabilities to direct all efforts towards this objective.

In the case of the Israeli response, these elements are conspicuous by their absence. "Destroying Hamas" is preferred to "eliminating the threat." These are two different things. As I wrote back in 2003, the Israelis are killing people, but not the Palestinians' will to resist, which should be their objective. On the contrary, one would think they go out of their way to create terrorism.

---

618. Ethan Bronner, "Israel Reminds Foes That It Has Teeth," *The New York Times*, December 28, 2008 (https://www.nytimes.com/2008/12/29/world/middleeast/29assess.html).

## Civilian Victims of Israeli Operation SWORDS OF IRON

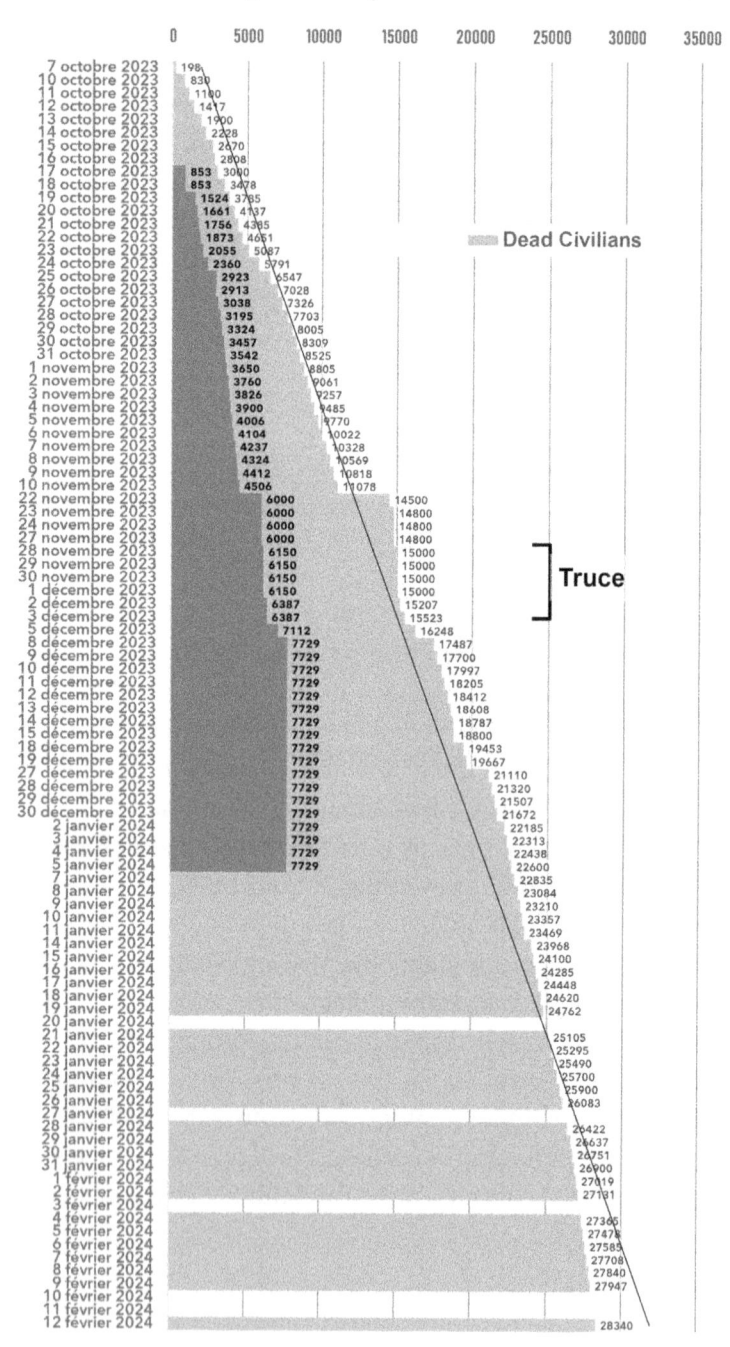

Figure 123—Number of civilian victims of Israeli strikes since October 7, 2023.
[Source: https://www.ochaopt.org/updates]

In the age of social networking, the exactions committed by soldiers looting Palestinian homes, stealing jewelry and ransacking toy stores give an even more disastrous image of the Israeli army. The very fact that these same soldiers publish these videos shows that they are both undisciplined and misbehaving.

Targeting does not take into account the presence of civilians. In an investigation conducted by the Israeli media *Local Call* and *+972 Magazine*, Israeli journalist Yuval Abraham revealed in November 2023 that the definition of targets in Gaza has four categories:

- Tactical objectives, i.e., positions identified by Palestinian fighters (firing positions, fortified positions, etc.).
- Tunnels and underground networks, the location of which is not always known with certainty, and the destruction of which can also mean the destruction of residential buildings.
- Objectives whose destruction should put pressure on the Palestinian (or Hamas) leadership. These objectives, known as "*power objectives*," are intended to shock the civilian population into "*putting pressure on Hamas.*" In other words, the aim is not to target militants, Hamas members or terrorists, but buildings and infrastructure likely to incite the population to rebel against Hamas. According to +972, these targets can be inhabited:

*[The source] confirmed that for the vast majority of potential targets in Gaza—including homes—the Israeli army has files indicating the number of civilians likely to be killed in an attack on a given target. This number is calculated and known in advance by the army's intelligence units, who also know, shortly before launching an attack, how many civilians are certain to be killed.*

- The homes and residences of Hamas members or their families.

These targets are selected in part using artificial intelligence software called *Habsora* (The Gospel).[619] But this system seems to have only limited intelligence, as it has led to targeting locations where there were no fighters. The reason is that this system does not choose its targets

---

619. Yuval Abraham, "'A mass assassination factory': Inside Israel's calculated bombing of Gaza," *+972 Magazine*, November 30, 2023 (https://www.972mag.com/mass-assassination-factory-israel-calculated-bombing-gaza/)

based on intelligence that would place a Hamas militant in a particular location, but based on the frequency of use of a cell phone.

The system uses metadata collected by service providers and passed on to intelligence services. They are associated with characteristic "profiles," established by mathematical algorithms that are supposed to represent the typical behavior of terrorists. Thus, to put it simply, a phone that frequently connects with phones suspected of belonging to terrorists, or located in areas where terrorists are present, will be considered to belong to a terrorist. It will be targeted without knowing who its actual user is at the time, or the identity of the people around it (e.g., a family), who are automatically considered terrorists.

The Americans used a similar system in Iraq and Afghanistan. It produced very poor results, killing over 90% of innocent victims.[620] Apparently, the Israeli system performs no better. The problem is that targeting is not based on the situation as it is, but on how we imagine it could be. It is, as the Israeli journalist puts it, "*a mass murder factory.*" In other words, claims of targeted fire are misleading. The shootings are not targeted because Israeli intelligence services have been unable to locate Hamas cadres who might constitute targets.

By comparison, in October 2023, a Ukrainian military officer told the British *Times* newspaper that the Russians were dropping 25-30 guided bombs a day in the Orekhov-Rabotino sector.[621] In Gaza, between October 7 and 14, the Israeli air force dropped 6,000 guided bombs on Gaza, i.e., 1,000 bombs a day, on an area mainly populated by civilians. On October 16, the American media outlet *Business Insider* noted that in 6 days, Israel had already dropped more bombs on Gaza than the United States had done in any month of its campaign against the Islamic State.[622]

---

620. "The Drone Papers," *The Intercept* (https://theintercept.com/drone-papers/); Andrew Blake, "Obama-led drone strikes kill innocents 90% of the time: report," *The Washington Times*, October 15, 2015.
621. Maxim Tucker, "'Our allies ask us to advance with a gun at our backs,'" *The Times*, October 4, 2023 (https://www.thetimes.co.uk/article/our-allies-ask-us-to-advance-with-a-gun-at-our-backs-vrjdnx2hv)
622. Jake Epstein & Lloyd Lee, "Israel dropped more bombs on Gaza in 6 days than the US-led coalition dropped in any month fighting ISIS," *Business Insider*, October 14, 2023 (https://www.businessinsider.com/israel-palestine-confilct-bombing-gaza-strip-hamas-united-states-isis-2023-10?amp)

On December 22, 2023, according to *CNN*, Israeli strikes on Gaza totaled 29,000 bombs.[623] On that day, the total number of civilian deaths reached 19,000. In other words, the Israeli army fired 1.5 bombs for every civilian killed. It is hard to say whether the Israeli army is the most moral army in the world, but it is certainly the most deadly for civilians and the least effective at eliminating its adversaries.

In the Israeli army, those planning strikes may be authorized to cause collateral damage, depending on the importance of the target. There is a scale for determining the number of "acceptable" collateral casualties for a given target.

Thus, according to the United Nations, between February 24, 2022 and October 8, 2023, the Russian offensive caused the death of 560 children in areas controlled by the Ukrainian government.[624] Between October 7 and 27, 2023, according to the Palestinian authorities in Gaza, the Israeli army killed 2,665 children.[625] In other words, the Russians killed 7 children a week, while the Israelis killed nearly 890.

In terms of "civilians," Israel killed as many in three weeks as the Russians did in 20 months of war in Ukraine. To the Israelis' credit, the distinction between "civilians" and "combatants" is trickier in Palestine.

*Comparison of Mortality Rates in the Ukraine and Gaza Conflicts*

| Conflict | From | Visit | Number of days | Civilians killed | Average per day | Children killed | Average per day |
|---|---|---|---|---|---|---|---|
| Ukraine | 24.02.2022 | 08.10.2023 | 591 | 7 649 | 13 | 560 | 0,95 |
| Gaza | 07.10.2023 | 03.11.2023 | 28 | 9 257 | 330 | 3 826 | 137 |

*Figure 124—As we can see, on the European continent, military personnel tend to respect civilian populations. The situation changes completely when these same soldiers are deployed on other continents. In Israel, the military do not have the culture of the area they claim to come from, but behave like their Western counterparts: without any respect for life. It is this brutality that is behind the terrorists' determination to strike at us in Europe.*

---

623. Tamara Qiblawi, Allegra Goodwin, Gianluca Mezzofiore & Nima Elbagir, "'Not seen since Vietnam': Israel dropped hundreds of 2,000-pound bombs on Gaza, analysis shows," *CNN*, December 22, 2023 (https://edition.cnn.com/gaza-israel-big-bombs/index.html)
624. https://ukraine.un.org/en/248799-ukraine-civilian-casualties-8-october-2023
625. https://www.aa.com.tr/fr/monde/le-minist%C3%A8re-de-la-sant%C3%A9-de-gaza-publie-une-liste-de-6-747-noms-de-palestiniens-tu%C3%A9s-depuis-le-d%C3%A9but-de-la-guerre-/3033868

The problem with Western forces is that they seek victory through *firepower superiority*. This was the way war was waged in 1914-1918, in a highly symmetrical situation with virtually no strategy. Today, in an asymmetrical conflict, it often leads to transgressing the rules of the law of war, without leading to victory.

## *Justifying the Use of Violence*

Surprisingly enough, in France the logic of our journalists in relation to Israel's war crimes always follows the same path:

### *The Law of Talion according to our Media*

|   | Arguments put forward by our media | International humanitarian law |
|---|---|---|
| Historical justification | Allied bombing of German populations in World War II was justified. No one has condemned Western bombing of civilian populations in Afghanistan, Iraq, Libya and Syria to fight the Islamic State, so bombing civilians in Palestine is legitimate. | No crime can justify another. Following this argument, we accept the law of retaliation. This would, for example, justify the terrorist attacks in France in 2015-2016, which were perpetrated after France. went to bomb populations in Iraq, then Syria. Moreover, some journalists who propose this argument justify Ukrainian terrorist acts against Russia. |
| Justification by the need to punish | Hamas militants committed criminal acts on October 7, 2023, so there is no reason to take any more precautions. | As before, whatever the horror of October 7, it does not justify further crimes. In all cases, the principle of proportionality applies. On the other hand, the refusal to take precautions to protect the civilian population, for example by using very large-caliber bombs, means that the punishment intended for Hamas is inflicted on the civilian population. We are therefore in a situation of "collective punishment," prohibited by Article 33 of the Fourth Geneva Convention and Article 4 of the Second Additional Protocol. |
| Justification by the right to defend oneself | Israel has the right to defend itself. | This is incorrect. Israel has the right to defend itself, but not under Article 51 of the UN Charter, which only applies between countries. Israel has the right—and the duty—to protect its population. It could therefore invoke the responsibility to protect. But it does not, because this duty also requires it to protect the Palestinian population as the occupying power. In any case, the right to defend oneself can only be exercised within the framework of international law. Israel is not allowed to use all possible means. |

*Figure 125—In the West, and in France in particular, our commentators justify the use of disproportionate violence by referencing situations such as the bombing of Dresden (1945) or strikes against the Islamic State. In so doing, they adopt exactly the same logic and arguments as the latter.*

The problem here is that anti-Semitism is not caused by Israel's actions *per se*, but by the fact that these actions can be carried out without being allowed to be questioned and criticized.

Cutting off supplies of electricity, drinking water and fuel,[626] as of October 10, on the pretext that Hamas might use them, constitutes a war crime. The assumption that some civilians might resell the food they are given to Hamas is not an argument for not giving it to them.

A war crime is a war crime, and contrary to what our journalists claim, there is never a good reason to commit a war crime or genocide. In the end, Israeli statements played down on *LCI*, *BFMTV* or *CNews* were accepted by the ICJ as evidence against Israel, as evidence of genocidal "intent."

## *Human Shields*

The practice of using human shields is to place civilians against their will in the vicinity of targets in order to induce the adversary not to target them. This practice is totally illegal under IHL[627] and Israel regularly accuses Hamas of using it, as we have seen. Excusing the brutality of its action by invoking the use of "human shields" is the excuse of someone who does not known how to get around this problem and find the right strategy, because the presence of civilians and innocents is inherent to this type of conflict.

An examination of strikes on Gaza, particularly since 2008, shows that this accusation is irrelevant as far as Hamas is concerned, for several reasons.

The first is that, by its very nature, a resistance movement evolves within a population, like "*a fish in water*," as Mao Zedong put it. This was the case for the Resistance in France, or in the rest of Europe, and it is the case for the Palestinian resistance. So that is one of the facts of the problem. To solve it, it is up to the State, the occupier or the aggressor to choose the right strategy. Israel has never done so, as we shall see, but has drawn inspiration from the way in which the United States, Great Britain and France have fought against opposition to their presence in the Middle East, Central Asia and North Africa.

Note here that in the 1960s-1980s, the British had the same problem in Northern Ireland, the Spanish in the Basque Country and the Italians in

---

626. https://youtu.be/zWuMUsZqajw
627. https://ihl-databases.icrc.org/fr/ihl-treaties/gciv-1949/article-28

Northern Italy, at a time when smart weapons did not exist, and they did not need to decimate civilian populations to defeat terrorism.

The second is that human shields can only be used if civilians are kept within the danger zone of the enemy's weapons. Since Israel attacks Hamas almost exclusively from the air, the danger zone of projectiles is expressed in terms of CEP. *CEP*, or *Circular Error Probable*, expresses the dispersion of a projectile around the target point.

When civilians are deliberately placed close to an objective, at a distance less than or equal to the CEP of the weapons used by the adversary, this can be considered as the use of human shields. If the effects of the explosion endanger civilians, this means that the adversary has chosen the wrong strategy and cannot invoke the existence of human shields. Thus, when Israel uses 1,000 kg bombs with a lethal radius of 300-400 m, it cannot invoke the existence of human shields.

### *Human Shields and CEP Weapons*

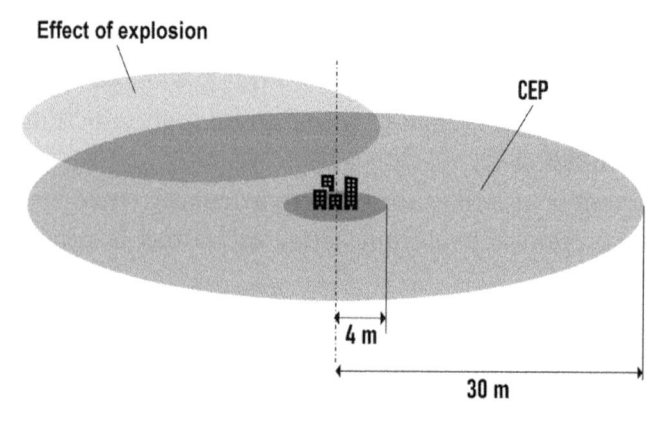

*Figure 126—Israel uses the notion of human shields as a justification for using bombs indiscriminately, and our media relay this message in support of its policy. But the use of human shields can be determined by technical criteria. For example, civilians would have to be kept at a distance of less than 4 m if Israel were to use precision weapons (to eliminate a Hamas cadre, for example), or 30 m if Israel wanted to bomb a large target with unguided bombs. However, it is clear that Hamas practice does not correspond to the claims made by the Israeli authorities.*

The CEP of Israeli bombs and missiles ranges from around 0.9 to 4 m for guided systems, to 30 m for unguided bombs. Since the Israeli army is targeting the Hamas leadership, it is reasonable to assume that it is using weapons with a CEP of around 1-2 m. Consequently, if civilians are found at a distance of 0.9-4 m from a clear target, we can speak of human shields.

### The CEP for Israeli Precision Weapons

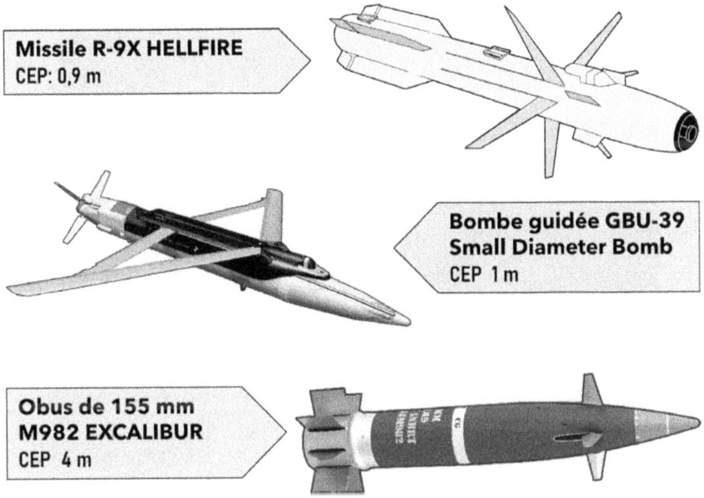

Missile R-9X HELLFIRE
CEP: 0,9 m

Bombe guidée GBU-39
Small Diameter Bomb
CEP 1 m

Obus de 155 mm
M982 EXCALIBUR
CEP 4 m

*Figure 127—Given Israel's stated objectives, Hamas can be accused of using human shields if it deliberately keeps civilians between 90 cm and 4 m from a target.*

The third reason is that the use of human shields only works with an adversary who respects IHL. The Palestinians are well placed to know that Israel does not respect IHL as a matter of principle, so this strategy would be useless. The facts show that Hamas is very rational in its decisions.

The fourth reason is that whatever Hamas's practice, it does not justify Israel's firing. Indeed, according to the Protocol Additional to the Geneva Conventions of August 12, 1949, and relating to the Protection of Victims of International Armed Conflicts (Protocol I), of June 8, 1977:

> *8. No violation of these prohibitions relieves the Parties to the conflict of their legal obligations towards the civilian population and individual civilians.*[628]

---

628. https://ihl-databases.icrc.org/fr/ihl-treaties/api-1977/article-51

## The Notion of "Human Shields" Overused

### The Indonesian Hospital 2023

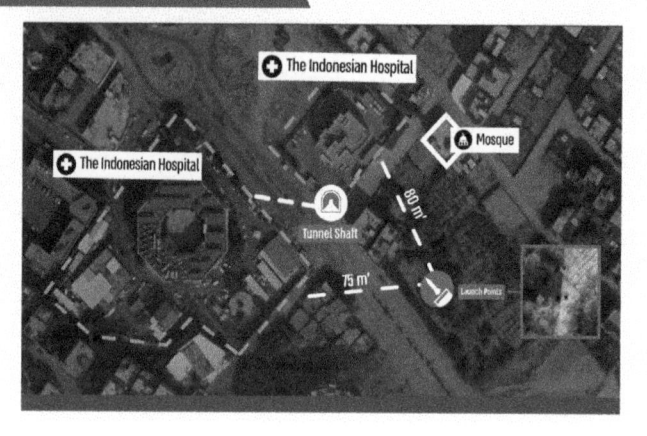

*Figure 128—On November 5, 2023, the Israeli army spokesman justified the assault on the Indonesian hospital by citing the presence of launchers 75 and 80 m from its premises and the use of human shields. However, this distance is more than twice the CEP of the unguided bombs used by Israel. Consequently, the accusation of human shields is nothing but a fallacious pretext. [Source: The Times of Israel]*

In other words, as we have said several times in this book, no matter what our journalists and politicians say, one crime cannot justify another.

The *"human shield"* issue is nothing more than a propaganda ploy, used to justify the targeting of the civilian population. Even if this were true, and even more so if the population were being held hostage by Hamas, bombing them makes no sense at all, because a self-respecting army should seek to minimize the number of innocent victims.

On October 29, 2023, on *LCI*, French actor Bernard-Henri Lévy claimed that Hamas had set up "checkpoints" in the Gaza Strip to prevent the civilian population from leaving areas threatened by Israeli bombardment. Yet, according to *Washington Post* journalists on the ground, *"civilians who have fled south since Friday told the Post they had not seen Hamas fighters in the streets."*[629] No comment.

---

629. Loay Ayyoub, Susannah George & Cate Brown, "Hundreds of thousands flee south in Gaza after Israel orders evacuation," *The Washington Post*, October 14, 2023 (https://www.washingtonpost.com/world/2023/10/14/gaza-evacuation-israel-hamas-war/)

From an operational point of view, if we look at the map of fighting since the start of Operation SWORDS OF IRON in Gaza, and then in Khan Yunis, we can see that the Palestinians have drawn the Israelis into areas that have been emptied of their inhabitants. In other words, Palestinian fighters are seeking to avoid areas where the civilian population would become an obstacle to their actions.

Palestinian fighters also use a network of tunnels to carry out their attacks. These networks are separate from the areas where the civilian population lives. The excuse of "human shields" is merely a reflection of the Israelis' inability to adapt to a form of combat they have always avoided by striking Palestinians from a distance.

In reality, it is the Israelis who are using the civilian populations with the settlements in the West Bank and Gaza envelope as a screen between the Palestinians and the Israeli army. This is why there were so many Israeli civilian casualties on October 7, 2023. We will come back to this later. In addition, numerous testimonies indicate that Israeli soldiers use children to precede them into areas suspected of being mined or booby-trapped.[630]

## Poor Tactics

The Israelis seek "*absolute operational control*" of the areas of the Gaza Strip they occupy. But the videos we have seen show that this is far from the case. As in Lebanon in 2006, they have underestimated the level of defensive preparations made by the Palestinian fighters. The latter manage to emerge behind their lines and carry out deadly attacks against their tanks and troops.

The intermingling of Israeli and Palestinian troops makes air support very difficult, and despite Israeli technology, the forces are at parity on this terrain. In view of the preparations, it seems highly likely that the Palestinians had anticipated an Israeli intervention, and Operation AL-AQSA FLOOD was probably intended to draw it into their territory.

---

630. "Israeli soldiers convicted for using child as human shield," *France 24*, October 3, 2010 (https://www.france24.com/en/20101003-israeli-soldiers-convicted-using-child-human-shield-palestinian-territories)

The intervention in northern Gaza is led by the Golani division, one of the oldest and most prestigious formations in the Israeli army. But at the end of December 2023, the Israeli government sought to give its Operation SWORDS OF IRON a religious dimension and decided to change its name to reflect this.

The Golani division was replaced by Brigade 900 "Kfir," which included Battalion 97 "Netsakh Yehuda" (Eternal Judea). This is a unit of Orthodox Jews, operating according to the imperatives and traditions of the Hebrew religion. It is a unit that has become infamous for its many abuses in the West Bank.

## Lack of Victories

Faced with worldwide criticism of the savagery of its action against civilian populations, the growing number of wounded and dead within its army and internal opposition, the Israeli government must demonstrate success.

But the Palestinians dominate the narrative. The successes announced by the Israeli leadership concerning Hamas headquarters and the tunnels turn out to be crude fabrications, and clearly do not undermine the determination and capabilities of the Palestinian resistance fighters.

At the beginning of January 2024, three months after the Hamas offensive, the Israeli army was struggling to claim success, despite massive destruction, with civilian casualties unprecedented in history.

"Too many children killed," according to Blinken. "The number of children killed is far too high."[631] What does "too many" mean? What is the acceptable number of children killed? But of course, Blinken is from the same culture as Netanyahu—without the slightest regard for human life.

---

631. James Gregory & Anthony Zurcher. "Israel-Gaza war: Blinken says cost of conflict on children 'far too high,'" *Radio New Zealand*, January 10, 2024 (https://www.rnz.co.nz/news/world/506418/israel-gaza-war-blinken-says-cost-of-conflict-on-children-far-too-high)

## Reactions inside Israel

In Israel, the news of the Hamas attack, followed by allegations of massacre, hit like a bombshell. Opposition to Benjamin Netanyahu quickly melted away, giving way to what one would see anywhere in such circumstances: a demonstration of national unity. Some even saw this as the reason for ignoring warnings of a Hamas operation to neutralize the opposition to the government that took to Israeli streets in 2023. Was this the case? We do not know.

But this does not mean that the entire Israeli population supports the government's policy. So much so that measures have to be taken to crack down on those who criticize the Israeli response. Arab Israelis, Palestinians and left-wing Jews are suspended from their studies, fired or arrested at night, for posting their opinions on social media.[632] Even in universities, left-wing students are suspended or arrested.[633]

Later, with the multiplication of testimonies from freed hostages, the course of events on October 7 appeared more and more to be the result of a total inability to manage the crisis.

## Genocide, Ethnic Cleansing or Crimes Against Humanity?

As soon as the situation of the Palestinians is mentioned, the terms that emerge are heavy and inevitably take us back to the fate of the Jews in the 1940s. We have got into the habit of using these terms without really thinking about their real meaning. For example, the word "genocide" is used to describe Vladimir Putin's decisions in Ukraine.[634] In fact, it is simply a matter of giving the most negative connotation possible to any activity, even if it is about sheltering children from war.

The problem is that today we realize that these terms can be applied to the country least likely to be guilty of them—Israel.

---

632. Ghousoon BISHARAT, Oren ZIV & Baker ZOUBI, "'This is political persecution': Israel cracks down on internal critics of its Gaza war," *+972 Magazine*, October 17, 2023 (https://www.972mag.com/israel-gaza-war-political-persecution/)

633. Mariam FARAH, "Israeli academia joins the crackdown on dissent," *+972 Magazine*, December 3, 2023 (https://www.972mag.com/israeli-academia-crackdown-palestinian-students/)

634. https://apnews.com/article/putin-genocide-icc-ukraine-house-3c353a93f4a6e-605fe8054cb387ef3d4

It is therefore important to review these terms and understand them in terms of international humanitarian law (IHL). IHL is a body of law comprising a whole series of conventions and treaties, which govern the way conflicts are conducted so as to limit their impact on civilian populations.

### *Ethnic Cleansing*

Ethnic cleansing is not considered an autonomous crime under IHL. It has been defined on the basis of activities carried out during various conflicts. According to the United Nations,[635] it can be defined as follows:

> *... to make an area ethnically homogeneous by using force or intimidation to remove people belonging to specific groups from the area in question.*[636]
> *... a deliberate policy conceived by an ethnic or religious group aimed at eliminating, through the use of violence and terror, civilian populations belonging to a distinct ethnic or religious community from certain geographical areas.*[637]

Ethnic cleansing may or may not be carried out as part of genocide. For many years, Israeli policy towards the occupied territories has been to encourage Palestinians to leave their territory. This policy has been strengthened and confirmed by the arrival in power of ultra-nationalist ministers. Thus, in 2020, Bezalel Smotrich, Minister of Transport, clearly stated his policy of expelling Arab populations from their territory, quoting the Bible:[638]

> *If you do not drive out the inhabitants of this land, those you allow to remain will become prickles in your eyes and thorns in your sides.*

The Palestinian question revolves entirely around respect for international law, which is refuted by Israel and supported by the United States and its Western "followers."

---

635. https://www.un.org/fr/genocideprevention/ethnic-cleansing.shtml
636. https://undocs.org/fr/S/25274
637. https://undocs.org/fr/S/1994/674
638. https://www.timesofisrael.com/smotrich-appears-to-post-support-for-expulsion-of-arab-israelis/

An essential notion for understanding the Palestinian question is that the Israelis' constant strategy from the outset has been to expel the Arab population from Palestine. In technical and legal terms, this is known as ethnic cleansing.[639]

Back in 1940, long before the creation of the State of Israel, the Zionists' vision went beyond what would be proposed seven years later by the United Nations:

> *It must be clear that there is no space in the country for two peoples... If the Arabs leave, the country will become wide and spacious for us... The only solution after the end of the Second World War is the Land of Israel at least the western part of the Land[640] without Arabs. There can be no compromise on this point. There is no other way than to transfer the Arabs from here to neighboring countries, to transfer them all, except perhaps those in Bethlehem, Nazareth and Old Jerusalem. Not one village must remain, not one Bedouin tribe. The transfer must be organized to Iraq, Syria and even Transjordan. Funds must be found for this purpose... And only after this transfer will the country be able to welcome millions of our brothers, and the Jewish problem will cease to exist.[641]*

On October 30, 2023, an Israeli media outlet published a document drawn up on the 13th by the *Ministry of Intelligence,* which proposed a strategy to the Israeli government,[642] the main elements of which were:

> *5. the three options examined are as follows*
> *a. Option A: maintaining the population of Gaza under the control of the Palestinian Authority (PA).*
> *b. Option B: keeping the population in Gaza and creating a local Arab authority.*

---

639. https://www.ohchr.org/en/press-releases/2023/10/un-expert-warns-new-instance-mass-ethnic-cleansing-palestinians-calls
640. N.d.A.: i.e. Palestine west of the Jordan River
641. Joseph Weitz, December 1940, quoted by Benny Morris, in *The Birth of the Palestinian Refugee Problem 1947-1949*, Cambridge University Press, 1987, p. 27, and by Dominique Vidal, *Le péché originel d'Israël*, Éditions Ouvrières, Paris, 1998, p. 99.
642. https://www.scribd.com/document/680677071/תופולח-הביטקרידל-תינידמ-היסולכואל-היחרזאה- בזעה-4-0#

> c. Option C: evacuation of the civilian population from Gaza to Sinai.
> 6. an in-depth examination of the options leads to the following conclusions:
> a. Option C—The option that will produce positive long-term strategic results for Israel, and is achievable. It requires determination at the political level in the face of international pressure, with an emphasis on mobilizing the support of the United States and other pro-Israeli countries for the undertaking.
> b. Options A and B have significant weaknesses, particularly with regard to their strategic repercussions and long-term unrealism. None of them will have the necessary deterrent effect, will not bring about a change of mindset, and could lead in a few years' time to the same problems and threats that Israel has had to face from 2007 to the present day.
> c. Option A is the riskiest; the division between the Palestinian population of Judea and Samaria (West Bank) and that of Gaza is one of the main obstacles to the creation of a Palestinian state.

As we can see, the aim here is not to protect the Palestinian population, but to make the creation of a Palestinian state impossible. That said, Arab countries are unwilling to accept Palestinian refugees for several reasons:

- It is a way for Israel to offload its obligations as occupying power and seek a political solution to the problem.
- This would be a way of ratifying the occupation, or even annexation, of the Gaza Strip, which would be contrary to international law in general and to United Nations Security Council Resolution 242 (1967).
- This would be a form of support for a policy of ethnic cleansing.[643]
- This would lead to a problem for neighboring Arab countries with Israel, rather like Lebanon, from where Palestinian resistance fighters carry out cross-border raids on northern Israel.

The argument put forward by Israeli propaganda and some journalists that this is simply a matter of protecting the population is fallacious. In

---

643. https://www.ohchr.org/en/press-releases/2023/10/un-expert-warns-new-instance-mass-ethnic-cleansing-palestinians-calls

fact, the Ministry of Intelligence document clearly establishes the displacement of the Gazan population towards Sinai:

> *[Dedicated] campaigns will have to be run for Gazans themselves to encourage them to accept this plan—the messages must revolve around the loss of land, making it clear that there is no hope of returning to the territories Israel will soon occupy, whether this is true or not. The image should be: "Allah has caused you to lose this land because of the Hamas leadership—there is no choice but to settle elsewhere with the help of your Muslim brothers."*

Israel's response to the AL-AQSA FLOOD operation is in line with this logic. The aim is not only to punish Hamas by affecting the civilian population, but also to dissuade them from living in Gaza, as Bezalel Smotrich, Israel's Finance Minister, has stated.[644] At the end of January 2024, testimonies collected by the *Haaretz* newspaper showed that Israeli troops were systematically burning down intact Palestinian homes, to prevent people from returning to live there.[645]

In fact, Israel has entered into negotiations with the Democratic Republic of Congo to accept Palestinian emigrants. Israel's Minister of Intelligence explains:

> *The problem of Gaza is not only ours. The world should support humanitarian emigration, because it is the only solution I know of.*[646]

---

644. "'100-200,000, Not Two Million': Israel's Finance Minister Envisions Depopulated Gaza," *Haaretz*, December 31, 2023 (https://www.haaretz.com/israel-news/2023-12-31/ty-article/100-200-000-not-two-million-israels-finance-minister-envisions-depopulated-gaza/0000018c-bfe8-d6c4-ab8d-fffc0b910000)

645. Yaniv Kubovich, "Israeli Army Occupies Gaza Homes—Then Burns Them Down," *Haaretz*, January 31, 2024 (https://www.haaretz.com/israel-news/2024-01-31/ty-article/.premium/israeli-army-occupies-gaza-homes-then-burns-them-down/0000018d-6021-d16e-a39f-7f3f01e30000)

646. "Israeli officials said in talks with Congo, others on taking in Gaza emigrants," *The Times of Israel*, January 3, 2024 (https://www.timesofisrael.com/liveblog_entry/israeli-officials-said-in-talks-with-congo-others-on-taking-in-gaza-emigrants/)

## Genocide

The notion of genocide has been widely evoked in relation to the situation of Palestinians in Gaza. To speak of genocide here should not be a gratuitous accusation, but the result of a factual analysis of the criteria that define this notion. These are to be found in the *Convention on the Prevention and Punishment of the Crime of Genocide* (CPRCG), which was unanimously approved by the United Nations General Assembly on December 9, 1948 and came into force on January 12, 1951. It forms part of international law and declares:

> *Article 2.*
> *In the present Convention, genocide means any of the following acts committed with intent to destroy, in whole or in part, a national, ethnical, racial or religious group, as such:*
> *a) Murder of group members;*
> *b) serious harm to the physical or mental integrity of group members;*
> *c) intentional subjection of the group to conditions of existence likely to bring about its total or partial physical destruction;*
> *d) measures to prevent births within the group;*
> *e) forced transfer of children from one group to another.*[647]

Two fundamental elements characterize the notion of genocide:
- The intention and targeting of individuals as members of a group.
- Actions are decisive, not results.

Our media and authorities do their utmost to maintain confusion about the notion of genocide in order to justify Israel's actions and minimize their scope. They try to make people believe that genocide consists in the rapid mass elimination of large numbers of people. In fact, international law does not define a temporal criterion, but describes what belongs to a process.

A central element in identifying a case of genocide is obviously the expression of intent. This expression obviously has a different weight if it is the opinion of a passer-by in the street or if it is the statements of a political decision-maker. Throughout Russia's Special Operation in Ukraine, Vladimir Putin's every response to Western threats to use

---

647. https://www.ohchr.org/fr/instruments-mechanisms/instruments/convention-prevention-and-punishment-crime-genocide

nuclear weapons has been presented as the Russians' willingness to use nuclear weapons. In Israel today, Minister Amichai Eliyahu's threat to use nuclear weapons on the Palestinian population has—by contrast—been kept very quiet in the Western media.[648] It is, however, far more serious because it illustrates an intention. Thus, in November 2023, Ben Gvir, the Minister of Security, declared:

> *To be clear, when we say that Hamas must be eliminated, we also mean those who sing, those who support and those who hand out sweets. All are terrorists. And they must be eliminated.*[649]

### *No Alternative to Destroying the Whole of Gaza*

*Figure 129—On British media outlet LBC, Israel's ambassador to the UK sees no alternative to destroying the whole of Gaza. [Source: https://twitter.com/LBC/status/1742628517966229662]*

---

648. Michael BACHNER, "Far-right minister says nuking Gaza an option, PM suspends him from cabinet meetings," *The Times of Israel*, November 5, 2023 (https://www.timesofisrael.com/far-right-minister-says-nuking-gaza-an-option-pm-suspends-him-from-cabinet-meetings/)
649. Antonio PITA, "In Israel, support for the war soars," *El Pais*, December 11, 2023 (https://english.elpais.com/international/2023-12-11/in-israel-support-for-the-war-soars.html)

We are no longer at the level of the man in the street, but at that of the decision-makers. The intention here is clear. Indeed, the same intention was expressed by Tzipi Hotovely, Israel's ambassador to the UK, on LBC media in early January 2024.

Clearly, Article 2 of the Convention applies to the situation of the Palestinians, particularly those in Gaza. One crime cannot justify another, but when a population is forced into a genocidal situation, those responsible should expect a desperate response. One would have to be either stupid or so full of one's own superiority not to understand this. Moreover, by refusing to implement international law and obey UN injunctions for over 75 years, Israel has turned Palestine into a kind of lawless zone, of which it is a victim today.

### Beyond Emotion, the Criteria for Genocide

| Convention criteria | Facts observed in Palestine |
|---|---|
| a) Murder of group members; | Targeted elimination and child elimination[650] The enemy is not Hamas, it is Gaza[651] |
| b) Serious harm to the physical or mental integrity of group members; | Bombing of Gaza with inappropriate weapons (including white phosphorus weapons)[652] and with disproportionate weapons[653] and threat to use nuclear weapons[654] Elimination of children.[655] |
| c) Intentional subjection of the group to conditions of existence likely to bring about its total or partial physical destruction; | Blockade of the Gaza Strip since 2007, with restrictions on trade, work, access to food, etc.[656] Threat of extermination. |

---

650. https://www.ohchr.org/Documents/HRBodies/HRCouncil/CoIOPT/A_HRC_40_74.pdf
651. https://youtu.be/sCug7kNJdOg
652. Philibert Slibert & Marija Ristic, "Identifying the Israeli army's use of white phosphorus in Gaza," *Amnesty International*, October 13, 2023 (https://citizenevidence.org/2023/10/13/israel-opt-identifying-the-israeli-armys-use-of-white-phosphorus-in-gaza/)
653. Tamara Qiblawi, Allegra Goodwin, Gianluca Mezzofiore & Nima Elbagir, "'Not seen since Vietnam': Israel dropped hundreds of 2,000-pound bombs on Gaza, analysis shows," *CNN*, December 22, 2023 (https://www.cnn.com/gaza-israel-big-bombs/index.html)
654. Michael Bachner, "Far-right minister says nuking Gaza an option, PM suspends him from cabinet meetings," *The Times of Israel*, November 5, 2023 (https://www.timesofisrael.com/far-right-minister-says-nuking-gaza-an-option-pm-suspends-him-from-cabinet-meetings/)
655. Tovah Lazaroff, "UN: IDF deliberately shot children on Gaza border in apparent war crime," *The Jerusalem Post*, March 1, 2019 (https://www.jpost.com/middle-east/unhrc-idf-may-have-committed-war-crimes-in-quelling-gaza-border-protests-582043)
656. "Israel must lift illegal and inhumane blockade on Gaza as power plant runs out of fuel," *Amnesty International*, October 12, 2023 (https://www.amnesty.org/en/latest/news/2023/10/israel-opt-israel-must-lift-illegal-and-inhumane-blockade-on-gaza-as-power-plant-runs-out-of-fuel/)

| | |
|---|---|
| d) Measures to prevent births within the group; | Malnutrition because of Israel's restrictions on food imports, impacting the birth rate.[657] Targeted attacks on hospitals and schools.[658] |
| e) Forced transfer of children from one group to another. | Arrests of children without charges.[659] Forced transfer of children from the Gaza Strip without informing parents.[660] |

*Figure 130—Ultimately, it is the ICJ that will determine whether Israel is committing genocide or not. Examination of the criteria set out in the Convention explains why the ICJ saw the plausibility of genocide.*

Israeli analyst Eliyahu Yossian says all Gazans, including women, babies and children, should be treated as enemies:

*Hamas does not control Gaza and is not the enemy. Gaza includes Hamas. So Hamas is not the enemy here, but Gaza is the enemy. As soon as you change the terminology, the reading of the situation changes too, and the definition of the enemy is different. So, it doesn't matter who you warn or who you evacuate from an area. This is what we call flattening an area, razing it to the ground. You ask me what I'd do, and my answer is simply to flatten it and kill as many of them as possible. Because the woman is an enemy, the baby is an enemy, the schoolboy is an enemy, the Hamas militant is an enemy, and the pregnant woman is an enemy, because we can see it with our own eyes. Why can't they absorb Western values? Because their logic is blurred. Why, because we see a little boy with a chocolate in his hand, but that same child is going to learn how to handle a Kalashnikov in elementary school. He's a terrorist even if he's a child.[661]*

---

657. Enas A. Assaf, Haleama Al Sabbah & Ayoub Al-Jawadleh, "Analysis of the nutritional status in the Palestinian territory: a review study," *Frontiers in Nutrition / National Library of Medicine*, July 18, 2023 (https://www.ncbi.nlm.nih.gov/pmc/articles/PMC10391640/#)
658. "Gaza: UN experts decry bombing of hospitals and schools as crimes against humanity, call for prevention of genocide," *UN OHCHR*, October 19, 2023 (https://www.ohchr.org/en/press-releases/2023/10/gaza-un-experts-decry-bombing-hospitals-and-schools-crimes-against-humanity)
659. "Number of Palestinian Children (12-17) in Israeli Military Detention," *Defense for Children International—Palestine*, December 2, 2023 (https://www.dci-palestine.org/children_in_israeli_detention)
660. "Fate of baby and other Palestinian children is unknown after Israeli army forcibly transfers them out of Gaza Strip [EN/AR]," *Euro-Med Monitor/Reliefweb*, January 2, 2024 (https://reliefweb.int/report/occupied-palestinian-territory/fate-baby-and-other-palestinian-children-unknown-after-israeli-army-forcibly-transfers-them-out-gaza-strip-enar)
661. https://youtu.be/sCug7kNJdOg

That said, Eliyahu Yossian is not a policy-maker. Therefore, this quotation is only representative of a way of thinking in the Israeli population, but does not constitute proof of genocide *per se*.

### The 10 Stages of Genocide According to Holocaust Memorial Day (HMD)[662]

| Step | Description (according to HMD) | Example in Palestine |
|---|---|---|
| Classification | There is a division between "us" and "them," which can be achieved by stereotyping or by excluding those perceived as different. | The definition of Israel as a "Jewish state" has resulted in a classification between "Jews" and "non-Jews".[663] This classification led to different laws for Jewish and non-Jewish citizens. |
| Symbolization | It is a visual manifestation of hatred. In Nazi Europe, Jews were forced to wear yellow stars to show that they were "different." | This symbolization is carried out in the occupied territories, where Palestinian access is restricted to certain areas only. In the occupied territories (which are in essence Palestinian), Palestinians can only enter certain areas with a special permit. |
| Discrimination | The dominant group denies civil rights or even citizenship to identified groups. The Nuremberg Laws of 1935 stripped Jews of their German citizenship, forbidding them to work in many professions or to marry non-Jewish Germans. | For some, the definition of the State of Israel as a "Jewish state" already establishes discrimination. In a democratic state, the state is for all citizens, not just a few.[664] Discrimination between Jewish and non-Jewish Israelis is established through a number of laws, which impose restrictions on marriage or the acquisition of real estate, as well as settlement in Jewish neighborhoods, which may be refused by residents.[665] This discrimination also affects Christian Arabs.[666] |

---

662. https://www.hmd.org.uk/learn-about-the-holocaust-and-genocides/what-is-genocide/the-ten-stages-of-genocide/
663. https://www.graduateinstitute.ch/fr/news-events/news/la-nouvelle-loi-israelienne-est-contraire-au-droit-international
664. Aaron BOXERMAN, "New 'citizenship law' moves forward," *The Times of Israel*, January 10, 2022 (https://fr.timesofisrael.com/la-nouvelle-loi-sur-la-citoyennete-avance/)
665. "Israel: Two new laws marginalize Palestinian Arab citizens," *Human Rights Watch*, March 30, 2011 (https://www.hrw.org/fr/news/2011/03/30/israel-deux-nouvelles-lois-marginalisent-les-citoyens-arabes-palestiniens)
666. Jean-Michel HAUTEVILLE, "Israël: une loi établit une distinction entre Arabes chrétiens et musulmans," *Jeune Afrique*, February 26, 2014 (https://www.jeuneafrique.com/165270/politique/isra-l-une-loi-tablit-une-distinction-entre-arabes-chr-tiens-et-musulmans/)

| | | |
|---|---|---|
| Dehumanization | People perceived as "different" are treated without any form of human rights or personal dignity. During the genocide against the Tutsis in Rwanda, the Tutsis were called "cockroaches"; the Nazis called the Jews "vermin." | Defense Minister Yoav Gallant: "We are fighting human animals."[667] Arabs are "cockroaches."[668] |
| Organization | Genocide is always planned. Regimes of hatred often train those who will go on to destroy a people. | The evictions of Palestinians from East Jerusalem and villages in the West Bank are intended to weaken them and remove all economic activity. France is contributing to this by punishing those who support the BDS initiative. |
| Polarization | Propaganda starts to be disseminated by hate groups. | The people of Gaza[669] and Hamas[670] are likened to Nazis. |
| Preparation | The perpetrators plan the genocide. They often use euphemisms such as the Nazi expression "final solution" to conceal their intentions. They create fear within the victim group, by forming armies and using weapons. | Justifying the destruction of the Palestinians by comparing them to the biblical tribe of "Amalek." The war on Gaza thus becomes a kind of holy war.[671] David Azoulai, mayor of Metula, proposes razing the Gaza Strip to the ground and turning it into an Auschwitz.[672] |

667. Emanuel FABIAN, "Defense minister announces 'complete siege' of Gaza: No power, food or fuel," *The Times of Israel*, October 9, 2023 (https://www.timesofisrael.com/liveblog_entry/defense-minister-announces-complete-siege-of-gaza-no-power-food-or-fuel/)

668. Odeh BISHARAT, "The Fate of the Arabs: Like Drugged Cockroaches in a Bottle," *Haaretz*, February 6, 2018 (https://www.haaretz.com/opinion/2018-02-06/ty-article-opinion/.premium/the-fate-of-the-arabs-like-drugged-cockroaches-in-a-bottle/0000017f-dbb4-d3a5-af7f-fbbea9dd0000)

669. Carrie KELLER-LYNN & Jacob MAGID, "'There are 2 million Nazis' in West Bank, says far-right Finance Minister Smotrich," *The Times of Israel*, November 28, 2023 (https://www.timesofisrael.com/there-are-2-million-nazis-in-west-bank-says-far-right-finance-minister-smotrich/)

670. "Nobel Prize-winning writer Elfriede Jelinek compares Hamas to the Nazis," *franceinfo Culture / AFP*, November 14, 2023 (https://www.francetvinfo.fr/culture/livres/l-ecrivaine-elfriede-jelinek-prix-nobel-de-litterature-compare-le-hamas-aux-nazis_6183426.html)

671. Joshua KRUG, "Comparing Hamas to Amalek, our biblical nemesis, will ultimately hurt Israel," *The Jewish News of Northern California*, November 2, 2023 (https://jweekly.com/2023/11/02/comparing-hamas-to-amalek-our-biblical-nemesis-will-ultimately-hurt-israel/)

672. Canaan LIDOR, "Israeli mayor calls for turning Gaza into 'Auschwitz-like' museum, prompting rebuke," *The Times of Israel*, December 18, 2023 (https://www.timesofisrael.com/liveblog_entry/israeli-mayor-calls-for-turning-gaza-into-auschwitz-like-museum-prompting-rebuke/)

| | | |
|---|---|---|
| Persecution | Victims are identified on the basis of their ethnic or religious affiliation, and lists of people to be shot are drawn up. | Palestinians are confined to the occupied territories and can only leave with special permits, the rules for which change without notice.[673] |
| | Populations are sometimes herded into ghettos, deported or starved, and property is often expropriated. Genocidal massacres begin. | The case of the Gaza Strip. |
| Extermination | The hate group murders its identified victims in a deliberate and systematic campaign of violence. | This is the policy of "mowing the lawn" at regular intervals in Gaza, for example.[674] |
| Denial | The perpetrators or subsequent generations deny the existence of any crime. | Commemorations of the 1948 Nakba are punishable by law.[675] |

*Figure 131—The ten stages of genocide as seen in the occupied Palestinian territories. [Source: https://www.hmd.org.uk/learn-about-the-holocaust-and-genocides/what-is-genocide/the-ten-stages-of-genocide/]*

In the occupied territories, 59% of Palestinian children are arrested at night by armed men. Under-age children are tried by military courts.[676] While the Israeli government is inspired by Western standards when it comes to the bombing of civilian populations, we are a long, long way from them when it comes to the treatment of minors.

To those who claim that the Israeli government is doing everything to spare the population of Gaza, the question is: assuming that Hamas leaders are hiding on Israeli territory, would the Israeli army have the same policy of massive bombardment?

---

673. https://www.amnesty.org/en/location/middle-east-and-north-africa/israel-and-occupied-palestinian-territories/report-israel-and-occupied-palestinian-territories/
674. https://en.wikipedia.org/wiki/Mowing_the_grass
675. https://www.adalah.org/en/law/view/496
676. Henriette CHACAR, "For Palestinians arrested under occupation, a childhood disrupted," *Reuters*, December 30, 2023 (https://www.reuters.com/world/middle-east/palestinians-arrested-under-israeli-occupation-childhood-disrupted-2023-12-30/)

## Children Incarcerated in Israel

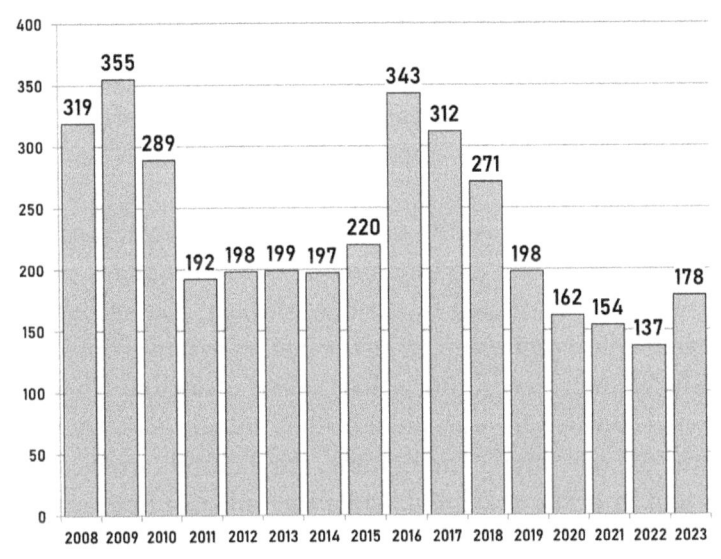

Figure 132—Average annual number of children (aged 12-17) incarcerated in Israeli prisons. There are a total of around 700 children per year in Israeli prisons. [Source: https://www.dci-palestine.org/children_in_israeli_detention]

| Year | Number |
|---|---|
| 2008 | 319 |
| 2009 | 355 |
| 2010 | 289 |
| 2011 | 192 |
| 2012 | 198 |
| 2013 | 199 |
| 2014 | 197 |
| 2015 | 220 |
| 2016 | 343 |
| 2017 | 312 |
| 2018 | 271 |
| 2019 | 198 |
| 2020 | 162 |
| 2021 | 154 |
| 2022 | 137 |
| 2023 | 178 |

## Incitement to Genocide

It is quite disturbing—but not really surprising—to note that our media are completely uncritical of the way Israel (but also Western countries and France in particular) fights terrorism. Our journalists seem intellectually incapable of imagining the fight against resistance as anything other than the crushing of a population by bombs or eliminations in sovereign countries.[677] In fact, they think exactly like terrorists, and their way of thinking inevitably leads to genocidal tendencies. Moreover, these journalists have never condemned the Ukrainian terrorist attacks in Russia.

While claiming to be the spokespersons for the defenders of rights and humanity, our media relay genocidal statements without batting an eyelid. On October 8, 2023, on FOX News, Nikki Haley, former U.S. ambassador to the UN and candidate in the 2024 U.S. presidential election, exclaimed about the Palestinians, *"Finish them all."*[678] On NBC

---

677. https://youtu.be/FvOH9S9amQk
678. https://youtu.be/NLe4j9Koxjw

News, during a primary debate, Republican Senator Ron DeSantis, Governor of Florida, said: *"Finish them all once and for all with these Hamas butchers."*[679]

In France, the debate is not much higher, and the critical stance of the left-wing party *La France Insoumise* (LFI) is seen as terrorism. Singer Enrico Macias, for example, declared that they should be *"physically disemboweled."*[680]

To be clear, the mood is one of revenge. Even Israeli doctors[681] and rabbis[682] were calling for the bombing of Gaza's hospitals, particularly Al-Shifa, in letters co-signed by dozens of them. The response of the Palestinian medical profession, in an open letter to Israeli doctors, is on a completely different level: it shows that the role of doctors, whatever their convictions, is not to wage war, and that their mission goes beyond that.[683]

Whatever the outcome of the fighting, the Palestinians won on moral grounds and in terms of dignity, while the Israelis unfortunately have learned nothing from history.

## South Africa's Lawsuit

Faced with the brutality of Operation SWORDS OF IRON, the Western world says nothing, despite pressure from the street, which notes that Israel's response is both disproportionate and inadequate to resolve the problem. As a signatory to the Genocide Convention, South Africa decided to appeal to the International Court of Justice in The Hague.

The ICJ is not a criminal court, but rather a tribunal that arbitrates disputes between countries, in this case between South Africa and Israel. South Africa was acting as a signatory to the Convention, taking its responsibilities to prevent genocide. The first question to be answered by the ICJ is whether there is in fact a dispute between the two countries. South Africa says there is a dispute about how to apply the Convention to which both countries are signatories. Israel argues that there is no

---

679. https://www.youtube.com/watch?v=VECQLkK5vcg
680. Maxime POUL, "Attaque du Hamas contre Israël: Enrico Macias appelle à 'dégommer' LFI 'physiquement,' la justice saisie," *Le Parisien*, October 11, 2023 (https://www.leparisien.fr/international/israel/video-attaque-du-hamas-contre-israel-enrico-macias-appelle-a-degommer-lfi-physiquement-la-justice-saisie-11-10-2023-76Z2FKBKJZHCFI5M4JZBBKEHDQ.php)
681. https://www.bhol.co.il/news/1613301
682. https://twitter.com/Nimrod_Flash/status/1719080045887521054
683. Julia CONLEY, "Doctors in Gaza Respond to Israeli Doctors Who Endorsed Bombing of Hospitals," *Common Dreams*, November 6, 2023 (https://www.commondreams.org/news/gaza-doctors-letter)

dispute with South Africa, and that the case should therefore be dropped. In the end, the Court decided that there is a dispute.

Secondly, as Hamas is neither a country nor a signatory to the Genocide Convention, it does not fall within the ICJ's jurisdiction. The ICJ cannot therefore issue an injunction. Furthermore, the case brought by South Africa before the ICJ and the accusation of genocide only concerns Israel. But a ceasefire concerns two parties. Since the ICJ cannot demand a ceasefire from Hamas, it has preferred to impose an *immediate* ceasefire on Israel.

Israel was obviously worried about the ICJ's decision, which is why it put pressure on the judges.[684] According to the American media outlet *Axios*, the Israeli Foreign Ministry sent a cable to all its delegations instructing diplomats to convey the following message to their host authorities:

> *We request an immediate and unequivocal public statement along the following lines: Declare publicly and clearly that YOUR COUNTRY rejects the most outrageous, absurd and baseless allegations made against Israel.*[685]

The stakes for Israel were obviously high, but would it not be simpler to adopt policies that are in harmony with IHL?

## *Order of the International Court of Justice (ICJ)*

On January 26, 2024, the International Court of Justice (ICJ) published its decision on the complaint lodged by South Africa against Israel. At this stage, the ICJ was not called upon to rule on the merits of the question, i.e., whether Israel was committing genocide, but had to determine the *plausibility* of genocide, in order to decide on provisional measures to prevent it.

It should be remembered here that the ICJ is a court that arbitrates disputes between states. As Hamas is not a state, it is not subject to the jurisdiction of the ICJ. The ICJ therefore arbitrated a dispute between South Africa, which claimed that Israel is violating the provisions of the

---

684. Jake JOHNSON, "Israel Accused of 'Effort to Intimidate the Judges' Ahead of Genocide Hearings," *Common Dreams*, January 7, 2024 (https://www.commondreams.org/news/israel-south-africa-genocide)
685. https://www.axios.com/2024/01/05/south-africa-gaza-genocide-icj-israel-plan

Convention on the Prevention of Genocide. Israel tried to evade the ICJ by declaring that it had no dispute with South Africa, but the court decided otherwise, a serious setback for Israel.

Our media were pleased to note that the ICJ did not demand a ceasefire, and saw this as a success for the Hebrew state. This is not the case. To understand this, we need to remember that the court's task is to rule on the plausibility of genocide, not on the conflict between Israel and Hamas. In other words, it is not a question of settling the dispute between Israel and Hamas, but of determining whether the way in which Israel conducts its operations is not genocidal in nature. The question of what Hamas is doing is therefore not discussed here (in any case, one crime can never justify another). Nor does the ICJ's judgment aim to resolve the conflict. That is why it did not call for a "ceasefire."

Thus, the order enjoins Israel to take six provisional measures:
1) The State of Israel shall, with respect to the Palestinians of Gaza, take all measures in its power to prevent the commission of all acts falling within the scope of Article II of the Genocide Convention, in particular:
(a) kill group members;
(b) seriously harm the physical or mental integrity of group members;
(c) deliberately subjecting the group to conditions of life calculated to bring about its physical destruction in whole or in part; and
(d) impose measures to prevent births within the group.
2) The State of Israel shall ensure with immediate effect that its military does not commit acts contrary to the first measure.
3) The State of Israel shall take all measures in its power to prevent and punish direct and public incitement to commit genocide against members of the Palestinian group in the Gaza Strip.
4) The State of Israel takes immediate and effective measures to enable the provision of urgently needed basic services and humanitarian aid to the Palestinians of the Gaza Strip, in order to alleviate the adverse living conditions they face.
5) The State of Israel shall take effective measures to prevent the destruction and ensure the preservation of evidence related to alleged acts under Articles II and III of the Convention on the Prevention and Punishment of the Crime of Genocide against members of the Palestinian group in the Gaza Strip.

(6) The State of Israel shall submit to the Court a report on all measures taken to give effect to this Order within one month from the date of this Order.[686]

At the time of writing, the ICJ's final decision is not yet known, and it will no doubt be months before it is, given what is at stake. But this is a case known in Anglo-American law as a *"prima facie"* case, which establishes that the court has sufficient elements to produce a judgment and prove that the accused (in this case Israel) is guilty.

Importantly, the order mentions elements that were not mentioned in South Africa's complaint, such as statements by Israeli ministers and other officials, the content of which is genocidal in nature. This means that the ICJ has understood that we are dealing with a serious case, which should worry *all those who deny* Israel's crimes.

The ICJ's decision is *"erga omnes,"* i.e., it obliges all parties to the Convention to support Israel's efforts to implement these provisional measures. This means that the *"unconditional support"* for Israel promised by Germany,[687] Austria,[688] the European Union, through the contested voice of Ursula von der Leyen[689] and of course the United States[690] will have to be called into question. Countries that actively support Israel in its "violation of the Genocide Convention," such as the USA and Germany, notably by providing military support, could show greater restraint, which would provide leverage over Israel's handling of the problem.

This is a serious blow against Israel and its strategy, which could already have an impact on its foreign policy. If the ICJ subsequently confirms this guilt in a final judgment, Israel's position on the international stage could take a decisive turn. For then, Israel would be forced to behave like a state

---

686. https://www.icj-cij.org/sites/default/files/case-related/192/192-20240126-ord-01-00-en.pdf
687. https://www.theguardian.com/commentisfree/2023/nov/13/germany-jewish-criticise-israel-tv-debate
688. Askin KIYAGAN, "Austrian activist slams government's unconditional support for Israel," *Anadolu Ajansi*, November 6, 2023 (https://www.aa.com.tr/en/europe/austrian-activist-slams-government-s-unconditional-support-for-israel/3045412)
689. Aurélie PUGNET & Davide BASSO, "EU staff criticise von der Leyen over Israel stance," *Euractiv.com*, October 20, 2023 (updated 25 October 2023) (https://www.euractiv.com/section/global-europe/news/eu-staff-criticise-von-der-leyen-over-israel-stance/)
690. Oliver EAGLETON, "Joe Biden's Unconditional Support for Israel Risks Creating a Regional War," *Jacobin*, January 5, 2024 (https://jacobin.com/2024/01/joe-biden-israel-support-war-gaza-regional-war-houthis-middle-east-palestine)

like any other. This is probably why the reaction in Israel was to declare the ICJ anti-Semitic.[691]

To what extent this judgment could open the door to criminal proceedings against the journalists, media and other commentators on our TV screens who, since October 7, have endeavored to justify a clearly disproportionate Israeli response that does not comply with IHL is an open question, but one that would help clean up our media landscape.

Once again, Hamas is just the tip of the iceberg. The issue is not its "ideology," as we hear on French TV, but the spirit of resistance. As long as there are occupied territories, and as long as Israel treats its occupiers like "human animals," there will be "Hamas" under this or any other name. The problem will not be solved by deporting the Gazan population to Egypt or the Congo in the modern version of cattle cars.

## The Israeli Response

### Benjamin Netanyahu's statements

Even before the ICJ decision, Benjamin Netanyahu had declared that he would not respect it. On January 13, 2024, in a televised address, he declared:

> *No one will stop us, not The Hague, not the Axis of Evil, not anyone.*[692]

Israel's argument is its right to defend itself. As we have seen, the question is not really whether it has the right to protect itself against hostile acts, but rather the method it uses to do so. This is exactly what I wrote in 2003, but Israel has only one strategy in mind: to crush the Palestinians with bombs. And therein lies the problem.

The ICJ decision is a severe blow against Israel. For the first time since the Second World War—with the notable exception of Rwanda—we are witnessing plausible genocide. The blow is all the stronger for the fact that Israel was previously seen as a victim. This is no longer the case.

---

691. Bethan McKernan, "Israeli officials accuse international court of justice of antisemitic bias," *The Guardian*, January 26, 2024 (https://www.theguardian.com/world/2024/jan/26/israeli-officials-accuse-international-court-of-justice-of-antisemitic-bias)
692. "Netanyahu declares no one can halt Israel's war to crush Hamas, including international court," *PBS.org*, January 13, 2024 (https://www.pbs.org/newshour/world/netanyahu-declares-no-one-can-halt-israels-war-to-crush-hamas-including-international-court)

But the ICJ decision does not discourage this government, whose genocidal statements upheld by the Court have not been condemned by any Western government or mainstream media. Not surprisingly, Itamar Ben Gvir, Minister of Security, declared the ICJ "anti-Semitic."[693]

*Mortality in Gaza after the ICJ Decision*

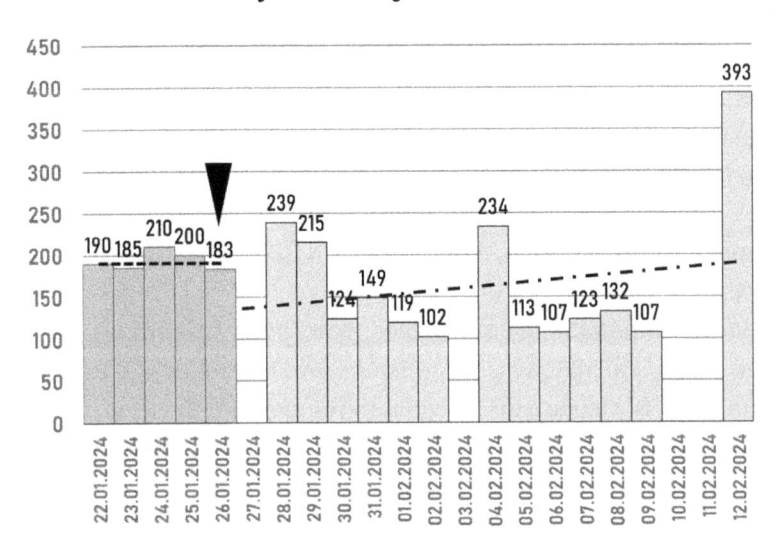

*Figure 133—Number of people killed in Israeli operations in Gaza between January 22 and February 5. The high figures for January 28, February 4 and February 12 are because of the absence of published figures for the preceding days. The daily average is 194 deaths just before January 26. After this date, the number of deaths fell, but the trend is up again. The drop observed after January 26 is due more to the nature of the operations than to a change in Israeli policy towards the Palestinians. Clearly, Israel did not change its policy after the ICJ order, which seems to confirm the apprehensions of the international community.*
*[Source: https://www.ochaopt.org/updates]*

On January 27, Benjamin Netanyahu declared that the government "decides and acts according to what is necessary for the country's security" and that it would continue to do so until a complete victory.[694] In other words, it does not recognize the authority of the ICJ as the expres-

---

693. Sam Sokol, "Netanyahu instructs cabinet members to refrain from responding to ICJ ruling, to no avail," *The Times of Israel*, January 26, 2024 (https://www.timesofisrael.com/liveblog_entry/netanyahu-instructs-cabinet-members-to-refrain-from-responding-to-icj-ruling-to-no-avail/)
694. "Defiant Netanyahu declares Israel's goal is 'complete victory' in Gaza after UN court ruling," *PBS.org*, January 27, 2024 (https://www.pbs.org/newshour/world/defiant-netanyahu-declares-israels-goal-is-complete-victory-in-gaza-after-un-court-ruling)

sion of a law that is binding on States. Exactly like France or the United States, it considers national security to be superior to international law. The problem with this thinking is that international law is there precisely to guarantee everyone's security. Provided, however, that everyone abides by the same rules. Israel will have no security as long as it flouts international law, as it has done since 1947. Terrorism and the repeated "9/11s" suffered by Western countries are simply the result of their inability to respect international law. Islamist terrorism is always a response.

That said, Israeli military actions caused slightly fewer civilian casualties from the end of January 2024. Claims that Israel caused more casualties after the ICJ decision are false.

**The Elimination of UNRWA, A Measure that Reinforces the Accusation of Genocide**

The *United Nations Relief and Works Agency for Palestine Refugees in the Near East* (UNRWA) was established on December 8, 1949 by UN Resolution 302(IV) to care for Palestinian refugees. At the time, the *Office of the* United Nations *High Commissioner for Refugees* (UNHCR) did not yet exist (it would not be created until December 1950), and the ethnic cleansing (*Nakba*) carried out by Jewish militias from 1947 onwards, then by the State of Israel from 1948 onwards, drove hundreds of thousands of Palestinians onto the roads.

Today, UNRWA has field offices in all the countries that have taken in Palestinian refugees since then: Lebanon, Syria, Jordan, the West Bank and Gaza. It employs 30,000 people (mainly local staff), including around 13,000 in Gaza. It provides the basic services required for the survival of a society: food supplies, education, social aid, medical assistance, etc.

In Gaza, UNRWA works with all the humanitarian organizations on the ground, which certainly includes the aid organizations associated with Hamas. Hamas employs almost 50,000 people in aid activities, whom the Israelis regard as terrorists, even if they are not involved in armed activities.

This approach is of course echoed by unenlightened Western minds. For example, in December 2023, at the instigation of David Zuberbühler, a far-right parliamentarian and member of the "Suisse-Israel" group, a pro-Israeli lobby, the lower house of the Swiss parliament (National Council) voted to stop funding UNRWA activities.[695]

---

695. https://www.jforum.fr/le-parlement-suisse-decide-de-cesser-de-financer-lunrwa.html

The Swiss parliamentarians based their decision on a report by an Israeli NGO, IMPACT-se, which claims that UNRWA is close to Hamas, based on the school textbooks used.[696] Yet according to the Brussels-based *European Middle East Project* (EuMEP), registered with the European Union,[697] IMPACT-se's allegations "are not credible" and marred by "methodological *deficiencies.*"[698] Indeed, in 2018, Alistair Burt, then Minister of State for the Middle East and North Africa, expressed *"concern"* about the IMPACT-se report, which *"was not objective in its conclusions and lacked methodological rigor."*[699] Similarly, a study by the Georg-Eckert-Institut (GEI) in Germany shows that the IMPACT-se report is partisan and misleading.[700]

In the end, the upper house of the Swiss Parliament (Council of States) decided against the idea of cutting this funding, and the discussion ended with a compromise, cutting financial support for UNRWA by half.[701] Moreover, this debate, which is essentially based on the issue of school textbooks, illustrates the intellectual inability of our parliamentarians to understand the situation. To think that Palestinian anger towards Israel is motivated by textbooks rather than by the daily injustices and humiliations Palestinians suffer under occupation is simply idiotic.

The decision to cut off official and verifiable funding to the Palestinians is part of Israel's policy of making it impossible for Palestinians to live in the occupied territories. But it also has the effect of pushing the Palestinians to find clandestine sources of funding. If we consider Hamas to be a terrorist organization, then we are in a situation that runs exactly counter to any counter-terrorist strategy. The problem is not the fight against terrorism, but an approach aimed at ethnic cleansing, to put it mildly. But our parliamentarians—in all European countries, including Switzerland—have never been particularly enlightened in this area, and have largely contributed to the development of terrorism in our countries and elsewhere.

---

696. https://www.timesofisrael.com/swiss-parliament-votes-to-cut-funding-for-unrwa-amid-incitement-allegations/
697. https://ec.europa.eu/transparencyregister/public/consultation/displaylobbyist.do?id=733135223769-69
698. https://eumep.org/wp-content/uploads/EuMEP-briefing-on-Palestinian-textbooks-21-07.pdf
699. https://questions-statements.parliament.uk/written-questions/detail/2018-09-07/171640
700. https://www.gei.de/forschung/projekte/analyse-palaestinensischer-schulbuecher-paltex
701. https://www.rts.ch/info/suisse/14572098-le-parlement-adopte-le-budget-2024-apres-un-compromis-sur-le-financement-de-lunrwa.html

On January 26, 2024, in the hours following the publication of the ICJ decision,[702] Israel made a bombshell accusation that 12 employees of the United Nations Relief and Works Agency for Palestine Refugees in the Near East (UNRWA) (i.e., between 0.04% and 0.1%) had participated in the Hamas attack of October 7, 2023.[703]

On January 29, according to *Reuters,* Israel distributed a 6-page report alleging that 190 UNRWA employees (i.e. 0.6%—1.4%), including teachers, were also hardcore Hamas members.[704] Based on the same report, the *Wall Street Journal* claimed that 10% of UNRWA staff (i.e., 1,300—3,000 people) have contacts with Hamas, that 6 of its employees took part in the October 7 attack, and that two of them even helped kidnap Israelis.[705]

However, their role is not specified. Did they follow the movement out of curiosity? Were they drawn in against their will? We do not know.

In addition, the information came from the interrogation of prisoners captured in Gaza. Given Israel's regular use of torture,[706] the reliability of these accusations is questionable.

But a close look at the file shows that the accusations are highly questionable. Firstly, there is no evidence to support the allegations. Secondly, it seems that the report's assertions concern those who may simply have had sporadic contact (for example, through a family member with links to Hamas). In fact, Hamas has mutual aid structures, notably for victims of bombardments or the reconstruction of housing destroyed by Israeli strikes. It is therefore plausible that there are contacts between UNRWA and these structures. The problem is that Israel considers these structures to be terrorist organizations.

---

702. Jason Burke, "UN agency investigates staff suspected of role in 7 October attack on Israel," *The Guardian,* January 26, 2024 (https://www.theguardian.com/world/2024/jan/26/unrwa-investigation-staff-7-october-attack-israel)

703. Hira Humayun, "UN agency fires staff members allegedly involved in October 7 attacks," *CNN,* January 26, 2024 (https://edition.cnn.com/2024/01/26/middleeast/unrwa-fires-staff-members-october-7-attacks-intl/index.html)

704. Dan Williams & Gabrielle Tétrault-Farber, "Israel accuses 190 UN staff of being 'hardened' militants," *Reuters,* January 29, 2024 (https://www.reuters.com/world/middle-east/israeli-intelligence-accuses-190-gaza-un-staff-hamas-islamic-jihad-roles-2024-01-29/)

705. Carrie Keller-Lynn & and David Luhnow, "Intelligence Reveals Details of U.N. Agency Staff's Links to Oct. 7 Attack," *The Wall Street Journal,* January 29, 2024 (https://www.wsj.com/world/middle-east/at-least-12-u-n-agency-employees-involved-in-oct-7-attacks-intelligence-reports-say-a7de8f36)

706. https://www.omct.org/en/resources/blog/its-now-even-more-official-torture-is-legal-in-israel

On top of this, Israel has been trying to stop UNRWA's work for several years. During his term in office, Donald Trump tried to cut funding to the agency.

For the Israelis, UNRWA is Israel's "original sin:" successive generations who benefit from the agency's services remain refugees. This status is perpetuated from generation to generation, and Israel sees it as the cause of terrorism. Thus, on January 4, 2024, at a hearing in the Knesset, Noga Arbell, a former official in Israel's Ministry of Foreign Affairs, declared:

> *I think we should start recognizing that UNRWA represents an existential threat that needs to be addressed.*
> 
> *Our main objective in war is to eliminate the threat, not neutralize it. And we know how to eliminate terrorists. It's harder for us with an idea. UNRWA came up with the idea. The idea is that more and more terrorists are being born by all sorts of methods, and that it will be impossible to win the war if we don't destroy UNRWA. And this destruction must begin immediately. There's no point talking about the day after. We must act now to face these threats. If we don't, we will miss the window of opportunity, as we have already done several times here.*[707]

In reality, they remain refugees because they are waiting for Israel to fulfill its obligations under international law and let them return to their homes and the territory taken from them by force.

Israel's "strategy" to combat Palestinian resistance is a snake biting its own tail. Israel's treatment of Palestinian refugees as *"human animals"* has forced Palestinian organizations to set up self-help structures. Today, we find it hard to understand counter-insurgency as anything other than extermination. But in Vietnam in the 1960s, one of the tasks of the Special Forces (the famous "Green Berets") was to create mutual aid structures in the Viet Cong zones, in order to win the loyalty of the population and dissuade them from joining the Communist ranks.

At the end of January 2024, UNRWA's main donors suspended their contributions in response to the Israeli allegations. It should be recalled that the ICJ order called for six measures to be taken by Israel, including

---

707. https://www.youtube.com/watch?v=h0bMANfC0BQ

the preservation of access to humanitarian aid and the integrity of the Palestinians in Gaza. By causing UNRWA in Gaza to cease payments and thus operations, Israel is in a way subcontracting the plausible genocide underway to the contributing countries. These eighteen countries thus become accomplices in the genocide of which Israel is accused.

The problem is that the information provided by the Israelis is unproven and unverifiable. The *New York Times* points out that the American decision to suspend its contribution is based solely on the plausibility of the accusations, but that not even the American services have been able to confirm them.[708] Similarly, according to the *Washington Post*:

> *The U.S. has not independently verified Israel's claims, which are based on phone intercepts, metadata, interrogations of Hamas fighters and documents the Israeli army found in the Gaza Strip, officials said. The Washington Post reviewed a document that has been shared with the US and other governments, containing the names, UN positions and alleged Hamas roles of these 12 individuals, but was unable to corroborate the information.*[709]

For in fact, if these countries had really wanted to protect the Palestinians, they would first have demanded a thorough investigation into these cases, before demanding dismissal or criminal proceedings against the culprits, if any. But they did not, and simply stopped their contribution at a critical moment when the ICJ explicitly asked not to interrupt humanitarian aid to Gaza.

---

708. Ronen BERGMAN & Patrick KINGSLEY, "Details Emerge on U.N. Workers Accused of Aiding Hamas Raid," *The New York Times*, January 28, 2024 (https://www.nytimes.com/2024/01/28/world/middleeast/gaza-unrwa-hamas-israel.html)
709. Shane HARRIS, John HUDSON, Karen DEYOUNG & Souad MEKHENNET, "Israeli intelligence prompted U.S. to quickly cut Gaza aid funding," *The Washington Post*, January 30, 2024 (updated January 31, 2024) (https://www.washingtonpost.com/national-security/2024/01/30/unrwa-gaza-israel-aid/)

## Countries Suspending their Contributions to UNRWA (January 30, 2024)

| Contributing country | Amount [millions of US dollars] |
|---|---|
| United States[710] | 343,900 |
| Germany[711] | 202,100 |
| European Union[712] | 114,100 |
| Sweden[713] | 61,000 |
| Japan[714] | 30,200 |
| France[715] | 343,900 |
| Switzerland[716] | 202,100 |
| Canada[717] | 114,100 |
| United Kingdom[718] | 61,000 |
| Netherlands | 30,200 |
| Australia[719] | 13,800 |
| Italy[720] | 18,000 |
| Austria[721] | 8,100 |
| Finland[722] | 7,800 |
| New Zealand[723] | 0,5608 |
| Iceland[724] | 0,5587 |
| Romania[725] | 0,2107 |
| Estonia[726] | 0,9000 |
| Total | 921,7302 |

*Figure 134—Some countries have stopped their contribution, others are waiting for more details before continuing. All have taken a decision without waiting for proof of Israel's allegations, and none has protested against the massacre of civilians in Gaza.[727]*

---

710. https://www.state.gov/statement-on-unrwa-allegations/
711. https://twitter.com/GermanyDiplo/status/1751584759782813884
712. https://ec.europa.eu/commission/presscorner/detail/en/ip_24_505
713. https://www.dn.se/sverige/sverige-stoppar-bistandspengar-till-unrwa/
714. https://www.mofa.go.jp/press/release/pressite_000001_00122.html
715. https://www.diplomatie.gouv.fr/en/country-files/israel-palestinian-territories/news/2024/article/israel-palestinian-territories-unrwa-28-jan-2024#:~:text=France%20has%20not%20planned%20any,are%20properly%20taken%20into%20account.
716. https://www.swissinfo.ch/eng/politics/swiss-aid-payments-for-unrwa-are-in-doubt/49164836
717. https://twitter.com/HonAhmedHussen/status/1751000728057876899
718. https://www.gov.uk/government/news/statement-on-allegations-about-unrwa-staff-and-7-october-attacks#:~:text=The%20UK%20is%20appalled%20by,we%20review%20these%20concerning%20allegations
719. https://twitter.com/SenatorWong/status/1751103658509644035
720. https://twitter.com/ItalyMFA_int/status/1751198588300829045
721. https://www.bmeia.gv.at/en/ministerium/presse/aktuelles/2024/01/austria-is-suspending-payments-to-unrwa
722. https://um.fi/current-affairs/-/asset_publisher/gc654PySnjTX/content/suomi-keskeyttaa-tukensa-yk-n-palestiinalaispakolaisjarjesto-unrwa-lle
723. https://www.rnz.co.nz/news/political/507907/no-more-aid-for-un-aid-agency-until-peters-satisfied-luxon
724. https://unric.org/en/unrwa-finland-and-iceland-suspend-contributions-the-3-scandinavian-countries-continue/
725. https://twitter.com/MAERomania/status/1751926826841018626
726. https://twitter.com/Tsahkna/status/1751620436629049462
727. "List of Countries Suspending UNRWA Funding," *UNWatch*, January 29, 2024 (https://unwatch.org/updated-list-of-countries-suspending-unwra-funding/)

The paradox of this situation is that the issue of possible bridges between the Palestinian resistance and the United Nations is not new. In order to prevent this problem, UNRWA regularly carries out security checks involving staff, donors and entities, beneficiaries, implementing partners, vendors, suppliers and recipients of UNRWA payments.[728] Thus,

- all contributions to UNRWA must comply with UNRWA's due diligence and verification policy, overseen by the Strategic Partnerships Division and, ultimately, by the Chief of Staff;
- the names of all potential suppliers and other beneficiaries are checked against the consolidated UN sanctions list;
- the names of all staff, donor entities, beneficiaries, vendors and suppliers are checked every six months against the consolidated UN sanctions list.

What is more, these checks are regularly shared with the Israeli authorities, who therefore know every detail about UNRWA staff on an ongoing basis. The Israeli authorities' accusations are all the more opaque in that the complete intelligence file has not been shared with the authorities of the United Nations and donor countries.[729]

However, this was not the case for Belgium, which preferred to wait for confirmation and clarification of the case before taking the decision to suspend its contributions.[730] The following day, this decision was criticized by the *Coordinating Committee of Jewish Organizations in Belgium* (CCOJB),[731] and the building housing the *Belgian Development Agency* (ENABEL) and the offices of the NGO *Handicap International* was destroyed by a strike.[732] This strike aroused international condemnation and illustrated the way in which Israel is conducting this war: with accusations that it is unable to substantiate with evidence and that prove false over time, and pressure on its allies to support its actions, in defiance of

---

728. https://www.unrwa.org/vetting
729. https://www.france24.com/en/middle-east/20240205-as-donors-suspend-critical-funding-to-unrwa-allegations-against-staff-remain-murky
730. Pauline Hofmann, "Guerre Israël-Hamas: le gouvernement belge maintient les financements de l'Unrwa," *Le Soir/Belga*, January 31, 2024 (https://www.lesoir.be/565057/article/2024-01-31/guerre-israel-hamas-le-gouvernement-belge-maintient-les-financements-de-lunrwa)
731. "Jewish organisations regret Belgium's decision to maintain UNRWA funding," *Belga*, February 1, 2024 (https://www.belganewsagency.eu/jewish-organisations-regret-belgiums-decision-to-maintain-unrwa-funding)
732. "Handicap International and Belgian Development Agency offices destroyed in same bombing," *RTBF*, February 2, 2024 (https://www.rtbf.be/article/guerre-israel-gaza-les-bureaux-de-handicap-international-et-de-l-agence-belge-de-developpement-ont-ete-detruits-dans-le-meme-bombardement-11323173)

international law. It was yet another manifestation of what dramatically fuels anti-Semitism around the world: impunity.[733]

The Israeli accusations seem more like a call to end all discussion than a documented accusation. In parallel with this procedure, the Israelis are blocking the passage of humanitarian aid trucks into Gaza at the Karem Abu Salam checkpoint.

## Military Operations Despite Suspicions of Genocide

On January 24, 2024, in one of the areas declared "safe" by the Israeli army, a group of Palestinians waved a white flag to fetch the rest of their families and bring them to "safety." The man holding the flag was shot in the head by an Israeli sniper.[734] On January 26, the day the ICJ issued its order in Gaza, a grandmother and grandson trying to reach an area declared "safe" and waving a white flag were shot dead in the street by Israeli soldiers.[735]

On January 30, *Mista'aravim* fighters broke into a hospital in Jenin, West Bank, to eliminate three Palestinian activists.[736]

In addition to these military operations, the Israeli army carried out summary executions of prisoners. At the beginning of February 2024, after the withdrawal of Israeli troops, Palestinians discovered a mass grave in the courtyard of an elementary school in Beit Lahia (North Gaza), which contained some thirty bodies,[737] blindfolded and with their hands tied behind their backs, placed in plastic bags with inscriptions in Hebrew.[738] The media supporting genocide in Gaza made no mention

---

733. Jake JOHNSON, "Israel Bombed Belgian Aid Office in Gaza After Nation Refused to Halt UNRWA Funding," *Common Dreams*, February 2, 2024 (https://www.commondreams.org/news/israel-belgium-unrwa)

734. Yasmine SALAM & Caroline RADNOFSKY, "A group of Palestinian men waving a white flag is shot at, killing 1," *NBC News*, January 24, 2024 (https://www.nbcnews.com/news/world/gaza-palestinian-israel-white-flag-shot-dead-killed-rcna135419)

735. Clarissa WARD, Brent SWAILS, Kareem KHADDER & Eliza MACKINTOSH, "She was fleeing with her grandson, who was holding a white flag. Then she was shot," *CNN*, January 26, 2024 (https://www.cnn.com/2024/01/26/middleeast/hala-khreis-white-flag-shooting-gaza-cmd-intl/index.html)

736. "Cisjordanie: un commando israélien tue trois membres du Hamas et du Jihad islamique dans un hôpital," *franceinfo / AFP*, January 30, 2024 (https://www.francetvinfo.fr/monde/proche-orient/israel-palestine/cisjordanie-occupee-trois-terroristes-palestiniens-tues-dans-un-raid-israelien-sur-un-hopital_6334144.html)

737. Brett WILKINS, "Bound and 'Executed' Palestinians Found at Gaza School After IDF Exit," *Common Dreams*, February 1, 2024 (https://www.commondreams.org/news/israel-executions)

738. Sharon ZHANG, "Palestinians Uncover Dozens Killed Execution-Style in Schoolyard in Gaza," *Truthout*, February 2, 2024 (https://truthout.org/articles/palestinians-uncover-dozens-killed-execution-style-in-schoolyard-in-gaza/)

of this crime, which is part of the South African initiative described as *"terrible, awful, scandalous"* by Manuel Valls on *LCI*.[739]

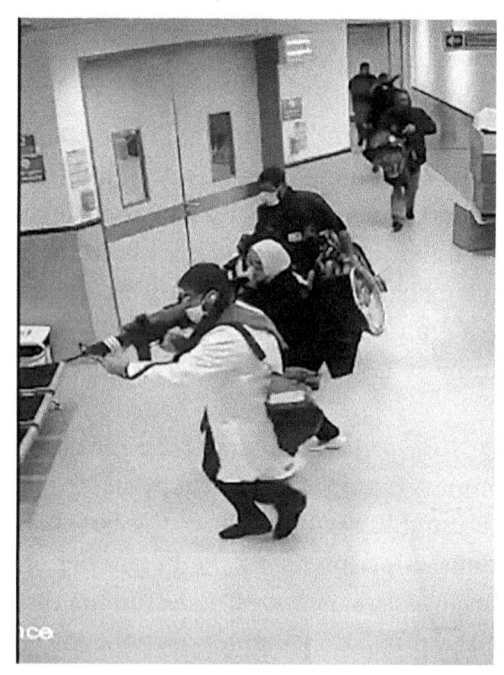

## The Action of the Mista'aravim

*Figure 135—The intervention of armed men to go and execute a Palestinian, one of whom was paralyzed, in a Jenin hospital illustrates the sense of impunity that reigns in Israel, particularly when what is a war crime is carried out four days after the ICJ has issued its order.*

As long ago as December 16, 2023, the *Office of the United Nations High Commissioner for Human Rights* published a report alleging the responsibility of Israeli forces for mass detentions, ill-treatment and the *"possible enforced disappearance of thousands of Palestinian men and boys, as well as a number of women and girls,"* in the northern Gaza Strip.[740]

---

739. https://www.tf1info.fr/replay-lci/video-le-20h-darius-rochebin-du-samedi-20-janvier-2283433.html
740. https://reliefweb.int/report/occupied-palestinian-territory/un-human-rights-office-opt-disturbing-reports-north-gaza-mass-detentions-ill-treatment-and-enforced-disappearances-possibly-thousands-palestinians

What seems scandalous is the lack of reaction from Manuel Valls. As Jean-Yves Le Drian, then Minister of Foreign Affairs, used to say: "Failure to react is tantamount to condoning."[741]

## Negotiations and Concessions

The idea that we should not negotiate with a terrorist group is absurd. Firstly, because the designation "terrorist" is purely political, and does not meet any internationally recognized criteria. Thus, movements such as Hamas and Hezbollah are qualified as terrorists by only a fraction of the international community.

Obviously, you cannot negotiate with a gun to your head. It was complicated to negotiate with movements like the Red Brigades in Italy, or other movements of the 1960s-1980s that sought to dismantle the state. It is easier to negotiate with autonomist or even separatist movements, because there are solutions that do not call into question the state, just the way it works. With resistance movements, whose existence is caused by the presence of an entity on a territory that is not its own, negotiation is even easier. Unless you want to make the territory your own for good.

That is why the media and commentators only mention the 1988 Hamas Charter and never the 2017 one: it is simply to justify the refusal of dialogue. In fact, Israel has never really been interested in negotiating with the Palestinians. In 2012, Yuval Diskin, former head of SHABAK, the Israeli *Security Service,* declared:

> *Forget the stories you hear about Mr. Abbas not being interested in negotiations... We are not talking to the Palestinians because this government is not interested in negotiating.*[742]

This is why designating a group as "terrorist" makes little sense, especially for countries not directly involved, as it reduces their capacity to mediate and tends to prohibit any dialogue or negotiated solution. This

---

741. "Plane diverted by Belarus: 'Russia's lack of reaction is worth guaranteeing,' believes Jean-Yves Le Drian," francetvinfo.fr, May 26, 2021
742. Barak Ravid, "Former Shin Bet Chief: Netanyahu Not Interested in Peace Talks," *Haaretz*, April 28, 2012 (https://www.haaretz.com/2012-04-28/ty-article/former-shin-bet-chief-netanyahu-not-interested-in-peace-talks/0000017f-df36-db5a-a57f-df7e9c230000)

is why, on October 11, 2023, the British *BBC* declared that it was abandoning these labels, in order to have more distance in its judgement.[743]

Let us not forget that if we never negotiated with terrorists, the State of Israel would not exist. So, we have to be careful with the terms. France went to fight against "terrorists" in Iraq (2014) and Syria (2015), and its only benefit was the attacks of 2015 and 2016. I am always surprised that victims' associations never point out the French government's responsibility, and are content with vengeful judgments and statements. Perhaps this is because their members feel remorse for not having reacted *before* going to bomb men, women and children in the Middle East. Terrorism is not inevitable. It never will be.

Westerners, and the US administration in particular,[744] fear a ceasefire in Gaza for the rather surreal reason that such a pause would allow journalists to go into Gaza and witness the extent of the destruction and thus the war crimes we support.[745]

This being the case, we need to consider two levels of negotiation at this stage:
- achieve a pause in the Gaza crisis, which is working against Israel, and return to a kind of "normal flow";
- find a long-term solution to the Palestinian question, which has existed since 1947.

Today, after the warlike declarations and bravado of Israeli leaders, the tone seems to have lesseened. The ICJ decision, the growing number of testimonies concerning the crimes committed by Israel, and the growing mobilization in the Middle East are weakening Israel's credibility.

It is certainly not without reason that at the end of January 2024, Israel was seeking an agreement for the release of the prisoners and looking for a way out of a conflict that is beginning to resemble a quagmire: the army has failed to free a single "hostage" and, on the contrary, has killed around 60 of them by shelling, direct fire or by poisoning them. Prisoners and hostages were obviously part of the negotiation. At the time, the

---

743. Ian YOUNGS & Paul GLYNN, "BBC defends policy not to call Hamas 'terrorists' after criticism," *BBC News*, October 11, 2023 (https://www.bbc.com/news/entertainment-arts-67076341)
744. "US Biden admin concerned about journalists exposing devastation in Gaza amid ceasefire with Israel," *Middle East Monitor*, November 22, 2023 (https://www.middleeastmonitor.com/20231122-us-biden-admin-concerned-about-journalists-exposing-devastation-in-gaza-amid-ceasefire-with-israel/)
745. Tori OTTEN, "The Grotesque Reason Why Some Biden Officials Don't Want a Cease-fire," *The New Republic*, November 22, 2023 (https://newrepublic.com/post/177077/grotesque-reason-biden-officials-dont-want-ceasefire)

Palestinians were still holding a few civilians (hostages), but mostly sol-diers (prisoners of war), apparently including high-ranking military person-nel (one or two generals were mentioned?).

Representatives of the Israeli, Egyptian, Qatari and American intelligence services met discreetly in France to negotiate an agreement. A proposal drawn up by Israel for a two-month prisoner exchange with a truce was submitted to Hamas. After a week, Hamas responded with a counter-proposal. The plan consisted of three stages, each lasting a maximum of 45 days:

Step one:
- A prisoner/hostage exchange,
- a partial withdrawal of Israeli forces from the Gaza Strip,
- the start of rebuilding hospitals and vital infrastructure,
- the start of ceasefire negotiations.

Step 2:
- A second exchange of prisoners/hostages,
- Full withdrawal of Israeli forces from the Gaza Strip.

Step three:
- Exchange of the remaining prisoners/hostages and the bodies of the deceased,
- continued reconstruction efforts.

This proposal was obviously rejected by Israel in early February, but it has the merit of offering a concrete roadmap that Israel—the occupying power—has been unable to produce. It also sheds light on the Hamas doctrine, which adopts the notion of a "permanent *tadiyah*" (military truce) as an intermediate stage before the "*hudna*" (armistice).

Hamas was not asking Israel to withdraw from the Gaza Strip, for the simple reason that it understands that the only way to exert pressure on Israel is for it to be there. Israel's tactical thinking is matched by the Palestinians' strategic thinking.

As for the long-term solution to the Israeli-Palestinian conflict, this is obviously a complex issue that goes beyond the scope of this book. The two-state solution is the one envisaged by the United Nations in 1947, assuming that this solution is revived on the basis of the June 4, 1967 borders, as Hamas suggests; how will the problem of settlements in the West Bank be resolved?

And if we were to move towards a one-state, two-peoples solution, as also proposed by the Palestinians, including Hamas, would the

Israeli government be prepared to give up the very idea of a "Jewish state?"

We do not have these answers, and it is up to the Israeli and Palestinian peoples to make their own choices, and probably up to us to accompany them, without making decisions for them, as we have done until now. In any case, the solution to this conflict will not be a military one, and must involve a phase of dialogue. We have dialogued with Israel, which was born of terrorism. There is no reason why we can not do the same with the Palestinians. By breaking so many rules of law and humanity, the risk Israel runs at the moment is that its support in the world will diminish to the point where no one will want to help it in the event of a *truly* existential threat.[746]

---

746. Anna GORDON, "New Polling Shows How Much Global Support Israel Has Lost," *Time Magazine*, January 17, 2024 (https://time.com/6559293/morning-consult-israel-global-opinion/)

# 7. Israel and its Neighbors

## Israeli Security Policy

With undefined borders and the ever-present idea of a "Greater Israel" which—at the very least—must extend from the Mediterranean to the Jordan,[747] a genuine policy of peace and regional integration seems difficult.

Israeli strategy—and foreign policy—have found expression less in diplomacy than in arms. Despite numerous Arab attempts, Israel has never counted on friendly relations with its neighbors, because everyone knows that Israel's borders are destined to change. Not without pragmatism, Israel has always believed that its security depended more on rivalries between Arab countries than on cooperation with them. This explains why its security policy has always sought to exploit the internal dissensions of its neighbors.

Thanks to the unconditional support of the United States and its role as "guarantor," Israel has been able to take actions in its neighboring countries that no other country in the world could have done. This "spoiled child" situation has been known for a long time, but the new configuration the world is taking on tends to sound the end of the playground for Israel. For a long time, Israel has been the country most condemned by United Nations resolutions, but also the one which makes the least effort to respect them.

---

747. "Israel's new deputy foreign minister: 'This land is ours. All of it is ours,'" *AP/The Guardian*, May 22, 2015 (https://www.theguardian.com/world/2015/may/22/israels-new-deputy-foreign-minister-this-land-is-ours-all-of-it-is-ours)

## United Nations Resolutions

| Period | Resolutions concerning Israel | Resolutions concerning the rest of the world |
|--------|-------------------------------|----------------------------------------------|
| 2021   | 15                            | 5                                            |
| 2022   | 15                            | 13                                           |
| 2023   | 14                            | 7                                            |

*Figure 136—Because Israel continues not to respect the resolutions adopted since 1948, it remains condemned every year by the United Nations. The lack of will on the part of Western countries to encourage it to respect its obligations has the effect of generating a feeling of impunity. It is this impunity towards a country that does not respect international law that generates anti-Semitism in our countries.*

In 2012, Yuval Diskin, former head of SHABAK, the Israeli *Security Service*, observed:

> *Over the past 10 to 15 years, Israel has become increasingly racist. All the studies show this. It's racism against Arabs and foreigners, and we've also become a more bellicose society.*[748]

It is symptomatic that members of the Jewish community who try to explain the events of October 7, 2023 refer exclusively to religious precepts and the Bible to justify the failure to comply with international law.[749]

Whereas the Palestinian argument systematically refers to international law, Israel's can only be religious. The problem is that international relations in the 21st century cannot be based on local beliefs, but only on universally accepted principles. This is the role of IHL.

---

748. Barak RAVID, "Israel's Former Shin Bet Chief: I Have No Confidence in Netanyahu, Barak," *Haaretz*, April 28, 2012 (https://www.haaretz.com/2012-04-28/ty-article/israels-former-shin-bet-chief-i-have-no-confidence-in-netanyahu-barak/0000017f-df32-d3ff-a7ff-ffb239f90000)
749. Lorenzo KAMEL, "The Roots of Israel's Annexation Policy," Carnegie Endowment for International Peace, August 6, 2020 (https://carnegieendowment.org/sada/82425)

## A Less-Than-Faithful Ally

Israel is a country which, as all other countries should, acts in its own national interest. The problem is that it tends to give precedence to its own interests over those of its partners, even at the cost of being unfaithful to them. A partnership is always two-way: every alliance is an exchange. This means that both parties accept a form of compromise in view of the gains to be made from the partnership. But you still have to "play the game."

Between 1946 and 1948, the USSR had been one of the staunchest supporters of the creation of the State of Israel, notably by supplying arms to the terrorists who made up the groups fighting against the British occupation. But once independence was achieved, Israel turned its back on its ally and chose the Western camp, triggering Stalin's wrath and purges among the Soviet Union's cadres to keep Jews out.

In the early 1950s, the United States was tempted to support nationalist, pan-Arab regimes in Egypt and Syria, while Great Britain sought to disengage from the Middle East. Israel felt its security threatened and sought to prevent the formation of an Arab coalition against it. In 1954, it launched Operation SUSANNAH, conceived and executed by Israel's military intelligence service (Agaf Modiin or AMAN). The aim was to carry out terrorist attacks against British, American and Egyptian targets, in order to pin the blame on the Muslim Brotherhood and provoke Anglo-American intervention. Uncovered by Egyptian security, the operation ended in a fiasco, leading to the resignation of Pinhas Lavon, Israel's Defense Minister at the time.[750] The "Lavon Affair" provoked a wave of indignation that resulted in the expulsion of Jews from Egypt.[751] As is often the case, the real causes of anti-Semitic acts are glossed over, turning them into an inescapable problem that can only be explained by religion.[752]

In the same spirit, the double attack on French and American contingents in Beirut on October 23, 1983, which killed almost 300 people,

---

750. Mitch GINSBURG, "Affaire Lavon: revelations that raise new questions," *The Times of Israel*, May 12, 2015.
751. See Wikipedia, "Lavon Affair" article.
752. See, for example Jean-Marc LILING, "La confiscation des biens juifs en pays arabes," *Pardès*, 2003/1, no. 34 (pages 159-179) (www.cairn.inforevue-pardes-2003-1-page-159.htm); François SWEYDAN, "Le dernier khamsin des juifs d'Égypte ou le deuxième Exode," *dreuz.info*, October 19, 2019.

was apparently known to the Israeli services in advance. Victor Ostrovsky, a former Mossad agent, later revealed that the Israelis were aware of the attack, but did not inform the Americans, in order to encourage them to become involved in the conflict.[753] The strategy is one of chaos.

Espionage activities against the United States in the 1960s[754] ("friends don't spy on friends"), the sinking of the *USS Liberty* in 1967, the Beirut bombing of 1983 and the Jonathan Pollard affair of the spy who spied for Israel within the American services, have left a bitter taste and continue to feed a deep-seated anti-Israeli sentiment that is still very present among American military personnel.[755]

These examples are largely ignored by our media, but remain very much alive with the American military, for example. They mean that our ties with Israel are often more constrained than anything else. It would be important for Israel to realize this, because as the reactions to its action in Gaza show, it could well find itself very isolated at a critical moment that could be very close at hand.

## American Presence in the Middle East

The role of the United States in the Near and Middle East can be summed up as ensuring Israel's strategic depth. Indeed, it has been a constant feature of Israeli policy since the 1950s to push for greater US involvement in the Near and Middle East. American and Western interventions in Kuwait, Iraq, Libya and Syria were applauded in Tel Aviv. Yet not only were they failures, they also contributed significantly to destabilizing the region.

The American military are a kind of "human red line" for the State of Israel, which has always seen the balance of power as the source of its security, but lacks the means to do so. In the closed world of intelligence and behind the scenes, Israel's role is generally very poorly perceived. Symptomatically, Dr. Michael Scheuer, former head of the CIA's Osama

---

753. Ostrovsky, Victor & Claire Hoy, *By Way of Deception*, New York, St. Martin's Press, 1990, p. 321.
754. Rupert Cornwell, "US accuses Israel of 'alarming, even terrifying' levels of spying," www.independent.co.uk, May 8, 2014.
755. Donald Neff, "Israel Charged With Systematic Harassment of U.S. Marines," leatherneck.com, June 28, 2004 (https://www.wrmea.org/1995-march/israel-charged-with-systematic-harassment-of-u.s.-marines.html)

bin Laden cell between 2001 and 2004, told a congressional committee hearing:[756]

*If it were up to me, I'd give up on the Israelis tomorrow!*

This is why the Palestinian offensive has triggered a whole series of strikes against US bases in Iraq and Syria. Between October 7, 2023 and January 28, 2024, the latter launched some 170 attacks against US bases in Iraq and Syria.[757]

On January 28, one of these attacks killed three soldiers at a secret site designated TOWER 22, on Jordanian territory. This site adjoins the Al-Tanf base just across the border in Syria. For many Americans, this incident was a reminder that their country is illegally occupying Syria. On the Jordanian side, the government initially denied that these soldiers had died on its territory,[758] as the American presence is very unpopular in the country.

These attacks triggered a series of 85 U.S. retaliatory strikes in Syria and Iraq, which left almost 40 people dead on February 2.[759] Despite the presence of two naval air groups and an amphibious assault group brought into the area in October 2023, the United States is uneasy. They are beginning to realize that the Arab world's exasperation with their presence and Israel's attitude is driving them out of the region.

As with Israel, their military successes can only be measured in terms of the number of civilians killed, but their political gains are nil.

Ridiculed in Afghanistan, unable to achieve their objectives in Ukraine, the Americans and their Western allies are beginning to understand that they are betting on the wrong horses, and that getting involved alongside Israel is far from in their best interests. Chinese, Russian and Iranian diplomacy is proving highly effective against Western gunboat policy. Aid to Ukraine and Israel is becoming increasingly difficult to get through our parliaments.

---

756. "I'd Dump the Israelis Tomorrow --Ex-CIA Michael Scheuer Tells Congress," *YouTube*, October 9, 2013 (https://youtu.be/rDlTSFBp9ds)
757. https://www.understandingwar.org/backgrounder/iran-update-january-28-2024
758. https://www.agenzianova.com/en/news/giordania-tre-militari-statunitensi-uccisi-e-25-feriti-in-un-attacco-con-droni-il-portavoce-del-governo-non-e-avvenuto-nel-nostro-territorio/
759. Alexandra Hutzler, "Biden's retaliatory strikes in Middle East come with significant political risk: Experts," *ABC News*, February 2, 2024 (https://abcnews.go.com/Politics/bidens-planned-retaliatory-strikes-middle-east-significant-political/story?id=106895901)

U.S. congressmen are asking the administration to justify bypassing the parliamentary processes that authorize arms deliveries to Israel, and are concerned about whether these deliveries *"comply with humanitarian principles and U.S. law, and whether they promote or undermine U.S. national security."*[760]

In presenting its case to the ICJ, South Africa states that Israel "has violated and continues to violate" the Convention on the Prevention of Genocide. *No one* has disputed this statement. This means that supporting Israel is increasingly tantamount to supporting a genocidal policy. This is why, at his election rallies, Joe Biden is systematically interrupted by Democratic activists who call him "Genocide Joe."[761]

## Syria

The idea of breaking up Syria emerged in February 1982, with the Yinon Plan, published under the aegis of the *World Zionist Organization*, under the title, *A Strategy for Israel in the 1980s*.[762] In its original form, this "plan" never constituted an official element of Israeli policy, but it does shed light on Israel's understanding of its strategic environment:

> *The dissolution of Syria and, later, Iraq into ethnically and religiously unique areas, as in Lebanon, is Israel's primary long-term objective on its eastern front, while the dissolution of the military power of these states is a primary objective in the short term. Syria will break up according to its ethnic and religious structures into several states, as is currently the case in Lebanon, with a Shiite Alawite state along the coast, a Sunni state in the Aleppo region, another Sunni state in Damascus, hostile to its northern neighbor, and the Druze who will establish their state, perhaps even in our Golan Heights, in the*

---

760. Jennifer Hansler, "Group of Democrats call on Blinken to provide answers on bypassing Congress to approve arms sales to Israel," *CNN*, January 30, 2024 (https://edition.cnn.com/2024/01/30/politics/democrats-letter-blinken-israel-arms-sale/index.html)
761. Ingrid Jacques, "Biden tries to shake off 'Genocide Joe' epithet, but it could be the issue that sinks him," *USA Today*, February 7, 2024 (https://www.usatoday.com/story/opinion/columnist/2024/02/07/biden-israel-gaza-genocide-democrats-2024-election/72480021007/)
762. Oded Yinon, "A Strategy for Israel in the Nineteen Eighties," KIVUNIM (Directions), *A Journal for Judaism and Zionism*; Issue No, 14--winter, 5742, Department of Publicity/The World Zionist Organization, Jerusalem, February 1982.

*Hauran and in northern Jordan. This configuration will guarantee peace and security in the long term, and this goal is already achievable today.*[763]

It served as the basis for another document drawn up in 1996 by an American think tank for the Israeli Prime Minister, Benjamin Netanyahu, outlining an Israeli strategy:[764] destabilization of the region, including the overthrow of the Iraqi and Syrian governments, instead of general peace; increased right of pursuit and intervention in the Palestinian territories; and enhanced cooperation with the USA. This plan, too, was never officially adopted by Netanyahu. But its authors, widely represented in the Bush administration, would later draw on it to shape US policy in the Middle East,[765] and it would form the backbone of the policy applied by governments led by Benjamin Netanyahu.[766]

Moreover, Israel's support for the Syrian opposition was aimed at keeping its neighbor in an unstable equilibrium in the medium and long term. This is why, for Israel, the Islamic State (IS) is a bulwark against Iranian influence and an ally in the fight against Hezbollah. This is confirmed by an Israeli think tank—funded (among other things) by NATO as part of its *Mediterranean Dialogue*[767]—in a report entitled, *Destroying the Islamic State is a Strategic Mistake*, in which it postulates that the Islamic State "*can be a useful instrument for weakening Tehran's ambitious plan to dominate the Middle East.*"[768] This is in line with the intellectual continuity of the Yinon report. So, while Israel certainly did not create the IS, it sees its presence as consistent with its own security policy.

A secret report from the U.S. *Defense Intelligence Agency* (DIA) on the situation in Syria, dated August 5, 2012, clearly identified the advantage of supporting Syrian Islamists, despite the risks of an Islamic State emerging:

---

763. Oded YINON, *A Strategy for Israel in the Nineteen Eighties*, Association of Arab-American University Graduates, Inc. Belmont, Massachusetts, 1982, Special Document No. 1.
764. "A Clean Break: A New Strategy for Securing the Realm," *The Institute for Advanced Strategic and Political Studies*, July 1996.
765. Brian WHITAKER, "Playing skittles with Saddam," *The Guardian*, September 3, 2002.
766. Oded YINON, "Une stratégie persévérante de dislocation du monde arabe," *Confluences Méditerranée*, vol. 61, no 2, 2007, p. 149-164 (DOI: https://doi.org/10.3917/come.061.0149)
767. http://besacenter.org/about/international-support/#.XTX2cegzaUk
768. Prof. Efraim INBAR, *The Destruction of Islamic State is a Strategic Mistake*, Begin-Sadat Center for Strategic Studies, Perspectives Paper No. 352, August 2, 2016.

*If the situation allows, there is the possibility of establishing a declared or undeclared Salafist principality in eastern Syria (Hasaka and Deir ez-Zor), and this is exactly what the countries supporting the opposition want in order to isolate the Syrian regime, which is seen as the strategic depth of Shiite expansion (Iraq and Iran).*[769]

The key to this strategy is a partition of Syria, of which there are several models. The most frequently evoked is that of a break-up of Syria into a Kurdish state in the north-east, a Sunni state in the south-east and a Christian-Alawite state in the west of the country, on the coast. It is reminiscent of the 1982 Yinon plan and explains the convergence of Western and Israeli strategies. This idea originated in Israel, but our media, such as *Le Figaro*[770] or *France 24*,[771] prefer to attribute it to the Syrian government. Yet the Syrian leader has never spoken of partitioning his country, and is seeking on the contrary to restore its integrity.[772]

That is why, contrary to widespread opinion, Westerners have not really been fighting the Islamic State. If we superimpose the map of Western strikes counted by the *Airwars.org* website[773] and that of the territories still held by the IS published by the *BBC*,[774] we can see that until 2017 there were no strikes in the IS's regrouping areas in southeastern Syria and that the coalition clearly sought to "channel" it towards this area. In fact, the coalition is strangely inactive when it comes to preventing the group from pushing towards Damascus.[775] Occasionally, the Western coalition even strikes the Syrian army or Christian allied forces facing the IS.

---

769. Brad Hoff, "West will facilitate rise of Islamic State 'in order to isolate the Syrian regime': 2012 DIA document," *Foreign Policy Journal*, May 21, 2015; see also: http://www.judicialwatch.org/wp-content/uploads/2015/05/Pg.-291-Pgs.-287-293-JW-v-DOD-and-State-14-812-DOD-Release-2015-04-10-final-version11.pdf

770. Isabelle Lasserre, "Khaddam: 'Assad is planning the partition of Syria," lefigaro.fr, January 25, 2012.

771. Amara Makhoul-Yatim, "Towards a partition of Syria?" (part two), *France 24*, May 17, 2013 (updated May 31, 2013).

772. Margaret Brennan, "If Syria cease-fire fails, is there a Plan-B?," *CBS News*, February 25, 2016.

773. See airwars.org

774. Islamic State and the crisis in Iraq and Syria in maps, BBC News, March 28, 2018 (www.bbc.com/news/world-middle-east-27838034)

775. James Dobbins, Jeffrey Martini & Philip Gordon, "A Peace Plan for Syria," *Rand Corporation*, 2015 (Document PE-182-RC); Jeff Mackler, "The US Plan to Partition Syria," *Counterpunch*, February 9, 2018; Nafeez Mosaddeq Ahmed, "US military document reveals how the West opposed a democratic Syria," mondiplo.com, September 24, 2018

What is more, the issue of the Golan Heights, illegally occupied by Israel, continues to divide the two countries. However, in the late 1990s, to resolve the Golan question, a peace process between Syria and Israel was initiated by Hafez al-Assad. An agreement was close at the time, but Assad's death in June 2000, the start of the second Intifada in Israel in September, the election of President Bush in the United States in November, the arrival of Ariel Sharon to power in Israel in March 2001 and, finally, 9/11, all combined to nip in the bud these attempts at peace, which Israel did not want to pursue.

The problem was exacerbated by Donald Trump's recognition of Israel's annexation of the Golan Heights. The latter is illegal under international law, but the United States does not obey international law, preferring to play by the rules it sets itself. As noted by the Atlanticist *Carnegie Endowment for International Peace*, Israel's policy of annexing territory is imbued with a biblical vision that takes precedence over international law.[776] For Israel, peace is a component of its security policy only insofar as it consolidates a strategic gain, but never as a principle.

The reintegration of Syria into the Arab League in May 2023 and the handshake between Iran and Saudi Arabia in March 2023 are two major events in the Middle East. Israel probably underestimated their importance because of the Abraham Accords, which were intended to consolidate its position in the Middle East. But in January 2024, the picture is less clear. Syria enjoys the support of Russia and, indirectly, China; in other words, with countries whose credibility has grown at the expense of that of Western countries and the United States.

## Iran

Iran is a country traditionally benevolent towards the West. Ethnically distinct from the Arabs, its population is strongly influenced by Indian culture and practices a Shiite Islam that is fundamentally more liberal than the Sunni Islam of Saudi Arabia. Iran has no tradition of warlike expansion, and has not attacked any country since 1798.

---

776. Lorenzo Kamel, "The Roots of Israel's Annexation Policy," *Carnegie Endowment for International Peace*, August 6, 2020 (https://carnegieendowment.org/sada/82425)

From 1976, the Carter administration's focus on human rights issues prompted the Shah to diversify his alliances, and he increased his military cooperation with Israel. Documents seized from the American embassy in Tehran in 1979 revealed that Israel had developed a nuclear missile which it was preparing to sell to Iran (Operation TZOR).[777]

The arrival of Khomeini in power in 1979 changed Iranian attitudes, but the decades of military and intelligence cooperation with Israel were not forgotten. Iran suffered the war against Iraq—largely supported by the West—and chemical attacks carried out with the blessing of the United States.[778] At that time, Israel saw Iran as a kind of "strategic counterweight" to the pressure from Arab countries and supported it. In particular, it bombed the Tuwaitha research center near Baghdad (September 30, 1980), then the Osirak nuclear power plant in Iraq (June 7, 1981). Israel's enemy was Iraq, which has been home to several Palestinian movements since the mid-1970s.

Negotiations for the release of the 52 hostages from the American Embassy in Tehran led to the signing of the Algiers Agreements on January 19, 1981, which stipulated, among other things, that:[779]

> *The United States pledges that, from now on, its policy will be not to intervene, directly or indirectly, politically or militarily, in Iran's internal affairs.*

... a commitment the Americans never kept.

Since the end of the Cold War, Iran has been striving to improve its relations with the West. Its neutrality during the first Gulf War (1990-1991) was a key to the success of the international coalition in Iraq. In this shifting geostrategic balance, Iran took the opportunity to extend its hand to the Europeans, but under American pressure, they failed to grasp it.

After 9/11, the government of President Mohammed Khatami expressed its condolences to the American people and supported American intervention in Afghanistan. Following the Taliban assassination of nine

---

777. Ronen BERGMAN, *The Secret War with Iran*, Oneworld, Oxford, 2008 (p. 5)
778. Shane HARRIS & Matthew M. AID, "Exclusive: CIA Files Prove America Helped Saddam as He Gassed Iran," *Foreign Policy*, August 26, 2013.( https://foreignpolicy.com/2013/08/26/exclusive-cia-files-prove-america-helped-saddam-as-he-gassed-iran/)
779. *Algiers Accords—Declaration of the Government of the Democratic and Popular Republic of Algeria*, January 19, 1981, para 1.

Iranian diplomats in 1998, tensions between the two countries increased, and Iran provided significant intelligence support to the Americans at the start of Operation ENDURING FREEDOM. Iran also financed and trained Ahmed Shah Massoud's Northern Alliance, which overthrew the Taliban and seized power in Kabul on November 14, 2001. In December 2001, at the Bonn Conference, American negotiator James Dobbins thanked Iran for having convinced its Afghan allies to join the coalition of national unity. But one month later, on January 29, 2002, during his State of the Union address, the American President, for all his thanks, included Iran in the "Axis of Evil."

As early as 2001, it was the West's mistakes and lack of strategic vision that gave Iran its role as a regional power, as confirmed by former Israeli Foreign Minister Shlomo Ben-Ami:[780]

> *Iran supported the United States in the first Gulf War, but was excluded from the Madrid conference. Iran also sided with the US administration in the war against the Taliban in Afghanistan. And when US forces routed Saddam Hussein's army in the spring of 2003, the defensive Iranians proposed a "comprehensive pact" that would put all points of contention on the table, from the nuclear issue to Israel, from Hezbollah to Hamas. The Iranians also pledged to stop obstructing the Arab-Israeli peace process. But American neo-conservative arrogance—"We don't talk to the Axis of Evil"— prevented a pragmatic response to the Iranian approach.*

By intervening in Iraq in 2003, with the support of the country's Shiite majority, American strategists failed to realize that they were creating a continuous axis between Iran and Lebanon, which they reinforced by isolating Syria after 2005. This created a sense of encirclement among the Gulf monarchies, as evidenced by a SECRET e-mail from the US embassy in Ryadh, dated March 22, 2009.[781] This led Saudi Arabia and Qatar to reassert their Sunni influence by supporting the "Arab revolutions." The West perceived them as democratic outbursts, whereas they were essentially a defensive reaction by the Gulf monarchies, which felt all the more

---

780. Shlomo BEN-AMI, former Israeli Foreign Minister, *Le Figaro*, September 19, 2007.
781. *Saudi Intelligence Chief Talks Regional Security with Brennan Delegation*, March 22, 2009 (https://wikileaks.org/plusd/cables/09RIYADH445_a.html)

threatened because most of their oil wealth is located in areas where their Shiite minorities are in the majority.

At the same time, relations between Iran and Israel changed radically. With the disappearance of Iraq as its main threat, Israel aligned itself with its American protector and adopted Iran as its "preferred enemy." This paranoia had proved unfounded in the case of Iraq, and is just as unfounded today in the case of Iran, but the Israelis see this threat as the key to American support.

On April 21, 2004, President George Bush declared: *"We're going to take care of Iran,"*[782] placing Iran in the crosshairs of the United States, with a view to imposing regime change.[783] This led Iran to announce, in February 2005, that it was beginning preparations to counter a possible American aggression. According to Philip Giraldi, a former CIA executive, the Americans then had a plan for a nuclear and conventional attack, with 450 strategic targets to be destroyed in Iran.[784] This explicit American threat strengthened national unity in favor of the "hardliners" and to the detriment of the reformers, despite opposition to the regime. This is what brought Mahmoud Ahmadinejad to the Iranian presidency on August 3, 2005.

In 2006, the USA began subversion operations in Syria. In 2007, President George W. Bush signed a *Presidential Finding* authorizing clandestine operations in Iran,[785] and Congress voted a $400 million appropriation to bring about regime change.[786] For Tehran, Syria is a kind of last bastion, the only ally in the region capable of preventing it from being strategically encircled: the Damascus-Tehran axis is growing stronger. American-Israeli policy in the Middle East is marked by a profound lack of vision and a total misunderstanding of the region's mentalities. Paradoxically, this illustrates that the State of Israel is an "off-ground" state, a Western appendage in a world and territory that are totally foreign to it.

The Palestinian cause is not an Iranian cause. It is an issue that the Arab countries have made their own, and which they do not want to share with the Iranians:[787]

---

782. Mike ALLEN, "Iran 'Will Be Dealt With,' Bush Says," *The Washington Post*, April 22, 2004.
783. "Sharon says U.S. should also disarm Iran, Libya and Syria," *Haaretz*, September 30, 2004.
784. Philip GIRALDI, "Deep Background," *The American Conservative*, August 1st, 2005.
785. Brian ROSS & Richard ESPOSITO, "Bush Authorizes New Covert Action Against Iran," *ABC News*, May 23, 2007.
786. Seymour M. HERSH, "Preparing the Battlefield," *The New Yorker*, June 29 2008.
787. *Washington Post*, May 19, 2007.

*Prince Turki al-Faysal has harsh words for Iran, saying that this predominantly Persian country has nothing to do with Israeli-Palestinian peace. "This is an Arab affair that must be resolved within the Arab fold."*

But today, we are trying to lump all the "bad guys" together in some kind of logic. Our learned experts repeat over and over that Iran finances and directs Hamas[788] and, like journalist Anne Sinclair, we declare loud and clear that the Islamic State is Hamas,[789] while other "experts" see in the October 7 operation the expression of a civilizational struggle.[790] This is total fantasy. On January 8, 2024, the Islamic State spokesman condemned Hamas[791] and claimed responsibility[792] for the January 2 attack[793] on the commemoration of the death of General Soleimani in Iran.[794] The Western narrative and that of our "experts" is caught up in a kind of infernal circle at the center of which is Hamas. In fact:

- Hamas is not associated with Iran, as we have seen.
- The Islamic State was not created by Israel, but it is not hostile to it and Israel does not consider it a threat.[795]
- The Islamic State sees Hezbollah and its Iranian backing as threats, as they are—along with Syria—the main obstacle to its project for a caliphate between Iraq and Syria.
- Hamas is perceived as an enemy by the Islamic State, because it is not fighting for Islamic values, but for territory.

---

788. https://youtu.be/9j9Gs0PdXzU
789. https://www.dailymotion.com/video/x8p2qe3
790. Gaétan SUPERTINO, "Hugo Micheron, spécialiste du djihadisme: 'Depuis le 7 octobre, l'EI et Al-Qaida cherchent à se saisir de l'engouement déclenché par le Hamas contre Israël," *Le Monde*, November 5, 2023 (updated November 8, 2023) (https://www.lemonde.fr/le-monde-des-religions/article/2023/11/05/hugo-micheron-specialiste-du-djihadisme-depuis-le-7-octobre-l-ei-et-al-qaida-cherchent-a-s-emparer-de-l-engouement-declenche-par-le-hamas-contre-israel_6198310_6038514.html)
791. https://shorturl.at/inF58
792. Parisa HAFEZI, Elwely ELWELLY & Clauda TANIOS, "Islamic State claims responsibility for deadly Iran attack, Tehran vows revenge," *Reuters*, January 4, 2024 (https://www.reuters.com/world/middle-east/iran-vows-revenge-after-biggest-attack-since-1979-revolution-2024-01-04/)
793. https://www.longwarjournal.org/archives/2024/01/islamic-state-announces-new-global-campaign-to-rally-members-and-supporters.php
794. https://www.reuters.com/world/middle-east/iran-vows-revenge-after-biggest-attack-since-1979-revolution-2024-01-04/
795. Efraim INBAR, "ISIS No Threat to Israel," *POV—Boston University*, September 18, 2015 (https://www.bu.edu/articles/2015/pov-isis-no-threat-to-israel/)

Against this backdrop, from the outset of the Hamas operation, our media have been peddling conspiracy theories, suggesting the involvement of Iran. True or false? We do not know precisely at this stage, but one thing is certain: apart from our own prejudices, there is nothing to indicate that Iran was involved in the preparation, organization and launching of the Hamas operation.

In Switzerland, on October 12, *RTS* raised the idea that Iran had actively contributed to the operation,[796] had helped train microlight pilots,[797] and even suspected that it was *"behind the massacres [of October 7],"*[798] thus justifying Israeli strikes against Syria.

In keeping with its anti-Arab tradition, the Swiss media, some of whose journalists defend conspiracy theories against Muslims, is lying once again. Four days earlier, on October 8, Anthony Blinken had declared in the *Washington Post* that *"we don't yet have proof that Iran directed or was behind this particular attack."*[799] The following day, Israeli journalist Yossi Melman declared:[800]

> *IDF spokesman Brigadier General Danny Hagari said there was no indication of Iranian involvement in the war in Gaza.*

Even *Reuters* declared on October 11 that, according to US intelligence, Iran had been surprised by the Hamas attack.[801] In other words, once again our media are not looking for appeasement, but show a deliberate desire to polarize and radicalize opinions, and make things worse.

---

796. https://www.rts.ch/info/monde/14384696-mahmoud-abbas-exige-la-fin-immediate-de-lagression-contre-le-peuple-palestinien.html
797. https://www.rts.ch/info/monde/14381098-le-hamas-affirme-avoir-libere-une-otage-et-ses-deux-enfants.html
798. https://www.rts.ch/play/tv/redirect/detail/14386304
799. John Hudson & Ellen Nakashima, "Biden administration scrambles to deter wider Mideast conflict," *The Washington Post*, October 8, 2023 (https://www.washingtonpost.com/national-security/2023/10/08/israel-hamas-intelligence-middle-east/)
800. https://twitter.com/yossi_melman/status/1711253641573584970
801. Jonathan Landay & Matt Spetalnick, "Hamas attack surprised some Iranian leaders, says US source, citing initial intelligence," *Reuters*, October 11, 2023 (https://www.reuters.com/world/initial-us-intelligence-shows-hamas-attack-surprised-iranian-leaders-ny-times-2023-10-11/)

## Lebanon

The main reason for linking Iran to international terrorism is its support for Lebanese Hezbollah. But these accusations are fueled more by our ignorance than by clear facts.

Hezbollah's origins date back to the Israeli intervention of 1982. After the 1967 war and the events of September 1970 in Jordan, some 300,000 Palestinian refugees settled in southern Lebanon. This presence destabilized the local economy, and affected the Shiite population, who lived in peace with their Israeli neighbor, but suffered the consequences of the conflict. The installation of PLO command in Beirut and frequent Feddayin incursions along the Lebanese border prompted Israel to intervene in Lebanon in June 1982. Operation PEACE IN GALILEE aimed to *"exterminate"*[802] the terrorists of Yasser Arafat's *Palestine Liberation Organization* (PLO).

The Lebanese Shiite population welcomed the Israelis with enthusiasm and *"a shower of grains of rice."*[803] But instead of relying on this population and intra-Arab dissensions to fight against the PLO, the Israelis fought indiscriminately against Lebanese Shiites and Palestinian Sunnis, quickly creating unanimity against them. Israeli intelligence services failed to grasp the situation, and the troops were caught up in a spiral of violence.[804] The result was a negative reaction from the American Jewish community, which threatened to stop supporting Israeli policy.[805] It was at this point that—according to intelligence sources—the Rue des Rosiers bombing in Paris (August 9, 1982) took place, in order to recreate unity around Israeli policy.

In September 1982, following the ceasefire agreements between Israel and the PLO, a *Multinational Security Force* (MNF) was deployed in Beirut. It was based on Security Council Resolution 521, which provided for aid to the Lebanese government to protect the population. In the following year, American forces were the target of a series of skirmishes

---

802. "134. Statement to the Knesset by Prime Minister Begin on the terrorist raid and the Knesset resolution, 13 March 1978," *mfa.gov.il*
803. Greg Myre, "Israelis in a Shiite Land: Hard Lessons From Lebanon," *The New York Times*, April 27, 2003.
804. Ronen Bergman, *The Secret War with Iran*, Oneworld, Oxford, 2008 (p. 58)
805. Dov Waxman, *Trouble in the Tribe: The American Jewish Conflict over Israel*, Princeton University Press, 2016 (pp. 316)

attributed to Israeli commandos.[806] On April 18, 1983, a bomb attack on the American embassy in Beirut killed 63 people. The *Islamic Jihad Organization* (IJO) claimed responsibility.

On October 23, 1983, two attacks hit the MNF: the first killed 241 people at US Marine headquarters, and the second, two minutes later, destroyed the "Drakkar," killing 58 French paratroopers.

The reasons for and sequence of events leading up to the attack on the French paratroopers have been the subject of various speculations, linked to the Iran-Iraq war. It is plausible, but not very realistic. The most likely explanation is simpler. It has to do with Western strategy in Beirut. The MNF was a security force, supposed to be impartial. However, in September 1983, the intervention of American naval artillery led to an intensification of the war. The MNF exceeded the limits of its original mandate. The decision to conduct joint patrols with the Lebanese army made France a party to the conflict. The United States was more critical of the government's strategy, and of Special Representative Robert McFarlane's decision to support the Lebanese army.[807] This is why the Italian contingent—deployed between the American and French sectors—remained in its original role, and was not targeted by attacks. Victor Ostrovsky, a former Mossad agent, would later reveal that the Israelis were aware of this attack, but did not inform the Americans, in order to push them into getting involved in the conflict.[808]

Both attacks were then attributed to the ODI, but they were claimed by the *Free Islamic Revolution Movement* (MRIL),[809] which was unknown at the time. However, the Americans immediately associated it with Iran, without any factual elements—it was the enemy of the moment. It was only later, in order to place the blame on a known entity, that Israel and several Western countries, including the United States and Great Britain, would accuse *Hezbollah,* claiming that it had been founded in 1982.

---

806. Donald Neff, "Israel Charged with Systematic Harassment of U.S. Marines," *Washington Report on Middle East Affairs*, March 1995, pp. 79-81.
807. Nir Rosen, "Lesson Unlearned," *Foreign Policy*, October 29, 2009.
808. Ostrovsky, Victor & Claire Hoy, *By Way of Deception*, New York, St. Martin's Press, 1990, p. 321.
809. Journal télévisé de 20h, *Antenne 2*, October 23, 1983; William E. Farrell, "Unanswered Question: Who Was Responsible?," *The New York Times*, October 25, 1983.

In 1982, Hezbollah did not exist.[810] Its creation was marked by the establishment of its charter on February 16, 1985,[811] as Israel completed the first phase of its withdrawal from Lebanon.[812] Prior to this date, no Lebanese armed group referred to or defined itself in relation to the *Party of God (Hezbollah)*. The main Shiite resistance group at the time was the ODI, a vague entity whose make-up was never precisely defined, rather like "al-Qaeda" twenty years later. Backdating the creation of Hezbollah made it possible to "label" individuals with suspected ODI links, such as Imad Mougnieh.[813] It was the same stratagem that American jurists would use twenty years later with "al-Qaeda" to circumvent the limits of the only anti-terrorism law they had at the time: the Organized Crime Act. More on this later.

In September 2001, Caspar Weinberger, who was Secretary of Defense in 1983, said in an interview:

> *We still don't know who carried out the bomb attack on the Marine barracks at Beirut airport, and we certainly didn't know it at the time.*[814]

In 2009, President Obama was criticized for not mentioning Hezbollah at a commemoration of the attack.[815] But the reason for this "omission" is very simple: to this day, with the exception of Pascal Boniface and *Conspiracy Watch*, who probably have more information than the American President, nobody knows exactly who carried it out.

## *Hezbollah's Raison d'Être*

Hezbollah is not a revolutionary organization, but a resistance organization created by and after the Israeli offensive of 1982. Its aim is to restore the integrity of Lebanese territory as it was in 1978.

---

810. Nir ROSEN, "Lesson Unlearned," *Foreign Policy*, October 29, 2009.
811. https://www.cia.gov/library/readingroom/docs/DOC_0000361273.pdf; Jonathan MASTERS & Zachary LAUB, "Hezbollah," *Council on Foreign Relations*, January 3, 2014; "Profile: Lebanon's Hezbollah movement," *BBC News*, March 15, 2016.
812. Jean-Jacques MÉVEL, "L'UE place le Hezbollah sur la liste noire du terrorisme," *lefigaro.fr*, July 22, 2013.
813. He was mysteriously assassinated in Damascus in 2008.
814. Frontline—Target America, Interview: Caspar Weinberger, (http://www.pbs.org/wgbh/pages/frontline/shows/target/interviews/weinberger.html) (accessed August 16, 2019)
815. https://www.govinfo.gov/content/pkg/PPP-2009-book2/pdf/PPP-2009-book2-doc-pg1581-2.pdf

Meyer Habib's claim that Israel *"has taken every inch of Lebanon out of its territory"*[816] is an outright lie.

There are several border lines between Lebanon and Israel: the one drawn in 1923 (for the partition between France and Great Britain), which was largely taken up again in 1949 to mark the "official" border ("green line"); the Israeli withdrawal line of 1978 and the "blue line" of the 2000 withdrawal. However, these lines do not coincide exactly. Although the blue line was drawn with the help of the United Nations, Lebanon still disputes 13 sectors of it,[817] not to mention the maritime borders, which Israel has extended to include underwater hydrocarbon reserves.

Israel still occupies the "Shebaa Farms" area, a territory of some 25 km2 on the borders of Israel, Lebanon and Syria; as well as numerous small portions of territory along the Israeli-Lebanese border, behind the Blue Line. These tiny territories are at the root of almost every incident between the two countries. For example, the tunnels discovered by Israel in 2018 in southern Lebanon linked these disputed areas to Lebanon, and not the "real" Israeli territory as claimed.

In July 2006, it was in one of these areas, unilaterally annexed by Israel and whose sovereignty is disputed, that Hezbollah kidnapped Israeli soldiers on patrol, triggering the war ("Harb Tamouz"). Naturally, our media systematically fail to mention these illegally annexed territories,[818] and after the arrest of the Israeli soldiers, Hezbollah was immediately blamed.

We interpret Hezbollah's intransigence as a manifestation of aggression towards Israel. But the Israeli army's daily provocations against the Lebanese population are regularly overlooked. According to the *Air Pressure* website, between 2007 and 2022, Israel violated Lebanese airspace[819] more than 22,000 times: 8,231 combat aircraft and 13,102 drones.[820] These violations (sometimes even in supersonic mode, genera-

---

816. "Habib: 'We're not calling for a boycott of a friendly country!,'" *Europe 1/YouTube*, June 4, 2015 (03'40").
817. Amos HAREL, "Thirteen Israeli Border Points Raising Tensions With Lebanon," *Haaretz*, February 27, 2018.
818. Nicolas FALEZ, "Ten years after the Israeli withdrawal from southern Lebanon, tensions persist," *RFI*, May 24 2010.
819. Anna AHRONHEIM, "Israel flew in Lebanese airspace over 22,000 times in last 15 years—study," *The Jerusalem Post*, June 12, 2022 (https://www.jpost.com/israel-news/article-709182)
820. https://www.airpressure.info/

ting a "bang" designed to frighten the civilian population)[821] are regularly reported by the UN forces deployed in southern Lebanon, but are never condemned by the international community.

Presented in the West as a terrorist organization, Hezbollah is a complex one. It includes a social aid structure, the *Mou'assat al-Shahid* ("Institution of the Martyr"), which helps the physical and social victims of war. It also has a specialized body for the reconstruction of infrastructure destroyed by Israel, the *Jihad al-Binah* ("Effort for Reconstruction"), which receives most of its funding from Iran.[822] It had rebuilt the road network in southern Lebanon, and built and managed 5 hospitals, 14 clinics and 12 schools, before the Israelis destroyed this infrastructure in 2006.

Its military wing is essentially a territorial resistance ("al-Muqawama"), which Israel and some Western countries describe as "terrorist." Yet it is organized and equipped for defensive operations, not for an invasion of Israel. The Israeli army had bitter experience of this in 2006: its military intelligence service, AMAN, had failed to detect the complex network of trenches and concrete forts built for defensive combat in anticipation of an Israeli invasion.

The Muqawama was formed with the assistance of instructors from the Al-Quds units, elite formations of the *Revolutionary Guards*. Better known as the *Pasdaran, these* units report to the Iranian Ministry of the Interior and are responsible for territorial defense and the fight against terrorism, much like the Gendarmerie in France. This training activity has earned them the reputation of being "terrorists," but in reality, no attack can be attributed to them.

In 2012, with the emergence of Sunni militias on the Lebanese border, Hezbollah decided, in agreement with the Syrian government, to deploy troops in Syria. It was not until 2014 that it had a structured "expeditionary corps" capable of operating with the Syrian army. In fact, once again, the West and the Israelis are behind the development of their "threat."

It is obviously convenient to refer to Hezbollah as a terrorist organization in order to justify Israel's almost daily operations in Lebanon.

---

821. "Israeli jets said to cause sonic boom over Lebanon," *The Times of Israel/AFP*, September 10, 2017.
822. *Jihad al-Bina Association in Lebanon: A Hezbollah social foundation engaged in construction and social projects among the Shiite community, being a major component in Hezbollah's civilian infrastructure*, The Meir Amit Intelligence and Terrorism Information Center, June 23, 2019.

### *Is Hezbollah a Terrorist Organization?*

The terrorist nature of Hezbollah is the subject of endless debate in the West. Israel, and therefore the United States, Canada and the Netherlands, consider Hezbollah to be a terrorist movement.

In addition to the October 1983 bombings, the U.S. State Department attributes to it the hijacking of TWA flight 847 in Beirut, which was intended to free 700-800 Shiites detained in Israel in violation of the Geneva Conventions.[823] But in fact, no one knew the identity of the terrorists, who claimed to be members of the *Organization of the Oppressed of the Earth*. At the time, the press spoke only of *"Shiite Muslims"*[824] and sometimes mentioned the Amal militia, led by Nabih Berri.[825]

On March 10, 2005, less than a month after the assassination attempt on Rafik Hariri in Beirut, in a resolution adopted by 473 votes to 33, the European Parliament *"considers that there is irrefutable evidence of terrorist action by Hezbollah and that the Council should take all necessary measures to put an end to this action."*[826] But here again, decisions with far-reaching consequences were taken on the basis of supposition alone. In fact, the investigation showed the good personal relations between Hassan Nasrallah, Secretary General of Hezbollah, and Rafic Hariri, who met on numerous occasions and set up a joint committee before the 2005 parliamentary elections,[827] making the accusation extremely shaky.[828]

Following the attack on Israeli tourists in Burgas, Bulgaria, on July 18, 2012, Hezbollah was immediately accused, without any real proof of responsibility. France, through its Foreign Minister Laurent Fabius, then declared Hezbollah's armed wing a terrorist and requested its inclusion on the EU's list of terrorist organizations,[829] which was done in

---

823. The 1949 Geneva Convention relative to the Protection of Civilian Persons in Time of War prohibits a state from transferring combatants who are prisoners on its territory. Despite international protests and those of the International Red Cross, Israel obviously denied violating international law. But President Reagan, in his press conference of June 18, 1985, acknowledged that Israel had violated the Convention.
824. Rosenberg, Howard, Terrorism as Theater: TV Covers a Hijacking, *Los Angeles Times*, June 18 1985.
825. "Document—Hijacking, June 18, 1985, Transcript," *danratherjournalist.org*
826. Pascal Priestley, "Liban: le Hezbollah, l'état dans l'état," *information.tv5monde.com*, January 31, 2011 (updated April 7, 2013)
827. *Bulletin of the Special Tribunal for Lebanon*, December 2014—January 2015, Information and Communication Section of the Special Tribunal for Lebanon (www.stl-tsl.org/fr/media/stl-bulletin/3795-stl-bulletin-december-2014-january-2015)
828. Nicholas Blanford, "Did Hezbollah Kill Hariri?," *Foreign Policy*, April 1, 2010.
829. "Pour Paris, la branche armée du Hezbollah est un groupe terroriste," *AFP/France 24*, May 23, 2013.

July 2013.[830] But in 2018, the Bulgarian public prosecutor's investigation failed to demonstrate any responsibility on the part of Hezbollah, and its name disappeared from the indictment.[831] In 2019, this did not prevent the ARTE channel, in a documentary entitled, *Le Liban, otage du Moyen-Orient*, from asserting that Hezbollah was responsible for the attack![832]

Terrorism always has a concrete objective. It is Western discourse that seeks to "derationalize" it, often in favor of accusatory rhetoric and to justify aggressive policies.

On April 8, 2019, President Donald Trump declared the Pasdaran a terrorist organization, but it was Benjamin Netanyahu who asked him to do so, as he boasted in a tweet in Hebrew (probably to show his own electorate that Trump was "eating out of his hand," without making the American president uncomfortable in relation to his public).[833] This is a political maneuver, not an informed decision.

But the American decision was rejected by Iraqi Prime Minister Adel Abdul Mahdi and by Hadi al-Amiri, ex-Minister of Transport who heads the Badr Organization, an Iraqi Shiite organization: the Iraqi militias were able to defeat the Islamic State thanks to the support of the Pasdaran.[834] The vagaries of the "ménage à trois." Naturally, the French mainstream media largely relayed Trump's decision, but none noted the Iraqi reaction and its reasons. On April 24, 2019, Iran provided a response to end all discussion by declaring the US military a "*terrorist organization*,"[835] which is not completely untrue, by the way, since the US military supports, arms and trains Islamist fighters. American special forces and Israeli Mossad agents have been working with armed groups in Iran since 2005, supporting Salafist groups such as Jundallah.[836]

---

830. Benjamin BARTHE and Philippe RICARD, "Le Hezbollah classé organisation terroriste par l'UE," *Le Monde*, July 23, 2013.
831. Yonah JEREMY BOB, "Hezbollah role unmentioned in charges for 2012 Bulgaria terrorist attack," *The Jerusalem Post*, January 31, 2018.
832. Michael RICHTER, "Le Liban, otage du Moyen-Orient," www.arte.tv, (12'50") (broadcast on Arte on September 24 at 22h25) (withdrawn on December 22, 2019)
833. https://twitter.com/netanyahu/status/1115265423673573379
834. "Iraqi militias reject U.S. naming of Iran's Guards as terrorist group," *Reuters*, April 13, 2019.
835. "Iran's parliament approves bill labelling US army as 'terrorist,'" *Al-Jazeera*, April 24, 2019.
836. Brian ROSS & Christopher ISHAM, "The Secret War against Iran," *ABC News*, April 3, 2007; Aram MIRZAEI, "Jundallah: the US-backed Salafi Terrorists Operating in Iran," *Mint Press News*, April 8, 2019; (Editor's note: In 2008, Jundallah split into two groups: Harakat Ansar Iran and Jaish ul-Adl).

## Hezbollah's Reaction After October 7, 2023

The Palestinian question is a territorial problem that is not an issue for either Iran or Hezbollah.

That said, Arab countries are keeping a low profile, and were it not for the courage of the Houthis, no Arab country has shown any real commitment to the Palestinians. Iran has therefore slowly taken up a place that was literally empty, and has become the defender of the Palestinian cause, more for foreign policy reasons than for operational purposes. To repeat, Iran has no motive for attacking Israel, but it does support the Shiite community, which is regularly attacked by Israel in southern Lebanon.

With the deterioration of relations with Israel, support for the Palestinian cause gives it two levers in line with support for the Lebanese Shiite community: the first is support for the small Shiite community that exists, notably in Gaza, and the second is a response to Israel's action in supporting (along with the USA) terrorist movements in Iran. This explains the attack on a Mossad station in Iraqi Kurdistan, carried out by the Revolutionary Guards in January 2024, in response to the attack on the celebration of the death of General Soleimani.[837]

Ties between Iran and the Palestinians developed after the PLO recognized the state of Israel in November 1988. But despite Israel's efforts to convince Westerners of this, there is no evidence that Iran supports terrorist activities. The Israeli authorities repeatedly mention the incident involving the cargo ship *Karine A*, intercepted in the international waters of the Red Sea in January 2002, which was allegedly transporting Iranian weapons for the Palestinian Authority. The Israeli version, however, presents a number of implausibilities: in fact, the weapons were destined for the Lebanese Hezbollah.[838] At the time, there was no reason for Iran to support Hamas. All the more so as President Khatami's policy at the time was geared towards dialogue and appeasement with Israel.

Since the early 2000s, Israeli propaganda has been desperately trying to equate Hezbollah with Hamas. In reality, Palestinians and Lebanese Shiites have different goals. This explains why, during the brutal Israeli interventions in Gaza, notably in December 2008 and July 2014,

---

837. Parisa Hafezi & Timour Azhari, "Iran says Revolutionary Guards attack Israel's 'spy HQ' in Iraq, vow more revenge," *Reuters*, January 16, 2024 (https://www.reuters.com/world/middle-east/irans-revolutionary-guards-say-they-have-attacked-espionage-centers-iraqs-erbil-2024-01-15/)
838. Brian Whitaker, "The strange affair of Karine A," *The Guardian*, January 21, 2002.

Hezbollah did not attack the Jewish state from the north, contrary to what many "experts" had "predicted."

October 7, 2023 was no exception. Our difficulty in understanding what is happening along Israel's northern border is because of the very sketchy nature of the information provided by our media. In fact, Israel carries out air raids or reconnaissance flights over Syria and Lebanon on an almost daily basis. This means that potentially every day these countries have reason to retaliate against Israel. In the days leading up to October 7, Israel carried out several air raids against Hezbollah and southern Lebanon, and in September, the *Washington Institute* raised the question of a possible war between Israel and Lebanon.[839] It is therefore difficult to distinguish between what is related to these regular fever rises and what could be linked to the Palestinian operation.

The problem is that Israel is not a rational actor. On November 12, General Austin, US Secretary of Defense, called Yoav Gallant, his Israeli counterpart, to express the White House's growing concern that Israeli military action in Lebanon is exacerbating tensions along the border. Members of the Biden administration fear that Israel is seeking to provoke Hezbollah and create a pretext for a wider war that could draw the United States into a regional conflict.[840]

On January 2, 2024, the assassination of Saleh Al-Arouri in Beirut, by an Israeli terrorist attack, illustrates this irrationality. For Israel seems—once again—incapable of assessing its adversaries. Thus, this assassination triggered a spiral of retaliation:

- Hezbollah carried out a strike against the electronic warfare station at Mount Meron (Har Miron) in northern Israel. Interestingly, Hamas did not announce a response to this attack, but Hezbollah did. The reason for this response was that the Israelis had violated Lebanese airspace, and not to react would have meant giving Israel carte blanche to carry out further operations of this type.
- This strike was followed by the elimination of Wassim Al-Tawil, a Hezbollah commander, near Khirbet Selm, in southern Lebanon, on January 8.[841]

---

839. https://www.washingtoninstitute.org/policy-analysis/new-israel-hezbollah-war-looming
840. https://www.axios.com/2023/11/12/israel-lebanon-lloyd-austin-yoav-gallant-military
841. Laila Bassam & Maya Gebeily, "Israeli strike kills a Hezbollah commander in Lebanon," *Reuters*, January 8, 2024 (https://www.reuters.com/world/middle-east/israeli-strike-lebanon-kills-senior-commander-elite-hezbollah-unit-security-2024-01-08/)

- Hezbollah then retaliated with a strike against the Israeli Northern Sector headquarters in Safad.[842]

Israel has probably begun to realize that the situation is no longer in its favor. The Israeli Ministry of Health has asked medical facilities in the north of the country to raise their level of preparedness and be ready to treat thousands of victims.[843]

In early January 2024, exchanges between Hezbollah and Israel continued. Hezbollah seeks to attack the Iron Dome system, which provides air protection for the country, as well as surveillance installations in the northern sector.

At the end of January 2024, the exchange of fire increased. At the time, Israel was in trouble in Gaza, where the plausibility of genocide had been established by the ICJ, while its practice of firing on its own troops had triggered widespread public protests in the country's major cities. The temptation to regain national unity in a new conflict with Lebanon is therefore tempting. Hezbollah fired FALAQ-1 and BURQAN missiles against Israeli military installations in the Northern Sector.

### AL-ARQAB Cruise Missile

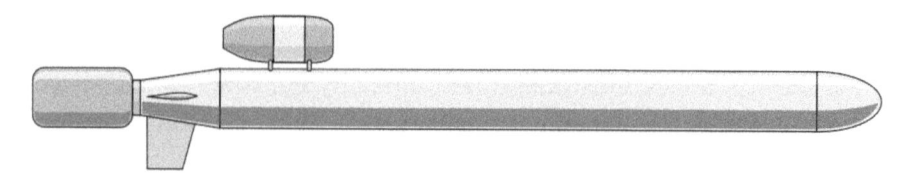

*Figure 137—The firing of a cruise missile against Israel marked a significant evolution. As with the missiles launched by the Houthis in the Red Sea, it testified to an essential change in the capabilities of the various resistance groups in the Near and Middle East.*

On the other hand, the Israeli and Western media were very discreet about another event. On January 8, the *Islamic Resistance in Iraq*[844] claimed responsibility for firing an Al-Arqab missile against a strategic installation near the Israeli city of Haifa, a distance of over 400 km. The

---

842. https://www.timesofisrael.com/liveblog_entry/hezbollah-claims-to-target-idf-northern-command-hq-with-drones-no-comment-from-army/
843. https://www.palestinechronicle.com/israel-orders-hospitals-to-prepare-for-treating-thousands-of-wounded/
844. NOA: The term "*Islamic Resistance in Iraq*" refers collectively to a whole range of resistance groups in Iraq, but there is no longer a group specifically bearing this designation in Iraq today.

reason why nobody wanted to talk about this firing is probably so as not to be forced to retaliate and engage in a worsening of the situation, which could well be unfavorable to Israel.

These actions indicate that Israel's neighbors are no longer afraid of it, and are ready to confront it. This means that Israel's strategy based on the balance of power is becoming obsolete. For a "normal" government, this should signal a change in strategic approach. A comparison with the security policy of another small country, such as Switzerland, is probably not without lessons.

## Comparing the Security Policies of two Small Countries

Switzerland and Israel have much in common. While today Switzerland is in a friendly strategic environment, it has long been in a situation similar to that of Israel: a small country surrounded by potentially hostile great powers.

While maintaining a strong defense policy, Switzerland has based its security policy on cooperation, independence and the promotion of international law. After it began acquiring nuclear weapons in the 1960s, Switzerland decided to join international disarmament efforts. Its security policy has historically been based on cooperation and stability in its strategic environment.

Israel also has a strong army, based on citizen involvement, a model that is quite similar to that of Switzerland. But for the rest, the philosophy is radically different. Believing that its future lies in a "Greater Israel" (Eretz Israel), it has never defined its borders and has sought to extend them since its creation in 1948.[845] This is why it encourages terrorism among its neighbors[846] while "nibbling" away at their territories. Based on the idea that if its larger neighbors were divided, they would be less of a threat, Israel's security policy is based on the division

---

845. https://www.c-r.org/accord/lebanon/boundaries-and-demarcation-delimiting-and-securing-lebanons-borders
846. Judah ARI GROSS, "IDF chief finally acknowledges that Israel supplied weapons to Syrian rebels," *The Times of Israel*, January 14, 2019 (https://www.timesofisrael.com/idf-chief-acknowledges-long-claimed-weapons-supply-to-syrian-rebels/)

and instability of its neighbors.[847] This explains its support for Salafist groups against Syria from 2011.[848]

Both countries have a conscript army deeply rooted in national culture. But that is where the similarities end. Whereas in its 750-year history, Switzerland has grown by association with its neighbors in order to pool defense capabilities, Israel has grown in 75 years by the strength of its army. In Israel, the army has slowly become the center of gravity of an aggressive nationalism that does not exist in Switzerland.

Unlike Switzerland, Israel's security policy is based on the notion of a balance of power, and it has acquired nuclear weapons, while counting on the protection of the United States. It is for this reason that Operation AL-AQSA FLOOD is perceived in Israel as a chink in its armor that neighboring countries might wish to exploit. As we saw above, this no doubt partly explains the brutality of the response against Gaza.

***Comparison of Swiss and Israeli Security Policies***

| Switzerland | Israel |
| --- | --- |
| A small country surrounded by great powers ||
| Defense based on a strong, popular army ||
| Defensive strategy based on protecting the population | Offensive strategy based on nuclear deterrence |
| Security policy based on cooperation and environmental stability | Security policy based on the balance of power and the instability of its neighbors |
| Independence from the great powers | Dependence on a major power (the United States) |
| Non-interference in the internal affairs of neighboring countries | Interference in the internal affairs of neighboring countries |
| Respect for international law | Respect for international law is subordinate to the country's interests |

*Figure 138—Two small countries with similar characteristics, but whose regional integration has followed diametrically opposed paths.*

---

847. Yinon ODED, "Une stratégie persévérante de dislocation du monde arabe," *Confluences Méditerranée*, 2007/2 (N°61), p. 149-164. (https://www.cairn.info/revue-confluences-mediterranee-2007-2-page-149.htm)
848. Elizabeth TSURKOV, "Inside Israel's Secret Program to Back Syrian Rebels," *Foreign Policy*, September 6, 2018.

To what extent this role of Switzerland will be confirmed in the future, after it was one of the three main countries to impose sanctions on Russia, is an open question. The fact remains that, until now at least, the international community has seen Switzerland as a solution in case of problems, whereas Israel is generally perceived as a problem in itself.

Switzerland's policy is to ensure that it is a recourse in the event of difficulties, and not part of the problem. With this in mind, it represents US interests in Iran and Iranian interests in Washington. The same applied to Cuba, until Barack Obama opened it up in 2014. On February 25, 2022, the day after the Russian offensive was launched, Volodymyr Zelenski turned to Switzerland to begin a negotiation process.

# 8. The Significance of the Palestinian Conflict for our Security

The relationship between European societies and their Jewish minorities has always been a complex one. Between pogroms and expulsions, Jewish populations have often been the object of hatred whose origins are sometimes difficult to understand.

At first, the lessons of the Second World War seemed to have borne fruit. The creation of Israel had given these minorities a "national home," in the words of the Balfour Declaration, which would guarantee them security. Yet, as time progressed, animosity towards Jewish populations did not diminish. Quite the contrary, in fact.

The reason is essentially twofold. On the one hand, Israel's security policy, which has been confrontational since 1947 (even before the creation of the State of Israel), and on the other, the world's growing empathy for the Palestinian cause. The latter has two origins: the ever-increasing presence of populations of Arab origin in our societies, sensitive to the Palestinian question, and the radicalization to the right observed in Israel since the early 2000s.

On October 9, 2023, on the *LCI* channel, journalist Ruth Elkrief recalled her arrival in France on the occasion of the Yom Kippur War and launched a message for politicians to assume their responsibilities: "*Respect principles: a life is a life, you don't attack civilians and you don't justify barbarism.*"[849] She was right, but at the time she did not yet realize that she would have to demonstrate the same rigor and respect for principles when her country massacred more than 25,000 civilians, 70% of

---

849. https://youtu.be/IU1irXjvt_w

them women and children. She did not, and that is probably where the problem lies.

Everyone recognizes a country's right to protect its population against terrorism, but the real question is: "How and within what limits?" Since 1948, Israel has applied the same, unchanged method to combat Palestinian resistance: the use of disproportionate violence as a deterrent. But it does not work. Terrorism is not inevitable, and if the strategy to eradicate it does not work, we probably need to move on to another strategy. But this has never been done, even after the Oslo Accords. Remember that it was the massacre of Palestinians at the Tomb of the Patriarchs on February 25, 1994, and the glorification of its perpetrator Baruch Goldstein,[850] that marked the beginning of Hamas suicide attacks.

Thus, Ruth Elkrief is right, but the principle of *"a life is a life"* is only valid when we believe that every life is worth another. But when her compatriots shoot children in the back with *impunity*[851] and make them prime targets,[852] or break the bones of trapped children with stones,[853] she does not seem to be moved nor does she condemn. Yet this is a situation in which the Israelis themselves are making themselves contemptible. During the war in Northern Ireland, British soldiers also had to deal with stones and Molotov cocktails thrown by children, yet there was a massacre of children as in Palestine.[854]

In the West Bank, where Hamas's presence is very weak, Palestinians are sometimes even shot for no reason.[855] Madame Elkrief's *"a life is a life"* principle only makes sense if we do not consider the other as a *"human animal."*

---

850. Tzvi Joffre, "10% of Israeli Jews think terrorist Baruch Goldstein is a 'national hero'—poll," *The Jerusalem Post*, March 6, 2023 (https://www.jpost.com/israel-news/article-733523)
851. Nick Logan, "Killings of Palestinian children are soaring in the West Bank. Advocates say it happens with impunity," *CBC News*, December 20, 2023 (https://www.cbc.ca/news/world/israel-palestinian-children-west-bank-1.7062531)
852. David Palumbo-Liu, "Palestinian children have suffered disproportionately as a result of the Israeli Occupation," *Salon*, July 29, 2015 (https://www.salon.com/2015/07/29/palestinian_children_have_suffered_disproportionately_as_a_result_of_the_israeli_occupation/)
853. "Colonel Says Rabin Ordered Breaking of Palestinians' Bones," *Los Angeles Times*, June 22, 1990 (https://www.latimes.com/archives/la-xpm-1990-06-22-mn-431-story.html)
854. https://youtu.be/vgjlkrTkH6A
855. "Video appears to show the Israeli army shooting Palestinians without provocation, killing 1 and wounding 2 others," *PBS.org*, January 10, 2024 (https://www.pbs.org/newshour/world/video-appears-to-show-the-israeli-army-shooting-palestinians-without-provocation-killing-1-and-wounding-2-others)

## The Impact of the Situation in Palestine on Security in France

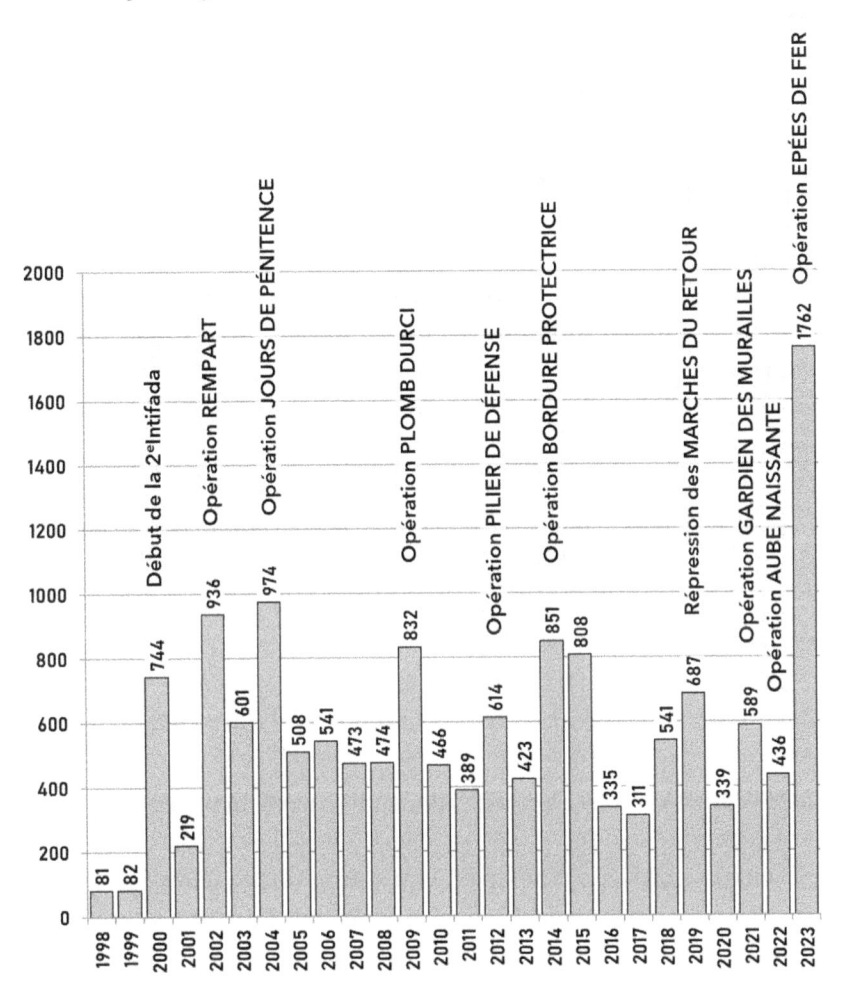

*Figure 139—The number of anti-Semitic acts against property and people in France (1998-2023) shows a strong correlation with events in the occupied Palestinian territories. The low values (the "troughs") no doubt largely reflect latent anti-Semitism, while the peaks are very clearly linked to the situation in Palestine. One possible strategy for combating anti-Semitism would be to dissociate what is religious from what is linked to Israeli politics.*
*[Figures: https://www.antisemitisme.fr/]*

An honest journalist would have called for an impartial investigation into what happened on October 7, to find out who killed the 1,200 Israelis, so as to make fair accusations and not simply to express revenge. But that is what our journalists have done: justify one crime with another. Our values are not those of vengeance, but those of the law, based on facts, findings and evidence, not perceptions. The weakness of our journalist's reasoning is that they forget that barbarism did not start on October 7, but 75 years earlier. What we are seeing is just the tip of an iceberg. We are simply in an "action-reaction" loop that no one has ever wanted to end. It is the scale of the Israeli reaction that highlights how wrong we were in thinking Israel was reasonable.

Let us not forget that Hamas is an expression of "resistance;" in other words, a response to action. Is its method the right one? That is debatable; but what is indisputable is that it is a reaction.

In his book, *Leaderless Jihad*, Dr Marc Sageman, sociologist, psychiatrist and former member of the CIA, after studying 500 cases of jihadist terrorists, finds that the three main reasons for an individual's radicalization process are:[856]

> *1—A feeling of anger stemming from his perception of the suffering endured by his co-religionists around the world;*
> *2—How the individual places this anger in the context of a more global war against Islam;*
> *3—Whether this "anger" echoes personal experience in Western society (such as discrimination or difficulties integrating).*

This process is observable for all the "radicalized" in the context of two types of crime:
- Communitarian crimes, of which the most striking examples in France are those of Mohammed Merah (2012), the murder of Samuel Paty (2019) or that of Dominique Bernard (2023).
- Crimes of a terrorist nature, such as the 2015-2016 attacks carried out by the Islamic State.

Dr. Sageman's scenario is repeated time and time again: the polarization of Western discourse on the Middle East conflict gives rise to a feeling of injustice, which translates into violent action against those perceived as "most guilty." Since 2015, in France, "Islamologists" "psychiatrists" "(Christian) experts" have been invoking all sorts of smoky theories and offering highly-paid services for solutions that deliberately ignore the heart of the problem: our murderous interventions in Muslim countries.

---

856. Marc SAGEMAN, *Leaderless Jihad: Terror Networks in the Twenty First Century*, University of Pennsylvania Press, 2008, 208 pages.

The brutal repression carried out by Israel in the occupied territories, and particularly in Gaza, goes unnoticed in Western circles, but resonates strongly in our Muslim immigrant communities. The intensity of Operation SWORDS OF IRON and the acceptance of its disproportionality by our countries has exacerbated the feeling of injustice and the profound contempt our authorities (and our mainstream media, without exception) have for Arab populations.

## Radicalization Fueled by our Policies

The problem today is that our silence, in the face of Israel's clearly inadequate strategy for resolving the Palestinian question and responding to the attack it suffered on October 7, 2023, echoes irrational domestic politics.

Whether we like it or not, the way our societies perceive the world's problems is influenced by the values and reference points brought by immigrant populations. In the past, we could go and massacre "natives" on the other side of the world without being bothered. Today, as a consequence of our multicultural society, a significant part of our society feels compassion for these "natives," and is increasingly at odds with the elites who govern us without any life experience, and who have never left the national soil. On October 17, *Le Figaro* noted that "*for part of the population, anything perceived as an insult to Islam is unacceptable.*"[857] We can deplore it, but it is a reality.

Radicalization and terrorism do not just fall from the sky. They are the consequence of foreign policies, such as the operations in Iraq, Syria and Libya,[858] which have never taken this societal change into account.

One only has to look at the comments made by our journalists, polemicists and other intellectuals on television to see their inability to understand conflicts holistically. Those who believe that history began on September 11, 2001, January 7, 2015, February 24, 2022 or October 7, 2023, and that nothing that came before played a role, deserve what has happened.

---

857. "Attentat à Bruxelles: 'Pour une partie de la population, tout ce qui est perçu comme une insulte envers l'islam est inacceptable,'" *Le Figaro*, October 17, 2023 (updated October 18, 2023) (https://www.lefigaro.fr/vox/monde/attentat-a-bruxelles-pour-une-partie-de-la-population-tout-ce-qui-est-percu-comme-une-insulte-envers-l-islam-est-inacceptable-20231017)
858. "Libye: BHL s'est engagé 'en tant que juif,'" *Le Figaro/AFP*, November 20, 2011.

We have systematically swept under the carpet clumsy decisions, often useless and illegal, but always illegitimate and murderous, that nothing obliged us to take. We have thus unleashed murderous and reprehensible anger, but in response to legitimate grievances.

The result has been to systematically find alternative explanations for this anger. Prisons, Iran, Russia, the Muslim Brotherhood or the burkini are alternately evoked as the cause of terrorism and Islamism. Our fight against terrorism has been conducted in all directions, without objectives and without results.

Israel is no exception to the rule. After September 11, 2001 and the war on terror unleashed by the Bush administration, the Israeli government sought to equate the Palestinian cause with jihadist terrorism. This had several aims:

- Moving away from the "occupier-occupied" relationship, to which international humanitarian law gives a clear status.
- Withdraw the legitimacy of UN Resolution 45/130 of 1990 from the Palestinian resistance.
- Get carte blanche to treat the Palestinian question as the West has treated al-Qaeda, i.e., with brutality.
- Exclude any negotiating mechanism with the Palestinians.

However, the root of the problem and the reason for Palestinian resistance is quite simply that Israel has never respected international law. For obscure reasons, our governments prefer to turn a blind eye to these repeated violations. In many ways, this is the wrong strategy:

- Israel's impunity for crimes that have been recognized and condemned by the international community creates a sense of injustice that is expressed with every outbreak of violence in the occupied territories.
- This undermines international law and turns Palestine into a lawless zone that legitimizes terrorism.
- It encourages the Hebrew state to commit new crimes.
- By keeping Israel's crimes quiet, we let rumors influence the crowd, which only fuels anti-Semitism around the world.

Our governments should help and support Israel to integrate into its geostrategic environment so that its security is guaranteed. But this is not what we do. On the contrary, we encourage it to distance itself from its regional and international community. The Jews created their state in 1948 because they were kept apart from our societies, but today we support a state whose security policy has not favored its regional integration, either.

To get people to think of Israel as a "normal" country, we need to encourage it to comply with international law and behave as such.

Conversely, labelling anyone who criticizes Israeli policy as anti-Semitic tends to weaken the scope of its meaning. Paradoxically, those who think they are fighting anti-Semitism by trying to give it a more exceptional dimension than other forms of racism tend to weaken it.

In addition to the enormous disproportion between Israeli and Palestinian casualties, there have been repeated violations of international law against civilian populations. Tsahal, which had built its reputation on daring successes, is now dishonored by disproportionate actions against the Palestinian population. It is no longer enough to declare the IDF the *"most moral army in the* world,"[859] one has to prove it.

## Anti-Semitism

The question of the relationship between Israel and the rest of the world, and the very narrow band separating myth from reality, oblige us to treat this chapter with caution.

It is important to understand the nature of anti-Semitism. First coined in the 19th century, the term has had trouble freeing itself from an emotional dimension. In 2018, the *Centre National de Ressources Textuelles et Lexicales* defined anti-Semitism as...

> *Hostility to the Jewish race, which sometimes became a doctrine or a movement calling for exceptional measures against Jews.*[860]

A definition that is open to question, since the very notion of "race" is disputed by scientists, as demonstrated by the controversy sparked by politician Nadine Morano, who referred to France as a "white race"

---

859. Gideon ALON, "PM: IDF Is Still Most Moral Army in World," *Haaretz*, December 9, 2004 (https://www.haaretz.com/2004-12-09/ty-article/pm-idf-is-still-most-moral-army-in-world/0000017f-e852-d62c-a1ff-fc7b1ce50000)
860. http://www.cnrtl.fr/definition/antisémitisme

country.[861] Whatever the case, Jews are probably less a "race," or even an ethnic group, than an identity forged by cultural ties and based on religion.[862]

Moreover, while the term "anti-Semitic" seems to refer to Semitic peoples in general (and therefore also to Arabs), its use in relation to the Jewish community has become established fairly quickly. We will use it accordingly. Furthermore, without entering into a discussion that would go beyond the scope of this book, we will remember that anti-Semitism is hostility towards a group, and not necessarily towards a single individual, unless he or she is "targeted" in the name of his or her community. This is why, before being defined as such, acts that appear anti-Semitic must be carefully contextualized.

Recently, not only have anti-Semitic acts multiplied, but the meaning given to the word "anti-Semitic" has broadened considerably. There is probably a correlation between these two developments, because the difficulty of combating this phenomenon stems from a confusion between three things:

- what is associated with Judaism ("Jewish"), which is essentially religious in nature;
- what belongs to the state of Israel ("Israeli") and is linked to its institutions;
- which is linked to Jewish nationalism ("Zionism"), which is a political movement.

Between these three notions, the message is totally blurred, and very few commentators seek to clarify it. In January 2016, when Manuel Valls, then Prime Minister, lamented that

> *Criticism of Israel's policies has been transformed into an "anti-Zionism" that almost systematically conceals anti-Semitism.*[863]

He was probably right about the first part of the proposition, but the second—whether intentionally or not—creates real confusion. *The Petit Robert* dictionary defines anti-Zionism as *"hostility against the State of*

---

861. "'ONPC'—Nadine Morano: la France, un pays 'de race blanche'", *Le Point.fr*, September 28, 2015 (https://www.lepoint.fr/economie/onpc-nadine-morano-la-france-un-pays-de-race-blanche-27-09-2015-1968451_28.php)
862. Europe-Israel News, "Culture: Jew was never a race, it's a people," August 22, 2013.
863. Manuel VALLS, at an evening organized by the "Friends of the CRIF," January 18, 2016.

*Israel.*" But this is also inaccurate, because while Israel's leaders have been predominantly Zionist until now, this situation is likely to change. In fact, anti-Zionism is more a hostility to the policies of the State of Israel. It is possible to be opposed to its government (and to be anti-Zionist) without being opposed to the state itself.

Zionism emerged with the emergence of nationalism in Europe in the 19th century, and has been the ideological foundation of Israeli governments since 1948. Today, the Zionist movement extends beyond the Jewish community to include Christians, such as Stephen Bannon, Donald Trump's former head of strategy, who declares himself a *"Christian Zionist."*[864] Even Joe Biden declares himself a Zionist, at the risk of highlighting a bias in his foreign policy that could hurt him in the 2024 presidential election.[865]

Christian Zionists are evangelicals who see the Jewish state as the fulfillment of a biblical prophecy. Derived from the *Apocalypse* of John, it predicts the return of the Jews to Jerusalem as a prelude to a conflict that should destroy Israel and allow the return of the Messiah.[866] It is therefore a complex ideology, more religious than political, fueled by a Christian identity rooted in Judaism and a form of "millenarian anti-Semitism." A paradoxical position, which remains debated within the American Zionist (Jewish) community, but is dealt with pragmatically: Zionists are a valuable ally of the State of Israel in the USA.[867] Indeed, it was this movement that prompted President Trump to recognize Jerusalem as Israel's capital.[868]

Anti-Zionism has essentially two dimensions:
- The first is carried exclusively by certain Orthodox Jews, who regard Zionism as an ideology contrary to the teachings of the Torah. They do not reject the existence of a Jewish state *per se*, but believe that such a state should have come into being after a period of redemption. This movement is very strong in the United

---

864. Ben SALES, "Stephen Bannon: 'I'm proud to be a Christian Zionist," *Jewish Telegraphic Agency*, November 13, 2017.
865. By Matt SPETALNICK, Jeff MASON, Steve HOLLAND & Patricia ZENGERLE, "'I am a Zionist:' How Joe Biden's lifelong bond with Israel shapes war policy," *Reuters*, October 21, 2023 (https://www.reuters.com/world/us/i-am-zionist-how-joe-bidens-lifelong-bond-with-israel-shapes-war-policy-2023-10-21/)
866. Pascal RICHÉ, "Why the American religious right supports Israel," *L'Obs*, May 14, 2018.
867. Alana GOODMAN, "Israel's Most Hated Friend," *jewishpost.com*, accessed August 2018.
868. Noah BIERMAN, "Who really wants Trump to recognize Jerusalem? His evangelical supporters at home," *Los Angeles Times*, December 6, 2017.

States, as evidenced by the large gatherings of ultra-Orthodox *Naturei Karta* activists in New York.[869] This rejection of Zionism by the Jews themselves was evident right from the start, in 1897, when 78 of the 80 German rabbis opposed the holding of the first World Zionist Congress in Munich, forcing Theodore Herzl to organize it in Basel, Switzerland.[870]

- The second is political and secular. It is not new, and has been manifest since the beginning of the 20th century, particularly in Palestine. It became much more pronounced with the Israeli repression of the first Intifada (1987-2000). It is also supported by Jews and Israelis—and is therefore not opposed to the existence of a Jewish state—but sees Zionism as a policy, which some Jews even consider anti-Semitic.[871]

On November 10, 1975, the United Nations General Assembly adopted Resolution 3379, entitled, *"Elimination of all forms of racial discrimination,"* which stated that *"Zionism is a form of racism and racial discrimination."* However, this resolution was revoked in December 1991 (Resolution 46/86) at Israel's request, in exchange for its participation in the Madrid Peace Conference,[872] which led to the Oslo process.

In recent years, in order to combat the rise in criticism of Israeli policy in the occupied territories, official discourse has tended to equate anti-Zionism with anti-Semitism and opposition to the very existence of the State of Israel. The claim that anti-Zionism is the *"denial of any state right to the Jewish people"*[873] is simply false. Even the new Hamas charter, published in May 2017, clearly distinguishes between the *"Zionist entity"* (the Israeli government and the instruments of its power) and the *"Israeli entity"* (Israel), whose borders it accepts. The problem, then, is neither the existence of Israel nor the right of the Jewish people to have a state, but the way in which it exercises that right.

---

869. See Danielle ZIRI, "Tens of Thousands of Ultra-Orthodox Jews in New York Protest IDF Draft Law," *The Jerusalem Post*, June 12, 2017.
870. See Shlomo SAND, *Comment le peuple juif fut inventé*, Paris, Éditions Fayard, September 3, 2008.
871. Matthew GINDIN, "The Latest Trend in Zionism? Anti-Semitism," *Forward.com*, February 16, 2017.
872. See Wikipedia, article "United Nations General Assembly Resolution 3379."
873. Richard Abitbol, president of the Confédération des Juifs de France et des amis d'Israël (CJ-FAI) in "Le face-à-face—Résolution Maillard, l'antisionisme est-il un antisémitisme?," *RTFrance/YouTube*, December 3, 2019, (03'20")

In 2019, speaking from the Elysée Palace after the desecration of a Jewish cemetery in Quatzenheim (Bas-Rhin), Emmanuel Macron spoke out against criminalizing anti-Zionism.[874] A few days later, however, he backtracked at the dinner of the *Conseil Représentatif des Institutions Juives de France* (CRIF), where he declared:

*Anti-Zionism is one of the modern forms of anti-Semitism.*[875]

Finally, he announced that France would associate itself with the definition of anti-Semitism recommended by the *International Holocaust Remembrance Alliance*, which refers to anti-Zionism.[876] In so doing, he is following in the footsteps of his predecessors.

By confusing criticism of Israel with anti-Semitism, we have made the state of Israel and the Jewish community vulnerable to any small incident. Our passivity in the face of Israeli policy has slowly created a convergence between anti-Semitism, anti-Judaism, anti-Zionism and the fight "against the system." In France, this trend expresses itself in a rough, even violent way, as witnessed by the inscription on some "yellow vests" the equation "*Macron = Drahi = Jew*" during the "Yellow Vest" crisis.[877] Instead of compartmentalizing the problems, we connected them and made them interdependent. It is a strategic error that could cost the Jewish community as a whole dearly.

Another problem with this amalgam is that it makes it impossible to decipher "anti-Semitic" acts, and tends to stimulate them.[878] There are no statistics to differentiate between anti-Israeli, anti-Zionist and anti-Jewish acts: everything is lumped together under the "anti-Semitic" label. It is therefore impossible to define an angle of attack against the problem. Like terrorism, anti-Semitism is seen as an inevitability, a kind of curse that cannot be prevented, only punished.

---

874. "Emmanuel Macron: 'I don't think penalizing anti-Zionism is a good solution,'" *BFMTV*, February 19, 2019.
875. Emmanuel Macron, CRIF dinner, Paris, February 20, 2019.
876. "France to implement definition of anti-Semitism incorporating anti-Zionism," *France 24*, February 21, 2019.
877. Jérôme Lefilliâtre, "Ces journaux qui en pincent pour Macron," liberation.fr, July 12, 2016; "De l'Institut Montaigne à Patrick Drahi, les puissants soutiens d'Emmanuel Macron," blogs.mediapart.fr/Revue Frustration, March 24, 2017.
878. Peter Beinart, "No, anti-Zionism isn't anti-Semitism," *Haaretz*, March 30, 2016 (https://www.haaretz.com/opinion/2016-03-30/ty-article/.premium/no-anti-zionism-isnt-anti-semitism/0000017f-e323-d804-ad7f-f3fb29bd0000).

A 2018 European poll commissioned by *CNN* showed that a third of Europeans believe that the label "anti-Semitic" is used to neutralize criticism of Israeli policy towards Palestinians.[879] The same poll established that for 28% of Europeans, anti-Semitism is linked to the actions of the State of Israel, while 54% (and 66% in Poland) believe that the existence of the State of Israel is legitimate. In other words, there is no objective link between the legitimacy of Israel and criticism of the government's policies: it is artificially created. The inability to deal effectively with anti-Semitism is therefore a deliberate choice.

The situation in Palestine has deteriorated because Western countries have deliberately refused to enforce UN resolutions. There is a glaring disproportion between the silence surrounding the Palestinian question and the omnipresence of the "Shoah" in the media. According to the *CNN* poll, 35% of Europeans surveyed believe that Israel exploits it to justify its actions, just over 31% believe that Israel uses the Holocaust to achieve its goals, and just over 30% believe that Holocaust commemorations only serve to mask "*other atrocities and injustices today.*"[880] A survey carried out in the USA by YouGov.com in December 2023 showed that 40% of young people aged between 18 and 29 believe that Israel is trying to exterminate the Palestinians, and 36% believe that Israel exploits the Holocaust to justify its crimes.[881] This led one young student to make a Freudian slip and provoke laughter by declaring before the Burlington City Council in the USA that:

> *I am appalled that the Holocaust should be mentioned. Don't use other genocides to describe this one.*[882]

The reactions of some Jews to the pro-Palestinian demonstrations in the United States show that there is a profound confusion affecting the Jewish population and causing a deep sense of insecurity. Being pro-Palestinian does not mean being "anti-Jewish" or anti-Semitic, but that is apparently how some people perceive it. Being pro-Palestinian, on the

---

879. Richard ALLEN GREENE, "CNN poll reveals depth of anti-Semitism in Europe," *CNN/ComRes*, 2018 (http://edition.cnn.com/interactive/2018/11/europe/antisemitism-poll-2018-intl/)
880. Richard ALLEN GREENE, "CNN poll reveals depth of anti-Semitism in Europe," *CNN/ComRes*, 2018 (Table 50) (http://edition.cnn.com/interactive/2018/11/europe/antisemitism-poll-2018-intl/)
881. https://today.yougov.com/politics/articles/48112-increasing-numbers-of-americans-say-antisemitism-is-a-serious-problem
882. https://uk.news.yahoo.com/not-other-genocides-describe-one-103008220.html

other hand, is more likely to be linked to anti-Zionism. Creating confusion between what one is (Jewish) and what one does (Zionist policy) tends to increase tensions between communities. Various attempts to criminalize criticism of Zionism, notably in France,[883] will only increase anti-Semitism.

As we have seen, anti-Semitism is not a driving force behind jihadist terrorism, as evidenced by the links between Israel and jihadist movements.[884] On the other hand, it is present in many acts of hatred and is a "facilitating factor" in jihadist terrorism. The fight against anti-Semitism helps to reduce the number of factors that push people towards violence, but is not enough to solve the problem. Crimes such as those committed by Mohammed Merah in March 2012 undoubtedly have more to do with our handling of the Israeli-Palestinian conflict than with global jihadism.

In France, Islamophobia and anti-Semitism are intimately linked, feed each other and will probably never be completely eradicated.[885] The only way to reduce their influence on violent extremism is to deal with them dispassionately, which is far from being the case today: current strategies to combat anti-Semitism only generate it.

For several decades now, Israeli behavior has been politically linked to Zionism. The Likud party is itself heir to the most extremist factions of Zionism. Thus, the equivalence between "Zionist" and "Jew" leads to the equation "Israel = Zionism = Jew." Extending the definition of anti-Semitism to include anti-Zionism allows Zionist governments to hide behind the Jewish community. This is why Rony Braumann, former president of the NGO Médecins sans Frontières, stated:

> *Israel today endangers the Jews... I am a Jew; I consider that Israel endangers me. Israel is not only the place where Jews are the most endangered in the world, but Israel endangers the Jews of the world.*[886]

---

883. Jannick ALIMI, "MPs condemn anti-Zionism," *Le Parisien*, December 3, 2019 (https://www.leparisien.fr/politique/les-deputes-condamnent-l-antisionisme-03-12-2019-8209341.php)
884. Elizabeth TSURKOV, "Inside Israel's Secret Program to Back Syrian Rebels," *Foreign Policy*, September 6, 2018.
885. Pamela DUNCAN, "Europeans greatly overestimate Muslim population, poll shows," *The Guardian*, December 13, 2016.
886. https://youtu.be/Mzxmt0nJKjY

Anti-Semitism is largely because of *our* incoherence, which our governments and that of Israel do accentuate. For example, they accept as logical the fact that the Gazan population, which voted in favor of Hamas in 2006, bears the same responsibility as the organization itself. Does this mean that, if the State of Israel behaves like a terrorist state, we are entitled to hold the Jews responsible too? Of course not! So why should what we accept for Israel not be valid for the Palestinians?

*Anti-Semitic Acts in France since October 7*

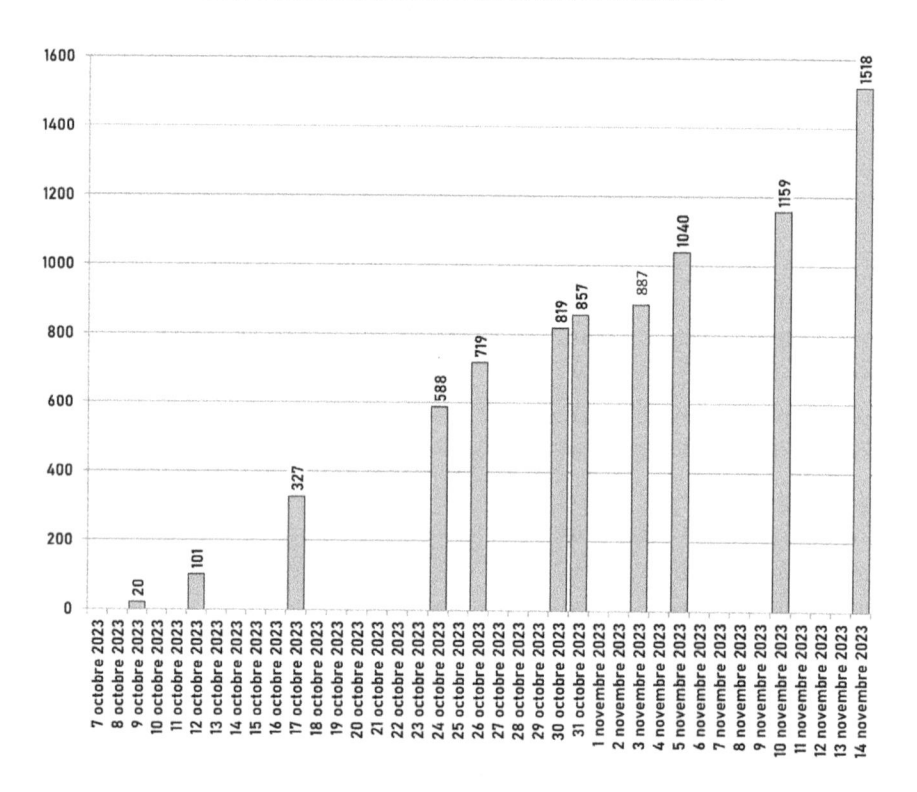

*Figure 140—Number of anti-Semitic acts in France according to the Ministry of the Interior. These are in addition to the number of anti-Semitic acts committed before October 7 (around 430). We will not go into the criteria defining these acts here. It should be noted that they did not begin on October 7, but a little later, around October 9, when there was already talk of a disproportionate response and Western countries were declaring their unconditional support for Israel.[887] [Source: Ministry of the Interior]*

---

887. "Unconditional Western support for Israel, UN calls emergency meeting," *Euronews*, October 8, 2023 (https://fr.euronews.com/2023/10/08/soutien-inconditionnel-des-occidentaux-envers-israel-lonu-convoque-une-reunion-durgence)

The source of anti-Semitism probably lies less in Israel's actions than in its impunity. Even if they do not accept it, our populations probably tolerate the way Israel reacts better than the injustice of not being punished.

Today, the fight against anti-Semitism inevitably requires a more critical stance towards Israeli policy and greater determination to impose international law in this context. The policy of *fait accompli*, camouflaged by a rewriting of history, has enabled Israel to free itself from its international obligations, creating a legitimate sense of injustice. It is this sense of injustice that fuels anti-Semitism today. More than Israel's mistakes, it is the fact that we accept them and prevent its criticism that creates indignation.

In 2008, a classified report by the British Security Service (MI5) warned that too much support for the Jewish community could lead to more anti-Semitism.[888] Against this backdrop, the French government has made just about every possible mistake, placing the Jewish community in the terrorist crosshairs.

Thus, Prime Minister Manuel Valls's overt and assertive link with the Jewish community[889] has undoubtedly had more tragic consequences than we can imagine, as the Islamic State itself explains:

> *Manuel Valls declares that the Jews of France are the vanguard of the Republic, so they must die first in the war pitting Islam and the Caliphate against France. This was clearly understood by the brothers Muhammad Merah and Amedy Coulibaly.*[890]

By ostensibly displaying a personal and privileged link with the Jewish community, Valls has undermined the impartiality of the government (secularism), which fuels communitarianism in France. What is more, he has reinforced existing anti-Semitism by superimposing his government's unpopularity, suggesting collusion between the Jewish community and France's involvement in the Middle East. He thus made the Jewish community appear to be a central player in the war against Muslims, making it "more guilty" than the others: by unnecessarily

---

888. *Behavioural Science Unit Operational Briefing Note: Understanding radicalisation and violent extremism in the UK*, Security Service—MI5 (UK RESTRICTED), Report BSU 02/2008, June 12 2008.
889. See https://www.youtube.com/watch?v=Y9Bs3tF1jj0.(video removed from *YouTube*)
890. "The history of France's enmity towards islâm," *Dar al-Islam*, no. 2, February 2015, p. 10 (NDA: the author of the article refers to Manuel Valls' speech of March 19, 2014, in Paris).

overexposing it, he placed it in the crosshairs of terrorists. The best is the enemy of the good.

But apparently, French ministers find it hard to learn from the past. Such was the case with Interior Minister Gérard Darmanin's association of soccer player Karim Benzema with the Muslim Brotherhood,[891] following a tweet expressing his sympathy for the victims in Gaza.

### Karim Benzema's Tweet

**Karim Benzema** ✓
@Benzema

Suivre

Toutes nos prières pour les habitants de Gaza victimes une fois de plus de ces bombardements injustes qui n'épargnent ni femmes ni enfants.

5:55 PM · 15 oct. 2023 · **43,1 M** vues

*Figure 141—"Our prayers go out to the people of Gaza, victims once again of unjust bombardments that spare neither women nor children." This is a far cry from incitement to hatred. Assuming that Hamas is indeed the perpetrator of the crimes of which it is accused, this in no way justifies retaliating against the Gazan civilian population. The reaction of the French authorities shows that one crime can justify another. In other words, the French government is using the same logic as certain terrorist movements. The most sensible reaction from the government would have been to say nothing.*

Anti-Semitism is a complex phenomenon that cannot be reduced to the extreme right. In France, this easy link has been widely used to try and contain the rise of the Front/Rassemblement National. But by focusing our attention on *"nazillons"* (as Bernard-Henri Lévy calls them),[892] we miss the real issue. In 2014, a study carried out in Germany on almost 14,000 letters with anti-Semitic content received by the Israeli Embassy and the *Central Council of Jews in Germany*[893] showed that only 3% came from the far right.[894] In fact, most came from liberal

---

891. "Gérald Darmanin links Karim Benzema to the Muslim Brotherhood, the Ballon d'Or winner plans to lodge a complaint," *Le Monde / AFP*, October 19, 2023 (https://www.lemonde.fr/politique/article/2023/10/19/gerald-darmanin-lie-karim-benzema-aux-freres-musulmans-le-ballon-d-or-envisage-de-porter-plainte_6195369_823448.html)
892. Tweet from Bernard-Henri Lévy, February 16, 2019.
893. Zentralrat der Juden in Deutschland (ZDJ)
894. Ofer ADERET, "Study: In Germany, anti-Semitic Hate Mail Doesn't Come From Far-right," *Haaretz*, February 25, 2014.

or moderate left-wing circles.[895] "Traditional" prejudices are therefore completely outdated.

This hypersensitivity tends to disrupt the common sense of our politicians. Thus, the video of a Gilet jaune doing the Roman salute while shouting "Ave Macron" was relayed by Naima Moutchou (who is rapporteur for the anti-fake news law!) suggesting that it was a Nazi salute. Her tweet was deleted shortly afterwards, but a debate ensued on the nature of the "salute." In fact, the question is specious, as it was not about glorifying Nazis, but making fun of "Jupiter!"[896] The "Gilet jaune" in question was therefore not a Nazi. This incident shows the incompetence and stupidity of the politician. For decades, it is this lack of judgment and simplistic assertions that have created the ultra-right and stimulated anti-Semitism.

On February 17, 2019, interviewed on the Israeli channel *i24News* the day after he was verbally assaulted by "Gilets jaunes," the philosopher Alain Finkielkraut quite rightly remarked that the situation is very different from that of the 1930s, as he was not assaulted because of his Jewish origin, but

> *because of my alleged links with a state described by some as criminal and even genocidal.*[897]

Indeed, among the insults directed at him, one distinctly heard: "*racist*" and "*anti-Semite!*,"[898] which seems paradoxical, but reflects an increasingly widespread perception. The media's silence on these details tends to be counter-productive. Linking contemporary anti-Semitism (or anti-Zionism) mechanically to Nazism, as Bernard-Henri Lévy does,[899] is simplistic and sterile. Today, anti-Semitism results more from what Israel does than from what it is. From a positive point of view, this means that

---

895. Patrick Grosse, "Anti-Semitic online harassment in Germany on the rise, study finds," *Deutsche Welle*, July 18, 2018.
896. Emma Donada, "Did a yellow vest make a Nazi salute on the CHAMPS-ÉLYSÉES?," www.liberation.fr, November 26, 2018.
897. i24NEWS, "Alain Finkielkraut looks back on the verbal assault he was the victim of," *YouTube*, February 17, 2019.
898. "Agression Finkielkraut: De la confusion naquit la haine—L'info du vrai du 18/02—CANAL+," *YouTube*, February 18, 2019.
899. Europe 1, "BHL reacts to Alain Finkielkraut's anti-Semitic attack: 'No one has a monopoly on the people," *YouTube*, February 17, 2019.

anti-Semitism is not inevitable, but that there are rational elements that can be acted upon to combat it.

There is a thin layer of anti-Semitism in society, fuelled by religious conservatism and "traditional" prejudice: it is the most persistent, but the least virulent. The spectacular increase in anti-Semitic acts—observed since the early 2000s[900]—is the product of other societal factors, including, but not limited to, immigration. Clearly, Islamization is playing a growing role in the way our societies view the Palestinian crisis. While Westerners tend to lose interest in this conflict, the immigrant population feels more concerned. This would be all the more reason to help Israel resolve the issue fairly and in accordance with international law, but that is not what we are doing. We turn a blind eye to Israel's violations of international law.

The problem is that we think that by covering up Israel's mistakes we will prevent criticism of Israel and thus anti-Semitism. But this is a rather simple analysis. In reality, as the Gaza crisis shows, more than Israel's mistakes or crimes, it is the impunity that surrounds it that generates anti-Semitism. The problem is therefore less the fault itself than the absence of justice.

Anti-Semitism is neither certain nor inevitable; but by fighting it in stupid ways, we amplify it. Like terrorism, anti-Semitism is a plural phenomenon, largely fueled by perceptions, but also by facts. We fight them in the same way: by focusing on their symptoms, not their causes; by seeing them as we would like them to be, not as they are. We fail to eradicate it because we are afraid to do so.

When researchers' work collides with official discourse, they are immediately ostracized. This is where the notions of anti-Semitism and anti-Zionism collide: the most assiduous critics of Israeli policy are Jewish intellectuals, often descendants of Holocaust survivors. Such is the case of intellectuals like Noam Chomsky and Norman Finkelstein, both American Jews, who were even banned from entering Israel.[901]

In France, the fight against anti-Semitism remains highly emotional, dogmatic, detached from the facts and often a street fight. With their lack of sensitivity and intellectual rigor, its "tenors," such as BHL and Meyer Habib, do it a disservice; while some, such as Éric Zemmour and Alain Finkielkraut, have traded credibility for media coverage. In the United States, on the other hand, it is more subtle, more intelligent,

---

900. See Dominique SCHNAPPER (C pol, "C Politique—Dominique Schnapper—17/02/19", YouTube, 18 février 2019 (40'00"))
901. Ali WAKED, "Noam Chomsky denied entry to Israel," YNet.com, May 17 2010.

more strategic and more factual. Its proponents are Jewish intellectuals, often also descendants of Holocaust victims, such as Noam Chomsky, Norman Finkelstein, Seymour Hersh, Max Blumenthal, Aaron Maté and Ben Norton, to name but a few.

Democracy is only as strong as the debates it is capable of conducting. Prohibiting divergent ideas only weakens it and strengthens those who think the democratic system is "rotten." What is more, as in a "pressure cooker," these dark forces are allowed to build up, without a "safety valve," risking their release with fatal and destructive violence, as was the case in the 1930s. There will be no significant progress until criticism (but not insult) of Israeli policy is unrestricted. When the international community has the courage to treat Israel as a normal country and make it respect the United Nations resolutions it has voted for, then anti-Semitism will weaken.

## Mohammed Merah's Attacks in 2012

According to Europol,[902] between 1997 and March 2012, numerous individuals suspected of belonging to (foreign) terrorist networks were arrested, but no jihadist terrorist attacks were prepared, prevented or carried out in France. So, did the jihadists take a break from their "fight against democracy" and their conquest of the West? In fact, at this stage, France was not in the jihadists' sights.

In March 2012, the crimes of Mohammed Merah ushered in a period in which two distinct phenomena were manifesting themselves in parallel in France: communitarian violence and terrorist attacks. These two phenomena have different origins and aims, but draw their perpetrators from the same social pool.

According to Merah himself, these attacks had two targets: France and Israel. The assassination of three French soldiers (March 11 and 15, 2012) was clearly motivated by the war the French army was waging in Afghanistan. Merah filmed these attacks and launched:[903]

*You kill my brothers, I kill you!*

---

902. See TESAT reports 2007-2017, Europol (www.europol.europa.eu/newsroom)
903. Maxime DE VALENSART, "Merah filmed the murders: 'You kill my brothers, I kill you," *7sur7.be*, March 22, 2012.

The reasons behind the attack on the Ozar Hatorah Jewish school in Toulouse (March 19, 2012) were never really detailed in the media and were immediately placed under the label of anti-Semitism. In fact, we have simply adopted a rhetoric that satisfies Jewish (or, more accurately, Zionist) organizations. But there is a danger in this: it obscures the real reasons and prevents adequate preventive solutions from being found.

Merah was undoubtedly an anti-Semite, but it was probably not anti-Semitism that was at the heart of his approach. His reasons for committing the crime were more specific. In fact, they were to be found in Gaza at the beginning of the month, as he himself explained by telephone to Ebba Kalondo, editor-in-chief at *France 24*:

> *The Jews killed our brothers and sisters in Palestine!*[904]

It refers to the Israeli strike on March 9, 2012 (Operation ECHO BACK) carried out against Zohair al-Qaisi, Secretary General of the *Popular Resistance Committees (PRC)*, killing some fifteen innocent civilians.[905] This triggered Palestinian rocket fire, which was met by further air strikes. In all, 23 Palestinians were killed and 74 wounded, while 23 Israelis were injured.[906]

The event seemed fairly "banal" and—as usual—the French media remained discreet about it. The question is, why did they trigger Merah's desire for revenge? The answer probably lies in the French government's reaction, which did not go unnoticed. The Foreign Affairs communiqué of March 10, 2012 neither mentions nor condemns the initial Israeli strike, but only the Palestinian rocket fire that followed:[907]

> *We condemn the rocket fire and the humanitarian consequences of this violence, and deplore the civilian casualties. France urges a return to calm and restraint in order to avoid an escalation that could again affect civilians. Our Consul General in Tel Aviv will be*

---

904. "The killer contacted France 24: 'This is just the beginning,' he claimed," *France 24*, March 21, 2012.
905. *The Guardian* and *The Washington Post*, March 10, 2012.
906. See Article "March 2012 Gaza-Israel clashes," *Wikipedia*
907. "Press release—Israel and occupied Palestinian territories. All parties must protect civilians in Gaza and Israel following ceasefire announcement," *Amnesty International*, March 13, 2012.

*visiting Ashdod and Ashkelon on Sunday morning to express his solidarity.*[908]

Given the sensitivities of part of the French population, we could have imagined a more measured and balanced reaction, or even none at all.

Two years later, on July 9, 2014, during Operation PROTECTIVE EDGE, François Hollande repeated the same error with a message to Benjamin Netanyahu stressing that *"it is up to the Israeli government to take all measures to protect its population in the face of threats,"*[909] thus demonstrating his support for the application of the *Dahiya doctrine*. Despite a timid correction from the Élysée Palace a few days later, this initial "cry from the heart" was hardly appeasing, and will remain in the memory of a large part of the French population.[910]

To what extent this partisan stance helped trigger Merah's criminal madness by provoking his outrage will remain a mystery, and emotion will label his crimes as "terrorist." Yet, technically, they are not associated with a process of recurrent violence aimed at exerting pressure to achieve something, nor are they part of a political process with concrete, expressed objectives. In fact, they are essentially vengeful and communitarian in nature.

Seen through the eyes of the intelligence community, Merah's crimes herald a number of problems that remain unresolved in France ten years on. Firstly, this case shows that there has been little reflection at the head of the French state on the integration of Muslim sensitivities into its foreign policy decisions. Merah was just the tip of the iceberg of a population that feels—rightly or wrongly—an enemy in its own country, and that provided the perpetrators of the 2015-2019 attacks.

---

908. Alain GRESH, "Gaza, Palestine et apartheid," *Le Monde diplomatique*, March 11, 2012 (http://blog.mondediplo.net/2012-03-11-Gaza-Palestine-et-apartheid) (Original link to Foreign Affairs press release: http://www.diplomatie.gouv.fr/fr/pays-zones-geo/israel-territoires-palestiniens/la-france-et-les-territoires/situation-dans-la-bande-de-gaza/article/nouvel-episode-de-violence-a-gaza

909. *Libération*, July 22, 2014.

910. Grégoire BISEAU and Jonathan BOUCHET-PETERSEN, "Soutien à Israël: Hollande ou le péché originel," *Libération*, July 22, 2014; "Le soutien de Hollande à Israël agace une partie de la gauche," *Le JDD*, July 11, 2014.

As *Le Figaro* put it, the Palestinian cause functions as a "mirror cause" with the immigrant population.[911] We can deplore this, but it is a reality that is further exacerbated by the policies of ministers like Manuel Valls or Gérald Darmanin, who have understood absolutely nothing.

An objective, dispassionate understanding of the reasons why Merah and others committed their crimes does not excuse them, but it could have helped to better prepare the strategic context for intervention in Iraq, and then Syria, in order to guard against the attacks of 2015-2016, and the communitarian crimes of 2019-2020. By adapting its language concerning Israel, the French government could have mitigated the exacerbation of the feeling of solidarity of certain radical French Muslim elements.

---

911. Ronan PLANCHON. "La question palestinienne functions among young French Muslims as a mirror cause," *Le Figaro*, December 19, 2023 (https://www.lefigaro.fr/vox/societe/la-question-palestinienne-fonctionne-chez-les-jeunes-musulmans-francais-comme-une-cause-miroir-20231219)

# 9. Conclusions

Masked by the conflict in Ukraine and buried with the Abraham Accords, the Palestinian question has returned to the center of the international agenda. This was one of the objectives of Hamas and the organizations participating in the Joint Operations Room (JOR), and it will remain the main consequence of this phase of the conflict. The latter began on October 7, 2023, but it is only the consequence of short-term strategies and practices that have only been possible because the international community, lined up behind the United States, has accepted that international law has been flouted since 1947.

Israelis and Westerners alike confuse tactics with strategy. During the 1960s and 1980s, terrorism in the West came from within: movements seeking to transform Western societies and overturn the principles that governed them. In Palestine, until the first Intifada, Palestinian resistance was part of a general liberation movement against Western imperialism, whose strategy had been outlined at the 1966 Tri-Continental Conference in Havana.

The collapse of the Communist world in the late 1980s changed everything. European terrorism shrank considerably and gradually became marginal.

Without the counterweight of the Communist bloc, the West adopted more aggressive foreign policies and embarked on military operations with disastrous consequences. Since the 1990s, *all* the Islamist terrorist acts that have affected us are responses to these actions in the Near and Middle East. Instead of prompting us to rethink our approaches, these terrorist acts have pushed us to outdo each other. September 11, 2001 has become the pretext for the most imbecilic strategies that civilized countries can take—without hindsight, without reflection, without concrete objectives and without humanity.

In Palestine, orphaned by the Warsaw Treaty, resistance movements have drawn on an Islamic culture to underpin their doctrine of struggle. This change has fueled an Israeli rhetoric that assimilates the Palestinian approach to that of movements like "Al-Qaeda," not to better understand the logic of terrorism and combat it strategically, but to justify a more brutal response, in the image of what the West has done, and combat it tactically.

Palestinian resistance has nothing to do with hatred of Jews, but with hatred of the occupier and the refusal of the law of the strongest. The order created in 1945—largely because of what had happened to the Jewish population—was intended precisely to prevent abuses that could affect populations in a weak position. It is the failure to respect the rules of international law that fuels the spirit of the Palestinian resistance and led to the launch of Operation AL-AQSA FLOOD.

## The October 7th Response

Israel's response to Operation AL-AQSA FLOOD is the culmination of an approach to combating Palestinian resistance that has fueled the cycle of violence for 75 years. Masked by the Western media, Israel's repeated violations of international law have created an environment where such law no longer exists. Why should a non-state entity respect a right that the occupying power itself does not respect? How does one assert legitimate claims in the face of an occupying power that refuses to engage in dialogue?

Israel has created a situation in which the use of force is the only way to impose dialogue. A good counter-insurgency strategy must inevitably offer a way out. The problem is that the exit offered by Israel's strategy is simply to leave the territories it occupies. We just go around in circles.

The strength of the Palestinian leadership lies in their strategic approach to the struggle. As I noted back in 2003,[912] the Palestinians function like chess players and the Israelis like gunslingers. The response to the Palestinian operation is a perfect illustration of this observation.

Only an international, impartial and independent inquiry can determine whether the Palestinians have committed the crimes attributed to them.

---

912. Jacques BAUD, *La Guerre asymétrique ou la Défaite du vainqueur*, Éditions du Rocher, 2003.

Failing that, these accusations are merely a pretext for a disproportionate response. The testimonies filtering through the Israeli media tend to show that this is indeed the case. The Israelis are in much the same situation as the Americans in the aftermath of 9/11: having built up a reputation for invincibility and power, they are now being mocked for the disproportionate nature of their response and the meagre results it has produced.

By hiding the facts behind accusations of anti-Semitism or conspiracy, we do Israel a disservice. Quite the contrary, in fact.

South Africa's complaint to the ICJ will take months at best, and probably years, to reach a verdict. But it does have the merit of forcing us to acknowledge the plausibility of genocide, and to point the finger at those who think that the Hamas attack justifies all responses, as we have heard on media such as *LCI* or *BFMTV*. Incitement to genocide is also punishable.

## The Absence of European Diplomacy

For fear of being accused of anti-Semitism, Western countries have preferred to let Israel move in the wrong direction rather than criticize its approach to the conflict. In the end, it was South Africa that had the courage to say "Stop!," and the ICJ that established the "plausibility of genocide." When you knowingly let your friend go in the wrong direction, you are not really his friend. In reality, very few countries think that Israel is in the right, but they do not dare face American sanctions. Israel should ponder this, because the ICJ ruling could well mean that they have been complicit in genocide.

As always, we always think that a crisis begins when its effects are felt. But it begins long before that, and we know it. Why did we not encourage and help Israel to fulfill its obligations? Why do we wait until it is in a critical situation to rant against its adversaries without offering a solution?

Israel cannot base its security policy on coerced support. This is why South Africa's move is so important, and marks an essential change for Israel's future. Until now, the United States could support Israel despite its deviations from international law because it knew that the international community would not react. Today, the situation has changed: the "rest of the world" has the courage to raise its voice.

In NATO member Turkey, Erdogan held Benjamin Netanyahu responsible for the situation in Gaza and recalled his ambassador to Tel Aviv.[913] Other Latin American countries such as Bolivia, Chile and Colombia did the same.[914] In Europe, the situation is very different. Ursula von der Leyen has declared Europe's unconditional support for Israel, while the question of a possible genocide is already up in the air, a notion that has no real hold on her, probably for family reasons.[915] But this is not the opinion of Josep Borrell, the EU's Foreign Affairs "minister," who declares that Israel's action is illegal[916] and that the Union is divided on the question of Gaza.[917] Perhaps this explains why, despite Josep Borrell's declarations in favor of Palestinian rights, European diplomacy is nowhere to be seen.

Like its American allies, the EU does not defend an international order based on law, but one based on rules. It is the reign of arbitrariness and discretionary decisions.

As with the Ukrainian crisis, the Gaza crisis reveals that the West has lost the upper hand. The Americans were the keystone of the balance of power in the Middle East, and the promoters of several peace initiatives in the 1970s-1990s; today, they are despised and have lost all credibility, even with Israel, which refuses to be guided by Joe Biden, nicknamed "Genocide Joe" in the United States.[918] U.S. ambassadors to the Middle East have joined forces to warn the Biden administration that a "fury" against the U.S. is rising in the Arab world.[919]

---

913. Dmitry ZAKS, "Turkey recalls envoy to Israel, 'writes off' Netanyahu," *Yahoo News*, November 4, 2023 (https://news.yahoo.com/turkey-recalls-envoy-israel-blasts-132041480.html)
914. https://apnews.com/article/israel-bolivia-colombia-chile-argentina-brazil-4cc038c-0dbe1de9b5e4118e2ceac2181
915. https://www.euractiv.com/section/global-europe/news/eu-staff-criticise-von-der-leyen-over-israel-stance/
916. Andrew GRAY, "EU's Borrell: Israeli moves in Gaza break international law," *Reuters*, October 10, 2023 (https://www.reuters.com/world/spain-opposes-suspending-aid-palestinian-territories-2023-10-10/)
917. Burak BIR, "Top EU diplomat says bloc divided over Gaza," *Anadolu Agency*, February 2, 2024 (https://www.aa.com.tr/en/europe/top-eu-diplomat-says-bloc-divided-over-gaza/3126374)
918. https://www.c-span.org/video/?c5103727/genocide-joe-yelled-president-biden-campaign-event-virginia
919. Priscilla ALVAREZ & Alex MARQUARDT, "Biden administration privately warned by American diplomats of growing fury against US in Arab world," *CNN*, November 10, 2023 (https://www.cnn.com/2023/11/09/politics/biden-diplomats-warn-middle-east-fury/index.html)

## An Arab World that has Forgotten its Brothers

The most conspicuous absentee from this crisis is the Arab world. Operation AL-AQSA FLOOD was named to remind them that Jerusalem's holy sites are in danger under the ultra-religious government currently in place in Jerusalem. Completely ignored in the Abraham Accords, the Palestinians wanted to remind their Gulf brothers that they share common goals. But so far, only the Houthis in Yemen, the Lebanese and the Iraqi government have reacted.

On November 11, 2023, the countries of the *Arab League* (AL) and the *Organization of Islamic Cooperation* (OIC) met to discuss options for resolving the Gaza crisis. Unlike the Western countries, which launched into massive and ineffective action from the outset of the Ukrainian crisis, the Arab countries opted for a more gradual approach. They rejected the option of an embargo on petroleum products, which would have given the impression that they were siding with Hamas, thus undermining the credibility of their action. They also rejected the idea of closing airspace to American military aircraft, which would have been premature at this stage of the crisis.

Cautiously, the Arab countries opted for institutional work at the level of the UN Security Council and General Assembly, whose inaction they deplored. In fact, the Arab countries' strategy is to take back the American mediation initiative in the conflict, in order to give it to the United Nations. But they have also decided to take the matter to the International Criminal Court (ICC) to condemn the Israeli leaders.[920] Their approach is more oriented towards resolving the Palestinian question than the humanitarian crisis.

## Why are We Always Wrong?

It seems that the West goes from failure to failure. Iraq, Afghanistan, Syria, Ukraine and Palestine are all examples of where it has committed itself by convincing itself that it has understood the situation. We do not

---

920. Peter BEAUMONT, "Why Israel fears the ICC war crimes investigation," *The Guardian*, March 3, 2021 (https://www.theguardian.com/law/2021/mar/03/israeli-officials-start-to-feel-the-impact-of-icc-investigation)

analyze conflicts; we try to make them fit our prejudices. This is what our media and their henchmen, such as *Conspiracy Watch*, do: instead of leading us down the right path, they reinforce our error, until the narrative collides with the reality of the facts.

This can be seen in our support for the Ukrainian conflict, which was a vehicle for Western values, but which was quickly abandoned[921] in favor of Israel, which is now accused of genocide. American munitions destined for the Ukraine are redirected to Israel. Volodymyr Zelensky rightly deplored this, and sought an invitation to Jerusalem to try to unite his cause with that of Israel. But Netanyahu refused; he thought he had his moment of glory, and he did not want to share it.

However, it shows that Zelensky was right: Ukraine is in a situation comparable to that of Israel, while the Palestinians are in the same situation as Russia. In both cases, the attacks of February 24, 2022 and those of October 9, 2023 could have been avoided if the attacked countries had respected their obligations under international law: the Minsk agreements for Ukraine and 75 years of UN resolutions for Israel. In both cases, the day of the attack was not a point of departure, but a point of arrival. In both cases, it was the flouting of a people's right to self-determination that was at the root of the attacks. In both cases, Westerners could have prevented them. In both cases, they did not. In both cases, they sought to protect their narrative of the problem at the expense of those they wanted to help.

Our perception of the conflict is built on the belief that Hamas committed the worst atrocities on October 7. We know that the Israeli narrative supports a strategy that clearly targets the civilian population. But, as the weeks went by and we heard from witnesses, we also know that most of the deaths on October 7 were not the result of the "pogroms" proclaimed by our propagandists, but of exchanges of fire between combatants; that the firepower of Israeli weapons, combined with poor leadership, was the cause of most of the destruction observed.

The Gaza war did not start on October 7, but in 1947. The lesson that Germany and other countries learned from the Second World War was to support the Jewish people, even when they violated international law. Gnawed by the guilt of having participated in the Holocaust, Western countries—led by France and Germany—refused to help Israel stay on

---

921. "Gaza conflict 'taking away focus' from Ukraine, Zelensky says," *France 24*, November 4, 2023 (https://www.france24.com/en/europe/20231104-gaza-conflict-taking-away-focus-from-ukraine-zelensky-says)

the path of the rule of law, preferring to turn a blind eye to its repeated violations of international law. However, its members, such as Germany—for whom the notion of genocide no longer holds any secrets—not only support Israel, but also frantically arm it.[922]

We have learned nothing and understood nothing.

The question is not whether one is for or against Israel or the Jews, but whether one is for or against international law. The lesson the world had to learn from the Second World War was twofold: respect for law and humanity, and the will to say "Stop!" Post-war international law was built around these two "ideas."

But we have learned nothing. Under the pretext of not contradicting Israel, we let it infringe international law and violate the obligations it is reminded of year after year by the United Nations. These obligations are far from extravagant, and are simply the application of the UN Charter. But for the West, *international order based on rules* has replaced *international order based on law*.

The part of the world that understood the lessons of the Second World War is what is now scornfully referred to as the "rest of the world." South Africa did what any state convinced it was a state governed by the rule of law should have done: it said, "Stop!"

In the Red Sea, the Houthis declared a blockade against Israel until it agrees to a ceasefire in Gaza, and are attacking ships bound for its ports with missiles. This blockade does not affect other ships, and even the ships of their Saudi enemy can pass through.[923] They have done exactly what the West does with other countries, but with their own means. American and British retaliation to force through the Houthi blockade has had no deterrent effect: President Biden admits that their strikes against Yemen are ineffective, but he will continue to order them.[924]

---

922. "German military exports to Israel up nearly 10-fold as Berlin fast-tracks permits," *Reuters*, November 8, 2023 (https://www.reuters.com/world/europe/german-military-exports-israel-up-nearly-10-fold-berlin-fast-tracks-permits-2023-11-08/)

923. https://www.reuters.com/world/middle-east/yemens-houthis-say-they-do-not-seek-expand-red-sea-attacks-2024-01-19/

924. Oren Liebermann & Nikki Carvajal, "Biden concedes Houthis haven't been deterred from carrying out attacks as US launches further strikes," *CNN*, January 18, 2024 (https://edition.cnn.com/2024/01/18/politics/biden-houthi-strikes/index.html)

In other words, the United States is no longer scary. Iraq has once again asked them to leave the country. This time, the US has agreed to negotiate a withdrawal plan.[925]

One can certainly question the way in which the Houthis are seeking to impose a ceasefire, but in fact, unlike Westerners like Germany, France and the United States who treat the massacre of Palestinians as a "detail of history," the Houthis are taking action.

The African continent is giving us a masterly lesson in courage, and showing the planet just how cowardly and corrupt our Western world really is. Our so-called "elites" are worthless. October 7th is only the temporary culmination of a situation that we—and Israel in particular—have allowed to fester. In France, the communitarian rhetoric that drives our media is part of this blindness, which was already apparent during the Ukrainian conflict.

When it comes to the situation in Gaza, Israel hides behind the terrorist designation of Hamas to justify its violations of international law, including against civilians. Yet Israel's leaders support Hamas underhandedly, in order to justify their strategy against the Palestinians.

While in the West the blame is systematically and unmistakably placed on the Palestinians, the British *Telegraph* reports that almost 80% of Israelis blame Netanyahu for the crisis.[926]

Thus, we are not supporting the Israeli people, but a radical minority who see the Palestinian question in terms of a balance of power. Yet what Hamas and other Palestinian organizations have brutally exposed is the profound injustice and inhumanity affecting the Palestinian population. In 2017, a report published by the *Brand Israel Group*, an organization specializing in monitoring Israel's image around the world, already showed Jewish students' disaffection with Israel and growing sympathy for the Palestinian cause. The report found that between 2010 and 2016, young American Jews' support for Israel had fallen by 27%.[927] Young American Jews feel a growing divergence between the values of the two

---

925. Tara Copp & Qassim Abdul-Zahra, "Iraq, US agree to start talks on phased withdrawal of US-led military coalition," *The Times of Israel*, January 25, 2024 (https://www.timesofisrael.com/iraq-us-agree-to-start-talks-on-phased-withdrawal-of-us-led-military-coalition/)
926. Verity Bowman, "Netanyahu is to blame for Hamas war, say four out of five Israelis," *The Telegraph*, October 20, 2023 (https://www.telegraph.co.uk/world-news/2023/10/20/netanyahu-to-blame-war-gaza-say-israelis/)
927. Jonathan Cook, "Can young Jews in US turn tide against Israel?," *The National*, June 26, 2017.

countries.[928] It is a real trend reversal.[929] Today, the Democratic electorate, which includes a majority of Jews from major metropolises such as New York, and which is traditionally very supportive of Israel, is withdrawing its support for the Hebrew state.[930]

The trend was confirmed by the tragic repression of the Marches of Return in Gaza in 2018. Israel had then shown its true face and lost the support of American Jewish youth,[931] and older people, too.[932]

The American political world—with its aversion to Trump—has become much more critical of Israeli policy. For example, Democratic Senator Dianne Feinstein has condemned the Israeli government's brutal land appropriation policy.[933] In the United States, more and more citizens are questioning the legality of aid granted to Israel, and calling for the application of the *International Security Assistance and Arms Export Control Act* passed by Congress in 1976. This prohibits the United States from granting financial aid to countries with nuclear arsenals that are not signatories to the *Non-Proliferation Treaty* (NPT).[934]

Israel continues to see its victory in the total destruction of its adversary, the Palestinians. It may succeed. But victory without peril is triumph without glory. What Israel gains militarily, it loses politically. And this at a time when the influence of its allies is waning in the world and the Arab world is growing stronger. Israel's strategy is therefore a failure.

Much of this failure is because of its inability to accept criticism of its policies. In France, criticism of Israel inevitably leads to anti-Semitism. In reality, anti-Semitism stems more from Israel's impunity than from any

---

928. Amanda BORSCHEL-DAN, "'Devastating' survey shows huge loss of Israel support among Jewish college students," *The Time of Israel*, June 21, 2017.
929. Yasmeen SERHAN, "The American Public's Views on Israel Are Undergoing a Profound Shift. Washington Hasn't Caught Up," *TIME Magazine*, July 19, 2023 (https://time.com/6295703/israel-herzog-visit-washington/)
930. Ron KAMPEAS, "Polls show lower support for Israel among young Americans amid war against Hamas," *The Times of Israel*, November 3, 2023 (https://www.timesofisrael.com/polls-show-lower-support-for-israel-among-young-americans-amid-war-against-hamas/)
931. "As Israel turns 70, many young American Jews turn away," *The Conversation*, May 3, 2018 (https://theconversation.com/as-israel-turns-70-many-young-american-jews-turn-away-95271)
932. Dina KRAFT, "Not Just Millennials: These Older U.S. Jews Are Disillusioned by Israel Too," *Haaretz*, September 20, 2018 (https://www.haaretz.com/us-news/2018-09-20/ty-article/.premium/not-just-millennials-these-older-u-s-jews-are-disillusioned-by-israel-too/0000017f-f909-d47e-a37f-f93db1d90000)
933. Amir TIBON, "Democratic Jewish Senator Feinstein Blasts Israel Over 'Brutal' Land-grab Law," *Haaretz*, February 8, 2017.
934. JTA, "Lawsuit claims US aid to Israel violates nuclear pact," *The Times of Israel*, August 12, 2016.

mention of its crimes. People think that by sweeping these crimes under the carpet, they wil not exist, and that Israel is right. We think we absolve Israel of its crimes by condemning its enemies. The ICJ reminds us that we are mistaken, and that our narrative is being overtaken by reality. As in Ukraine, we have made the illusion of victory seem real.

In the past, the term anti-Semitism meant a sickly hatred of the Jew. Today, it means protesting against the bombing of women and children.

Israel's security will be guaranteed as long as it applies the rules accepted by all. Israel has always sought to impose itself by force, and this strategy is not a winning one. Today, the Palestinian David is defeating the Israeli Goliath.

But the West pretends not to notice. As with all the conflicts of the last thirty years, we believe that reality can be contained by narrative. This may satisfy some in the West, but not the "rest of the world," which is giving us a lesson in humanity.

Israel alone does not merit criticism.

# Appendix 1—The Hamas Charter

## A document of general principles and policies

Praise be to Allah, the Lord of the worlds. May Allah's peace and blessings be upon Muhammad, the master of messengers and leader of the Mujahideen, and upon his family and all his companions.

**Preamble:**
Palestine is the land of the Palestinian Arab people, from which it originates, to which it adheres and belongs, and about which it extends and communicates.

Palestine is a land whose status has been elevated by Islam, a faith that holds it in high esteem, imbues it with its spirit and just values, and lays the foundations for the doctrine of its defense and protection.

Palestine is the cause of a people who have been let down by a world that fails to guarantee their rights and restore what was usurped from them, a people whose land continues to suffer one of the world's worst types of occupation.

Palestine is a land that has been seized by a racist, inhuman and colonial Zionist project, based on a false promise (the Balfour Declaration), the recognition of a usurping entity and the imposition of a fait accompli by force.

Palestine symbolizes the resistance that will continue until liberation is achieved, until return is realized and until a fully sovereign state is established with Jerusalem as its capital.

Palestine is the true partnership between Palestinians of all affiliations for the sublime goal of liberation.

Palestine is the spirit of the Ummah and its center of attention.

**Movement:**

1. The Islamic Resistance Movement "Hamas" is a Palestinian Islamic liberation and national resistance movement. Its aim is to liberate Palestine and confront the Zionist project. Its frame of reference is Islam, which determines its principles, objectives and means.

**The Land of Palestine:**

2. Palestine, stretching from the Jordan River in the east to the Mediterranean in the west, and from Ras Al-Naqurah in the north to Umm Al-Rashrash in the south, constitutes an integral territorial unit. It is the land and home of the Palestinian people. The expulsion and banishment of the Palestinian people from their land, and the establishment of the Zionist entity on it, do not nullify the right of the Palestinian people to the whole of their land, nor do they confer any right on the usurping Zionist entity.

3. Palestine is an Arab-Islamic land. It is a sacred and blessed land that holds a special place in the heart of every Arab and Muslim.

**The Palestinian people:**

4. Palestinians are those Arabs who lived in Palestine until 1947, whether they were expelled or remained there; and anyone born of a Palestinian Arab father after that date, whether in Palestine or outside, is a Palestinian.

5. Palestinian identity is authentic and timeless; it is transmitted from generation to generation. The catastrophes that have befallen the Palestinian people as a result of the Zionist occupation and its policy of displacement cannot erase or deny the identity of the Palestinian people. A Palestinian will not lose his national identity or his rights by acquiring a second nationality.

6. The Palestinian people is one people, composed of all Palestinians, inside and outside Palestine, whatever their religion, culture or political affiliation.

**Islam and Palestine:**

7. Palestine is at the heart of the Arab and Islamic Ummah and enjoys a special status. In Palestine, there is Jerusalem, whose precincts are blessed by Allah. Palestine is the Holy Land that Allah has blessed for mankind. It is the first Qiblah of Muslims and the destination of the night

journey of the Prophet Muhammad, peace be upon him. It is the place from which he ascended to the higher heavens. It is the birthplace of Jesus Christ, peace be upon him. Its soil contains the remains of thousands of prophets, companions and mujahideen. It is the land of people determined to defend the truth—in and around Jerusalem—who are neither deterred nor intimidated by those who oppose them and those who betray them, and they will continue their mission until Allah's promise is fulfilled.

8. By virtue of its justly balanced middle way and moderate spirit, Islam—for Hamas—offers a comprehensive way of life and an order suited to its purpose at all times and in all places. Islam is a religion of peace and tolerance. It provides a framework for followers of other faiths and religions to practice their beliefs in safety. Hamas also believes that Palestine has always been and will always be a model of coexistence, tolerance and civilizational innovation.

9. Hamas believes that the message of Islam upholds the values of truth, justice, freedom and dignity, prohibits all forms of injustice and incriminates oppressors regardless of religion, race, gender or nationality. Islam opposes all forms of religious, ethnic or sectarian extremism and sectarianism. It is the religion that inculcates in its followers the importance of resisting aggression and supporting the oppressed; it motivates them to give generously and make sacrifices to defend their dignity, their land, their peoples and their holy places.

**Jerusalem:**

10. Jerusalem is the capital of Palestine. Its religious, historical and civilizational status is fundamental to Arabs, Muslims and the world at large. Its Islamic and Christian holy sites belong exclusively to the Palestinian people and to the Arab and Islamic Ummah. Not a single stone of Jerusalem can be surrendered or abandoned. Measures taken by the occupiers in Jerusalem, such as Judaization, settlement building and the establishment of facts on the ground, are fundamentally null and void.

11. The blessed mosque of Al-Aqsa belongs exclusively to our people and our Ummah, and the occupation has no right to it. The occupation's plots, measures and attempts to Judaize and divide Al-Aqsa are null, void and illegitimate.

**Refugees and the right to return:**

12. The Palestinian cause, in its essence, is the cause of an occupied land and a displaced people. The right of Palestinian refugees and displaced persons to return to their homes from which they were banished or to which they were forbidden to return—whether in the lands occupied in 1948 or in 1967 (i.e. the whole of Palestine), is a natural right, both individual and collective. This right is confirmed by all divine laws, as well as by the fundamental principles of human rights and international law. It is an inalienable right and no party, whether Palestinian, Arab or international, can renounce it.

13. Hamas rejects all attempts to erase the rights of refugees, including attempts to settle them outside Palestine and through alternative homeland projects. The compensation of Palestinian refugees for the harm they have suffered as a result of their banishment and the occupation of their lands is an absolute right that goes hand in hand with their right to return. They must receive compensation on their return, and this neither cancels nor diminishes their right to return.

**The Zionist project:**

14. The Zionist project is a racist, aggressive, colonial and expansionist project based on the seizure of other people's property; it is hostile to the Palestinian people and their aspiration to freedom, liberation, return and self-determination. The Israeli entity is the plaything of the Zionist project and its base of aggression.

15. The Zionist project does not only target the Palestinian people; it is the enemy of the Arab and Islamic Ummah, posing a grave threat to its security and interests. It is also hostile to the Ummah's aspirations to unity, rebirth and liberation, and has been the main source of its troubles. The Zionist project also constitutes a danger to international security and peace, as well as to humanity, its interests and stability.

16. Hamas claims that its conflict is with the Zionist project, not with Jews because of their religion. Hamas is not fighting against Jews because they are Jews, but against the Zionists who occupy Palestine. Yet it is the Zionists who constantly identify Judaism and Jews with their own colonial project and illegal entity.

17. Hamas rejects the persecution of any human being or any infringement of their rights for nationalistic, religious or sectarian reasons. Hamas believes that the Jewish problem, anti-Semitism and the perse-

cution of Jews are phenomena fundamentally linked to European history and not to the history of Arabs and Muslims or their heritage. The Zionist movement, which has been able to occupy Palestine with the help of the Western powers, is the most dangerous form of colonial occupation, which has already disappeared from a large part of the world and must disappear from Palestine.

**The position towards occupation and political solutions:**

18. The following are considered null and void: the Balfour Declaration, the British Mandate Document, the UN Resolution on the Partition of Palestine, and all resolutions and measures deriving from them or similar to them. The creation of "Israel" is totally illegal and contravenes the inalienable rights of the Palestinian people and goes against their will and that of the Ummah; it is also a violation of the human rights guaranteed by international conventions, foremost among which is the right to self-determination.

19. There will be no recognition of the legitimacy of the Zionist entity. Everything that has happened to the land of Palestine in terms of occupation, settlement building, Judaization or changes in its characteristics or falsification of facts is illegitimate. Rights are never extinguished.

20. Hamas believes that no part of the land of Palestine should be compromised or conceded, whatever the causes, circumstances and pressures, and however long the occupation. Hamas rejects any alternative to the full liberation of Palestine, from the river to the sea. However, without compromising its rejection of the Zionist entity and without renouncing any Palestinian right, Hamas envisages the creation of a fully sovereign and independent Palestinian state, with Jerusalem as its capital, on the model of June 4 1967, with the return of refugees and displaced persons to their homes from which they were expelled, as a formula for national consensus.

21. Hamas affirms that the Oslo Accords and their addenda contravene the rules governing international law insofar as they generate commitments that violate the inalienable rights of the Palestinian people. The Movement therefore rejects these agreements and all that follows from them, such as obligations detrimental to the interests of our people, including security coordination (collaboration).

22. Hamas rejects all settlement agreements, initiatives and projects that aim to undermine the Palestinian cause and the rights of our Palestinian

people. in this regard, any political stance, initiative or program must in no way violate these rights and must not contravene or contradict them.

23. Hamas stresses that the transgression against the Palestinian people, the usurpation of their land and their banishment from their homeland, cannot be called peace. Any settlement reached on this basis will not lead to peace. Resistance and jihad for the liberation of Palestine will remain a legitimate right, a duty and an honor for all the sons and daughters of our people and our Ummah.

**Resistance and Liberation:**

24. The liberation of Palestine is the duty of the Palestinian people in particular and the duty of the Arab and Islamic Ummah in general. It is also a humanitarian obligation made necessary by the imperatives of truth and justice. Agencies working for Palestine, whether national, Arab, Islamic or humanitarian, complement each other and are harmonious and not in conflict with each other.

25. Resisting occupation by all means and methods is a legitimate right guaranteed by divine laws and international norms and laws. At the heart of these issues lies armed resistance, seen as the strategic choice to protect the principles and rights of the Palestinian people.

26. Hamas rejects all attempts to undermine the resistance and its weapons. It also affirms the right of our people to develop the means and mechanisms of resistance. The management of resistance, in terms of escalation or de-escalation, or in terms of diversification of means and methods, is an integral part of the conflict management process and must not be at the expense of the principle of resistance.

**The Palestinian political system:**

27. A true State of Palestine is a liberated State. There is no alternative to a fully sovereign Palestinian state on all Palestinian national soil, with Jerusalem as its capital.

28. Hamas believes and adheres to managing its relations with Palestine on the basis of pluralism, democracy, national partnership, acceptance of the other and the adoption of dialogue. The aim is to strengthen unity of ranks and joint action in order to achieve national objectives and meet the aspirations of the Palestinian people.

29. The PLO is a national framework for the Palestinian people inside and outside Palestine. It must therefore be preserved, developed

and rebuilt on a democratic basis to ensure the participation of all constituents and forces of the Palestinian people, so as to safeguard Palestinian rights.

30. Hamas stresses the need to build Palestinian national institutions on the basis of sound democratic principles, foremost among which are free and fair elections. Such a process must be based on a national partnership and in line with a clear program and strategy that respects rights, including the right of resistance, and responds to the aspirations of the Palestinian people.

31. Hamas asserts that the role of the Palestinian Authority should be to serve the Palestinian people and safeguard their security, rights and national project.

32. Hamas stresses the need to maintain the independence of the Palestinian national decision-making process. Outside forces should not be allowed to intervene. At the same time, Hamas affirms the responsibility of Arabs and Muslims, and their duty and role in liberating Palestine from Zionist occupation.

33. Palestinian society is enriched by its eminent figures, personalities, dignitaries, civil society institutions, youth, students, trade unionists and women's groups who work together to achieve national goals and build society, pursue resistance and achieve liberation.

34. The role of Palestinian women is fundamental in the process of building the present and the future, just as it has always been in the process of writing Palestinian history. They play a central role in the project of resistance, liberation and the construction of a political system.

**The Arab and Islamic Ummah:**

35. Hamas considers the Palestinian question to be the central cause of the Arab and Islamic Ummah.

36. Hamas believes in the unity of the Ummah with all its diverse components and is aware of the need to avoid anything that could fragment the Ummah and undermine its unity.

37. Hamas believes in cooperation with all states that support the rights of the Palestinian people. It opposes any interference in the internal affairs of any country. It also refuses to be drawn into disputes and conflicts between different countries. Hamas adopts a policy of openness to the various states of the world, in particular to Arab and Islamic states. It strives to establish balanced relations based on a combination of the

requirements of the Palestinian cause and the interests of the Palestinian people, on the one hand, and the interests of the Ummah, its revival and its security, on the other.

**The humanitarian and international aspect:**

38. The Palestinian question has major humanitarian and international dimensions. Supporting and backing this cause is a humanitarian and civilizational task which is required by the preconditions of truth, justice and common humanitarian values.

39. From a legal and humanitarian point of view, the liberation of Palestine is a legitimate activity, an act of self-defense and an expression of the natural right of all peoples to self-determination.

40. In its relations with the nations and peoples of the world, Hamas believes in the values of cooperation, justice, freedom and respect for the will of peoples.

41. Hamas salutes the positions of States, organizations and institutions that support the rights of the Palestinian people. It salutes the free peoples of the world who support the Palestinian cause. At the same time, it denounces the support given by any party to the Zionist entity or attempts to conceal its crimes and aggressions against the Palestinians, and calls for the prosecution of Zionist war criminals.

42. Hamas rejects attempts to impose hegemony on the Arab and Islamic Ummah, just as it rejects attempts to impose hegemony on the rest of the nations and peoples of the world. Hamas also condemns all forms of colonialism, occupation, discrimination, oppression and aggression throughout the world.

May 2017

Source: http://hamas.ps/ar/uploads/documents/06c-77206ce934064ab5a901fa8bfef44.pdf; alternative site: https://www.middleeasteye.net/news/hamas-2017-document-full

# Appendix 2—United Nations Resolutions Condemning Israel

*The term "rogue state" refers to the idea of a state that does not respect the most basic international laws, organizes or supports attacks, or systematically violates the most basic human rights.*
[Wikipedia]

| | Resolutions | Significant extracts |
|---|---|---|
| 1 | Resolution 57 (1948) | "Deeply shocked by the tragic death of the United Nations mediator in Palestine, Count Folke Bernadotte, following a cowardly act that appears to have been committed by a criminal group of [Zionist] terrorists in Jerusalem." |
| 2 | Resolution 89 (1950) | Calls for attention to the expulsion of "thousands of Arabs from Palestine," noting that Israel has announced it will withdraw to the armistice lines. |
| 3 | Resolution 93 (1951) | Israeli air strikes on Syria constitute "a violation of the ceasefire," and decide that Arab civilians who have fled or been forcibly expelled from the demilitarized zone by Israel should be allowed to return. |
| 4 | Resolution 100 (1953) | He made "special reference to the recent acts of violence, and in particular to the Qibya incident on October 14 and 15, 1953" and to the continuing Israeli actions in the demilitarized zone. (Note: The Qibya massacre took place when Israeli troops under the command of Ariel Sharon attacked the West Bank village of Qibya. At least sixty-nine Palestinian villagers were killed, two-thirds of them women and children. Forty-five houses, a school and a mosque were destroyed). |
| 5 | Resolution 101 (1953) | Considers that the Israeli attack on Qibya (see above), in the West Bank, on October 14 and 15, 1953, constitutes a violation of the cease-fire and "expresses its strongest reprobation of this action."—underlining the impact of such actions on a potential peaceful resolution. |
| 6 | Resolution 106 (1955) | Condemns Israel's attack on Egyptian forces in the Gaza Strip on February 28, 1955, which broke the ceasefire. |
| 7 | Resolution 111 (1956) | Condemns the Israeli attack on Syria on December 11, 1955 as "a flagrant violation of the ceasefire" and the armistice agreement and "according to the report of the Chief of Staff, this Israeli action was a deliberate violation of the provisions of the general armistice agreement between Israel and Syria." |
| 8 | Resolution 119 (1956) | Declares that a "grave situation has been created" by the attack on Egypt by Great Britain, France and Israel. |
| 9 | Resolution 171 (1962) | "Determines that the Israeli attack of March 16 and 17, 1962, constitutes a flagrant violation of this resolution, and calls upon Israel scrupulously to refrain from any such action in the future."—reaffirming resolution 111 (January 19, 1956). |

| | | |
|---|---|---|
| 10 | Resolution 228 (1966) | "Deplores the loss of human life and the heavy material damage resulting from Israel's action in the southern zone of Hebron on November 13, 1966, and condemns Israel for this large-scale military action in violation of the United Nations Charter and the armistice agreement between Israel and Jordan. |
| 11 | Resolution 237 (1967) | "Calls on the government of Israel to ensure the safety, well-being and security of the inhabitants of areas where military operations have taken place and to facilitate the return of inhabitants who have fled these areas since the beginning of hostilities," referring to the war launched by Israel on June 5, 1967. |
| 12 | Resolution 242 (1967) | Calls for "the withdrawal of Israeli armed forces from the territories occupied during the recent conflict; (ii) the cessation of all claims or states of belligerence and respect for and recognition of the sovereignty, territorial integrity and political independence of all states in the region." Emphasizes that member states are committed to respecting the United Nations Charter. |
| 13 | Resolution 248 (1968) | Notes that the Israeli attack on Jordan "was carried out on a large scale and carefully planned," "deplores the loss of human life and the heavy material damage," "condemns the military action launched by Israel in flagrant violation of the United Nations Charter and ceasefire resolutions" and "calls on Israel to desist" from any further violation of resolution 237. |
| 14 | Resolution 250 (1968) | Considers "that the holding of a military parade in Jerusalem will aggravate tensions in the region and have a negative effect on the peaceful settlement of problems in the region" and "calls upon Israel to refrain from holding the military parade in Jerusalem which is envisaged" for May 2, 1968. |
| 15 | Resolution 251 (1968) | Recalls resolution 250 and "strongly deplores Israel's organization of the military parade in Jerusalem" on May 2, 1968 "in defiance" of resolution 250. |
| 16 | Resolution 252 (1968) | Deplores Israel's failure to comply with the above-mentioned General Assembly resolutions;<br>Considers that all legislative and administrative measures and provisions taken by Israel, including the expropriation of land and property, which tend to change the legal status of Jerusalem are invalid and cannot change that status;<br>Urgently calls upon Israel to rescind all such measures already taken and to refrain immediately from any further action that would alter the status of Jerusalem; |
| 17 | Resolution 256 (1968) | I. Reaffirms its resolution 248 (1968) in which, inter alia, it declares that serious violations of the cease-fire cannot be tolerated and that the Council should study new and more effective provisions as envisaged in the Charter to ensure against the recurrence of such acts:<br>2. Deplores the loss of life and property:<br>3. Considers that premeditated and repeated military attacks endanger peacekeeping:<br>4. Condemns the new military attacks by Israel in flagrant violation of the Charter of the United Nations and of resolution 248 (1968) and warns that should such attacks be repeated, the Council will take due account of any failure to comply with this resolution. |
| 18 | Resolution 259 (1968) | Deploring the delay in the implementation of resolution 237 (1967) because of Israel's continuing conditions for receiving a special representative of the Secretary-General.<br>1. Requests the Secretary-General urgently to send a special representative to the Arab territories occupied militarily by Israel following the hostilities of June 5, 1967, and to report on the implementation of resolution 237 (1967);<br>2. Requests the Government of Israel to receive the Special Representative of the Secretary-General, to cooperate with him and to facilitate his task. |
| 19 | Resolution 262 (1968) | Noting that the military action taken by the Israeli armed forces against Beirut's civilian international airport was premeditated, large-scale and carefully prepared, |

| 20 | Resolution 265 (1969) | Noting with deep concern that the recent air attacks against villages and other populated areas in Jordan were prepared in advance, in violation of resolutions 248 (1968) of March 24, 1968 and 256 (1968) of August 16, 1968, Gravely concerned by the deteriorating situation, which is endangering peace and security in the region, 1. Reaffirms resolutions 248 (1968) and 256 (1968); 2. Deplores the loss of civilian lives and property; 3. Condemns the recent premeditated Israeli air attacks on villages and populated areas in Jordan in flagrant violation of the UN Charter and ceasefire resolutions, and warns once again that should such attacks be repeated, the Security Council should meet to consider new and more effective measures, as provided for in the Charter, to ensure that such attacks are not repeated. |
|---|---|---|
| 21 | Resolution 267 (1969) | 2. Deplores Israel's disregard of the above-mentioned General Assembly and Security Council resolutions; 3. Censures in the strongest terms all measures taken to modify the status of the city of Jerusalem; 4. Confirms that all legislative and administrative measures and provisions taken by Israel which have the effect of altering the status of Jerusalem, including the expropriation of land and property, are invalid and cannot alter that status; 5. Urgently calls once again upon Israel to rescind forthwith all measures taken by it which may tend to change the status of the city of Jerusalem and to refrain in future from any measures likely to have such an effect; |
| 22 | Resolution 270 (1969) | 1. Condemns the premeditated Israeli air attack on villages in southern Lebanon in violation of its obligations under the Charter and Security Council resolutions; 2. Deplores all violent incidents in violation of the ceasefire; 3. Deplores the extension of the combat zone; 4. Declares that such acts of military reprisals and other serious violations of the ceasefire cannot be tolerated and that the Security Council should consider new and more effective measures, as provided for in the Charter, to ensure that such acts are not repeated. |
| 23 | Resolution 271 (1969) | 3. Notes that the abhorrent act of violation and desecration of the Holy Al Aqsa Mosque underscores the immediate need for Israel to desist from acting in violation of the above-mentioned resolutions and to immediately rescind all measures and actions taken by it which tend to alter the status of Jerusalem; 4. Calls upon Israel to observe scrupulously the provisions of the Geneva Conventions13 and of international law governing military occupation, and to refrain from interfering in any way with the exercise of the functions that belong to the Supreme Muslim Council of Jerusalem, including any cooperation the Council may wish to obtain from countries with predominantly Muslim populations and Muslim communities regarding its plans for the maintenance and repair of the Islamic Holy Places of Jerusalem; 5. Condemns Israel's failure to comply with the above-mentioned resolutions, and calls upon it to implement the provisions of said resolutions immediately |
| 24 | Resolution 279 (1970) | Demands the immediate withdrawal of all Israeli armed forces from Lebanese territory. |
| 25 | Resolution 280 (1970) | 1. Deplores Israel's failure to comply with Security Council resolutions 262 (1968) and 270 (1969); 2. Condemns Israel for its premeditated military action in violation of its obligations under the Charter of the United Nations; 3. Declares that these armed attacks cannot be tolerated any longer and reiterates to Israel its solemn warning that, should it reoffend, the Security Council will consider taking, in accordance with resolution 262 (1968) and the present resolution, appropriate and effective measures or steps under the relevant Articles of the Charter to implement its resolutions; 4. Deplores the loss of life and damage to property resulting from violations of Security Council resolutions. |
| 26 | Resolution 285 (1970) | Demands the complete and immediate withdrawal of all Israeli forces from Lebanese territory. |

| | | |
|---|---|---|
| 27 | Resolution 298 (1971) | 1. Reaffirms the provisions of its resolutions 252 (1968) and 267 (1969); 2. Deplores the fact that Israel has not complied with the resolutions previously adopted by the United Nations concerning the measures and steps taken by Israel to change the status of the city of Jerusalem; 3. Confirms in the most explicit terms that all legislative and administrative measures taken by Israel to change the status of the city of Jerusalem, including the expropriation of land and property, the transfer of populations and legislation to incorporate the occupied part, are totally null and void and cannot change the status of the city; |
| 28 | Resolution 313 (1972) | The Security Council Demands that Israel immediately renounce and refrain from any military action on land and in the air against Lebanon, and immediately withdraw all its military forces from Lebanese territory. |
| 29 | Resolution 316 (1972) | Deploring the tragic loss of human life resulting ‹from all acts of violence and reprisals, Gravely concerned by Israel's failure to comply with Security Council resolutions 262 (1968), 270 (1969), 280 (1970), 285 (1970) and 313 (1972) of December 31, 1968, August 26, 1969, May 19 and September 5, 1970, and February 28, 1972, respectively, calling upon Israel to immediately renounce any violation of Lebanon's sovereignty and territorial integrity, l. Calls on Israel to comply strictly with the above-mentioned resolutions and to refrain from any military action against Lebanon; 2. Condemns, while deeply deploring all acts of violence, the repeated attacks by Israeli forces against the territory and people of Lebanon in violation of the principles of the United Nations Charter and the obligations Israel has assumed thereunder; |
| 30 | Resolution 317 (1972) | 1. Reaffirms resolution 316 (1972), adopted by the Security Council on June 26, 1972; 2. Deplores the fact that, despite these efforts, the strong desire of the Security Council to see all Syrian and Lebanese military and security personnel abducted by the Israeli armed forces on June 21, 1972 on Lebanese territory released as soon as possible has not yet been carried out; 3. Requests Israel to return the above-mentioned personnel without delay; |
| 31 | Resolution 332 (1973) | 2. Condemns Israel's repeated military attacks against Lebanon and its violation of Lebanon's territorial integrity and sovereignty, which are contrary to the Charter of the United Nations, the General Armistice Agreement between Israel and Lebanon and the Council's ceasefire resolutions; 3. Calls on Israel to immediately renounce all military attacks against Lebanon. |
| 32 | Resolution 337 (1973) | Recalling its resolutions 262 (1968) of December 31, 1968 and 286 (1970) of September 9, 1970, 1. Condemns the Government of Israel for violating the sovereignty and territorial integrity of Lebanon and for the hijacking and forcible capture by the Israeli air force of a Lebanese aircraft in Lebanese airspace; 2. Considers that these acts of Israel constitute a violation of the 1949 General Armistice Agreement between Israel and Lebanon, of the ceasefire resolutions adopted by the Security Council in 1967, of the provisions of the Charter of the United Nations, of the international conventions relating to civil aviation and of the principles of international law and morality; |
| 33 | Resolution 347 (1974) | 1. Condemns Israel's violation of Lebanon's territorial integrity and sovereignty, and once again calls on the Israeli Government to refrain from further military actions and threats against Lebanon; 2. Condemns all acts of violence, particularly those which result in the tragic deaths of innocent civilians, and urges all concerned to refrain from further acts of violence; 3. Calls upon all governments concerned to respect their obligations under the Charter of the United Nations and international law; 4. Calls on Israel to immediately release and return to Lebanon the abducted Lebanese civilians; |

| 34 | Resolution 425 (1978) | 1. Calls for strict respect for the territorial integrity, sovereignty and political independence of Lebanon within its internationally recognized borders;<br>2. Calls on Israel to cease immediately its military action against the territorial integrity of Lebanon and to withdraw without delay its forces from all Lebanese territory;<br>3. Decides, taking into account the request of the Government of Lebanon, to establish immediately under its authority a United Nations interim force for southern Lebanon for the purpose of confirming the withdrawal of Israeli forces, restoring international peace and security and assisting the Government of Lebanon in ensuring the restoration of its effective authority in the region, such force to be composed of personnel provided by Member States; |
|---|---|---|
| 35 | Resolution 427 (1978) | 3. Calls on Israel to complete its withdrawal from all Lebanese territory without further delay; |
| 36 | Resolution 446 (1979) | Affirming once again that the Geneva Convention relative to the Protection of Civilian Persons in Time of War, of August 12, 1949, is applicable to the Arab territories occupied by Israel since 1967, including Jerusalem,<br>1. Considers that the Israeli policy and practice of establishing settlements in the Palestinian and other Arab territories occupied since 1967 has no validity in law and is a serious obstacle to the establishment of a comprehensive, just and lasting peace in the Middle East;<br>2. Deeply deplores Israel's failure to comply with Security Council resolutions 237 (1967), 252 (1968) and 298 (1971) of June 14, 1967, May 21, 1968 and September 25, 1971, respectively, as well as with the consensus statement made by the President of the Council on November 11, 1976) and with General Assembly resolutions 2253 (ES-V) and 2254 (ES-V), 32/5 and 33/113 of July 4 and 14, 1967, October 28, 1977 and December 18, 1978, respectively;<br>3. Calls once again upon Israel, as the occupying Power, to abide scrupulously by the Geneva Convention relative to the Protection of Civilian Persons in Time of War, of August 12, 1949, to rescind the measures that have already been taken and to refrain from any measures that would alter the legal status and geographical character of the Arab territories occupied since 1967, including Jerusalem, and materially affect their demographic composition, and, in particular, not to transfer elements of its own civilian population into the occupied Arab territories; |
| 37 | Resolution 450 (1979) | 1. Deeply deplores the acts of violence against Lebanon which have led to the displacement of civilians, including Palestinians, and caused destruction and loss of innocent life;<br>2. Calls on Israel to cease immediately its actions against the territorial integrity, unity, sovereignty and political independence of Lebanon, in particular its incursions into Lebanon and its continued support for irresponsible armed groups;<br>3. Also calls upon all parties involved to refrain from activities incompatible with the objectives of the United Nations Interim Force in Lebanon and to cooperate in the achievement of these objectives; |
| 38 | Resolution 452 (1979) | Deeply deploring Israel's lack of cooperation with the Commission,<br>Considering that Israel's policy of establishing settlements in the occupied Arab territories has no validity in law and constitutes a violation of the Geneva Convention relative to the Protection of Civilian Persons in Time of War, of August 12, 1949,<br>Deeply concerned by the way in which the Israeli authorities are implementing this colonization policy in the occupied Arab territories, including Jerusalem, and by its consequences for the local Arab and Palestinian population<br>(...)<br>3. Calls on the Israeli Government and people to urgently cease establishing, building and planning settlements in the Arab territories occupied since 1967, including Jerusalem. |

| 39 | Resolution 465 (1980) | Deeply deploring Israel's refusal to cooperate with the Commission and regretting that it has formally rejected resolutions 446 (1979) and 452 (1979), Affirming once again that the Geneva Convention relative to the Protection of Civilian Persons in Time of War, of August 12, 1949, is applicable to the Arab territories occupied by Israel since 1967, including Jerusalem. Deploring the Israeli government's decision to officially support the settlement of Israelis in the Palestinian and other Arab territories occupied since 1967, Deeply concerned by the way in which the Israeli authorities are implementing this policy of colonization in the occupied Arab territories, including Jerusalem, and by its consequences for the local Arab and Palestinian population,<br>5. Considers that all measures taken by Israel to modify the physical character. demographic composition. institutional structure or status of the Palestinian and other Arab territories occupied since 1967. or any part thereof have no validity in law, and that Israel's policy and practice of settling elements of its population and new immigrants in these territories constitute a flagrant violation of the Geneva Convention relative to the Protection of Civilian Persons in Time of War, and moreover seriously impede the establishment of a comprehensive, just and lasting peace in the Middle East:<br>6. Deeply deplores Israel's persistence and obstinacy in these policies and practices and calls upon the Government and people of Israel to report these measures. to dismantle existing settlements and. in particular. to urgently cease establishing. building and planning settlements in the Arab territories occupied since 1967, including Jerusalem:<br>7. Calls on all states not to provide Israel with any assistance that would be used specifically for settlements in the occupied territories: |
| 40 | Resolution 467 (1980) | 2. Condemns all actions contrary to the provisions of the above-mentioned resolutions and, in particular, strongly deplores:<br>(a) Any violation of Lebanon's sovereignty and territorial integrity;<br>(b) Israel's military intervention in Lebanon;<br>(c) All acts of violence committed in violation of the General Armistice Agreement between Israel and Lebanon; |
| 41 | Resolution 468 (1980) | Deeply concerned by the expulsion by the Israeli military occupation authorities of the mayors of Hebron and Halhoul and the Islamic judge of Hebron,<br>1. Calls upon the Government of Israel, in its capacity as Occupying Power, to rescind these illegal measures and to facilitate the immediate return of the expelled Palestinian notables, so that they may resume the functions to which they were elected or appointed; |
| 42 | Resolution 469 (1980) | Recalling the Geneva Convention relative to the Protection of Civilian Persons in Time of War, of August 12, 1949, and in particular Article I, which states that "The High Contracting Parties undertake to respect and to ensure respect for the present Convention in all circumstances," and Article 49, which states that "Individual or mass forcible transfers, as well as deportations of protected persons from occupied territory to the territory of the Occupying Power or to that of any other state, occupied or not, are prohibited, whatever the motive,"<br>1. Deeply deplores the failure of the Israeli Government to implement resolution 468 (1980);<br>2. Reiterates its call upon the Government of Israel, in its capacity as the occupying Power, to rescind the illegal measures taken by the Israeli military occupation authorities in expelling the mayors of Hebron and Halhoul and the Islamic judge of Hebron, and to facilitate the immediate return of the expelled Palestinian notables, so that they may resume the functions to which they were elected or appointed; |

| 43 | Resolution 471 (1980) | Recalling once again the Geneva Convention relative to the Protection of Civilian Persons in Time of War, of August 12, 1949, and in particular article 27, which states in particular:<br>.. Protected persons are entitled, in all circumstances, to respect for their person... They shall at all times be treated humanely and protected in particular against any act of violence or intimidation....,"<br>(...) Appalled by the assassination attempts on the mayors of Nablus, Ramallah and Al Bireh,<br>Deeply concerned by the fact that Jewish settlers in the occupied Arab territories are allowed to carry weapons, enabling them to commit crimes against the Arab civilian population,<br>I. Condemns the assassination attempts against the mayors of Nablus, Ramallah and Al Bireh and calls for the immediate arrest and prosecution of the perpetrators of these crimes;<br>2. Expresses its deep concern at the failure of Israel, as the occupying Power, to provide adequate protection for the civilian population of the occupied territories, in accordance with the provisions of the Geneva Convention relative to the Protection of Civilian Persons in Time of War;<br>3. Calls on the Israeli Government to adequately compensate the victims for the harm they have suffered as a result of these crimes;<br>4. Reiterates its call on the Israeli Government to respect and apply the provisions of the Geneva Convention relative to the Protection of Civilian Persons in Time of War and the relevant Security Council resolutions;<br>5. Calls once again on all states not to provide Israel with any assistance that would be used specifically for settlements in the occupied territories;<br>6. Reaffirms the vital need to end the prolonged occupation of Arab territories occupied by Israel since 1967, including Jerusalem; |
|---|---|---|
| 44 | Resolution 476 (1980) | Reaffirming that the acquisition of territory by force is inadmissible. (...)<br>2. Deeply deplores the continued refusal of Israel, the occupying Power, to comply with the relevant resolutions of the Security Council and the General Assembly;<br>3. Reaffirms that all legislative and administrative measures and actions taken by Israel, the occupying Power, aimed at altering the character and status of the Holy City of Jerusalem have no validity in law and constitute a flagrant violation of the Geneva Convention relative to the Protection of Civilian Persons in Time of War, and furthermore gravely impede the achievement of a comprehensive, just and lasting peace in the Middle East;<br>4. Reaffirms that all measures which have altered the geographical, demographic and historical character and status of the Holy City of Jerusalem are null and void and must be rescinded in accordance with the relevant Security Council resolutions;<br>5. Urges Israel, the occupying Power, to comply with the present resolution and previous resolutions of the Security Council and to cease immediately the implementation of policies and measures affecting the character and status of the Holy City of Jerusalem; |

| 45 | Resolution 478 (1980) | Reaffirming that the acquisition of territory by force is inadmissible. Deeply concerned by the promulgation of a "fundamental law" by the Israeli Knesset proclaiming a change in the character and status of the Holy City of Jerusalem, with its implications for peace and security, Noting Israel's failure to comply with resolution 476 (1980), Reaffirming its determination to consider practical ways and means, in accordance with the relevant provisions of the Charter of the United Nations, to ensure the full implementation of resolution 476 (1980), in the event of non-compliance by Israel, 1. Condemns in the strongest terms Israel's enactment of the "Basic Law" on Jerusalem and its refusal to comply with the relevant Security Council resolutions; 2. Affirms that the promulgation of the "Basic Law" by Israel constitutes a violation of international law and does not affect the continued application of the Geneva Convention relative to the Protection of Civilian Persons in Time of War, of August 12, 1949, in the Palestinian and other Arab territories occupied since June 1967, including Jerusalem; 3. Determines that all legislative and administrative measures and actions taken by Israel, the occupying power, which have altered or purport to alter the character and status of the Holy City of Jerusalem, and in particular the recent "Basic Law" on Jerusalem, are null and void and must be rescinded forthwith; 4. Affirms also that this action constitutes a serious obstacle to the achievement of a comprehensive, just and lasting peace in the Middle East; 5. Decides not to recognize the "Basic Law" or any other action by Israel which, as a result of this law, seeks to alter the character and status of Jerusalem and calls: a) All Member States to accept this decision; b) States that have established diplomatic missions in Jerusalem to withdraw these missions from the Holy City; |
|---|---|---|
| 46 | Resolution 484 (1980) | Expressing its grave concern at Israel's expulsion of the mayor of Hebron and the mayor of Halhoul, l. Reaffirms the applicability of the Geneva Convention relative to the Protection of Civilian Persons in Time of War, of August 12, 1949, to all Arab territories occupied by Israel in 1967; 2. Calls upon Israel, the occupying Power, to comply with the provisions of the Convention; 3. Declares that 'ii is of imperative necessity that the mayor of Hebron and the mayor of Halhoul be able to return to their homes and resume their office; |
| 47 | Resolution 487 (1981) | Deeply concerned by the danger to international peace and security caused by Israel's premeditated air attack on Iraq's nuclear facilities on June 7, 1981, which could at any moment trigger an explosion in the region with grave consequences for the vital interests of all states, Whereas, under the terms of paragraph 4 of Article 2 of the Charter of the United Nations, "Members shall refrain in their international relations from the use of force against the territorial integrity or political independence of any state, or in any other manner inconsistent with the Purposes of the United Nations," l. Strongly condemns the military attack carried out by Israel in flagrant violation of the United Nations Charter and international standards of conduct; 2. Calls upon Israel to refrain in the future from perpetrating such acts or from threatening to do so; 3. Further considers that the said attack constitutes a serious threat to the entire safeguards system of the International Atomic Energy Agency, on which the Treaty on the Non-Proliferation of Nuclear Weapons is based; |

| 48 | Resolution 497 (1981) | Reaffirming that the acquisition of territory by force is inadmissible, in accordance with the United Nations Charter, the principles of international law and the relevant Security Council resolutions,<br>1. Decides that Israel's decision to impose its laws, jurisdiction and administration in the occupied Syrian territory of the Golan Heights is null and void and without international legal effect;<br>2. Demands that Israel, the occupying power, rescind its decision without delay;<br>3. Declares that all the provisions of the Geneva Convention relative to the Protection of Civilian Persons in Time of War, of August 12, 1949, continue to apply to the Syrian territory occupied by Israel since June 1967; |
|---|---|---|
| 49 | Resolution 501 (1982) | I. Reaffirms its resolution 425 (1978), which reads as follows:<br>(...)1. Calls for strict respect for the territorial integrity, sovereignty and political independence of Lebanon within its internationally recognized borders;<br>2. Calls on Israel to cease immediately its military action against the territorial integrity of Lebanon and to withdraw without delay its forces from all Lebanese territory; |
| 50 | Resolution 509 (1982) | Reaffirming the necessity of strict respect for the territorial integrity, sovereignty and political independence of Lebanon within its internationally recognized borders,<br>I. Demands that Israel immediately and unconditionally withdraw all its military forces to the internationally recognized borders of Lebanon; |
| 51 | Resolution 515 (1982) | Referring to the humanitarian principles of the Geneva Conventions of 1949 and the obligations arising from the regulations annexed to the Hague Convention of 1907,<br>Recalling its resolutions 512 (1982) and 513 (1982),<br>I. Demands that the Government of Israel immediately lift the blockade of the city of Beirut so as to enable the dispatch of supplies to meet the urgent needs of the civilian population and to permit the distribution of relief supplies provided by United Nations agencies and non-governmental organizations, in particular the International Committee of the Red Cross; |
| 52 | Resolution 517 (1982) | Deeply shocked and alarmed by the deplorable consequences of Israel's invasion of Beirut on August 3, 1982,<br>I. Reconfirms its resolutions 508 (1982), 509 (1982), 512 (1982), 513 (1982), 515 (1982) and 516 (1982);<br>2. Confirms once again that it demands an immediate ceasefire and the immediate withdrawal of Israeli forces from Lebanon;<br>3. Blames Israel for failing to comply with the above-mentioned resolutions;<br>4. Calls for the prompt retreat of Israeli troops who advanced after 1:25 p.m. New York summer time on August 1, 1982;<br>5. Takes note of the decision of the Palestine Liberation Organization to withdraw the Palestinian armed forces from Beirut; |
| 53 | Resolution 518 (1982) | 1. Demands that Israel and all parties to the conflict strictly respect the terms of the Security Council resolutions concerning the immediate cessation of all military activities in Lebanon, and in particular in and around Beirut;<br>2. Demands that all restrictions imposed on the city of Beirut be lifted immediately to allow the free entry of supplies to meet the urgent needs of the civilian population of Beirut; |

| 54 | Resolution 520 (1982) | Condemning the assassination of Bechir Gemayel, the President whom Lebanon had elected in accordance with its constitution, as well as any effort to use violence to disrupt the re-establishment of a strong and stable government in Lebanon, Having heard the statement by the Permanent Representative of Lebanon, Noting Lebanon's determination to ensure the withdrawal of all non-Lebanese forces from Lebanon, 1. Reaffirms its resolutions 508 (1982), 509 (1982) and 516 (1982) in their entirety; 2. Condemns the recent Israeli incursions into Beirut, which constitute a violation of ceasefire agreements and Security Council resolutions; 3. Demands the immediate return to the positions occupied by Israel before September 15, 1982, as a first step towards the full implementation of the Security Council resolutions; 4. Reiterates its demand for strict respect for the sovereignty, territorial integrity, unity and political independence of Lebanon, under the sole and exclusive authority of the Lebanese Government, exercised through the Lebanese army throughout Lebanon; |
|---|---|---|
| 55 | Resolution 521 (1982) | Struck with horror by the massacre of Palestinian civilians in Beirut, Having heard the report of the Secretary-General at its 2396th meeting Noting that the Lebanese government has agreed to send UN observers to the areas of greatest suffering and loss of life in and around Beirut, l. Condemns the criminal massacre of Palestinian civilians in Beirut; 2. Reaffirms once again its resolutions 512 (1982) and 513 (1982), which call for respect for the rights of civilian populations without any discrimination, and repudiates all acts of violence against these populations; |
| 56 | Resolution 573 (1985) | Having noted with concern that the Israeli attack has caused numerous casualties and considerable material damage, Whereas, under the terms of paragraph 4 of Article 2 of the Charter of the United Nations, the Members of the Organization shall refrain in their international relations from the threat or use of force against the territorial integrity or political independence of any state, or in any other manner inconsistent with the Purposes of the United Nations, Gravely concerned by the threat to peace and security in the Mediterranean region caused by Israel's air attack on the Hammam Plage area in the southern suburbs of Tunis on October 1, 1985, Drawing attention to the grave consequences that Israel's aggression and all acts contrary to the Charter cannot fail to have for any initiative aimed at establishing a just and lasting peace in the Middle East, Whereas the Israeli government claimed responsibility for the attack as soon as it occurred, l. Strongly condemns the act of armed aggression perpetrated by Israel against Tunisian territory, in flagrant violation of the United Nations Charter and international law and standards of conduct; 2. Demands that Israel refrain from perpetrating such acts of aggression or from threatening to do so; |
| 57 | Resolution 592 (1986) | Gravely concerned by the situation in the Palestinian and other Arab territories occupied by Israel since 1967, including Jerusalem, Bearing in mind the special status of Jerusalem, 1. Reaffirms that the Geneva Convention relative to the Protection of Civilian Persons in Time of War is applicable to the Palestinian and other Arab territories occupied by Israel since 1967, including Jerusalem; 2. Deeply deplores the actions of the Israeli army which, having opened fire, killed or wounded defenceless students; 3. Calls upon Israel to comply immediately and scrupulously with the Geneva Convention relative to the Protection of Civilian Persons in Time of War; 4. Also calls upon Israel to release all those arrested following the latest events at Bir Zeit University, in violation of the above-mentioned Geneva Convention; |

| 58 | Resolution 605 (1987) | Considering that the current policies and practices of Israel, the occupying power, in the occupied territories will inevitably seriously undermine efforts to achieve a comprehensive, just and lasting peace in the Middle East,<br>1. Strongly deplores these policies and practices of Israel. Occupying Power, which violate the human rights of the Palestinian people in the occupied territories. in particular the fact that the Israeli army has opened fire. killing or wounding defenseless Palestinian civilians;<br>2. Reaffirms that the Geneva Convention relative to the Protection of Civilian Persons in Time of War of August 12, 1949, applies to the Palestinian and other Arab territories occupied by Israel since 1967, including Jerusalem;<br>3. Calls once again upon Israel. Occupying Power, to comply immediately and scrupulously with the Geneva Convention relative to the Protection of Civilian Persons in Time of War, and to put an immediate end to its policies and practices which are contrary to the provisions of the Convention: |
| --- | --- | --- |
| 59 | Resolution 607 (1988) | Having learned of the decision by Israel, the occupying power, to "continue to expel" Palestinian civilians from the occupied territories,<br>Recalling the Geneva Convention relative to the Protection of Civilian Persons in Time of War, of August 12, 1949, in particular articles 47 and 49,<br>1. Reaffirms once again that the Geneva Convention relative to the Protection of Civilian Persons in Time of War, of August 12, 1949, applies to the Palestinian and other Arab territories occupied by Israel since 1967, including Jerusalem;<br>2. Calls upon Israel to refrain from expelling Palestinian civilians from the occupied territories;<br>3. Urgently calls upon Israel, the occupying Power, to abide by its obligations under the Convention; |
| 60 | Resolution 608 (988) | Deeply deploring that Israel, the occupying power, has, in defiance of this resolution, expelled Palestinian civilians,<br>l. Calls on Israel to rescind the expulsion order against Palestinian civilians and to ensure the immediate and safe return to the occupied Palestinian territories of those who have already been expelled;<br>2. Requests Israel to cease immediately the expulsion of further Palestinian civilians from the occupied territories; |
| 61 | Resolution 611 (1988) | Having noted with concern that the aggression perpetrated on April 16, 1988 in the locality of Sidi Bou Saïd caused loss of life, particularly the assassination of Mr. Khalil Al-Wazir,<br>Gravely concerned by this act of aggression, which constitutes a serious and renewed threat to peace, security and stability in the Mediterranean region,<br>1. Strongly condemns the aggression perpetrated on April 16, 1988 against the sovereignty and territorial integrity of Tunisia, in flagrant violation of the United Nations Charter and international law and standards of conduct;<br>2. Urges Member States of the United Nations to take measures to prevent such acts against the sovereignty and territorial integrity of all States; |
| 62 | Resolution 636 (1989) | 1. Deeply regrets that Israel, the occupying power, continues to expel Palestinian civilians;<br>2. Calls on Israel to ensure the immediate and safe return of the expelled persons to the occupied Palestinian territories and to cease immediately the expulsion of other Palestinian civilians;<br>3. Reaffirms that the Geneva Convention relative to the Protection of Civilian Persons in Time of War of August 12, 1949 applies to the Palestinian territories occupied by Israel since 1967, including Jerusalem, as well as to the other occupied Arab territories; |

| 63 | Resolution 641 (1989) | 1. Deplores the fact that Israel, the occupying power, continues to expel Palestinian civilians;<br>2. Calls upon Israel to ensure the immediate and safe return of the expelled persons to the occupied Palestinian territories and to cease immediately the expulsion of other Palestinian civilians;<br>3. Reaffirms that the Geneva Convention relative to the Protection of Civilian Persons in Time of War, of August 12, 1949, applies to the Palestinian territories occupied by Israel since 1967, including Jerusalem, as well as to the other occupied Arab territories; |
|---|---|---|
| 64 | Resolution 672 (1990) | 1. Expresses its alarm at the violence unleashed on October 8 in Al-Haram Al-Sharif and other holy places in Jerusalem, which left more than twenty Palestinians dead and more than one hundred and fifty wounded, including Palestinian civilians and innocent people who had gone to prayer;<br>2. Condemns in particular the acts of violence committed by the Israeli security forces, which have resulted in death and injury;<br>3. Calls upon Israel, the occupying power, to comply scrupulously with its legal obligations and responsibilities under the Geneva Convention relative to the Protection of Civilian Persons in Time of War, of August 12, 1949, which is applicable to all territories occupied by Israel since 1967; |
| 65 | Resolution 673 (1990) | Expressing concern that the Israeli Government has rejected resolution 672 (1990) and refuses to receive the Secretary-General's mission,<br>Taking into consideration the statement of the Secretary-General concerning the purpose of the mission he is sending to the region, brought to the attention of the Council by the President on October 12, 1990,<br>Deeply concerned that the situation continues to deteriorate in the occupied territories,<br>1. Deplores the refusal of the Government of Israel to receive the Secretary-General's mission to the region;<br>2. Urges the Government of Israel to reverse its decision and insists that it comply scrupulously with resolution 672 (1990) and allow the mission to fulfil its mandate; |
| 66 | Resolution 681 (1990) | 2. Expresses its deep concern at Israel's rejection of its resolutions 672 (1990) of September 27, 1990 and 671 (1990) of October 12, 1990;<br>3. Deplores the decision by Israel, the occupying power, to once again expel Palestinian civilians from the occupied territories;<br>4. Calls upon the Government of Israel to recognize the de jure applicability of the Geneva Convention relative to the Protection of Civilian Persons in Time of War, of August 12, 1949, to all territories occupied by Israel since 1967 and to comply scrupulously with the provisions of the Convention;<br>5. Calls upon the High Contracting Parties to the said Convention to ensure that Israel, the occupying Power, fulfils its obligations under Article I of the Convention; |
| 67 | Resolution 694 (1991) | Deeply concerned and dismayed to learn that Israel, in violation of its obligations under the Geneva Convention relative to the Protection of Civilian Persons in Time of War, of August 12, 1949, and acting against the relevant Security Council resolutions and to the detriment of efforts to achieve a comprehensive, just and lasting peace in the Middle East, expelled four Palestinian civilians on May 18, 1991,<br>1. Declares that in expelling four Palestinian civilians on May 18, 1991, the Israeli authorities acted in violation of the Geneva Convention relative to the Protection of Civilian Persons in Time of War, of August 12, 1949, which is applicable to all Palestinian territories occupied by Israel since 1967, including Jerusalem;<br>2. Deplores this action and reaffirms that Israel, the occupying power, must refrain from expelling Palestinian civilians from the occupied territories and guarantee the immediate and safe return of all those expelled; |

| 68 | Resolution 726 (1992) | 1. Strongly condemns Israel, the occupying power, for its decision to carry out renewed expulsions of Palestinian civilians;<br>2 Reaffirms that the Geneva Convention relative to the Protection of Civilian Persons in Time of War, of August 12, 1949, applies to all Palestinian territories occupied by Israel since 1967, including Jerusalem;<br>3. Calls on Israel, the occupying power, to refrain from expelling Palestinian civilians from the occupied territories;<br>4. Also calls upon Israel, the occupying Power, to ensure the immediate and safe return of all expelled persons to the occupied territories; |
|---|---|---|
| 69 | Resolution 799 (1992) | 1. Strongly condemns these expulsions of hundreds of Palestinian civilians by Israel, the occupying power, and declares its firm opposition to such expulsions by Israel;<br>2. Reaffirms that the Fourth Geneva Convention of August 12, 1949 applies to all Palestinian territories occupied by Israel since 1967, including Jerusalem, and stresses that the expulsion of civilians contravenes Israel's obligations under the Convention;<br>3. Also reaffirms the independence, sovereignty and territorial integrity of Lebanon;<br>4. Demands that Israel, the occupying power, guarantee the immediate and safe return to the occupied territories of all those who have been expelled; |
| 70 | Resolution 904 (1994) | 1. Strongly condemns the Hebron massacre and its aftermath, which claimed the lives of more than 50 Palestinian civilians and left several hundred injured;<br>2. Calls upon Israel, the occupying power, to continue to take and implement measures, including, inter alia, the confiscation of weapons, to prevent illegal acts of violence by Israeli settlers;<br>3. Calls for measures to ensure the safety and protection of Palestinian civilians throughout the occupied territory […].<br>(Note: on February 25, 1994 Baruch Goldstein, a Jewish settler from the colony of Kiryat Arba, massacred 29 people praying in a mosque. His grave is now a place of pilgrimage, where Minister Itamar Ben-Gvir speaks). |
| 71 | Resolution 1073 (1996) | "Expressing its deep concern at the tragic events in Jerusalem, in the Nablus, Ramallah and Bethlehem areas and in the Gaza Strip, which have resulted in a large number of deaths and injuries among the Palestinian civilian population, and also concerned at the clashes between the Israeli army and the Palestinian police, which have resulted in casualties on both sides," and<br>"Calls for the security and protection of the Palestinian civilian population to be ensured." |
| 72 | Resolution 1322 (2000) | 1. Deplores the act of provocation committed on September 28, 2000, at the Haram al-Sharif in Jerusalem, as well as the violence that subsequently took place there and at other holy sites and in other areas throughout the territories occupied by Israel since 1967, which caused the death of more than 80 Palestinians and many other victims;<br>2. Condemns the acts of violence, particularly the excessive use of force against Palestinians, which have resulted in injuries and loss of life;<br>3. Calls upon Israel, the occupying power, to comply scrupulously with its legal obligations and responsibilities under the Fourth Geneva Convention relative to the Protection of Civilian Persons in Time of War, of 12 August 1949;<br>4. Demands that the violence cease immediately and that all necessary measures be taken to ensure that the violence ceases, that no further provocative acts take place, and that normalcy returns in a way that improves the prospects for the Middle East peace process; |

| | | |
|---|---|---|
| 73 | Resolution 1402 (2002) | Expressing grave concern that the situation has deteriorated further, notably as a result of the recent suicide bombings in Israel and the military offensive against the headquarters of the President of the Palestinian Authority,<br>1. Calls on both parties to achieve an immediate and genuine cease-fire; calls for the withdrawal of Israeli troops from Palestinian cities, including Ramallah; and calls on the parties to cooperate fully with Special Envoy Zinni, and others, in implementing the Tenet security work plan as a first step towards implementing the Mitchell Committee recommendations, with the aim of resuming negotiations on a political settlement;<br>2. Reiterates its demand in resolution 1397 (2002) of 12 March 2002 for the immediate cessation of all acts of violence, including all acts of terror, provocation, incitement and destruction; |
| 74 | Resolution 1403 (2002) | Deeply concerned by the worsening situation on the ground, and noting that resolution 1402 (2002) has not yet been implemented.<br>1. Demands the immediate implementation of its resolution 1402 (2002); |
| 75 | Resolution 1405 (2002) | Concerned by the appalling humanitarian situation of the Palestinian civilian population, in particular by reports from the Jenin refugee camp of an unknown number of deaths and destruction,<br>Calling for the lifting of restrictions imposed, particularly in Jenin, on the activities of humanitarian organizations, including the International Committee of the Red Cross and the United Nations Relief and Works Agency for Palestine Refugees in the Near East,<br>Emphasizing the need for all parties concerned to ensure the safety of civilians and respect universally accepted norms of international humanitarian law |
| 76 | Resolution 1435 (2002) | Condemning all terrorist attacks against any civilian, including the terrorist bombings directed against Israel on September 18 and 19, 2002, and against a Palestinian school in Hebron on September 17, 2002,<br>Gravely concerned by the reoccupation of the headquarters of the President of the Palestinian Authority in the city of Ramallah on September 19, 2002, and demanding that it be brought to an immediate end,<br>Alarmed by the reoccupation of Palestinian towns and the severe restrictions on the freedom of movement of people and goods, and gravely concerned by the humanitarian situation facing the Palestinian people,<br>Reiterating the need to respect international humanitarian law in all circumstances, including the Fourth Geneva Convention relative to the Protection of Civilian Persons in Time of War of August 12, 1949, |
| 77 | Resolution 1544 (2004) | Reaffirming that Israel, the occupying power, must scrupulously respect its legal obligations and responsibilities under the Fourth Geneva Convention relative to the Protection of Civilian Persons in Time of War, of August 12, 1949,<br>Calling on Israel to meet its security needs within the limits of international law,<br>Expressing its grave concern at the continuing deterioration of the situation on the ground in the territory occupied by Israel since 1967,<br>Condemning the deaths of Palestinian civilians in the Rafah area,<br>Gravely concerned by the recent destruction of homes by Israel, the occupying power, in the Rafah refugee camp,<br>Recalling the obligations imposed by the Roadmap on the Palestinian Authority and the Israeli Government,<br>Condemning all acts of violence, terror and destruction, Reaffirming its support for the Road Map, which it endorsed in resolution 1515 (2003),<br>1. Calls on Israel to respect its obligations under international humanitarian law, and stresses in particular its obligation not to engage in the destruction of homes, which is contrary to that law;<br>2. Expresses its grave concern at the humanitarian situation of Palestinians deprived of their shelters in the Rafah area, and appeals for emergency aid to be provided; |

| 78 | Resolution 1701 (2006) | 3. Stresses the importance of the Government of Lebanon extending its authority over all Lebanese territory, in accordance with the provisions of resolutions 1559 (2004) and 1680 (2006), and the relevant provisions of the Taif Accords, in order to exercise its full sovereignty therein, so that no weapons are present without the consent of the Government of Lebanon and no authority is exercised therein other than that of the Government of Lebanon;<br>4. Reaffirms its strong support for strict adherence to the Blue Line;<br>5. Reaffirms also its firm attachment, as recalled in all its previous resolutions on this question, to the territorial integrity, sovereignty and political independence of Lebanon within its internationally recognized borders, as provided for in the Israeli-Lebanese General Armistice Agreement of March 23, 1949; |
|---|---|---|
| 79 | Resolution 1860 (2009) S/RES/1860 (2009) | 1. Emphasizes the urgency of and calls for an immediate, durable and fully respected ceasefire leading to the full withdrawal of Israeli forces from Gaza;<br>2. Calls for the unimpeded provision and distribution throughout Gaza of humanitarian aid, including food, fuel and medical treatment;<br>3. Welcomes initiatives to create and open humanitarian corridors and other mechanisms to ensure the uninterrupted flow of humanitarian aid;<br>4. Calls on all Member States to support international efforts to improve the humanitarian and economic situation in Gaza, in particular by making urgently needed additional contributions to UNRWA and through the Ad Hoc Liaison Committee;<br>5. Condemns all violence and hostilities directed against civilians, as well as all acts of terrorism; |
| 80 | Resolution 2334 (2016) | 1. Reaffirms that Israel's establishment of settlements in the Palestinian Territory occupied since 1967, including East Jerusalem, has no basis in law and constitutes a flagrant violation of international law and a major obstacle to the realization of the two-State solution and the establishment of a comprehensive, just and lasting peace;<br>2. Reiterates its demand that Israel immediately and completely cease all settlement activities in the Occupied Palestinian Territory, including East Jerusalem, and comply fully with all its legal obligations in this regard;<br>3. Stresses that it will not recognize any changes to the June 4, 1967 borders, including Jerusalem, other than those agreed upon by the parties through negotiations |
| 81 | A/C.4/78/L.13 (2023) | 2. Reiterates its demand that Israel, the occupying Power, cooperate with the Special Committee in the performance of its mandate, in accordance with its obligations as a State Member of the United Nations, and regrets the continued lack of cooperation in this regard;<br>3. Deplores the policies and practices of Israel that violate the human rights of the Palestinian people and other Arabs of the occupied territories, as stated in the report of the Special Committee on the period under review;<br>4. Expresses its grave concern at the crisis situation created in the Occupied Palestinian Territory, including East Jerusalem, by illegal Israeli practices and measures, condemns in particular all Israeli settlements and the construction of the wall, the blockade of the Gaza Strip and the excessive and indiscriminate use of force and military operations against the civilian population, the acts of violence committed by settlers, the provocations and incitements surrounding the Holy Places, the destruction and confiscation of property, the forced displacement of civilians, the detention and imprisonment of thousands of civilians and all collective punishments against the Palestinian civilian population, and calls for the immediate cessation of these actions; |

| 82 | A/C.4 /78/L.14 (2023) | 1. Calls upon Israel, the occupying Power, to comply with the resolutions concerning the occupied Syrian Golan, in particular Security Council resolution 497 (1981), in which the Council decided, inter alia, that the decision by Israel to impose its laws, jurisdiction and administration on the occupied Syrian Golan was null and void and without international legal effect, and demanded that Israel, the occupying Power, rescind forthwith this decision;<br>2. Also calls upon Israel to refrain from changing the physical character, demographic composition, institutional structure and legal status of the occupied Syrian Golan and, in particular, to refrain from establishing settlements there; |
|---|---|---|
| 83 | A/C.4 /78/L.15 a (2023) | 1. Reaffirms that Israeli settlements in the Occupied Palestinian Territory, including East Jerusalem, and in the occupied Syrian Golan are illegal and constitute an obstacle to peace and to economic and social development;<br>2. Demands that Israel recognize the de jure applicability of the Geneva Convention relative to the Protection of Civilian Persons in Time of War, of August 12, 1949, to the Occupied Palestinian Territory, including East Jerusalem, and to the other Arab territories occupied by Israel since 1967, including the occupied Syrian Golan, scrupulously respect its provisions, in particular article 49, comply with all its obligations under international law, and immediately cease all actions which result in the alteration of the character, status or demographic composition of the Occupied Palestinian Territory, including East Jerusalem, and the occupied Syrian Golan;<br>3. Demands once again the immediate and complete cessation of all Israeli settlement activities throughout the Occupied Palestinian Territory, including East Jerusalem, and the occupied Syrian Golan, and calls in this regard for the full implementation of all relevant Security Council resolutions, including resolutions 446 (1979), 452 (1979) of 20 July 1979, 465 (1980), 476 (1980), 478 (1980), 1515 (2003) of 19 November 2003 and 2334 (2016);<br>4. Stresses that a complete halt to all Israeli settlement activity is essential to safeguard the two-state solution based on the pre-1967 borders; |
| 84 | A/C.4 /78/L.11 (2023) | Expressing its deep concern in particular at the serious humanitarian and socio-economic situation of Palestine refugees in the Gaza Strip, and stressing the importance of emergency humanitarian aid and urgent reconstruction work, Noting that the Government of Israel and the Palestine Liberation Organization signed the Declaration of Principles on Interim Self-Government Arrangements3 on September 13, 1993, as well as subsequent implementation agreements,<br>1. Notes with regret that neither the repatriation nor the compensation of the refugees provided for in paragraph 11 of its resolution 194 (III) has yet taken place and that, as a result, the situation of the Palestine refugees remains a matter of grave concern and that they continue to require assistance to meet their basic health, education and subsistence needs;<br>2. Notes with regret that the United Nations Conciliation Commission for Palestine has been unable to find a way to advance the implementation of paragraph 11 of its resolution 194 (III), and reiterates its request to the Commission to continue its efforts in this direction and to report, as appropriate, to the General Assembly no later than 1 September 2024;<br>3. Emphasizes the need for the continuation of the work of the United Nations Relief and Works Agency for Palestine Refugees in the Near East and the importance of its unimpeded operations and services, including emergency assistance, for the well-being, protection and human development of the Palestine refugees and for the stability of the region, pending the just resolution of the question of the Palestine refugees; |

| 85 | A/C.4/78/L.10 (2023) | 38. Calls upon Israel, the occupying Power, to comply fully with the provisions of the Geneva Convention relative to the Protection of Civilian Persons in Time of War, of August 12, 1949;<br>39. Also calls upon Israel to comply with Articles 100, 104 and 105 of the Charter of the United Nations and with the Convention on the Privileges and Immunities of the United Nations in order to ensure in all circumstances the safety of the staff of the Agency, the protection of its institutions and the security of its installations in the Occupied Palestinian Territory, including East Jerusalem;<br>40. Urges the Government of Israel to promptly reimburse the Agency for all transit costs and other financial losses incurred as a result of the delays and restrictions on freedom of movement and access imposed by Israel;<br>41. Calls in particular on Israel to cease obstructing the movement and access of the Office's personnel, vehicles and supplies and to stop levying taxes, additional duties and fees, which are detrimental to the Office's activities;<br>42. Reiterates its call on Israel to fully lift restrictions hindering or delaying the import of construction materials and supplies needed for the reconstruction and repair of still-damaged or even destroyed refugee housing and for the implementation of outstanding civil infrastructure projects that are sorely lacking in the refugee camps of the Gaza Strip, noting the alarming figures contained in the August 26, 2016 and July 2017 reports of the United Nations country team, entitled respectively "Gaza: two years after" and "Gaza ten years later" |
|---|---|---|
| 86 | A/C.4/78/L.12 (2023) | 1. Reaffirms that the Palestine refugees are entitled to the enjoyment of their property and the proceeds thereof, in accordance with the principles of equity and justice;<br>2. Requests the Secretary-General, in consultation with the United Nations Conciliation Commission for Palestine, to take all necessary measures to protect Arab property, assets and property rights in Israel;<br>3. Calls once again upon Israel to provide the Secretary-General with all facilities and forms of assistance for the implementation of the present resolution;<br>4. Calls upon all parties concerned to communicate to the Secretary-General all relevant information at their disposal concerning Arab property, assets and property rights in Israel which would assist him in the implementation of the present resolution |
| 87 | A/C.1/78/L.2 (2023) | Recalling that Israel remains the only state in the Middle East not yet party to the Treaty,<br>(...)<br>5. Reaffirms the importance of Israel's accession to the Treaty on the Non-Proliferation of Nuclear Weapons and the placement of all its nuclear facilities under comprehensive International Atomic Energy Agency safeguards in order to achieve the goal of universal adherence to the Treaty in the region; |

| 88 | A/C.2/78/L.21 (2023) | Noting with great concern the ecological disaster caused by the destruction by the Israeli air force, on July 15, 2006, of fuel tanks in the immediate vicinity of the Jiyeh power plant (Lebanon), which resulted in an oil slick covering the entire Lebanese coastline and extending as far as the Syrian coastline, hampering efforts to achieve sustainable development, as already emphasized in resolutions 61/194, 62/188, 63/211, 64/195, 65/147, 66/192, 67/201, 68/206, 69/212, 70/194, 71/218, 72/209, 73/224, 74/208, 75/209, 76/199 and 77/157, Noting that the Secretary-General was deeply concerned by the Israeli Government's failure to acknowledge its responsibility to provide reparations and compensation to the Lebanese and Syrian Governments and peoples affected by the oil slick, Recalling that in paragraph 5 of its resolution 77/157, it reiterated its request to the Government of Israel to assume its responsibility to provide prompt and adequate compensation to the Government of Lebanon and other countries directly affected by the oil slick, such as the Syrian Arab Republic, whose coasts have been partially polluted, and noting that the Secretary-General has noted that this request has not yet been met, (...) 5. Reiterates in this regard its call upon the Government of Israel to assume its responsibility to compensate promptly and adequately the Government of Lebanon for the above-mentioned damage, as well as other countries directly affected by the oil spill, such as the Syrian Arab Republic, whose coasts were partially polluted, for the expenses incurred in repairing the ecological damage caused by the destruction of the reservoirs, including the restoration of the marine environment, in particular in view of the conclusion drawn in the Secretary-General's report that the non-implementation of the relevant provisions of his resolutions concerning compensation and restitution to the Governments and peoples of Lebanon and the Syrian Arab Republic affected by the oil spill remains a matter of grave concern; |
|---|---|---|
| 89 | A/C.2/78/L.44 (2023) | 5. Calls upon Israel, the occupying Power, to abide scrupulously by its obligations under international law, including international humanitarian law, and to cease immediately and completely all policies and measures aimed at altering the character and status of the Occupied Palestinian Territory, including East Jerusalem; 6. Also calls upon Israel, the occupying Power, to cease all actions, including those of Israeli settlers, that damage the environment in the Occupied Palestinian Territory, including East Jerusalem, and in the occupied Syrian Golan, in particular the dumping of all kinds of waste materials, which gravely threaten the natural resources of these territories, namely water and land resources, and which endanger the environment and sanitation, as well as the health of the civilian population; |
| 89 | A/C.2/78/L.44 (2023) | 7. Further calls on Israel to put an end to the destruction of essential facilities, including water, sanitation and electricity networks, and to the demolition and confiscation of Palestinian homes, civil infrastructure, agricultural land and wells, which, among other things, degrade the natural resources of the Palestinian people, Insists on the urgent need to advance reconstruction and development projects in this regard, particularly in the Gaza Strip, and calls for support for the necessary efforts in this regard, in line with the commitments made inter alia at the Cairo International Conference on Palestine, entitled "Rebuilding Gaza," held on October 12, 2014; 8. Calls upon Israel, the occupying Power, to remove all obstacles to the implementation of essential environmental projects, including the construction of sewage treatment plants in the Gaza Strip and the reconstruction and improvement of water supply infrastructure, including the Gaza Strip desalination plant project; |

| 90 | A/C.3 /78/L.24 (2023) | Recalling further the advisory opinion given on July 9, 2004 by the International Court of Justice on the legal consequences of the construction of a wall in the Occupied Palestinian Territory7, and noting in particular the Court's response, notably on the right of peoples to self-determination, which is a right opposable erga omnes, <br> Recalling the conclusion of the Court, in its Advisory Opinion of 9 July 2004, that the construction of the wall by Israel, the occupying Power, in the Occupied Palestinian Territory, including East Jerusalem, in addition to measures previously taken, severely impedes the exercise by the Palestinian people of its right to self-determination <br> 1. Reaffirms the right of the Palestinian people to self-determination, including their right to an independent State of Palestine; |
|---|---|---|
| 91 | A/78/L.22 (2023) | Considering that development is difficult under a regime of occupation, and that it is best served by peace and stability, <br> Noting the serious economic and social problems facing the Palestinian people and their leaders, (...) <br> Expressing its deep concern at the gravity of the humanitarian situation in the Gaza Strip, and stressing the importance of humanitarian aid and emergency relief and the need to make progress in the reconstruction of the Gaza Strip, (...) <br> Reaffirming the need to achieve a comprehensive settlement of the Arab-Israeli conflict in all its aspects, on the basis of the relevant Security Council resolutions, in particular resolutions 242 (1967) of November 22, 1967, 338 (1973) of October 22, 1973, 1397 (2002) of March 12, 2002, 1515 (2003) of November 19, 2003, 1850 (2008) of December 16, 2008 and 1860 (2009), as well as the terms of reference of the Madrid Conference and the principle of land for peace, to achieve a political settlement corresponding to the two-state solution: Israel and a contiguous, independent, democratic, sovereign and viable Palestinian state, living side by side in peace, security and mutual recognition, |
| 92 | A/RES /78/11 (2023) | 1. Declares that Israel has still not complied with Security Council resolution 497 (1981); <br> 2. Also declares that the decision of December 14, 1981, by which Israel imposed its laws, jurisdiction and administration on the occupied Syrian Golan, is null and void and has no validity whatsoever, as confirmed by the Security Council in its resolution 497 (1981), and calls upon Israel to rescind it; <br> 3. Reaffirms its determination that all relevant provisions of the Regulations annexed to the Hague Convention of 1907 and of the Geneva Convention relative to the Protection of Civilian Persons in Time of War, of August 12, 1949, continue to apply to the Syrian territory occupied by Israel since 1967, and calls upon the parties to these instruments to respect and to ensure respect in all circumstances for the obligations arising therefrom; <br> 4. Notes once again that the continued occupation of the Syrian Golan and its de facto annexation are obstacles to the establishment of a just, comprehensive and lasting peace in the region; <br> 5. Calls on Israel to relaunch the Syrian and Lebanese tracks of the talks and to respect the guarantees and commitments previously entered into; 6. Demands once again that, in application of the relevant Security Council resolutions, Israel withdraw from all the occupied Syrian Golan up to the line of June 4, 1967; |

| 93 | A/ES-10/L.25 (2023) | Condemning all acts of violence directed against Palestinian and Israeli civilians, including all acts of terrorism and indiscriminate attacks, as well as acts of provocation, incitement and destruction, (...) 5. Also calls for the rescinding of the order given by Israel, the occupying Power, to Palestinian civilians and United Nations personnel, as well as humanitarian and medical workers, to evacuate all areas of the Gaza Strip north of Wadi Gaza and to relocate to the southern Gaza Strip, recalls and reaffirms that civilians are protected under international humanitarian law and must receive humanitarian aid wherever they are, and recalls the importance of taking appropriate measures to guarantee the safety and well-being of civilians, in particular children, and their protection, and to allow their free movement; 6. Firmly rejects any attempt at forced transfer of the Palestinian civilian population; 7. Calls for the immediate and unconditional release of all civilians illegally held in captivity, demands that their safety and well-being be ensured and that they be treated humanely, in accordance with international law; |
|---|---|---|
| 94 | A/ES-10/L.27 (2023) | 1. Demands an immediate humanitarian ceasefire; 2. Reiterates its demand that all parties comply with their obligations under international law, including international humanitarian law, in particular with regard to the protection of civilians; 3. Demands the immediate and unconditional release of all hostages and the assurance of humanitarian access; |

# Appendix 3—Use of the Veto by the USA

|    | Date       | Proposal        | File      | Agenda item |
|----|------------|-----------------|-----------|-------------|
| 1  | 10.09.1972 | S/10784         | S/PV.1662 | Situation in the Middle East |
| 2  | 26.07.1973 | S/10974         | S/PV.1735 | Situation in the Middle East |
| 3  | 08.12.1975 | S/11898         | S/PV.1862 | Situation in the Middle East |
| 4  | 26.01.1976 | S/11940         | S/PV.1879 | Situation in the Middle East and the Palestinian question |
| 5  | 25.03.1976 | S/12022         | S/PV.1899 | Request by Libya and Pakistan for consideration of the serious situation resulting from recent developments in the occupied Arab territories |
| 6  | 29.06.1976 | S/12119         | S/PV.1938 | The question of the Palestinian people's exercise of their inalienable rights |
| 7  | 30.04.1980 | S/13911         | S/PV.2220 | The question of the Palestinian people's exercise of their inalienable rights |
| 8  | 20.01.1982 | S/14832/Rev.1   | S/PV.2329 | Situation in the occupied Arab territories |
| 9  | 02.04.1982 | S/14943         | S/PV.2348 | Situation in the occupied Arab territories |
| 10 | 20.04.1982 | S/14985         | S/PV.2357 | Situation in the occupied Arab territories |
| 11 | 08.06.1982 | S/15185         | S/PV.2377 | Situation in the Middle East |
| 12 | 26.06.1982 | S/15255/Rev.2   | S/PV.2381 | Situation in the Middle East |
| 13 | 06.08.1982 | S/15347/Rev.1   | S/PV.2391 | Situation in the Middle East |
| 14 | 02.08.1983 | S/15895         | S/PV.2461 | Situation in the occupied Arab territories |
| 15 | 06.09.1984 | S/16732         | S/PV.2556 | Situation in the Middle East |
| 16 | 12.03.1985 | S/17000         | S/PV.2573 | Situation in the Middle East |
| 17 | 13.09.1985 | S/17459         | S/PV.2605 | Situation in the occupied Arab territories |
| 18 | 17.01.1986 | S/17730/Rev.2   | S/PV.2642 | Situation in the Middle East |
| 19 | 30.01.1986 | S/17769/Rev.1   | S/PV.2650 | Situation in the occupied Arab territories |
| 20 | 18.01.1988 | S/19434         | S/PV.2784 | Situation in the Middle East |
| 21 | 01.02.1988 | S/19466         | S/PV.2790 | Situation in the occupied Arab territories |
| 22 | 15.04.1988 | S/19780         | S/PV.2806 | Situation in the occupied Arab territories |
| 23 | 10.05.1988 | S/19868         | S/PV.2814 | Situation in the Middle East |

| | | | | |
|---|---|---|---|---|
| 24 | 14.12.1988 | S/20322 | S/PV.2832 | Situation in the Middle East |
| 25 | 17.02.1989 | S/20463 | S/PV.2850 | Situation in the occupied Arab territories |
| 26 | 09.06.1989 | S/20677 | S/PV.2867 | Situation in the occupied Arab territories |
| 27 | 07.11.1989 | S/20945/Rev.1 | S/PV.2889 | Situation in the occupied Arab territories |
| 28 | 31.05.1990 | S/21326 | S/PV.2926 | Situation in the occupied Arab territories |
| 29 | 17.05.1995 | S/1995/394 | S/PV.3538 | Situation in the Middle East and the Palestinian question |
| 30 | 07.03.1997 | S/1997/199 | S/PV.3747 | Situation in the Middle East and the Palestinian question |
| 31 | 21.03.1997 | S/1997/241 | S/PV.3756 | Situation in the Middle East and the Palestinian question |
| 32 | 27-28.03.2001 | S/2001/270 | S/PV.4305 | Situation in the Middle East and the Palestinian question |
| 33 | 14-15.12.2001 | S/2001/1199 | S/PV.4438 | Situation in the Middle East and the Palestinian question |
| 34 | 20.12.2002 | S/2002/1385 | S/PV.4681 | Situation in the Middle East and the Palestinian question |
| 35 | 16.09.2003 | S/2003/891 | S/PV.4828 | Situation in the Middle East and the Palestinian question |
| 36 | 14.10.2003 | S/2003/980 | S/PV.4842 | Situation in the Middle East and the Palestinian question |
| 37 | 25.03.2004 | S/2004/240 | S/PV.4934 | Situation in the Middle East and the Palestinian question |
| 38 | 05.10.2004 | S/2004/783 | S/PV.5051 | Situation in the Middle East and the Palestinian question |
| 39 | 13.07.2006 | S/2006/508 | S/PV.5488 | Situation in the Middle East and the Palestinian question |
| 40 | 11.11.2006 | S/2006/878 | S/PV.5565 | Situation in the Middle East and the Palestinian question |
| 41 | 18.02.2011 | S/2011/24 | S/PV.6484 | Situation in the Middle East and the Palestinian question |
| 42 | 18.12.2017 | S/2017/1060 | S/PV.8139 | Situation in the Middle East and the Palestinian question |
| 43 | 01.06.2018 | S/2018/516 | S/PV.8274 | Situation in the Middle East and the Palestinian question |
| 44 | 18.10.2023 | S/2023/773 | S/PV.9442 | Situation in the Middle East and the Palestinian question |
| 45 | 08.12.2023 | S/2023/970 | S/PV.9499 | Situation in the Middle East and the Palestinian question |

# Appendix 4—Definition of Apartheid

[Source: https://treaties.un.org/doc/Publication/UNTS/Volume%20 1015/volume-1015-I-14861-French.pdf]

Article II—(...) the expression "crime of apartheid," (...) designates the inhuman acts indicated below, committed with a view to establishing or maintaining the domination of one racial group of human beings over any other racial group of human beings and to systematically oppressing the latter:

- a) Denying a member or members of a racial group or groups the right to life and personal liberty:
- 1) By taking the lives of members of one or more racial groups;
- 2) By seriously impairing the physical or mental integrity, liberty or dignity of members of one or more racial groups, or by subjecting them to torture or to cruel, inhuman or degrading treatment or punishment;
- 3) By arbitrarily arresting and illegally imprisoning members of one or more racial groups;
- b) To deliberately impose on a racial group or groups conditions of life calculated to bring about their physical destruction, in whole or in part;
- c) Take legislative or other measures designed to prevent a racial group or groups from participating in the political, social, economic and cultural life of the country, and deliberately create conditions which impede the full development of the group or groups concerned, in particular by depriving the members of a racial group or groups of fundamental human rights and freedoms, including the right to work, the right to form recognized trade unions, the right to education, the right to leave and return

to one's country, the right to a nationality, the right to freedom of movement and residence, the right to freedom of opinion and expression, and the right to freedom of peaceful assembly and association;

d) Take measures, including legislative measures, to divide the population along racial lines by creating separate reservations and ghettos for members of one or more racial groups, by prohibiting marriages between persons belonging to different racial groups, and by expropriating land belonging to one or more racial groups or to members of such groups;

e) Exploiting the labor of members of one or more racial groups, in particular by subjecting them to forced labor;

f) Persecute organizations or individuals, depriving them of fundamental rights and freedoms, because they oppose apartheid.